THE REVISED COMPLEAT

Sinatra

DISGOGRAPHY
FILMOGRAPHY
TELEVISION APPEARANCES
MOTION PICTURE APPEARANCES
RADIO APPEARANCES
CONCERT APPEARANCES
STAGE APPEARANCES

By: Albert I. Lonstein
Vito R. Marino

I

II

DEDICATIONS

For Mom, Sondy, Herbert, Wayne, Wendy and Elizabeth
A.I.L.

For my mother Mary and my father Nunzio
V.R.M.

Cover reproduced from an original sketch by Gene Locklear.
   Gene is a full-blooded Lumbee Indian from Pembroke, North Carolina who has been sketching since early childhood.
   He also is a major-league baseball player having played with the New York Yankees, Cincinnatti Reds and the San Diego Padres; who's ultimate aim is to become the great painter that one can admire, appreciate and criticize with pleasure.
   His paintings have been displayed in various exhibits throughout the United States and in 1975 he was honored by President Carter exhibiting a painting at the White House.

TABLE OF CONTENTS

Acknowledgements and Preface .... VII & VIII

Instrumental, Label and Miscellaneous Abbreviations .... IX & X

Forward   Bill Zietung XI

Introduction   The Authors..................................... XIV

Chapter I   In the Beginning 1-3

Chapter II   Harry James 4-9

Chapter III   With the Sentimental Gentleman 10-26

Chapter IV   Four for Bluebird .... 27 & 28

Chapter V   Appearances at the Paramount Theater 29-41

                   Song Index for First Five Chapters
                   Index of Orchestra's, Arrangers, Composers,
                   Soloists, Vocalists, and Vocal Groups for First
                   Five Chapters.

Chapter VI   The Columbia Years 42-108

                   Song Index for Chapter VI, Index of Orchestras,
                   Arrangers, Composers, Soloists, Vocalists, and
                   Vocal Groups for Chapter VI.

Chapter VII   V-Discs...................................... 109-123

                   Song Index for Chapter VII

Chapter VIII   A Fresh Start - Capitol Records 124-175

                   Song Index for Chapter VIII, Index of Orchestras,
                   Arrangers, Composers, Soloists, Vocalists and
                   Vocal Groups for Chapter VIII

Chapter IX   On His Own - Reprise Records 176-244

                   Song Index for Chapter IX, Index of Orchestras,
                   Arrangers, Composers, Soloists, Vocalists and Vocal
                   Groups for Chapter IX

Chapter X   Television Appearances....................... 245-296

                   Song Index for Chapter X, Index of Orchestras,
                   Arrangers, Composers, Soloists, Vocalists and Vocal
                   Groups for Chapter X

Chapter XI   Motion Pictures.................................. 297-374

        Song Index for Chapter XI

Air Checks
Chapter XII   Air Checks 375-485

        Song Index for Chapter XII, Index of Orchestras,
        Arrangers, Composers, Soloists, Vocalists and Vocal
        Group for Chapter XII

Chapter XIII   Concert Appearances 486-534

        Song Index for Chapter XIII, Index of Orchestras,
        Arrangers, Composers, Soloists, Vocalists and Vocal
        Groups for Chapter XIII

Chapter XIV   Album Index 535-605

Chapter XV   Select Bibliography 606-612

Chapter XVI   Major Awards 613-616

Chapter XVII   Looking Back - Harvey Geller.................. 617-679

    Addenda & Errata 680-702

ACKNOWLEDGMENTS

This manuscript could never have been compiled without the vast amount of help received from many sources. The authors are particularly indebted to Bob Chiappari, Frank Driggs and Katherine Peart for their invaluable aid and for the following for the loan of pictures and assistance in compiling this book:

Harry Gittleson of R.K.O. Radio Pictures, Frank J. Gillhause of United World Films, Inc., Phil Bernstein of A.B.C., Doris Ieda, Walter Siegal and Diane Ognibene of C.B.S., Leonard Meyers of N.B.C., Norman Kaphan of M.G.M., Steven Schumach of United Artists Corp., Sue Round of Capitol Records, Jerry Miller of R.C.A. Victor Records, Mike Berman of Paramount Pictures, John Sutherland of Warner Bros. and Reprise Records, Sara Pentz and Jane Gallagher of T.V. Guide, Willard Alexander, Inc., Columbia Pictures and Twentieth Century Fox.

ALSO

Daniel H. Baer of the Academy of Motion Picture Arts and Sciences, Barbara McCarthy, Catherine D'Addetta, Angela Farinola, Kay Cerelli, Mike Milo, Jacob Schneider, Anthony Colello, Pat Caporino, Kiers Photos, Milton Lichenstein of Metronome, Louis Baricelli, Bob Sherrick, Dick Partee, Henry Beau, Verna Hazel, Lola Dishek, Mary Alice Watring, Ruth Arnowitz, Arthur Mallon, Robert Harrigan and John Haviland.

and

Very special thanks to John Brady and Jack M. Launer

Preface

This, our second edition of "The Compleat Sinatra", is different in many ways from the first. We have received numerous letters of praise and criticism and of course, many helpful suggestions on how we could have made it a much more "complete" listing of Mr. Sinatra's achievements. On the whole, the criticisms were aimed at the ommissions of certain performances such as concert dates or radio air-checks and one complete session missing from a Capitol recording date (which was totally inexcusable). Others pointed out that we did not include a usable and useful song index which is quite necessary to locate a particular performance, and still more complainants were noting that none of the photographs had identifying dates or names. It was, as Bill Weedon so aptly stated "A field day for the vultures," but there is one "principle" that we will defend. We have been criticized for including many television performances of which nobody seems to own or know about. These listings were given to us by the various networks on duplicated work sheets from the individual shows and coupled with our own previous findings, they are thus presented. We have tried in this book to correct all of these problems along with our aim to expand, compile and include a considerable amount of new informaiton. In this respect we believe our first four chapters to be as complete as can be, but from then on a great difficulty arises. As an example, at one time we were offered the Paramount Theater files in a verbal discussion and a few days later that offer was withdrawn and subsequently we did not want to include songs on his later appearances without verification. The Columbia Recording files were at our complete disposal thanks to Mr. Frank Driggs, but Capitol and Reprise Records are extremely reticent concerning any information to be given out and we painstakingly had to obtain as best as possible what we present here. To make things easier we have included song indexes for each main chapter except for the first four which have a comprehensive index. The songs listed are followed by their respective composers and dates of performances or recording sessions. With the exception of one chapter (concert appearances) *All* of the dates for each song is given. In the case of the concert appearance there were many songs that were repeated too often and to list every date would have been a waste of time and space. What we have done in this particular index is to list at least the first and last date of performance and to include one date for each different year in between. The index of orchestras, arrangers, etc., lists only those who actually perform with Sinatra in that particular chapter musically, thus there is no listing of actors and actresses who perform on dramatic shows or Motion Pictures. The Bibliography chapter has expanded quite a bit as many new books and articles have appeared since our first publication, and we have also included a Major Awards chapter along with whatever useful information we thought would be of interest to you, the Frank Sinatra fan.

INSTRUMENTAL, LABEL AND MISCELLANEOUS ABBREVIATIONS

ALT.	- Alto Saxophone
BAR.	- Baritone Saxophone
CLT.	- Clarinet
DR.	- Drums
G.	- Guitar
F.	Flute
P.	- Piano
RDS.	- Reeds
TEN. SAX.	- Tenor Saxophone
TBN.	- Trombone
TPT.	- Trumpet
TU.	- Tuba
VIB.	- Vibraphone
VIA.	- Viola
VIN.	- Violin
H.	- Harp
A.C.	- Air Check
AFRS.	- Armed Forces Radio Service Record
AV. INT.	- Avenue International Album
Bb.	- Bluebird Records
BR.	- Brunswick Records
CAL.	Camden Long Playing Record
CAM.	- Cameron Long Playing Record
T., W., SCO., STFL., DKAO., SW., DQBO, DNFR.	- Capitol Long Playing Record
MFC., MFP.	- English Capitol Long Playing Record
CH.	- Chairman Long Playing Record
COB.	- Cobra Long Playing Record
C., SL.	- Columbia Long Playing Record
P., P2M., CZ.	- Columbia Special Products Record
CX.	- Coronet Long Playing Record
C.C.	- Curtain Calls Album
HL., HS.	Harmony Long Playing Record
	- Here's To Veterans Album
	- Ho-Ho-Ho Long Playing Record
SM.	- Joker Long Playing Record
	- Joyce Long Playing Record
	- Larynx Long Playing Record
SYMS.	- Longines Long Playing Record
PRO.	- Magnovox Long Playing Record
M & M	- M & M Long Playing Record
	- My Way Long Playing Record
	- Oscar Long Playing Record
RC., SPC.	Pickwick Long Playing Record

PRM.	- RCA Custom Album
LPM., VPM	- RCA Long Playing Record
RD., RDA.	- Reader's Digest Long Playing Record
SD.	- English RCA Long Playing Box Set
LPV.	- RCA Vintage Long Playing Record
R., R.S., F., F.S.	- Reprise Long Playing Record
K.	- English Reprise Long Playing Record
	- Show Business Long Playing Record
T.	- Tobey Music Long Playing Record
U.R.	- Universal International Promotional
	- Vine Land Long Playing Record
V.D.	- V-Discs (Army & Navy Recordings)
T.P.	- World Record Club (English Capitol)
W.	- Windmill Long Playing Record
N.R.	- Not Released
B.	- Columbia 45 Rpm Extended Play
EAP.	- Capitol 45 Rpm Extended Play
ACC.	- Accompanied (by); Accompanist
ARR.	- Arranged (By); Arranger
REV.	- Reverse (Side)
VCL.	Vocal; Vocalist

Foreword

The modern-day singer of popular songs is the victim of an unpredicatable species; in a large part he is pushed rapidly into prominence by a momentary whim of taste and just as rapidly, when that taste has been satisfied, he is back where he started, living out the remainder of his career in a sort of musical limbo. There he remains, perhaps not entirely ignored by the public, but passed over in favor of someone new; someone who may not have an equal amount of talent, but who is the possessor of a different talent, sounding gimmick, one which captures the vagaries of public attention for a few fleeting seconds. This is the general pattern of success in popular musical circles but as in the conjugation of French verbs, there are exceptions. Certainly, one of the most obvious of these is the career of Frank Sinatra, truly a fabulous figure in any compendium of American musical history. Unchanged and unchanging, Frank has altered his style not one whit from the days when he was occupying more musical space than the president of the United States, when teenagers were falling over themselves to get glimpses of this romantic figure. Frank has not changed and public acceptance of his vocal styling has changed even less.

Bill Zeitung
(Copyright 1954 - R.C.A. Victor)

Sinatra at the age of three - 1918.

The "Sportsman" in 1924.

Jersey Shore — Belmar with friends.

With his mother Dolly in 1925.

Introduction

Hoboken, New Jersey - December 12, 1915. A cold, wintry, snow-flurried day.

That night the famed Hippodrome in New York City was jammed to capacity. The occasion was a farewell to Vernon Castle who was ending his fabulous dancing career with his wife, Irene, to return home and join the British Air Corps. Earlier that same day an equally historic event occured - Francis Albert Sinatra was born. He was an only child, son of Natalie and Martin Sinatra.

Natalie ("Dolly" to her many friends) was born in Genova, Italy, was active in politics at the time of Frank's birth. Before that she has worked in her husband's tavern and also had become a trained practical nurse. Martin had been a professional fighter for a while, and boxed under the name Marty O'Brien.

He was Sicilian born (in Cantania) and he and Natalie had been married six years before young Frank was born. Young Sinatra's birth was a difficult one - because of his size, and the necessity of an instrument delivery - and his left ear, neck and a small portion of his face were permanently scarred.

Frank's early years were spend mostly with his maternal grandmother, Rosa Garavanti, because Natalie had little time to devote at home.

Being an only child, he was doted on and always received an ample allowance, though these were hard times, they never affected him financially. What did affect him, though, was the constant bickering between the different nationalities that populated the Hoboken area. He was to return this feeling of racial discrimination to his early adulthood and fought against it at every opportunity.

ALBERT I. LONSTEIN
VITO R. MARINO

Chapter I
1930 - 1938

There is no way of pin-pointing the exact year that the young Frank Sinatra decided to become a vocalist, but it is known that seeing Bing Crosby on the movie screen and one eventful night in person certainly spurred his tentative feelings about the music business.

Sinatra was sixteen when "Der Bingles" early films were being featured at the Loews theatre in Jersey City, New Jersey, and Bing impressed him. His lifestyle had always been a notch or two above his young teenage pals even though it was the height of depression, and this enabled him to pursue his musical inclinations, although both his parents were initially against it.

He enjoyed singing in the Demerest High School (now Hoboken High) Glee Club, but was restless and decided to quit in his senior year. He began singing in social clubs and at political rallies (his mother aided him considerably here), and made the rounds of every Hoboken night spot he could - often for little monetary compensation. Then came an important opportunity. He had teamed up with three friends also from Hoboken, at the instigation of Major Bowes for whom they had all gone separately to audition. Mr. Bowes also gave them their name - "The Hoboken Four" and on September 8, 1935, at the Capitol Theatre in New York City, the group, with 19 year old Sinatra as lead, sang "Shine" and won first prize. First prize was a travelling tour across the nation, with each member receiving $50 a week plus meals. They travelled as far west as Hollywood and Oakland, but on the return trip east the group broke up and got the giggles in the middle of a song. An irate Major Bowes fired them all. Frank returned to Hoboken and began singing at local clubs. Although he was working steadily and branching out to other towns (such as Union City and Jersey City), he got the feeling that he was going nowhere.

One good and steady job was at the Union Club on Hudson Street in Hoboken where he was making $40 a week; but when an attempt to persuade owner Joseph Samperi to install a radio wire failed, he quit. Realizing he needed air exposure, Sinatra visited every station in New Jersey and New York City and offered his services for nothing. And that's almost what he received at station WNEW, where he filled in on open periods or whenever no one else showed up. He also sang on station WAAT in Newark for carfare.

In the Fall of 1937, through the efforts of musician friends and perhaps the interjection of his mother, he landed a job that at the time seemed like a dream come true. Harold Arden was the bandleader at the Rustic Cabin in Englewood, New Jersey. Arden listened and liked what he heard; he also found this young vocalist professional and dedicated. For Sinatra it meant achieving two immediate goals - singing in front of a larger orchestra, and, most important, being heard over the air-waves during prime time via the Club's nightly broadcasts.

For a year and a half Sinatra sang and emceed - first with Arden, then with Bill Henri and His Headliners and a vocal group called the Three Flashes. His starting salary was $15 per week, and eventually grew to $25.

Frank, meantime, had been going steady with his childhood sweetheart, Nancy Barbato. They wanted to get married, but - though she was working as a

With Hoboken Four and Major Bowes — 1935.

On tour with local theater mgr. — 1935. (Left to right - Jimmy Petrozelli, Patty Prince, Mgr., Fred Tamburro, F.S.)

secretary in nearby Elizabeth - they were faced with a grim financial situation. They decided to get married anyway, and on February 4, 1939, in a double-ring ceremony at Our Lady of Sorrows Church in Jersey City, the young couple were wed. Frank had also decided that if things did not look brighter soon, he would quit the music business and apply his energies to a "legitimate" job.

Once again, when the situation looked bleak, fate stepped in. In April of 1939, WNEW initiated a program called "WNEW's Dance Parade", which featured live musical broadcasts from all the local night clubs, including the Rustic Cabin. We shall see in the following chapter how these live musical broadcasts affected, furthered and caused a continuance of a great career.

Recordings made from this period are:

The Hoboken Four	September 8, 1935
Shine	Chairman-6008
Sinatra Dub Recording	1938
Unknown Backing	
Our Love	No number

With Patti Prince and friend — 1934.

Chapter II

Harry James   June 1939 - December 1939

Harry James' career in 1939 was in many ways similar to Frank Sinatra's. Of course, he had been well known and even idolized while playing fiery trumpet for one of the nation's top swing orchestras - Benny Goodman - but now on his own he couldn't quite hit the right combination for success. He had made some great recordings under his own name with all-star musicians in 1937 and 1938; and also with his own band since February 1939 but the fans weren't attending his personal appearances, nor were they buying his records, in large numbers.

He and the band had been playing at the Paramount Theatre to sparse crowds, and he was trying to evaluate what was wrong with his orchestra. He concluded there were too many jump or up-tempo arrangements in his band's book, and, although he loved playing them, he had to slow things down a bit.

Early in May, 1939, he added a female vocalist to the band - Connie Haines - and was shopping around for a romantic male vocalist. Then he heard one of the nightly broadcasts aired from the Rustic Cabin. Stories differ as to what Sinatra was singing when James first heard the broadcast, but the next night when Harry went to see him in person, he asked Sinatra to sing "Begin the Beguine".

The thin vocalist impressed him. Harry signed him on at $75 a week. Frank had been trying to get into the Bob Chester organization, but immediately accepted James' offer. He also signed a two-year contract, and couldn't wait to get home to tell Nancy.

He rehearsed with the band for a full week before his first singing engagement at the Hippodrome Theatre in Baltimore, the week of June 30, 1939. While there he sang two songs, "Wishing" and "My Love For You", which he never recorded. This was followed by a short stint at the Roseland Ballroom on Broadway in New York City, then quickly on to the Steel Pier in Atlantic City, a favorite spot for big bands in the thirties and forties.

His first two sides were out on the Brunswick label, a subsidiary of Columbia Records. It is interesting to note that although Connie Hainess recorded two sides before Sinatra, she left the band in early August. There were rumors that she and Frank never got along but he has denied this consistently, and when they reunited later with Tommy Dorsey's Orchestra, all went smoothly.

All through August and part of September, the band alternated between Roseland and the New York World's Fair, and public response to the band was improving and Frank received his first critical appraisal - from the former Metronome writer and editor George T. Simon.

In mid-September, the band travelled to Chicago and appeared in the Panther Room of the Hotel Sherman. In a few months the band continued westward, specifically the Palomar Ballroom in Los Angeles where it had a booking, but when the band arrived it was almost burned to the ground. The band took a substitute engagement at Victor Hugo's in Beverly Hills, a disastrous mistake. The crowd did not enjoy hard swing and loud jazz; it was accustomed to society bands that played syrupy dance music. Things grew worse; the management refused to pay; and Nancy, who had made the trip west, was sent back home as she was expecting her first child.

Very first recording — 1939.

At the Rustic Cabin, N.J. — 1938

While in California, Sinatra cut his last sides with James.

At the end of November when the band again went into the studios to record four more sides, they were all instrumentals. It is also interesting to note that throughout his tenure with James, there was an ASCAP radio ban which precluded any song licensed by that performing society from receiving any airplay; subsequently, none of the recordings became popular until later when Frank reached his first zenith with Tommy Dorsey.

When Sinatra's recordings with Dorsey started to cause some commotion in the early forties, Columbia Records began digging out the sides Frank had made with James. At first, they released them as they originally were, without changing the label credits, but as the young crooner's career spiraled, they decided it would be advantageous to give him top billing. Manie Sacks, who was to play an important role in both performers' careers, asked Harry if it was all right to feature Siantra's name over his on reissue pressings. James (who was, and is, one of the most gracious people in the music business) said okay - especially if it could help Sinatra in any way.

"All Or Nothing At All" thus reissued, became a hit, as did a few others also re-released. Sinatra and James have remained close friends through the years, and when they appeared together at Caesar's Palace in 1968, Harry introduced him as "my original boy singer". Frank, in turn, thanked him for launching his career into the music world.

Recordings made from this period are:

HARRY JAMES AND HIS ORCHESTRA   July 13, 1939, New York
Arrangements by Andy Gibson

(Tpt) Harry James, Jack Schaeffer, Claude Bowen, Jack Palmer; (Tbn) Russell Brown, Truett Jones; (Sax) Dave Mathews, Claude Lackey, Bill Luther, Drew Page; (Piano) Jack Gardner; (Guitar) Bryan "Red" Kent; (Bass) Thurman Teague; (Drums) Ralph Hawkins.

B 25057	From The Bottom Of My Heart	Brunswick 8443, S3L - 42
B 25059	Melancholy Mood	Brunswick 8443, S3L - 42

Orchestra The Same   August 17, 1939, New York
Arrangements by Gibson

Orchestra The Same   August 17, 1939, New York
Arrangements by Gibson

B 25212	My Buddy	COL 35242, 37520, S3L - 42
B 25215	It's Funny To Everyone But Me	COL 35209, 36738, HL - 7159

Orchestra The Same   August 31, 1939, New York
Arrangements by Gibson

B 25285	Here Comes The Night	COL 35227, S3L - 42

B 25288	All Or Nothing At All	COL 35587, CL - 2630, CS 9430,
		C2L - 6, SM 3055

Orchestra The Same   September 14, 1939
Air checks from New York's World Fair

	All Or Nothing At All	Chairman - 6008
	To You	JA - 31
	From The Bottom Of My Heart	JA - 31

Orchestra The Same   October 13, 1939, Chicago
Arrangements by Gibson

WC 2798	On A Little Street In Singapore	COL 35261, 36700,
		HL 7159, HL 7255
WC 2799	Who Told You I Cared	COL 35261, P2M 5267

HARRY JAMES AND HIS ORCHESTRA   November 8, 1939, Hollywood
Arrangements by Gibson

(Tpt) Harry James, Jack Palmer, Claude Bowen, Jack Schaeffer; (Tbn) Truett
Jones, Dalton Rizzotto, Bruce Squires; (Alto Sax) Dave Mathews; (Tenor Sax)
Claude Lackey, Drew Page, Bill Luther; (Piano) Jack Gardner; (Guitar) Bryan
"Red" Kent; (Bass) Thurman Teague; (Drums) Michael Scrima.

LA 2046	Ciribiribin	COL 35316, 37141, C2L - 6
LA 2047	Every Day Of My Life	COL 35531, 36700

For the collector who is interested in the original couplings, we present them
in the order of their release.

FRANK SINATRA - HARRY JAMES - COUPLINGS

From The Bottom Of My Heart	F.S. B.R. 8443
REV. Melancholy Mood	F.S. BR. 8443

My Buddy	F.S. COL 35242
REV. Willow Weep For Me	INST. COL 35242

NOTE: On the re-issue of "My Buddy" it was coupled with "Prince Charming",
a Harry James Instrumental on COL 37520.

It's Funny To Everyone But Me	F.S. COL 35209
REV. Vol Vistu Gailey Star	J.P. COL 35209

NOTE: On the re-issue of "It's Funny To Everyone But Me" it was coupled with
"Don't Take You Love From Me" a vocal by Lynn Richards who recorded it with
James on August 4, 1941 on COL 36738.

Here Comes The Night	F.S. COL 35227
REV. Feet Draggin' Blues	INST. COL 35227

With Harry James in Atlantic City — 1939.

With Harry James — Radio Broadcast.

All Or Nothing At All   F.S. COL 35587
REV. Flash   INST. COL 35587

On A Little Street In Singapore   F.S. COL 35261
REV. Who Told You I Cared   F.S. COL 35261

NOTE: "On A Little Street In Singapore" was later re-issued and coupled with "Every Day Of My Life" on COL 36700.

Ciribiribin   F.S. COL 35316
REV. Avalon   INST. COL 35316

NOTE: "Ciribiribin" was later re-issued and coupled with "Sleepy Lagoon", a Harry James Instrumental on COL 37141.

Every Day Of My Life   F.S. COL 35531
REV. Cross Country Jump   INST. COL 35531

NOTE: "Every Day Of My Life" was later re-issued and coupled with "On A Little Street In Singapore" on COL 36700.

Chapter III

With The Sentimental Gentlemen   Tommy Dorsey
                                    February 1, 1940 - September 30, 1942

Frank Sinatra still had over a year to go on his contract with Harry James as he and the band headed East to Chicago, but events that were to change the 24-year-old singer's entire career began formulating that cold December of 1939. Jack Leonard, Tommy Dorsey's star vocalist and hit-maker, had a disagreement with the bandleader, which developed into an irreparable parting. Leonard rejoined the band for a few nights, but found himself sharing vocal chores with Allan DeWitt; and when the latter recorded three sides with the band in January, 1940, Leonard decided to make the split permanent. Dorsey, a perfectionist, was not completely satisfied with the replacement and heeded the advice of Jimmy Hilliard, CBS's musical supervisory in Chicago: to audition the "Skinny Kid" appearing with Harry James at the Panther Room. Bobby Burns, then manager of the Dorsey band, contacted Sinatra and asked him to call the trombonist. The next day at the Palmer House, Frank sang "Marie" with the band - and Tommy was pleased. So pleased, in fact, that he offered him $150 a week plus a three-year contract if he could get out of his present contract with James.

When Sinatra approached Harry James, the bandleader graciously ignored his contract and wished him luck and success. This was a real turning point in his ever-spiralling career because Dorsey was already an established hit with the public, and Sinatra's subsequent experience and exposure with the Dorsey band would prove priceless. He first appeared with the band at Rockford, Illinois, January 25, 1940, and tapes from a broadcast that night have him singing two of Jack Leonard's hits, "Marie" and "My Prayer." Jo Stafford, a member of the Pied Pipers vocal group who had also recently joined the band, was impressed with his smooth delivery. Frank, who was never officially a member of the Pipers, worked hard to achieve a perfect blend whenever they sang or recorded together. On February 1, 1940, Sinatra recorded "The Sky Fell Down" and "Too Romantic," his first sides with the Dorsey organization.

The next day, the band opened at the Lyric Theatre in Indianapolis and one can also hear on an air-check, among other things, a comedy routine built around the tune "South Of The Border." The band's next engagement was at New Jersey's famed Meadowbrook where on February 20, 1940, Sinatra performed a haunting "A Lover Is Blue", a beautiful song that went unrecorded.

From the Meadowbrook the band went to the Astor Roof in New York. Air-check listings indicate they travelled from city to city, cross-country and back, and Sinatra sang a number of additional songs that he and the band never recorded commercially. (These are of a special interest to collectors and one wishes that RCA would issue more of them instead of letting bootleggers take the initiative.)

On April 23, 1940, in New York City, Frank, the band and the Pied Pipers were in the studios once more. After two tunes were completed, they attempted to record the lovely "I'll Never Smile Again" written by Ruth Lowe after the death of her husband. Fred Stulce had penned a beautiful arrangement with Joe

First recording with Tommy Dorsey — 1941.

With Tommy Dorsey — 1941.

Bushkin on celeste, Tommy on trombone, and Frank and the Pipers softly blending their voices trying to mold it into the classic it has become. But after two attempts, they shelved it, feeling it was not completely right. Exactly one month later, it was done for the third time, and this is the take that was released. Many consider it to be the most musically satisfying side Frank ever recorded with Dorsey.

The Dorsey bandstand became a dream setting for the young vocalist. Besides featuring musicians of all-star calibre such as Bunny Berigan, Ziggy Elman, Joe Bushkin, Babe Russin, Buddy Rich and a host of others, it also had an incredible arranging staff. This was most important to Sinatra for seldom did one orchestra have the writing talent that Tommy employed. Paul Weston, Axel Stordahl, Deane Kincaide, Fred Stulce, Heinie Beau, and the outstanding Sy Oliver were with the band during Frank's stay and contributed heavily to the success of all involved. There have been many stories written about how Dorsey was beginning to resent the increasing popularity of his vocalist and also the mounting dissention from some of his sidemen, especially Buddy Rich. Buddy and Frank did have a little feud going that did erupt one night, but this soon passed over and in later years they were to become extremely close friends and Tomy was astute enough as a businessman to know he had a gem of an attraction.

Frank in turn admired Dorsey's talent. The way he breathed while playing trombone fascinated Sinatra so much that he worked hard at developing his own lung capacity so that he too could produce those long, easy, seemingly effortless musical phrases.

While some of the jazz-inclined musicians were occasionally perturbed at so many ballads being sung, Sinatra's dedication did gain their respect. He was very worried that one of the other popular band vocalists would branch out before him. He especially respected Bob Eberly who was singing with Jimmy Dorsey and feared that if Bob made the move first, it would hurt his chances considerably. He had become close to arranger Axel Stordahl, and on January 19, 1942, he and Axel recorded four tunes without Dorsey. The band appeared in a movie, "Las Vegas Nights," and in May of 1942, it again went to the studios to make "Ship Ahoy". But increasingly Frank had the urge to try it out on his own. Sinatra soon expressed his desire to leave the orchestra, but Dorsey held firm and reminded him that he still had time left on his contract. Not until Frank came up with some cash and a percentage of future earnings did Tommy reluctantly agree to give him his release. Although there is an air-check recording which has Sinatra speaking a farewell to the band on September 3, 1942, he did not officially leave the band for at least another month. Thus, another chapter came to a close for Sinatra. Dick Haymes, who had replaced him in the Harry James orchestra, became the new vocalist with the Dorsey Band.

Recordings from this period are:

Tommy Dorsey And His Orchestra   February 1, 1940, Chicago

(Tpt) Zeke Zarchey, Lee Castle, Jimmy Blake; (Tbn) Tommy Dorsey, Ward Silloway, Elmer Smithers, Dave Jacobs; (Saxes) Fred Stulce, Johnny Mince,

Tony Zimmers, Deane Kincaide; (Piano) Howard Smith; (Guitar) Carmen Mastren; (Bass) Gene Traxler; (Drums) Buddy Rich.

| BSO44680-1 | The Sky Fell Down | Vic 26518, Lpv 583,
SD 1000 |
| BSO44682-1 | Too Romantic | Vic 26500, CAL 650,
SM 3055, SD 1000 |

Tommy Dorsey And His Orchestra   February 26, 1940, New York

(Tpt) Ray Linn replaces Castle; (Tbn) Lowell Martin replaces Smithers; Dave Jacobs out; (Saxes) Stulce, Mince, Les Robinson, Paul Mason, Babe Russin; (Piano) Bob Kitses; (Guitar) Benney Heller; (Bass and Drums) Same.

BSO47706-1	Shake Down The Stars	Vic 26525, Lpm 6702 SD 1000
BSO47707-1	Moments In The Moonlight	Vic 26525, SD 1000
BSO47708-1	I'll Be Seeing You	Vic 26539, Lpm 1632 RD25K, SD 1000

Tommy Dorsey And His Orchestra   March 4, 1940, New York

(Tpt) Bunny Berigan added; (Tbn) George Arvs replaces Silloway; Jacob returns; (Saxes) Hymie Schertzer replaces Robinson; (Guitar) Al Viola replaces Heller; (Bass) Ray Leatherford replaces Traxler.

| BSO47746-1 | Say It | Vic 26535, Lpm 1569,
SD 1000 |
| BSO47747-1 | Polka Dots And Moonbeams | Vic 26539, Lpm 1569,
RDA-76, Lpv 583,
SD 1000 |

Tommy Dorsey And His Orchestra   March 12, 1940, New York

(Tpt) Bob Condelman replaces Zarchey; Linn out; (Tbn) Les Jenkins replaces Martin, Arvs out; (Saxes) Don Lodice replaces Russin; Schertzer out; (Bass) Sid Weiss replaces Leatherford.

| BSO48129-1 | The Fable Of The Rose | Vic 26555, SD 1000 |
| BSO48130-1 | This Is The Beginning Of
The End | Vic 26555, Lpm 1632,
PRM 182, SD 1000 |

Tommy Dorsey And His Orchestra   March 25, 1940, New York

(Tbn) George Arus; (Sax) Hymie Schertzer returns; (Guitar) Benny Heller replaces Viola.

| BSO48430-1 | Imagination | Not Released |
| BSO48430-1 | Yours Is My Heart Alone | Not Released |

Orchestra Same.		March 29, 1940, New York
BSO48430-1	Hear My Song Violetta	Vic 26616, Sm 3055, SD 1000
BSO48479-2	Hear My Song Violetta	
BSO48480-1	Fools Rush In	Vic 26593, Lpm 1632 RD25K, Lpv 583, SD1000
BSO48481-1	Devil May Care	Vic 26593, Lpm 1569

Tommy Dorsey And His Orchestra		April 10, 1940, New York

(Tpt) Berigan, Linn, Blake, John Dilliard; (Tbn) Dorsey, Jenkins, Arus, Martin; (Saxes) Schertzer, Stulce, Mason, Mince, Russin; (Piano) Joe Bushkin; (Guitar) Clark Yocum; (Bass) Sid Weiss; (Drums) Buddy Rich.

BSO48758-1	April Played The Fiddle	Vic 26606, SD 1000, AI-1001
BSO48766-1	I Haven't Time To Be A Millionaire	Vic 26606, SD 1000 AI-1001
BSO48431-3	Yours Is My Heart Alone	Vic 26616, RD4-92, SM3055, Lpv 583, SD 1000

Tommy Dorsey And His Orchestra		April 23, 1940, New York

(Sax) Don Lodice returns.

BSO48938-1	You're Lonely And I'm Lonely	Vic 26596, SD 1000

The Dorsey Sentimentalists		Same Date

(Tpt) Berigan; (Tbn) Dorsey; (Clt) Mince; (Sax) Stulce; (Piano) Bushkin; (Guitar) Yocum; (Bass) Weiss; (Drums) Rich.

BSO48939-1	East Of The Sun - (1)-(A)	BB-B 10726, Lpm 1433, Rd4-92, Vpm 6038, SD 1000
BSO48940-1	Head On My Pillow	BB-B 10726, Lpm 1643, Rd4-92, SD 1000
BSO48941-1	It's A Lovely Day Tomorrow	Vic 26596, SD 1000
BSO48942-1-2	I'll Never Smile Again	Not Released

(1) With Vocal Chorus by members of the band.
(2) Arranged by Sy Oliver.

Tommy Dorsey And His Orchestra		May 23, 1940, New York

(Tpt) Leon Debrow replaces Dilliard.

BSO48942-4	I'll Never Smile Again (1)-(A)	Vic 26628, 27521, PRM 261, Lpm 1229, RD4-92, Sm 3055, Vpm 6038
BSO50852-1	All This And Heaven Too	Vic 26652, SD 1000
BSO50853-1	Where Do You Keep Your Heart	Vic 26653, SD 1000

(1) With the Pied Pipers.
(A) Arranged by Fred Stulce.

Tommy Dorsey and His Sentimentalists		June 13, 1940, New York

(Tpt) Ray Linn, Jimmy Blake, Bunny Berigan, Clyde Hurley; (Tbn) Tommy Dorsey; (Clt) Johnny Mince; (Piano) Joe Bushkin; (Guitar) Clark Yocum; (Bass) Sid Weiss; (Drums) Buddy Rich; (Saxes) Schertzer, Lodice, Mason.

BSO51279-1	Whispering - (1)	BB-B 10771, Lpm 1632, RD4-92, Sm 3055, Vpm 6038, SD 1000

(1) With the Pied Pipers.

Tommy Dorsey And His Orchestra		June 27, 1940, New York

(Tpt) Ray Linn, Jimmy Blake, Bunny Berigan, Clyde Hurley; (Tbn) Lowell Martin, George Arvs, Les Jenkins, Tommy Dorsey; (Saxes) Fred Stulce, Johnny Mince, Hymie Schertzer, Paul Mason, Don Lodice; (Piano) Joe Bushkin; (Guitar) Clark Yocum; (Bass) Sid Weiss; (Drums) Buddy Rich.

BSO51579-1	Trade Winds	Vic 26666, SD 1000
BSO51581-1	The One I Love - (1)-(A)	Vic 26660, Lpm 1433, RD4-92, Vpm SD 1000

(1) With the Pied Pipers.
(A) Arranged by Sy Oliver.

Tommy Dorsey And His Orchestra		July 17, 1940, New York

(Tpt) Bunny Berigan out.

BSO51874-1	The Call Of The Canyon	Vic 26678, Cal 650, SD 1000
BSO51875-1	Love Lies	Vic 26678, SD 1000
BSO51876-1	I Could Make You Care	Vic 26717, Lpm 1569, Lpv 583, SD 1000

BSO51877-1	The World Is In My Arms	Vic 26717, SD 1000

Tommy Dorsey And His Orchestra   August 29, 1940, New York

(Tpt) Ziggy Elman added; (Sax) Heinie Beau for Mason.

BSO55543-1	Our Love Affair	Vic 26736, Lpm 1569, Vpm 6038, SD 1000
BSO55563-1	Looking For Yesterday	Vic 26738, SD 1000
BSO55564-1	Tell Me At Midnight	Vic 26747, Lpm 1632, SD 1000
BSO55565-1	We Three - (A)	Vic 26747, Lpm 1632, SD 1000

(A) Arranged by Sy Oliver.

Tommy Dorsey And His Orchestra   September 9, 1940, New York

(Tpt) Charles "Chuck" Peterson replaces Blake.

BSO55690-1	Whey You Awake	Vic 26764, SD 1000
BSO55961-1	Anything	Vic 27208, Lpm 1569, SD 1000

Tommy Dorsey And His Orchestra   September 17, 1940, New York

(Tpt) Clyde Hurley out.

BSO56131-1	Shadows On The Sand	Vic 26761, SD 1000
BSO56133-2	You're Breaking My Heart All Over Again	Vic 26761, SD 1000
BSO56133-1	I'd Know You Anywhere	Vic 26770, CAL 800, SD 1000

Orchestra Same.   October, 16, 1940, Hollywood

PBSO55110-1	Do You Know Why?	Vic 26798, CAL 800, SD 1000

The next two items are air checks and are listed in this section because they were released by RCA.

Orchestra Same.   October 17, 1940, Hollywood

Marie - (A)

(A) Arranged by Fred Stulce.

Orchestra Same.		November 7, 1940, Hollywood
	Yearning	Vic Lpm 6003
Orchestra Same.		November 11, 1940, Hollywood
PBSO55157-2	Not So Long Ago	Vic 27219, SD 1000
PBSO55157-1	Not So Long Ago	
PBSO55158-1	Stardust - (1)-(A)	Vic 27233, 27520, Lpm 1229, RD4-92, Vpm 6038, SD 1000

(1) With the Pied Pipers.
(A) Arranged by Paul Weston.

Air Check - Orchestra Same.		November 28, 1940, Hollywood
	How Am I To Know	Vic Lpm 6003
Tommy Dorsey And His Orchestra		January 6, 1941, New York

(Tpt) Ziggy Elman, Bob Alexy, Lee Castle, Jimmy Blake; (Tbn) Tommy Dorsey, Les Jenkins, George Arvs, Dave Jacobs; (Saxes) Fred Stulce, Johnny Mince, Paul Mason, Bill Shine, Don Lodice; (Piano) Joe Bushkin; (Guitar) Clark Yocum; (Bass) Sid Weiss; (Drums) Buddy Rich.

BSO58760-1	Oh Look At Me Now - (1)-(A)	Vic 27274, Lpm 1569, SM 3055, SD 1000
BSO58761-1	You Might Have Belonged To Another - (1)	Vic 27274, SD 1000

(1) With Connie Haines and the Pied Pipers.
(A) Arranged by Sy Oliver.

Tommy Dorsey And His Orchestra		January 15, 1941, New York

(Tpt) Ray Linn, Chuck Peterson replace Alexy and Castle; (Tbn) Lowell Martin replaces Jacobs; (Saxes) Heinie Beau replaces Shine.

BSO58877-1	You Lucky People, You - (A)	Vic 27350, SD 1000
BSO58879-1	It's Always You	Vic 27345, Lpv 583, SD 1000

(A) Arranged by Sy Oliver

Orchestra Same.		January 20, 1941, New York
BSO60346-1	I Tried	Vic 27317, Lpv 583, SD 1000, AI-1001
BSO60347-1	Dolores - (1)-(A)	Vic 27317, RD25K, RD4-92, SD 1000

CSO60349-2	Without A Song - (A)	Vic 36396, PRM182, RD4-92, Lpv 583, SD 1000

(1) With the Pied Pipers.
(A) Arranged by Sy Oliver.

Orchestra Same.   February 7, 1941, New York

BSO60626-1	Do I Worry? - (1)	Vic 27338, RD-76, SD 1000
BSO60628-1	Everything Happens To Me	Vic 27359, Lpm 1432, PRM 182, Lpv 583, SD 1000

(1) With the Pied Pipers.

Orchestra Same.   February 17, 1941, New York

BSO60902-1	Let's Get Away From It All, Part II - (1)-(A)	Vic 27377, Lpm 6702, RDA-76, SD 1000

(1) With Connie Haines, Joe Stafford and the Pied Pipers. Although sometimes billed as a member of the Pied Pipers, Sinatra is featured as a solo only on Part II.

(A) Arranged by Sy Oliver.

Tommy Dorsey And His Orchestra   May 28, 1941, New York

(Tpt) Shorty Sherock replaces Linn; (Tbn) Walter Mercurio replaces Jenkins; (Saxes) Hymie Schertzer, Manny Gershman replace Mince and Beau; (Bass) Jack Kelleher replaces Weiss.

BSO65913-1	I Never Let A Day Pass By	Vic 27461, SD 1000
BSO65915-1	Love Me As I Am	Vic 27483, SD 1000
BSO65917-1	This Love Of Mine - (A)	Vic 27508, Lpm 1569, RD4-92, Lpv 583, Vpm, SD 1000

(A) Arranged by Axel Stordahl.

Tommy Dorsey And His Orchestra   June 27, 1941, New York

(Tbn) Dave Jacobs for Mercurio; (Sax) Bruce Snyder for Hymie Schertzer; (Bass) Sid Weiss returns in place of Kelleher.

BSO66430-1	I Guess I'll Have To Dream The Rest - (1)-(B)	Vic 27525, lpm 1569, RD4-92, SD 1000
BSO66431-1	You And I - (A)	Vic27532, RD25K, SD 1000

—18—

| BSO66432-2 | Neiani - (1)-(B) | Vic 27508, SD 1000, AI-1001 |
| BSO66432-2 | Free For All - (1) | Vic 27532, SD 1000 |

(1) With the Pied Pipers.
(A) Arranged by Sy Oliver.
(B) Arranged by Axel Stordahl.

Tommy Dorsey And His Orchestra   July 15, 1941, New York

(Tpt) Al Stearns for Sherock.

| BSO66923-1 | Blue Skies - (1)-(A) | Vic 27566, Lpm 1433, SM 3055, Vpm SD 1000 |

(1) With Vocal Chorus by members of the band.
(A) Arranged by Sy Oliver.

Tommy Dorsey And His Orchestra   August 19, 1941, New York

(Tbn) Walter Mercurio for Martin.

BSO67651-1	Two In Love	Vic 27611, SD 1000, AI-1001
BSO67652-1	Violets For Your Furs - (A)	Lpm 1433, Lpv 583
BSO67653-1	The Sunshine Of Your Smile	Not Released.
BSO67654-1	Pale Moon	Vic27591, SD 1000

(A) Arrangement by Heinie Beau.

Tommy Dorsey And His Orchestra   September 18, 1941, New York

(Tbn) Johnny Skiles for Mercurio.

BSO67913-1	I Think Of You	Vic 27701, SD 1000
BSO67914-1	How Do You Do Without Me	Vic 27710, Lpm 1569, SD 1000
BSO67915-1	A Sinner Kissed An Angel	Vic 27611, CAL 650, SM 3055, Lpv 538, SD 1000

Orchestra Same.   September 26, 1941, New York

| BSO67652-3 | Violets For Your Furs | Vic 27690, SD 1000; |
| BSO67653-2 | The Sunshine Of Your Smile | Vic 27638, SD 1000 |

Tommy Dorsey And His Orchestra   December 22, 1941, Hollywood

(Bass) George Boehm for Weiss.

| PBSO61991-1 | How About You? | Vic 27749, Lpm 1569, RD4-92, Lpv 583, SD 1000 |

NOTE: See Section "Four For Bluebird" for next chronological listings at this point.

Orchestra Same.   February 19, 1942, Hollywood

PBSO72107-1	Snootie Little Cutie - (1)-(A)	Vic27876, CAL 800, RD4-92, SD 1000
PBSO72108-1	Poor You - (B)	Vic 27849, SD 1000
PBSO72109-1	I'll Take Tallulah - (2)-(A)	Vic 27869, SM3055, SD 1000
PBSO72110-1	The Last Call For Love - (3)-(B)	Vic 27840, SD 1000

(1) With Connie Haines and the Pied Pipers.
(2) With Jo Stafford, Tommy Dorsey and the Pied Pipers.
(3) With the Pied Pipers.
(A) Arranged by Sy Oliver.
(B) Arranged by Axel Stordahl.

Tommy Dorsey And His Orchestra   March 19, 1942, Hollywood

(Tpt) Mannie Klein for Stearns; (Piano) Milt Raskin for Bushkin; (Bass) Phil Stevens for Boehm.

| PBSO72171-1 | Somewhere A Voice Is Calling (A) | Vic 27887, RD4-92, SM3055, SD 1000 |

(A) Arranged by Sy Oliver.

Air Check - Orchestra Same.   May 13, 1942, New York

| | My Melancholy Baby | Vic Lpm 6003 |

Tommy Dorsey And His Orchestra   May 18, 1942, New York

(Tpt) Ziggy Elman, Chuck Peterson, Jimmy Blake, Jimmy Zito; (Tbn) Tommy Dorsey, George Arvs, Jimmy Skiles, Dave Jacobs; (Saxes) Fred Stulce, Harry Schuchman, Heinie Beau, Bruce Snyder, Don Lodice; (Strings) Leonard Atkins, Seymour Miroff, William Ehrenkranz, Leonard Posner, Paul Pollakin, Sam Ross, Bernard Tinterow, Harold Bemke; (Harp) Ruth Hill; (Piano) Milt Raskin; (Guitar) Clark Yocum; (Bass) Phil Stevens; (Drums) Buddy Rich.

| BSO75204-1 | Just As Though You Were Here - (1)-(A) | Vic 27903, CAL 800, SD 1000 |
| BSO75205-1 | Street Of Dreams - (1)-(A) | Vic 27903, Lpm 1433, RD4-92, RDA-76, Vpm 6038, SD 1000 |

(1) With the Pied Pipers.
(A) Arranged by Axel Stordahl.

Orchestra Same.   June 9, 1942, New York

BSO75264-1   Take Me - (A)   Vic 27923, SD 1000

BSO75265-1   Be Careful, It's My Heart - (A)   Vic 27923, CAL 650,
                                                       Lpv 583, SD 1000

              (A) Arranged by Axel Stordahl.

Orchestra Same.   June 17, 1942, New York

BSO75282-1   In The Blue Of Evening - (A)   Vic 27947, Lpm 6702,
                                                       Lpv 583, SD 1000

BSO75285-1   Dig Down Deep - (1)   Vic 20-1539, Lpm 1632,
                                                       SD 1000

              (1) With the Pied Pipers.
              (A) Arranged by Axel Stordahl.

Orchestra Same.   July 1, 1942, New York

BSO75400-1   There Are Such Things - (1)-(A)   Vic 27974, Lpm 1569,
                                                       PRM182, RD4-92,
                                                       SM3055, Vpm 6038,
                                                       PRS383, SD 1000

BSO75402-1   Daybreak - (A)   Vic 27974, SD 1000,
                                                       AI-1001

BSO75403-1   It Started All Over Again - (1)-(A)Vic 20-1522, Lpm 1632,
                                                       SD 1000

              (1) With the Pied Pipers.
              (A) Arranged by Axel Stordahl.

Tommy Dorsey And His Orchestra   July 2, 1942, New York

(Sax) Danny Vanelli added.

BSO75407-1   Light A Candle In The Chapel-(A)Vic 27941, SD 1000

              (A) Arranged by Axel Stordahl.

Air Check - Orchestra Same.   July 30, 1942, New York

              I'll Take Tallulah   Vic Lpm 6003

Air Check - Orchestra SAme.   September 3, 1942, New York

              The Song Is you - (A)   Vic Lpm 6003

Sinatra's farewell speech to the Dorsey band and an introduction of his replacement in the band - Dick Haymes.

(A) Arranged by Axel Stordahl.

Air Check - Orchestra assumed the same as last   Late 1942, Hollywood

I've Got A Restless Spell   CX 186

Is There A Chance For Me   CX 186

For a listing of the couplings as they were released by RCA and additional information pertaining to the reverse sides of these couplings, we present the following.

Frank Sinatra - Tommy Dorsey Couplings

The Sky Fell Down	F.S.	VIC 26518
REV. What Can I Say After		
I've Said I'm Sorry	P.P.	VIC 26518
Too Romantic	F.S.	VIC 26500
REV. Sweet Potato Piper	P.P.	VIC 26500
Shake Down Stars	F.S.	VIC 26525
REV. Moments In The Moonlight	F.S.	VIC 26525
I'll Be Seeing You	F.S.	VIC 26539
REV. Polka Dots and Moonbeams	F.S.	VIC26539
Say It	F.S.	VIC 26535
REV. My My	P.P.	VIC 26535
The Fable Of The Rose	F.S.	VIC 26555
REV. This Is The Beginning		
Of The End	F.S.	VIC 26555
Imagination	F.S.	VIC 26581
REV. Charming Little Faker	P.P.	VIC 26581
Yours Is My Heart Alone	F.S.	VIC 26616
REV. Hear My Song Violetta	F.S.	VIC 26616
Fools Rush In	F.S.	VIC 26593
REV. I Haven't Time To Be		
A Millionaire	F.S.	VIC 26606
You're Lonely and I'm Lonely	F.S.	VIC 26596
REV. It's A Lovely Day	F.S.	VIC 26596
Tomorrow		
East Of The Sun	F.S. & Chorus	Bb-B 10726
REV. Head On my Pillow	F.S.	Bb-B 10726
I'll Never Smile Again	F.S. & P.P.	VIC 26628
REV. Marcheta	T.D. & Inst. VIC 26628	
All This And Heaven Too	F.S.	VIC 26653

REV. Where Do You Keep Your Heart	F.S.	VIC 26653
Whispering	F.S. & P.P.	Bb-B 10771
REV. Funny Little Pedro	P.P.	Bb-B 10771

(NOTE: "Whispering" was also re-issued and coupled with a Tommy Dorsey Instrumental, "Not So Quite Please," on VIC 20-1579.)

Trade Winds	F.S.	VIC26666
REV. Only Forever	A.S.	VIC 26666
The One I Love	F.S. & P.P.	VIC 26660
REV. And So Do I	C.H.	VIC26660
The Call Of The Canyon	F.S.	VIC 26678
REV. Love Lies	F.S.	VIC 26678
I Could Make You Care	F.S.	VIC 26717
REV. The World Is In My Arms	F.S.	VIC 26717
Our Love Affair	F.S.	VIC 26736
REV. That's For Me	C.H.	VIC 26736
Looking For Yesterday	F.S.	VIC 26738
REV. I Wouldn't Take A Million	C.H.	VIC 26738
Tell Me At Midnight	F.S.	VIC 26747
REV. We Three	F.S.	VIC 26747
When You Awake	F.S.	VIC 26764
REV. Two Dreams Met	C.H.	VIC 26764
Anything	F.S.	VIC 27208
REV. Another One Of Them Things	T.D. INST. VIC 27208	
Shadows On The Sand	F.S.	VIC 26761
REV. You're Breaking My Heart All Over Again	F.S.	VIC 26761
I'd Know You Anywhere	F.S.	VIC 26770
REV. You've Got Me This Way	P.P.	VIC 26770
Do You Know Why?	F.S.	VIC 26798
REV. Isn't That Just Like Love	P.P.	VIC 26798
Not So Long Ago	F.S.	VIC 27219
REV. You Say The Sweetest Things	C.H. & P.P.	VIC 27219
Stardust	F.S. & P.P.	VIC 27233
REV. Swanee River	T.D. INST.	VIC 27233
Oh Look At Me Now	F.S., C.H. & P.P.	VIC 27274
REV. You Might Have Belonged To Another	F.S., C.H. & P.P.	VIC 27274

(NOTE: "Oh Look At Me Now" was later re-issued and coupled with "Little Man With A Candy Cigar" sung by Jo Stafford on VIC 20-1578.)

You Lucky People, You	F.S.	VIC 27350
REV. You're Dangerous	C.H.	VIC 27350

It's Always You	F.S.	VIC 27345
REV. Birds Of A Feather	C.H. & Chorus	VIC 27345

(NOTE: "It's Always You" was later re-issued and coupled with "In The Blue Of Evening" on VIC 20-1530.)

I Tried	F.S.	VIC 27317
REV. Dolores	F.S. & P.P.	VIC 27317
Without A Song (12 inch)	F.S.	VIC 36396
REV. Deep River	T.D. INST.	VIC 36396
Do I Worry	F.S. & P.P.	VIC 27338
REV. Little Man With A Candy Cigar	J.S.	VIC 27338
Everything Happens To Me	F.S.	VIC 27359
REV. Whatcha Know Joe	P.P. & J.S.	VIC 27359
Let's Get Away From It All - 1	J.S. & P.P.	VIC 27377
REV. Let's Get Away From It All - 2	F.S., C.H., J.S. & P.P.	VIC 27377
I Never Let A Day Pass By	F.S.	VIC 27461
REV. Kiss The Boys Goodbye	C.H.	VIC 27461
Love Me As I Am	F.S.	VIC 27483
REV. Nine Old Men	P.P.	VIC 27483
This Love Of Mine	F.S.	VIC 27508
REV. Neiani	F.S. & P.P.	VIC 27508
I Guess I'll Have To Dream The Rest	F.S. & P.P.	VIC 27526
REV. Loose Lid Special	T.D. INST.	VIC 27526
You And I	F.S.	VIC 27532
REV. Free For All	F.S. & P.P.	VIC 27532
Blue Skies	F.S. & Chorus	VIC 27566
REV. Backstage At The Ballet	T.D. INST.	VIC 27566
A Sinner Kissed An Angel	F.S.	VIC 27611
REV. Two In Love	F.S.	VIC 27611
Violets For Your Furs	F.S.	VIC 27690
REV. Somebody Loves Me	P.P.	VIC 27690
The Sunshine Of Your Smile	F.S.	VIC 27638
REV. Embraceable You	J.S. & P.P.	VIC 27638
Pale Moon	F.S.	VIC 27591
REV. Hallelujah	T.D. INST.	VIC 27591
I Think Of You	F.S.	VIC 27701
REV. Who Can I Turn To?	J.S.	VIC 27701
How Do You Do Without Me?	F.S.	VIC 27710
REV. It Isn't A Dream Anymore	J.S.	VIC 27710
How About You	F.S.	VIC 27749
REV. Winter Weather	P.P.	VIC 27749
Poor You	F.S.	VIC 27849
REV. The Last Call For Love	F.S. & P.P.	VIC 27849

With Tommy Dorsey, The Pied Pipers and Jo Stafford.

Publicity shot — 1942.

I'll Take Tallulah	F.S., C.H., T.D. & P.P.	VIC 27869
REV. Not So Quite Please	T.D. INST.	VIC 27869
Snootie Little Cutie	F.S., C.H. & P.P.	VIC 27876
REV. Moonlight On The Ganges	T.D. INST.	VIC 27876

(NOTE: "Snootie Little Cutie" also re-issued and coupled with "Tom Foolery" on VIC 20-2116.)

Somewhere A Voice Is Calling	F.S.	VIC 27887
REV. Well Get It	T.D. INST.	VIC 27887
Just As Though You Were Here	F.S. & P.P.	VIC 27903
REV. Street Of Dreams	F.S. & P.P.	VIC 27903
Take Me	F.S.	VIC 27923
REV. Be Careful, It's My Heart	F.S.	VIC 27923
In The Blue Of Evening	F.S.	VIC 27947
REV. A Boy In Khaki, A Girl In Lace	J.S.	VIC 27947
Dig Down Deep	F.S. & P.P.	VIC 27974
REV. Daybreak	F.S.	VIC 27974
It Started All Over Again	F.S. & P.P.	VIC 20-1522
REV. Mandy Make Up Your Mind	T.D. INST.	VIC 20-1522
Light A Candle In The Chapel	F.S.	VIC 27941
REV. He's My Guy	J.S.	VIC 27941

With Dorsey, Buddy Rich, Ziggy Elman, Jo Stafford and The Pied Pipers — 1942.

— 26 —

Chapter IV

Four For Bluebird   **Axel Stordahl**

Frank Sinatra made four sides for Bluebird, a subsidiary of R.C.A. Victor, while still under contract with Tommy Dorsey. Tommy was very angry at the time. Frank wanted to see how he would sound outside of the context of the Dorsey band with a different setting and tailor made arrangements.

He also wanted to know if he could sell recordings on his own without the Dorsey name on the label. Both questions were answered and when he got the first "dub" pressings, he played them over and over by himself and with friends and most agreed that he was polished enough to venture out as a single. The sales figures for the two recordings were heartening even though they were at a cheaper price than the parent label. The four sides do show a different Sinatra for here he is backed by a small string section augmented with several woodwinds and tempered rhythm. The over-all result differs greatly from the familiar surroundings of a big band and this new approach is highly personal — one that appealed just as much to women at that time as it still does today.

It is as though he were singing to an individual girl and each one listening was dead certain that she alone was that one girl.

THE FOUR SIDES ARE LISTED BELOW

Frank Sinatra with Axel Stordahl as Arranger and Conductor
Jaunary 12, 1942, Hollywood

(Violins) Harry Bluestone, Mischa Russell, Nick Pisani, Sami Freed Jr.; (Cello) Cy Bernard; (Oboe) Charles Strickfaden; (Harp) Ann Mason; (Bass) Henry Stern; (Guitar) Clark Yocum; (Piano) Skitch Henderson; (Saxes) Manny Gershman, Fred Stulce, Don Lo Gindice, Henry Beau.

PBSO 72042-1	The Night We Called It A Day	Bb-B11463, LPM 1623, EPA 5147
PBSO 72043-1	The Lamplighter's Serenade	Bb-B11515, EPA 5147, LPM 1623
PBSO 72044-1	The Song Is You	Bb-B11515, EPA 5147, LPM 1623
PBSO 72045-1	Night And Day	Bb-B11463, EPA 5147, LPM 1623, PR 112, LOP 1509, ANLI-1586

A and R man was Harry Meyerson and the recording contractor was former band leader - Louis Bring. The original work sheet lists Axel Stordahl's real name - ODD Stordahl.

First recording for Bluebird — 1942.

"Frankie" among his fans.

Chapter V

FRANK SINATRA - APPEARANCES AT PARAMOUNT THEATRE

1. **March 13, 1940 - Tommy Dorsey and Orchestra**
   4 Weeks

   My Prayer
   Careless
   All The Things You Are
   South Of The Border
   Marie
   Trombone Man Is The Best Man In The Band

2. **December 18, 1940 - Tommy Dorsey and Orchestra**
   4 Weeks - "Love Thy Neighbor"

   Begin The Beguine
   I'll Never Smile Again - (Pied Pipers)
   South Of The Border

3. **August 27, 1941 - Tommy Dorsey and Orchestra**
   3 Weeks - "Alohma Of The South Seas"

   Without A Song
   This Love Of Mine
   Lets Get Away From It All - (Pied Pipers)
   I Guess I'll Have To Dream The Rest - (Pied Pipers)
   I'll Never Smile Again - (Pied Pipers)
   South Of The Border
   Blue Skies
   Free For All

4. **April 1, 1942 - Tommy Dorsey and Orchestra**
   4 Weeks - "My Favorite Blond"

   Night and Day
   Ol' Man River
   The One I Love - (Pied Pipers)
   South Of The Border
   I'll Never Smile Again - (Pied Pipers)
   I'll Take Tallulah - (P.P., T.D., C.H., J.S.)

   First Solo Appearance

5. **December 30, 1942 - Benny Goodman and Orchestra**
   4 Weeks - "Star Spangled Rhythm"

   Where Or When
   There Are Such Things
   When The Lights Go On Again

On stage at the Paramount — 1944.

Rio Bomba Night Club with friends from Hoboken — (Left to right: Dominic Caporino, Augie Delano, Fred Tamburro, F.S., Mrs. Tamburro, Mrs. Delano).

Paramount Theater — 1944.

Sinatra's last appearance at the Paramount — 1956.

She's Funny That Way
For Me and My Gal
I Had The Craziest Dream

6. **February 2, 1943 - Johnny Long and Orchestra**
   4 Weeks

   Where Or When
   You'd Be So Nice To Come Home To
   She's Funny That Way
   For Me and My Gal
   I Had The Craziest Dream
   There Are Such Things

7. **May 26, 1943 - Gracie Barrie and Orchestra**
   4 Weeks - "Five Graves To Cairo"

   Dancing In The Dark
   Wrong (Can It Be Wrong To Love)
   I Only Have Eyes For You
   Lets Get Lost
   All Or Nothing At All
   That Old Black Magic
   Night And Day

8. **October 11, 1944 - Raymond Paige and Orchestra**
   3 Weeks - "Our Hearts Were Young And Gay"

9. **November 28, 1945 - Jan Savitt and Orchestra**
   1 Week - "Hold That Blonde"

10. **May 5, 1951 - Orchestra Conducted By Joe Bushkin**
    1 Week

11. **July 24, 1956 - The Orchestra Of Tommy and Jimmy Dorsey**
    2 Weeks - "Johnny Concho"

SONG INDEX
FOR

CHAPTER I   IN THE BEGINNING

CHAPTER II   HARRY JAMES

CHAPTER III   TOMMY DORSEY

CHAPTER IV   BLUEBIRD RECORDINGS

CHAPTER V   PARAMOUNT APPEARANCES

All or Nothing At All (Jack Lawrence - Arthur Altman) August 31, 1939 Harry James, September 14, 1939, Harry James, May 26, 1943 Paramount.

All The Things You Are (Jerome Kern - Oscar Hammerstein II) March 13, 1940 (Paramount)

All This And Heaven Too (Eddie De Lange - Jimmy Van Heusen) May 3, 1940 Tommy Dorsey

Anything (Phil Napolean - Frank Signorelli - Roy Jacobs) September 9, 1940 Tommy Dorsey

April Played The Fiddle (Johnny Burke - James Monaco) April 10, 1940 Tommy Dorsey

Be Careful Its My Heart (Irving Berlin) June 9, 1942 Tommy Dorsey

Begin The Beguine (Cole Porter) December 18, 1940 Paramount

Blue Skies (Irving Berlin) July 15, 1941 Tommy Dorsey, August 27, 1941 Paramount

Call Of The Canyon, The - (Billy Hill) July 17, 1940 Tommy Dorsey

Careless (Lew Quadling - Eddy Howard - Dick Jurgens) March 13, 1940

Ciribiribin (Harry James - Jack Lawrence - Pestalozza) November 8, 1939 Harry James

Dancing In The Dark (Arthur Schwartz - Howard Dietz) May 26, 1943 Paramount

Daybreak (Ferde Grofe - Harold Adamson) July 1, 1942 Tommy Dorsey

Devil May Care (Johnny Burke - Harry Warren) March 29, 1940 Tommy Dorsey

Dig Down Deep (Hirsch - Marks - Sano Marco) June 17, 1942 Tommy Dorsey

Dolores (Frank Loesser - Louis Alter) January 20, 1941 Tommy Dorsey

Do I Worry (Stanley Cowan - Bobby Worth) February 7, 1941 Tommy Dorsey

Do You Know Why (Johnny Burke - Jimmy Van Heusen) September 17, 1940 Tommy Dorsey

East Of The Sun (Brooks Bowman) April 23, 1940 Tommy Dorsey

Everyday Of My Life (Harry James - Morty Berk - Billy Hays) November 8, 1939

Everything Happens To Me (Matt Dennis - Tom Adair) February 7, 1941 Tommy Dorsey

Fable Of The Rose, The (Bickley Reichner - Josef Myrow) March 12, 1940 Tommy Dorsey

Fools Rush In (Johnny Mercer - Rube Bloom) March 29, 1940 Tommy Dorsey

For Me And My Gal (Edgar Leslie - Ray Goetz - George Meyer) December 30, 1942, February 2, 1943 both Paramount

Free For All (Matt Dennis - Tom Adair) May 21, 1941, June 27, 1941 Both Tommy Dorsey, August 27, 1941 Paramount

From The Bottom Of My Heart (Harry James - Billy Hays - Albert Gibson - Morty Berk) July 13, 1939 Harry James, August 1939 Harry James

Head On My Pillow (Bissell Palmer - Fred Norman) April 23, 1940 Tommy Dorsey

Hear My Song Violetta (Buddy Bernier - Bob Emmerich - Othmar Klase - Rudolph Lukesch) March 29, 1940 Tommy Dorsey

Here Comes The Night (Loesser - Edelstein - Hohengarten) April 31, 1939 Harry James

How About You (Arthur Freed - Burton Lane) September 18, 1941 Tommy Dorsey

How Am I To Know (Dorothy Parker - Jack King) November 28, 1940 Tommy Dorsey

How Do You Do Without Me (Joe Bushkin - John De Vries) September 18, 1941 Tommy Dorsey

I Could Make You Care (Sammy Cahn - Saul Chaplin) July 17, 1940 Tommy Dorsey

I'd Know You Anywhere (Johnny Mercer - Jimmy McHugh) September 17, 1940 Tommy Dorsey

I Guess I'll Have To Dream The Rest (Mickey Stoner - Martin Block - Harld Green) June 27, 1941 Tommy Dorsey, August 27, 1941 Paramount

I Had The Craziest Dream (Mack Gordon - Harry Warren) December 30, 1942, February 2, 1943 both Paramount

I Haven't Time To Be A Millionaire (Johnny Burke - James Monaco April 10, 1940 Tommy Dorsey

I'll Be Seeing You (Sammy Fain - Irving Kahal) February 26, 1940 Tommy Dorsey

I'll Never Let A Day Pass By (Frank Loesser - Victor Schertzinger) May 28, 1941 Tommy Dorsey

I'll Never Smile Again (Ruth Lowe) April 23, 1940, May 23, 1940 both Tommy Dorsey, December 18, 1940, August 27, 1941, April 1, 1942 all Paramount

I'll Take Tallulah (Yip Harburg - Burton Lane) February 19, 1942, July 30, 1942 Both Tommy Dorsey, April 1, 1942 Paramount.

Imagination (Johnny Burke - Jimmy Van Heusen) March 25, 1940, April 10, 1940 both Tommy Dorsey

In The Blue Of Evening (Tomy Adair - Alfred D'Artega) June 17, 1942 Tommy Dorsey

I Only Have Eyes For You (Aldubin - Harry Warren) May 26, 1943 Paramount

Is There A Chance For Me Late 1942 Tommy Dorsey

I Think Of You (Jack Elliot - Don Macotte) September 18, 1941 Tommy Dorsey

I Tried (Nutter - Hand - Dennis) January 20, 1941 Tommy Dorsey

It's A Lovely Day Tomorrow (Irving Berlin) April 23, 1940 Tommy Dorsey

It's Always You (Johnny Burke - Jimmy Van Heusen) January 15, 1941 Tommy Dorsey

It's Funny To Everyone But Me (Jack Lawrence) April 17, 1939 Harry James

It Started All Over Again (Carl Fischer - Bill Carey) July 1, 1942 Tommy Dorsey

I've Got A Restless Spell Late 1942 Tommy Dorsey

Just As Though You Were Here (Eddie De Lange - John Brooks) May 18, 1942 Tommy Dorsey

Lamplighters Serenade, The (Paul Webster - Hoagy Carmichael) January 19, 1942 Bluebird

Last Call For Love, The (Yip Harburg - Margery Cummings - Burton Lane) February 19, 1942 Tommy Dorsey

Lets Get Away From It All (Matt Dennis - Tom Adair) February 17, 1941, Tommy Dorsey, August 27, 1941 Paramount

Let's Get Lost (Frank Loesser - Jimmy McHugh) May 26, 1943 Paramount

Light A Candle In The Chapel (Harry Pease - Ed Nelson - Robert Leonard) July 2, 1942 Tommy Dorsey

Looking For Yesterday (Eddie DeLange - Jimmy Van Heusen) August 29, 1940 Tommy Dorsey

Love Lies (Carl Sigman - Ralph Freed - Joseph Meyer) July 17, 1940 Tommy Dorsey

Love Me As I Am (Frank Loesser - Louis Alter) May 28, 1941 Tommy Dorsey

Marie (Irving Berlin) March 13, 1940 Paramount, October 17, 1940 Tommy Dorsey

Melancholy Mood (Vick Knight - Walter Schuman) July 13, 1939 Harry James

Moments In The Moonlight (Richard Himber - Irving Gordon - Al Kaufman) February 26, 1940 Tommy Dorsey

My Buddy (Walter Donaldson) August 17, 1939 Harry James

My Melancholy Baby (George Norton - Ernie Burnett) May 3, 1941 Tommy Dorsey

My Prayer (Jimmy Kennedy - George Boulanger) March 13, 1940 Paramount

Neiani (Axel Stordahl - Sy Oliver) June 27, 1941 Tommy Dorsey

Night And Day (Cole Porter) January 19, 1942 Bluebird, April 1, 1942, May 26, 1942 both Paramount

Night We Called It A Day, The (Matt Dennis - Tom Adair) January 19, 1942 Bluebird

Not So Long Ago (Bickley Reichner - Clay Boland) November 11, 1940 Tommy Dorsey

Oh Look At Me Now (Joe Bushkin - John Devries) January 6, 1941 Tommy Dorsey

Ol' Man River (Jerome Kern - Oscar Hammerstein II) April 1, 1942 Paramount

On A Little Street In Singapore (Peter De Rose - Billy Hill) October 13, 1939 Harry James

One I Love, The (Gus Kahn - Isham Jones) June 27, 1940 Tommy Dorsey, April 1, 1942 Paramount

Our Love (Larry Clinton - Buddy Bernier - Bob Emmerich) 1938 Private recording in the beginning

Our Love Affair (Arthur Freed - Roger Edens) August 29, 1940 Tommy Dorsey –

Pale Moon (Jesse Glick - Frederick Logan) August 19, 1941 Tommy Dorsey

Polka Dots and Moonbeams (Johnny Burke - Jimmy Van Heusen) March 4, 1940 Tommy Dorsey

Poor You (Yip Harburg - Burton Lane) February 19, 1942 Tommy Dorsey

Say It (Frank Loesser - Jimmy Mc Hugh) March 4, 1940 Tommy Dorsey

Shadows On The Sand (Stanley Adams - Cross) September 17, 1940 Tommy Dorsey

Shake Down The Stars (Eddie De Lange - Jimmy Van Heusen) February 26, 1940 Tommy Dorsey

She's Funny That Way (Neil Moret - Richard Whiting) December 30, 1942, February 2, 1943 both Paramount

Shine (Cecil Mack - Lew Brown - Ford Dabney) September 8, 1935 In The Beginning

Sinner Kissed An Angel, A (Mack David - Ray Joseph) September 18, 1941 Tommy Dorsey

Sky Fell Down, The (Edward Heyman - Louis Alter) February 1, 1940 Tommy Dorsey

Snootie Little Cutie (Bobby Troup) March 19, 1942 Tommy Dorsey

Somewhere A Voice Is Calling (Eileen Newton - Arthur Tate) March 19, 1942 Tommy Dorsey

Song Is You, The (Jerome Kern - Oscar Hammerstein II) January 19, 1942 Bluebird, September 3, 1942 Tommy Dorsey

South Of The Border (Jimmy Kennedy - Michael Carr) March 13, 1940, December 18, 1940, August 27, 1941, April 1, 1942 All Paramount

Stardust (Hoagy Carmichael - Mitchell Parish) November 11, 1940 Tommy Dorsey

Street Of Dreams (Victor Young - Sam Lewis) May 18, 1942 Tommy Dorsey

Sunshine Of Your Smile, The (Leonard Cooke - Lillian Ray) August 19, 1941, August 26, 1941 both Tommy Dorsey

Take Me (Rube Bloom - Mack David) June 9, 1942 Tommy Dorsey

Tell Me At Midnight (Bickley Reichner - Boland) August 29, 1940 Tommy Dorsey

That Old Black Magic (Johnny Mercer - Harold Arlen) May 26, 1943 Paramount

There Are Such Things (Stanley Adams - Abel Baer - George Meyer) July 1, 1942 Tommy Dorsey, December 30, 1942, February 2, 1943 both Paramount

This Is The Beginning Of The End (Mack Gordon) March 12, 1940 Tommy Dorsey

This Love Of Mine (Sol Parker - Hank Sanicola - Frank Sinatra) May 28, 1941 Tommy Dorsey, August 27, 1941 Paramount

Too Romantic (Johnny Burke - James Monaco) February 1, 1940 Tommy Dorsey

To You (John Stokes) August 1939

Trade Winds (Cliff Friend - Charles Tobias) June 27, 1940 Tommy Dorsey

Trombone Man Is The Best Man In The Band March 13, 1940 Paramount

Two In Love (Meredith Wilson) August 19, 1941 Tommy Dorsey

Violets For Your Furs (Matt Dennis - Tom Adair) August 19, 1941 Tommy Dorsey

We Three (Dick Robertson - Nelson Gogane - Sammy Mysels) August 29, 1940 Tommy Dorsey

When The Light Go On Again (Eddie Seiler - Sol Marcus - Bennie Benjamin) December 30, 1942 Paramount

When You Awake (Henry Nemo) September 9, 1940 Tommy Dorsey

Where Do You Keep Your Heart (Al Stillman - Fred Ahlert) May 23, 1940 Tommy Dorsey

Where Or When (Richard Rodgers - Lorenz Hart) December 30, 1942, February 2, 1943 both Paramount

Whispering (John Schonenburger - Richard Coburn - Vincent Rose) June 13, 1940 Tommy Dorsey

Who Told You I Cared (George Whiting - Reisfel) October 13, 1939 Harry James

Without A Song (Vincent Youmans - Billy Rose - Edward Eliscu) January 20, 1941 Tommy Dorsey, August 27, 1941 Paramount

World Is In My Arms, The (Yip Harburg - Burton Lane) July 17, 1940 Tommy Dorsey

Wrong (Can It Be Wrong To Love) (Kim Gannon - Max Steiner) May 26, 1943 Paramount

Yearning (Benny Davis - Joe Burke) November 7, 1940 Tommy Dorsey

You And I (Meredith Wilson) June 27, 1941 Tommy Dorsey

You'd Be So Nice To Come Home To (Cole Porter) February 2, 1943 Paramount

You Lucky People You (Johnny Burke - Jimmy Van Heusen) January 15, 1941 Tommy Dorsey

You Might Have Belonged To Another (Pat West - Lucille Hermon) January 6, 1940 Tommy Dorsey

You're Breaking My Heart All Over Again (James Cavanaugh - John Redmond - Arthur Altman) September 17, 1940 Tommy Dorsey

You're Lonely And I'm Lonely (Irving Berlin) April 23, 1940 Tommy Dorsey

Yours Is My Heart Alone (Frank Lehar - Ludwig Herzer - Fritz Lohner) March 25, 1940, April 10, 1940 both Tommy Dorsey

ORCHESTRA'S, ARRANGERS, COMPOSERS, SOLOISTS, VOCALISTS AND VOCAL GROUP INDEX - CHAPTER I, CHAPTER II, CHAPTER III, CHAPTER IV, CHAPTER V

Arden, Harold   - Orchestra Leader
Autumn, 1937   (Rustic Cabin)

Barrie, Grace   - Orchestra Leader
May 26, 1943   (Paramount Theatre)

Beau, Heinie   - Arranger, Tenor Sax
1941, 1942   (Dorsey Orchestra)

Berigan, Bunny   - Trumpet Soloist
April 23, 1940   (Dorsey Orchestra)

Bushkin, Joe   - Piano, Celeste, Composer, Conductor
1940, 1941, 1942   (Dorsey Orchestra)

Dorsey, Jimmy   - Orchestra Leader, Alto Sax
July 24, 1956   (Paramount Theater)

Dorsey, Tommy   - Orchestra Leader, Trombone,
January 1940   Arranger
through October
1942   - (RCA and Bluebird Records)
July 24, 1956   - (Paramount Theater)

Elman, Ziggy   - Trumpet Soloist
October 17, 1940, February 17, 1941, July 15, 1941, February 19, 1942, July 30, 1942 (Dorsey Orchestra)

Gibson, Andy   - Composer, Arranger
1939   (Harry James Orchestra)

Goodman, Benny   - Orchestra Leader, Clarinet
December 30, 1942   (Paramount Theater)

Haines, Connie   - Vocalist
January 6, 1941, February 17, 1941, March 19, 1942 (Dorsey Orchestra)

Henri and His Head Liners, Bill   - Orchestra Leader
1937, 1938   (Rustic Cabin)

Hoboken Four   - Vocal Group (Fred Tamburro, Jimmy
Petrozelli, Patty Principi - Sinatra was the Fourth)
September 8, 1935   (Major Bowes Show)

James, Harry   - Orchestra Leader, Trumpet Soloist,
Composer, Arranger.
June 1939 through December 1939 (Brunswick and Columbia Records)

Kincaide, Deane   - Arranger, Saxaphone
1940, 1941, 1942   (Dorsey Orchestra)

Long, Johnny   - Orchestra Leader
February 2, 1943   (Paramount Theater)

Lowe, Ruth   - Composer
1940 (I'll Never Smile Again)

Major Bowes   - Talent Scout, Coordinator
1935 (Amateur Hour Show)

Oliver, Sy   - Arranger, Composer, Trumpeter
1940, 1941, 1942   (Dorsey Orchestra)

Paige, Raymond   - Orchestra Leader
October 11, 1944   (Paramount Theater)

Pied Pipers, The   - Vocal Group (Jo Stafford - Chuck
Lowrey - Clark Yokum - Floyd Huddleston)
1940, 1941, 1942   (Dorsey Orchestra)

Rich, Buddy   - Drummer
1940, 1941, 1942   (Dorsey Orchestra)

Russin, Babe   - Sax Soloist
1940, 1941   (Dorsey Orchestra)

Savit, Jan   - Orchestra Leader
November 28, 1945   (Paramount Theater)

Stafford, Jo   - Vocalist
November 11, 1940, February 17, 1941, February 19, 1942, July 30, 1942
(Dorsey Orchestra)

Stulce, Fred   - Arranger, Saxaphone
May 23, 1940   (Dorsey Orchestra)

Stordahl, Axel   - Arranger, Composer, Conductor
1940, 1941, 1942   (Dorsey Orchestra)
                                           (Stordahl Orchestra)

Three Flashes, The   - Vocal Trio
1937, 1938   (Rustic Cabin)

Weston, Paul   - Arranger, Composer
1941, 1942   (Dorsey Orchestra)

We would like to add our comments at the end of every chapter concerning each segment of Sinatra's career. We believe that although no one could ever hope to match his consistantly high level performances for so long a period of time, there could have been so much more. The chapter's we are dealing with now, were not, for the most part, left up to his discretion and the Dorsey era was very gratifying. The only improvement we can think of is that there should have been more duets with Jo Stafford and of course with Berigan. Also, some of the air checks with the band have Frank singing marvelous songs that were never recorded. Not too much to say about the James recordings because he was actually feeling his way at that time and they still sound fairly good.

Chapter VI

The Columbia Years   June 7, 1943 - September 17, 1952

In August of 1942, A.F.M.'s President James C. Petrillo instituted a recording ban for all its musicians which lasted until November 1943. Thus, Sinatra did not record more sides with Dorsey after his last session on July 2, 1942; or even after he left the band to go out on his own. Frank kept busy, though, and went to the West Coast in December, hoping to obtain a job as staff singer for NBC. While this did not materialize, he did get a small part in a musical made by Columbia Pictures called "Reveille With Beverly" and sang one song, "Night And Day." (Years later when he achieved stardom, the movie was re-released "starring" Frank Sinatra.)

He returned to New York where on December 30, 1942, backed by the great Benny Goodman orchestra, he appeared as a solo act for the first time at the Paramount Theatre. Paramount's booking manager had been presuaded to give him a visit. He noticed that although the young singer wasn't packing the house, the people that were there, especially the younger girls were enthusiastic with their applause.

What happened at the Paramount was totally unexpected. The movie was "Star Spangled Rhythm," and the star in-person attraction was, naturally, Benny Goodman. After the last tune by the band, Benny turned around and introduced Sinatra and when he appeared from a side entrance, all bedlam broke loose, causing Goodman to remark "What the hell is that?" Frank broke into a grin and began singing "For Me and My Gal".

This marked the beginning of the mass hysteria that was to follow in later engagements. He continued there for eight solid weeks, the last four backed by Johnny Long and his orchestra. The two leading musical magazines, *Metronome* and *Downbeat* both presented him with their awards as the nation's number one male vocalist. In March RKO signed him up to star in their new film "Higher and Higher," and Arthur Jarwood, owner of the Riobamba night club brought him in to co-star with veteran performer Walter O'Keefe on the night of March 11, 1943. Sinatra outlasted his co-star and stayed for eight more successful weeks. On May 5, 1943, he opened at Frank Dailey's Terrace Room in Newark. During this engagement CBS premiered (on Friday, May 14) a radio series entitled "The Broadway Bandbox." This was a 45 minute late-evening variety show that experimented with time formerly devoted to dance band remotes. The network felt that coupling songs by Sinatra with music by Raymond Scott would have a strong dial draw. (On July 19, 1943, Axel Stordahl replaced Scott.) Meanwhile, Sinatra again played the Paramount, backed by the Gracie Barrie Orchestra, but with two other important differences: 1.) In his two previous engagements, he had received second billing, but now he was getting star-billing; and 2.) his weekly stipend was raised from $1,000 to $7,500. Then came Columbia Records.

Manie Sacks, Columbia's top executive, saw great possibilities in the young crooner and quickly signed him to a long-term contract before RCA Victor knew what was happening. His relationship with Sacks turned out to be a long and fruitful collaboration, as was most of his association with the recording

First recording for Columbia Records — 1943

Recording with Axel Stordahl — 1944

company. Due to the recording ban, Sinatra's first eight records on Columbia were with vocal chorus background (at least three of the vocal arrangements from the pen of Alec Wilder).

"The Voice," as he was now called, was riding high. He was a smash hit at all his personal appearances and his recordings, past and present, were among the top sellers across the country. The musicians recording ban was finally over and on November 14, 1943, he cut his first sides with orchestral backing and, of course, featuring arrangements by Axel Stordahl. Axel, who had left Dorsey, continued providing him with lush, simple, unobtrusive backgrounds and Sinatra's voice began to take on a slightly deeper, more mature sound. His choice of tunes was always tasteful now that he had almost complete control. (This control was to diminish in the latter part of his tenure with Columbia). Jazz critic Barry Ulanov states in his *A History of Jazz in America,* that "Frank Sinatra made perhaps the definitive recordings of Try A Little Tenderness, Why Shouldn't I, and Paradise, and did as much for Cole Porter's I Concentrate On You". He goes on to laud "the sustained notes and the delicate scoops of pitch that has brilliant moments on some of Sinatra's earlier Columbia sides". Frank had been on two other shows in early '43, one called "Songs By Sinatra" and the famous "Your Hit Parade." Mark Warnow was the conductor and Frank shared vocal honors with Joan Edwards and a vocal group called "The Lucky Strike Hit Paraders." He was never too happy with the songs he had to sing on the Hit Parade and continuously fought with the powers that be to improve the format. He brought in Dick Jones, whom he had known from his Dorsey days, and later on Stordahl also joined him.

Sinatra's third appearance at the Paramount was on October 11, 1944 and the "bobby soxers" came out in force, often lining up five or six hours before show time to ensure getting a seat. Throughout the city and neighboring towns, there were reports of truancy from the school boards who began to object that Sinatra was the major cause of it all. Mayor LaGuardia had to impose a nine o'clock curfew to curtail the mobs lining up around the entire block of the theatre.

The movie industry's cartoons also got into the act. Who can forget Merrie Melodies and Loony Tunes depicting a skinny young man with a large bow-tie being pulled down a soda straw by suction, and one particular farce that masqueraded him as a chicken and whenever he crooned, the hens would lay huge amounts of eggs.

Although Sinatra's income at this time was astronomical, his new booking agency, M.C.A., discovered that he was making plenty of money for other people. They quickly settled his former contractural obligations with his previous agency, G.A.C. and even managed to square things with Tommy Dorsey. Sinatra moved to Hasbrouk Heights, a residential area of Passaic Valley, New Jersey, but before he could settle in the comfortable Cape Cod cottage, his fans discovered the address and engulfed the area, much to the consternation of the local police. Even the news that Nancy was expecting another child did not deter his avid followers. When he journeyed West to make his first film for RKO, five thousand screaming fans met him at the railroad station in Pasadena. Like millions of others, Sinatra reported to his draft board and was given a 1-A classification - but after his physical examination, it was determined that he had a punctured ear drum and was reclassified 4-F. This news met with much criticism throughout the land and many accused him of gold-bricking or of buying himself out of the service. Those close to him knew otherwise, they also knew how deeply disappointed Sinatra was, and how he even tried to join the Navy, to no avail. To compensate, he began making U.S.O. tours knowing that the majority of the servicemen would heckle him unmercifully. But, he never failed to entertain them, and, armed with a program of songs coupled with a comedy routine in which he poked fun at his own shortcomings, he succeeded in eventually winning them over. When he returned from a six-week tour of military bases in Europe and Africa, he complained bitterly to the press that most of the facilities and entertainment were second-rate. This brought an irate response from Marlene Dietrich who reportedly said "What does he expect, the Paramount?" (Many years later they became the best of friends and she has been quoted recently on what a gentleman Sinatra is.) He appeared on numerous Armed Forces Radio programs with a bevy of stars, among them Bob Hope and Bing Crosby; and listening to tapes of these broadcasts one can hear a warm, relaxed, splendidly-voiced entertainer who also showed a flair for comedy. Despite all the success and a seemingly happy marriage (Frank, Jr. had been born on January 10, 1944) all was not well in the Sinatra household.

Nancy and Frank agreed to a mutual parting. Sinatra came back to New York on December 15, 1946 to record with the Metronome All-Stars (he was named top male vocalist again) and spent the entire month, including the holidays with Nancy and the two children. This reconciliation lasted for over two years, and on June 20, 1948, their second daughter, Christine (Tina), was born.

During these years, there began to emerge the side of Sinatra that was to become as famous to the world as his vocal and acting talents. He became disenchanted with much of the recording scene and let loose a blast at the popular hits of the day. He especially blasted the music publishers for not buying the better music and accused them of going after the fast buck. Though continuing to record the songs he considered worthwhile, he also tried some of the newer ones, and, restless, recorded with different conductors other than Stordahl. He refused, however, to record many of the top hits such as "Near You," "I'm Looking Over A Four Leaf Clover," "Apple Blossom Wedding," etc., and openly stated that "they were so decadent, they were bloodless." Many of the sides Frank did record during this period, though not best sellers, are nevertheless some of the best made for Columbia: "Why Remind Me," "(We've Got A) Sure Thing," "Where Is The One," "If I Ever Love Again," and the emotional "I'm A Fool To Want You," which was done in one take. One story concerning this particular recording session describes how distraught Frank was. Ben Barton, a close friend, claims that Sinatra walked out of the studio after the completion of the one take. The late Mathew (Matty) Golizio, guitarist on the date, and a childhood friend from Hoboken, adds that Sinatra did indeed walk out, but soon came back and did another emotional tune - "Love Me" - also in one take. Again he walked out and no one saw him for two days. Sinatra even missed the rehearsal for a CBS television show to be aired on the 31st with Peggy Lee.

Although he had been linked romantically with Lana Turner, Marilyn

Recording with the Charioteers — 1945

Conducting with Alex Wilder — 1945

Maxwell and a host of other lovely starlets, it became increasingly apparent that Frank Sinatra was infatuated with Ava Gardner and Nancy could not ignore this any longer. In February of 1950, she announced that "her married life with Frank had become unhappy and, therefore, they would separate." A few days later, Frank went into the studios to record "Kisses And Tears" and "When The Sun Goes Down."

A year later, Nancy filed for a divorce and at the same time MGM released Sinatra from his contract. To make matters worse, he began disagreeing with the new A & R man at Columbia - Mitch Miller - who persuaded him to bark like a dog on a duet recording with Dagmar entitled "Mama Will Bark."

A session with Harry James' orchestra followed, but one can discern a noticeable strain in his voice on these three takes. Ray Conniff, who was James' trombonist and arranger, was on the session and states that Frank was enthusiastic about reuniting with his old boss, and possibly tried too hard.

His next assignment was the soundtrack for "Meet Danny Wilson," a movie that could have been an artistic and financial success if done properly with a higher budget, for it was a perfect vehicle for him. On November 7, 1951, he married Ava Gardner. The marriage was scheduled for the night before, but such was their stormy relationship, that they quarreled at the last minute and everything was postponed until the next day. Ava's career was speedily ascending and even though he had a new radio show - "Light Up Time" - his voice was feeling the strain of his emotions and on one disastrous evening at the Copacabana, it failed him completely. As he was rapidly approaching 34 his career was going completely downhill.

His further disagreements with Mitch Miller and his poor sales for Columbia led to a final recording session for that company. On September 17, 1952, after nine years and over 300 recordings, Frank Sinatra recorded, prophetically, a tune called "Why Try To Change Me Now"? Indicative of the times, he had to share the session with another vocalist, Mindy Carson.

Recordings from this period are:

NOTE: Because of the musicians union ban on recording activity from the Fall of 1942 to the Fall of 1944, his first eight sides are made with choral background.

FRANK SINATRA - COLUMBIA RECORDS

June 7, 1943 - September 17, 1952

June 7, 1943, New York

No Musicians - Bobby Tucker Singers used as vocal background for Sinatra.

Fay Devlin, Mary Jane Watkins, Rae Whitney, Ruth Doring, Marshall Hall, Robert Miller, Ray Charles, Dick Byron, John Hubert, Edward Constantine, James Ballister, Frank Raye.

CO 33249-3A	Close To You	COL 36678, B2626 S3L42
CO 33250	People Will Say We're In Love*	UNISSUED

| CO 33251-3D | You'll Never Know | COL 36678, B 1984,
B 2614, CL 606, C2L 6 |

*Arrangement by Alec Wilder

June 22, 1943, New York

Marshall Hall out. Add Floyd Sherman and Bob Lyon.

CO 33268-2A	Sunday, Monday Or Always*	COL 36679, CL 2474
CO 33269-1	If You Please	COL 36679, MM-1
CO 33250	People Will Say We're In Love*	UNISSUED Remake

* Arrangement by Alec Wilder

August 5, 1943, New York

Frank Raye, Henry Rosenblatt, Thomas Foster, George Kirk, Kenneth Schon, Norman Horn, Ray Charles, Robert Miller, Edward Constantine, Fay Devlin, Mary Jane Watkins, Rae Whitney, Ruth Doring.

| CO 33250-6A | People Will Say We're In Love | COL 36682, B 2515,
Cl-2572, -3rd REMAKE
KH 30318 |
| CO 33283-1A | Oh What A Beautiful Morning* | COL 36682, B 1608,
B 2515, SM 3634 |

* Arrangements by Alec Wilder

November 3, 1943, New York

Jewel Bowman, Pauline Dugart, Mary Mullen, Kathleen Mullen, Kathleen Carnes, Ruth Doring, Rae Whitney, Fay Devlin, Ernest Anderson, Jack Lathrop, Elwin Carter, Ed Hayes, James Ballister, Travis Johnson, Richard Stokes, John Hubert, Thomas Foster.

| CO 33368-1A | I Couldn't Sleep A Wink Last
Night | COL 36687, B 2515,
CL 2572, CL 2913,
HS 11277 |
| CO 33369-PB | The Music Stopped | COL - CL 2913 |

New York, November 10, 1943

Bobby Tucker Singers - Same as previous session except James Ballister, Richard Stokes and John Hubert are replaced by Norman Luboff, Harold Branch and John Neher.

| CO 33373-3 | A Lovely Way To Spend An

Evening | COL 36687, B 2515,

CL 2913 |
| CO 33374-3 | The Music Stopped | HL 7405 |

Orchestra Under The Direction Of Axel Strodahl - Arrangements by Stordahl.

November 14, 1944, New York

(Tpt) M. Solomon, C. Poole, S. Shapiro; (Tbn) C. Small, A. Russo, J. D'Agostino; (F.H.) K. Chlupsa; (Sax) B. Kaufman, R. Pumiglio, H. Rose, H. Feldman, A. Baker; (Violins) F. Buldrini, G. Poliakins, S. Harris, L. Kantor, S. Mirroff, B. Kundell, G. Orloff, W. Lockwood, H. Micklin, J. Brand, A. Loeserman, M. Kellner; (Violas) M. Kohn, S. Rumberg, S. Pfaff; (Cellos) R. Poliakin, E. Gara, A. Twerdowsky; (Harp) R. Hill; (Piano) W. Rowland; (Guitar) M. Golizio; (Brass) W. Lay; (Drums) J. Blowers.

CO 33808-2	If You Are But A Dream	COL 36756, COL 36814, B 2559, C2L 6, CL 2474, CL 2474, KH 30318
CO 33809-1	Saturday Night	COL 36762, COL 50069, CL 1241, CL 2474, KH 31318
CO 33810-1A	There's No You	COL 36797, S3L 42
CO 33811-1	White Christmas (1)	COL 36756, COL 36860, 38257, COL 37152, CL 1032, B167, HL 7400, CL 2542, CL 6019, P 11417

(1) Vocal Chorus by Bobby Tucker Singers:
Jewel Bowman, Claude Reese, Pauline Dugart, Rae Whitney, Kathleen Garnes, Phil Reep, Darrel Woodyard and John Hubert.

NOTE: Also last two titles minus French Horn - K. Chlupsa.

Orchestra Under The Direction Of Axel Stordahl - Arrangements by Stordahl
December 1, 1944, New York

(Tpt) Same; (Tbn) Small and Russo out, A. Mastren and A. Koty in; (F.H.) Same; (Sax) Rose out, W. Tannebaum in; (Violins) Kellner, Loeserman, Miroff, Kundell, Lockwood and Micklin out. Z. Kaufman, B. Levitsky, L. Gabowitz, K. Rebe and M. Bornstein in; (Violas) T. Adoff, Sidney Brecher, H. Dickler; (Cellos) Gara and Twerdowsky out. A. Kaproff and A. Shapinsky in; (Harp) R. Berman; (Piano) D. Mann; (Guitar) Same; (Bass) Same; (Drums) Same.

CO 33928-1	I Dream Of You	COL 36762, CL 1136, B2626
CO 33929-1A	I Begged Her	COL 36774, CL2913
CO 33930-2	What Makes The Sunset	COL 36774, CL 2913
CO 33931-1	I Fall In Love Too Easily (1)	COL 36830, HL 7405, CL 2913

(1) Piano Solo by Dave Mann

Orchestra Under The Direction of Axel Stordahl - Arrangements by Stordahl.
December 3, 1944, New York

(Tpt) M. Solomon, C. Poole, B. Butterfield; (Tbn) C. Small, W. Rauch, S. Koty;
(F.H.) K. Chlupsa; (Sax) H. Shertzer, B. Kaufman, N. Chiazza, F. Pfeifer,
E. Caceres; (Violins) Same as last; (Violas) Adoff out, S. Rumberg in; (Cellos)
G. Poliakin, S. Barab, A. Twerdowsky; (Harp) M. Rosen; (Piano) Same; (Guitar)
Same; (Bass) J. Kimmel; (Drums) Same.

CO 33932-1	Nancy (With The Laughing Face)	UNISSUED
CO 33933-1	The Cradle Song	COL 36868, CL 1448
XCO 33934-1	Ol' Man River (12 inch)	COL 55037, C2L 6, B1702 B2564, CL 2572, KH 30318
XCO 33935-1	Stormy Weather (12 inch)	(1) COL 55037, C2L 6
CO 33936-1	The Charm Of You	COL 36830, B 2626, S3L 42, CL 2913

(1) Ken Lane Singers: Ernest Seckler, Mack McLean,
Marvin Charles Bailey, Lee Gotch, Charles Schrousder,
Betty Allan, Norma Larsen, Dorothy Compton, Thora
Thora Matthiason and Kermit Lane.

(1) Muted trumpet solo on Stormy Weather by Billy
Butterfield.

NOTE: Last title only - complete trumpet and trombone section out.

Orchestra Under The Direction Of Axel Stordahl - Arrangements by Stordahl
December 19, 1944, Los Angeles, California

(Tpt) L. Mack, C. Griffard, W. Macy; (Tbn) J. Skiles, E. Smithers, C. Loeffler;
(F.H.) J. Stagliano; (Sax) F. Stulce, H. Beau, H. Lawson, D. Lo Giudice,
L. Hartmen, (Violins) M. Russell, V. Arno, D. Frisana, N. Pisani, P. Ellils,
A. Perrotti, G.B. Joyce, T. Rosen, O. Vail, S. Lindler, R. Barena, G. Kast;
(Violas) D.A. Sterkin, G. White, A. Harshman; (Cellos) F.F. Goerner, A. Kafton,
J.T. Sewell; (Harp) I.L. Clow; (Piano) M.W. McIntyre; (Guitar) D.M. Barbour;
(Bass) P. Stephens; (Drums) R.T. Hagan.

HCO 1183-1	Embraceable You	COL 37259, Cl 1359, B1673, CL 6087, B2626
HCO 1184-1	When Your Lover Has Gone	COL 36791, CL 1448 S3L 42
HCO 1185-1B	Kiss Me Again	COL 38287, AI 1013

| HCO 1186-1 | She's Funny That Way | COL 37259, CL 743, B7432, CL 6087, HS 11390 |

Orchestra Under The Direction Of Axel Stordahl - Arrangements by Stordahl
January 29, 1945, Los Angeles, California

(Tpt) C. Griffard, L. Mack, D. Anderson; (Tbn) J. Skiles, J. Yukl, C. Loeffler; (Sax) E. Gershman, H. Beau, D. Lo Giudice, H. Lawson, L. Hartmen; (Violins) S. Freed, P. Ellis, N. Pisani, S. Kindler, M. Russell, G.B. Joyce, S. Levine, G. Kast, O. Vail, A. Perrotti, T. Rosen, V. Arno; (Violas) D.A. Sterkin, A. Harshman, G. White; (Cellos) F.F. Goerner, J.T. Sewell, A. Kafton; (F.H.) J. Stagliano; (Harp) I.L. Clow; (Piano) M.W. McIntyre; (Guitar) D.M. Barbour; (Bass) A. Shapiro; (Drums) R.T. Hagen.

HCO 1257-1B	My Melancholy Baby	COL 38287, CL 1359
HCO 1258-1	Where Or When (1)	COL 38685, CL 6096, 5-1040, CL 1448, HS 11390
HCO 1259-1A	All The Things You Are (1)	COL 37258, CL 6087, B1702, CL 1448
HCO 1260-1	Mighty Lak' A Rose	COL 36860, CL 1448

(1) Ken Lane Singers as previous accompaniment on Stormy Weather.

Orchestra Under The Direction Of Axel Stordahl - Arrangements by Stordahl
March 6, 1945, Los Angeles, California

(Tpt) C. Griffard, L. Mack, D. Anderson; (Tbn) J. Skiles, J. Wirkle, C. Loeffler; (F.H.) J. Stagliano; (Sax) E. Gershman, H. Beau, H.M. Haymer, H. Lawson, L. Hartman; (Violins) S. Freed, Jr., N. Pisani, P. Ellis, S. Kindler, M. Russell, G.B. Joyce, S. Levine, G. Kast, I. Vail, A Perrotti, T. Rosen, V. Arno; (Violas) D.A. Sterkin, A. Harshman, G. White; (Cellos) F.F. Goerner, A. Kafton, J.T. Sewell; (Harp) I.L. Clow; (Piano) M.W. McIntyre; (Guitar) D.M. Barbour; (Bass) A. Shapiro; (Drums) R.T. Hagen.

HCO 1286-1	I Should Care	COL 36791, B 2559, S3L 42
HCO 1287-1	Home Sick - That's All (1)	COL 36830, SM 3631
HCO 1288-1	Dream (1)	COL 36797, CL 1136, C1 2474, 40522
HCO 1289-1	A Friend Of Yours (1)	COL 36820, S3L 42

(1) With the Ken Lane Singers

Orchestra Under The Direction Of Axel Stordahl - Arrangements By Stordahl
May 1, 1945, Los Angeles, California

Personnel same as March 6, 1945 session.

HCO 1377-1	Put Your Dreams Away	COL 36814, B 2614, CL 1136, C2L 6, HS 11277
HCO 1378-1	Over The Rainbow (1)	COL 37258, B 7433, CL 6087, CL 743, C2-a
HCO 1379-1	You'll Never Walk Alone (1)	COL 36825, COL 50066, B 1620, B 2464, CL 6212, C2L 6
HCO 1380-1	If I Loved You	COL 36825, COL 50066, B 419, B1620, CL 2539, CL 6290, C2L 6, SM 3632

(1) With Vocal Chorus (Unknown but presumably Ken Lane Singers)

May 16, 1945, Los Angeles, California

Accompanied by: (Tpt) Loring (Red) Nichols; (Clt) J. Mayhew; (Piano) J. Sherman; (Guitar) D.M. Barbour; (Bass) P. Stevens; (Drums) N. Fatool.

HCO 1395-1B	Lilly Belle (1)	COL 36854, MM-1
HCO 1396-1	Don't Forget Tonight Tomorrow (1)	COL 36854, MM-1
HCO 1397-1	I've Got A Home In That Rock (1)	COL 37853
HCO 1398-1	Jesus Is The Rock (In The Weary Land) (1)	COL 37853

(1) With vocal group - The Chariotteers: James Sherman, Edward Jackson, Ira Williams, Wilfred Williams, Howard Daniels.

NOTE: On the last two titles - Piano, bass and drums only.

Xavier Cugat and his Orchestra   May 24, 1945, New York

(Tpt) George Lopez, Norman Sandow; (Tbn) James Curry; (Sax) Candido Dimanlig, William Hobbs, Robert Mosca, Reuben Moss, Max Nadell; (Violins) Marty Gold, Horacio Zito, Sal Picardi, Alfred Rickey, Nicholas Ragusa, David Oristein, William Brailowsky, Saul Grant, Myron Romas, Joseph Spallino, Harry Urbont, Joseph Livolsi; (Violas) Virgil Alonge, Max Serbin; (Cellos) Leo Rostal, Joseph Benavente; (Guitar) Herman Bogart; (Marimba) Raymond Gonzales; (F.H.) Richard Moore; (Bass) Simon Madera; (Drums) Albert

Calderon; (Congo Drum) Antonio Lopez; (Piano) Raul Soler; (Maracas) Angelo Santos.

| CO 34817-1 | Stars In Your Eyes | COL 36842 |
| CO 34818-1 | My Shawl | CO 36842, S3L 42 |

Orchestra Under The Direction of Axel Stordahl - Arrangements by Stordahl
July 30, 1945
Los Angeles, California

(Violins) M. Russell, D. Frisana; (Violas) S. Freed, Jr.; (Cello) f. Goerner; (Piano) M. McIntyre; (Bass) J. Ruan; (Drums) R. Hagan; (Guitar) G. Van Eps; (Flute) J. Mayhew.

HCO 1499-1	Someone To Watch Over Me	COL 36921, B 112, CL 6001, CL 6339, HS 11277, CL 1359
HCO 1500-1	You Go To My Head	COL 36918, B 112, CL 6001, C2L 6
HCO 1501-1	These Foolish Things	COL 36919, B 112, CL 6001, CL 743
HCO 1502-1A	I Don't Know Why (I Just Do)	COL 36918, B 112 CL 6001, CL 743

Orchestra Under The Direction Of Axel Stordahl - Arrangments by Stordahl
August 22, 1945,
Los, Angeles, California

(Tpt) Uan Ramsey, L. Mack, B. Hudson; (Tbn) P.R. Beilman, E. Smithers, C. Loeffler; (Sax) F. Stulce, H. Beau, D. Lo Giudice, H. Lawson, L. Hartman; (F.H.) J. Stagliano; (Violins) S. Freed, Jr., N. Pisani, P. Ellis, S. Kindler, M. Russell, G.G. Joyce, S. Levine, H.C. Halbert, D. Frisana, A. Perrotti, W. Edelstein, W. Bloom; (Violas) D.A. Sterkin, M. Permutter, A. Harshman; (Cellos) C. Bernard, J. Sewell, A. Kafton; (Harp) A. Mason; (Guitar) P. Botkin; (Piano) F. Leithner; (Bass) J.H. Ryan; (Drums) R. Hagan.

HCO 1519-1	The House I Live In	COL 36886, C2L 6, CL 2474, CL 2913, KH 30318
HCO 1520-1	Day By Day	COL 36905, COL 40565 CL 1359, CL 2572
HCO 1521-1A-2A	Nancy (With The Laughing Face)	COL 36868, COL 50053 CL 606, C2L 6, CL 2474, S3L 42, KH 30318
HCO 1522-1	You Are Too Beautiful	COL 36947, S3L-42

NOTE: Re-issues of Day By Day have bongos dubbed in. Also, on all re-issues of "Nancy", Sinatra sings "I've Got A Terrible Case" instead of "Believe Me, I've Got A Terrible Case."

Orchestra Under The Direction of Axel Stordahl - Arrangements by Stordahl

August 27, 1945

Los Angeles, California

(Tpt) C. Griffard, L. Mack, B. Hudson; (Tbn) J. Skiles, C. Loeffler, E. Smithers; (Sax) E. Gershman, H. Beau, D. Lo Giudice, H. Lawson, L. Hartman; (F.H.) J. W. Cave; (Violins) S. Freed, Jr., O. Vail, P. Ellis, M. Russell, S. Kindler, D. Frisana, N. Pisani, S. Levine, V. Arno, A. Perrotti, G. Kast, W. Edelstein; (Violas) D. Sterkin, M. Permutter, G. White; (Cellos) F. Goerner, J. Sewell, N. Ochialbi; (Harp) L. McFarland; (Piano) M. McIntyre; (Guitar) D. Barbour; (Bass) J.H. Ryan; (Drums) R. Hagan.

HCO	1525-1	American The Beautiful (1)	COL 36886
HCO	1526-1B	Silent Night, Holy Night (1)	COL 37145, COL 50079 CL 2542, CL 6019 CL 1032, HL 7400
HCO	1527-1	The Moon Was Yellow (1)	COL 38683, CL 6096 CL 2572
HCO	1528-1	I Only Have Eyes For You (1)	COL 38550, CL 6290, CL 606, HS 11390

(1) With the Ken Lane Singers:
Kermet Lane, Ruth Clark, Norma Larsen, Elva Kellog, Dudley, Kuzell, Sydney Pepple, Orville Race, Raymond Clark, John Glaha, Flora Mathiason, Ken Cameron, Stewart Bair.

Orchestra Under The Direction of Mitch Miller - Arrangements by Miller

November 15, 1945, New York

(Clarinets) J. Baker, E. Powell, B. Kaufman; (Bass Clarinet) H. Berv; (Oboe) P.J. Ricci; (Flutes) R. Merrill, A. Geltzer; (Bassoon) H. Holtzer; (Tbn) W. Bradley, W. Pritchard, A. Russo; (F.H.) L. Plato; (Guitar) A. Ryerson; (Piano) W. Clifton; (Bass) F. Sirava; (Drums) N. Polen.

CO	35426-1B	Old School Teacher	V-Disc, G14, MM-1
CO	35427-1C	Just An Old Stone House	COL 38809

Orchestra Under The Direction Of Axel Stordahl - Arrangements by Stordahl

November 19, 1945, New York

(Tpt) G. Griffin, L. Vunk, M. Solomon; (Tbn) W. Rauch, L. Altpeter, A. Russo; (Sax) H. Shertzer, W. Versaci, G. Desinger, E. Brown, R. Ekstrand; (Violins) C. Powers, L. Posner, M. Bornstein, R. Poliakin, B. Altman,

G. Orloff, A. Eidus, Z. Smirnoff, S. Caplan, J. Augustine, L. Gabowitz, M. Lomask; (Violas) S. Brecker, A. Loft, II. Dickler; (Cellos) A. Sophos, G. Poliakin, R. Anastasio; (Bass) F. Sirava; (Piano) H. Smith; (Guitar) M. Golizio; (Drums) N. Polen, H.E. Ricci; (F.H.) K. Chlupsa.

| CO 35441-2 | Full Moon And Empty Arms | COL 36947, CL 902, CL 2572 |
| CO 35442-2 | Oh What It Seemed To Be | COL 36905, CL 606, HS 11390, SM 3631 |

Orchestra Under The Direction Of Axel Stordahl - Arrangements by Stordahl
November 30, 1945, New York

(Tpt) B. Wallace in for Griffin; (Tbn) W. Pritchard, S. Slaffer, H. Winfield: (Sax) M. Yaner, B. Kaufman, W. Tannenbaum, H. Feldman, A. Baker; (Violins) Orloff, Eidus, Smirnoff, Caplan, Augustine, Gabowitz and Lomask out: H. Azen, S. Finglel, S. Harris, W. Hagen, H. Micklin and F. Orlewitz in; (Violas) T. Adoff in for Loft; (Cellos) F. Carmelia in for R. Anastasio; (Piano) H. Clifton; (Harp - Guitar - F.H. - Drums) Same as last session; (Bass) S. Shoobe.

| CO 35484-1 | I Have But One Heart (O Marenariollo) | COL 37554, CL 1136, CL 2572, HS 11277 KH 30318 |

Sinatra Conducts Alex Wilder ..... December 5, 1945

Orchestra Under The Direction Of Axel Stordahl - Arrangements by Stordahl
December 7, 1945, New York

(Violins) R. Poliakin, L. Posner; (Viola) S. Brecker; (cello) A. Sophos; (Oboe) M. Miller; (Guitar) M. Golizio; (Piano) W. Clifton; (Bass) F. Sirava; (Drums) N. Polen.

CO 35496-1	A Ghost Of A Chance	COL 36919, B 112, B 7431, CL 743, CL 6001, SM 3632
CO 35497-1	Why Shouldn't I?	COL 36920, B 1815, B 112, CL 6001, S3L 42
CO 35498-1	Try A Little Tenderness	COL 36920, COL 39498 B 112, CL 6001, CL 743, HL 7405
CO 35499-1	Paradise	COL 36921, B 112, CL 6001, CL 743

Sinatra Conducts Alec Wilder .....December 10, 1945

Orchestra Under The Direction of Axel Stordahl - Arrangements by Stordahl
February 3, 1946

Los Angeles, California

(Tpt) I.N. Parker, M. Herman, R.S. Linn; (Tbn) H.H. Bohannon, L. Jenkins,
E. Smithers; (Sax) H.J. Beau, A.C. Smith, H.M. Haymer, H. Schuchman, J.
Kinsler; (F.H.) R.E. Perissi; (Violins) M. Russell, S. Levine, G. Kast, G.G.
Joyce, S. Middleman, S. Kindler, W. Bloom, M. King, E. Powers, S. Freed, Jr.,
H. Blostein, N. Pisani; (Violas) D.A. Sterkin, A. Neiman, L. Selic; (Cellos) F.F.
Goerner, J. Sewell, J. Tannenbaum; (Harp) M.H. Cambern; (Piano) M.
McIntyre; (Guitar) D.M. Barbour); (Bass) P. Stephens; (Drums) R. Hagan.

HCO 1674-2	All Through The Day	COL 36962, SM 3634
HCO 1674-3	All Through The Day	COE DB 2227 - English Issue, MM-1
HCO 1675-1	One Love	COL 37054, S3L 42
HCO 1676-2	Two Hearts Are Better Than One (1)	COL 36962
HCO 1677-1	How Cute Can You Be (2)	COL 37048, CL 606

(1) Violins, Violas, Cellos and Harp out.

(2) This title only has the following personnel:
(Sax) Henry Beau, Arthur Smith, Herbert Haymer,
Harry Schuchman; (Tpt) Ray Linn; (Tbn) Hoyt Bohan-
non; (Bass) Phil Stephens; (Drums) Raymond Hagan;
(Piano) Mark Mc Intyre; (Guitar) David Barbour.

Orchestra Under The Direction Of Axel Stordahl-Arrangements by Stordahl
February 24, 1946, Los Angeles, California

(Tps) R. Linn, M. Herman, E. Klein; (Tbn) H. Bohannon, E. Smithers,
L. Jenkins; (Sax) H. Beau, J. Kinsler, A. Smith, H. Haymer, H. Schuchman;
(Violins) M. Russell, S. Levine, G. Kast, G. Joyce, S. Middleman, S. Kindler,
W. Bloom, H. Blostein, N. Pisani, O. Vail, S. Freed, Jr., M. King; (Violas)
D. Sterkin, A. Neiman, L. Selic; (Cellos) F. Goerner, J. Sewell, J. Tannenbaum;
(F.H.) R. Parisi; (Harp) M. Cambern; (Guitar) G. Van Eps; (Piano) M. McIntyre;
(Bass) P. Stephens; (Drums) R. Hagan.

HCO 1733-1	From This Day Forward	COL 36987
HCO 1734-1	Where Is My Bess	COL 37064, B 1673, CL 1297
HCO 1735-1	Begin The Beguine	COL 37064, C2L 6, HS 11390, SM 3631
HCO 1736-1	Something Old-Something New	COL 36987, S3L 42

NOTE: HCO 1736 ("Something Old - Something New") was originally titled "Here Comes The Bride - She Said Yes" on Columbia work sheet.

Orchestra Under The Direction Of Axel Stordahl - Arrangements by Stordahl
March 10, 1946, Los Angeles, California

(Tps) R. Linn, M. Herman, R. Zarchy; (Tbn) H. Bohannon, L. Jenkins, E. Smithers; (Sax) H. Beau, J. Kinsler, A. Smith, H. Haymer, H. Schuchman; (F.H.) R. Perissi; (Violins) M. Russell, S. Levine, G. Kast, G. Joyce, S. Middleman, S. Kindler, W. Bloom, H. Blostein, N. Pisani, G. Powers, O. Vail, S. Freed, Jr.; (Violas) D. Sterkin, A. Neiman, L. Selic; (Cellos) F. Goerner, J. Sewell, J. Tannenbaum; (Harp) M. Cambern; (Bass) P. Stephens; (Guitar) D. Barbour; (Piano) M. McIntyre; (Drums) R. Hagan.

HCO 1748-1	They Say It's Wonderful	COL 36975, CL 2539, CL 6290, CL 1297, SM 3632
HCO 1749-1	That Old Black Magic	COL 37257, CL 6087, CL 743
HCO 1750-1A	The Girl That I Marry	COL 36975, 50053, CL6290, Cl 1136, CL 1297, CL 2474, HS 11277, KH 30318, SM 3632
HCO 1751-1	I Fall In Love With You Everyday	COL 39493, SM 3634
HCO 1752-1	How Deep Is The Ocean	COL 37257, CL 6087, C2L 6
HCO 1753-1	Home On The Range	England - COE DC 385, MM-1

Orchestra Under The Direction Of Axel Stordahl - Arrangements by Stordahl
April 7, 1946, New York

(Tps) C. Poole, L. Vunk, M. Solomon; (Tbn) J. Satterfield, A. Russo, H. Hubble; (Sax) V. Abato, F. Pfeifer, A. Drelinger, B. Kaufman, H. Shertzer; (F.H.) J. Singer; (Violins) G. Ockner, B. Steinberg, N. Kaproff, N. Bielski, M. Bornstein, M. Hershaft, P. Winter, B. Altman, A. Loeserman, F. Orlewitz, B. Levitzky, B. Sheppard; (Violas) A. Loft, H. Dickler, S. Brecker; (Cellos) G. Poliakin, D. Soyer, M. Prinz; (Harp) D. Johnson; (Guitar) M. Golizio; (Piano) J. Bushkin; (Bass) S. Weiss; (Drums) J. Blowers

XCO 36056-1	Soliloquy Part I	C2L 6
XCO 36057-1	Soliloquy Part II	C2L 6

Orchestra Under The Direction Of Axel Stordahl - Arrangements b Stordahl
May 28, 1946, Los Angeles, California

(Tpt) R. Zarchy, R. Linn, El Klein; (Tbn) W. Schaefer, L. Jenkins, S. Zentner; (Sax) H. Beau, J. Kinsler, F. Stulce, H. Haymer, F. Dornbach; (F.H.) J. Stagliano; (Violins) M. Russell, S. Cytron, G. Kast, S. Middleman, S. Kindler, W. Bloom, N. Pisani, O. Vail, E. Powers, G. Vinci, D. Frisana, S. Freed; (Violas) D. Sterkin, G. Nuttycomb, G. Serulnic; (Cellos) F. Goerner, J. Sewell, J. Tannenbaum; (Guitar) A. Reuss; (Piano) M. McIntyre; (Bass) A. Shapiro; (Harp) M. Cambern; (Drums) R. Hagan

XHCO 1849-1	Soliloquy Part I	M 7492, B 1620, B 2564
XHCO 1850-1	Soliloquy Part II	M 7492, B 1620, B 2564
HCO 1851-1	Somewhere In The Night	COL 37054, AI 1013
HCO 1852-1	Could 'Ja (1)	COL 38608
HCO 1853-1	Five Minutes More	COL 37048, COL 50069 B 2517, CL 2521
HCO 1853-2	Five Minutes More *	CL 1241, CL 2474, KH 30318

(1) With the Pied Pipers

* On HCO 1853-2 --- The re-issues CL 1241, CL 2474, the first few bars of rhythm are cut out before the singing starts

NOTE: Violins, Violas, Cellos and Harp out for last two titles and personnel as listed below:
(Tpt) Ray Linn; (Sax) Henry Beau, Fred Stulce, Herbert Haymer, Fred Dornbach; (Tbn) William Schaefer; 4 Rhythm the same.

Orchestra Under The Direction Of Axel Stordahl - Arrangements by Stordahl
July 24, 1946, Los Angeles, California

(Tpt) R. Zarchy, D. Anderson, R. Linn;)Tbn) W. Schaefer, R. Kuczborski, L. Jenkins; (Sax) H. Beau, F. Stulce, J. Kinsler, H. Haymer, F. Dornbach; (Violins) M. Russell, S. Cytron, G. Kast, S. Middleman, B. Bluestone, O. Vail, S. Freed, S. Callios, W. Bloom, M. King, P. Ellis, G. Joyce, (Violas) D. Sterkin, R. Robyn, S. Spiegelman; (Cellos) C. Bernard, F. Goerner, J. Sewell; (Piano) M. McIntyre; (Bass) P. Stephens; (Guitar) D. Barbour; (Drums) R. Hagan; (F.H.) R. Perissi; (Harp) M. Cambern.

NOTE: On HCO 1925 Ray Linn plays Clovis and Fred Dornbach plays Maracas.

| HCO 1922-1 | The Things We Did Last Summer | COL 37089, CL 1136 |
| HCO 1923-1 | You'll Know When It Happens | UNISSUED in U.S. |

		Australia DO-3041, MM-1, WMD-200
HCO 1924-1	This Is The Night	COL 37193, COL 38853
HCO 1925-1	The Coffee Song	COL 37089
HCO 1925-2	The Coffee Song*	CL 2474

***NOTE:** On HCO 1925-2, the re-issue CL2474, Sinatra sings "Put Coffee In The Java In Brazil". The original take on COL 37089 has "Put Coffee In The Coffee In Brazil". Also, on second take, the rhythm seems off.

Orchestra Under The Direction Of Axel Stordahl-Arrangements by Stordahl
July 30, 1946, Los Angeles, California

(Tpt) R. Zarchy, E. Klein, C. Hurley,; (Tbn) H. Bohannon, L. Jenkins, E. Kuczborski; (Sax) H. Klee, J. Kinsler, H. Haymer, F. Dornbach; (Violins) M. Russell, S. Freed, E. Lamas, W. Bloom, S. Kindler, H. Habort, W. Callies, D. Lube, D. Frisana, W. Edelstein, G. Vinci, M. King; (Violas) A. Hochstein, S. Spiegelman, A. Newman; (Cellos) F. Goerner, J. Sewell, J. Tannenbaum; (F.H.) R. Perissi; (Piano) M. McIntyre; (Harp) A. Mason; (Guitar) D. Barbour; (Bass) P. Stephens; (Drums) R. Hagan.

HCO 1930-1A	Among My Souvenirs	COL 37161, COL 50003 CL 1359, HS 11390
HCO 1931-1	I Love You	COL 38684, CL 6096, HS 11277, SM 3632
HCO 1932-1	September Song	COL 37161, COL 50003 CL 1359, CL 2572
HCO 1933-1	Blue Skies	CL 902, B 1524, B 9021, S3L 42, AI-1014
HCO 1934-1	Guess I'll Hang My Tears Out To Dry	COL 38474, CL 6059, S3L 42

Orchestra Under The Direction Of Axel Stordahl - Arrangements by Stordahl
August 8, 1946, Los Angeles, California

(Tpt) R. Linn in, C. Hurley out; (Tbn) Same; (Sax) H. Klee out, F. Stulce, J. Dumont in; (Violins) E. Lamas, W. Bloom, H. Halbort, D. Frisana, W. Edelstein and G. Vinci out; H. Bluestone, M. Sosson, P. Ellis, G. Kast, G. Joyce and S. Middleman in; (Violas) A. Hochstein and A. Neiman out; D. Sterkin and P. Robyn in; (Cellos) J. Tannenbaum out; C. Bernard in; (Piano) - Bass - Drums - Guitar - F.H. - Harp) Same as last session.

HCO 1945-1	Adeste Fidelis (O Come All Ye Faithful)	COL 37145, COL 50079 CL 6019, CL 1032, HL 7400

HCO 1946-1C	Lost In The Stars	COL 38650, CL 1136, CL 1297
HCO 1947-1	Jingle Bells (1)	COL 37152, CL 2542, CL 6019. CL 1032, HL 7400
HCO 1948-1	Falling In Love With Love	CL 606, B 1872, B 1984

(1) With Ken Lane Singers - Same as last.

Orchestra Under The Direction Of Axel Stordahl - Arrangements by Stordahl
August 22, 1946, Los Angeles, California

(Tpt) R. Zarchy, R. Linn, D. Anderson; (Tbn) H. Bohannon, L. Jenkins, E. Smithers; (Sax) J. Dumont, F. Stulce, J. Kinsler, F. Dornbach, H. Haymer; (F.H.) J. Cave; (Violins) M. Russell, H. Bluestone, M. Sasson, P. Ellis, G. Kast, M. King, G. Joyce, S. Middleman, E. Lamas, W. Gallies, S. Freed, Jr., F. Slatkin; (Violas) D. Sterkin, P. Robyn, S. Spiegelman; (Cellos) F. Goerner, J. Sewell, J. Tannenbaum; (Harp) M. Cambern; (Piano) M. McIntyre; (Guitar) A. Reuss; (Bass) A. Shapiro; (Drums) R. Hågan.

HCO 1969-1B	Hush-A-Bye Island	COL 37193
HCO 1970-1	So They Tell Me	MM-1
HCO 1971-1	There's No Business Like Show Business (1)	CL 1297
HCO 1972-1E	(Once Upon) A Lovely Moonlight Night	COL 38316

(1) Vocal Chorus; Richard Davis, Mack McLean, Gil Mershon, Ernest Newton, David Knight, Robert Stevens, E. William Seckler and Marvin Bailey.

Orchestra Under The Direction Of Axel Stordahl - Arrangements by Stordahl
October 15, 1946, Los Angeles, California

(Tpt) Same; (Tbn) W. Schaefer and F. Howard in; H. Bohannon and E. Smithers out; (Sax) H. Beau in, J. Dumont out; (Violins) G. Kast, S. Middleman, E. Lamas, W. Gallies and F. Slatkin out; W. Bloom, W. Edelstein, N. Pisani, V. Arno and O. Vail in; (Cellos) J. Tannenbaum out, C. Bernard in; (Harp) K. Thompson; (Piano) L. Berman; (Guitar) V. Mumolo; (Bass) Same; (Drums) Same; (F.H.) J. McGee.

HCO 2090-1	Strange Music	UNISSUED
HCO 2091-1	Poinciana (Song Of The Tree)	Foreign Issue Only DB 2357
HCO 2092	The Music Stopped	UNISSUED

| HCO 2093-1A | Why Shouldn't It Happen To Us | COL 37251, S3L 42 |

| HCO 2094-1 | None But The Lonely Heart | UNISSUED |

Orchestra Under The Direction of Axel Stordahl - Arrangements by Stordahl
October 24, 1946, Los Angeles, California

(Tpt) R. Linn, R. Zarchy, D. Anderson; (Tbn) W. Schaefer, L. Jenkins, D. Hallett; (Sax) F. Stulce, H. Haymer, J. Kinsler, F. Dornbach, H. Beau; (F.H.) F. Fox; (Violins) M. Russell, G. Kast, N. Pisani, S. Cytron, S. Middleman, M. Sosson, A Olson, W. Edelstein, M. King, P. Ellis, H. Bluestone, E. Bergman, F. Slatkin, E. Powers, W. Gallies; (Violas) M. Perlmutter, P. Lowenkron, P. Robyn, A. Harshman; (Cellos) N. Ochialbi, A. Kafton, F. Goerner, J. Sewell; (Bass) P. Stephens; (Piano) M. McIntyre, (Guitar) A. Reuss, (Drums) R. Hagan.

| HCO 2116-1 | Time After Time | COL 37300, CL 606, CL 2572, CL 2913, KH 30318 |

| HCO 2117-1 | It's The Same Old Dream (1) | COL 37288, S3L 42, CL 2913 |

| HCO 2118-1 | I'm Sorry I Made You Cry | COL 37256, CL 6087, AI 1013 |

(1) With Four Hits And A Miss: William Seckler, Mack McLean, Lee Gotch, Marvin Bailey and Beverly Mahr.

Orchestra Under The Direction Of Axel Stordahl - Arrangements by Stordahl
October 31, 1946, Los Angeles, California

(Tpt) M. Klein, R. Linn, R. Zarchy, P. Ceil, (Tbn) E. Kuczborski, W. Schaefer, S. Zentner, C. Coolidge; (Sax) J. Dumont, H. Klee, M. Beriov, B. Russin, H. Schuchman; (Violins) M. Russell, G. Kast, N. Pisani, S. Cytron, S. Middleman, M. Sosson, F. Olson, W. Edelstein, P. Ellis, H. Bluestone, J. Quadri, F. Slatkin, W. Callies, D. Lube, A. Mierlot; (Violas) M. Perlmutter, P. Lowenkron, P. Robyn, A. Harshman; (Cellos) F. Goerner, J. Sewell, J. Saxon, N. Ochialbi; (F.H.) R. Perissi; (Guitar) A. Reuss; (Piano) M. Raskin; (Drums) R. Hagan; (Harp) C. Scott.

| HCO 2094-2 | None But The Lonely Heart | UNISSUED |

| HCO 2121-1 | The Brooklyn Bridge | COL 37288, CL 2913 |

Orchestra Under The Direction Of Axel Stordahl - Arrangements by Stordahl
Same Date, Los Angeles, California

(Tpt) E. Klein, R. Linn, R. Zarchy; (Tbn) E. Kuczborski, W. Schaefer, S. Zentner; (Sax) J. Dumont, H. Klee, M. Bercov, B. Russin, H. Schuchman; (Bass) P. Stephens; (Guitar) A. Reuss, (Piano) M. Raskin; (Drums) R. Hagan.

| HCO 2122-1 | I Believe | COL 37300, CL 2913 |

Same Date

(Tpt) P. Ceil in; (Sax) M. Bercov out; (Tbn) E. Kuczborski and Zentner out.

| HCO 2123-1 | I Got A Gal I Love | COL 37231, CP 12-76 |

Orchestra Under The Direction Of Axel Stordahl - Arrangements by Stordahl
November 7, 1946, Los Angeles, California

(Tpt) R. Linn, R. Zarchy, E. Klein, C. Hurley; (Tbn) W. Atkinson, H. Bohannon, L. Jenkins; (Sax) J. Dumont, H. Beau, J. Kinsler, B. Russin, F. Stulce, F. Dornbach; (Bass) P. Stephens; (Piano) M. McIntyre; (Guitar) A. Reuss; (Drums) N. Fatool.

| HCO 2134-1 | The Dum Dot Song (1) | COL 37966 |
| HCO 2135-1 | All Of Me (Arranged by George Siravo) | Foreign Issue only COE DB 2330 |

(1) With the Pied Pipers

Same Session: (Tpt) R. Linn out; (Tbn - Sax - Bass) Same; (Drums) R. Hagan; (Guitar) Same; (Piano) Same. ADD: (Violins) M. Russell, F. Slatkin, M. Sosson, W. Bloom, S. Freed, H. Halbert, W. Edelstein, O. Vail, F. Olson, G. Vinci, G. Joyce, M. King, D. Lube, W. Callies, S. Kindler; (Violas) B. Smon, D. Sterkin, A. Harshman, M. Perlmutter; (Cellos) F. Goerner, J. Sewell, C. Bernard, N. Albi; (F.H.) V. De Rosa.

| HCO 2136-1 | It's All Up To You (1) * | MM-1, WMD-200 |
| HCO 2137-1 | My Romance (1) | UNISSUED |

(1) With Dinah Shore

NOTE: On Master HCO 2136, the orchestra is given as Kay Kyser but upon investigation turns out to be Axel Stordahl's studio orchestra. Since it was a promotional record especially recorded for the Good Health League and given away free in North Carolina, the inclusion of Mr. Kyser's name might have been for publicity purposes.

Orchestra Under The Direction Of Axel Stordahl - Arrangements by Stordahl
December 15, 1946, New York

(Tpt) A. Ferretti, N. Solomon, J. Maxwell; (Tbn) W. Covington, A. Russo, W. Heins, Jr.; (F.H.) J. Singer; (Sax) A. Baker, W. Tannenbaum, V. Abato, G. Tudor, J. Fulton; (Violins) M. Hershaft, P. Frank, S. Mirroff, E. Magazines, B. Altman, M. Schwartz, N. Brusiloff, J. Margolies, M. Pitt, A. Micci, B. Sheppard, G. Ockner; (Violas) R. Reilich, S. Rumberg, W. Schoen; (Cellos) B. Greenhouse, D. Soyer, M. Bialkin; (Bass) H. Alpert; (Piano) S. Freedman; (Harp) E. Ricci; (Guitar) M. Golizio; (Drums) J. Blowers.

Recording with the Metronome All-Stars (left to right: Coleman Hawkins, John-ny Hodges, Harry Carney, F.S., Buddy Rich, Lawrence Brown, Eddie Safranski, Bob Ahern, Sy Oliver) — 1946.

With Dinah Shore celebrating their "Tea For Two" recording — 1947.

CO 37161-1	Always *	ISSUED IN AUSTRALIA
CO 37162-1	I Want To Thank Your Folks	COL 37251, CP 12-76

PAGE CAVANAUGH TRIO - Arrangements by P. Cavanaugh
Same Date As Above

(Piano) Page Cavanaugh; (Guitar) Al Viola; (Bass) Loyd Pratt

CO 37163-1	That's How Much I Love You	COL 37231, CL 2521
CO 37164-1	You Can Take My Word For It Baby	COL 40229, S3L 42

* Mr. Bill Weeden of Australia has purchased the 78 released there and states that there is distinct difference between this version and the take HCO 2181-1A.

METRONOME ALL STARS - Arrangements by Sy Oliver
Same Date As Last - New York

(Tpt) Charlie Shavers; (Tbn) Laurence Brown; (A. Sax) Johnny Hodges; (Bar. Sax) Harry Carney; (Piano) Nat Cole; (Guitar) Bob Ahern; (Bass) Eddie Safranski; (Drums) Buddy Rich.

CO 37177-1	Sweet Lorraine	COL 37293, CL 2528
CO 37177-2	Sweet Lorraine	COL 37293, HL 7044, S3L 42

NOTE: All previous discographies list the Metronome All Star session as December 17, 1946, but the actual Columbia worksheet lists it on the 15th.

Orchestra Under The Direction Of Axel Stordahl - Arrangements by Stordahl
January 9, 1947, Los Angeles, California

(Sax) F. Stulce, H. Haymer, F. Dornbach, H. Beau, H. Lawson; (Violins) G. Kast, S. Cytron, A. Beller, M. King, D. Jeselson, O. Tomasso, E. Powers, G. Joyce, M. Russell, H. Bluestone, F. Slatkin, N. Pisani; (Violas) W. Hymanson, W. Spear, D. Sterkin; (Cellos) C. Bernard, F. Goerner, J. Sewell; (Harp) M. Cambern; (Guitar) A. Reuss; (Piano) M. McIntyre, (Bass) J. Ryan; (Drums) R. Hagan.

HCO 2181-1A	Always	COL 38686, B 1524, CL 6096, CL 1359, CP 12-76

Same Session - ADD: (Tpt) R. Zarchy, R. Linn, L. Mack; (Tbn) P. Pederson, L. Jenkins, D. Hallett; (F.H.) R. Perissi.

HCO 2182-1B	I Concentrate On You	COL 37256, CL6087, C2L 6

| HCO 2183-1 | My Love For You | COE DB 2388, MM-1, AI 1013 |

Orchestra Under The Direction Of Axel Stordahl - Arrangements by Stordahl
March 11, 1947, Los Angeles, California

(Tpt) R. Zarchy, L. Mack, R. Linn; (Tbn) P. Pederson, D. Hallett, L. Jenkins; (Sax) F. Stulce, J. Kinsler, H. Beau, H. Haymer, F. Dornbach; (Violins) G. Kast, S. Cytron, M. Russell, W. Callies, H. Bluestone, S. Freed, N. Pisani, G. Joyce, O. Vail, G. Vinci, M. King, P. Ellis; (Violas) W. Hymanson, M. Perlmutter, W. Spear; (F.H.) V. De Rosa; (Harp) M. Cambern; (Guitar) A. Reuss; (Piano) M. McIntyre; (Bass) P. Stephens; (Drums) R. Hagan.

HCO 2256-1A	Mam'selle	COL 37343, CL 1136, HL 7405
HCO 2257-1A	Aintcha Ever Comin' Back (1)	COL 37554, CL 1136
HCO 2258-1A	Stella By Starlight	COL 37343, CL 1448, HS 11277

(1) With the Pied Pipers.

Orchestra Under The Direction Of Axel Stordahl - Arrangements by Stordahl
March 31, 1947, Los Angeles, California

(Tpt) R. Zarchy, D. Anderson, R. Linn; (Tbn) W. Schaefer, D. Hallett, L. Jenkins; (Sax) F. Stulce, J. Kinsler, H. Beau, H. Haymer, L. Hartman; (F.H.) V. DeRosa; (Violins) G. Kast, S. Cytron, M. Russell, G. Vinci, H. Bluestone, F. Slatkin, N. Pisani, G. Joyce, O. Vail, S. Freed, M. King, M. Sosson, (Violas) A. Harshman, D. Sterkin, W. Hymanson; (Cellos) F. Goerner, J. Sewell, C. Bernard, (Harp) M. Cambern; (Guitar) A. Reuss; (Piano) M. McIntyre; (Bass) P. Stephens; (Drums) R. Hagan.

| HCO 2280-1A | There But For You Go I | COL 37382, CL 1297 |
| HCO 2281-2A | Almost Like Being In Love | COL 37382, B 1986, CL 606 |

Orchestra Under The Direction Of Axel Stordahl - Arrangements by Stordahl
April 25, 1947, Los Angeles, California

(Tpt) E. Klein, I. Ransey, C. Griffard; (Tbn) P. Pederson, L. Jenkins, D. Hallett; (Sax) P. Pumiglio, D. Bonnee, B. Russin, J. Kinsler, H. Schuchman; (F.H.) V. DeRosa; (Violins) M. Russell, M. Sosson, F. Slatkin, S. Freed, J. Sclachter, G. Vinci, M. King, W. Miller, E. Powers, O. Tomasso, M. Haigh, A. Beller; (Violas) W. Hymanson, W. Spear, A. Harshman; (Cellos) F. Goerner, J. Sewell, C. Bernard; (Harp) M. Cambern; (Guitar) A. Reuss; (Piano) M. McIntyre; (Bass) P. Stephens; (Drums) R. Hagan.

| HCO 2310-1N | Tea For Two (1) | COL 37528, CP 12-76 |
| HCO 2311-1N | My Romance (1) - (2) | COL 37528, S3L 42 |

(1) Vocal Duet With Dinah Shore.

(2) Vocal Chorus: William Seckler, Lee Gotch, Conrad Taylor, Arthur Davies, Frank Holiday, Gil Mershon, Harry Stanton, Stewart Bair, Mack McLean.

Orchestra Under The Direction Of Axel Stordahl - Arrangements by Stordahl
June 26, 1747, Los Angeles, California

(Tpt) R. Zarchy, D. Anderson, R. Linn; (Tbn) P. Pederson, L. Jenkins, D. Hallett; (Sax) F. Stulce, H. Haymer, J. Kinsler, H. Beau, F. Dornbach; (F.H.) V. DeRosa; (Violins) G. Kast, S. Cytron, G. Joyce, W. Callies, M. Russell, H. Bluestone, O. Vail, A. Beller, F. Slatkin, M. Sosson, N. Pisani, S. Middleman; (Violas) W. Hymanson, D. Sterkin, M. Perlmutter; (Cellos) F. Goerner, J. Sewell, C. Bernard; (Harp) M. Cambern; (Guitar) D. Barbour; (Piano) M. McIntyre; (Bass) P. Stephens; (Drums) R. Hagan.

HCO 2419-1N	Have Yourself A Merry Little Christmas	CL 1032, HL 7400
HCO 2420-1N	Christmas Dreaming	CL 1032, HL 7400
HCO 2421-1N	The Stars Will Remember	UNISSUED

Orchestra Under The Direction Of Axel Stordahl - Arrangements by Stordahl
July 3, 1947, Los Angeles, California

Personnel same as last session.

HCO 2419-3N	Have Yourself A Merry Little Christmas	COL 38259, CL 6019
HCO 2420-2N	Christmas Dreaming	CO 37809
HCO 2421-2N	The Stars Will Remember	CO 37809, AI 1013
HCO 2433-1A	It All Came True	Foreign Issue DB 2381, SM 3634

Orchestra Under The Direction Of Axel Stordahl - Arrangements by Stordahl
August 11, 1947, Los Angeles, California

(Sax) H. Beau, H. Haymer; (Tpt) R. Zarchy; (Flute) J. Kinsler, (Also double on Sax); (Violins) M. Russell, F. Slatkin; (Viola) D. Sterkin; (Cello) F. Goerner; (Guitar) A. Reuss; (Piano) M. McIntyre; (Bass) P. Stephens; (Drums) R. Hagan.

HCO 2519-1	That Old Feeling	B 9021, CL 902, HL 7405
HCO 2520-1C	If I Had You	HL 7405
HCO 2521-1B	The Nearness Of You	B 9022, CL 902, HS 11277
HCO 2522-1D	One For My Baby (And One More For The Road)	COL 38474, COL 40373, B 455, B 1938, B 2614,

NOTE: On HCO 2519 and HCO 2520, SAX AND TRUMPET OUT.

On HCO 2521 and HCO 2522, Full Band Personnel

Orchestra Under The Direction Of Axel Stordahl - Arrangements by Stordahl
August 17, 1947, Los Angeles, California

(Tpt) R. Zarchy, E. Klein, R. Linn; (Tbn) P. Pederson, L. Jenkins, D. Hallett;
(Sax) F. Stulçe, H. Haymer, J. Kinsler, H. Beau, F. Dornbach; (F.H.) V. DeRosa;
(Violins) M. Russell, G. Kast, S. Cytron, W. Callies, H. Bluestone, O. Vail,
S. Middleman, N. Pisani, S. Freed, M. Sosson, B. Kundell, P. Ellis; (Violas)
W. Hymanson, D. Sterkin, A. Harshman; (Cellos) F. Goerner, J. Sewell,
C. Bernard; (Harp) M. Cambern; (Guitar) A. Reuss; (Piano) M. McIntyre; (Bass)
P. Stephens; (Drums) R. Hagan.

HCO 2538-1N	But Beautiful	COL 38053, CL 1448
HCO 2539-1N	A Fellow Needs A Girl	COL 37883, CL 902
HCO 2540-1N	So Far	COL 37883

ALVY WEST AND THE LITTLE BAND - Arrangement by West

September 23, 1947, Los Angeles, California

(Tpt) John Plonsky; (Accordion) Robert Candana; (Guitar) Trefoni Rizzi,
Alton Hendrickson; (Alto Sax) Alvy West; (Bass) Arthur Shapiro; (Drums)
Milton Holland.

HCO 2642-1N	It All Came True	COL 37966, S3L 42

Orchestra Under The Direction Of Axel Stordahl - Arrangements As Noted*
October 19, 1947, New York

(Tpt) A. Ferretti, M. Solomon, C. Griffan; (Tbn) W. Pritchard, G. Arus, A. Russo;
(Sax) M. Yaner, N. Mondello, W. Tannenbaum, H. Feldman, E. Caceres;
(Violins) Z. Smirnoff, R. Poliakine, L. Cruczek, F. Buldrini, S. Rand, M. Pitt,
M. Cappos, H. Kay, H. Katzman, J. Brand, B. Sheppard, K. Kieterle; (Violas) H.
Colletta, H. Furmansky, I. Zir; (Cellos) G. Ricci, M. Brown, C. Bernard;
(Harp) E. V. Ricci; (Piano) B. Leighton; (F.H.) J. Singer; (Guitar) M. Golizio;
(Bass) H. Alpert; (Drums) N. Shawker.

CO 38269-1	Can't You Just See Yourself	COL 37978, CL 1297	
CO 38270-1	You're My Girl (1)	COL 37978, CP 12-76	CL 1297
CO 38271-1	All Of Me (2)	COL 38163, CL 606, AI 1013	B 1985, HS 11277

(1) No Trumpets; plus Ken Lane on Piano.

(2) 6 Brass, 5 Sax, Piano, Bass, Guitar, Drums, No Strings, No French Horn, No Harp.

*CO 38269 - Arrangement by Dick Jones

CO 38270 - Arrangement by Axel Stordahl

CO 38271 - Arrangement by George Siravo

Orchestra Under The Direction of Axel Stordahl - Arrangements by Stordahl
October 22, 1947, New York

(Tpt) M. Solomon, H. Lawsen, A. Ferretti; (Tbn) W. Pritchard, A. Russo, G. Arus; (Sax) M. Yaner, T. Mondello, W. Tannenbaum, H. Feldman, E. Caceres; (F.H.) J. Singer; (Violins) L. Kruczek, R. Poliakin, Z. Smirnoff, F. Buldrini, H. Katzman, M. Pitt, K. Dieterle, E. Green, H. Kay, J. Brandt, S. Rand, M. Ceppos; (Violas) H. Coletta, S. Deutsch, I. Zir; (Cellos) C. Bernard, G. Ricci, M. Brown; (Harp) E. Vito Ricci; (Guitar) M. Golizio; (Piano) J. Guanieri; (Bass) H. Alpert; (Drums) N. Shawker.

CO 38272-1B	I'll Make Up For Everything	COL 38989
CO 38273-1	Strange Music	COL 38684, CL 6096, CL 1448, SM 3632
CO 38274-1	Laura	COL 38472, CL 6059, CL 743, C2L 6, HL 7405, SM 3632
CO 38275-1B	Just For Now	UNISSUED

NOTE: On CO 38272 Only - (Tpt) G. Griffin in, A. Ferretti out; (Tbn) W. Rauch in, G. Arus out.

On CO 38274 Trumpets and Trombones out.

With Trio Accompaniment - Arrangements by T. Mottola
October 24, 1947, New York

(Piano) John Guanieri; (Bass) Herman "Trigger" Alpert; (Guitar) Anthony "Tony" Mottola.

CO 38284-1A	My Cousin Louella	COL 38045, AI 1012
CO 38285-1	We Just Couldn't Say Goodbye	COL 38129, CP 12-76
CO 38286-1	S'Posin'	COL 38210, B 1985, CL 606

Orchestra Under The Direction of Axel Stordahl - Arrangements by Stordahl
October 26, 1947, New York

Personnel same as October 22, 1947 Session.

CO 38287-1C	None But The Lonely Heart	COL 38685, CL 6096, CL 1359
CO 38288-1B	The Song Is You	B 1702, CL 1136, SM 3631
CO 38275-1C	Just For Now (REMAKE)	COL 38225, AI 1012

Orchestra Under The Direction Of Axel Stordahl - Arrangements by Stordahl
October 29, 1947, New York

Personnel same as October 26, 1947 Session.

CO 38293-1A	What'll I Do	COL 38045, CP 12-76
CO 38294-1	Poinciana	COL 38829, B 9023, CL 902, S3L 42
CO 38295-1	Senorita	COL 38334, CL 2913
CO 38296-2	The Music Stopped	COL 38683, B 197, CL 6096, SM 3632

Orchestra Under The Direction of Axel Stordahl - Arrangements by Stordahl
October 31, 1947, New York

(Tpt) Gordon "Chris" Griffin; (Sax) Wolfe Tannenbaum; (Clarinet) Ernie Caceres; (Violins) R. Poliakin, Z. Smirnoff; (Viola) H. Coletta; (Cello) George Ricci; (Bass) Herman Alpert; (Piano) Johnny Guarnieri; (Guitar) Matty Golizio; (Drums) Norris Shawker.

CO 38301-1C	Mean To Me	B 9023, CL 902, CL 2572
CO 38302-1	Spring Is Here	COL 38473, CL 6059, CL 743, HL 7405
CO 38303-1	Fools Rush In	COL 38473, CL 6059, CL 743

NOTE: On last two titles there are no Trumpet, Clarinet and Sax. Add Mitchell Miller on Oboe.

Orchester Under The Direction Of Axel Stordahl - Arrangements by Stordahl
November 5, 1947, New York

(Violins) R. Poliakin, Z. Smirnoff; (Viola) H. Coletta; (Cello) G. Ricci; (Flute) B. Kaufman; (Oboe) M. Miller; (Guitar) M. Golizio; (Piano) R. Ketsis; (Bass) H. Alpert; (Drums) J. Blowers.

| CO 38331-1 | When You Awake | COL 38475, CL 6059, AI 1014 |
| CO 38332-1 | It Never Entered My Mind | COL 38475, CL 6059, |

Same Date:

Rhythm accompaniment, strings and Bobby Hacket (Tpt).

CO   38333-1   I've Got A Crush On You   COL 38151, COL 50028,
                                                       B 419, B 1673, B 2517,
                                                       CL 2539, CL 6290, C2L 6,
                                                       CL 2474, SM 3632

Orchestra Under The Direction Of Axel Stordahl - Arrangements by Stordahl
November 9, 1947, New York

(Tpt) A. Ferretti, J. Lawsen, M. Solomon, R. Hacket; (Tbn) G. Arus, W. Pritchard, A. Russo; (Sax) N. Mondello, M. Yaner, W. Tannenbaum, H. Feldman, E. Caceres; (F.H.) J. Singer; (Violins) Z. Smirnoff, R. Poliakin, M. Herslaft, L. Kruczek, J. Slacter, S. Kirsner, M. Zeppos, H. Katzman, M. Pitt, H. Kay, S. Rand, F. Buldrini; (Violas) H. Coletta, I. Zir, H. Furmansky; (Cellos) G. Ricci, M. Brown, A. Kaproff; (Harp) E.V. Ricci; (Guitar) M. Golizio; (Piano) R. Ketsis; (Bass) H. Alpert; (Drums) J. Blowers.

CO   38369-1A   Body And Soul (1)   COL 38472, CL 6059,
                                                       CL 6254, CL 607,
                                                       CL 1448, S3L 42

CO   38370-1   I'm Glad There Is You   COL 40229, C2L 6,
                                                       HS 11390

         (1)   Featuring Trumpet Solo by Bobby Hacket.

Orchestra Under The Direction Of Axel Stordahl - Arrangements by Stordahl
November 25, 1947, New York

(Tpt) B. Previn, D. McNickle, J. Lausen; (Tbn) W. Pritchard, J. D'Agostino, G. Arus; (Sax) H. Shertzer, J. Muenzenberger, W. Tannenbaum, A. Drellinger, S. Webb; (Guitar) M. Golizio; (Piano) R. Ketsis; (Bass) J. Lessberg; (Drums) J. Blowers.

CO   38408-1A   I Went Down To Virginia   COL 38163, S3L 42

CO   38409-1B   If I Only Had A Match   COL 38053, S3L 42

Orchestra Under The Direction Of Axel Stordahl - Arrangements by Stordahl
December 4, 1947, New York

(Tpt) G. Griffin, A. Ferretti, D. McNickle; (Tbn) W. Pritchard, G. Arus, J. D'Agostino; (Sax) H. Shertzer, B. Kaufman, W. Tannenbaum, F. Pfeifer, E. Caceres; (F.H.) K. Chupsa; (Violins) R. Poliakin, B. Sheppard, M. Pitt, M. Hersdaft, M. Ceppos, J. Zayde, F. Orlewitze, S. Morris, M. Kellner, H. Urbont, H. Nosco, H. Azen; (Violas) S. Deutsch, G. Brown, D. Markowitz; (Cellos) A. Kaproff, M. Prinz, F. Miller; (Harp) E.V. Ricci; (Guitar) M. Golizio,

B. Mortell; (Piano) R. Kitsis; (Bass) F. Carroll; (Drums) J. Blowers.

CO 38482-1A	If I Steal A Kiss	COL 38334, CL 2913
CO 38483-1B	Autumn In New York	COL 38316, CL 902, HS 11390
CO 38484-1B	Everybody Loves Somebody	COL 38225, S3L 42

Orchestra Under The Direction of Axel Stordahl - Arrangements by Sy Oliver   December 8, 1947, New York

(Tpt) M. Solomon; (Clarinet) J. Muenzenberger; (Tenor Sax) A. Drellinger; (Guitar) C. Mastren; (Piano) B. Kyle; (Bass) H. Alpert; (Drums) J. Crawford.

| CO 38496-1A | A Little Learnin' Is A Dangerous Thing (1) | COL 38362, B 2542 |
| CO 38497-1A | A Little Learnin' Is A Dangerous Thing (1) | COL 38362, B 2542 |

(1) Vocal Duet with Pearl Bailey

Same Session - Big Band Personnel as CO 38484
Arrangement by Axel Stordahl

| CO 38498-1A | Ever Homeward | COL 38151 |
| CO 38498-PB | Ever Homeward | CL 2913 |

Orchestra Under The Direction of Axel Stordahl - Arrangements by Stordahl
December 26, 1947,
Los Angeles, California

(Tpt) R. Zarchy, G. Seaberg, L. Mack; (Tbn) W. Schaefer, P. Pederson, E. Smithers; (Sax) F. Stulce, M. Clark, A. Gershinoff, H. Haymer, L. Hartman; (F.H.) J. McGee; (Violins) O. Vail, G. Kast, G. Vinci, S. Cytron, D. Frisana, W. Callies, S. Middleman, S. Freed, D. Lube, P. Ellis, W. Bloom, J. Gootkin, G. Joyce; (Violas) M. Perlmutter, G. White, D. Sterkin; (Cellos) F. Goerner, C. Bernard, J. Sewell; (Harp) A. Mason; (Guitar) A. Reuss; (Piano) M. Raskin; (Bass) J. Ryan; (Drums) R. Hagan.

HCO 3052-1N	But None Like You	COL 38129
HCO 3053-1	Catana	MM-1
HCO 3054-1	Why Was I Born	SM 3632

Orchestra Under The Direction of Axel Stordahl - Arrangements by Stordahl
December 28, 1947
Los Angeles, California

(Tpt) G. Wendt, R. Linn, L. Mack; (Tbn) S. Zentner, H. Bohannon, E.

Kuczborski; (Sax) F. Stulce, J. Kinsler, M. Clark, T. Nash, H. Schuchman; (F.H.) J. McGee; (Violins) M. Russell, G. Kast, W. Callies, N. Pisani, D. Frisana, W. Edelstein, E. Buano, D. Lube, M. Levant, S. Freed, Jr., A. Murray, S. Cytron; (Violas) M. Perlmutter, G. White, D. Sterkin; (Cellos) F. Goerner, J. Sewell, E. Slatkin; (Harp) L. McFarland; (Guitar) A. Reuss; (Piano) M. McIntyre; (Bass) A. Shapiro; (Drums) R. Hagan.

HCO 3067-1N	O Little Town of Bethlehem (1)	COL 38258, CL 2542, CL 6019, CL 1032, HL 7400
HCO 3068-1N	It Came Upon The Mid-night Clear (1)	COL 38258, CL 2542, CL 6019, CL 1032, HL 7400
HCO 3069-1N	White Christmas (2)	COE (DB 3745, CP 12-76
HCO 3070-1N	For Every Man There's A Woman	COL 38089, B 9023, CL 902
HCO 3071-1N	Help Yourself To My Heart	MM-1
HCO 3072-1N	Santa Claus Is Coming To Town	COL 38259, CL 2542, CL 6019, CL 1032, HL 7400

(1) With The Ken Lane Singers

(2) On this version no Ken Lane Singers

NOTE: Also on this same session:

HCO 3054-3	Why Was I Born (REMAKE)	COL 38686, B 9023, CL 6096, C2L 6, HS 11390

On HCO 3072 only: 3 (Tpt); 3 (Tbn); 5 (Sax); 4 (Rhythm); (Violin); (Viola); (Cello); (Harp); (F.H.) Out.

Orchestra Under The Direction of Axel Stordahl - Arrangements by Stordahl
December 30, 1947,
Los Angeles, California

Personnel Same as Last Session (Full Band including strings)

HCO 3089-1N	If I Forget You	COL 41133, CL 1136
HCO 3090-1	Where Is The One	COL 38421, CP 12-76
HCO 3091-1	When Is Sometime	COL 38417, AI 1012

Orchestra Under The Direction Of Axel Stordahl - Arrangements by Stordahl
March 16, 1948
Los Angeles, California

(Tpt) M. Solomon, G. Griffin, J. Lausen; (Tbn) W. Pritchard, A. Russo, R.

Dupont; (F.H.) A. Miranda; (Violins) H. Azen, B. Sheppard, J. Held, S. Kirsner, H. Urbont, R. Poliakin, F. Orlewitz, M. Hershaft, S. Harris, H. Shomer, M. Pitt, M. Ceppos; (Violas) S. Deutsch, R. Hersh, L. Frengat; (Cellos) G. Ricci, A. Kaproff, H. Shapiro; (Sax) J. Muenzenberger, B. Kaufman, W. Tannenbaum, H. Feldman, E. Caceres; (Harp) E.V. Ricci; (Guitar) M. Golizio; (Piano) R. Kitsis; (Bass) H. Alpert; (Drums) J. Blowers.

HCO 3224-1A   It Only Happens When I Dance   COL 38192, AI 1012
                        With You

HCO 3225-1A   A Fellow With An Umbrella   COL 38192, AI 1012

NOTE: The background for the above two tunes was cut in Hollywood in December 9, 1947 and Sinatra simply dubbed his voice in on March 16, 1948. A background of a tune called "Miracle Of The Bells" was also cut, but Sinatra never sang the tune or recorded it.

Jeff Alexander - Leader and Vocal Arranger
Los Angeles, California   April 10, 1948

Jeff Alexander Choir: Twelve male voices and eight female voices - no orchestra.

HCO 3250-1A   Nature Boy   COL 38210, CL 1448

Orchester Under The Direction of Mitchell Ayres - Arrangements by Ayres
                                       December 15, 1948, New York

(Tpt) M. Solomon, J. Maxwell, C. Poole; (Tbn) M. Morrow, W. Rauch, J. D'Agostino; (Sax) H. Terrill, P. Zolkind, J. Small, H. Feldman, H. Ross; (Piano) H. Rowland; (Bass) R. Haggart; (Guitar) H. White; (Drums) T. Snyder.

CO 40254-1A   Once In Love With Amy   COL 38291, CL 902

NOTE: On this session, Sinatra recorded in New York City and flew to California and promptly recorded another session upon arriving there. This is the only explanation we can obtain for the same date in two separate cities. According to Columbia work sheets, the New York session started at 9:30 A.M. to 12:30 P.M.; the California session started at 9:30 P.M. to 11:30 P.M.

PHIL MOORE FOUR - Arrangements by Moore
Los Angeles, California   December 15, 1948

(Piano) Phil Moore; (Sax) Marshall Royal; (Guitar) Robert Bain; (Bass) Ernest Sheppard, Jr.; (Drums) Leonidas

HCO 3475-1N   Why Can't You Behave?   COL 38393, B 1815,
                                            CL 1297

HCO 3476-1N   Bop Goes My Heart   COL 38421, AI 1012

Accompaniment Unknown
Los Angeles, California   December 16, 1948

Personnel Unknown

| HCO 3467-1C | Sunflower | COL 38391, CL 6057, AI 1012 |

NOTE: No one seems to know who the leader, arranger or accompaniment is on this session and it sounds like a single guitar. Also the master number (HCO 3467) is lower than the last session (HCO 3475 - HCO 3476) which should indicate that it was recorded before them, but Columbia work sheet has this date although it lacks all other information. The dates Dec. 15, 1948 and Dec. 16, 1948 are certainly baffling to say the least.

Orchestra Under The Direction Of Axel Stordahl - Arrangements by Stordahl
December 19, 1948
Los Angeles, California

(Tpt) R. Zarchy, G. Seaberg, Z. Elman; (Tbn) W. Schaefer, R. McGanty, L. Jenkins; (Sax) F. Stulce, H. Beau, A. Gershinoff, H. Haymer, M. Colani, F. Chase; (F.H.) V. DeRosa; (Violins) M. Russell, G. Kast, S. Cytron, N. Pisani, D. Middleman, M. Kellner, O. Vail, J. Sclackter, R. Poliakin, D. Karpilowsky; (Violas) M. Perlmutter, P. Robyn, G. White; (Cellos) E. Slatkin, J. Sewell, C. Bernard; (Harp) M. Cambern; (Guitar) A. Reuss; (Piano) M. McIntrye; (Bass) P. Stephens; (Drums) R. Hagan.

HCO 3479-1A	Comme Ci, Comme Ca	COL 38407, S 3L 42
HCO 3480-1N	No Orchids For My Lady	COL 38393, SM 3634, CP 12-76
HCO 3481-1N	While The Angelus Was Ringing	COL 38407, AI 1012

PHIL MOORE FOUR - Arrangements by Moore
Los Angeles, California
January 4, 1949

(Piano) and (Leader) Phil Moore; (Sax) Marshall Royal; (Guitar) Robert Bain; (Bass) Ernest Sheppard, Jr.; (Drums) Oscar Lee Bradley.

| HCO 3511-1P | If You Stub Your Toe On The Moon | COL 38417, S 3L 42, AI 1012 |
| HCO 3512-1 | Kisses And Tears | MM-1 |

NOTE: This version of Kisses and Tears does not have Jane Russell.

Orchestra Under The Direction Of Axel Stordahl - Arrangements by Stordahl
February 28, 1949,
Los Angeles, California

(Sax) F. Stulce, H. Haymer, A. Gershinoff, H. Beau, F. Chase, M. Cohan; (F.H.) V. DeRosa; (Violins) M. Russell, N. Pisani, R. Poliakin, J. Sclackter, D. Frisana, W. Callies, G. Kast, D. Karpilowsky, S. Middleman, G. Vinci, O. Vail, M. Kellner; (Violas) M. Perlmutter, G. White, P. Robyn; (Cellos) C. Bernard, E. Slatkin, J. Sewell; (Harp) M. Cambern; (Bass) P. Stephens; (Guitar) A. Reuss;

(Piano) M. McIntyre; (Drums) R. Hagan.

| HCO 3617-1 | Some Enchanted Evening | COL 38446, B 1608, CL 1297 |
| HCO 3618-1 | Bali Ha'i * (1) | COL 38446, B 1608, CL 1297 |

(1) With Vocal Chorus

NOTE: On HCO 3618 add three unknown Steel Guitars.

Orchestra Under The Direction Of Axel Stordahl - Arrangements by Stordahl
March 3, 1949,
Los Angeles, California

(Sax) F. Stulce, H. Haymer, A. Gershinoff, H. Beau, F. Chase, M. Cohan; (F.H.) V. DeRosa; (Violins) M. Russell, N. Pisani, R. Poliakin, J. Schackter, D. Frisana, W. Callies, G. Kast, D. Karpilowsky, S. Middleman, G. Vinci, O. Vail, M. Kellner; (Violas) M. Perlmutter, G. White, P. Robyn; (Cellos) C. Bernard, E. Slatkin, J. Sewell; (Harp) M. Cambern; (Bass) P. Stephens; (Guitar) A. Reuss; (Piano) M. McIntyre; (Drums) R. Hagan.

| HCO 3635-1N | The Right Girl For Me | COL 38456, S 3L 42, CL 2913 |
| HCO 3636-1N | Night After Night | COL 38456 |

Orchester Under The Direction Of Axel Stordahl - Arrangements by Stordahl
April 10, 1949,
Los Angeles, California

(Tpt) G. Seaberg, L. Mack, R. Zarchy, Z. Elman; (Tbn) S. Zentner, R. McGarity, L. Jenkins; (Sax) F. Stulce, H. Beau, H. Haymer, A. Gershinoff, M. Cohan, F. Chase; (Guitar) A. Reuss; (Piano) M. McIntyre; (Harp) M. Cambern; (Bass) P. Stephens; (Drums) R. Hagan.

| HCO 3692-1N | The Huckle Buck (1) | COL 38486, CL 2521, S 3L 42 |
| HCO 3693-1N | It Happens Every Spring | COL 38486, AI 1013 |

(1) With The Ken Lane Quintet

Orchestra Under The Direction Of Axel Stordahl - Arrangements by Stordahl
May 6, 1949,
Los Angeles, California

(Sax) F. Stulce, D. Bonnee, B. Russin, M. Cohan, A. Gershinoff; (Violins) G. Kast, S. Cytron, R. Poliakin, S. Middleman, W. Callies, G. Vinci, M. Russell, D. Frisana, N. Kellner; (Violas) M. Perlmutter, G. White; (Cellos) C. Bernard, J. Sewell; (Bass) P. Stephens; (Guitar) A. Reuss; (F.H.) V. DeRosa, (Harp) A. Mason; (Piano) M. McIntyre; (Drums) R. Hagan.

With Doris Day
— 1949.

With Rosemary Clooney — 1950.

| HCO 3748-1N | Let's Take An Old Fashioned Walk (1) | COL 38513 |
| HCO 3749-1N | (Just One Way To Say) I Love You | COL 38513 |

(1) Vocal Duet With Doris Day

HUGO WINTERHALTER AND ORCHESTRA - Arrangements by Winterhalter
July 10, 1949, New York

(Tpt) C. Pool, M. Solomon, J. Lausen; (Tbn) M. Morrow, J. D'Agostino, W. Pritchard; (Sax) E. Caceres, S. Cooper, W. Tannenbaum, N. Mondello, H. Ross; (Piano) J. Guarniere; (Guitar) A. Caiola; (Bass) H. Alpert; (Drums) T. Snyder.

CO 40951-1	It All Depends On You	COL 38550, CL 6143, CL 606
CO 40952-1B	Bye Bye Baby (1)	COL 38556, CL 1241
CO 40953-1B	Don't Cry Joe (1)	COL 38555, B 9021, CL 902

(1) With Vocal Group - The Pastels.

HUGO WINTERHALTER AND ORCHESTRA - Arrangements by Winterhalter
July 14, 1949, New York

(Sax) H. Ross, S. Cooper, N. Mondello, A. Drellinger, I. Horowitz; (Violins) L. Kruczek, M. Ceppos, S. Shulman, F. Buildrini, F. Orlewitz, J. Zayde; (Violas) I. Zir, H. Kay; (Cello) M. Brown; (Harp) E.V. Ricci; (F.H.) T. Miranda; (Piano) B. Leighton; (Guitar) A. Gottuso; (Bass) H. Alpert; (Drums) T. Snyder.

CO 40970-1A	Every Man Should Marry	UNISSUED
CO 40971-1A	If I Ever Love Again (1)	COL 38572, S 3L 42, AI 1013
CO 40972-1A	Just A Kiss Apart	UNISSUED

(1) With The Double Daters

Orchestra Under The Direction Of Morris Stoloff - Arrangements by Stoloff
July 21, 1949,
Los Angeles, California

(Sax) F. Stulce, H. Beau, A. Gershinoff, H. Schuman, B. Russin; (Violins) M. Sosson, F. Slatkin, M. Russell, N. Pisani, D. Lube, D. Karpilowsky; (Violas) D. Sterkin, M. Perlmutter; (Cello) C. Bernard; (F.H.) V. DeRosa; (Bass) P. Stephens; (Piano) M. McIntyre; (Guitar) A. Reuss; (Harp) L. McFarland; (Drums) R. Hagan.

| HCO 3853-1N | Just A Kiss Apart | COL 38556 |

| HCO 3854-1N | Every Man Should Marry | COL 38572 |
| HCO 3855-1N | The Wedding Of Lili Marlene | COL 38555, CP 12-76 |

Orchestra Under The Direction Of Jeff Alexander - Arrangements by
Alexander   September 15, 1949
                                                  Los Angeles, California

(Tpt) G. Seaberg, V. Mangano, Z. Elman; (Tbn) R. McGarity, G. Arus, P.
Weigand; (Sax) E. Callen, H. Schuchman, P. Shuken, A. Raskin, L. Palange;
(F.H.) V. DeRosa; (Guitar) A. Reuss; (Piano) K. Lane; (Bass) P. Stephens; (Harp)
R. Maxwell; (Drums) R. Hagan.

| HCO 3903-1 | That Lucky Old Sun (1) | COL 38608, B 9022, CL 902 |

             (1) With Vocal Chorus

(Tpt) Out; (Tbn) Out; (Sax) Same; (Harp) Same; (Rhythm) Same; Add: (Violins)
R. Poliakin, W. Miller, V. Arno, J. Shulman, M. Russell, D. Lube; (Violas) J.
DeFiore, A. Weiss; (Cellos) C. Bernard, E. Slatkin.

| HCO 3904-1 | Mad About You | COL 38613, CL 953, B 9533 |

(Tpt) Out; (Tbn) Out; (Sax) Out; (Violins) Same; (Bass) Same; (Harp) Same;
Add: (Alto Flute) L. Palange; (2 Mandolins) M. Gralnick, J. Rose; (2 Guitars) A.
Reuss, B. Kessel; (Accordion) M. Delugg.

| HCO 3905-1 | (On The Island Of) Stromboli | COL 38613, CL 953, B 9533 |

Orchestra Under The Direction Of Axel Stordahl - Arrangements by Stordahl
                                                  October 30, 1949,
                                                  Los Angeles, California

(Sax) F. Stulce, H. Beau, B. Russin, J. Kinsler, L. Hartman; (Violins) R.
Poliakin, M. Russell, N. PIsani, F. Slatkin, M. Sosson, W. Callies; (Violas) G.
White, M. Perlmutter; (Cello) C. Bernard; (Harp) A. Stockton; (Guitar) A.
Reuss; (Piano) K. Lane; (Bass) P. Stephens; (Drums) R. Hagan. NO TRUM-
PETS OR TROMBONES.

| RHCO 3937-1B | The Old Master Painter (1) | COL 38650, AI 1012 |
| RHCO 3938-1N | Why Remind Me (1) | COL 38662, S 3L 42 |

        (1) With the Modernaires: Paula Kelly, Allan Copeland,
           Hal Dickinson, Francis Scott, Johnny Drake.

Orchestra Under The Direction Of Axel Stordahl - Arrangements by Stordahl
                                                  November 8, 1949,
                                                  Los Angeles, California

(Tpt) Z. Elman, G. Seaberg, R. Zarchy, M. Klein; (Tbn) L. McGarity, W.

Schaefer, G. Arus, E. Smithers; (Sax) F. Stulce, J. Kinsler, E. Gershman, B. Russin, L. Hartman; (Harp) A. Mason; (Guitar) A. Reuss; (Piano) K. Lane; (Bass) P. Stephens; (Drums) R. Hagan.

RHCO 3939-1N	Sorry (1)	COL 38662, B 9533, CL 953
RHCO 3940-1N	Sunshine Cake (2)	COL 38705, S 3L 42
RHCO 3941-1N	(We've Got A) Sure Thing (3)	COL 38705, S 3L 42

(1) With the Modernaires (as last session)

(2) With Paula Kelly only

(3) With the Ken Lane Singers

Orchestra Under The Direction Of Axel Stordahl - Arrangements by Stordahl
January 12, 1950,
Los Angeles, California

(Tpt) Z. Elman; (Tbn) R. L. McGarity; (Sax) F. Stulce, H. Beau, J. Kinsler, B. Russin, L. Hartman; (Violins) R. Poliakin, D. Frisana, M. Russell, N. Pisani, G. Kast, S. Cytron; (Violas) M. Perlmutter, G. White; (Cello) C. Bernard; (F.H.) J. Cave, V. DeRosa; (Harp) A. Mason; (Piano) K. Lane; (Guitar) A. Reuss; (Bass) P. Stephens; (Drums) R. Hagan.

RHCO 3999-1A	God's Country (1)	COL 38708
RHCO 4000-2C	Sheila (1)	COL 40565
RHCO 4001-1D	Chattanooga Shoe Shine Boy (1)	COL 38708, AI 1012

(1) With Jeff Alexander Choir

NOTE: On Master RHCO 4001 only - 3 woodwinds, 4 rhythm, trumpet and trombone.

Orchestra Under The Direction Of Axel Stordahl - Arrangements by Stordahl
February 23, 1950,
Los Angeles, California

(Tpt) Z. Elman, G. Seaberg, R. Zarchy, R. Brooks; (Tbn) R.L. McGarity, G. Arus, E. Kuczborski, E. Smithers; (Sax) F. Stulce, H. Beau, B. Russin, J. Kinsler, L. Hartman; (Piano) K. Lane; (Guitar) A. Reuss; (Bass) P. Stephens; (Drums) R. Hagan.

RHCO 4020-1A	Kisses And Tears (1)	COL 38790, CL 2530, CP 12-76
RHCO 4021-1N	When The Sun Goes Down (2)	COL 38790, CL 1359

(1) Vocal Duet with Jane Russell and the Modernaires

(2) With the Modernaires (as last session)

Orchestra Under The Direction Of Mitch Miller - Arrangement by Miller
March 10, 1950, New York

(Tpt) B. Butterfield, H. Freistadt; (Tbn) W. Bradley, L. Altpeter; (Sax) E. Powell, V. Abato, R. Banzer, S. Amata; (Guitar) A. Ryerson; (Piano) S. Freeman; (Bass) F. Carroll; (Drums) T. Snyder.

| CO 42967-1B | American Beauty Rose | COL 38809, COL 40522, CL 6119, CL 1241 |

Orchestra Under The Direction Of George Siravo - Arrangements by Siravo
April 8, 1950, New York

(Tpt) G. Griffin, P. Savitt, R. Weinstein, R. Trent; (Tbn) G. Arus, R. Cutshall; (Sax) A. Klink, E. Callan, H. Shertzer, L. Hartman, B. Russin; (Piano) K. Lane; (Bass) P. Stephens; (Guitar) A. Reuss; (Drums) M. Purtill.

| CO 43100-1D | Peach Tree Street (1) | COL 38853, CP 12-76 |

| CO 43101-1 | There's Something Missing | UNISSUED |

(1) Vocal Duet With Rosemary Clooney

Orchestra Under The Direction Of George Siravo - Arrangements by Siravo
April 14, 1950, New York

(Tpt) B. Butterfield, C. Poole, P. Savitt; (Tbn) G. Arus, B. Rauch; (Sax) H. Shertzer, E. Callen, L. Hartman, B. Russin, E. Caceres; (Piano) K. Lane; (Bass) P. Stephens; (Guitar) A. Reuss; (Drums) J. Blowers.

| CO 43126-1 | Should I | COL 38998, CL 6143, CL 1241 |

| CO 43127-1 | You Do Something To Me | COL 38999, B 419, B 1815, CL 2539, CL 6143, CL 6290, CL 1241, SM 3632 |

| CO 43128-1 | Lover | COL 38996, B 1872, B 7433, CL 6143, CL 743 |

Orchestra Under The Direction Of George Siravo - Arrangements by Siravo
April 24, 1950, New York

(Tpt) C. Griffin, S. Lipkis, B. Butterfield, P. Savitt; (Tbn) G. Arus, B. Mano; (Sax) H. Shertzer, A. Drellinger, J. Jerone, B. Russin, J. Horvath; (Piano) B. Leighton; (Bass) P. Stephens; (Guitar) A. Reuss; (Drums) J. Blowers.

| CO 43180-1 | When You're Smiling | COL 38996, CL 6143, CL 1242 |

| CO 43181-1 | It's Only A Paper Moon | COL 38997, CL 6143, |

Recording with the Whipporwills vocal quintet — 1950.

Recording with Dagmar — 1951.

		CL 953, B 9533, S 3L 42
CO 43182-1	My Blue Heaven	COL 38892, CL 6143, CL 1241, S3L 42
CO 43182-3	My Blue Heaven	COE DB 2737
CO 43183-2	The Continental	COL 38997, CL 6143, CL 1241

Mitch Miller - Leader and Arranger

June 28, 1950, New York

(Organ) Lou White; (Bass) Frank Carroll; (Guitar) Mundell Lowe.

CO 44015-1	Goodnight Irene	COL 38892, CL6150, CL 1448
CO 44015-3	Goodnight Irene	COE DB 2737
CO 44016-1A	Dear Little Boy Of Mine (1)	COL 38960, CL 1448

(1) With the Ken Lane Singers

Orchestra Under The Direction Of Percy Faith - Arrangements by Faith

August 2, 1950, New York

Personnel not exactly known, but similar to next session.

CO 44185-1	Life Is So Peculiar (1)	COL 38960, AI 1012

(1) With Helen Carroll and the Swantones

Orchestra Under The Direction Of Axel Stordahl - Arrangements by Stordahl

September 18, 1950, New York

(Tpt) D. McNickle, T. Faso, J. Owens; (Tbn) B. Rausch, G. Arus, W. Heins; (Sax) P. Ricci, J. Small, J. Lytell, A. Drellinger; (F.H.) A. DeRosa; (Violins) R. Poliakin, A. Smirnoff, J. Brandt, M. Heischaft, R. Lynch, B. Taylor; (Violas) I. Zir, S. Deutsch; (Cello) G. Ricci; (Oboe) I. Horowitz; (Harp) E. Vito; (Piano) G. Forbes; (Bass) F. Carroll; (Guitar) M. Golizio; (Drums) J. Blowers.

CO 44366-1	Accidents Will Happen	COL 39014
CO 44367-1	One Finger Melody	COL 39013, 1013

Orchestra Under The Direction Of Axel Stordahl - Arrangements by Stordahl

September 21, 1950, New York

(Tpt) C. Griffin, T. Faso, J. Owens; (Tbn) B. Morrow, B. Rausch, G. Arus; (Sax) H. Shertzer, B. Kaufman, J. Lytell, W. Tannenbaum, J. Greenberg; (F.H.) J. Barrow; (Violins) R. Poliakin, Z. Smirnoff, M. Heischaft, J. Brandt, H. Urbont, M. Lomask; (Violas) H. Colletti, S. Deutsch; (Cello) F. Miller;

(Harp) E.V. Ricci; (Piano) G. Forbes; (Guitar) M. Golizio; (Bass) F. Carroll; (Drums) J. Blowers.

CO 44376-1A	Remember Me In Your Dreams (1)	COL 39069, CL 541, B-363, CI 1014
CO 44377-1N	If Only She'd Look My Way	B 9533, CL 953, AI 1013
CO 44378-1C	London By Night	COL 39592, AI 1013
CO 44379-1N	Meet Me At The Copa	MM-1

(1) With the Whipporwills Vocal Quintet - Marilyn Sullivan, Gordon Thorin, John Ackerman, Frank Howren, David O'Hern

NOTE: Masters CO 44377 and CO 44378 were issued in England with spoken introduction by Prince Phillip for special proceeds for a playing field for youngsters.

Orchestra Under The Direction Of Axel Stordahl
Arrangements by Stordahl   October 9, 1950, New York

(Tpt) B. Butterfield, C. Griffin, J. Owens; (Tbn) L. Altpeter, G. Arus, W. Rausch; (Sax) H. Shertzer, W. Versaci, A. Drellinger, E. Gershman, H. Feldman; (F.H.) Q. Schuller; (Violins) R. Poliakin, F. Buldrini, M. Hershaft, J. Held, R. Lynch, J. Brandt; (Violas) S. Deutsch, L. Drusinsky; (Cello) G. Ricci; (Harp) E.V. Ricci; (Piano) G. Forbes; (Guitar) M. Golizio; (Bass) H. Alpert; (Drums) J. Blowers.

CO 44427-1	Come Back To Sorrento (Torna A. Surriento)	COL 39118, CL 1359
CO 44428-1A	April In Paris	COL 39592, CL 6290, C2L 6
CO 44429-1	I Guess I'll Have To Dream The Rest (1)	COL 39044, CL 953
CO 44430-1	Nevertheless (2)	COL 39044, CL 953, S3L 42

(1) With the Ken Lane Singers

(2) Featuring Billy Butterfield on Trumpet Solo

Orchestra Under The Direction Of Axel Stordahl
Arrangements by Stordahl   November 5, 1950, New York

(Tpt) D. McNickle, J. Owens, T. Lawson; (Tbn) R. Dupont, G. Arus, B. Rank; (Sax) H. Shertzer, H. Feldman, B. Kaufman, M. Gershamn, A. Richman; (F.H.) J. Barrows; (Violins) Z. Smirnoff, J. Brandt, M. Hershoft, A. Eidus, J. Held, H. Hoffman; (Violas) S. Deutsch, H. Formasky; (Cello) G. Poliakin;

(Harp) E.V. Ricci; (Guitar) M. Golizio; (Piano) G. Forbes; (Bass) F. Carroll; (Drums) J. Blowers.

| CO 44615-1B | Let It Snow, Let It Snow, Let It Snow, (1) | COL 39069, CL 1032, CL 2521 |

(1) With the Ken Lane Singers

Orchestra Under The Direction Of Axel Stordahl
Arrangements by Stordahl   November 16, 1950, New York

(Tpt) L. Castle, D. McNickle, J. Owens; (Tbn) W. Rausch, B. Rank, G. Arus; (Sax) H. Shertzer, B. Kaufman, A. Drellinger, M. Gershman, H. Feldman; (F.H.) J. Barrows; (Violins) R. Poliakin, M. Lomask, M. Hershaft, L. Brandt, H. Katzman, J. Jeld; (Violas) I. Zir, S. Deutsch; (Cello) G. Poliakin; (Harp) E.V. Ricci; (Piano) G. Forbes; (Guitar) M. Golizio; (Bass) F. Carroll; (Drums) J. Blowers.

CO 44634-1	Take My Love	COL 39118, B 9532, CL 953
CO 44635-1A	I Am Loved	COL 39079, B 9532, CL 953
CO 44636-1C	You Don't Remind Me	COL 39079
CO 44637-1A	You're The One	UNISSUED

Orchestra Under The Direction Of Axel Stordahl
Arrangements by Stordahl   December 11, 1950, New York

(Tpt) C. Griffin; (Sax) H. Shertzer, T. Mondello, M. Gershman, H. Feldman, A. Drellinger; (Piano) G. Forbes; (Guitar) M. Golizio; (Bass) F. Carroll; (Drums) J. Blowers.

| CO 44714-1B | Love - Means - Love (1) | COL 39141 |
| CO 4415-1A | Cherry Pies Ought To Be You (1) | COL 39141 |

(1) Vocal Duet with Rosemary Clooney

Orchestra Under The Direction Of Axel Stordahl
Arrangements by Stordahl   January 16, 1951, New York

(Tpt) T. Faso, D. McNickle, J. Owens; (Tbn) W. Rausch, G. Arus, L. McGarity; (Sax) H. Shertzer, B. Kaufman, A. Drellinger, M. Gershman, E. Brown; (F.H.) D. Rattner; (Violins) G. Ockner, H. Katzman, R. Lynch, J. Brandt, M. Lomask; (Violas) S. Deutsch, T. Adoff; (Cello) G. Poliakin; (Harp) E. V. Ricci; (Guitar) M. Golizio; (Piano) S. Freeman; (Bass) F. Caroll; (Drums) J. Blowers.

| CO 45111-1B | Faithful (1) | COL 39213 |
| CO 45112-1D | You're The One | COL 39213, S 3L 42 |

| CO 45113-1C | There's Something Missing (A)-(1) (REMAKE) | MM-1 |

(1) With Unknown Vocal Chorus - probably the Ken Lane Singers

(A) Arranged by George Siravo

Orchestra Under The Direction Of Axel Stordahl
Arrangements by Stordahl   March 2, 1951, New York

(Tbn) G. Arus, T. Satterfield; (Woodwinds) B. Stegmeyer, B. Kaufman, A. Drellinger, M. Gershman, H. Feldman; (F.H.) J. Barrows; (Violins) R. Poliakin, Z. Smirnoff, R. Lynch, M. Hershaft, H. Katzman, M. Lomask, F. Orlewitz, H. Melinkoff, A. Eidus; (Violas) I. Zir, S. Deutsch; (Cellos) G. Poliakin, A. Borodkin; (Harp) E.V. Ricci; (Guitar) M. Golizio; (Piano) G. Forbes; (Bass) F. Carroll; (Drums) J. Blowers.

| CO 45156-1F | Hello Young Lovers | COL 39294, B 1984, CL 606 |
| CO 45157-1E | We Kiss In A Shadow | COL 39294, B 9531, CL 953 |

Orchestra Under The Direction Of Axel Stordahl
Arrangements by Stordahl   March 27, 1951, New York

(Tbn) G. Arbus, W. Rausch; (Woodwinds) B. Kaufman, M. Gershman, H. Terril, F. Glantz, H. Keinz; (F.H.) J. Burrows; (Violins) H. Katzman, T. Lassoff, R. Lynch, F. Buldrini, J. Shacter, M. Lomask, A. Eidus, M. Ceppos, M. Green; (Violas) I. Zir, H. Furmansky; (Cellos) G. Poliakin, F. Miller; (Harp) V. Salvi; (Guitar) M. Golizio; (Piano) G. Forbes; (Bass) F. Carroll; (Drums) J. Blowers.

CO 45184-1	I Whistle A Happy Tune	COL 39346, CL 1297,
CO 45185-1D	I'm A Fool To Want You	COL 39425, COL 41133, B 2559, CL 2572, S3L 42
CO 45186-1	Love Me	COL 39346, B 9532 CL 953, S3L 42

Orchestra Under The Direction Of Axel Stordahl
Arranger Unknown   May 10, 1951, New York

(Tpt) C. Griffin; (Tbn) W. Rausch; (Sax) H. Shertzer, A. Klink, B. Kaufman, M. Gershman, E. Caceres; (Guitar) M. Golizio; (Piano) G. Forbes; (Bass) F. Carroll; (Drums) J. Blowers.

| CO 45819-1A | Mama Will Bark (1) | COL 39425 |

CO 45820-1G   It's A Long Way (From Your   COL 39493
                     House To My House)

                     (1) With Vocal Duet With Dagmar
                     Dog Imitations by Donald Bain

HARRY JAMES AND HIS ORCHESTRA - Arranger Unknown*
Los Angeles, California   July 9, 1951

(Tpt) Jarry James, Nick Buono, Philip Cook, Evertt McDonald, Ralph Osborn;
(Tbn) Lewis McCreary, Ray Conniff, Jimmy Priddy; (Bass Tbn) Hal Smith;
(Alto Sax) Frank Polifroni, Rene Block; (Tenor Sax) Herbie Steward; (Baritone
Sax) Robert Poland; (Piano) Bruce McDonald; (Guitar) Allen Reuss; (Bass)
Edward Mikelitch; (Drums) Jackie Mills.

RHCO 4561-1D   Castle Rock   COL 39527, C2L 6,
                                                         B 2542

RHCO 4562-1   Farewell, Farewell To Love   CL 1242, B 2542

RHCO 4563-1   Deep Night   COL 39527, CL 1241

*Presumed to be Ray Conniff.

Orchestra Under The Direction Of Joseph Gershenson
Arrangements by Gershenson   October 16, 1951, Hollywood

Orchestra personnel unknown. Taken from the original soundtrack of the
Universal-International film "Meet Danny Wilson".

RHCO 10022-1   A Good Man Is Hard To Find (1)UR 179178*

RHCO 10022-1   A Good Man Is Hard To Find (1)MM-1, UR 179178

                     All Of Me, Lonesome Man Blues UR 179178

                     When You're Smiling, She's   UR 179178
                     Funny That Way   UR 179178

(1) Vocal Duet with Shelly Winters

NOTE: UR 179178 is a promotional disc released by Universal-International
of songs recorded for the film "Meet Danny Wilson."

Orchestra Under The Direction Of Axel Stordahl
Arrangements by Stordahl   January 7, 1952,
                                                  Los Angeles, California

(Tpt) Rubin Zarchy; (Tbn) Jimmy Priddy, George Arus; (Sax) Jack Dumont,
Morris Bercov, Babe Russin, Emanuel Gershman, Leonard Hartman; (Violins)
Mischa Russell, Harry Bluestone, Irving Prager, David Frisana, John
Augustine, Murray Kellner; (Violas) David Sterkin, Maurice Perlmutter; (Cello)
Cy Bernard; (Harp) Ann Stockton; (Bass) John Ryan; (Guitar) Allan Reuss;

(Piano) William Miller; (Drums) Nick Fatool.

RHCO 10081-1C	I Could Write A Book (1)	COL 39652, B 2559, CL 953
RHCO 10082-1A	I Hear A Rhapsody (1)	COL 39652, B 419,
		CL 2539, CL 6290 CL 1359, SM 3632
RHCO 10083-1N	Walking In The Sunshine (1) With The Jeff Alexander Choir	COL 39726, S3L 42

Orchestra Under The Direction Of Axel Stordahl
Arrangements by Stordahl   February 6, 1952,
                                        Los Angeles, California

(Tpt) R. Zarchy; (Tbn) J. Priddy, G. Arus; (Sax) F. Stulce, E. Callen, B. Russin,
E. Gershman, L. Hartman; (Violins) M. Sosson, M. Russell, D. Lube, J.
Augustine, I. Prager, N. Pisana; (Violas) D. Sterkin, S. Harris; (Cello) E. Slatkin;
(Harp) A. Stockton; (Guitar) A. Reuss; (Piano) W. Miller; (Bass) J. Ryan;
(Drums) R. Hagan.

RHCO 10110-1A	My Girl	COL 39726, CL 1297, AI 1013
RHCO 10115-1N	Feet Of Clay	COL 39687
RHCO 10115-1N	Don't Ever Be Afraid To Go Home	COL 39687

Orchestra Under The Direction Of Axel Stordahl
Arrangements by Stordahl   June 3, 1952,
                                        Los Angeles, California

(Tpt) R. Zarchy, C. Gozzo, J. Best; (Tbn) D. Noel, J. Priddy, G. Arus; (Sax)
L. Robinson, F. Stulce, B. Russin, T. Nash, C. Gentry; (Guitar) A. Ruess;
(Steel Guitar) W. West; (Piano) W. Miller; (Bass) J. Ryan; (Drums) A. Stoller,
J. Siracusa.

RHCO 10178-1N	Luna Rosa (1)	COL 39787, CL 1359
RHCO 10179-1N	The Birth Of The Blues (A)	COL 39882, COL 50028, CL 2521, C2L 6, S3L 42
RHCO 10180-1A	Azure-Te (Paris Blues)	COL 39819, S3L 42
RHCO 10181-1B	Tennessee Newsboy	COL 39787, SM 3634
RHCO 10190-1A	Bim Bam Baby	COL 39819, CL 2521, CL 1241

(1) With the Norman Luboff Choir

(A) Arranged by Heinie Beau

Recording at Columbia — late 1952.

PERCY FAITH AND ORCHESTRA - Arrangement by Faith
September 17, 1952, New York

(Tbn) G. Satterfield, C. Butterfield, P. Giardina; (Woodwinds and Sax) V. Abato, A. Freistadt, J. Fulton, R. Banzer, H. Feldman; (Violins) M. Lomask, G. Ockner, E. Green, S. Carmell, C. Orloff, A. Cores, H. Katzman, H. Hoffman, B. Erle; (Violas) R. Dickler, S. Brecher; (Cello) B. Greenhouse; (Piano) S. Freeman; (Guitar) A. Ryerson; (Bass) F. Carroll; (Harp) E. Druzinski; (Drums) P. Kraus.

CO 48181-1A   Why Try To Change Me Now   COL 39882, S3L 42

NOTE: Remainder of this session by Mindy Carson.

Recording with Axel Stordahl and A & R man Mitch Miller — 1952.

SONG INDEX
COLUMBIA RECORDS - CHAPTER VI

Accidents Will Happen - (Johnny Burke - Jimmy Van Heusen)
September 18, 1950

Adeste Fidelis - (Reading)
August 8, 1946

Ain'tcha Ever Comin' Back - (Paul Weston - Axel Stordahl - I. Taylor)
March 11, 1947

All Of Me - (Seymour Simons - Gerald Marks)
November 7, 1946 - October 16, 1951

All The Things You Are - (Jerome Kern - Oscar Hammerstein II)
January 29, 1945

All Through The Day - (Jerome Kern - Oscar Hammerstein II)
February 3, 1946

Almost Like Being In Love - (Alan J. Lerner - Frederick Lowe)
March 31, 1947

Always - (Irving Berlin)
December 15, 1946 - January 9, 1947

American Beauty Rose - (Ray Evans - Mack David - Arthur Altman)
March 10, 1950

America The Beautiful - (Katherine Bates - Samuel Ward)
August 27, 1945

Among My Souveniers - (Edgar Leslie - Horatio Nicholls)
July 30, 1946

April In Paris - (Vernon Duke - Yip Harburg)
October 9, 1950

Autumn In New York - (Vernon Duke)
December 4, 1947

Azure-Te - (Jack Wolf - Mack Davis)
June 3, 1952

Bali Hai - (Richard Rodgers - Oscar Hammerstein II)
February 28, 1949

Begin The Beguine - (Cole Porter)
February 24, 1946

Bim Bam Baby - (George Mysels)
June 3, 1952

Birth Of The Blues, The - (Buddy DeSylva - Lew Brown - Ray Henderson)
June 3, 1952

Blue Skies - (Irving Berlin)
July 30, 1946

Body And Soul - (Edward Heyman - Robert Sour - Frank Eyton - Johnny
   Green)
November 9, 1947

Bop Goes My Heart - (Walter Bishop - Jule Styne)
December 15, 1948

Brooklyn Bridge - (Sammy Cahn - Jule Styne)
October 31, 1946

But Beautiful - (Johnny Burke - Jimmy Van Heusen)
August 17, 1947

But None Like You - (Ray Noble)
December 26, 1947

Bye, Bye Baby - (Leo Robin - Jule Styne)
July 10, 1949

Can't You Just See Yourself - (Sammy Cahn - Jule Styne)
October 19, 1947

Castle Rock - (Irwin Drake - Jimmy Shirl - Al Sears)
July 9, 1951

Catana - (Alfred Newman - Eddie DeLange)
December 26, 1947

Charm Of You, The - (Sammy Cahn - Jule Styne)
December 3, 1944

Chattanoogie Shoe Shine Boy - (Henry Stone - Jack Stupp)
January 12, 1950

Cherry Pies Ought To Be You - (Cole Porter)
December 11, 1950

Christmas Dreaming - (Mack Gordon - Lester Lee)
June 26, 1947 - July 3, 1947

Close To You - (Al Hoffman - Jerry Livingston - Carl Lampl)
June 7, 1943

Coffee Song, The - (Bob Hilliard - David Miles)
July 24, 1946

Come Back To Sorrento - (DeCurtis - DeCurtis)
October 9, 1950

Comme Ci, Comme Ca - (Alex Kramer - Joan Whitney - Piere Dudan - Bruno Coquatrix)
December 19, 1948

Continental, The - (Con Conrad - Herb Magidson)
April 24, 1950

Could'ja - (Bill Carey - Carl Fischer)
May 28, 1946

Cradle Song, The - (Brahms Lullaby) - (Johannes Brahms)
December 3, 1944

Day By Day - (Sammy Cahn - Axel Stordahl - Paul Weston)
August 22, 1945

Dear Little Boy Of Mine - (Ernest Ball - John Brennan)
June 28, 1950

Deep Night - (Rudy Vallee - Charlie Henderson)
July 9, 1951

Don't Cry Joe - (Joe Marsala)
July 10, 1949

Don't Ever Be Afraid To Go Home - (Bob Hilliard - Carl Sigman)
February 6, 1952

Don't Forget Tonight, Tomorrow - (Jay Milton - Mamy Sherwin)
May 16, 1945

Dream - (Johnny Mercer)
March 6, 1945

Dum, Dot Song, The - (Kay)
November 7, 1946

Embraceable You - (George Gershwin - Ira Gershwin)
December 19, 1944

Ever Homeward - (Sammy Cahn - Jule Styne - Kasimierz Lubomirski)
December 8, 1947

Everybody Loves Somebody - (Irving Taylor - Ken Lane)
December 4, 1947

Every Man Should Marry - (Benny Davis - Abner Silver)
July 14, 1949 - July 21, 1949

Faithful - (Leo Robin - Ralph Rainger)
January 16, 1951

Falling In Love With Love - (Richard Rodgers - Lorenz Hart)
August 8, 1946

Farewell, Farewell To Love - (Jack Wolf - George Siravo)
July 9, 1951

Feet Of Clay - (Bob Hilliard - Carl Sigman)
February 6, 1952

Fella With An Umbrella, A - (Irving Berlin)
March 16, 1948

Fellow Needs A Girl, A - (Richard Rodgers - Oscar Hammerstein II)
August 17, 1947

Five Minutes More - (Sammy Cahn - Jule Styne)
May 26, 1946

Fools Rush In - (Rube Bloom - Johnny Mercer)
October 31, 1947

For Every Man There's A Woman - (Leo Robin - Harold Arlen)
December 28, 1947

Friend Of Yours, A - (Johnny Burke - Jimmy Van Heusen)
March 6, 1945

From This Day Forward - (Eddie Greene - Leigh Harline)
February 24, 1946

Full Moon And Empty Arms - (Buddy Kaye - Ted Mossman)
November 19, 1945

Ghost Of A Chance, A - (Bing Crosby - Ned Washington - Victor Young)
December 7, 1945

Girl That I Marry, The - (Irving Berlin)
March 10, 1946

God's Country - (Harold Arlen - Yip Harburg)
January 12, 1950

Good Man Is Hard To Find, A - (Eddie Greene)
October 16, 1951

Goodnight Irene - (Huddie Leadbetter - John Lomax)
June 28, 1950

Guess I'll Hang My Tears Out To Dry - (Sammy Cahn - Jule Styne)
July 30, 1946

Have Yourself A Merry Little Christmas - (Hugh Martin - Ralph Blane)
June 26, 1947 - July 3, 1947

Hello Young Lovers - (Richard Rodgers - Oscar Hammerstein II)
March 2, 1951

Help Yourself To My Heart - (Kaye - Timberg)
December 28, 1947

Home On The Range - (Traditional)
March 10, 1946

Homesick That's All - (Gordon Jenkins)
March 6, 1945

House I Live In, The - (Lewis Allen - Earl Robinson)
August 22, 1945

How Cute Can You Be - (Carl Fischer - Bill Carey)
February 3, 1946

How Deep Is The Ocean - (Irving Berlin)
March 10, 1946

Huckle Buck, The - (Roy Alfred - Andy Gibson)
April 10, 1949

Hush-A-Bye Island - (Harold Adamson - Jimmy McHugh)
August 22, 1946

I Am Loved - (Cole Porter)
November 16, 1950

I Begged Her - (Sammy Cahn - Jule Styne)
December 1, 1944

I Believe - (Sammy Cahn - Jule Styne)
October 31, 1946

I Concentrate On You - (Cole Porter)
January 9, 1947

I Couldn't Sleep A Wink Last Night - (Harold Adamson - Jimmy McHugh)
November 3, 1943

I Could Write A Book - (Richard Rodgers - Lorenz Hart)
January 7, 1952

I Don't Know Why - (Roy Turk - Fred Ahlert)
July 30, 1945

I Dream Of You - (Marjorie Goetschius - Edna Osser)
December 1, 1944

I Fall In Love To Easily - (Sammy Cahn - Jule Styne)
December 1, 1944

I Fall In Love With You Every Day - (Mamy Sherwin - Frank Loesser)
March 10, 1946

If I Ever Love Again - (Carlyle - Reynolds)
July 14, 1949

If I Forget You - (Irving Caesar)
December 30, 1947

If I Had You -(Ted Shapiro - Jimmy Campbell - Reg Connelly)
August 11, 1947

If I Loved You - (Richard Rodgers - Oscar Hammerstein II)
March 6, 1945

If I Only Had A Match - (Lee Morris - Arthur Johnston - Joseph Meyer)
November 25, 1947

If I Steal A Kiss - (Edward Heyman - Lew Brown)
December 4, 1947

If Only She'd Look My Way - (Novello - Melville)
September 21, 1950

If You Are But A Dream - (Moe Jaffe - Jack Fulton - Nathaniel Bonx)
November 14, 1944

If You Please - (Johnny Burke - Jimmy Van Heusen)
June 22, 1943

If You Stub Your Toe On The Moon - (Johnny Burke - Jimmy Van Heusen)
January 4, 1949

I Got A Gal I Love - (Sammy Cahn - Jule Styne)
October 31, 1946

I Guess I'll Have To Dream The Rest - (Michey Stoner - Martin Block -
   Harold Green)
October 9, 1950

I Have But One Heart - (Marty Symes - Johnny Farrow)
November 30, 1945

I Hear A Rhapsody - (George Fragos - Jack Baker - Dick Gasparre)
January 7, 1952

I'll Make Up For Everything - (Ross Parker)
October 22, 1947

I Love You - (Edvard Grieg - Robert Wright - George Forrest)
July 30, 1946

I'm A Fool To Want You - (Jack Wolf - Herron - Frank Sinatra)
March 27, 1951

I'm Glad There Is You - (Paul Madeira - Jimmy Dorsey)
November 9, 1947

I'm Sorry I Made You Cry - (Clesi)
October 24, 1946

I Only Have Eyes For You - (Al Dubin - Harry Warren)
August 27, 1945

I Should Care - (Sammy Cahn - Axel Stordahl - Paul Weston)
March 6, 1945

It All Came True - (Sammy Skylar)
September 23, 1947 - August 11, 1947

It All Depends On You - (Buddy DeSylva - Lew Henderson - Ray Brown)
July 10, 1949

It Came Upon A Midnight Clear - (Willis)
December 28, 1947

It Happens Every Spring - (Mack Gordon - Josef Myrow)
April 10, 1949

It Never Entered My Mind - (Richard Rodgers - Lorenz Hart)
November 5, 1947

It Only Happens When I Dance With You - (Irving Berlin)
March 16, 1948

It's All Up To You - (Sammy Cahn - Jule Styne)
November 7, 1946

It's A Long Way From Your House To My House - (Sid Tepper - Nick Brodsky)
May 10, 1951

It's Only A Paper Moon - (Harold Arlen - Billy Rose - Yip Harburg)
April 24, 1950

It's The Same Old Dream - (Sammy Cahn - Jule Styne)
October 24, 1946

I've Got A Crush On You - (George Gershwin - Ira Gershwin)
November 5, 1947

I've Got A Home In That Rock - (Traditional)
May 16, 1945

I Want To Thank Your Folks - (Bennie Benjamin - George Weiss)
December 15, 1946

I Went Down To Virginia - (Ray Evans - Paul Mann)
November 25, 1947

I Whistle A Happy Tune - (Richard Rodgers - Oscar Hammerstein II)
March 27, 1951

Jesus Is A Rock In The Weary Land - (Traditional)
May 16, 1945

Jingle Bells - (James Pierpont)
August 8, 1946

Just A Kiss Apart - (Leo Robin - Jule Styne)
July 21, 1949

Just An Old Stone House - (Alec Wilder)
November 15, 1945

Just For Now - (Dick Redmond)
October 22, 1947 - October 26, 1947

Just One Way To Say (I Love You) - (Irving Berlin)
May 6, 1949

Kisses And Tears - (Sammy Cahn - Jule Styne)
January 4, 1949 - February 23, 1950

Kiss Me Again - (Victor Herbert - Henry Blossom)
December 19, 1944

Laura - (Johnny Mercer - David Raskin)
October 22, 1947

Let It Snow, Let It Snow - (Sammy Cahn - Jule Styne)
November 5, 1950

Let's Take An Old Fashioned Walk - (Irving Berlin)
May 6, 1949

Life Is So Peculiar - (Johnny Burke - JImmy Van Heusen)
August 2, 1950

Lilly Belle - (Dave Franklin - Irving Taylor)
May 16, 1945

Little Learnin' Is A Dangerous Thing, A - (Sy Oliver - Al Jacobs)
December 8, 1947

London By Night - (Carroll Coates)
September 21, 1950

Lonesome Man Blues - (Sy Oliver)
October 16, 1951

Lost In The Stars - (Maxwell Anderson - Kurt Weill)
August 8, 1946

Lovely Moonlight Night, A (Once Upon) - (Sidney Clare - Irving Bibo)
August 22, 1946

Lovely Way To Spend An Evening, A - (Harold Adamson - Jimmy McHugh)
November 10, 1943

Love Me - (Ned Washington - Victor Young)
March 27, 1951

Love Means Love - (Arthur Lake - Carl Sigman)
December 11, 1950

Lover - (Richard Rodgers - Lorenz Hart)
April 14, 1950

Luna Rosa - (Vincenzo DeCrescenzo - Vian)
June 3, 1952

Mad About You - (Ned Washington - Victor Young)
September 15, 1949

Mama Will Bark - (Dick Manning)
May 10, 1951

Mam'selle - (Mack Gordon - Edmund Goulding)
March 11, 1947

Mean To Me - (Roy Turk - Fred Ahlert)
October 31, 1947

Meet Me At The Copa - (Sammy Cahn - Axel Stordahl)
September 21, 1950

Mighty Lak' A Rose - (Ethelbert Nevin - Frank Stanton)
January 29, 1945

Moon Was Yellow, The - (Fred Ahlert - Edgar Leslie)
August 27, 1945

Music Stopped, The - (Harold Adamson - Jimmy McHugh)
November 10, 1943 - October 15, 1946 - October 29, 1947

My Blue Heaven - (Walter Donaldson - Richard Whiting)
April 24, 1950

My Cousin Louella - (Bernard Bierman - Jack Manos)
October 24, 1947

My Love For You - (Eddie Heyman - Harry Jacobson)
January 9, 1947

My Melancholy Baby - (George Norton - Ernie Burnett)
January 29, 1945

My Romance - (Richard Rodgers - Lorenz Hart)
November 7, 1946 - April 25, 1947

My Shawl - (Stanley Adams - Xavier Cugat)
May 24, 1945

Nancy - (Phil Silvers - Jimmy Van Heusen)
December 3, 1944 - August 22, 1945

Nature Boy - (Eden Ahbez)
April 10, 1948

Nearness Of You, The - (Hoagy Carmichael - Ned Washington)
August 11, 1947

Nevertheless - (Bert Kalmar - Harry Ruby)
October 9, 1950

Night After Night - (Sammy Cahn - Axel Stordahl - Paul Weston)
March 3, 1949

None But The Lonely Heart - (Tchaikovsky) - (Brandt)
October 31, 1946 - October 26, 1947

No Orchids For My Lady - (Stranks - Jack Strachey)
December 19, 1948

Oh What A Beautiful Morning - (Richard Rodgers - Oscar Hammerstein II)
August 5, 1943

Oh What It Seemed To Be - (George Weiss - Frankie Carle - Bennie Benjamin)
November 19, 1945

Old Master Painter, The - (Haven Gillespie - Beasley Smith)
October 30, 1949

Old School Teacher -
November 15, 1945

O' Little Town Of Bethlehem - (Phillip Brooks - Lawrence Rodner)
December 28, 1947

Ol' Man River - (Jerome Kern - Oscar Hammerstein II)
December 3, 1944

Once In Love With Amy - (Frank Loesser)
December 15, 1948

One Finger Melody - (Al Hoffman - Kermitt Goell - Frederic Speilman)
September 18, 1950

One For My Baby - (Harold Arlen - Johnny Mercer)
August 11, 1947

One Love - (Leo Robin - Billy Rose)
February 3, 1946

On The Island Of Stromboli - (Irving Taylor - Ken Lane)
September 15, 1949

Over The Rainbow - (Yip Yarburg - Harold Arlen)
May 1, 1945

Paradise - (Nacio Herb Brown - Gordon Clifford)
December 7, 1945

Peach Tree Street - (Joseph Davis - Jack Mason - Frank Sinatra)
April 8, 1950

People Will Say We're In Love - (Richard Rodgers - Oscar Hammerstein II)
June 7, 1943 - June 22, 1943 - August 5, 1943

Poinciana - (Buddy Bernier - Nat Simon)
October 15, 1946 - October 29, 1947

Put Your Dreams Away - (Ruth Lowe - Stephen Weiss - Paul Mann)
May 1, 1945

Remember Me In Your Dreams - (Morty Nevins - Hal David)
September 21, 1950

Right Girl For Me, The - (Betty Comden - Roger Edens - Adolph Green)
March 3, 1949

Santa Claus Is Coming To Town - (Haven Gillespie - Fred Coots)
December 28, 1947

Saturday Night - (Sammy Cahn - Jule Styne)
November 14, 1944

Senorita - (Edward Hayman - Nacio Herb Brown)
October 29, 1947

September Song - (Kurt Weill - Maxwell Anderson)
July 30, 1946

Sheila - (Howard - Frank Sinatra - Staver)
January 12, 1950

She's Funny That Way - (Neil Moret - Richard Whiting)
December 19, 1944

Should I - (Nacio Brown - Arthur Freed)
April 14, 1950

Silent Night - (Franz - Gruber)
August 27, 1945

So Far - (Richard Rodgers - Oscar Hammerstein II)
August 17, 1947

Soliloquy - (Richard Rodgers - Oscar Hammerstein II)
April 7, 1946 - May 28, 1946

Some Enchanted Evening - (Richard Rodgers - Oscar Hammerstein)
February 28, 1949

Someone To Watch Over Me - (George Gershwin - Ira Gershwin)
July 30, 1945

Something Old, Something New - (Ramez Idrees - George Tibbles - Eddy Howard)
February 24, 1946

Somewhere In The Night - (Mack Gordon - Joseph Myrow)
May 28, 1946

Song Is You, The - (Jerome Kern - Oscar Hammerstein II)
October 26, 1947

Sorry - (Buddy Pepper - Richard Whiting)
November 8, 1949

So They Tell Me - (
August 22, 1946

S'posin' - (Paul Denniker - Andy Razaf)
October 24, 1947

Spring Is Here - (Richard Rodgers - Lorenz Hart)
October 31, 1947

Stars In Your Eyes - (Gabriel Ruiz - Mort Greene)
May 24, 1945

Stars Will Remember - (Don Pelosi - Leo Towers)
June 26, 1947 - July 3, 1947

Stella By Starlight - (Ned Washington - Victor Young)
March 11, 1947

Stormy Weather - (Harold Arlen - Ted Koehler)
December 3, 1944

Strange Music - (Robert Wright - George Forrest - Edvard Grieg)
October 15, 1946 - October 22, 1947

Sunday, Monday Or Always - (Johnny Burke - Jimmy Van Heusen)
June 22, 1943

Sunflower - (Mack David)
December 16, 1948

Sunshine Cake - (Johnny Burke - Jimmy Van Heusen)
November 8, 1949

Sure Thing, A (We've Got) - (Johnny Burke - Jimmy Van Heusen)
November 8, 1949

Sweet Lorraine - (Mitchell Parish - Cliff Burell)
December 15, 1946

Take My Love - (Jack Wolf - Herron - Frank Sinatra)
November 16, 1950

Tea For Two - (Vincent Youmans - Irving Caesar)
April 25, 1947

Tennessee Newsboy - (Bob Manning - Percy Faith)
June 3, 1952

That Lucky Old Sun - (Haven Gillespie - Beasley Smith)
September 15, 1949

That Old Black Magic - (Johnny Mercer - Harold Arlen)
March 10, 1946

That Old Feeling - (Lew Brown - Sammy Fain)
August 11, 1947

That's How Much I Love You - (Eddie Arnold - Wally Fowler - Graydon Hall)
December 15, 1946

There But For You Go I - (Alan J. Lerner - Frederick Lowe)
March 31, 1947

There's No Business Like Show Business - (Irving Berlin)
August 22, 1946

There's No You - (Hal Hopper - Bullets Durgom - Tom Adair)
November 14, 1944

There's Something Missing - (
April 8, 1950 - January 16, 1951

These Foolish Things - (Jack Strachey - Harry Link - Holt Marvel)
July 30, 1945

They Say It's Wonderful - (Irving Berlin)
March 10, 1946

Things We Did Last Summer, The - (Sammy Cahn - Jule Styne)
July 24, 1946

This Is The Night - (Redd Evans - Lewis Bellin)
July 24, 1946

Time After Time - (Sammy Cahn - Jule Styne)
October 24, 1946

Try A Little Tenderness - (Harry Woods - Jimmy Campbell - Reg Connelly)
December 7, 1945

Two Hearts Are Better Than One - (Johnny Mercer - Jerome Kern)
February 3, 1946

Walking In The Sunshine - (Bob Merrill)
January 7, 1952

Wedding Of Lille Marlene - (Connor - Rerne)
July 21, 1949

We Just Couldn't Say Goodbye - (Harry Woods)
October 24, 1947

We Kiss In A Shadow - (Richard Rodgers - Oscar Hammerstein II)
March 2, 1951

What'll I Do - (Irving Berlin)
October 29, 1947

What Makes The Sunset - (Sammy Cahn - Jule Styne)
December 1, 1944

When Is Sometime - (Johnny Burke - Jimmy Van Heusen)
December 30, 1947

When The Sun Goes Down - (Walter O'Keefe - Orton)
February 23, 1950

When You Awake - (Henry Nemo)
November 5, 1947

When You're Smiling - (Larry Shay - Mark Fisher - Joe Goodwin)
April 24, 1950 - October 16, 1951

When Your Lover Has Gone - (Eddie Swan)
December 19, 1944

Where Is My Bess - (George & Ira Gershwin - Dubose Heyward)
February 24, 1946

Where Is The One - (Alex Wilder - Bill Finkle)
December 30, 1947

Where Or When - (Richard Rodgers - Lorenz Hart)
January 29, 1945

While The Angelus Was Ringing - (Dick Manning - Jean Villiard)
December 19, 1948

White Christmas - (Irving Berlin)
November 14, 1944 - December 28, 1947

Why Can't You Behave - (Cole Porter)
December 15, 1948

Why Remind Me - (Wilner - Doris Tauber)
October 30, 1949

Why Shouldn't I - (Cole Porter)
December 7, 1945

Why Shouldn't It Happen To Us - (Mann Holiner - Alberta Nichols)
October 15, 1946

Why Try To Change Me Now - (Cy Coleman - Joseph McCarthy)
September 17, 1952

Why Was I Born - (Jerome Kern - Oscar Hammerstein II)
December 26, 1947 - December 28, 1947

You Are Too Beautiful - (Richard Rodgers - Lorenz Hart)
August 22, 1945

You Can Take My Word For It Baby - (Ticker Freeman - Irving Taylor)
December 15, 1946

You Do Something To Me - (Cole Porter)
April 14, 1950

You Don't Remind Me - (Cole Porter)
November 16, 1950

You Go To My Head - (Haven Gillespie - Fred Coots)
July 30, 1945

You'll Know When It Happens - (Lombard - John Loeb)
July 24, 1946

You'll Never Know - (Mack Gordon - Harry Warren)
June 7, 1943

You'll Never Walk Alone - (Richard Rodgers - Oscar Hammerstein II)
May 1, 1945

You're The One - (Ned Washington - Victor Young)
November 16, 1950 - January 16, 1951

ORCHESTRAS, ARRANGERS, COMPOSERS, SOLOISTS, VOCALISTS AND VOCAL GROUP INDEX - COLUMBIA RECORDS - CHAPTER VI

Ahern, Bob - Guitar Soloist
December 15, 1946

Alexander, Jeff - Orchestra Leader and Arranger
April 10, 1948, September 15, 1949

Alexander Choir, Jeff - Vocal Group
April 10, 1948, January 12, 1950, January 7, 1952

Ayres, Mitchel - Orchestra Leader and Arranger
December 15, 1948

Bailey, Pearl - Vocalist
December 8, 1947

Bain, Donald - Imitation of Dog Barking
May 10, 1951

Baker, Julius - Flute Soloist

Beau, Heinie - Arranger, Saxaphonist
June 3, 1952

Bobby Tucker Singers, The - Large Vocal Group
June 7, 1943, June 22, 1943, August 5, 1943, November 3, 1943, November 10, 1943, November 14, 1944

Brown, Lawrence - Trombone Soloist
December 15, 1946

Butterfield, Billy - Trumpet Soloist
December 3, 1944, October 9, 1950

Carney, Harry - Baritone Sax Soloist
December 15, 1946

Cavanaugh, Page - Instrumental and Vocal Trio
December 15, 1946

Charioteers, The - Vocal Group
May 16, 1945

Clooney, Rosemary - Vocalist
April 8, 1950, December 11, 1950

Cole, Nat - Piano Soloist
December 15, 1946

Conniff, Ray - Arranger
July 9, 1951

Cugat, Xavier - Orchestra Leader
May 24, 1945

Dagmar - Vocalist
May 10, 1951

Day, Doris - Vocalist
May 6, 1949

Double Daters, The - Vocal Group
July 14, 1949

Faith, Percy - Orchestra Leader and Arranger
August 2, 1950, September 17, 1952

Four Hits and A Miss - Vocal Group
October 24, 1946

Freeman, Stan - Pianist

Gershenson, Joseph - Arranger, Composer
October 16, 1951

Goltzer, Harold - Bassoon Soloist
December 5, 1945

Guanieri, Johnny - Pianist
October 24, 1947

Hacket, Bobby - Trumpet Soloist
November 5, 1947, November 9, 1947

Helen Carroll and The Swan Tones - Vocal Group
August 2, 1950

Hodges, Johnny - Alto Sax Soloist
December 15, 1946

James, Harry - Orchestra Leader
July 9, 1951

Jones, Dick - Arranger
October 19, 1947

Kelly, Paula - Vocalist
November 8, 1949

Ken Lane Singers, The - Vocal Group
December 3, 1944, January 29, 1945, March 6, 1945, August 27, 1945, August 8,
1946, December 28, 1947, April 10, 1949, November 8, 1949, June 28, 1950,
October 9, 1950, November 5, 1950, January 16, 1951

Keyser, Kay - Orchestra Leader
November 7, 1946

Mann, Dave - Piano Soloist
December 1, 1944

Metronome All Stars, The - All Star Jazz Musicians
December 15, 1946

Miller, Mitch - Orchestra Leader, Arranger, R.R. Man, Oboe and English Horn
November 15, 1945, October 31, 1947, March 10, 1950, June 28, 1950

Modernaires, The - Vocal Group
October 30, 1949, November 8, 1949, February 23, 1950

Moore, Phil - Instrumental Quartet, Pianist, Composer, Arranger
December 15, 1948, January 4, 1959

Mottola, Tony - Guitarist, Arranger
October 24, 1947

Norman Luboff Choir, The - Vocal Choir
June 3, 1952

Oliver, Sy - Arranger
December 15, 1946, December 8, 1947

Pastels, The - Vocal Group
July 10, 1949

Pied Pipers, The - Vocal Group
May 28, 1946, November 7, 1946, March 11, 1947

Rich, Buddy - Drum Soloist
December 15, 1946

Russell, Jane - Vocalist
February 23, 1950

Safranski, Eddie - Bass Soloist
December 15, 1946

Shavers, Charlie - Trumpet Soloist
December 15, 1946

Shore, Dinah - Vocalist
November 7, 1946, April 25, 1947

Siravo, George - Orchestra Leader, Arranger
October 19, 1947, April 8, 1950, April 14, 1950, April 24, 1950, January 16, 1951

Stoloff, Morris - Orchestra Leader, Arranger
July 21, 1949

Stordahl, Axel - Orchestra Leader, Arranger, Conducted and Arranged Most Sessions, from November 14, 1944 through June 3, 1952 and his musical contributions and personal assistance were major factors to Sinatra's early success.

West, Alvy - Instrumental Group
September 23, 1947

Whipporwills Quartet, The - Vocal Group
September 21, 1950

Wilder, Alec - Composer, Conductor, Arranger
June 5, 1943, June 22, 1943, August 5, 1943, December 5, 1945, December 10, 1945

Winter Halter, Hugo - Orchestra Leader, Arranger
July 14, 1949

Winters, Shelly - Vocalist
October 16, 1951

COMMENTS

Imagine the possibilities in this phase of his career.

Sinatra singing with The Woody Herman Orchestra to a Ralph Burns Arrangement, or Dukes Big Band, the one with Louis Bellson on Drums or the lightly swingin' band of Les Brown. Instead we have one session with Harry James that must have been put together in a hurry, for neither sounds relaxed and Harry had a great band at that time. What about a session with The Fine Sounding Claude Thornhill? The vocal duets should have included many more with Doris Day. (They were made for each other) some with Sarah Vaughan, Frankie Laine or Buddy Clark. Its nice to speculate and Sinatra **did** record many classics for Columbia but oh to be able to turn back the clock and do it again.

Chapter VII

V-DISCS

The V-Discs produced during World War II were made specifically for the armed forces and are the property of the United States Government. They were forbidden, by law, to be sold to the public, but since many are available and can be purchased, we have decided to list them. The music branch of the War Department's Special Services Division issued 905 V-Discs for the listening pleasure of American Servicemen.

Sinatra contributed ninety-five performances on fifty-three discs. Forty-five tunes were taken directly from Columbia masters, seven from RCA and the remaining forty-three were extracted from Armed Forces Radio Broadcasts, concerts and the War Department recording sessions. The Army and the Navy issued their own separate V-Discs which will be noted, the Army number will appear first followed by the Navy number which will be in parenthesis.

For those collectors who are interested, we have listed the complete information relating to the reverse sides and also the Lp release numbers that some of them have been reissued on.

#1 Blue Skies - Frank Sinatra with Tommy Dorsey and his orchestra - Same as Vic. 27566 (BS 066923) 7/15/41.

> **REV.** - Put Your Arms Around Me/Comin' In On A Wing And A Prayer - Bea Wain, Acc. by unknown orchestra.

#18 In The Blue of Evening - Frank Sinatra with Tommy Dorsey and his orchestra - Same as Vic. 27947 (075282) 6/17/42.

> **REV.** - Boogie Woogie - Tommy Dorsey and his orchestra.

#25 Night and Day/The Song Is You - Frank Sinatra with orchestra arranged Axel Stordahl - Same as Bluebird B 111463 and Bluebird B 111515 1/19/42.

#33 Without A Song - Frank Sinatra with Tommy Dorsey and his orchestra - Same as Vic. 36396 (060349) 1/20/41.

#42 (262) Put Your Dreams Away/And Then You Kissed Me - Frank Sinatra with orchestra arranged and conducted by Axel Stordahl. First title not the released Columbia pressing. Second title made originally for film "Step Lively" but not included in released version. Both were recorded in released version. Both were recorded in Spring or Summer of 1944.

> **REV.** - I'll Be Seeing You/Someone To Love - Jo Stafford acc. by Paul Weston.

#72 (103) I Only Have Eyes For You (with spoken intro)/Kiss Me Again/ There's Gonna Be A Hot Time In The Town of Berlin - Frank Sinatra with orchestra arranged and conducted by Axel

Stordahl. None of these titles are the Released Columbia Pressings. They were recorded sometime in late 1944 or early 1945. (On Navy disc "Nancy" replaces "I Only Have Eyes For You.")

#116 The Music Stopped/I Couldn't Sleep A Wink Last Night/The Way You Look Tonight - Frank Sinatra with orchestra arranged and conducted by Axel Stordahl. Vocal chorus - The Ken Lane Singers. None of these titles are the released Columbia Pressings. They were recorded sometime in early 1945.

#124 I'll Be Around/You've Got A Hold On Me/A Lovely Way To Spend An Evening/She's Funny That Way - Frank Sinatra with orchestra arranged and conducted by Axel Stordahl. None of these titles are the released Columbia Pressings. They were recorded sometime in mid 1945.

#138 Ciribiribin - Frank Sinatra with Harry James and his orchestra. Same as Columbia 35316 (LA 2046) 11/8/39, Carnival of Venice.

REV. - Easter Parade/Backbeat Boogie - with Harry James and his orchestra.

#154 Speak Low/Close To You - Frank Sinatra with orchestra arranged and conducted by Axel Stordahl. None of these titles are the released Columbia Pressings. They were recorded in late 1945.

REV. - The Whiffenpoof Song - Lieutenant Rudy Vallee with the U.S. Coast Guard Band and Choir.

#159 (868) Silent Night/Adestes Fidelis/O Little Town Of Bethlehem/ It Came Upon A Midnight Clear/Jingle Bells/Santa Claus Is Coming To Town - Frank Sinatra with orchestra arranged and conducted by Axel Stordahl. Vocal Chorus - Ken Lane Singers. Same as Columbia Pressings - CO 37145 (HCO 1526) 8/27/45; CO 37145 (HCO 1945) 8/8/46; CO 37152 (HCO 1947) 8/8/46; CO 38258 (HCO 3067) 12/28/47; CO 38258 (HCO 3068) 12/28/47; CO 38259 (HCO 3072) 12/28/47.

#160 I Don't Know Why/Aren't You Glad You're You - Frank Sinatra with orchestra arranged and conducted by Axel Stordahl. None of these titles are the released Columbia Pressings.

#166 (109) My Shining Hour/Long Ago and Far Away - Frank Sinatra with orchestra arranged and conducted by Axel Stordahl. These recordings made especially for V-Discs and never commercially released. Probably made in 1945.

REV. - Darling Je Vous Ame Beaucoup/By The Light Of The Silvery Moon - Bing Crosby

#241 (21) Some Other Time/Come Out Wherever You Are - Frank Sinatra with orchestra arranged and conducted by Axel Stordahl. These sound like they were taken directly from the soundtrack of the film "Step Lively". Probably recorded in early 1944.

> **REV.** - Amor/It Could Happen To You - Bing Crosby.

#262 (See Number 42)

#287 (67) All Of Me/All The Things You Are - Frank Sinatra with orchestra arranged and conducted by Axel Stordahl. None of these titles are the released columbia Pressings. Recorded around mid 1946.

> **REV.** - Pennies From Heaven - Bing Crosby acc. by John Scott Trotter. I'm In The Mood For Love - Frances Langford.

#310 (90) Mighty Lak' A Rose - Frank Sinatra with orchestra arranged and conducted by Axel Stordahl. This is not the commercially released Columbia Pressing. Recorded around late 1946.

> **REV.** - My Reverie/Blow Gabriel, Blow - Bea Wain with Vaughn Monroe's orchestra.

#323 Nancy - Frank Sinatra with orchestra arranged and conducted by Axel Stordahl. This is not the commercially released Columbia Pressing. Recorded around early 1945.

> **REV.** - Happiness Is A Thing Called Joe - Frances Wayne with Woody Herman's orchestra.

#351 (131) Let Me Move You Tonight/Just Close Your Eyes - Frank Sinatra with orchestra arranged and conducted by Axel Stordahl. Made especially for V-Discs and not recorded commercially. Recorded in 1946.

> **REV.** - My Blue Heaven/When I Marry - Billy Williams and Instrumental Trio.

#378 (155) There's No You/Someone To Watch Over Me - Frank Sinatra with orchestra arranged and conducted by Axel Stordahl. None of the titles are the released Columbia Pressings. Recorded in 1945.

> **REV.** - Carry Me Back To Old Virginny - Jo Stafford with Paul Weston's orchestra.

#393 (173) If You Are But A Dream/Saturday Night - Frank Sinatra with orchestra arranged and conducted by Axel Stordahl. Same as Columbia CO 36756 (CO 33808) 11/14/44 and CO 36762 (CO 33809) 11/14/44.

> **REV.** - I Didn't Know About You/Tumbling Tumble Weeds - Jo Stafford with Paul Weston's orchestra.

#405 (185) What Makes The Sunset/I Begged Her - Frank Sinatra with orchestra arranged and conducted by Axel Stordahl. Same as columbia CO 36774 (CO 33930) 12/1/44; CO 36774 (CO 33929) 12/1/44.

REV. - Two Little Fishes and Five Loaves of Bread - Evelyn Knight. Too-Ra-Loo-Ra-Loo-Ra, That's An Irish Lullaby - Herman Chittison Trio.

#434 (214) The Lamplighters Serenade - Frank Sinatra with orchestra arranged and conducted by Axel Stordahl. Same as Bluebird B 11515 (PBSO 72043) 1/19/42.

The Sunshine Of Your Smile - Frank Sinatra with Tommy Dorsey's orchestra. Same as Vic. 27638 (BSO 67653) 8/26/41.

REV. - Sometimes I Feel Like A Motherless Child - Mildred Bailey with Paul Baron's orchestra.

#460 (240) Ol' Man River - Frank Sinatra with orchestra arranged and conducted by Axel Stordahl. Not the same as the Columbia commercial release. Recorded about the middle of 1945.

REV. - Jimmy's Blues/Take Me Back Baby - Jimmy Rushing with Count Basie's orchestra.

#467 (247) When Your Lover Has Gone/Falling In Love With Love - Frank Sinatra with orchestra arranged and conducted by Axel Stordahl. Not the same as the Columbia commercial releases. Recorded about the middle of 1946.

REV. - Baby Won't You Please Come Home - Jo Stafford and her V-Disc Jazz Boys, - B. Butterfield, H. Damico, L. McGarity, B. Richmond, B. Rowland, H. White, J. Lesberg, G. Wettling.

#494 None But The Lonely Heart - Frank Sinatra with orchestra arranged and conducted by Axel Stordahl. Not the same as the Columbia commercial release. Recording date unknown.

REV. - There'll Be A Jubilee - Mildred Bailey with Benny Goodman and The V-Disc All Stars.

#506 (266) Brahm's Lullaby/I'll Follow My Secret Heart - Frank Sinatra with orchestra arranged and conducted by Axel Stordahl. First title same as Columbia release CO 36868 (CO 33933) 12/3/44. Second title made only for V-Disc. Recording date unknown.

REV. - Goodnight Sweetheart/Shine On Harvest Moon - Connie Boswell and The V-Disc Fellows.

#521 My Shawl/Stars In Your Eyes - Frank Sinatra with Xavier Cugat and his orchestra. Same as columbia release CO 36842 (CO 34818) 5/24/45 and CO 35842 (CO 34817) 5/24/45.

 REV. - Jungle Drums/Casey Jones - Morton Gould.

#537 You'll Never Walk Alone/The Charm Of You - Frank Sinatra with orchestra arranged and conducted by Axel Stordahl. Same as Columbia release CO 36835 (HCO 1379) 5/1/45 and CO 36830 (CO 33936) 12/3/44.

 REV. - Bakery Blues - Jo Stafford and The V-Disc Playboys.

#564 Homesick That's All/ The Night Is Young And You're So Beautiful - Frank Sinatra with orchestra arranged and conducted by Axel Stordahl. First title same as Columbia release CO 36820 (HCO 1287) 3/6/45. Second title made only for V-Disc and his Dinah Shore sharing the vocal. Recording date unknown.

 REV. - For Musicians Only - Bud Freeman

#582 (102) I'll Never Smile Again/Without A Song - Frank Sinatra with orchestra arranged and conducted by Axel Stordahl, featuring Tommy Dorsey on Trombone and the Pied Pipers vocal group. this recording made especially for V-Disc. Recording date unknown. "I'll Never Smile Again" does not appear on Navy Disc.

 REV. - Two Sleepy People - Jack Leonard and Martha Tilton.

#594 Aren't You Glad You're You/You Brought A New Kind Of Love To Me - Frank Sinatra with orchestra arranged and conducted by Axel Stordahl. Made for V-Disc only. Recording date unknown.

 REV. - Love Letters - Perry Como with Lloyd Shaeffer and his orchestra. What A Deal - Martha Tilton.

#614 Old School Teacher/Oh What It Seemed To Be - Frank Sinatra with orchestra under the direction of Mitch Miller on first title. Same as Columbia Master (CO 35426). Never commercially released. Recorded 11/15/45. Second title same as Columbia release CO 36905 (CO 35442) 11/30/45. With orchestra arranged and conducted by Axel Stordahl.

 REV. - Frim Fram Sauce - King Cole Trio. Come To Baby Do - Lena Horne with Benny Goodman and his orchestra.

#625 I Have But One Heart - Frank Sinatra with orchestra arranged and conducted by Axel Stordahl. Same as Columbia release CO 37554 (CO 35484) 11/30/45.

 REV. - Lover Come Back To Me/Great Day - Eileen Barton with Jerry Jerome and his orchestra.

#635 Slow Dance/Contraptunal Variations - Frank Sinatra conducting the music of Alec Wilder.

#642 Piece For English Horn/Piece For Bassoon - Frank Sinatra conducting the music of Alec Wilder.

#645 My Romance - Frank Sinatra and Dinah Shore with orchestra arranged and conducted by Axel Stordahl. This version without vocal chorus and is the unissued Columbia Master (HCO 2137) 11/7/46.

> **REV.** - Amado Mio - Dick Haymes.
> Button Up Your Overcoat - Dick Haymes and Helen Forest.

#652 O Little Town Of Bethlehem/Joy To The World/White Christmas - Frank Sinatra with orchestra arranged and conducted by Axel Stordahl. Not the same as Columbia releases. "Joy To The World" has chorus only (No Sinatra). Recorded in 1946.

> **REV.** - Silent Night/O Come All Ye Faithful - Dick Haymes with Gordon Jenkins Orchestra and Chorus.

#663 Should I - Pied Pipers - Frank Sinatra has one line at the end - "Man they was way out, they ain't never gonna come back again" - with orchestra under the direction of Axel Stordahl. Recorded in 1946.

> **REV.** - I'm Beginning To See The Light - Art Tatum - 920 Special.

#670 They Say It's Wonderful/You Are Too Beautiful - Frank Sinatra with orchestra arranged and conducted by Axel Stordahl. Same as Columbia release CO 36975 (HCO 1748) 3/10/46 and CO 36947 (HCO 1522) 8/22/45.

> **REV.** - I Got Lost In His Arms/Its A Woman's Perogative - Marie Green with David Mann and his orchestra.

#679 The Girl That I Marry/Something Old, Something New - Frank Sinatra with orchestra arranged and conducted by Axel Stordahl. Same as Columbia release CO 36975 (HCO 1750) 3/10/46 and CO 36987 (HCO 1736) 2/24/46.

> **REV.** - Bewitched - Marie Green with David Mann and his orchestra. Introduction by Bob Hope.

#689 The Song Is You - Frank Sinatra with orchestra arranged and conducted by Axel Stordahl. Also an introduction by Bob Hope. Made especially for V-Disc in early 1947.

> **REV.** - Remember Me - Skinny Ennis.
> The Outlaw - Johnny Thompson.

#700 Come Rain Or Come Shine/You Go To My Head - Frank Sinatra with orchestra arranged and conducted by Axel Stordahl. First title made especially for V-Disc. Second title same as Columbia release CO 36918 (HCO 1500) 7/30/45.

> REV. - There's A Small Hotel - Bing Crosby with Eddie Duchin John Scott Trotter and Orchestra.

#711 Someone To Watch Over Me/I Don't Know Why - Frank Sinatra with orchestra arranged and conducted by Axel Stordahl. Same as Columbia release CO 3692 (HCO 1499) 7/30/45 and CO 36918 (HCO 1502) 7/30/45.

> REV. - I Don't Stand A Ghost Of A Chance With You/Jump For Joy - Herb Jeffries with Eddie Beal and His Group.

#722 That Old Black Magic/Begin The Beguine - Frank Sinatra with orchestra arranged and conducted by Axel Stordahl. Same as Columbia release CO 37257 (HCO 1749) 3/10/46 and CO 37064 (HCO 1735) 2/24/46.

> REV. - You Made Me Love You - Bea Wain with Ray Bloch and his orchestra.

#749 Soliloquy - Frank Sinatra with orchestra arranged and conducted by Axel Stordahl. Not the same as the Columbia release. Recording date unknown.

> REV. - Part II.

#754 Sweet Lorraine - Frank Sinatra with Metronome All Stars. Arranged by Sy Oliver. Same as Columbia release CO 37293 (CO 37177-1) 12/15/46; also Nat Meets June.

> REV. - How Are Things In Glocca Morra - Buddy Clark with Mitchell Ayres Orchestra. Buddy Hughes and Claude Thornhill Orchestra (Song Of Unknown Title).

#763 I Want To Thank Your Folks/You Can Take My Word For It Baby - Frank Sinatra with orchestra arranged and conducted by Axel Stordahl. Same as columbia release CO 37251 (CO 67162) 12/15/46. Second title accompanied by Page Cavanaugh Trio. Same as Columbia release CO 40229 (CO 37164) 12/15/46.

> REV. - Swanee - Al Jolson with Skitch Henderson and Orchestra/The One I Love Belongs To Somebody Else - Al Jolson with Bing Crosby.

#789 I Fall In Love With You Every Day/Where Is My Bess - Frank Sinatra with orchestra arranged and conducted by Axel Stordahl. Same as Columbia release CO 39493 (HCO 1751) 3/10/46 and CO 37064 (HCO 1734) 2/24/46.

REV. - Vingt Ans/Ma Pomme - Maurice Chevalier with Henri Reni and his orchestra.

#822 These Foolish Things/Over The Rainbow - Frank Sinatra with orchestra arranged and conducted by Axel Stordahl. Same as Columbia release CO 36919 (HCO 1501) 7/30/45 and CO 37458 (HCO 1378) 5/1/45.

> **REV.** - A Little Indiscretion - Dorothy Shay.
> Blue Turning Grey Over You - Harry James and his orchestra.

#831 One For My Baby - Frank Sinatra with orchestra arranged and conducted by Axel Stordahl. Not the same as Columbia commercial release. Recording date unknown.

> **REV.** - You Do - Dick Farney with Ray Bloch.
> Vine Street Boogie/Pagan Love Song - Harry James and his orchestra.

#839 Stormy Weather - Frank Sinatra with orchestra arranged and conducted by Axel Stordahl.   Same as Columbia release CO 55037 (XCO 33935) 12/3/44.

> **REV.** - Confessin' - Frankie Laine.
> San Francisco Fan - Cab Calloway and his orchestra.
> Ooh Looka There, Ain't She Pretty - Charioteers.

#851 That Old Feeling - Frank Sinatra with orchestra arranged and conducted by Alex Stordahl. Same as Columbia release CO B9021 (HCO 2519) 8/11/47.

> **REV.** - Song Of India - Tommy Dorsey and his orchestra.
> Neapolitan Nights - Jerry Wayne and The Dell Trio.
> Haunted Heart - Jo Stafford.

#859 Ever Homeward - Frank Sinatra with orchestra arranged and conducted by Axel Stordahl. Same as Columbia release CO 38151 (CO 39498) 12/8/47.

> **REV.** Carle Orchestra
> I've Only Myself To Blame - Doris Day.
> Ain't We Got Fun - Peanuts Hucko and Group.

#868 (See Number 159)

#879 Lost In The Stars - Frank Sinatra with orchestra arranged and conducted by Axel Stordahl. Same as Columbia release CO 38650 (HCO 1946) 8/8/46.

> **REV.** - Un Cantinko E Voce - Dick Farney with orchestra by Charles Lichter.

The Love I Long For - Mildred Bailey and Vernon Duke
at the piano.
All Star Strut - Metronome All Stars.

#904 Sunflower - Frank Sinatra with orchestra arranged and conducted by Axel Stordahl. Not the Columbia commercial release. Recording date unknown.

REV. - Black Coffee - Sarah Vaughn.
Sugar Blues - Johnny Mercer
I'll String Along With You - Buddy Clarke and Doris Day.

V-Disc #103.

V-Disc #21.

THE FOLLOWING IS A LISTING OF V-DISCS THAT HAVE BEEN ISSUED ON LONG PLAYING ALBUMS.

#42	Put Your Dreams Away	My Way 1002
#42	And Then You Kissed Me	My Way 1002
#72	I Only Have Eyes For You	My Way 1002
#72	A Hot Time In The Town Of Berlin	My Way 1002
#124	I'll Be Around	My Way 1001
#124	You've Got A Hold On Me	My Way 1001
#124	A Lovely Way To Spend An Evening	My Way 1001
#124	She's Funny That Way	My Way 1001
#241	Some Other Time	My Way 1001
#241	Come Out Wherever You Are	My Way 1001
#287	All Of Me	My Way 1002
#287	All The Things You Are	My Way 1002
#323	Nancy	My Way 1002
#351	Let Me Love You Tonight	My Way 1002
#351	Just Close Your Eyes	My Way 1002
#378	There's No You	My Way 1001
#378	Someone To Watch Over Me	My Way 1001
#460	Ol' Man River	My Way 1002
#467	When Your Lover Has Gone	My Way 1002
#467	Falling In Love With Love	My Way 1002
#506	I'll Follow My Secret Heart	My Way 1002
#564	The Night Is Young And You're So Beautiful	My Way 1002
#594	You Brought A New Kind Of Love	My Way 1001
#614	Old School Teacher	My Way 1002
#749	Soliloquy	My Way 1001
#831	One For My Baby	My Way 1001
#904	Sunflower	My Way 1001

SONG INDEX FOR CHAPTER VII - DISCS

Adeste Fidelis - (Reading)
#159

All Of Me - (Seymour Simins - Gerald Marks)
#287

All The Things You Are - (Jerome Kern - Oscar Hammerstein II)
#287

And Then You Kissed Me - (Sammy Cahn - Jule Styne)
#42

Aren't You Glad You're You - (Johnny Burke - Jimmy Van Heusen)
#160, #594

Begin The Beguine - (Cole Porter)
#722

Blue Skies - (Irving Berlin)
#1

Brahms Lullaby - (Johannes Brahms)
#506

Charm Of You, The - (Sammy Cahn - Jule Styne)
#537

Ciribiribin - (Harry James - Jack Lawrence - Pestalozza)
#138

Close To You - (Al Hoffman - Jerry Livingston - Carl Lampl)
#154

Come Out Wherever You Are - (Sammy Cahn - Jule Styne)
#24

Come Rain Or Come Shine - (Harold Arlen - Johnny Mercer)
#700

Ever Homeward - (Sammy Cahn - Jule Styne - Kasimierz Lubomirski)
#161, #859

Falling In Love With Love - (Richard Rodgers - Lorenz Hart)
#467

Girl That I Marry - (Irving Berlin)
#679

Homesick - That's All - (Gordon Jenkins)
#564

I Begged Her - (Sammy Cahn - Jule Styne)
#405

I Couldn't Sleep A Wink Last Night - (Jimmy McHugh - Harold Adamson)
#116

I Don't Know Why - (Roy Turk - Fred Ahlert)
#160, #711

I Fall In Love With You Every Day - (Mamy Sherwin - Arthur Altman)
#789

If You Are But A Dream - (Moe Jaffe - Jack Fulton - Nathaniel Bonx)
#393

I Have But One Heart - (Marty Symes - Johnny Farrow)
#625

I'll Be Around - (Alec Wilder)
#124

I'll Follow My Secret Heart - (Noel Coward)
#506

I'll Never Smile Again - (Ruth Lowe)
#582

In The Blue Of Evening - (Tom Adair - Alfred D'Artega)
#18

I Only Have Eyes For You - (Al Dubin - Harry Warren)
#72

It Came Upon A Midnight Clear - (Traditional)
#159

I've Got A Crush On You - (George & Ira Gershwin)
#161

I Want To Thank Your Folks - (Bennie Benjamin - George Weiss)
#763

Jingle Bells - (James Pierpoint)
#159

Just Close Your Eyes - (Bernice Petkere)
#351

Kiss Me Again - (Victor Herbert - Henry Blossom)
#72

Lamplighters Serenade, The - (Hoagy Carmichael - Paul Frances Webster)
#434

Let Me Love You Tonight - (Mitchell Parish - Rene Touzet)
#351

Long Ago And Far Away - (Jerome Kern - Ira Gershwin)
#166

Lost In The Stars - (Kurt Weill - Maxwell Anderson)
#879

Lovely Way To Spend An Evening, A - (Jimmy McHugh - Harold Adamson)
#124

Mighty Lak' A Rose - (Ethelbert Nevin - Frank Stanton)
#310

Music Stopped, The - (Jimmy McHugh - Harold Adamson)
#116

My Romance - (Richard Rodgers - Lorenz Hart0
#645

My Shawl - (Xavier Cugat - Stanley Adams)
#521

My Shining Hour - (Johnny Mercer - Harold Arlen)
#166

Nancy - (Phil Silvers - Jimmy Van Heusen)
#323

New Kind Of Love, A - (Irving Kahal - Sammy Fain - Pierre Norman)
#161, #594

Night And Day - (Cole Porter)
#25

Night Is Young And You're So Beautiful, The - (Billy Rose - Irving Kahal - Dana Suesse)
#564

None But The Lonely Heart - (Tchaikovsky - Brandt)
#494

Oh What It Seemed To Be - (Frankie Carle - George Weiss - Bennie Benjamin)
#614

Old School Teacher -
#614

O' Little Town Of Bethlehem - (Phillip Brooks - Lawrence Rodner)
#159, #652

Ol' Man River - (Jerome Kern - Oscar Hammerstein II)
#460

One For My Baby - (Harold Arlen - Johnny Mercer)
#831

Over The Rainbow - (Harold Arlen - Yip Harburg)
#822

Poinciana - (Nat Simon - Buddy Bernier)
#173

Put Your Dreams Away - (Ruth Lowe - Stephen Weiss - Paul Mann)
#42

Santa Claus Is Comin' To Town - (Haven Gillespie - Fred Coots)
#159

Saturday Night - (Sammy Cahn - Jule Styne)
#393

Should I - (Nacio Herb Brown - Arthur Freed)
#663

Silent Night - (Franz Gruber)
#159

Soliloquy - (Richard Rodgers - Oscar Hammerstein II)
#749

Someone To Watch Over Me - (George & Ira Gershwin)
#173, #378, #711

Some Other Time - (Sammy Cahn - Jule Styne)
#241

Something Old, Something New - (Ramez Idrees - George Tibbles)
#679

Song Is You, The - (Jerome Kern)
#25, #689

Speak Low - (Kurt Weill - Ogden Nash)
#154

Stars In Your Eyes - (Gabriel Ruiz - Johnny Green)
#521

Stormy Weather - (Harold Arlen - Ted Koehler)
#839

Sunflower - (Mack David)
#904

Sunshine Of Your Smile, The - (Lillian Ray - Leonard Cooke)
#434

Sweet Lorraine - (Mitchell Parish - Cliff Burwell)
#754

That Old Black Magic - (Johnny Mercer - Harold Arlen)
#722

That Old Feeling - (Lew Brown - Sammy Fain)
#851

There's Gonna Be A Hot Time In The Town Of Berlin - (Joe Bushkin - John Devries)
#72

There's No You - (Hal Hopper - Bullets Durgom - Tom Adair)
#378

These Foolish Things - (Jack Strachey - Harry Link - Holt Marvel)
#822

They Say It's Wonderful - (Irving Berlin)
#670

Way You Look Tonight, The - (Jerome Kern - Dorothy Fields)
#116

What Makes The Sunset - (Sammy Cahn - Jule Styne)
#405

When Your Lover Has Gone - (Edgar Swan)
#467

Where Is My Bess - (George & Ira Gershwin)
#789

White Christmas - (Irving Berlin)
#652

Without A Song - (Billy Rose - Edward Elisco - Vincent Youmans)
#33, #582

You Are Too Beautiful - (Richard Rodgers - Lorenz Hart)
#670

You Can Take My Word For It Baby - (Ticker Freeman - Irving Taylor)
#763

You Go To My Head - (Haven Gillespie - Fred Coots)
#700

You'll Never Walk Alone - (Richard Rodgers - Oscar Hammerstein II)
#537

Chapter VIII

A Fresh Start---Capitol Records
April 2, 1953 - March 6, 1962

Near the end of Sinatra's Columbia recording career, from 1948 to 1952, there was a marked change in public taste. The big bands, with the exception of a few hangers on and studio orchestras, had almost become extinct. The trend had turned to vocalists, and the wackier the song, the more chance it had to become a hit. Couple that with the ability to sing loud and you were a shoe-in for number one status.

The disc jockeys kept playing the likes of "Lavender Blue," "Hop Scotch Polka," "The Woody Wood Pecker Song," "Music, Music, Music," "My Truly Fair," and the public was buying. After the shouters came the vocal groups, who also sang out of tune and engaged in visual acrobatics. This was the period immediately preceeding Rock and Roll, or Rhythm and Blues. This was the era of Guy Mitchell, Teresa Brewer, Frankie Laine (a very able vocalist before Mitch Miller started to guide him to the top) and later Johnny Ray, who cried his way to huge sales and immense popularity.

From 1942 - 1947, Sinatra had grossed over $12,000,000, but almost as quickly as it happened, it was over. The "Sinatra Era" ended as abruptly as it began. In a candid moment of self-appraisal, he stated that he "was at the lowest point of his life, financially and spiritually, he felt mixed emotions that effected his singing."

Then came FROM HERE TO ETERNITY. The film was released on August 17, 1953 to much acclaim, and in 1954 received many awards. Frank was nominated for Best Supporting Actor, and he won. This was what he had scratched, clawed and worked for, and he had accomplished his goal to the amazement of everyone but himself and a few close friends who knew what a battler he was. He started on a new film, "Young At Heart," and he had already undertaken a new career in the recording studio.

In 1952 Sinatra contacted his old friend, Manie Sacks, now associated with RCA Victor. Manie did his best, but the label did not seem interested in Sinatra. Capitol records, which had begun operations in 1941, offered him a one-year contract, with options, and a flat 5% royalty. Sinatra wanted to bring in his old friend, Axel Stordahl, but the brass at Capitol immediately raised all kinds of objections. After much hasseling and haggling, a compromise was reached.

For his first recording session on April 2, 1953, Frank recorded three tunes - two with arrangements by Stordahl, and one, "Lean Baby," with an arrangement by Heinie Beau, who was with Frank in the Dorsey band back in the forties. The arrangement by Beau was in the style of the Billy May Orchestra, which was very popular at the time, and was released along with "I'm Walking Behind You" as his initial offering for his new label. The third tune recorded that day, "Don't Make A Beggar Of Me," was shelved and not until the late sixties was it finally released. Both sides of the single got good airplay and more than passing sales response.

The big hit of "I'm Walking Behind You" went to Eddie Fisher, which was not surprising; what was surprising was that Sinatra's recording of the same tune

First record with Capitol Records — 1953.

With Axel Stordahl recording - "I'm Walking Behind You" — 1953.

was a very close second.

Twenty eight days later, Frank again went into the Capitol studios to record. This time with a difference. His new producer, Voyle Gilmore, wanted to use one of Capitol's own staff arrangers, an ex-trombonist who already had two major hits to his credit: Nat "King" Cole's "Mona Lisa" and Ella Mae Morse's "Blacksmith Blues." He was Nelson Riddle.

Out of the four selections to be recorded that day, two were to have Bill May - styled arrangements and two were to be done in the Riddle manner. These were released before From Here To Eternity, and, although not selling in the millions, they made enough noise to tell Capitol that they had something substantially more than they had realized. In May another session included four ballads with Riddle - one the title song of his new movie, and one that was never released until much later. But the session that really made its impact was still to come.

On November 5 and 6, 1953, a milestone in the recording industry occurred; the invention of the long-playing album. At first, the companies made ten-inch discs with four tunes on each side. Capitol, eager to enter the new market, asked Sinatra and Riddle to do eight numbers specifically for this purpose.

Sinatra believed it should contain the kind of musical - melodic, rhythmic, romantic - that folks hadn't heard for quite some time. Frank also suggested that what was good in nightclubs would probably be good on records as well. This simple and reasonable thought was entirely novel to the recording business in 1953. It was then considered judicious to beef up both orchestra and vocalist. Gilmore agreed to visit a club in Las Vegas where Sinatra was appearing successfully. There he heard for himself what Frank was talking about. He was sold. He agreed that the smooth, uncluttered instrumentation of four string, four rhythm and two swing-bred saxaphonists was ideally suited to project the mood they wanted for an album of romantic songs. It was agreed that the arrangements permitted the desired flexible framework in which Sinatra could build his own distinctive interpretations. The important thing was to capture the same intimate mood that Frank easily achieved when he appeared in person on a nightclub floor. The songs they picked were good ones, tried, true, and familiar, but ones that had not been done to the death by every other entertainer. The album was called "Songs For Young Lovers" and was an immediate hit. It was a vindication of Sinatra's basic good taste and often expressed belief that popular music is still music, and must be treated with respectful consideration of rhythm, melody and phrasing.

Another milestone quickly followed. While making "Young At Heart" with Doris Day for Warner Bros. Capitol decided to have him record the title tune even though producer Gilmore did not think the song worthwhile. Nat Cole, Capitol's biggest selling artist at the time, had already rejected it, but Frank felt it had something, and on December 9, 1953, three days before his thirty-sixth birthday, he recorded what was to turn out to be his biggest selling single for Capitol. Another comment about this deceptively simple tune is that many of Sinatra's jazz-oriented fans considered it overly sentimental and commercial, yet it was written by one of Jazzdom's unsuing heroes, Johnny Richards, who penned many an exciting score for the great Stan Kenton orchestra. It wasn't long after "Songs For Young Lovers" was released that Capitol, naturally, began thinking about a new Sinatra album.

Branch managers, salesmen and dealers reported that Sinatra's fans had reappeared in sizeable droves and were making frequent requests for more recordings. In fact, they were demanding another Sinatra album just like the first one. However, Frank's Capitol advisers felt that a sequel would probably enjoy about the same success as the first one and they wanted to top the first album in sales. They met with him and asked his opinion. Several ideas were discussed and discarded. They agreed that the second album should be a contrast. The answer, then, seemed to be a more rhymthmic treatment of the songs. The next question was - how would they be orchestrated? Since Sinatra had proved with the first album that he knew what he was talking about when it came to instrumentation, they deferred to his opinion.

Frank had long been a fan of The Red Norvo-Mildred Bailey Band of the late thirties. They played over some of the old Norvo-Bailey records. Though the general style seemed a little dated for modern consumption, the mood of polite swing, which the old band purveyed, was exactly what Frank had in mind. Nelso Riddle was again called in and he worked out an arrangement that called for five reeds, four rhythm, one trumpet, three trombones and vibes. It was tested and discovered that this instrumentation provided the desired swing, but was not so obstrusive as to detract from the featured lyrics. The tunes for the second album were chosen by a process of elimination, Sinatra making the final choice on the basis of what he thought his fans would most enjoy. As in the first album, the songs had to stand the test of musical merit. They had to be songs which had not been overdone, and possess lyrics suited to the special Sinatra treatment. When the album "Swing Easy" was released, it too jumped onto the bestseller lists.

Just prior to the "Swing Easy" sessions, Frank had recorded three ballands - a slow version of "Day In, Day Out," "Three Coins In The Fountain," and a lovely song called "Last Night When We Were Young," which for some reason or another was not immediately released.

A full year later, Riddle and Sinatra decided on a ballad album. Frank again selected the tunes with care, and in four memorable sessions in February and March of 1955, made what is considered even to this day, the finest collection of mood songs ever recorded: "In The Wee Small Hours of the Morning".

It was still the era of the ten-inch album and all the tracks except one were issued on two long-playing records. Together they represent a supreme example of singer and arranger producing an album that is an entity in itself, thematically and musically. The songs were recorded at a time when Sinatra's voice still had a lilting quality, unbowed by the harshness of age. The effect is that while sadness is purveyed, desperation is not, and the album's beauty is even more enhanced. Sinatra's singing is perfect. When later on it became one twelve-inch Lp, "Last Night When We Were Young" was thankfully included. Nelson is always remembered as the arranger of numerous Sinatra sessions that swing; but knowledgeable fans and critics appreciate his warm and sensitive ballad accompaniments, too. When asked what his favorite albums with Frank were the arranger named "Only The Lonely" as one, and was quick to credit Sinatra, observing that "Frank gives more thought to a lyric than most other vocalists, and after sizing up a song this way and that, he uses all the tricks of the trade to accomplish his goals." Sinatra himself has been quoted as saying "Nelson is the greatest arranger in the world," and when further pressed

With Voyle Gilmore, Capitol record producer — 1954.

With Nelson Riddle — 1954.

to make a comparison with others who have backed him, he reflects: "Recording with Billy May is like having a bucket of cold water thrown in your face. Riddle will come to a session with all the arrangements carefully and neatly worked out beforehand. With Billy you sometimes don't get the copies of the next number until you've finished the one before. Billy and Nelson both work better under pressure. I, myself, work better under pressure. If there's too much time available, I don't like it - not enough stimulus, and I'll never record before eight in the evening. The voice is more relaxed then. Billy May is always driving while Nelson has more depth and with Gordon Jenkins, it's just plain beautiful and simple."

It was around the time that the so-called "Rat Pack" or "Clan" developed and at various times consisted of such names as Dean Martin, Sammy Davis, Jr., Peter Lawford, Joey Bishop, Shirley Maclaine, Jimmy Van Heusen, Sammy Cahn and Tony Curtis. They cavorted on stage and off and generally attracted unfavorable attention to their leader - nicknamed by WNEW disc jockey William B. Williams "The Chairman Of The Board". Music critics and fans acclaimed his vocal offerings, while the press dissected his social and private life. A musical peak of sorts was reached in 1956 when with Riddle once again at the helm of a swinging aggregation of outstanding jazz musicians, he recorded the album "Songs For Swingin' Lovers". Again the tunes were superior standards and the arrangements remarkable in that they completely reflected the bravado Frank displays on these selections. Even the strings swing, as do the two drummers who alternated during the different sessions - Irv Cottler and Alvin Stoller. Other instrumental highlights to be found are Harry Edison's muted trumpet solos and, of course, Juan Tizol's exciting trombone solo on the classic Riddle arrangement of "I've Got You Under My Skin".

Gone were the days when Frank could be asked to bark like a dog or sing opposite washboard. Here was a man who had risen to even greater musical heights. Sinatra often said "The trick is when you are down, do not quit".

The great albums and singles continued, and in May, 1956, Sinatra recorded for the very first time with his onetime idol, Bing Crosby.

One year later, he and Riddle recorded "Witchcraft", which rivaled "Young At Heart" in popularity. After collaborating with Gordon Jenkins on a sumptuous Christmas album, Sinatra found himself in the enviable position of having a single with both sides hitting the charts: on one side was "All The Way", backed with "Chicago". He had sung both in the movie "The Joker Is Wild". Other musical triumphs of the late fifties include the great "Only The Lonely" album, the equally superb "When No One Cares", and a host of beautiful singles. Sinatra was not satisfied with things at Capitol though, and for several reasons wanted to start his own label.

Capitol agreed to let him start his own company - on the condition that he record four more albums for them. Many of the songs he selected for these last efforts for Capitol were selections he had sung before on Columbia, and it was obvious that he was saving the newer, unrecorded songs for his own company. The "Nice And Easy" album maintains a leisurely, graceful manner and Riddle's backgrounds are elegant examples of jazz-tinged ballad orchestrations. Frank was also in superior voice on this one and on the "Point Of No Return" album he blends well with the trombones on the selection "A Million Dreams Ago' and even revives and strengthens the Don Raye, Gene DePaul and

Pat Johnson chestnut "I'll Remember April."

Yes, his Capitol days would soon be over and in retrospect, the eight years would be referred to as his "Swingin' Years" and gratifying years they were - to be sure.

With Red Buttons and Milton Berle — 1953.

Cover of recording with Ray Anthony — 1954.

April 2, 1953 - March 6, 1962

Orchestra Under The Direction of Axel Stordahl
Arrangements by Stordahl, except where noted.

April 2, 1953, Los Angeles

11394	Lean Baby (A)	CAP. 2450, W1429, WCO 1726, DNFR 7630, SPC 3457
11395	I'm Walking Behind You	CAP. 2450, H9115, TP 81, SYS 5637
11396	Don't Make A Beggar Of Me	CAP. T2602

(A) Arranged by Heinie Beau.

Orchestra Under The Direction of Nelson Riddle.
Arrangements by Riddle

April 30, 1953, Los Angeles

| 11504 | I've Got The World On A String | CAP. 2505, T768, WCO 1726, W 2123, SW90986, PC 3458 |
| 11511 | Don't Worry 'Bout Me | CAP. 2787, T768, PC 3458 |

On the next two titles, the label lists Billy May And His Orchestra, and although the band sounds like a May band, reliable information confirms our belief that it is Nelson Riddle leading the orchestra.   — The Editors

| 11512 | I Love You | CAP. 2638, W 1429, DQBO91261, DNFR7630 |
| 11513 | South Of The Border | CAP. 2638, T768, T2036, WCO 1726, DNFR 7630 |

Orchestra Under The Direction of Nelson Riddle
Arrangements By Riddle

May 2, 1953, Los Angeles

11524	Anytime, Anywhere	CAP. 2560, W 1164
11525	My One And Only Love	CAP. 2505, T768, W1432, PC 3458
11526	From Here To Eternity	CAP. 2560, T768, WCO 1726, DNFR 7630, PC 3458
11527	I Can Read Between The Lines	CAP. W1432, PC3452

Orchestra Under The Direction of Nelson Riddle
Arrangements By Riddle   November 5, 1953, Los Angeles

(Sax) Skeets Herfurt, Mahlon Clark; (Piano) Bill Miller; (Guitars) Al Hendrikson, Alan Reuss; (Bass) Joe Comfort; (Drums) Alvin Stoller; plus strings. strings.

11846	A Foggy Day	CAP. H488, W1432
11847	My Funny Valentine	CAP. H488, W1432, W1825
11852	They Can't Take That Away From Me	CAP. H488, W1432
11853	Violets For Your Furs	CAP. H488, W1432, WCO 1726, SM 3631

Accompaniment The Same.   November 6, 1953, Los Angeles

11858	Like Someone In Love	CAP. 2703, H488, W1432
11859	I Get A Kick Out Of You	CAP. H488, W1432, W2301
12033	Little Girl Blue	CAP. H488, W1432, W1825
12034	The Girl Next Door	CAP. H488, W1432, DQBO 91261, DNFR 7630, PC 3458

Orchestra Under The Direction of Nelson Riddle
Arrangements by Riddle   December 8, 1953, Los Angeles

12051	Take A Chance	CAP. 2703, SYS 5637
12052	Ya Better Stop	CAP. UNISSUED
12053	Why Should I Cry Over You (1)	CAP. 2703, 3050, W1429

(1) With Vocal Chorus.

Orchestra Under The Direction of Nelson Riddle

Arrangements by Riddle   December 9, 1953, Los Angeles

11991	Rain	CAP. 2816, T768
11992	Young At Heart	CAP. 2703, 6019, T768, W1762, T1488, WCO 1726, T2036, T2700, DQBO 91261, DKAO 2950, DNFR 7630
11993	I Could Have Told You	CAP. 2787, W1164

Accompaniment The Same.		March 1, 1954, Los Angeles
12365	Day In, Day Out	CAP. EAP-590, SYS 5637
12366	Last Night When We Were Young	CAP. W581, W2123
12367	Three Coins In The Fountain	CAP. 2816, T768, T2036, WCO 1726, T2700, DNFR 7630

Accompaniment The Same.		April 2, 1954, Los Angeles
12400	The Sea Song (1)	CAP. UNISSUED
	(1) With Vocal Chorus.	

Orchestra Under The Direction of Nelson Riddle
Arrangements by Riddle   April 7, 1954, Los Angeles

(TPT) Harry Edison; (TBN) Tommy Pederson, Ray Sims; (Bass TBN) George Roberts; (Alto Sax) Mahlon Clark, Skeets Herfurt; (Tenor Sax) Eddie Miller, Babe Russin; (Bar. Sax) Joe Koch; (Vibes) Frank Flyn; (Piano) Bill Miller; (Guitar) Allan Reuss; (Bass) Joe Comfort; (Drums) Alvin Stoller.

12430	Sunday	CAP. H528, W1429, DQBO 91261, DNFR 7630, SM 3631, MFP 5005
12431	Just One Of Those Things	CAP. H528, W1429, W2301, SPC 3457
12432	I'm Gonna Sit Right Down And Write Myself A Letter	CAP. H528, W1429
12433	Wrap Your Troubles In Dreams	CAP. H528, W1429, DNFR 7630

April 19, 1954, Los Angeles

Abe Most (Alto Sax) and Bob Bain (Guitar) replace Clark and Reuss.

12564	All Of Me	CAP. H528, W1429, WCO 1726
12565	Jeepers Creepers	CAP. H528, W1429, W1984, SPC 3457
12566	Get Happy	CAP. H528, W1429, W1429, W2123, SPC 3457, SM 3631

12567	Taking A Chance On Love	CAP. H528, W1429, DQBO 91261, DNFR 7630

Orchestra Under The Direction of Nelson Riddle
Arrangements By Riddle   May 13, 1954, Los Angeles

12642	The Gal That Got Away	CAP. 2864, T768, WCO1726, W2123, DQBO 91261, DNFR 7630, SM 3631
12643	Half As Lovely	CAP. 2864, W982
12644	It Worries Me	CAP. 2922, W1432, SW 90986

Orchestra Under The Direction of Nelson Riddle
Arrangements By Riddle   August 23, 1954, Los Angeles

12937	When I Stop Loving You (1)	CAP. 2922, W1164
12938	White Christmas (1)	CAP. 2954, T9030
12939	The Christmas Waltz (1)	CAP. 2954

     (1) With Vocal Chorus.

Accompaniment The Same.   September 23, 1954

12702	Don't Change Your Mind About Me (1)	CAP. 3050, EAP-629, SYS. 5637
12703	Someone To Watch Over Me	CAP. 2993, EAP-579, W1432
12704	You, My Love	CAP. 2993, EAP-571, W1164

     (1) With Vocal Chorus.

Ray Anthony And His Orchestra
Arrangements By Dick Reynolds   December 13, 1954, Los Angeles

(TPT) Ray Anthony, John Best, Conrad Gozzo, Manny Klein, Uan Rassey; (TBN) Ed Kusby, Tommy Pederson, Si Zentner, George Roberts; (Alto Sax) Skeets Herfurt, Willie Schwartz; (Tenor Sax) Morris Broov, Fred Fallensby; (Bar. Sax) Leo Anthony; (Piano) Paul Smith; (Guitar) Al Hendrickson; (Bass) Joe Comfort; (Drums) Alvin Stoller.

13141	Melody Of Love	CAP. 3018, EAP-590, T2602, DNFR 7630
13302	I'm Gonna Live Till I Die	CAP. 3018, EAP-590, W1164

Orchestra Under The Direction of Nelson Riddle
Arrangements By Riddle   February 8, 1955, Los Angeles

13556	Dancing On The Ceiling	CAP. W581, W1825, SPC 3457
13557	Can't We Be Friends	CAP. W581, W1919
13558	Glad To Be Unhappy	CAP. W581, W1825
13559	I'll Be Around	CAP. W581, W1825

Accompaniment The Same.   February 16, 1955

13457	What Is This Thing Called Love	CAP. W581, W2301
13458	Ill Wind	CAP. W581, W1919, W2123
13459	I See Your Face Before Me	CAP. W581
13523	Mood Indigo	CAP. W581, SW90986

Accompaniment The Same.   February 17, 1955

13460	I Get Along Without You Very Well	CAP. W581, PC3450 SW90986
13461	In The Wee Small Hours	CAP. W581, WCO 1726
13573	When Your Lover Has Gone	CAP. W581, W1919, WCO 1726
13574	This Love Of Mine	CAP. W581, DNFR 7630, PC 3458
13575	Soliloquy	CAP. UNISSUED

Accompaniment The Same.   March 4, 1955

13486	It Never Entered My Mind	CAP. W581, W1825, W1919, PC 3452
13487	Not As A Stranger	CAP. 3130, W1164
13585	Deep In A Dream	CAP. W581
13586	I'll Never Be The Same	CAP. W581, DNFR 7630, MFP-5005

Orchestra Under The Direction of Nelson Riddle
Arrangements By Riddle   March 7, 1955, Los Angeles

| 13594 | If I Had Three Wishes | CAP. 3102, W1164 |
| 13595 | How Could You Do A Thing Like That To Me | CAP. 3130, W1429 |

Recording with Dave Cavanaugh — 1955.

At Capitol with F.S., Danny Kaye, Gordon MacRae, Nat Cole, Dean Martin and Stan Freburg — 1955.

Accompaniment By Big Dave (Cavanaugh's) Music

Same Date As Last Session

| 13596 | Two Hearts, Two Kisses (1) | CAP. 3084, EAP-629, T2602 |
| 13597 | From The Bottom To The Top (1) | CAP. 3084, EAP-629, T2602 |

(1) With Vocal Group, The Nuggets.

Orchestra Under The Direction of Nelson Riddle
Arrangement By Riddle

March 23, 1955, Los Angeles

| 13628 | Learnin' The Blues | CAP. 3102, 6019, T768, T2036, WCO 1726, DNFR 7630 |

Accompaniment The Same.

July 29, 1955

| 14286 | Same Old Saturday Night | CAP. 3218, W1164 |
| 14288 | Fairy Tale | CAP. 3218, W1164 |

Accompaniment The Same.

August 15, 1955

14118	Look To Your Heart (1)	CAP. EAP-673, W1164
14119	Love And Marriage	CAP. 3260, EAP-673, T768, WCO 1726, T2036, DNFR7630
14120	The Impatient Years	CAP. 3260, EAP-673, W1164, DNFR 7630, MFP-5005
14121	Our Town	CAP. EAP-673, W1164

(1) With Vocal Chorus.

Soundtrack Recordings for 20th Century Fox Film "Carousel".
Orchestra Under The Direction of Alfred Newman - Vocal Director - Ken Darby.

August 20, 1955, Boothbay, Maine

| Soliloquy | 3 Takes UNISSUED |

August 21, 1955, Boothbay, Maine

| Soliloquy | 3 Takes, UNISSUED |

August 22, 1955, Boothbay, Maine

| Soliloquy | 3 Takes, UNISSUED |

If I Loved You   3 Takes, UNISSUED

August 24, 1955, Boothbay, Maine

If I Loved You   1 Take, UNISSUED

Orchestra Under The Direction of Nelson Riddle
Arrangements By Riddle   September 13, 1955, Los Angeles

| 14429 | The Tender Trap (Love Is) | CAP. 3290, T-768, WCO 1726, T2700, DNFR 7630 |
| 14430 | You'll Get Yours | CAP. 3350, T2602 |

Orchestra Under The Direction of Nelson Riddle
Arrangements By Riddle   October 17, 1955, Los Angeles

(TPT) John Best, Harry Edison, Shorty Sherock, Zeke Zarchey; (TBN) Dick
Noel, Jimmy Priddy, Paul Tanner, George Roberts; (Alto Sax) Mahlon Clark,
Willie Schwartz; (Tenor Sax) Justin Gordon, Warren Webb; (Bar. Sax) Bob
Lawson; (Vibes) Frank Flyn; (Piano) Bill Miller; (Guitar) George Van Epps;
(Bass) Joe Comfort; (Drums) Irv Cotter; plus Harp and Strings.

14287	You Forgot All The Words	CAP. 3552, EAP-800, W982
14633	Love Is Here To Stay	CAP. W653
14634	Weep They Will	CAP. 3290, W1919

January 9, 1956, Los Angeles

(TPT) Harry Edison, Conrad Gozzo, Manny Klein, Micky Mangano; (TBN)
Milt Bernhart, Joe Howard, Juan Tizol, George Roberts; (Alto Sax) Mahlon
Clark, Willie Schwartz; (Ten. Sax) Ted Nash, Babe Russin; (Bar. Sax)
Marty Friedman; (Vibes) Frank Flyn; (Piano) Bill Miller; (Guitar) George Van
Epps; (Bass) Joe Comfort; (Drums) Alvin Stoller; plus Harp and Strings.

14605	A New Kind Of Love	CAP. W653, PC3450
14606	I Thought About You	CAP. W653, W1984
14607	You Make Me Feel So Young	CAP. W653, DQBO 91261
14608	Memories Of You	CAP. SYS. 5637

Zeke Zarchey (TPT), Jimmy Priddy (TBN), Justin Gordon and Jim Williamson (Tenor Sax) replace Klein, Howard, Nash and Russin.

14613	Pennies From Heaven	CAP. W653
14614	How About You	CAP. W653, DQBO 91261, DNFR 7630, MFP-5005
14615	The Man With The Golden Arm	CAP. UNISSUED
14616	You're Getting To Be A Habit With Me	CAP. W653
14617	Together Again	CAP. UNISSUED

January 12, 1956, Los Angeles

Manny Klein (TPT) and Irv Cottler (Drums) replace Zarchey and Stoller.

14940	It Happened In Monterey	CAP. W653, DNFR 7630
14941	Swinging Down The Lane	CAP. W653, DQBO 91261, DNFR 7630
14942	Flowers Mean Forgiveness (1)	CAP. 3350, EAP-800, T2602
14943	I've Got You Under My Skin	CAP. W653, W2301

(1) With Vocal Chorus.

Orchestra The Same.   January 16, 1956

14956	Makin' Whoopee	CAP. W653, W1919
14957	Old Devil Moon	CAP. W653
14958	Anything Goes	CAP. W653, W2301
14959	Too Marvelous For Words	CAP. W653, W1984, SPC3457
14960	We'll Be Together Again	CAP. W653

Orchestra Under The Direction of Nelson Riddle
Add The Hollywood String Quartet.
Arrangements By Riddle   March 8, 1956, Los Angeles

| E15186 | Don't Like Goodbyes | CAP. W789, W2123 |

E15187	P.S. I Love You	CAP. W789, W1984
E15188	Love Locked Out	CAP. W789
E15189	If It's The Last Thing I Do	CAP. T2602

Accompaniment The Same.   April 4, 1956, Los Angeles

E15310	I've Had My Moments	CAP. W789
E15311	Blame It On My Youth	CAP. W789
E15312	Everything Happens To Me	CAP. W789
E15313	Wait Till You See Her	CAP. W1825

Accompaniment The Same.   April 5, 1956

| E15278 | End Of A Love Affair | CAP. W789 |
| E15296 | It Could Happen To You | CAP. W789, PC 3450 |

Same Date. Hollywood String Quartet out.

E15315	How Little We Know	CAP. 3423, EAP-800, EAP-800, W982, DQBO 91261, DNFR 7630
E15316	Johnny Concho Theme (Wait For Me)	CAP. 3469, W982
E15317	You're Sensational	CAP. 3469
E15318	There's A Flaw In My Flue	CAP. SYS. 5637, SM 3631

Same Date. Hollywood String Quartet back in.

| E15360 | With Every Breath I Take | CAP. W789 |

Orchestra Under The Direction of Nelson Riddle
Arrangements By Riddle   April 9, 1956, Los Angeles

(TPT) Harry Edison, Manny Klein, Ray Linn, Shorty Sherock; (TBN) Milt Bernhart, Ed Kusby, Jimmy Priddy, George Roberts; (Alto Sax) Harry Klee, Willie Schwartz; (Tenor Sax) Babe Russin, Warren Webb; (Bar. Sax) Chuck Gentry; (Piano) Bill Miller; (Guitar) George Van Epps; (Bass) Joe Comfort; (Drums) Alvin Stoller; plus Harp and Strings.

E15330	Five Hundred Guys	CAP. 3423, T611,* SYS. 5637
E15331	Something Wonderful Happens In Summer	CAP. UNISSUED
E15332	Hey Jealous Lover (1)	CAP. 3552, EAP-800,

		W982, WCO 1726, T2036, DKAO 2950, DNFR 7630
E15333	No One Ever Tells You	CAP. 4103, T803, PC3450, WCO 1726, SPC 3457

(1) With Vocal Chorus.

NOTE: British Release Lp - World Record Club.

The Metro-Goldwyn-Mayer Orchestra
Under The Direction of Johnny Green
Arrangements As Noted   April 20, 1956, Los Angeles

E15405	You're Sensational (A)	CAP. W750
E15406	Who Wants To Be A Millionaire- (1) - (B)	CAP. 3508, W750
E15407	Mind If I Make Love To You (C)	CAP. 3508, W750

(1) Vocal Duet with Celeste Holm.

(A) Arrangement by Nelson Riddle.

(B) Arrangement by Conrad Salinger.

(C) Arrangement by Nelson Riddle.

Accompaniment The Same.   May 7, 1956, Los Angeles

E15721	Well Did You Evah (1) - (D)	CAP. 3507, W750

(1) Vocal Duet with Bing Crosby.
(D) Arrangement by Skip Martin.

Orchestra Under The Direction of Nelson Riddle
Add The Hollywood String Quartet
Arrangements By Riddle   October 1, 1956, Los Angeles

E16159	I Couldn't Sleep A Wink Last Night	CAP. W789
E16160	It's Easy To Remember	CAP. W789, W1825, SW90986, SPC 3457
E16161	Close To You	CAP. W789, DNFR 7630, MFP 5005

Orchestra Under The Direction of Nelson Riddle
Arrangements By Riddle   November 15, 1956, Los Angeles

(TPT) Harry Edison, Conrad Gozzo, Micky Mangano, Shorty Sherock; (TBN) George Arvs, Ed Kusby, Dick Noel, George Roberts; (Alto Sax) Jack Dumont,

—141—

Mickey Mumolo; (Tenor Sax) Dan Raffael, Buck Skalak; (Bar. Sax) Bob Lawson; (Piano) Bill Miller; (Guitar) Nick Bonney; (Bass) Joe Comfort; (Drums) Alvin Stoller; plus Harp and Strings.

E16192	I've Got Plenty Of Nothin'	CAP. W803
E16193	I Won't Dance	CAP. W803
E16194	Stars Fell On Alabama	CAP. W803, PC 3452, SW90986

Orchestra Under The Direction of Nelson Riddle
Arrangements By Riddle   November 20, 1956, Los Angeles

Harry Klee, Willie Schwartz (Alto Sax); Jim Briggs, Ted Nash (Tenor Sax); Joe Koch (Bar. Sax); Irv Cottler (Drums); replace Dumont, Mumolo, Raffael, Skalak, Lawson and Stoller.

E16196	At Long Last Love	CAP. W803, W2301
E16197	I Guess I'll Have To Change My Plans	CAP. W803, T1919
E16198	I Wish I Were In Love Again	CAP. W803, W1825
E16199	Nice Work If You Can Get It	CAP. W803

November 26, 1956, Los Angeles

Ray Linn (TPT); Murry MacAhearn, Juan Tizol (TBN); Jules Kinsler, Jim Williamson (Ten. Sax); replace Gozzo; Arvs, Kusby, Nash and Briggs.

E16205	The Lady Is A Tramp	CAP. EAP-912, W1825
E16206	Night And Day	CAP. 6195, W803, T1919, W2301
E16207	The Lonesome Road	CAP. W803
E16208	If I Had You	CAP. W803, PQBO 91261, DNFR 7630, MFP 5005

Orchestra Under The Direction of Nelson Riddle
Arrangements By Riddle   November 28, 1956, Los Angeles

(TPT) Pete Candoli, Harry Edison, Ray Linn, Shorty Sherock; (TBN) Dick Nash, Tommy Pederson, Juan Tizol, George Roberts; (Alto Sax) Skeets Herfurt, Harry Klee; (Ten. Sax) Ted Nash, Jim Williamson; (Bar. Sax) Joe Koch; (Piano) Bill Miller; (Guitar) Nick Bonney; (Bass) Joe Comfort; (Drums) Alvin Stoller; plus Harp and Strings.

| E16209 | I Got It Bad | CAP. W803, T1919, DNFR 7630, MFP 5005 |

Recording with
Gordon Jenkins — 1956.

Recording with
Billy May — 1958.

E16210	From This Moment On	CAP. W803, T2301
E16211	Oh Look At Me Now	CAP. W803
E16212	You'd Be So Nice To Come Home To	CAP. W803, W2301

Accompaniment The Same		December 3, 1956, Los Angeles
E16217	Your Love For Me	CAP. 3608, T2602, DNFR 7630, PC 3458, MFP 5005
E16218	Can I Steal A Little Love	CAP. 3608, T2602

Orchestra Under The Direction of Nelson Riddle
Arrangements By Riddle — March 14, 1957, Los Angeles

| E16731 | So Long My Love | CAP. 3703, W982 |
| E16732 | Crazy Love | CAP. 3703, W982 |

Orchestra Under The Direction of Gordon Jenkins
Arrangements By Jenkins — April 10, 1957, Los Angeles

E16820	Where Is The One	CAP. W855
E16821	There's No You	CAP. W855, Playboy 1959
E16822	The Night We Called Is A Day	CAP. W855
E16823	Autumn Leaves	CAP. W855, W1984, WCO 1726, DNFR 7630

Accompaniment The Same		April 29, 1957, Los Angeles
E17008	I Cover The Waterfront	CAP. W855
E17009	Lonely Town	CAP. W855
E17010	Laura	CAP. W855, W1984, PC 3450, DNFR 7630, MFP 5005
E17011	Baby Won't You Please Come Home	CAP. W855, WCO 1726

Accompaniment The Same		May 1, 1957, Los Angles
E16863	Where Are You	CAP. W855, DNFR 7630
E16869	I Think Of You	CAP. W855

| E17040 | I'm A Fool To Want You | CAP. W855, DNFR 7630, PC 3458, MFP 5005 |
| E17041 | Maybe You'll Be There | CAP. W855 |

Orchestra Under The Direction of Nelson Riddle
Arrangements By Riddle · May 20, 1957, Los Angeles

E17069	Witchcraft	CAP. 3859, 6078, T1762, W1538, T2036, WCO 1726 STFL 2814, SW 90986, DKAO 2950, DNFR 7630
E17070	Something Wonderful Happens In Summer	CAP. 3744, W982, T1729
E17071	Tell Her You Love Her	CAP. 3859, T1919, DNFR 7630, PC 3458, MFP 5005
E17072	You're Cheatin' Yourself	CAP. 3744, W982

Orchestra Under The Direction of Gordon Jenkins
Arrangements By Jenkins · July 10, 1957, Los Angeles

E17289	It Came Upon A Midnight Clear (1)	CAP. W984
E17290	O, Little Town Of Bethlehem (1)	CAP. W894
E17291	Hark, The Herald Angels Sing (1)	CAP. W894
E17292	Adeste Fidelis (O, Come All Ye Faithful) (1)	CAP. W894

(1) With The Ralph Brewster Singers.

Accompaniment The Same. · July 16, 1957, Los Angeles

E17331	Jingle Bells (1)	CAP. W984
E17332	Have Yourself A Merry Little Christmas (1)	CAP. W984
E17334	The Christmas Waltz (1)	CAP. 3900, W984

(1) With The Ralph Brewster Singers.

Accompaniment The Same. · July 17, 1957, Los Angeles

E17339	Mistletoe And Holly (1)	CAP. 3900, W984
E17340	The Christmas Song (1)	CAP. W984
E17341	Silent Night (1)	CAP. W984

| E17342 | I'll Be Home For Christmas (1) | CAP. W984 |

(1) With The Ralph Brewster Singers.

Orchestra Under The Direction of Morris Stoloff
Arrangements By Nelson Riddle   August 13, 1957, Los Angeles

E17468	I Could Write A Book	CAP. EAP-912, W912
E17469	Bewitched	CAP. EAP-912, W912
E17471	There's A Small Hotel	CAP. W912

Orchestra Under The Direction of Nelson Riddle
Arrangements By Riddle   August 13, 1957, Los Angeles

| E17470 | All The Way | CAP. 3793, 6027, W1538, W1726, T2036, WCO 1726 T2700, STFL 2814, DKAO 2950, DNFR 7630 |
| E17472 | Chicago | CAP. 3793, 6078, W1729, T2602, DKAO 2950 |

Orchestra Under The Direction of Morris Stoloff
Arrangements By Riddle   September 25, 1957, Los Angeles

| E17553 | I Didn't Know What Time It Was | CAP. W912 |
| E17561 | What Do I Care For A Dame | CAP. W912 |

Orchestra Under The Direction of Billy May
Arrangements By May   October 1, 1957, Los Angeles

(TPT) Mannie Klein, Conrad Gozzo, Shorty Sherock, Pete Candoli; (TBN) Si Zentner, Murray MacAhearn, Tommy Pederson, Frank Howard; (Alto Saxz0 Skeets Herfurt, Buddy Collette; (Ten. Sax) Ted Nash, Jules Jacob; (Bar. Sax) Fred Fallensby; (Vibes) Frank Flyn; (Piano) Bill Miller; (Guitar) Al Hendrickson; (Bass) Joe Mondragon; (Tuba) Country Washburne; (Drums) Alvin Stoller; (Harp) Verle Mills.

E17639	On The Road To Mandalay	CAP. W920
E17640	Let's Get Away From It All	CAP. W920
E17641	Isle Of Capri	CAP. W920

October 3, 1957, Los Angeles

Gozzo, Candoli, Sherock, Pederson and Flyn out; Wilbur Schwartz (Alto Sax), Joe Kinsler (Ten. Sax) replace Collette and Nash. Add Strings.

| E17647 | Autumn In New York | CAP. W920 |
| E17648 | London By Night | CAP. W920, DNFR 7630 |

| E17649 | April In Paris | CAP. W920 |
| E17650 | Moonlight In Vermont | CAP. W920, PC 3452 |

Add Gozzo, Sherock, Mangano (TPT); Ed Kusby (TBN); Frank Flyn (Vibes); Harry Klee (Alto Sax); Buddy Collette (Tenor Sax) replace Herfurt and Kinsler.

October 8, 1957, Los Angeles

E17696	Blue Hawaii	CAP. W920, PC 3450
E17697	Come Fly With Me	CAP. W920, WCO 1726, DNFR 7630
E17698	Around The World	CAP. W920
E17699	It's Nice To Go Traveling	CAP. W920
E17700	Brazil	CAP. W920

Orchestra Under The Direction of Nelson Riddle
Arrangements By Riddle   November 25, 1957, Los Angeles

E17974	I Believe	CAP. W982
E17975	Everybody Loves Somebody	CAP. W982
W17976	It's The Same Old Dream	CAP. W982
E17977	Time After Time	CAP. 4155, W982, Playboy 1958

Accompaniment The Same.   December 11, 1957, Los Angeles

E18052	You'll Always Be The One I Love	CAP. 4466, W982
E18053	If You Are But A Dream	CAP. W982
E18054	Put Your Dreams Away	CAP. W982, WCO 1726, DKAO 2950, DNFR 7630

Orchestra Under The Direction of Billy May
Arrangements By May   March 3, 1958, Los Angeles

E18522	Nothin' In Common (1)	CAP. 3952
E18523	How Are You Fixed For Love (1)	CAP. 3952
E18524	The Same Old Song And Dance	CAP. 4003, T2602

(1) Vocal Duet with Keely Smith.

Orchestra Under The Direction of Felix Slatkin
Arrangements By Slatkin   May 29, 1958, Los Angeles

| E19230 | Song From "Kings Go Forth" (Monique) | CAP. 4003, W1729, T2700 |

E19231	Lush Life (1)	CAP. UNISSUED

(1) Frank sings part of the song then decides to forget the whole thing until a future date but never does record it.

Orchestra Under The Direction of Nelson Riddle
Arrangements By Riddle — Same Date As Last Session

E19240	Ebb Tide	CAP. W1053, PC 3452 STFL 2814, DNFR 7630
E19241	Angel Eyes	CAP. W1053, STFL 2814
E19242	Spring Is Here	CAP. W1053, STFL 2814, W1825, DNFR 7630, SPC 3457
E19255	Guess I'll Hang My Tears Out To Dry	CAP. W1053, STFL 2814
E19256	Only The Lonely	CAP. W1053, T2036, WCO 1726, STFL 2814, DNFR 7630, DKAO 2950
E19258	Willow Weep For Me	CAP. W1053, STFL 2814

Accompaniment The Same. — June 24, 1958, Los Angeles

E19478	Blues In The Night	CAP. W1053, W1984, W2123, STFL 2814
E19479	What's New	CAP. W1053, STFL 2814
E19480	Gone With The Wind	CAP. W1053, STFL 2814

Accompaniment The Same. — June 25, 1958, Los Angeles

E19420	Goodbye	CAP. W1053, STFL 2814
E19421	It's A Lonesome Old Town	CAP. W1053, T200, STFL 2814
E19422	One For My Baby	CAP. 6193, W1053, WCO 1726, W2123, STFL 2814, DNFR 7630

Orchestra Under The Direction of Nelson Riddle.
Arrangements By Riddle — September 11, 1958, Los Angeles

E30096	Mr. Success	CAP. 4070, W1729, DNFR 7630
E30097	Sleep Warm	CAP. 4070, W1538, STFL 2814

E30098	The Way I Love You	CAP. UNISSUED
E30099	Who's In Your Arms Tonight	CAP. UNISSUED
E30100	Where Or When	CAP. UNISSUED

Orchestra Under The Direction of Billy May
Arrangement By May   September 30, 1958, Los Angeles

| E30171 | It All Depends On You | CAP. SYS 5637 |

Orchestra Under The Direction of Billy May
Arrangement By May   October 1, 1958, Los Angeles

| E30178 | I Couldn't Care Less | CAP. SYS. 5637 |

Orchestra Under The Direction of Nelson Riddle
Arrangement By Riddle   December 5, 1958, Los Angeles

| E30380 | Song From "Some Came Running" (To Love and Be Loved) | CAP. 4103, W1538, STFL 2814, T2700, DNFR 7630 |

Orchestra Under The Direction of Billy May
Arrangements By May except where noted
                                                  December 9, 1958, Los Angeles

E30771	The Song Is You	CAP. W1069, STFL 2814
E30772	Something's Gotta Give	CAP. W1069, W1984, STFL 2814
E30773	Just In Time	CAP. W1069, STFL 2814

Accompaniment The Same.   December 22, 1958, Los Angeles

E30876	Day In, Day Out	CAP. W1069, W1984, STFL 2814
E30877	Baubles, Bangles and Beads	CAP. W1069, STFL 2814
E30878	Dancing In The Dark	CAP. W1069, STFL 2814
E30879	Saturday Night (A)	CAP. W1069, STFL 2814
E30880	Cheek To Cheek	CAP. W1069, STFL 2814

(A) Arranged By Heinie Beau.

Accompaniment The Same.   December 23, 1958, Los Angeles

E30887	Too Close For Comfort (A)	CAP. W1069, STFL 2814
E30888	I Could Have Danced All Night	CAP. W1069, STFL 2814
E30889	Come Dance With Me	CAP. W1069, T2036,

| | | WCO 1726, STFL 2814,
DKAO 2950, DNFR 7630 |
| E30890 | The Last Dance (A) | CAP. W1069, WCO 1726,
STFL 2814 |

(A) Arranged By Heinie Beau.

Orchestra Under The Direction of Nelson Riddle
Arrangements By Riddle   December 29, 1958, Los Angeles

E30893	The Moon Was Yellow	CAP. 4677, W1729
E30894	They Came To Cordura	CAP. 4284, W1729, T2700
E30895	All My Tomorrows	CAP. 4214, W1538, STFL 2814, T2700, DNFR 7630

Orchestra Under The Direction of Gordon Jenkins
Arrangements By Jenkins   March 24, 1959, Los Angeles

E31391	Ghost Of A Chance	CAP. W1221
E31392	Why Try To Change Me Now	CAP. W1221
E31393	None But The Lonely Heart	CAP. W1221
E31394	Stormy Weather	CAP. W1221, W2123

Accompaniment The Same.   March 25, 1959, Los Angeles

| E31421 | Here's That Rainy Day | CAP. W1221 |
| E31422 | The One I Love Belongs To
Somebody Else | CAP. SYS. 5637 |

Accompaniment The Same.   March 26, 1959, Los Angeles

E31424	I Can't Get Started	CAP. W1221, PC 3452, WCO 1726
E31425	Where Do You Go	CAP. W1221
E31426	A Cottage For Sale	CAP. W1221
E31427	Just Friends	CAP. W1221, DNFR 7630

Orchestra Under The Direction of Nelson Riddle
Arrangements By Riddle   May 8, 1959, Los Angeles

| E31632 | High Hopes (1) | CAP. 4214, 6027, W1538,
WCO 1726, T2700,
STFL 2814, SKAO 2950,
DNFR 7630 |
| E31633 | Love Looks so Well On You | CAP. W1729 |

(1) Vocal accompaniment with a
"bunch of kids" and Eddie Hodges.

Accompaniment The Same.		May 14, 1959, Los Angeles
E31679	This Was My Love	CAP. 4408, W1538, STFL 2814
E31682	Talk To Me	CAP. 4284, W1538, WCO 1726, STFL 2814, DNFR 7630

Orchestra Under The Direction of Gordon Jenkins
Arrangements By Jenkins

		May 14, 1959, Los Angeles
E31680	When No One Cares	CAP. W1221
E31681	I'll Never Smile Again	CAP. W1221, WCO 1726

Orchestra Under The Direction of Nelson Riddle
Arrangements By Riddle

		February 19, 1960, Los Angeles
E33339	It's All Right With Me	CAP. W1301, T2700
E33340	C'est Magnifique	CAP. W1301, T2700
E33341	I Love Paris (1)	CAP. W1301

(1) Vocal Duet with Maurice Chevalier and Chorus.

Accompaniment The Same.		February 20, 1960, Los Angeles
E33348	Let's Do It (1)	CAP. W1301
E33349	Montmart' (2)	CAP. W1301

(1) Vocal duet with Shirley MacLaine.
(2) Vocal Duet with Maurice Chevalier and Chorus.

Orchestra Under The Direction of Nelson Riddle
Arrangements By Riddle

		March 1, 1960, Los Angeles
E33350	You Go To My Head	CAP. W1417, STFL 2814
E33351	Fools Rush In	CAP. W1417, W1984, STFL 2814
E33352	That Old Feeling	CAP. W1417, STFL 2814, DNFR 7630
E33353	Try A Little Tenderness	CAP. W1417, PC 3452, STFL 2814, DQBO91261, DNFR 7630

Accompaniment The Same.		March 2, 1960, Los Angeles
E33364	She's Funny That Way	CAP. W1417, STFL 2814
E33365	The Nearness Of You	CAP. W1417, PC 3450, STFL 2814, SW 90986
E33366	Nevertheless	CAP. W1417, STFL 2814
Accompaniment The Same.		March 3, 1960, Los Angeles
E33363	Dream	CAP. W1417, WCO 1726, W1984, STFL 2814, SPC 3457
E33386	I've Got A Crush On You	CAP. W1417, STFL 2814
E33387	Embraceable You	CAP. W1417, STFL 2814
E33388	Mam'selle	CAP. W1417, STFL 2814, DQBO 91261, DNFR 7630
E33390	How Deep Is The Ocean	CAP. W1417, STFL 2814

Orchestra Under The Direction of Nelson Riddle
Arrangements By Riddle   April 12, 1960, Los Angeles

E33650	Nice 'N Easy	CAP. 4408, W1417, W2036, STFL 2814 DKAO 2950, DNFR 7630
E33651	River Stay Away From My Door	CAP. 4376, W1538, STFL 2814, DNFR 7630, MFP 5005
E33652	I Love Paris	CAP. 4815, W1729
E33653	It's Over, It's Over, It's Over (1)	CAP. 4376, W1538, STFL 2814, DNFR 7630
	(1) With Vocal Chorus.	

Orchestra Under The Direction of Nelson Riddle
Arrangements By Riddle   August 22, 1960, Los Angeles

(TPT) Mickey Mangano, Shorty Sherock; (TBN) Tommy Pederson, James Priddy; (Sax) Buddy Collette, Ronnie Lang; (Piano) Bill Miller; (Bass) Red Mitchell; (Drums) Alvin Stoller; plus Strings and others.

E34373	When You're Smiling	CAP. W1491, STFL 2814
E34374	I Concentrate On You	CAP. W1491, STFL 2814, W2301

Recording at Capitol — 1956.

E34375	You Do Something To Me	CAP. W1491, STFL 2814, W2301
E34376	Sposin'	CAP. W1491, STFL 2814, DQBO 91261
E34377	Should I	CAP. W1491, STFL 2814, DQBO 91261

Accompaniment The Same.		August 23, 1960, Los Angeles
E34386	My Blue Heaven	CAP. 4546, W1491, PC 3452, STFL 2814, DQBO 91261, DNFR 7630
E34387	I Can't Believe That You're In Love With Me	CAP. W1491, STFL 2814
E34388	Always	CAP. W1491, STFL 2814
E34389	It All Depends On You	CAP. W1491, STFL 2814

Accompaniment The Same.		August 31, 1960, Los Angeles
E34409	It's Only A Paper Moon	CAP. W1491, W2123, STFL 2814
E34410	September In The Rain	CAP. W1491, STFL 2814
E34411	Hidden Persuasion	CAP. 4815, W1729

Accompaniment The Same.		September 1, 1960, Los Angeles
E34413	Sentimental Baby	CAP. 4546, W1729
E34414	Old MacDonald	CAP. 4466, W1538, STFL 2814
E34415	Blue Moon	CAP. W1491, W1825, STFL 2814, DQBO 91261

At this stage in his recording career, Sinatra had formed his own record company which was called Reprise. He was still under contract to do more sides with Capitol and he received permission to record with his own label. Since it has been our aim to list his recordings for the various labels and break them down into individual chapters, we will continue to finish the Capitol sessions even though there were Reprise dates made in between.

Orchestra Under The Direction of Billy May
Arrangements By May except where noted

March 20, 1961, Los Angeles

E35576	On The Sunny Side Of The Street - (A)	CAP. W1594, DNFR 7630
E35577	Day By Day	CAP. W1594, DNFR 7630
E35578	Sentimental Journey (A)	CAP. 4615, W1594, SW SW 90986
E35579	Don't Take Your Love From Me (A)	CAP. W1594

(A) Arranged By Heinie Beau.

Accompaniment The Same.

March 21, 1961, Los Angeles

E35592	Yes Indeed	CAP. W1594
E35593	American Beauty Rose (A)	CAP. 4615, W1594
E35594	I've Heard That Song Before	CAP. 4677, W1594, DQBO 91261, DNFR 7630
E35595	That Old Black Magic (A)	CAP. W1594, W2123, SW 90986, PC 3450

(A) Arranged By Heinie Beau.

Accompaniment The Same.

March 22, 1961, Los Angeles

E35616	Five Minutes More	CAP. 4729, W1594, DQBO 91261
E35617	Almost Like Being In Love	CAP. W1594
E35618	Lover (A)	CAP. W1594, W1825, PC 3450
E35619	Paper Doll	CAP. W1594, PC 3452

(A) Arranged By Heinie Beau.

Orchestra Under The Direction of Axel Stordahl
Arrangements By Stordahl except where noted

September 11, 1961, Los Angeles

E36463	I'll Be Seeing You	CAP. W1676, STFL 2814
E36464	I'll See You Again	CAP. W1676, STFL 2814

E36465	September Song	CAP. W1676, STFL 2814, PC 3452
E36466	Memories Of You (A)	CAP. W1676, STFL 2814, DNFR 7630
E36471	There Will Never Be Another You	CAP. W1676, STFL 2814, DQBO 91261, SW 90986, DNFR 7630
E36472	When The World Was Young	CAP. W1676, STFL 2814, W1984

(A) Arrangement By Heinie Beau.

Accompaniment The Same.   September 12, 1961, Los Angeles

E36481	Somewhere Along The Way	CAP. W1676, STFL 2814
E36482	A Million Dreams Ago	CAP. W1676, STFL 2814, SW 90986
E36483	These Foolish Things	CAP. W1676, STFL 2814, SW 90986
E36484	As Time Goes By	CAP. W1676, STFL 2814
E36485	It's A Blue World (A)	CAP. W1676, STFL 2814, SW 90986
E36486	I'll Remember April (A)	CAP. 4729, W1676, STFL 2814

(A) Arranged By Heinie Beau.

Orchestra Under The Direction of Skip Martin
Arrangement By Martin   March 6, 1962, Los Angeles

E37303	I Gotta Right To Sing The Blues	CAP. W1729, W2123

Promo for
Hit Recording — 1957

Promo for
Hit Recording — 1957

SONG INDEX - CAPITOL RECORDS - CHAPTER VIII

Adeste Fidelis - (John Reading)
July 10, 1957

All My Tomorrows - (Sammy Cahn - Jimmy Van Heusen)
December 29, 1958

All Of Me - (Seymour Simons - Gerald Marks)
April 19, 1954

All The Way - (Sammy Cahn - Jimmy Van Heusen)
August 13, 1957

Almost Like Being In Love - (Alan Lerner - Frederick Lowe)
March 22, 1961

Always - (Irving Berlin)
August 23, 1960

American Beauty Rose - (Ray Evans - Mack David - Arthur Altman)
March 21, 1961

Angel Eyes - (Matt Dennis - Earl Brent)
May 29, 1958

Anything Goes - (Cole Porter)
January 16, 1956

Anytime, Anywhere - (Carpenter)
May 2, 1953

April In Paris - (Vernon Duke - Yip Harbourg)
October 3, 1957

Around The World - (Harold Adamson - Victor Young)
October 8, 1957

As Time Goes By - (Herman Hupfield)
September 12, 1961

At Long Last Love - (Cole Porter)
November 20, 1956

Autumn In New York - (Vernon Duke)
October 3, 1957

Autumn Leaves - (Joseph Kosman - Jacques Prevert - Johnny Mercer)
April 10, 1957

Baby Won't You Please Come Home - (Charles Warfield - Clarence Williams)
April 29, 1957

Baubles, Bangles And Beads - (Robert Wright - George Forrest)
December 22, 1958

Bewitched - (Richard Rodgers - Lorenz Hart)
August 13, 1957

Blame It On My Youth - (Oscar Levant - Edward Hayman)
April 4, 1956

Blue Hawaii - (Leo Robin - Ralph Rainger)
October 8, 1957

Blue Moon - (Richard Rodgers - Lorenz Hart)
September 1, 1960

Blues In The Night - (Harold Arlen - Johnny Mercer)
June 25, 1958

Brazil - (Ary Barroso - S. K. Russell)
October 8, 1957

Can I Steal A Little Love - (Phil Tuminello)
December 3, 1956

Can't We Be Friends - (Kay Swift - Paul James)
February 8, 1955

C'est Magnifique - (Cole Porter)
February 19, 1960

Cheek To Cheek - (Irving Berlin)
December 22, 1958

Chicago - (Fred Fisher)
August 13, 1957

Christmas Song, The - (Mel Torme - Bob Wells)
July 17, 1957

Christmas Waltz, The - (Sammy Cahn - Jule Styne)
August 23, 1954, July 16, 1957

Close To You - (Al Hoffman - Jerry Livingston - Carl Lampl)
October 1, 1956

Come Dance With Me - (Sammy Cahn - Jimmy Van Heusen)
December 23, 1958

Come Fly With Me - (Sammy Cahn - Jimmy Van Heusen)
October 8, 1957

Cottage For Sale, A - (Larry Conley - Willard Robinson)
March 26, 1959

Crazy Love - (Sammy Cahn - Phil Tuminello)
March 14, 1957

Dancing In The Dark - (Arthur Schwartz - Howard Dietz)
December 22, 1958

Dancing On The Ceiling - (Richard Rodgers - Lorenz Hart)
February 8, 1955

Day By Day - (Sammy Cahn - Axel Stordahl - Paul Weston)
March 20, 1961

Day In, Day Out - (Rube Bloom - Johnny Mercer)
March 1, 1954, December 22, 1958

Deep In A Dream -(Eddie DeLange - Jimmy Van Heusen)
March 4, 1955

Don't Change Your Mind About Me - (Adelson - Carpenter)
September 23, 1954

Don't Like Goodbyes - (Harold Arlen - Truman Capote)
March 8, 1956

Don't Make A Begger Of Me - (Sherman - Goodman)
April 2, 1953

Don't Take Your Love From Me - (Henry Nemo)
March 20, 1961

Don't Worry 'Bout Me - (Ted Koehler - Rube Bloom)
April 30, 1953

Dream - (Johnny Mercer)
March 3, 1960

Ebb Tide - (Carl Sigman - Robert Maxwell)
May 29, 1958

Embraceable You - (George Gershwin - Ira Gershwin)
March 3, 1960

End Of A Love Affair, The - (Redding)
April 5, 1956

Everybody Loves Somebody - (Irving Taylor - Ken Lane)
November 25, 1957

Everything Happens To Me - (Matt Dennis - Tom Adair)
April 4, 1956

Fairy Tale - (Jay Livingston - Dak Stanford)
July 29, 1955

First Noel - (Traditional)
July 16, 1957

Five Hundred Guys - (Canteen - Kosleff)
April 9, 1956

Five Minutes More - (Sammy Cahn - Jule Styne)
March 22, 1961

Flowers Mean Forgiveness - (White - Frisch - Wolfson)
January 12, 1956

Foggy Day, A - (George Gershwin - Ira Gershwin)
November 5, 1953

Fools Rush In - (Johnny Mercer - Rube Bloom)
March 1, 1960

French Foreign Legion - (Aaron Schroeder - Guy Wood)
December 29, 1958

From Here To Eternity - (Freddie Karger - Robert Wells)
May 2, 1953

From The Bottom To The Top - (Gee Wilson)
March 7, 1955

From This Moment On - (Cole Porter)
November 28, 1956

Gal That Got Away, The - (Harold Arlen - Ira Gershwin)
May 13, 1954

Get Happy - (Harold Arlen - Ted Koehler)
April 19, 1954

Ghost Of A Chance, A - (Bing Crosby-Ned Washington-Victor Young)
March 24, 1959

Girl Next Door, The - (Hugh Martin - Ralph Blane)
November 6, 1953

Glad To Be Unhappy - (Richard Rodgers - Lorenz Hart)
February 8, 1955

Gone With The Wind - (Herb Magidson - Allie Wrubel)
June 24, 1958

Goodbye - (Gordon Jenkins)
June 25, 1958

Guess I'll Hang My Tears Out To Dry - (Sammy Cahn - Jule Styne)
May 29, 1958

Half As Lovely - (Lew Spence - Sammy Gallop)
May 13, 1954

Hark, The Herald Angels Sing - (Felix Mendelsson)
July 10, 1957

Have Yourself A Merry Little Christmas - (Hugh Martin - Ralph Blane)
July 16, 1957

Here's That Rainy Day - (Johnny Burke - Jimmy Van Heusen)
March 25, 1959

Hey Jealous Lover - (Sammy Cahn - Bee Walker - Kay Twomey)
April 9, 1956

Hidden Persuasion - (Churchill Wainwright)
August 31, 1960

High Hopes - (Sammy Cahn - Jimmy Van Heusen)
May 8, 1959

How About You - (Arthur Freed - Burton Lane)
January 10, 1956

How Are You Fixed For Love - (Sammy Cahn - Jimmy Van Heusen)
March 3, 1958

How Could You Do A Thing Like That To Me - (Allan Roberts - Tyree
Glenn)
March 7, 1955

How Deep Is The Ocean - (Irving Berlin)
March 3, 1960

How Little We Know - (Philip Springer - Carolyn Leigh)
April 5, 1956

I Believe - (Sammy Cahn - Jule Styne)
November 25, 1957

I Can Read Between The Lines - (Getzov - Frank)
May 2, 1953

I Can't Believe That You're In Love With me - (Clarence Gaskill - Jimmy McHugh)
August 23, 1960

I Can't Get Started - (Vernon Duke - Ira Gershwin)
March 26, 1959

I Concentrate On You - (Cole Porter)
August 22, 1960

I Could Have Danced All Night - (Allen Lerner - Frederick Lowe)
December 23, 1958

I Could Have Told You - (Carl Sigman - Jimmy Van Heusen)
December 9, 1953

I Couldn't Care Less -
October 1, 1958

I Couldn't Sleep A Wink Last Night - (Jimmy McHugh - Harold Adamson)
October 1, 1956

I Could Write A Book - (Richard Rodgers - Lorenz Hart)
August 13, 1957

I Cover The Water Front - (Edward Heyman - John Green)
April 29, 1957

I Didn't Know What Time It Was - (Richard Rodgers - Lorenz Hart)
September 25, 1957

If I Had Three Wishes - (Lew Spence - Claude Baum)
March 7, 1955

If I Had You - (Ted Shapiro - Jimmy Campbell - Reg Connelly)
November 26, 1956

If I Loved You - Richard Rodgers - Oscar Hammerstein)
August 20, 1955

If It's The Last Thing I Do - (Sammy Cahn - Saul Chaplin)
March 8, 1956

If You Are But A Dream - (Moe Jaffe - Jack Fulton - Nat Bonx)
December 11, 1957

I Get A Kick Out Of You - (Cole Porter)
November 6, 1953

I Get Along Without You Very Well - (Hoagy Carmichael)
February 17, 1955

I Got It Bad - (Ben Webster - Duke Ellington)
November 28, 1956

I Got Plenty Of Nothin' - (George Gershwin - Ira Gershwin)
November 15, 1956

I Gotta Right To Sing The Blues - (Harold Arlen - Ted Koehler)
March 6, 1962

I Guess I'll Have To Change My Plans - (Harold Dietz - Arthur Schwartz)
November 20, 1956

I'll Be Around - (Alec Wilder)
February 8, 1955

I'll Be Home For Christmas - (Kim Gannon - Walter Kent - Buck Ram)
July 17, 1957

I'll Be Seeing You - (Irving Kahal - Sammy Fain)
September 11, 1961

I'll Never Be The Same - (Matty Malneck - Frank Signorelli - Gus Kahn)
March 4, 1955

I'll Never Smile Again - (Ruth Lowe)
May 14, 1959

I'll Remember April - (Don Raye - Gene DePaul - Pat Johnston)
September 12, 1961

I'll See You Again - (Noel Coward)
September 11, 1961

Ill Wind - (Harold Arlen - Ted Koehler)
February 16, 1955

I Love Paris - (Cole Porter)
February 19, 1959, April 12, 1960

I Love You - (Harold Archer - Harlan Thompson)
April 30, 1953

I'm A Fool To Want You - (Jack Wolf - Herron - Frank Sinatra)
May 1, 1957

I'm Gonna Live Till I Die - (Albert Hoffman - Walter Kent - Mann Curtis)
December 13, 1954

I'm Gonna Sit Right Down And Write Myself A Letter - (Fred Ahlert - Victor Young)
April 7, 1954

Impatient Years, The - (Sammy Cahn - Jimmy Van Heusen)
August 15, 1955

I'm Walking Behind You - (Billy Reid)
April 2, 1953

In The Wee Small Hours - (Dave Mann - Bob Hilliard)
February 17, 1955

I See Your Face Before Me - (Arthur Schwartz - Howard Dietz)
February 16, 1955

Isle Of Capri, The - (Will Croz - Jimmy Kennedy)
October 1, 1957

It All Depends On You - (Buddy DeSylva - Ray Henderson - Ray Brown)
September 30, 1958, August 23, 1960

It Came Upon A Midnight Clear - (Richard Wallis)
July 10, 1957

It Could Happen To You - (Johnny Burke - Jimmy Van Heusen)
April 5, 1956

It Happened In Monterey - (Mabel Wayne - Billy Rose)
January 12, 1956

I Think Of You - (Jack Elliot - Don Marcotte)
May 1, 1957

I Thought About You - (Johnny Mercer - Jimmy Van Heusen)
January 9, 1956

It Never Entered My Mind - (Richard Rodgers - Lorenz Hart)
March 4, 1955

It's A Blue World - (Chet Wright - Bob Forrest)
September 12, 1961

It's Alright With Me - (Cole Porter)
February 19, 1960

It's A Lonesome Old Town - (Harry Tobias - Charles Kisko)
June 25, 1958

It's Easy To Remember - (Richard Rodgers - Lorenz Hart)
October 1, 1956

It's Nice To Go Traveling - (Sammy Cahn - Jimmy Van Heusen)
October 8, 1957

It's Only A Paper Moon - (Harold Arlen- Billy Rose - Yip Harburg)
August 31, 1960

It's Over, It's Over, It's Over - (Matt Dennis - Dak Stanford)
April 12, 1960

It's The Same Old Dream - (Sammy Cahn - Jule Styne)
November 25, 1957

It Worries Me - (Fritz Schulz - Reichel - Carl Sigman)
May 13, 1954

I've Got A Crush On You - (George Gershwin - Ira Gershwin)
March 3, 1960

I've Got The World On A String - (Harold Arlen - Ted Koehler)
April 30, 1953

I've Got You Under My Skin - (Cole Porter)
January 12, 1956

I've Had My Moments - (Gus Kahn - Walter Donaldson)
April 4, 1956

I've Heard That Song Before - (Sammy Cahn - Jule Styne)
March 21, 1961

I Wish I Were In Love Again - (Richard Rodgers - Lorenz Hart)
November 20, 1956

I Won't Dance - (Jerome Kern - Dorothy Fields - Jimmy McHugh)
November 15, 1956

Jeepers Creepers - (Harry Warren - Johnny Mercer)
April 19, 1954

Jingle Bells - (James Pierpoint)
July 16, 1957

Just Friends - (John Klenner - Sam Lewis)
March 26, 1959

Just In Time - (Betty Comden - Adolph Green - Jule Styne)
December 9, 1958

Just One Of Those Things - (Cole Porter)
April 7, 1954

Lady Is A Tramp, The - (Richard Rodgers - Lorenz Hart)
November 26, 1956

Last Dance, The - (Sammy Cahn - Jimmy Van Heusen)
December 23, 1958

Last Night When We Were Young - (Yip Harburg - Harold Arlen)
March 1, 1954

Laura - (Johnny Mercer - David Raskin)
April 29, 1957

Lean Baby - (Billy May - Roy Alfred)
April 2, 1953

Learnin' The Blues - (Dolores Silvers)
March 23, 1955

Let's Do It - (Cole Porter)
February 20, 1960

Let's Get Away From It All - (Matt Dennis - Tom Adair)
October 1, 1957

Like Someone In Love - (Johnny Burke - Jimmy Van Heusen)
November 6, 1953

Little Girl Blue - (Richard Rodgers - Lorenz Hart)
November 6, 1953

London By Night - (Carroll Coates)
October 3, 1957

Lonely Town - (Betty Comden - Adolph Green - Leonard Bernstein)
April 29, 1957

Lonesome Road - (Gene Austin - Nathaniel Shilket)
November 26, 1956

Look To Your Heart - (Sammy Cahn - Jimmy Van Heusen)
August 15, 1955

Love And Marriage - (Sammy Cahn - Jimmy Van Heusen)
August 15, 1955

Love Is Here To Stay - (George Gershwin - Ira Gershwin)
October 17, 1955

Love Locked Out - (Ray Noble - Kester)
March 8, 1956

Love Looks So Well On You - (Lew Spence - Marilyn Keith - Alan Bergman)
May 8, 1959

Lover - (Richard Rodgers - Lorenz Hart)
March 22, 1961

Lush Life - (Billy Strayhorn)
May 29, 1958

Makin' Whoopee - (Walter Donaldson - Gus Kahn)
January 16, 1956

Mam'selle - (Mack Gordon - Edmund Goulding)
March 3, 1960

Man With The Golden Arm, The - (Sammy Cahn - Jimmy Van Heusen)
January 10, 1956

Maybe You'll Be There - (Rube Bloom - Sammy Gallop)
May 1, 1957

Melody Of Love - (Tom Glazer - Harry Engleman)
December 13, 1954

Memories Of You - (Andy Razaf - Eubie Blake)
January 9, 1956, September 11, 1961

Million Dreams Ago, A - (Lou Quadling - Eddy Howard - Dick Jurgens)
September 12, 1961

Mind If I Make Love To You - (Cole Porter)
April 20, 1956

Mistletoe And Holly - (Hank Sanicola - Dak Stanford - Frank Sinatra)
July 17, 1957

Monique - (Sammy Cahn - Elmer Bernstein)
May 29, 1958

Montmart' - (Cole Porter)
February 20, 1960

Mood Indigo - (Duke Ellington - Irving Mills - Barney Bigard)
February 16, 1955

Moonlight In Vermont - (John Blackburn - Karl Suessdorf)
October 3, 1957

Moon Was Yellow, The - (Edgar Leslie - Fred Ahlert)
December 29, 1958

My Success - (Grienes - Frank Sinatra - Hank Sanicola)
September 11, 1958

My Blue Heaven - (Walter Donaldson - George Whiting)
August 23, 1960

My Funny Valentine - (Richard Rodgers - Lorenz Hart)
November 5, 1953

My One And Only Love - (Guy Wood - Roberto Mellin)
May 2, 1953

Nearness Of You, The - (Hoagy Carmichael - Ned Washington)
March 2, 1960

Nevertheless - (Bert Kalmar - Harry Ruby)
March 2, 1960

Nice 'N Easy - (Marilyn Keith - Alan Bergman - Lew Spence)
April 12, 1960

Nice Work If You Can Get It - (George Gershwin - Ira Gershwin)
November 20, 1956

Night And Day - (Cole Porter)
November 26, 1956

Night We Called It A Day, The - (Matt Dennis - Tom Adair)
April 10, 1957

None But The Lonely Heart - (Tchaikovsky - Branot)
March 24, 1959

No One Ever Tells You - (Hub Atwood - Carroll Coates)
April 9, 1956

Not As A Stranger - (Kaye - Jimmy Van Heusen)
March 4, 1955

Nothing In Common - (Sammy Cahn - Jimmy Van Heusen)
March 3, 1958

Oh Look At Me Now - (John DeVries - Joe Bushkin)
November 28, 1956

Old Devil Moon - (Yip Harburg - Burton Lane)
January 16, 1956

Old McDonald - (Lew Spence - Marilyn Keith - Alan Bergman)
September 1, 1960

O Little Town Of Bethlehem - (Phillip Brooks - Lawrence Rodner)
July 10, 1957

One For My Baby - (Harold Arlen - Johnny Mercer)
June 25, 1958

One I Love, The - (Gus Kahn - Isham Jones)
March 25, 1959

Only The Lonely - (Sammy Cahn - Jimmy Van Heusen)
May 29, 1958

On The Road To Mandalay - (Rudyard Kipling - Oley Speaks)
October 1, 1957

On The Sunny Side Of The Street - (Dorothy Fields - Jimmy McHugh)
March 20, 1961

Our Town - (Sammy Cahn - Jimmy Van Heusen)
August 15, 1955

Paper Doll - (Johnny Black)
March 22, 1961

Pennies From Heaven - (John Burke - Arthur Johnston)
January 10, 1956

P.S. I Love You - (Gordon Jenkins - Johnny Mercer)
March 8, 1956

Put Your Dreams Away - (Ruth Lowe - Stephen Weiss - Paul Mann)
December 11, 1957

Rain - (Robert Mellin - George Finlay)
December 9, 1953

River Stay Away From My Door - (Mort Dixon - Harry Woods)
April 12, 1960

Same Old Saturday Night - (Sammy Cahn - Reardon)
July 29, 1955

Same Old Song And Dance - (Sammy Cahn - Jimmy Van Heusen - Worth)
March 3, 1958

Saturday Night - (Sammy Cahn - Jule Styne)
December 22, 1958

Sea Song, The - (By The Sea) - Howard Dietz - Arthur Schwartz)
April 2, 1954

Sentimental Baby - (Lew Spence - Marilyn Keith - Alan Bergman)
September 1, 1960

Sentimental Journey - (Bud Green - Les Brown - Ben Homer)
March 20, 1961

September In The Rain - (Al Dubin - Harry Warren)
August 31, 1960

September Song - (Kurt Weill - Maxwell Anderson)
September 11, 1961

She's Funny That Way - (Neil Moret - Richard Whiting)
March 2, 1960

Should I - (Nacio Herb Brown - Arthur Freed)
August 22, 1960

Silent Night - (Franz Gruber)
July 17, 1957

Sleep Warm - (Lew Spence - Marilyn Keith - Alan Bergman)
September 11, 1958

Soliloquy - (Richard Rodgers - Oscar Hammerstein II)
February 17, 1955, August 20, 1955

So Long My Love - (Sammy Cahn - Lew Spence)
March 14, 1957

Someone To Watch Over Me - (George Gershwin - Ira Gershwin)
September 23, 1954

Something's Gotta Give - (Johnny Mercer)
December 9, 1958

Something Wonderful Happens In Summer - (Joe Bushkin - John DeVries)
April 9, 1956, May 20, 1957

Somewhere Along The Way - (Sammy Gallop - Kurt Adams)
September 12, 1961

Song Is You, The - (Jerome Kern - Oscar Hammerstein II)
December 9, 1958

South Of The Border - (Jimmy Kennedy - Michael Carr)
April 30, 1953

S'posin' - (Andy Razaf - Paul Denniker)
August 12, 1960

Spring Is Here - (Richard Rodgers - Lorenz Hart)
May 29, 1958

Stars Fell On Alabama - (Mitchell Parish - Frank Perkins)
November 15, 1956

Stormy Weather - (Harold Arlen - Ted Koehler)
March 24, 1959

Sunday - (Con - Miller - Kruger - Styne)
April 7, 1954

Swingin' Down The Lane - (Gus Kahn - Isham Jones)
Janury 12, 1956

Take A Chance - (David Raskin - Dak Stanford)
December 8, 1953

Taking A Chance On Love - (John LaTouche - Vernon Duke - Ted Fetter)
April 19, 1954

Talk To Me - (Snyder - Kahan - Vallee)
May 14, 1959

Tell Her You Love Her - (Dennison - Parker - Halliday)
May 20, 1957

Tell Her You Love her Each Day - (Gil Ward)
May 20, 1957

Tender Trap, The - (Sammy Cahn - Jimmy Van Heusen)
September 13, 1955

That Old Black Magic - (Johnny Mercer - Harold Arlen)
March 21, 1961

That Old Feeling - (Lew Brown - Sammy Fain)
March 1, 1960

There's A Flaw In My Flue - (Sammy Cahn - Jule Styne)
April 5, 1956

There's A Small Hotel - (Richard Rodgers - Lorenz Hart)
August 13, 1957

There's No You - (Tom Adair - Hal Hopper - Bullets Durgom)
April 10, 1957

There Will Never Be Another You - (Mack Gordon - Harry Warren)
September 11, 1961

These Foolish Things - (Jack Strachey - Harry Link - Holt Marvel)
September 12, 1961

They Came To Cordura - (Sammy Cahn - Jimmy Van Heusen)
December 29, 1958

They Can't Take That Away From Me - (George Gershwin - Ira Gershwin)
November 5, 1953

This Was My Love - (Jim Harbert)
May 14, 1959

This Love Of Mine - (Sol Parker - Hank Sanicola - Frank Sinatra)
February 17, 1955

Three Coins In The Fountain - (Sammy Cahn - Jule Styne)
March 1, 1954

Time After Time - (Sammy Cahn - Jule Styne)
November 25, 1957

Together Again -
January 10, 1956

To Love And Be Loved - (Song From "Some Came Running") - (Sammy Cahn - Jimmy Van Heusen)
December 5, 1958

Too Close For Comfort - (Jerry Bock - Larry Holofcener - George Weiss)
December 23, 1958

Too Marvelous For Words - (Johnny Mercer - Richard Whiting)
January 16, 1965

Try A Little Tenderness - (Harry Woods - Jimmy Campbell - Reg Connelly)
March 1, 1960

Two Hearts, Two Kisses - (Henry Stone - Otis Williams)
March 7, 1955

Violets For Your Furs - (Tom Adair - Matt Dennis)
November 5, 1953

Wait For Me - (Theme From "Johnny Concho") - (Nelson Riddle - Dak Stanford)
April 5, 1956

Wait Till You See Her - (Richard Rodgers - Lorenz Hart)
April 4, 1956

Way I Love You, The -
September 11, 1958

Weep They Will - (Fischer - Carey)
October 17, 1955

We'll Be Together Again - (Frankie Laine - Carl Fischer)
January 16, 1956

Well Did You Evah - (Cole Porter)
May 7, 1956

What Do I Care For A Dame - (Richard Rodgers - Lorenz Hart)
September 25, 1957

What Is This Thing Called Love - (Cole Porter)
February 16, 1955

What's New - (Bob Haggart - Johnny Burke)
June 24, 1958

When I Stop Loving You - (Cates - Copeland - Greene)
August 23, 1954

When No One Cares - (Sammy Cahn - Jimmy Van Heusen)
May 14, 1959

When The World Was Young - (Philippe - Gerrard - Johnny Mercer)
September 11, 1961

When You're Smiling - (Mark Fisher - Joe Goodwin - Larry Shay)
August 12, 1960

When Your Lover Has Gone - (Edgar Swann)
February 17, 1955

Where Are You - (Harold Adamson - Jimmy McHugh)
May 1, 1957

Where Do You Go - (Alec Wilder - Arnold Sundagard)
March 26, 1959

Where Is The One - (Alec Wilder - Bill Finkle)
April 10, 1957

Where Or When - (Richard Rodgers - Lorenz Hart)
September 11, 1958

White Christmas - (Irving Berlin)
August 23, 1954

Who's In Your Arms Tonight -
September 11, 1958

Who Wants To Be A Millionaire - (Cole Porter)
April 20, 1956

Why Should I Cry Over You - (Miller - Conn)
December 8, 1953

Why Try To Change Me Now - (Cy Coleman - Joseph McCarthy)
March 24, 1959

Willow Weep For Me - (Ann Ronnell)
May 29, 1958

Witchcraft - (Carolyn Leigh - Cy Coleman)
May 20, 1957

With Every Breath I Take - (Leo Robin - Ralph Rainger)
April 5, 1956

Wrap Your Troubles In Dreams - (Ted Koehler - Harry Barris - Billy Moll)
April 7, 1954

Ya Better Stop - (Ferre - McIntyre)
December 8, 1953

Yes Indeed - (Sy Oliver)
March 21, 1961

You Brought A New Kind Of Love To Me - (Sammy Fain - Irving Kahal - Pierre Norman)
January 9, 1956

You'd Be So Nice To Come Home To - (Cole Porter)
November 28, 1956

You Do Something To Me - (Cole Porter)
August 22, 1960

You Forget All The Words - (Bernie Wayne - E.H. Jay)
October 17, 1955

You Go To My Head - (Haven Gillespie - Fred Coots)
March 1, 1960

You'll Always Be The One I Love - (Ticker Freeman - Sunny Skylar)
December 11, 1957

You'll Get Yours - (Jimmy Van Heusen - Dak Stanford)
September 13, 1955

You Make Me Feel So Young - (Mack Gordon - Josef Myrow)
January 9, 1956

You, My Love - (Mack Gordon - Jimmy Van Heusen)
September 23, 1954

Young At Heart - (Johnny Richards - Carolyn Leigh)
December 9, 1953

Your Cheating Yourself - (Al Hoffman - Dick Manning)
May 20, 1957

You're Getting To Be A Habit With Me - (Al Dubin - Harry Waren)
January 10, 1956

You're Sensational - (Cole Porter)
April 5, 1956, April 20, 1956

Your Love For Me - (Ross Parker)
December 3, 1956

Capitol Recording Session — 1959

ORCHESTRAS, ARRANGERS, COMPOSERS, SOLOISTS, VOCALISTS AND VOCAL GROUP INDEX - CAPITOL RECORDINGS - CHAPTER VIII

Anthony, Ray - Orchestra Leader
December 13, 1954

Beau, Heinie - Arranger, Saxaphone
December 22, 1958, December 23, 1958, March 20, 21, 22, 1961, September 11, 12, 1961

Brewster Singers, Ralph - Large Vocal Group
July 10, 16, 17, 1957

Cavanaugh, Big Dave - Arranger, Composer, Producer
March 7, 1955

Chavalier, Maurice - Vocalist, Actor
February 20, 1960

Crosby, Bing - Vocalist, Actor
May 7, 1956

Darby, Ken - Vocal Director
August 20, 21, 22, 23, 24, 1955

Edison, Harry - Trumpet Soloist
Appeared on most big band sessions on Capitol

Green, Johnny - Leader and Conductor of M.G.M. Orchestra
April 20, 1956, May 7, 1956

Hodges, Eddie - Vocalist, Actor
May 8, 1959

Hollywood String Quartet, The - Small String Section
March 8, 1956, April 4, 1956, April 5, 1956, October 1, 1956

Holm, Celeste - Vocalist, Actress
April 20, 1956

Jenkins, Gordon - Arranger, Conductor, Composer
April 10, 1957, April 29, 1957, May 1, 1957, July 10, 16, 17, 1957, March 24, 25, 26, 1959, May 14, 1959
Indispensable Ballad Arranger

MacLaine, Shirley - Vocalist, Actress
February 20, 1960

Martin, Skip - Arranger, Conductor
May 7, 1956, March 6, 1962

May, Billy - Arranger, Conductor
October 1, 3, 8, 1957, March 3, 1958, September 30, 1958, October 1, 1958, December 9, 1958, December 22, 23, 1958, March 20, 21, 1961 - Exuberant and Swinging.

Miller, Bill - Pianist
Most Capitol Sessions - Very Close Friend

Newman, Alfred - Arranger, Conductor
August 20, 21, 22, 23, 24, 1955

Nuggets, The - Vocal Group
March 7, 1955

Reynolds, Dick - Arranger
December 13, 1954

Riddle, Nelson - Arranger, Conductor
Starting on April 30, 1953, Sinatra's main arranger throughout his Capitol
career. A rewarding meeting of Giants.

Salinger, Conrad - Arranger
April 20, 1956

Slatkin, Felix - Arranger, Conductor
May 29, 1958

Smith, Keely - Vocalist
March 3, 1958

Stoller, Alvin - Drummer
On most Capitol Big Band Sessions

Stoloff, Morris - Arranger, Conductor
August 13, 1957, September 25, 1957 (Cond.)

Stordahl, Axel - Arranger, Conductor
April 2, 1953, September 11, 12, 1961

Tizol, Juan - Trombone Soloist
January 12, 1956 (Great solo on the memorable Riddle arrangement of "I've
Got You Under My Skin")

COMMENTS

If you realized the possibilities that could have been on Columbia Records,
multiply them ten-fold and apply them to Capitol Records. Sinatra and Nat
King Cole, Peggy Lee, Kay Starr, June Christy, The Four Freshman, The Stan
Kenton Orchestra, Benny Goodman, etc. etc. etc.

Again we would like to say that his Capitol tenure was extremely gratifying
as it was and I guess we are nitpicking to the point of fantasizing.

Chapter IX

On His Own - Reprise

February, 1961 ----

After eight highly successful years with Capitol, Sinatra felt restless and perhaps a little tied down. He was always looking for ways to improve his career and he felt that he could best do this on his own. In 1961, Sinatra freed himself from his recording contract with Capitol and initiated a life-long dream - the formation of his own company, Reprise Records. He had already tried to buy Verve Records from M.G.M. but was unable to pry the label loose, so here he was, ready, eager, ambitious and excited. He began to record with renewed enthusiasm and his first Reprise album with Johnny Mandel at the helm and a host of modern Jazz soloists set the mood - and it swung! Ring-a-ding-ding was followed by three singles, two of which were released - one a song named for his second daughter Tina. The new record company and especially its concepts attracted many established artists such as Sammy Davis, Jr., Dean Martin, Bing Crosby and Keely Smith, to name a few. Quality, not quantity was the byword. Sonny Burke becomes head producer and his long time experience with Decca (now M.C.A.) was a great asset to the fledgling label.

Frank himself was jubilant. Now he could make the albums he'd always wanted to without someone to preach economics. He had always believed that if the end product was good musically, it would sell despite changing fads. He asked old Tommy Dorsey arranger Sy Oliver to help recreate an album of Dorsey hits called *I Remember Tommy*. It became one of the most successful albums ever made by Frank for Reprise. (Today he feels that it contains some of the best work he's ever done.) Now the trade people were starting to take notice of the new label and after seeing that there was a two hundred thousand advance order, no longer dismissed the company as a joke.

Mo Ostin, general manager of Reprise, described the setup as a "better economic mousetrap for its artists." As if this new enterprise was not enough to keep Sinatra busy, he continued to make films *(Ocean's Eleven)* which bore the seal of his own production company, Dorchester; and, Sinatra was busy in other ways, too. Being closely involved with the Kennedy campaign, he had staged an Inaugeral Gala to surpass anything before and after and still managed to appear on three television specials. The Gala which was staged to wipe out the Democratic National Committee campaign deficit was a huge financial and artistic success. The lineup of artists appearing on one stage in one show surpassed promoter's wildest dreams: Nat "King" Cole, Gene Kelly, Kate Smith, Jimmy Durante, Ella Fitzgerald, Joey Bishop, Mahalia Jackson, Juliet Prowse, Peter Lawford, Milton Berle, Harry Belafonte, Bette Davis, Leonard Berstein, and, of course, Frank. All gave sterling performances prompting President-elect Kennedy to remark, "We are all indebted to a great friend, Frank Sinatra, and tonight we saw excellence."

After a short rest in Palm Beach, Sinatra staged another star-studded tribute, this time for Martin Luther King, at Carnegie Hall. Mr. King, then in a Georgia jail, was freed through the intervention of President Kennedy and appeared on stage. Sinatra's recording activities for his new record company from 1960 to mid 1962 were prolific. He appeared in 93 actual studio sessions, and although not all of them were released most critics agreed that he never

Reprise Session — 1961.

Sinatra in London recording with Robert Farnon — 1962.

sounded better.

He used eight different arrangers to instill freshness into each session. In November 1961, he recorded for the first time with Don Costa - a lovely album titled *Sinatra and Strings*. Many Sinatra admirers have often raised the question as to why two of the tunes recorded for this album were never released: "As You Desire Me" and "Don't Take Your Love From Me", both of which have been circulating among collectors who agree that they are especially beautiful. No one knows why they were held back. On June 12, 13 and 14, 1962, Frank went to England to record with the Robert Farnon Orchestra. In three separate sessions, eleven songs were recorded, but only ten were issued in an album titled *Great Songs From Great Britain*. ("Roses of Picardy" was deleted). The album was issued only in England, and it has been said that Sinatra was not entirely satisfied, and the masters were destroyed.

Sinatra's next major album project was hailed by the trade press as a meeting of giants. At last, Frank was to record with the swinging big band of Count Basie and there are some great musical moments to be cherished here if one takes the time to listen. Frank did exactly what Sy Oliver told him he should do twenty-one years earlier. Oliver told him to lie back on the beat, and not to push but to let the beat carry him along. Listen as he does just that on the tunes "I Won't Dance", "Pennies From Heaven", "Learnin' The Blues" and "My Kind Of Girl".

Around this time, too, an important film was released starring Sinatra: *The Manchurian Candidate* drew rave reviews for his stellar performance as Lieutenant Bennet Marco. The movie itself was well received, too.

In early 1963, Frank, Nelson Riddle, and some fifty musicians started the first of four sessions to record in a concert setting some of the songs Sinatra has considered great American standards. The album was expensive to produce and some consider the orchestrations a trifle ponderous, but two gems emerged in *The Concert Sinatra*: "I Have Dreamed" and "This Nearly Was Mine". In April, Sinatra and Nelson redid some of the older Capitol hits on *Sinatra's Sinatra*. Although he is in fine voice, and Riddle's backing is, as usual, exemplary, one is inclined to appreciate the original performances. He also embarked on a series of albums with others of the Reprise roster devoted to songs from great Broadway plays. Some of the duets - with Bing Crosby, Dean Martin, Keely Smith and Sammy Davis Jr. - are well worth hearing. In August of '63, Sinatra and Reprise merged with Warner Bros. Frank, still retaining one-third ownership of Reprise, was said to have profited handsomely.

Not all was rosy in 1963, however; on December 8, the singer received the horrible news of his son's kidnapping. Although Frank Jr. was freed after two days, and most of the ransom money was recovered, the ordeal touched Sinatra deeply.

The year 1964 began with Frank recording a swing album with Nelson Riddle and then another ambitious undertaking, this time with Fred Waring and Bing Crosby. After recording the soundtrack for his new movie, *Robin and the Seven Hoods*, he once again teamed up with Count Basie. The charts for *It Might As Well Be Swing* were arranged by Quincy Jones, who added strings to six of the selections. It met with mixed reviews among music critics, but nevertheless climbed to the top twenty in a few months.

Frank also kept busy by embarking on a tour with the Count Basie

Orchestra. In 1965 he recorded an album that won the Grammy Award - *The September Of My Years,* a poignant collection of songs, most of which reflect and recall the heartaches and happiness of a man's life. One thing was apparent: Sinatra at 50 was still singing a great song.

In order to celebrate reaching the half-century mark, Reprise issued both a standard and a limited-edition two-record set called *A Man and His Music* which contained a running narration by Sinatra with songs tracing his career from the James days to the present. In November of 1965, he recorded an album of "moon" songs titled *Moonlight Sinatra,* generally underrated by even staunch Sinatraphiles. His singing is superb, the songs are excellent standards and Nelson Riddle's arrangements have never sounded better.

After a tremendously successful engagement at the Sands Hotel in Las Vegas with Count Basie, Sinatra again collaborated with Riddle who utilized a swinging organ which resulted in a jazz adventure on several cuts for the album *Strangers In The Night.*

In 1967, another meeting of giants was preserved for all time on record - Frank with Antonois Carlos Jobim. This is great pop music, as was Sinatra's collaboration with Duke Ellington in December, 1967. Through the next few years Sinatra seemed to be heading in a slightly confused musical direction. He recorded again with Riddle and attempted to keep abreast of the newer pop favorites. And he did many beautiful things with Don Costa. The brooding *Watertown* album did not sell well, though critically acclaimed. *Cycles* contained some fine singing, as did the *My Way* LP. But they were uneven albums, and offered no central theme. *Sinatra and Company* was an attempt by Reprise to capitalize on his 1971 retirement, and it, too, is eclectic and musically uneven.

Sinatra's retirement statement shocked the world of music: "For over three decades I have had the great and good fortune to enjoy a rich, rewarding and deeply satisfying career as an entertainer and public figure. It has been a fruitful, busy, uptight, loose, sometimes boisterous, occasionally sad, but always exciting three decades. There has been at the same time little room or opportunity for reflection, reading, self-examination, and that need which every thinking man has for a fallow period, a long pause in which to seek a better understanding of changes occurring in the world. This seems a proper time to take that breather, and I am fortunate enough to be able to do so. I look forward to enjoying more time with my family and my dear friends, to writing a bit - perhaps even to teaching. Thank you." Following this April 1971 statement, Sinatra made what was to be his last public appearance at the Los Angeles Music Center in California. Prior to this engagement, he had received the Cecil B. DeMille Award for his contribution to entertainment and for bringing honor and distinction to the film industry. On April 15th he also received the Jean Hersholt Humanitarian Award from the Academy of Motion Pictures Arts and Sciences.

The supposedly final appearance took place on June 13, 1971 and was an emotional experience for those attending. With the last refrain from "Angel Eyes" - "S'cuse me while I disappear" - it was all over. Or seemed to be. Many doubted that this star among stars could stay away from the limelight he cherished so much: and Sammy Davis Jr. came out with the statement of truth ' "He'll be back." And back he came after two and a half years.

Recording with Count Basie — 1964.

Recording with Quincy Jones — 1964.

This time he was Ol' Blue-Eyes. A little tanner, a little heavier, but healthier than he had been in years. There had been rumors that his was a forced retirement due to health reasons; but this was not so. The first hint that there might be a second coming of Sinatra occurred on May 19, 1972 when he sang an altered rendition of "The Lady Is A Tramp" at a fund-raising benefit. On April 17, 1973 he entertained at President Nixon's State Dinner for Italian Prime Minister Guilio Andreotti singing many of the famous songs he had long been associated with. Some two months later he was in the studio again to record. It was June 4, 1973, and the first song selected was a tune his daughter, Nancy, had already recorded - "Bang Bang".

It was rejected as unsuitable and to this day has not been released. He kept recording in June, July and August and the selections that were approved made up the album - *Ol' Blue Eyes Is Back*. The voice was rusty but the old feeling was there and he knew what was needed - more work. He went to work immediately plunging into a television special; his co-star was Gene Kelly.

In January, 1974 he opened at Casesars Palace backed by the Nat Brandwynne orchestra under the guidance of Gordon Jenkins. Joey Heatherton was on the same bill, but it was Frank's night as everyone welcomed him back to the town he helped put on the map. On the 29th of January he hosted a special event on television - *The American Film Institute Salute to James Cagney*. By now Sinatra was in a new groove. He had trimmed down in weight, and radiated cheer and easy humor.

He kept moving. In April 1974 he starred at Carnegie Hall. Then he undertook a string of one-and two-nighters, ending the tour in the Chicago Stadium before resting a bit. At 59 he was working harder at his trade than when he was 29. His daughter Tina was married earlier in the year, January 26, 1974, and he was soon to become a grandfather: on May 22, 1974, Nancy Jr. gave birth to a baby girl named Angela Jennifer Lambert. He seemed to thrive on all the action and activity.

In the spring of 1974 Sinatra was in the recording studio at Burbank over a period of several months, working with producer Sonny Burke and arranger Gordon Jenkins on what was to be an album called either *She Shot Me Down* or *Saloon Songs*. Sinatra wanted to use some earlier tracks such as ("Bang Bang") and some new ones - among them "Empty Tables", the last song written by the late Johnny Mercer. He also recorded "If" and "The Summer Knows" in familiar, string-heavy, lamenting arrangements by Jenkins. The album looked promising - built as it was around Sinatra's familiar musical milieu: a saloon singer doing his thing.

But the idea got lost somewhere along the way - and when the album came out in the summer of '74 it was called *Some Nice Things I've Missed*. Though it included several takes intended for the saloon song collection, *Some Nice Things* for the most part is a gathering of pop songs made famous by other singers while Sinatra was in retirement. (One distinguishing feature of this LP, in addition to several fine takes by Sinatra - notably "If", "The Summer Knows" and a fun-but-bawdy "Satisfy Me One More Time" - are the album liner notes, by John Brady, which capture Sinatra in action at a recording session with both style and an eye for telling detail.)

After an infamous tour of Australia that summer - in which Sinatra pleased listeners but battled an arrogant press - the singer came home undaunted. He continued his concert tours that fall, and the daddy of them all was to be the much-heralded appearance at the new Madison Square Garden. "Sinatra - The Main Event" was also telecast to the world at large. He had been to the old Garden in March, 1943, when he sang "The Star Spangled Banner" for the fight between Tami Mauriello and Jimmy Bivens; but this was different. The entire spectacle was staged like a championship fight, and not even Howard Cosell's ramblings could diminish the electricity generated by Sir Francis. His voice was not up to par that particular evening, but his presence was not to be denied.

An album released by Reprise bearing the same name as the concert stated that it indeed was the event seen on television by millions. In fact it was not. Some of the selections were from other concerts; Reprise engineers wisely selected the best renditions from each appearance.

Sinatra concerts were sellouts wherever he appeared. He began putting more time into concerts, and less time in the recording studio - to the delight of fans who wanted to see him but to the consternation of listeners who wanted fresh sounds to play forever. His November 13-20, 1975 engagement at the London Palladium was sold out well in advance. Sinatra's co-stars on this trip were Sarah Vaughn and Count Basie. Many consider the two-week appearance at the Uris Theater his greatest recent triumph. Again, he was accompanied by Basie, and Ella Fitzgerald. The entire two weeks were sold out, grossing well over $1,000,000. What was more gratifying was that he was in excellent voice throughout - and even at $40 a seat, many returned for additional performances.

While in New York for this fantastically succssful engagement, Sinatra made an unprecedented bow on the Jerry Lewis Muscular Dystrophy Telethon. He appeared three separate times at his own expense, and in so doing solicited thousands of dollars for this great cause. In addition to paying for the musicians and studio time, he donated $25,000 in his grand-daughter's name and also pledged various amounts from close friends. And by appearing at ten o'clock in the morning, he drew an early audience that normally would not view at that time.

In January, 1976 he recorded the Barry Manilow hit - "I Write The Songs", written by Bruce Johnston, a member of the Beach Boys. He substitutes the word "sing" for "write" and it becomes more effective for his rendition. Sinatra has always had an uncanny knack for making a lyric initimately his own.

During the past two years Sinatra has spent time in the recording studio - usually sandwiched between personal appearances, "roasts", TV shows, and concert tours. But only a few singles have surfaced for release, such as a disco version of "All or Nothing At All". There has been talk of a Big Album on the horizon, with charts by Nelson Riddle - but until something is actually released, we can only view this chatter as idle (and idol) speculation.

Though Sinatra's range is not what it once was, there is still plenty of mood, vibrato, and intimacy in his voice to record with care. Our only hope as we go to press is that he does release more material for his devoted listeners, and that the songs are worthy of his attention. A dream album would be one filled with great standards that Sinatra has over-looked through the years - preferably one that would run to six or eight sides, with arrangements by Nelson Riddle. *That's* an album worth waiting in line for - and boy do we need it now.

REPRISE COMMENTS

Sinatra was now in complete control of all his recording activities and it seems he intended to overcome the restrictions that were imposed upon him in his previous alliances with Columbia and Capitol Records. We say intend because not all of what was planned materialized for one reason or another. A great number of sessions proved fruitful and rewarding yet a few that could have been more so fell far short of what was expected. The Count Basie and Duke Ellington collaborations suffered from either lack of preparation time or did not include the appropriate songs and it is a tribute to their inert professionalism that they still sound fairly good. Many projects that were in the making or planning stage were either discarded or lightly touched upon, such as collaborations with Ella Fitzgerald and Oscar Peterson.

The Italian Album never materialized and the Country Album along with the Saloon Songs set never were completed.

A second set with Ellington with more of Dukes Great Classics could have been greatly appreciated and also some more duets with Keely Smith and Rosemary Clooney.

Recording with Claus Ogerman and Antonios Carlos Jobim — 1967.

Recording with Antonios Carlos Jobim — 1967.

Recording with Bing Crosby and Dean Martin — 1963.

Orchestra Under The Direction of Johnny Mandel
Arrangements by Mandel   December 19, 1960,
                                                         Los Angeles

Personnel include: (Tpt) Don Fagerquist, John Anderson; (Tbn) Frank
Rosolino; (Flute) Bud Shank; (Vibes) Emil Richards; (Piano) Bill Miller, as
soloists; plus large orchestra.

100	Ring-A-Ding-Ding	Rep. R 1001, 2F 1016
101	Let's Fall In Love	Rep. R 1001
102	In The Still Of The Night	Rep. R 1001
103	A Foggy Day	Rep. R 1001
104	Let's Face The Music And Dance	Rep. R. 1001
105	You'd Be So Easy To Love	Rep. R 1001
106	A Fine Romance	Rep. R 1001

Accompaniment The Same.

                                                    December 20, 1960,
                                                         Los Angeles

107	The Coffee Song	Rep. R 1001
108	Be Careful, It's My Heart	Rep. R 1001
109	Have You Met Miss Jones	Rep. UNISSUED
110	I've Got My Love To Keep Me Warm	Rep. R 1001
111	Zing Went The Strings Of My Heart	Rep. UNISSUED
112	You And The Night And The Music	Rep. R 1001
113	When I Take My Sugar To Tea	Rep. R 1001

Orchestra Under The Direction of Felix Slatkin
Arrangements by Slatkin   December 21, 1960, Los Angeles

114	The Last Dance	Rep. UNISSUED
115	The Second Time Around	Rep. 20001, FS 5238
116	Tina	Rep. 20001, 20151, FS 5238

Orchestra Under The Direction of Sy Oliver
Arrangements by Oliver   March 20, 1961, Los Angeles

197	Take Me	Rep. UNISSUED
198	Without A Song	Rep. UNISSUED
199	Polka Dots And Moonbeams	Rep. UNISSUED

Accompaniment the Same.   March 21, 1961, Los Angeles

200	There Are Such Things	Rep. UNISSUED
201	In The Blue Of Evening	Rep. UNISSUED
202	I'll Be Seeing You	Rep. UNISSUED
203	I'm Getting Sentimental Over You	Rep. UNISSUED
204	Imagination	Rep. UNISSUED

Accompaniment The Same.   May 1, 1961, Los Angeles

233	I'll Be Seeing You	Rep. 20023, 20053, R 1003 2F 1016
234	I'm Getting Sentimental Over You	Rep. 20025, R 1003
235	Imagination	Rep. 20024, R 1003
236	Take Me	Rep. 20022, R 1003

Accompaniment The Same.   May 2, 1961, Los Angeles

237	Without A Song	Rep. 20026, 20053, R1003, R 1015
238	Polka Dots And Moonbeams	Rep. 20021, R 1003, 2F 1016
239	Daybreak	Rep. 20022, R 1003

Accompaniment The Same.   May 3, 1961, Los Angeles

240	The One I Love - (1)	Rep. 20023, R 1003, 2F 1016
241	There Are Such Things	Rep. 20021, R 1003, 2F 1016
242	It's Always You	Rep. 20024, R 1003
243	It Started All Over Again	Rep. 20025, R 1003

244	East Of The Sun	Rep. 20025, R 1003
	(1) Vocal Duet with Sy Oliver	

Orchestra Under The Direction of Billy May
Arrangements by May   May 17, 1961, Los Angeles

275	You're Nobody Till Somebody Loves You	Rep. UNISSUED
276	Don't Cry Joe	Rep. UNISSUED
277	Moonlight On The Ganges	Rep. UNISSUED
278	Granada	Rep. UNISSUED

Accompaniment The Same.   May 18, 1961, Los Angeles

279	The Curse Of An Aching Heart*	Rep. 20010, R 1002
280	Love Walked In	Rep. R 1002
281	Please, Don't Talk About Me When I'm Gone	Rep. R 1002
282	Have You Met Miss Jones	Rep. R 1002, R 1015

*NOTE: On the single release Reprise 20010, the recording is edited and
      shorter.

Accompaniment The Same.   May 19, 1961, Los Angeles

283	Don't Be That Way	Rep. R 1002
284	I Never Know	Rep. R 1002
285	Falling In Love With Love	Rep. R 1002
286	It's A Wonderful World	Rep. R 1002

Accompaniment The Same.   May 23, 1961, Los Angeles

287	Don't Cry Joe	Rep. R 1002
288	You're Nobody Till Somebody Loves You	Rep. R 1002
289	Moonlight On The Ganges	Rep. R 1002
290	Granada*	Rep. 20010, R 1002, FS 5250

*NOTE: On the single release Reprise 20010, the recording is edited and
      shorter.

Orchestra Under The Direction of Don Costa
Arrangement by Costa   November 20, 1961, Los Angeles

591	As You Desire Me	Rep. UNISSUED, Zv893
592	Stardust	Rep. 20059, R 1004
593	Yesterdays	Rep. R 1004, R 1015·
594	I Hadn't Anyone Till You	Rep. R 1004

Accompaniment The Same.   November 21, 1961, Los Angeles

595	It Might As Well Be Spring	Rep. R 1004
596	Prisoner Of Love	Rep. R 1004
597	That's All	Rep. R 1004
598	Don't Take Your Love From Me	Rep. UNISSUED
599	Misty	Rep. R 1004

Accompaniment The Same.   November 22, 1961, Los Angeles

600	Come Rain Or Come Shine	Rep. 20059, R 1004
601	Night And Day	Rep. R 1004, 2F 1016
602	All Or Nothing At All	Rep. R 1004, 2F 1016

Orchestra Under The Direction of Nelson Riddle
Arrangements by Riddle   November 23, 1961, Los Angeles

| 634 | Pocketful of Miracles | Rep. 20046, R 1010 |
| 635 | Name It And It's Yours | Rep. 20046, FS 5238 |

Orchestra Under The Direction of Gordon Jenkins
Arrangements by Jenkins   January 15, 1962, Los Angeles

740	The Song Is Ended	Rep. R 1007
741	All Alone	Rep. R 1007
742	Charmaine	Rep. R 1007
743	When I Lost You	Rep. R 1007

Accompaniment The Same.   January 16, 1962, Los Angeles

744	Remember	Rep. R 1007
745	Together	Rep. R 1007
746	The Girl Next Door	Rep. R 1007
747	Indiscreet	Rep. 20107, R 1007

Accompaniment The Same.   January 17, 1962, Los Angeles

748	What'll I Do	Rep. R 1007
749	Oh, How I Miss You Tonight	Rep. R 1007
750	Are You Lonesome Tonight	Rep. R 1007
751	Come Waltz With Me	Rep. UNISSUED

Orchestra Under The Direction of Neal Hefti
Arrangements by Hefti   February 27, 1962, Los Angeles

| 924 | Everybody's Twistin' | Rep. 20063, FS 5238 |
| 925 | Nothing But The Best | Rep. 20063, FS 5238 |

Orchestra Under The Direction of Neal Hefti
Arrangements by Hefti   April 10, 1962, Los Angeles

Personnel include: (Tpt) Conte Candoli; (Tenor Sax) Ben Webster; (Alto Sax) Joe Maini; (Bass) Al McKibbon; (Piano) Bill Miller; plus large orchestra.

1007	I'm Beginning To See The Light	Rep. R 1005
1008	I Get A Kick Out Of You	Rep. R 1005, PRO 573
1009	Ain't She Sweet	Rep. R 1005
1010	I Love You	Rep. R 1005
1011	They Can't Take That Away From Me	Rep. R 1005, R 1015
1012	Love Is Just Around The Corner	Rep. 20092, R 1005

Accompaniment The Same.   April 11, 1962, Los Angeles

1013	At Long Last Love	Rep. R 1005
1014	Serenade In Blue	Rep. R 1005
1015	Goody, Goody	Rep. 20092, R 1005
1016	Don'cha Go Away Mad	Rep. R 1005
1017	Tangerine	Rep. R 1005
1018	Pick Yourself Up	Rep. R 1005

Orchestra Under The Direction of Robert Farnon
Arrangements by Farnon   June 12, 1962, London, England

| 1023 | If I Had You | Eng. Rep. R 1006 |

Recording with Duke Ellington — 1967.

With daughter Nancy at recording session — 1967.

1024	The Very Thought Of You	Eng. Rep. R 1006
1025	I'll Follow My Secret Heart	Eng. Rep. R 1006
1026	Garden In The Rain	Eng.Rep. R 1006

Accompaniment The Same.   June 13, 1962, London, England

1027	London By Night	Eng. Rep. Ep 30087, R 1006
1028	The Gypsy	Eng. Rep. R 1006
1029	Roses Of Picardy	Eng. Rep. UNISSUED
1030	A Nightingale Sang In Berkley Square	Eng. Rep. R 1006

Accompaniment The Same.   June 14, 1962, London, England

1031	We'll Meet Again	Eng. Rep. R 1006
1032	Now Is The Hour	Eng. Rep. R 1006
1033	We'll Gather Lilacs	Eng. Rep. R 1006

Orchestra Under The Direction of Neal Hefti
Arrangements by Nelson Riddle   August 27, 1962, Los Angeles

| 1426 | The Look Of Love | Rep. 20107, F 1013, FS FS 5238 |
| 1427 | I Left My Heart In San Francisco* | Rep. 20107, FS 5238 |

*The single was withdrawn soon after release.

Count Basie And His Orchestra
Arrangements by Neal Hefti   October 2, 1962, Los Angeles

(Tpt) Thad Jones, Flip Richard, Sonny Cohn, Al Aarons, Al Porcino; (Tbn) Henry Coker, Rufas Wagner, Benny Powell; (Alto Sax) Marshall Roayl, Frank Wess; (Tenor Sax) Frank Foster, Eric Dixon; (Bar. Sax) Charlie Fowlks; (Piano) Count Basie; (Guitar) Freddie Greene; (Bass) Buddy Collette, (Drums) Sunny Payne.

1492	Nice Work If You Can Get It	Rep. R 1008, R 1015
1493	Please Be Kind	Rep. R 1008, FS 5240
1494	I Won't Dance	Rep. R 1008
1495	Learnin' The Blues	Rep. R 1008, 2F 1016

Accompaniment The Same.   October 3, 1962, Los Angeles

1496	I'm Gonna Sit Right Down And Write Myself A Letter	Rep. R 1008
1497	I Only Have Eyes For You	Rep. R 1008
1498	My Kind Of Girl	Rep. R 1008
1500 1499	Pennies From Heaven	Rep. R 1008
1500	Looking At The World Through Rose Colored Glasses	Rep. R 1008
1501	The Tender Trap	Rep. R 1008

Orchestra Under The Direction Of Billy May
Arrangements by May   October 22, 1962, Los Angeles

1509	Me And My Shadow - (1)	Rep. 20128, FS 5238

(1) Vocal Duet with Sammy Davis, Jr.

Orchestra Under The Direction Of Nelson Riddle
Arrangements by Riddle   January 21, 1963, Los Angeles

1671	Come Blow Your Horn	Rep. 20184, F 1013
1672	Call Me Irresponsible	Rep. 20151, R 1010, 2F 1016

Orchestra Under The Directio Of Nelson Riddle
Arrangements by Riddle   February 18, 1963, Los Angeles

1820	Lost In The Stars	Rep. R 1009, R 1015
1821	My Heart Stood Still	Rep. R 1009
1822	Ol' Man River	Rep. R 1009

Accompaniment The Same.   February 19, 1963, Los Angeles

1823	This Nearly Was Mine	Rep. 20184, R 1009
1824	You'll Never Walk Alone	Rep. R 1009
1825	I Have Dreamed	Rep. 20184, R 1009

Accompaniment The Same.   February 20, 1963, Los Angeles

1826	California	Rep. 20157 (Promotional Record)
1827	Bewitched	Rep. R 1009

| 1828 | America The Beautiful - (1) | Rep. 20157 (Promotional Record) |

(1) With Unknown Vocal Chorus

Accompaniment The Same.		February 21, 1963, Los Angeles
1829	Soliloquy	Rep. R 1009, 2F 1016
1830	You Brought A New Kind Of Love To Me	Rep. 20209, R 6167

Orchestra Under The Direction Of Nelson Riddle
Arrangements by Riddle.   April 29, 1963, Los Angeles

2023	In The Wee Small Hours	Rep. R 1010, 2F 1016
2024	Nancy	Rep. R 1010, 2F 1016, K 44145
2025	Young At Heart	Rep. R 1010, 2F 1016
2026	The Second Time Around	Rep. R 1010, 2F 1016
2027	All The Way	Rep. R 1010, 2F 1016, R 1011, K 44145, FS 5240

Accompaniment The Same.		April 30, 1963, Los Angeles
2028	Witchcraft	Rep. R 1010, 2F 1016
2029	How Little We Know	Rep. R 1010, 2F 1016
2030	Put Your Dreams Away	Rep. R 1010, 2F 1016, PRO 573
2031	I've Got You Under My Skin	Rep. R 1010, 2F 1016
2032	Oh, What It Seemed To Be	Rep. R 1010, 2F 1016

Orchestra Under The Direction Of Morris Stoloff
Arrangements by Billy May   July 10, 1963, Los Angeles

2149	We Open In Venice - (1)	Rep. R 2017, R 6188
2188	Guys And Dolls - (2)	Rep. R 2016, HS 11374

(1) With Dean Martin and Sammy Davis, Jr.
(2) With Dean Martin

Accompaniment The Same.
Arrangements By Nelson Riddle   July 18, 1963, Los Angeles

| 2161 | Old Devil Moon | Rep. R 2015, HS 11286 |

2166	When I'm Not Near The Girl I Love	Rep. 0398, R 2015, R 6167, HS 11286
2190	I've Never Been In Love Before	Rep. R 2016, R 6167, HS 11374

Accompaniment The Same.
Arrangements by Nelson Riddle   July 24, 1963, Los Angeles

2156	So In Love (Reprise) - (1)	Rep. R 2017
2180	Some Enchanted Evening (Reprise) - (2)	Rep. R 2018

(1) Vocal Duet with Keely Smith
(2) Vocal Duet with Rosemary Clooney

Accompaniment The Same.
Arrangements by Billy May   Same Date As Last

2193	Luck Be A Lady	Rep. R 2016, R 6167, R 1015, HS 11374, FS 5250, 2F 1016*

* Edited Version

2177-A	Guys And Dolls (Reprise) - (3)	Rep. R 2016

(3) Vocal Duet with Dean Martin

Accompaniment The Same.
Arrangements by Billy May   July 29, 1963, Los Angeles

2184	Fugue For Tinhorns - (1)	Rep. R 2016, HS 11374
2185	The Oldest Established - (1)	Rep. R 2016, 2F 1016, HS 11374

(1) With Bing Crosby and Dean Martin

Accompaniment The Same.
Arrangements by Nelson Riddle   July 31, 1963, Los Angeles

| 2171-B | Some Enchanted Evening | Rep. R 2018 |
| 2172 | Twin Soliloquys - (1) | Rep. R 2018 |

(1) With Keely Smith

Orchestra Under The Direction Of Marty Paich
Arrangements by Paich   Same Date As Last, Los Angeles

| 2203 | Here's To The Losers | Rep. R 1013, 20209 |
| 2204 | Love Isn't Just For The Young | Rep. R 1013, 20209 |

Orchestra Under The Direction of Gil Grau
Arrangements by Grau   October 13, 1963, Los Angles

2295	Have Yourself A Merry Little Christmas - (1)	Rep. 50001
2295	Have Yourself A Merry Little Christmas - (2)	Rep. 0243
2295	Have Yourself A Merry Little Christmas - (3)	CP 509

(1) On Reprise Premium Album

(2) Short Edited Version

(3) Long Edited Version on Colpix Album

Orchestra Under The Direction Of Don Costa
Arrangements by Costa   December 3, 1963, Los Angeles

| 2448 | Talk To Me Baby | Rep. 0249, R 1013 |
| 2449 | Stay With Me (Main theme From "The Cardinal") | Rep. 0249, R 1013, R 6167 |

Orchestra Under The Direction Of Nelson Riddle
Arrangements by Riddle   January 27, 1964, Los Angeles

2521	The Way You Look Tonight	Rep. R 1011
2522	Three Coins In The Fountain	Rep. R 1011
2523	Swinging On A Star	Rep. R 1011
2524	In The Cool, Cool, Cool Of Of The Evening	Rep. R 1011
2525	The Continental	Rep. R 1011

Accompaniment The Same.   January 28, 1964, Los Angeles

2526	It Might As Well Be Spring	Rep. R 1011
2527	Secret Love	Rep. R 1011
2528	Moon River	Rep. R 1011
2529	Days Of Wine And Roses	Rep. R 1011
2530	Love Is A Many Splendored Thing	Rep. R 1011

Orchestra Under The Direction of Fred Waring
Arrangements As Noted   February 4, 1964

2470   Let Us Break Bread Together - (1)Rep. R 2020, HS 30931

               (1) With Bing Crosby
               Arranged by Roy Ringwald

2471   You Never Had It So Good - (1) Rep. R 2020, HS 30931
               (1) With Bing Crosby
               Arranged by Jack Halloran

2472   The House I Live In   Rep. R 2020, 2F 1016,
                                               H 30931

               Arranged by Nelson Riddle

2473   You're A Lucky Fellow   Rep. R 2020, FS 5250,
                 Mr. Smith   H 30931

               Arranged by Jack Halloran

2474   Early American   Rep. R 2020

               Arranged by Nelson Riddle

Orchestra Under The Direction Of Don Costa
Arrangement by Costa   April 8, 1964

2577   I Can't Believe I'm Losing You Rep. 0380, F 1013,
                 (1)   FS 5250

               (1) Guitar over-dubbed (3/14/1968) for later single release -
               0677.

Orchestra Under The Direction Of Nelson Riddle
Arrangements by Riddle   Same Date As Last Los Angeles

2628   My Kind Of Town   Rep. 0279, F2021, R6167
                                               2F 1016, K44145

2629   I Like To Lead When I Dance   Rep. 0279, F 2021, R 6167

Orchestra Under The Direction of Nelson Riddle
Arrangements by Riddle   April 10, 1964, Los Angeles

2631	Style - (1)	Rep. F 2021
2632	Mister Booze - (2)	Rep. F 2021
2633	Don't Be A Do Badder (Finale) - (2)	Rep. F 2021

(1) With Bing Crosby and Dean Martin
(2) With Bing Crosby, Dean Martin, Sammy Davis, Jr.
Vocal Chorus.

Count Basie And His Orchestra
Arrangements by Quincy Jones   June 9, 1964, Los Angeles

(Tpt) Al Porcino, Don Rader, Wallace Davenport, Al Aarons, George Cohn, Harry Edison; (Tbn) Henry Coker, Grover Mitchell, Bill Hughes, Henderson Chambers, Kenny Shroyer; (Sax) Frank Foster, Charles Fowlkes, Marshall Royal, Frank Wess, Eric Dixon; (Vibes) Emil Richards; (Bass) George Callett; (Guitar) Freddie Green; (Drums) Sonny Payne; (Piano) Count Basie.

2809	The Best Is Yet To Come	Rep. R 1012, R 1015
2810	I Wanna Be Around	Rep. R 1012
2811	I Believe In You	Rep. R 1012
2812	Fly Me To The Moon	Rep. R 1012, 2F 1016, FS 5240

Add the following personnel: (Violins) Gerald Vinci, Israel Baker, Jacques Gasselin, Thelma Beach, Bonnie Douglas, Marshall Sosson, Erno Neufeld, Lou Raderman, Paul Shure, James Getzoff; (Violas) Virginia Majewski, Paul Robyn, Alvin Dinkin, Stan Harris; (Cellos) Edgar Lustgarten, Ann Goodman.

2814	Hello Dolly	Rep. R 1012, R 1015, K 44145
2815	The Good Life	Rep. R 1012
2816	I Wish You Love	Rep. R 1012

Accompaniment The Same.   June 12, 1964, Los Angeles

2817	I Can't Stop Loving You	Rep. R 1012
2818	More	Rep. R 1012
2819	Wives And Lovers	Rep. R 1012

Orchestra Under The Direction Of Fred Waring

June 16, 1964, Los Angeles

2453	An Old Fashioned Christmas	Rep. F 2022
2454	I Heard The Bells On Christmas Day	Rep. F 2022
2455	Carol Of The Drums (Little Drummer Boy)	Rep. F 2022

Accompaniment The Same.

June 17, 1964, Los Angeles

| 2457 | Go Tell It On The Mountain (1) | Rep. F 2022 |
| 2458 | We Wish You The Merriest (1) | Rep. F 2022 |

(1) Vocal Duet with Bing Crosby.

Orchestra Under The Direction Of Ernie Freeman
Arrangements by Freeman

June 19, 1964, Los Angeles

2888	Softly, As I Leave You	Rep. 0301, F 1013, 2F 1016, FS 1025
2889	And Suddenly Love	Rep. 0301, F 1013
2890	Since Marie Has Left Paree	Rep. UNISSUED
2891	Available	Rep. 0350, F 1013

Orchestra Under The Direction Of Billy May
Arrangement by May

October 4, 1964, Los Angeles

| 2980 | Pass Me By | Rep. F 1013 |

Orchestra Under The Direction of Nelson Riddle
Arrangements by Riddle

Same Date As Last, Los Angeles

| 2981 | Emily (1) | Rep. 0332, F 1013 |
| 2982 | Dear Heart | Rep. F 1013 |

(1) With Vocal Chorus.

Orchestra Under The Direction of Ernie Freeman
Arrangements by Freeman

November 11, 1964, Los Angeles

| 3046 | Somewhere In Your Heart (1) | Rep. 0332, R 6167, FS 1025 |
| 3047 | Anytime At All | Rep. 0350, R 6167 |

(1) With Vocal Chorus.

Orchestra Under The Direction of Gordon Jenkins
Arrangements by Jenkins   April 13, 1965, Los Angeles

H 3295	Don't Wait Too Long	Rep. F 1014
H 3296	September Song	Rep. F 1014
H 3297	Last Night When We Were Young	Rep. F 1014
H 3298	Hello Young Lovers	Rep. F 1014

Accompaniment The Same.   April 14, 1965, Los Angeles

H 3299	I See It Now	Rep. F 1014
H 3300	When The Wind Was Green	Rep. F 1014
H 3301	Once Upon A Time	Rep. F 1014
H 3302	How Old Am I	Rep. UNISSUED

Orchestra Under The Direction of Ernie Freeman
Arrangements by Freeman   Same Date As Last, Los Angeles

| HX 3320 | Tell Her (You Love Her Each Day) (1) | Rep. 0373, R 6167, F 1020 FS 1025 |
| HX 3321 | When Somebody Loves You (1) | Rep. 0373, R 6167, FS 1025 |

(1) With Vocal Chorus.

Orchestra Under The Direction of Gordon Jenkins
Arrangements by Jenkins   April 22, 1965, Los Angeles

H 3352	It Was A Very Good Year	Rep. 0429, F1014, FS1025
H 3353	The Man In The Looking Glass	Rep. F 1014
H 3354	This Is All I Ask	Rep. F 1014
H 3355	It Gets Lonely Early	Rep. F 1014
H 3302	Re: - How Old Am I (1)	Rep. F 1014, FS 5250

(1) Guitar over-dubbed (3/14/1968) for single reissue 0677.

Orchestra Under The Direction of Ernie Freeman
Arrangement by Freeman   May 6, 1965, Los Angeles

| HX 3417 | Forget Domani | Rep. 0380, FS 1025, FS 5238 |

Orchestra Under The Direction of Gordon Jenkins
Arrangement by Jenkins   May 27, 1965, Los Angeles

H 3442   The September of My Years   Rep. 0531, F 1014, 2F1016

Orchestra Under The Direction of Torrie Zito
Arrangements by Zito   August 23, 1965, Los Angeles

HX 3703   Everybody Has The Right To   Rep. 0410, F 1015
                      Be Wrong

HX 3704   I'll Only Miss Her When I   Rep. 0410, F 1015
                      Think Of Her

Arrangement by Riddle   Same Date As Last, Los Angeles

HX 3707   Golden Moment   Rep. F 1015

Orchestra Under The Direction of Nelson Riddle
Arrangement by Riddle   September 14, 1965, Los Angeles

HX 3728   Moment To Moment*   Rep. 0429, FS 5238

                      *This was just the orchestra alone with Sinatra doing
                      the voice over-dub on October 21, 1965.

Orchestra Under The Direction of Freddie Stultz
Arrangement by Stultz   October 11, 1965, Los Angeles

H 3767   I'll Never Smile Again* (1)   Rep. 2F 1016

                      (1) With Vocal Chorus.

Same Orchestra
Arrangement by Billy May   Same Date As Last, Los Angeles

H 3768   Come Fly With Me*   Rep. 2F 1016

Same Orchestra
Arrangements by Nelson Riddle   Same Date As Last, Los Angeles

H 3769   From Here To Eternity*   Rep. 2F 1016

H 3770   Love And Marriage*   Rep. 2F 1016

*NOTE: The above four tunes were also recorded by the band alone, with
       Sinatra doing the voice over-dubbing on October 21, 1965.

Live From Sands Hotel   Unknown Date, Probably November 1965

H 3824   The Summit (Comedy Routine   Rep. 2F 1016
                      With Martin & Sammy Davis)

Orchestra Under The Direction of Nelson Riddle
Arrangements by Riddle   November 29, 1965, Los Angeles

H 3892   Moon Song   Rep. R 1018

H 3893	Moon Love	Rep. R 1018
H 3894	The Moon Got In My Eyes	Rep. R 1018
H 3895	Moonlight Serenade	Rep. R 1018
H 3896	Reaching For The Moon	Rep. R 1018

Accompaniment The Same.

November 30, 1965, Los Angeles

H 3897	I Wished On The Moon	Rep. R 1018
H 3898	Moonlight Becomes You	Rep. R 1018
H 3899	Moonlight Mood	Rep. R 1018
H 3900	Oh You Crazy Moon	Rep. 0470, R 1018
H 3901	The Moon Was Yellow	Rep. R 1018

Count Basie And His Orchestra - Arranged by Quincy Jones
Live at the Sands Hotel in Las Vegas, Nevada.

January 26, 1966

J 4097	I've Got A Crush On You	2FS 1019
J 4098	I've Got You Under My Skin	2FS 1019
J 4099	The September Of My Years	2FS 1019, FS 1034

Same As Above.

January 27, 1966

J 4100	Street Of Dreams	2FS 1019, PRO 573
J 4101	You Make Me Feel So Young	0509, 2FS 1019
J 4102	The Shadow Of Your Smile	2FS 1019, FS 1032
J 4103	Luck Be A Lady	UNISSUED
J 4104	It Was A Very Good Year	2FS 1019
J 4105	Don't Worry 'Bout Me	2FS 1019

Same As Above.

January 28, 1966

J 4106	My Kind Of Town	2FS 1019, FS 5240
J 4106-A	My Kind Of Town (Reprise)	2FS 1019
J 4107	One For My Baby	2FS 1019
J 4108	Fly Me To The Moon	2FS 1019
J 4109	Get Me To The Church On Time	2FS 1019

Same As Last.   January 29, 1966

J 4110   Angel Eyes   2FS 1019

J 4111   Where Or When   2FS 1019

Same As Last.   February 1, 1966

J 4112   Come Fly With Me   2FS 1019, PRO 573

Orchestra Arranged and Conducted by Ernie Freeman
                                                  April 11, 1966, Hollywood

J 4195   Strangers In The Night   0470, FS 1017, FS 1025

Orchestra Arranged and Conducted by Nelson Riddle
                                                  May 11, 1966, Hollywood

J 4234   My Baby Just Cares For Me   FS 1017

J 4235   Yes Sir, That's My Baby   FS 1017

J 4236   You're Driving Me Crazy   FS 1017

J 4237   The Most Beautiful Girl In   FS 1017
                The World

Same As Above.   May 16, 1966

J 4238   Summer Wind   0509, 0710, FS 1017,
                                                 FS 1025

J 4239   All Or Nothing At All   FS 1017

J 4240   Call Me   FS 1017

J 4241   On A Clear Day   FS 1017

J 4242   Downtown   FS 1017

Next tune was taken directly from a radio station and supposedly released then
recalled.
                                                            June 10, 1966

J 4363   Gunga Din   UNISSUED?

Orchestra Unknown   August 25, 1966

J 4410   She Believes In Me   UNISSUED

J 4412   That's Life   UNISSUED

Orchestra Arranged and Conducted by Ernie Freeman
                                                  October 18, 1966, Hollywood

J 4569   That's Life   0531, FS 1020, FS 1025

Same As Last.		November 17, 1966
J 4661	Give Her Love	FS 1020
J 4662	What Now My Love	FS 1020, K 44145
J 4663	Somewhere My Love (Lara's Theme)	FS 1020
J 4664	Winchester Cathedral	FS 1020
Same As Above.		November 18, 1966
J 4665	I Will Wait For You	0561, FS 1020
J 4666	You're Gonna Hear From Me	FS 1020
J 4667	Sand And Sea	FS 1020
J 4668	The Impossible Dream	FS 1020

Orchestra Arranged and Conducted by Claus Ogerman

		January 30, 1967, Hollywood
K 4807	Baubles, Bangles And Beads (1)	FS 1021
K 4808	I Concentrate On You (1)	FS 1021
K 4809	Dindi	FS 1021
K 4810	Change Partners	FS 1021

(1) Vocal duet with Antonio Carlos Jobim.

Same As Above.		January 31, 1967, Hollywood
K 4811	Quiet Nights of Quiet Stars (Corcovado)	FS 1021
K 4812	If You Never Come To Me	FS 1021
K 4813	The Girl From Ipanema (1)	FS 1021
K 4814	Meditation	FS 1021

(1) Vocal duet with Antonio Carlos Jobim.

Same As Last.		February 1, 1967, Hollywood
K 4815	Once I Loved	FS 1021
K 4816	How Insensitive (1)	FS 1021
K 4817	Drinking Again	FS 1022

(1) Vocal duet with Antonio Carlos Jobim.

Orchestra Arranged and Conducted by Billy Strange

February 1, 1967, Hollywood

K 4818	Somethin' Stupid (1)	0561, FS 1022, FS 5250, R 6419

(1) Vocal duet with Nancy Sinatra.

Orchestra Arranged and Conducted as noted

June 29, 1967, New York City, N.Y.

K 5296	You Are There (1)	0610, FS 1022
K 5297	The World We Knew (2)	0610, FS 1022
K 5298	This Town (3)	UNISSUED

(1) Gordon Jenkins
(2) Arr. - Ernie Freeman; Con. - Billy Strange
(3) Billy Strange

Orchestra Arranged and Conducted as noted

July 24, 1967, Hollywood

K 6108	Born Free (1)	FS 1022, FS 1032
K 6109	This Is My Love (1)	0631, FS 1022
K 6110	This Is My Song (2)	FS 1022
K 6111	Don't Sleep In The Subway (2)	FS 1022
K 6112	Some Enchanted Evening (3)	FS 1022
K 6113	This Town (4)	0631, FS 1022

(1) Gordon Jenkins
(2) Ernie Freeman (Vocal Chorus on K 6111)
(3) H.B. Barnum
(4) Billy Strange

Orchestra Arranged and Conducted by Billy Strange

September 20, 1967, Hollywood

K 6159	Younger Than Springtime	FS 6277, FS 5250

Duke Ellington And His Orchestra
Arranged and Conducted by Billy May

December 11, 1967, Hollywood

(Tpt) Cootie Williams, Cat Anderson, Mercer Ellington, Herbie Jones; (Tbn) Lawrence Brown, Buster Cooper, Chuck Connors; (Cl) Jimmy Hamilton; (A.S.) Johnny Hodges, Russel Procope; (T.S.) Paul Gonsalves; (B.S.) Harry Carney; (P.) Duke Ellington; (B.) John Lamb; (D.) Sam Woodyard.

K 6319	All I Need Is The Girl	FS 1024
K 6320	Yellow Days	FS 1024
K 6321	Indian Summer	FS 1024
K 6322	Come Back To Me	FS 1024

Same As Above.   December 12, 1967

K 6323	Poor Butterfly	FS 1024
K 6324	Sunny	FS 1024
K 6325	I Like The Sunrise	FS 1024
K 6326	Follow Me	FS 1024

Orchestra Arranged and Conducted by Don Costa
July 24, 1968, New York City, N.Y.

L 5401	My Way Of Life	0764, FS 1027, K 44145
L 5402	Cycles	0764, FS 1027, K 44145, FS 1034
L 5403	What Ever Happened To Christmas	0790, FS 1026, P 12013

Orchestra Arranged and Conducted by Nelson Riddle
August 12, 1968, Hollywood

L 6755	The Twelve Days Of Christmas (1)	FS 1026
L 6756	The Bells Of Christmas (Greensleeves) (1)	FS 1026
L 6757	I Wouldn't Trade Christmas (1)	0790, FS 1026
L 6758	The Christmas Waltz	FS 1026

(1) With Frank Sinatra, Jr., Nancy Sinatra, Tina Sinatra and the Jimmy Joyce Singers

Orchestra Arranged and Conducted by Nelson Riddle
November 11, 1968, Hollywood

L 6927	Blue Lace	0817, FS 1032
L 6928	Star	0798, FS 5238, FS 1034

Orchestra Arranged by Don Costa and Conducted by Bill Miller
November 12, 1968, Los Angeles

L 6929	Little Green Apples	FS 1027, FS 1032, FS5328

L 6930	Gentle On My Mind	FS 1027, FS 1032
L 6931	By The Time I Get To Phoenix	FS 1027, K 44145
Same As Last.		November 13, 1968
L 6932	Moody River	FS 1027
L 6933	Pretty Colors	FS 1027
Same As Above.		November 14, 1968
L 6934	Rain In My Heart	0798, FS 1027
L 6935	Wandering	FS 1027
L 6936	Wait By The Fire	UNISSUED
L 6937	From Both Sides Now	FS 1027, FS 1032
Same As Above.		December 30, 1968
L 7053	My Way	0817, FS 1029, FS 1034, FS 1032, FS 5240

Orchestra Arranged by Eumer Deodato and Conducted by Morris Stoloff
February 11, 1969, Los Angeles

M 7141	One Note Samba	FS 1028 N.R., FS 1033
M 7142	Don't Ever Go Away	FS 1028 N.R., FS 1033
M 7143	Wave (Part I)	FS 1028, N.R., FS 1033
M 7144	Wave (Part II)	FS 1028, N.R., FS 1033
M 7145	Bonita	FS 1028 N.R., K 64039
	N.R. - Not Released	

Same As Above.		February 12, 1969, Los Angeles
M 7162	Someone To Light Up My Life	FS 1028 N.R., FS 1033
M 7163	Desafinad (Off Key)	FS 1028 N.R.
M 7164	Drinking Water (1)	FS 1028 N.R., FS 1033
	N.R. - Not Released (1) Vocal Duet with Antonio Carlos Jobim	

Same As Above.		February 13, 1969
M 7165	Song Of The Sabia	0970, FS 1028*, PRO 359, FS 5250
M 7166	This Happy Madness	FS 1028*, FS 1033

| M 7167 | Triste | FS 1028, FS 1033 |

*NOTE: This album number - **FS 1028** - was scheduled for release then cancelled, but a few 8 track tape albums slipped out before total recall was put in effect.

Orchestra Arranged and Conducted by Don Costa

February 13, 1969

| M 7180 | All My Tomorrows | FS 1029 |
| M 7181 | Didn't We | FS 1029, K 44145, FS5240 |

Same As Above   February 20, 1969, Los Angeles

M 7182	A Day In The Life Of A Fool	FS 1029
M 7183	Yesterday	FS 1029, FS 1032
M 7220	If You Go Away	FS 1029

Same As Above.   February 24, 1969

M 7221	Watch What Happens	FS 1029
M 7222	For Once In My Life	FS 1029, FS 1032
M 7223	Mrs. Robinson	RA 3401, FS 1029
M 7224	Hallelujah, I Love Her So	FS 1029

Same As Above.   February 25, 1969

| M 7225 | Shadow Of The Moon | RA 3401, FS 5238, W 54093 |

Same As Last.   March 19, 1969, Hollywood

M 7263	I've Been To Town	FS 1030
M 7264	Empty Is	FS 1030
M 7265	The Single Man	FS 1030
M 7266	Lonesome Cities	FS 1030

Same As Above.   March 20, 1969

M 7267	The Beautiful Strangers	FS 1030
M 7268	A Man Alone	0852, FS 1030, FS 5240, FS 1034
M 7269	A Man Alone (Reprise)	FS 1030
M 7270	Love's Been Good To Me	0852, FS 1030, FS 5240, FS 1034

Same As Above.   March 21, 1969

M 7271   Out Beyond The Window   FS 1030, FS 5240

M 7272   Night   FS 1030

M 7273   Some Traveling Music   FS 1030

M 7274   From Promise To Promise   FS 1030

Same As Above.   June 18, 1969, Hollywood

M 7431   Forget To Remember   0865, FS 5240

M 7432   Goin' Out Of My Head   0865, FS 5240, FS 1034

Orchestra Arranged and Conducted by Joseph Scott
                              July 14, 1969, New York City, N.Y.

(Trombones) Urban Green, Wayne Andre, Tony Studd, Warren Covington;
(Reeds) Romeo Penque, Philip Bodner, William Shapin, Walter Kane; (French
Horns) James Buffington, Ray Alonge; (Guitars) Jay Berliner, Vincent Bell;
(Piano) Dick Hyman; (Bass) Joseph Macho; (Drums) Alvin Rogers; (Percussion) David Carey; (Strings) Emanuel Green, Tosha Samaroff, George Ockner,
Max Pollikoff, Max Cahn, Henri Aubert, Joseph Malignarri, Rocco Pesile, Peter
Buonconsiglio, Raoul Poliakin, Julius Schacter, Julius Held, Alfred Brown,
Harold Coletta, Richard Dickler, Cal Fleisig, George Ricci, Harvey Shapiro,
Kermit Moore.

M 51586   I Would Be In Love   0895, FS 1031, K 44145

M 51587   The Train   0920, FS 1031

M 51588   Goodbye   FS 1031

M 51589   Watertown   0895, FS 1031

Orchestra Arranged and Conducted by Charles Calello
                              July 15, 1969, New York City, N.Y.

Musicians same as last except add - (Guitars) Stuart Scharf, Ralph Casale;
omit - Vincent Bell. Richard Davis replaces Joseph Macho on Bass. Add (Harp)
Margaret Ross. Strings same.

M 51591   Elizabeth   FS 1031

M 51592   Michael And Peter   UNISSUED

M 51594   She Says (1)   FS 1031

M 51596   What's Now Is Now (1)   0920, FS 1031, FS 1034

                (1) Arr. and Con. by Joseph Scott.

Orchestra Arranged and Conducted by Charles Calello
July 17, 1969, New York City, N.Y.

M 51636	For A While	UNISSUED
M 51637	Lady Day	UNISSUED
M 51638	What A Funny Girl	FS 1031

Orchestra Arranged and Conducted by Charles Calello
October 13, 1969, New York City, N.Y.

M 161492	Michael And Peter	FS 1031
M 161493	Lady Day	UNISSUED
M 161494	For A While	FS 1031

Orchestra Arranged and Conducted by Don Costa
November 7, 1969, Los Angeles

M 17803	Lady Day (3rd Remake)	0970, FS 1033

Orchestra Arranged and Conducted by Don Costa
October 26, 1970, Los Angeles

N 19254	I Will Drink The Wine (1)	FS 1033
N 19255	Bein' Green	0981, FS 1033, F 1034
N 19256	My Sweet Lady	FS 1033

(1) With Vocal Chorus.

Orchestra Arranged and Conducted by Don Costa
October 27, 1970, Los Angeles

N 19261	Sunrise In The Morning	FS 1033

Same As Above. October 28, 1970

N 19267	I'm Not Afraid	1011, FS 5250, FS 1034
N 19268	Something	0981, FS 5250, FS 1034

Same As Above. October 29, 1970

N 19269	Leaving On A Jet Plane	FS 1033
N 19270	Close to You	FS 1033

Same As Above. November 2, 1970

N 19276	Feelin' Kinda Sunday (1)	0980, FS 5250
N 19277	Life's A Trippy Thing (1)	1011, FS 5250

| N 19278 | The Game Is Over | UNISSUED |
| | (1) Vocal Duet with Nancy Sinatra. | |

Orchestra Arranged and Conducted by Gordon Jenkins

June 4, 1973, Hollywood

RCA 4011	Bang Bang	UNISSUED
RCA 4012	You Will Be My Music	1190, FS 2155, 72383
RCA 4013	Noah	FS2155

Same As Above.

June 5, 1973, Hollywood

| RCA 4014 | Nobody Wins | FS2155 |
| RCA 4015 | The Hurt Doesn't Go Away | RPS1327, W54093 |

Orchestra Arranged by Don Costa and Conducted by Gordon Jenkins

June 21, 1973, Hollywood

| RCA 4026 | Winners | 1190, FS2155 |
| RCA 4027 | Let Me Try Again | 1181, FS2155, 72383, K 64039 |

Orchestra Arranged and Conducted by Gordon Jenkins

June 22, 1973, Hollywood

RCA 4028	Empty Tables	RPS1343, W54093
RCA 4029	Walk Away	UNISSUED
RCA 4030	Send In The Clowns	1181, FS2155
RCA 4031	There Used To Be A Ball Park	FS2155

Orchestra Arranged and Conducted as Noted

August 20, 1973, Hollywood

RCA 4188	You're So Right (For What's Wrong In My Life) (1)	FS2155, 72383
RCA 4189	Dream Away (2)	FS2155, 72383
	(1) Arr. and Con. by Gordon Jenkins	
	(2) Arr. by Don Costa, Con. by Gordon Jenkins	

Orchestra Arranged and Conducted by Don Costa

December 10, 1973, Hollywood

| RCA 4523 | Bad, Bad Leroy Brown | 1196, FS2195, K64039 |
| RCA 4524 | I'm Gonna Make It All The Way | 1196, FS2195 |

Orchestra Arranged and Conducted by Gordon Jenkins
February 4, 1974, Hollywood

SCA 4720	Empty Tables	UNISSUED
SCA 4721	If	FS2195, K64093
SCA 4722	The Summer Knows	FS2195

Orchestra Arranged and Conducted by Don Costa
May 8, 1974, Hollywood

| SCA 4840 | Sweet Caroline | FS2195 |
| SCA 4841 | You Turned My World Around | 1208, FS2195 |

Orchestra Arranged and Conducted by Don Costa
May 9, 1974, Hollywood

| SCA 4842 | You Are The Sunshine Of My Life | FS2195, K64039 |

Same As Above.   May 21, 1974, Hollywood

SCA 4849	What Are You Doing The Rest Of Your Life	FS2195
SCA 4850	Tie A Yellow Ribbon 'Round The Old Oak Tree	FS2195
SCA 4851	Satisfy Me One More Time	1208, FS2195
SCA 4852	If You Could Read My Mind	UNISSUED

Orchestra Arranged and Conducted By Gordon Jenkins
September 24, 1974, Hollywood

?	Everything Happens To Me	UNISSUED
?	The Saddest Thing Of All	UNISSUED
?	Just As Though You Were Here	UNISSUED

Woody Herman And His Young Thundering Herd Orchestra
Recorded Live From Madison Square Garden
October 13, 1974, New York City

?	The Lady Is A Tramp	Reprise FS2207
?	I Get A Kick Out Of You	FS2207
?	Let Me Try Again	FS2207
?	Autumn In New York	FS2207
?	I've Got You Under My Skin	FS2207

?	Bad, Bad Leroy Brown	FS2207
?	Angel Eyes	FS2207
?	You Are The Sunshine Of My Life	FS2207
?	The House I Live In	FS2207
?	My Kind Of Town	FS2207
?	My Way	FS2207

We know that all of the selections listed here are not in fact from this specific date as Reprise states. However, since we cannot trace the exact concerts from where a few of these selections come from we will wait until we are positive and issue our findings in our first supplement.

Orchestra Arranged by Don Costa and Conducted by Bill Miller
December 4, 1974, Hollywood

| RCA 5292 | Anytime (I'll Be There) (1) Background Vocals by Rhodes, Chalmers and Rhodes | 1327, W54093 |

Sextet Arranged and Conducted by Don Costa
February 4, 1975, Hollywood

?	That Old Black Magic	UNISSUED
?	You Are The Sunshine Of Of My Life	UNISSUED
?	Oh Babe, What Would You Say	UNISSUED

Orchestra Arranged and Conducted By Don Costa
February 20, 1975, Los Angeles

| TCA 5325 | The Only Couple On The Floor | 1335, W54093 |

Orchestra Arranged and Conducted By Al Capps
February 24, 1975, Los Angeles

| TCA 5326 | I Believe I'm Gonna Love You | 1335, W54093, K64039 |

Orchestra Arranged and Conducted By Gordon Jenkins
September 1975, Hollywood

| TCA 5601 | The Saddest Thing Of All | 1343, W54093 |
| TCA 5602 | Grass | UNISSUED |

Orchestra Arranged and Conducted By Don Costa
October 16, 1975, Hollywood

| TCA 5717 | A Baby Just Like You | 1342, W54093 |

| TCA 5718 | Christmas Mem'ries | 1342, W54093 |
| TCA 5719 | My Little Angel | UNISSUED |

Orchestra Arranged and Conducted By Don Costa

January 21, 1976, Hollywood

| UCA 5873 | I Sing The Songs | 1347, W54093, K64039 |

No Orchestra - Only Bill Miller, Piano

Same Date As Last

| UCA 5874 | Empty Tables | 1347, K64039 |
| UCA 5875 | Send In The Clowns | 1382, K64039 |

Orchestra Arranged and Conducted By Billy May

May, 1976, Hollywood

| UCA 6205 | The Best I Ever Had (1) | 1364 |

(1) Tenor Sax Solo By Sam Butera

Orchestra Arranged by Don Costa, Conducted By Bill Miller

Same Date As Last

| UCA 6206 | Star Gazer (1) | 1364, K64039 |

(1) Tenor Sax Solo By Sam Butera

Orchestra Arranged by Don Costa, Conducted by Bill Miller

June 1976, Hollywood

| UCA 6251 | Dry Your Eyes | 1377 |

Orchestra Arranged and Conducted By Nelson Riddle

September 1976, Hollywood

| UCA 6590 | I Love My Wife | 1382 |

Orchestra Arranged and Conducted By Claus Ogerman

December 1976, Hollywood

| UNY 1180 | Like A Sad Song | 1377 |

Orchestra Unknown, Arranger Unknown

Late 1976, Hollywood

?	All By Myself	UNISSUED
?	The Hungry Years	UNISSUED
?	Never Gonna Fall In Love Again	UNISSUED

With composer Rod McCuen — 1969.

With Conductor Morris Stoloff — 1975.

Orchestra Arranged and Conducted By Charles Calello
January 17, 1977, Hollywood

?	Everybody Ought To Be In Love	UNISSUED
?	See The Show Again	UNISSUED

Orchestra Arranged and Conducted By Joe Beck
Early February, 1977, Hollywood

UNY 1197	Night And Day	1386
UNY 1198	All Or Nothing At All	UNISSUED
UNY 1199	Sorry Is The Hardest Word	UNISSUED

Orchestra Arranged and Conducted By Charles Calello
February 14, 1977, Hollywood

UNY 1288	Everybody Ought To Be In Love (1)	1386

(1) With Unknown Vocal Chorus

Orchestra Arranged and Conducted By Nelson Riddle
February 14 Through February 19, 1977, New York City

?	Here's To The Ladies	UNISSUED
?	Sweet Georgia Brown	UNISSUED
?	Nina Never Knew	UNISSUED
?	When Joanna Loved Me	UNISSUED
?	Linda	UNISSUED
?	Sweet Lorraine	UNISSUED
?	Emily	UNISSUED
?	Elizabeth	UNISSUED

Orchestra Same As Last.
March 9, 1977, New York City

?	Nancy	UNISSUED
?	Tina	UNISSUED
?	Barbara	UNISSUED
?	Laura	UNISSUED

The above twelve songs were recorded to be included in a two record set titled "Here's To The Ladies" and was given a release number - FSK2259. So far it has been shelved and there has been talk that Sinatra may leave Reprise and is presently negotiating with RCA Victor. He may bring these masters with him and release them for that company as he has been dissatisfied with the way Warners/Reprise has been handling his recordings.

Unknown Orchestra and Arrangement

March 11, 1977, Hollywood

?	I Can't Believe It's Over	UNISSUED

Orchestra Arranged and Conducted By Nelson Riddle

Mid-August, 1977, Hollywood

?	Josephine	UNISSUED
?	Stella By Starlight	UNISSUED
?	Ruby	UNISSUED
?	Michelle	UNISSUED
?	Lenora	UNISSUED

The above five songs were also scheduled to be in the album "Here's To The Ladies".

SONG INDEX FOR CHAPTER IX - REPRISE RECORDS

Ain't She Sweet (Milton Ager - Jack Yellin)
April 10, 1962

All Alone (Irving Berlin)
January 15, 1962

All By Myself (Eric Carmen)
Late, 1976

All I Need Is The Girl (Stephen Sondheim - Jule Styne)
December 11, 1967

All My Tomorrows (Sammy Cahn - Jimmy Van Heusen)
February 13, 1969

All Or Nothing At All (Jack Lawrence - Arthur Altman)
November 22, 1961; May 11, 1966

All The Way (Sammy Cahn - Jimmy Van Heusen)
April 29, 1963

America The Beautiful (Katherine Bates - Samuel Ward)
February 20, 1963

And Suddenly Love (Paul Vance - Howard)
June 1964

Angel Eyes (Matt Dennis - Earl Brent)
January 29, 1966; October 13, 1974

An Old Fashioned Christmas
June 16, 1964

Anytime (Paul Anka)
December 4, 1974

Anytime At All (Knight)
November 11, 1964

Are You Lonesome Tonight (Roy Turk - Lou Handman)
January 17, 1962

As You Desire Me (Allie Wrubel)
November 20, 1961

At Long Last Love (Cole Porter)
April 11, 1962

Autumn In New York (Vernon Duke)
October 13, 1974

Available (Sammy Cahn - Marks - Wynn)
June 19, 1964

Baby Just Like You, A (John Denver - John Henry)
October 16, 1975

Bad, Bad Leroy Brown (Jim Croce)
December 10, 1973; October 13, 1974

Bang Bang (Sonny Buono)
June 4, 1973

Barbara (Sammy Cahn - Jimmy Van Heusen)
March 9, 1977

Baubles, Bangles And Beads (Robert Wright - George Forrest)
January 30, 1967

Beautiful Strangers, The (Rod McKuen)
March 20, 1969

Be Careful Its My Heart (Irving Berlin)
December 20, 1960

Bein' Green (Joe Raposo)
October 26, 1970

Bells Of Christmas, The (Greensleeves) (Adapted by Sammy Cahn &
  Jimmy Van Heusen)
August 12, 1968

Best Is Yet To Come, The (Carolyn Leigh - Cy Coleman)
June 9, 1964

Best I Ever Had, The (Ruby Hice - Danny Hice)
May 7, 1976

Bewitched (Richard Rodgers - Lorenz Hart)
February 20, 1963

Blue Lace (Riz Ortolani - Patty Jacob)
November 11, 1968

Bonita (Antonio Carlos Jobim - Gene Lees - Ray Gilbert)
February 11, 1969

Born Free (John Barry - Stanley Black)
July 24, 1967

By The Time I Get To Phoenix (Jim Webb)
November 12, 1968

California (Sammy Cahn - Jimmy Van Heusen)
February 20, 1963

Call Me (Tony Hatch)
May 11, 1966

Call Me Irresponsible (Sammy Cahn - Jimmy Van Heusen)
January 21, 1963

Carol Of The Drums (Davis - Onerati - Simeone)
June 16, 1964

Change Partners (Irving Berlin)
January 30, 1967

Charmaine (Erno Rapee - Lew Pollack)
January 15, 1962

Christmas Mem'ries (Alan & Marilyn Bergman - Don Costa)
October 16, 1975

Christmas Waltz, The (Sammy Cahn - Jule Styne)
August 12, 1968

Close To You (Hal David - Burt Bacharach)
October 29, 1970

Coffee Song, The (Bob Hilliard - Dave Miles)
December 20, 1960

Come Back To Me (Alan Lerner - Burton Lane)
December 11, 1967

Come Blow Your Horn (Sammy Cahn - Jimmy Van Heusen)
January 21, 1963

Come Fly With Me (Sammy Cahn - Jimmy Van Heusen)
October 11, 1965; October 21, 1965; February 1, 1966

Come Rain Or Come Shine (Harold Arlen - Johnny Mercer)
November 22, 1961

Come Waltz With Me (Sammy Cahn - Jimmy Van Heusen)
January 17, 1962

Continental, The (Herb Magidson - Con Conrad)
January 27, 1964

Curse Of An Aching Heart, The (Henry Fink - Al Piantodosi)
May 18, 1961

Cycles (Gayle Caldwell)
July 24, 1968

Daybreak (Ferde Grofe - Harold Adamson)
May 2, 1961

Day In The Life Of A Fool, A (Carl Sigman - Luis Bonfa)
February 20, 1969

Days Of Wine And Roses, The (Johnny Mercer - Henry Mancini)
January 28, 1964

Dear Heart (Jay Livinston - Ray Evans - Henry Mancini)
October 4, 1964

Didn't We (Jim Webb)
February 13, 1969

Dindi (Antonio Carlos Jobim - Ray Gilbert)
January 30, 1967

Don't Be A Do-Badder (Sammy Cahn - Jimmy Van Heusen)
April 10, 1964

Don't Be That Way (Benny Goodman - Edgar Sampson - Mitchell Parish)
May 19, 1961

Don'cha Go Away Mad (Jimmy Munday - Al Stillman - Illinois Jacquet)
April 11, 1962

Don't Cry Joe (Joe Marsala)
May 17, 1961; May 23, 1961

Don't Ever Go Away (Antonio Carlos Jobim - Ray Gilbert - Duran)
February 11, 1969

Don't Sleep In The Subways (Tony Hatch - Jack Trent)
July 24, 1967

Don't Take Your Love From Me (Henry Nemo)
November 21, 1961

Don't Wait Too Long (Sunny Skylar)
April 13, 1965

Don't Worry 'Bout Me (Rube Bloom - Ted Koehler)
January 27, 1966

Downtown (Tony Hatch)
May 16, 1966

Dream Away (Paul Williams - John Williams)
August 20, 1973

Drinking Again (Johnny Mercer - Doris Tauber)
February 1, 1967

Drinking Water (Antonio Carlos Jobim - Gene Lees - Vinicius Demoraes)
February 12, 1969

Dry Your Eyes (Neil Diamond)
June, 1976

Early American (Johnny Burke - Jimmy Van Heusen)
February 4, 1964

East Of The Sun (Brooks Bowman)
May 3, 1961

Easy To Love (Cole Porter)
December 19, 1960

Elizabeth (Bob Gaudio - Jake Holmes)
July 15, 1969; February, 1977)

Emily (Johnny Mandel - Johnny Mercer)
October 4, 1964; February, 1977

Empty Is (Rod McKuen)
March 19, 1969

Empty Tables (Johnny Mercer - Jimmy Van Heusen)
June 27, 1973; February 4, 1974; January 21, 1976

Everybody Has The Right To Be Wrong (Sammy Cahn - Jimmy
Van Heusen)
August 23, 1965

Everybody Ought To Be In Love (Paul Anka)
January 17, 1977; February 14, 1977

Everybody's Twistin' (Rube Bloom - Ted Koehler)
February 27, 1962

Everything Happens To Me (Matt Dennis - Tom Adair)
September 24, 1974

Falling In Love With Love (Richard Rodgers - Lorenz Hart)
May 19, 1961

Feelin' Kinda Sunday (Kathy Wakefield - Annette Tucker - Nino Tempo)
November 2, 1970

Fine Romance, A (Dorothy Fields - Jerome Kern)
December 19, 1960

Fly Me To The Moon (Bart Howard)
June 9, 1964; January 28, 1966

Foggy Day, A (George & Ira Gershwin)
December 19, 1960

Follow Me (Alan Lerner - Frederick Loewe)
December 12, 1967

For A While (Bob Gaudio - Jake Holmes)
July 17, 1969; October 13, 1969

Forget Domani (Norman Newell - Riz Ortolani)
May 6, 1965

Forget To Remember (Teddy Randazzo - Vinny Pike)
June 18, 1969

For Once In My Life (Ronald Miller - Orlando Murden)
February 24, 1969

From Here To Eternity (Freddie Karger - Robert Wells)
October 11, 1965; October 21, 1965

From Both Sides Now (Joni Mitchell)
November 14, 1968

From Promise To Promise (Rod McKuen)
March 21, 1969

Fugue For Tin Horns (Frank Loesser)
July 29, 1963

Game Is Over, The
November 2, 1970

Garden In The Rain, A (James Dyrenforth - Carroll Gibbons)
June 13, 1962

Gentle On My Mind (John Hartford)
November 12, 1968

Get Me To The Church On Time (Alan Lerner - Frederick Loewe)
January 28, 1966

Girl From Ipanema, The (Antonio Carlos Jobim - Norman Gimbel - Vinicius Demoraes)
January 31, 1967

Girl Next Door, The (Hugh Martin - Ralph Blane)
January 16, 1962

Give Her Love (Jim Harbert)
November 17, 1966

Goin' Out Of My Head (Teddy Randazzo - Bobby Weinstein)
June 18, 1969

Golden Moment (Kenneth Jacobson - Rhoda Roberts)
August 23, 1965

Goodbye (She Quietly Says) - (Bob Gaudio - Jake Holmes)
July 14, 1969

Good Life, The (Jack Reardon - Sacha Distel)
June 10, 1964

Goody, Goody (Johnny Mercer - Matty Malneck)
April 11, 1962

Go Tell It On The Mountain
June 17, 1964

Granada (Augustin Lara - Dorothy Dodd)
May 17, 1961; May 23, 1961

Grass
September 4, 1975

Gunga Din (Sammy Cahn - Jimmy Van Heusen)
June 10, 1966

Guys And Dolls (Frank Loesser)
July 10, 1963

Guys And Dolls (Reprise) - (Frank Loesser)
July 24, 1963

Gypsy, The (Billy Reid)
June 13, 1962

Hallelujah, I Love Her So (Ray Charles)
February 24, 1969

Have You Met Miss Jones (Richard Rodgers - Lorenz Hart)
December 20, 1960; May 18, 1961

Have Yourself A Merry Little Christmas (Hugh Martin - Ralph Blane)
October 13, 1963

Hello Dolly (Jerry Herman)
June 10, 1964

Hello Young Lovers (Richard Rodgers - Oscar Hammerstein II)
April 13, 1965

Here's To The Ladies (Earl Brent)
February, 1977

Here's To The Losers (Bob Wells - Segal)
July 31, 1963

House I Live In, The (Lewis Allen - Earl Robinson)
February 4, 1964; October 13, 1974

How Insensitive (Antonio Carlos Jobim - Norman Gimbel - Vinicius
Demoraes
February 1, 1967

How Little We Know (Carolyn Leigh - Philip Springer)
April 30, 1963

How Old Am I (Gordon Jenkins)
April 14, 1965

Hungry Years, The (Neil Sadaka - Howard Greenfield)
Late 1976

Hurt Doesn't Go Away, The (Joe Raposo)
June 5, 1973

I Believe I'm Gonna Love You (Gloria Sklerov - Harry Lloyd)
February 24, 1975

I Believe In You (Frank Loesser)
June 9, 1964

I Can't Believe I'm Losing You (Don Costa - Zeller)
April 8, 1964

I Can't Believe It's Over (Frankie Randle)
March 11, 1977

I Can't Stop Loving You (Don Gibson)
June 12, 1964

I Concentrate On You (Cole Porter)
January 30, 1967

If (David Gates)
February 4, 1974

If I Had You (Ted Shapiro - Jimmy Campbell - Reg Connelly)
June 12, 1962

If You Could Read My Mind
May 21, 1974

If You Go Away (Rod McKuen - Jacques Brel)
February 20, 1969

If You Never Come To Me (Antonio Carlos Jobim - Ray Gilbert)
January 31, 1967

I Get A Kick Out Of You (Cole Porter)
April 10, 1962; October 13, 1974

I Hadn't Anyone Till You (Ray Noble)
November 20, 1961

I Have Dreamed (Richard Rodgers - Oscar Hammerstein II)
February 19, 1963

I Heard The Bells On Christmas Day (Johnny Marks - Henry Longfellow)
June 16, 1964

I Left My Heart In San Francisco (Doughlass Cross - George Cory)
August 27, 1962

I Like The Sunrise (Duke Ellington)
December 12, 1967

I Like To Lead When I Dance (Sammy Cahn - Jimmy Van Heusen)
April 8, 1964

I'll Be Seeing You (Sammy Fain - Irving Kahal)
March 21, 1961; May 1, 1961

I'll Follow My Secret Heart (Noel Coward)
June 12, 1962

I'll Never Smile Again (Ruth Lowe)
October 11, 1965; October 21, 1965

I'll Only Miss Her When I Think Of Her (Sammy Cahn - Jimmy Van Heusen)
August 23, 1965

I Love My Wife (Cy Coleman - Michael Stewart)
September, 1976

I Love You (Cole Porter)
April 10, 1962

Imagination (Johnny Burke - Jimmy Van Heusen)
March 12, 1961; May 1, 1961

I'm Beginning To See The Light (Harry James - Duke Ellington - Johnny Hodges - Don George)
April 10, 1962

I'm Getting Sentimental Over You (Ned Washington - George Bassman)
March 21, 1961; May 1, 1961

I'm Gonna Make It All The Way (Floyd Huddleston)
December 10, 1973

I'm Gonna Sit Right Down And Write Myself A Letter (Victor Young - Fred Ahlert)
October 3, 1962

I'm Not Afraid (Rod McKuen - Jacques Brel)
October 28, 1970

Impossible Dream, The (Mitch Leigh - Joe Darion)
November 18, 1966

Indian Summer (Victor Herbert - Al Dubin)
December 11, 1967

Indiscreet (Sammy Cahn - Jimmy Van Heusen)
January 16, 1962

I Never Knew (Gus Kahn - Ted Fiorita)
May 19, 1961

In The Blue Of Evening (Tom Adair - Alfred D'Artega)
March 21, 1961

In The Cool, Cool, Cool Of The Evening (Johnny Mercer - Hoagy
 Carmichael)
January 27, 1964

In The Still Of The Night (Cole Porter)
December 19, 1960

In The Wee Small Hours (Dave Mann - Bob Hilliard)
April 29, 1963

I Only Have Eyes For You (Al Dubin - Harry Warren)
October 3, 1962

I See It Now (Alec Wilder - Engvick)
April 14, 1965

I Sing The Songs (Bruce Johnston)
January 21, 1976

It Gets Lonely Early (Sammy Cahn - Jimmy Van Heusen)
April 22, 1965

It Might As Well Be Spring (Richard Rodgers - Oscar Hammerstein II)
November 21, 1961; January 28, 1964

It's Always You (Johnny Burke - Jimmy Van Heusen)
May 3, 1961

It's A Wonderful World (Jan Savitt - Harold Adamson - Leo Watson)
May 19, 1961

It Started All Over Again (Carl Fischer - Bill Carey)
May 3, 1961

It Was A Very Good Year (Irvin Drake)
April 22, 1965; January 27, 1966

I've Been To Town (Rod McKuen)
March 19, 1969

I've Got A Crush On You (George & Ira Gershwin)
January 26, 1966

I've Got My Love To Keep Me Warm (Irving Berlin)
December 20, 1960

I've Got You Under My Skin (Cole Porter)
April 3, 1963; January 26, 1966; October 13, 1974

I've Never Been In Love Before (Frank Loesser)
July 18, 1963

I Wanna Be Around (Johnny Mercer - Sadie Vimmerstedt)
June 9, 1964

I Will Drink The Wine (Paul Ryan)
October 26, 1970

I Will Wait For You (Michael Le Grand - Norman Gimbel)
November 18, 1966

I Wished On The Moon (Dorothy Parker - Ralph Rainger)
November 30, 1965

I Wish You Love (Charles Trenet - Albert Beach)
June 10, 1964

I Won't Dance (Jerome Kern)
October 2, 1962

I Would Be In Love (Anyway) (Bob Gaudio - Jake Holmes)
July 14, 1969

I Wouldn't Trade Christmas (Sammy Cahn - Jimmy Van Heusen)
August 12, 1968

Josephine
August, 1977

Just As Though You Were Here (Eddie De Lange - John Brooks)
September 24, 1974

Lady Day (Bob Gaudio - Jake Homes)
July 17, 1969; October 13, 1969; November 7, 1969

Lady Is A Tramp, The (Richard Rodgers - Lorenz Hart)
October 13, 1977

Last Dance, The (Sammy Cahn - Jimmy Van Heusen)
December 21, 1960

Last Night When We Were Young (Yip Harburg - Harold Arlen)
April 13, 1965

Laura (Johnny Mercer - David Raskin)
March 9, 1977

Learnin' The Blues (Dolores Vicki Silvers)
October 2, 1962

Leaving On A Jet Plane (John Denver)
October 29, 1970

Lenora (Sammy Cahn - Jimmy Van Heusen)
August, 1977

Let Me Try Again (Paul Anka - Michelle Caravelli - Sammy Cahn)
June 21, 1973; October 13, 1974

Lets Face The Music And Dance (Irving Berlin)
December 19, 1960

LEts Fall In Love (Harold Arlen - Ted Koehler)
December 19, 1960

Let Us Break Bread Together
February 4, 1964

Life's A Trippy Thing (Linda Laurie - Howard Greenfield)
November 2, 1970

Like A Sad Song (John Denver)
December, 1976

Linda (Jack Lawrence - Ann Ronell)
February, 1977

Little Drummer Boy (See Carol Of The Drums)

Little Green Apples (Bobby Russell)
November 12, 1968

London By Night (Carroll Coates)
June 13, 1962

Lonesome Cities (Rod McKuen)
March 19, 1969

Looking At The World Through Rose Colored Glasses (Jimmy Steiger -
 Tommy Malie)
October 3, 1962

Look Of Love, The (Sammy Cahn - Jimmy Van Heusen)
August 27, 1962

Lost In The Stars (Kurt Weill - Maxwell Anderson)
February 18, 1963

Love And Marriage (Sammy Cahn - Jimmy Van Heusen)
October 11, 1965; October 21, 1965

Love Is A Many Splendored Thing (Paul Frances Webster - Sammy Fain)
January 28, 1964

Love Is Just Around The Corner (Leo Robin - Lewis Gensler)
April 10, 1962

Love Isn't Just For The Young (Miller - Kane)
July 31, 1963

Love's Been Good To Me (Rod McKuen)
March 20, 1969

Love Walked In (George & Ira Gershwin)
May 18, 1961

Luck Be A Lady (Frank Loesser)
July 24, 1963; January 27, 1966

Man Alone, A (Rod McKuen)
March 20, 1969

Man Alone, A (Reprise) (Rod McKuen)
March 20, 1969

Man In The Looking Glass, The (Bart Howard)
April 22, 1965

Me And My Shadow (Al Jolson - Dave Dryer)
October 22, 1962

Meditation (Antonio Carlos Jobim - Norman Gimbel - Newton Mendonea)
January 31, 1967

Michael And Peter (Bob Gaudio - Jake Holmes)
July 15, 1969; October 13, 1969

Michelle (John Lennon - Paul Mc Cartney)
August, 1977

Mister Booze (Sammy Cahn - Jimmy Van Heusen)
April 10, 1964

Misty (Johnny Burke - Errol Garner)
November 21, 1961

Moment To Moment (Johnny Mercer - Henry Mancini)
September 14, 1965; October 21, 1965

Moody River (Gary Bruce)
November 13, 1968

Moon Got In My Eyes, The (Johnny Burke - Arthur Johnston)
November 29, 1965

Moonlight Becomes You (Johnny Burke - Jimmy Van Heusen)
November 30, 1965

Moonlight Mood (Harold Adamson - Peter De Rose)
November 30, 1965

Moonlight On The Ganges (Chester Wallace - Sherman Myers)
May 17, 1961; May 23, 1961

Moonlight Serenade (Mitchell Parish - Glenn Miller)
November 29, 1965

Moon Love (Mack David - Andre Kostelanetz) (Based on Theme of
Tschaikowsky)
November 29, 1965

Moon River (Johnny Mercer - Henry Mancini)
January 28, 1964

Moon Song (Arthur Johnston - Sam Coslow)
November 29, 1965

Moon Was Yellow, The (Edgar Leslie - Fred Ahlert)
November 30, 1965

More (Riz Ortolani - Oliviero)
June 12, 1964

Most Beautiful Girl In The World, The (Richard Rodgers - Lorenz Hart)
May 11, 1966

Mrs. Robinson (Paul Simon)
February 24, 1969

My Baby Just Cares For Me (Gus Kahn - Walter Donaldson)
May 11, 1966

My Heart Stood Still (Richard Rodgers - Lorenz Hart)
February 18, 1963

My Kind Of Girl (Leslie Bricusse)
October 3, 1962

My Kind Of Town (Sammy Cahn - Jimmy Van Heusen)
April 8, 1964; January 28, 1966; October 13, 1974

My Little Angel (John Denver)
October 16, 1975

My Sweet Lady (John Denver)
October 26, 1970

My Way (Paul Anka - C. Francois - Gilles Thibault - J. Revaix)
December 30, 1968, October 13, 1974

My Way Of Life (Bert Kaempfert - Carl Sigman - Herbert Rehbein)
July 24, 1968

Name It And It's Yours (Sammy Cahn - Jimmy Van Heusen)
November 23, 1961

Nancy (Phil Silvers - Jimmy Van Heusen)
April 29, 1963; March 9, 1977

Never Gonna Fall In Love Again (Eric Carmen)
Late, 1976

Nice Work If You Can Get It (George & Ira Gershwin)
October 2, 1962

Night (Rod McKuen)
March 21, 1969

Night And Day (Cole Porter)
November 22, 1961; February, 1977

Nightingale Sang In Berkley Square, The (Eric Maschwitz - Manning
Sherwin)
June 13, 1962

Nina Never Knew (Milton Drake - Louis Alter)
February, 1977

Noah (Joe Raposo)
June 4, 1973

Nobody Wins (Kris Kristofferson)
June 5, 1973

Nothing But The Best (Rotella)
February 27, 1962

Now Is The Hour (Maewa Kaihau - Dorothy Stewart - Clement Scott)
June 14, 1962

Off Key (Desafinado) (Antonio Carlos Jobim - Gene Lees - Newton
Mendonca)
February 12, 1969

Oh Babe What Would You Say (Hurricane Smith)
February 4, 1975

Oh How I Miss You Tonight (Benny Davis - Joe Burke - Mark Fisher)
January 17, 1962

Oh What It Seemed To Be (Stephan Weiss - Bennie Benjamin - Frankie Carle)
April 30, 1963

Oh You Crazy Moon (Johnny Burke - Jimmy Van Heusen)
November 30, 1965

Old Devil Moon (Yip Harburg - Burton Lane)
July 18, 1963

Oldest Established, The (Frank Loesser)
July 29, 1963

Old Fashioned Christmas, An
June 16, 1964

Ol' Man River (Jerome Kern - Oscar Hammerstein II)
February 18, 1963

On A Clear Day (Allan Lerner - Burton Lane)
May 16, 1966

Once I Loved (Antonio Carlos Jobim - Vinicius Demoraes - Norman Gimbel)
February 1, 1967

Once Upon A Time (Lee Adams - Charles Strouse)
April 14, 1965

One For My Baby (Harold Arlen - Johnny Mercer)
January 28, 1966

One I Loved, The (Gus Kahn - Isham Jones)
May 3, 1961

One Note Samba (Antonio Carlos Jobim - Newton Mendonca)
February 11, 1969

Only Couple On The Floor, The (John Durrill)
February 20, 1975

Out Beyond The Window (Rod McKuen)
March 21, 1969

Pass Me By (Carolyn Leigh - Cy Coleman)
October 4, 1964

Pennies From Heaven (Johnny Burke - Arthur Johnston)
October 3, 1962

Pick Yourself Up (Jerome Kern - Dorothy Fields)
April 11, 1962

Please Be Kind (Sammy Cahn - Saul Chaplin)
October 2, 1962

Please Don't Talk About Me When I'm Gone (Sam Stept - Sidney Clare)
May 18, 1961

Pocketful Of Miracles (Sammy Cahn - Jimmy Van Heusen)
November 23, 1961

Polka Dots and Moonbeams (Johnny Burke - Jimmy Van Heusen)
March 20, 1961; May 2, 1961

Poor Butterfly (John Golden - Raymond Hubbell)
December 12, 1967

Pretty Colors (Al Giorgoni - Chip Taylor)
November 13, 1968

Prisoner Of Love (Leo Robin - Clarence Gaskill - Russ Columbo)
November 21, 1961

Put Your Dreams Away (Ruth Lowe - Stephen Weiss - Paul Mann)
April 30, 1963

Quiet Nights Of Quiet Stars (Antonio Carlos Jobim - Gene Lees)
January 31, 1967

Rain In My Heart (Teddy Randazzo - Vinny Pike)
November 14, 1968

Reaching For The Moon (Irving Berlin)
November 29, 1965

Remember (Irving Berlin)
January 16, 1962

Ring-A-Ding Ding (Sammy Cahn - Jimmy Van Heusen)
December 19, 1960

Roses Of Picardy (Frederick Weatherly - Haydn Wood)
June 13, 1962

Ruby (Mitchell Parish - Heinz Roemheld)
August, 1977

Saddest Thing Of All, The (Michael Le Grand - Carl Sigman - Eddie Barclay)
September 24, 1974; September 4, 1975

Sand And Sea (Gilbert Becaud - Mike Vidalin - Mack David)
November 18, 1966

Satisfy Me One More Time (Floyd Huddleston)
May 21, 1974

Second Time Around, The (Sammy Cahn - Jimmy Van Heusen)
December 21, 1960; April 29, 1963

Secret Love (Paul Francis Webster - Sammy Fain)
January 28, 1964

See The Show Again (Barry Manilow)
January 17, 1977

Send In The Clowns (Stephen Sondheim)
June 22, 1973; January 21, 1976

September Of My Years, The (Sammy Cahn - Jimmy Van Heusen)
May 27, 1965; January 26, 1965

September Song (Kurtweill - Maxwell Anderson)
April 13, 1965

Serenade In Blue (Mack Gordon - Harry Warren)
April 11, 1962

Shadow Of Your Smile, The (Paul Francis Webster - Johnny Mandel)
January 27, 1966

She Says (Bob Gaudio - Jake Holmes)
July 15, 1969

She Believes In Me (Baker Knight)
August 25, 1966

Since Marie Has Left Paree
June 19, 1964

Single Man, The (Rod McKuen)
March 19, 1969

Softly, As I Leave You (Hal Shaper - Angelo De Vita - Nick Calabrese)
June 19, 1964

So In Love (Cole Porter)
July 24, 1963

Sololoquy (Richard Rodgers - Oscar Hammerstein II)
February 21, 1963

Some Enchanted Evening (Richard Rodgers - Oscar Hammerstein II)
July 24, 1963; July 31, 1963; July 24, 1967

Someone To Light Up My Life (Antonio Carlos Jobim - Gene Lees - Vinicius Demoraes)
February 12, 1969

Something (George Harrison)
October 28, 1970

Something Stupid (C. Carson Parks)
February 1, 1967

Some Traveling Music (Rod McKuen)
March 21, 1969

Somewhere In Your Heart (Russell Faith - Clarence Kehner)
November 11, 1964

Somewhere My Love (Lara's Theme) (Paul Francis Webster - Maurice Jarre)
November 17, 1966

Song Is Ended, The (Irving Berlin)
January 15, 1969

Song Of The Sabia, The (Antonio Carlos Jobim - Norman Gimbel - Chico Hollanda)
February 13, 1969

Sorry Is The Hardest Word
Early February 1977

Star (Sammy Cahn - Jimmy Van Heusen)
November 11, 1968

Stardust (Verse only) (Hoagy Carmichael - Mitchell Parish)
November 20, 1961

Stargazer (Neil Diamond)
May 7, 1976

Stay With Me (Theme from "The Cardinal") (Carolyn Leigh - Jerome Moross)
December 3, 1963

Stella By Starlight (Ned Washington - Victor Young)
August, 1977

Strangers In The Night (Bert Kaempfert - Charles Singleton - Eddie Synder)
April 11, 1966

Street Of Dreams (Sam Lewis - Victor Young)
January 27, 1966

Style (Sammy Cahn - Jimmy Van Heusen)
April 10, 1964

Summer Knows, The (Alan & Marilyn Bergman - Michel Le Grand)
February 4, 1974

Summer Wind, The (Johnny Mercer - Henry Mayer)
May 16, 1966

Summit, The (Comedy Routine)
November 18, 1965

Sunny (Bobby Hebb)
December 12, 1967

Sunrise In The Morning (Paul Ryan)
October 28, 1970

Sweet Caroline (Neil Diamond)
May 8, 1974

Sweet Georgia Brown (Ben Bernie - Maceo Pinkard - Kenneth Casey)
February, 1977

Sweet Lorraine (Mitchell Parish - Cliff Burwell)
February, 1977

Swinging On A Star (Johnny Burke - Jimmy Van Heusen)
January 27, 1964

Take Me (Rube Bloom - Mack David)
March 20, 1961; May 1, 1961

Talk To Me Baby (Johnny Mercer - Dolan)
December 3, 1963

Tangerene (Johnny Mercer - Victor Schertizinger)
April 11, 1962

Tell Her (You Love Her Each Day) (Gil Ward)
April 14, 1965

Tender Trap, The (Sammy Cahn - Jimmy Van Heusen)
October 3, 1962

That's All (Bob Haymes - Alan Brandt)
November 21, 1961

That's Life (Dean Kay - Kelly Gordon)
August 25, 1966; October 18, 1966

That Old Black Magic (Johnny Mercer - Harold Arlen)
February 4, 1975

There Are Such Things (George Meyer - Stanley Adams - Abel Baer)
March 21, 1961; May 3, 1961

There Used To Be A Ballpark (Joe Raposo)
June 22, 1973

The Can't Take That Away From Me (George & Ira Gershwin)
April 10, 1962

This Happy Madness (Antonio Carlos Jobim - Gene Lees - Vinicius Demoraes)
February 13, 1969

This Is All I Ask (Gordon Jenkins)
April 22, 1965

This Is My Love (Jim Harbert)
July 24, 1967

This Is My Song (Charles Chaplin)
July 24, 1967

This Nearly Was Mine (Richard Rodgers - Oscar Hammerstein II)
February 19, 1963

This Town (Lee Hazelwood)
June 29, 1967; July 24, 1967

Three Coins In The Fountain (Sammy Cahn - Jule Styne)
January 27, 1964

Tie A Yellow Ribbon 'Round The Old Oak Tree (Irwin Levine - L. Russell
 Brown)
May 21, 1974

Tina (Sammy Cahn - Jimmy Van Heusen)
December 21, 1960; March 9, 1977

Together (Buddy De Sylva - Lew Brown - Ray Henderson)
January 16, 1962

Train, The (Bob Gaudio - Jake Holmes)
July 14, 1969

Triste (Antonio Carlos Jobim)
February 13, 1969

Twelve Days Of Christmas, The (Traditional - Adopted by Sammy Cahn &
 Jimmy Van Heusen)
.August 12, 1968

Twin Soliloquies (Wonder How It Feels) (Richard Rodgers - Oscar
Hammerstein II)
July 31, 1963

Very Thought Of You, The (Ray Noble)
June 12, 1962

Wait By The Fire
November 14, 1968

Walk Away
June 22, 1973

Wandering (Gayle Caldwell)
November 14, 1968

Watch What Happens (Michel Le Grand - Norman Gimbel)
February 24, 1969

Watertown (Bob Gaudio - Jake Holmes)
July 14, 1969

Where Or When (Richard Rodgers - Lorenz Hart)
January 29, 1966

Winchester Cathedral (Geoff Stephens)
November 17, 1966

Winners (Joe Raposo)
June 21, 1973

Witchcraft (Carolyn Leigh - Cy Coleman)
April 30, 1963

Without A Song (William Rose - Edward Eliseu - Vincent Youmans)
March 20, 1961; May 2, 1961

Wives And Lovers (Hal David - Burt Bacharach)
June 12, 1964

World We Knew, The (Bert Kaempfert - Carl Sigman - Herbert Rehbein)
June 29, 1967

Yellow Days (Alvarro Carrillo - Alan Bernstein)
December 11, 1967

Yes Sir, That's My Baby (Gus Kahn - Walter Donaldson)
May 11, 1966

Yesterday (John Lennon - Paul Mc Cartney)
February 20, 1969

Yesterday's (Jerome Kern - Otto Harbach)
November 20, 1961

You And The Night And The Music (Howard Dietz - Arthur Schwartz)
December 30, 1960

You Are There (Harry Sukeman - Paul Francis Webster)
June 29, 1967

You Are The Sunshine Of My Life (Steve Wonder)
May 19, 1974; February 4, 1975; October 13, 1974

You Brought A New Kind Of Love To Me (Irving Kahal - Sammy Fain)
February 21, 1963

You'll Never Walk Alone (Richard Rodgers - Oscar Hammerstein II)
February 19, 1963

You Make Me Feel So Young (Mack Gordon - Joseph Myrow)
January 27, 1966

You Never Had It So Good (Sammy Cahn - Jimmy Van Heusen)
February 4, 1964

Wave (Parts I and II) (Antonio Carlos Jobim)
February 14, 1969

Way You Look Tonight, The (Jerome Kern - Dorothy Fields)
January 27, 1964

We'll Gather Lilacs In The Spring (Ivor Novello)
June 14, 1962

We'll Meet Again (Parker - Charles)
June 14, 1962

We Open In Venice (Cole Porter)
July 10, 1963

We Wish You The Merriest (Les Brown)
June 17, 1964

What A Funny Girl You Used To Be (Bob Gaudio - Jake Holmes)
July 17, 1969

What Are You Doing The Rest Of Your Life? (Alan & Marilyn Bergman -
Michel Le Grand)
May 21, 1974

Whatever Happened To Christmas (Jimmy Webb)
July 24, 1968

What'll I Do (Irving Berlin)
January 17, 1962

What Now My Love (Carl Sigman - Peter De Lanoe - Gilbert Becaud)
November 17, 1966

What's Now Is Now (Bob Gaudio - Jake Holmes)
July 15, 1969

When I Lost You (Irving Berlin)
January 15, 1962

When I'm Not Near The Girl That I Love (Yip Harburg - Burton Lane)
July 18, 1963

When I Take My Sugar To Tea (Sammy Fain - Irving Kahal - Pierre Norman)
December 20, 1960

When Joanna Loved Me
February, 1977

When Somebody Loves You (Sammy Fain - Irving Kahal - Pierre Norman)
April 14, 1965

When The Wind Was Green (Don Hunt)
April 14, 1965

Young At Heart (Carolyn Leigh - Johnny Richards)
April 29, 1963

Younger Than Springtime (Richard Rodgers - Oscar Hammerstein II)
September 20, 1967

You're A Lucky Fellow Mr. Smith (Sonny Burke - Raye - Prince)
February 4, 1964

You're Driving Me Crazy (Walter Donaldson)
May 11, 1966

You're Gonna Hear From Me (Dory Previn - Andre Previn)
November 18, 1966

You're Nobody Till Somebody Loves You (Russ Morgan - Larry Stock - James Cavanaugh)
May 17, 1961; May 23, 1961

You're So Right (For Whats Wrong In My Life) - (Teddy Randazzo - V. Pike)
August 20, 1973

You Turned My World Around (Bert Kaempfert - Herbert Rehbein - Kim Carnes - Dave Ellingson)
May 8, 1974

You Will Be My Music (Joe Raposo)
June 4, 1973

Zing, Went The Strings Of My Heart (James Hanley)
December 20, 1960

INDEX OF ORCHESTRAS, ARRANGERS, COMPOSERS, SOLOISTS, VOCALISTS AND VOCAL GROUPS
CHAPTER IX - REPRISE RECORDINGS

Barnum, H.B. - Arranger, Conductor
July 24, 1967

Basie, Count (William) - Orchestra Leader, Pianist
October 2, 3, 1962; June 9, 10, 1964; January 26, 27, 28, 1966

Beck, Joe - Arranger, Conductor
February, 1977

Brown, Lawrence - Trombone
December 11, 12, 1967

Butera, Sam - Tenor Sax Soloist
May 1976

Calello, Charles - Arranger, Conductor
July 15, 17, 1969; October 13, 1969; January 17, 1977; February 14, 1977

Candoli, Conte - Trumpet
April 10, 11, 1962

Capps, Al - Arranger, Conductor
February 24, 1975

Clooney, Rosemary - Vocalist
July 24, 1963

Costa, Don - Arranger, Conductor, Composer
November 20, 21, 22, 1961; December 3, 1963; April 18, 1964; July 24, 1968;
November 12, 13, 14, 1968; December 30, 1968; February 13, 20, 24, 1969;
March 19, 20, 21, 1969; June 18, 1969; November 7, October 26, 27, 28, 29, 1970;
June 21, August 20, December 10, 1973; May 8, 9, 21, 1974; December 4, 1974;
February 4, 20, 1975; October 16, 1975; January 21, 1976

Crosby, Bing - Vocalist
July 29, 1963; February 4, 1964; April 10, 1964; June 17, 1964

Davis, Sammy - Vocalist
July 10, 1963; April 10, 1964

Deodato, Eumer - Arranger
February 11, 12, 13, 1969

Dixon, Eric - Tenor Sax
October 2, 3, 1962, June 9, 19, 1964

Edison, Harry - Trumpet Soloist
June 9, 10, 1964

Ellington, Duke (Edward) - Orchestra Leader, Composer
December 11, 12, 1967

Fagerquist, Don - Trumpet Soloist
December 19, 20, 1960

Farnon, Robert - Arranger, Conductor
June 12, 13, 14, 1962

Foster, Frank - Tenor Sax
October 2, 3, 1962; June 9, 10, 1964

Freeman, Ernie - Arranger, Conductor
June 19, November 11, 1964; April 14, May 6, 1965; April 11, 1966; October 18, 1966; November 17, 18, 1966; June 29, 1967; July 24, 1967

Gonsalves, Paul - Tenor Sax Soloist
December 11, 12, 1967

Grau, Gil - Arranger, Conductor
October 13, 1963

Greene, Freddy - Guitar
October 2, 3, 1962, June 9, 10, 1964

Halloran, Jack - Arranger
February 4, 1964

Hefti, Neal - Arranger, Conductor
February 27, 1962; April 10, 11, 1962; August 27, 1962

Herman, Woody - Orchestra Leader
October 13, 1974

Hodges, Johnny - Alto Sax Soloist
December 11, 12, 1967

Jenkins, Gordon - Arranger, Conductor, Composer
January 15, 16, 17, 1962; April 13, 14, 22, 1965; May 27, 1965; June 29, 1967; July 24, 1967; June 4, 5, 21, 22, 1973; August 20, 1973; February 4, 1974; September 24, 1974; September 1975

Jobim, Antonio Carlos - Vocalist, Composer
January 30, 31, 1967; February 1, 1967; February 12, 1969

Jones, Quincy - Arranger, Conductor
June 9, 10, 1964, January 26, 27, 28, 1966

Jones, Thad - Trumpet
October 2, 3, 1962

Joyce Singers, Jimmy - Vocal Group
August 12, 1968

Maini, Joe - Alto Sax
April 10, 11, 1962

Mandel, Johnny - Arranger, Conductor, Composer
December 19, 1960; December 20, 1960

Martin, Dean - Vocalist
July 10, 24, 29, 1963; April 10, 1964

May, Billy - Arranger, Conductor
May 17, 18, 19, 23, 1961; October 22, 1962; July 10, 24, 19, 1963; October 4, 1964;
October 11, 1965; December 11, 12, 1967; May 1976

McKibbon, Al - Bass
April 10, 11, 1962

Miller, Bill - Pianist, Conductor
Pianist on most sessions; Conductor on few occasions

Ogerman, Claus - Arranger, Conductor
January 30, 31, 1967; February 1, 1967; December 1976

Oliver, Sy - Arranger, Vocalist, Conductor
March 21, 1961; May 1, 2, 3, 1961

Paich, Marty - Arranger, Conductor
July 31, 1963

Payne, Sunny - Drums
October 2, 3, 1962; June 9, 10, 1964

Rhodes, Chalmus, Rhodes - Vocal Group
December 4, 1974

Richards, Emil - Vibraphonist
December 19, 20, 1960

Riddle, Nelson - Orchestra Leader, Arranger, Conductor
November 23, 1961; January 21, 1963; February 18, 19, 20, 21, 1963; April 29, 30,
1963; July 18, 24, 29, 31, 1963; January 27, 28, 1964; April 8, 10, 1964; October 4,
1964; August 23, 1965; September 14, 1965; October 11, 1965; November 29, 30,
1965; May 11, 16, 1966; August 12, 1968; November 11, 1968; September, 1976
February 14, 1977; March 9, 1977; August, 1977

Ringwald, Roy - Arranger
February 4, 1964

Rosolino, Frank - Trombone
December 19, 20, 1960

Scott, Joseph - Arranger, Conductor, Composer
July 14, 15, 1969

Shank, Bud - Flute, Alto Sax
December 19, 20, 1960

Sinatra, Frank, Jr., - Vocalist
August 12, 1968

Sinatra, Nancy - Vocalist
August 12, 1968; November 2, 1970

Sinatra, Tina - Vocalist
August 12, 1968

Slatkin, Felix - Conductor, Arranger
December 21, 1960

Smith, Keely - Vocalist
July 24, 1963; July 31, 1963

Stoloff, Morris - Conductor, Arranger
July 10, 1963; February 11, 12, 13, 1969

Strange, Billy - Arranger, Conductor
February 1, 1967; June 29, 1967; July 24, 1967; September 20, 1967

Stulz, Freddie (same as Freddie Stulce from Dorsey days?) - Arranger
October 11, 1965

Waring, Fred - Orchestra Leader
February 4, 1964; June 16, 17, 1964

Webster, Ben - Tenor Sax
April 10, 11, 1962

Wess, Frank - Tenor Sax, Flute Soloist
October 2, 3, 1962; June 9, 10, 1964

Zito, Torrie - Arranger, Conductor
August 23, 1965

Chapter X

TELEVISION APPEARANCES

May 27, 1950	**Television Debut**	NBC

"Star Spangled Revue" - Sinatra is guest star along with Bob Hope and Beatrice Lillie.

October 7, 1950	**"The Frank Sinatra Show"**	CBS

Orchestra Conducted by Axel Stordahl

This first show of his own on television was a half-hour variety series which were sponsored by Bulova Watch Corporation. Later in 1951, the show was expanded to a full hour and sponsored by Echo Housewares. The opening show had Perry Como as special guest star along with J. Carol Nash.

October 14, 1950 - With Brian Aherne, Condos and Brandon.
October 21, 1950 - With Mary McCarty, Lou Wills and Vocal Group, The The Whippoorwills
October 28, 1950 - With Kay Thompson, Buster Shaver, The Blue Family and Mary Mayo.
November 4, 1950 - With Nancy Walker, Teddy Hale.
November 11, 1950 - With The Whippoorwills
November 18, 1950 - With The Whippoorwills
November 25, 1950 - With Sarah Vaughan, Johnny Coy.

November 28, 1950	**"Texaco Star Theatre"**	NBC

At this point Sinatra appears in a light comedy sketch with Milton Berle and Tallulah Bankhead.

Back to **"Frank Sinatra Show"** on CBS

December 2, 1950 - With Whippoorwills
December 9, 1950 - With Jackie Gleason, Joe Bushkin
December 16, 1950 - With Phil Silvers and Whippoorwills
December 23, 1950 - With Whippoorwills
December 30, 1950 - With Gary Moore

January 6, 1951 - With June Hutton, Buster West and Vocal Group, The Heathertones. *
January 13, 1951 - With Jackie Gleason, June Hutton and the Heathertones. *

* This vocal quintet has been called The Hutton Tones in some publications, but in correspondence with musicians and going through actual CBS listings we find that this is the correct name.

January 16, 1951 -	**"Texaco Star Theatre"**	NBC

Sinatra again appears on Milton Berle Show.

Debut of "The Frank Sinatra Show" — 1950.

T.V. special "Our Town" — 1955.

Back again to "Frank Sinatra Show" on CBS

January 20, 1951   - With Phil Foster, Leo Durocher
January 27, 1951   - With Phil Silvers, June Hutton and Ollie.

There'll Be Some Changes Made
Comedy Sketch (with Silvers)
Lets Take An Old Fashioned Walk (with June Hutton)
No Business, Like Show Business (with Phil Silvers)
I'm Always Chasing Rainbows
I'm No Pretender (with Phil Silvers)
They Didn't Believe Me

January 28, 1951 -   **"The Jack Benny Show"**

As special guest along with Faye Emerson and Frank Fontaine.

Again to "Frank Sinatra Show" on CBS

February 3, 1951 -   With Jackie Gleason, June Hutton

It Had To Be You
Take My Love
Zip-A-Dee-Do-Da
Comedy Sketch (with Hutton and Gleason)
Everything Happens To Me
Comedy Sketch (with Gleason)
You'd Be So Nice To Come Home To (with Hutton)

February 10, 1951 -   With Barbara Birtton, June Hutton.

I Love You (with June Hutton)
Comedy Sketch (with Britton)
I've Got A Crush On You
Just Say I Love Her (with Heathertones)
The Night Is Young and You're So Beautiful
   (with June Hutton)

February 17, 1951 -   With Faye Emerson, Skitch Henderson,   Irving
                Kupcinet.

Them There Eyes
If
These Foolish Things
Without A Song
Get Happy
Comedy Sketch (with entire cast)
Why Shouldn't I
Bess, Oh Where's My Bess

February 24, 1951   - With Jean Carroll, Douglas Fairbanks
March 3, 1951   - With Joan Blondell, Don Ameche

March 10, 1951	- With Perry Como, Frankie Laine
March 17, 1951	- With Jackie Gleason, Mary McCarty

It's The Same Old Shillelagh
A Little Bit of Heaven (with June Hutton)
That Old Black Magic
Walking My Baby Back Home
Comedy Sketch (with Gleason and McCarty)
Faithful (with The Heathertones)
Get Happy

March 24, 1951	- With Denise Darcel, Basil Rathbone
March 31, 1951	- With Peggy Lee, Conrad Nagel
April 7, 1951	- With Dagmar, Frank Fontaine, Harry Slate
April 14, 1951	- With Rudy Vallee, The Pied Pipers
April 21, 1951	- With Smith and Dale, Al Bernie
April 28, 1951	- With Dagmar, Frank Fontaine
May 5, 1951	- With Dagmar, Eileen Barton, Joe Bushkin, Tim Herbert, Don Saxon

When You're Smiling
My Romance (with June Hutton)
Comedy Sketch (with Dagmar)
Hello Young Lovers
Oh Look At Me Now
Comedy Sketch (with Rest of Cast)
If

May 12, 1951	- With Jackie Gleason

I Whistle A Happy Tune
Comedy Sketch (with Gleason)
We Kiss In The Shadows
She's Funny That Way

May 19, 1951	- With Phil Silvers, June Hutton
May 26, 1951	- J. Carroll Nash, Phil Foster
June 2, 1951	- With Phil Silvers, June Hutton
June 9, 1951	- With June Hutton, The Heathertones
October 9, 1951	- With Frankie Laine, Perry Como, Andrew Sisters
October 16, 1951	- With Jackie Gleason, Anne Jeffries
October 23, 1951	- With Jack Leonard, Dagmar, Mary McCarty
October 30, 1951	- With Jules Munshin, Georgia Gibbs, Eddie Mayoff
November 6, 1951	- With Jackie Gleason, Pert Kelton
November 13, 1951	- With Jack Benny, Larry Griswald
November 20, 1951	- With Arlene Dahl, George Tobias, Mike Mazurki, Marie Blanchard, Larry Kert, Jimmy Boyd
November 27, 1951	- With Lorraine Day, Leo Durocher

| December 4, 1951 | - With Marie Wilson, June Hutton |
| December 11, 1951 | - With Andrew Sisters, Roger Price |

December 20, 1951   **"The Alan Young Show"**   CBS

Sinatra as special guest.

Back to "Frank Sinatra Show" on CBS

December 25, 1951   - With Edmund Gwenn, Marilyn Maxwell, Jimmy Boyd

January 1, 1952   - With Louis Armstrong, Yvonne De Carlo, and The Three Stooges

Great Day
Comedy Sketch (with The Three Stooges)
Getting To Know You (with Yvonne De Carlo)
Oh Look At Me Now
Lonesome Man Blues (with Louis Armstrong)
Sketch (with entire cast)

January 8, 1952   - With Tennessee Ford, Jimmy Boyd, Alan Young

Lover
Comedy Sketch (with June Hutton)
Penthouse Serenade (with June Hutton)
That Old Black Magic
I'm Gonna Live Till I Die
Comedy Sketch (with entire cast)

January 15, 1952	- With Denise Darcel, Frank Fontaine, Sammy Davis Jr.
January 22, 1952	- With George McManus, Beatrice Kay, Buster Keaton
January 29, 1952	- With Dick Haymes, Tom D'Andrea
February 5, 1952	- With Diana Lynn, Frank Fontaine, Ann Tricola
February 12, 1952	- With Zsa Zsa Gabor, Buster Keaton, and the Delta Rhythm Boys
February 19, 1952	- With James Mason, Jackie Coogan
February 26, 1952	- With Zsa Zsa Gabor, Yma Sumac, Frank Fontaine
March 4, 1952	- With Cass Daley, Liberace

March 6, 1952   **"The Dinah Shore Show"**   NBC
Sinatra as special guest.

Back to "Frank Sinatra Show" on CBS

| March 11, 1952 | - With Andrew Sisters, Jimmy Boyd |
| March 18, 1952 | - With Victor Borge, The Nicholas Bros., Borrah Minevitch and the Harmonica Rascals. |

March 22, 1952   **"The Nick Kenny Show"**   NBC
Sinatra as special guest.

Back to Final "Frank Sinatra Show" on CBS

April 1, 1952 — With Frank Fontaine, Bill Bailey

June 21, 1952 **Bob Hope-Bing Crosby Telecast for** NBC
United States Olympic Committee
With Sinatra as guest.

October 18, 1952 **"All Star Revue"** NBC
Starring Jimmy Durante with Sinatra as special guest.

November 25, 1952 **"Texaco Star Theatre"** NBC
Once again on Milton Berle Show.

June 15, 1953 **"Fords 50th Anniversary Program"** CBS
Sinatra sings "You Go To My Head" on film.

September 29, 1953 **"The Buick Berle Show"** NBC
Sinatra as special guest.

I've Got The World On A String
This Can't Be Love (with M. Berle)
September Song Sketch (with M. Berle)
Lets Do The Town Tonight (with M. Berle, T. Bankhead)
Comedy Sketch (with T. Bankhead)

November 8, 1953 **"Colgate Comedy Hour"** NBC
Orchestra conducted by Al Goodman - starring Ethel Merman. Sinatra plays
Harry Dane in skit "Anything Goes".

You Do Something To Me (with Ethel Merman)
I Get A Kick Out Of You
You're The Top (with Ethel Merman)
Just One Of Those Things
All Through The Night
I Get A Kick Out Of You (with Ethel Merman)

December 25, 1953 **"The Bob Hope Show"**

Jingle Bells
Comedy Sketch (with Bob Hope)
South Of The Border

March 25, 1954 **"26th Annual Academy Awards Presentation"**

Sinatra receives award for best supporting actor of the year for his role of
Maggio in "From Here To Eternity."

November 7, 1954 **"Fanfare"** NBC

The Gal That Got Away
Violets For Your Furs
When I Stop Loving You

March 30, 1955 **"27th Annual Academy Awards"** NBC

April 24, 1955   **"Kaleidoscope"**   NBC
Presented by Max Liebman - Color.
    I'm Gonna Live Till I Die
    When Your Lover Has Gone
    Learnin' The Blues
    Wrap Your Troubles In Dreams
    Comedy Sketch

September 18, 1955   **"The Dean Martin and Jerry Lewis Show"** NBC
For Colgate. Sinatra heard via audio only as he sings a song written especially for the show, a humorous ditty called "Yetta I Can't Forget Her".

September 19, 1955   Producers Showcase Presents - **"Our Town"** NBC
In color. Sinatra plays the key role of stage manager who narrates the story and uses songs to skillfully integrate and express the high points of mood and action. Written by Thorton Wilder, produced by Fred Coe and directed by Valerie Betts. Music by James Van Heusen, Lyrics by Sammy Cahn. Orchestrations by Nelson Riddle.

    Our Town
    Grovers Corners (with Paul Hartman, Ernest Truex)
    The Impatient Years
    Our Town (with chorus)
    Love and Marriage
    Look To Your Heart

December 2, 1955   **"Wide Wide World"**   CBS
    The Tender Trap
    Love and Marriage
Speaks on the International Goodwill Service Cause.

August 19, 1956   **"The Steve Allen Show"**   NBC
Sinatra as guest performer, however, laryngitis prevents him from singing and he pantomines one of his own records.

September 15, 1956   **"The Edward R. Murrow Show"**   CBS
Interview with Sinatra.

October 5, 1956   **"The Chevy Show"**   NBC
Starring Dinah Shore and Dizzy Dean with Sinatra as special guest star - color.

    Ding Dong Ding (with Dinah Shore)
    Hey Jealous Lover
    Smack Dab In The Middle (with Shore and Dean)
    Two Sleepy People (with Shore)
    Remember Me (with Shore)
    You Make Me Feel So Young
    Them There Eyes (with Shore)

April 15, 1957   **"The Bob Hope Show"**

With Sinatra as special guest.

October 13, 1957   **"The Edsel Show"**   CBS

SINATRA MEDLEY -All The Way
Love and Marriage
Baby Won't You Please Come Home
South of the Border

SINATRA - CROSBY MEDLEY - I Love Paris
Sweet Lei Lani
The Road To Morocco

SINATRA - CROSBY MEDLEY - The Sweetheart of Sigma Chi
September Song
There's A Long Long Trail
The Birth of The Blues (with Louis Armstrong)

SINATRA, CROSBY, ROSEMARY CLOONEY MEDLEY
Where The Blue of The Night
I'm Always Chasing Rainbows
I've Got You Under My Skin
I Can't Give You Anything But Love
You Go To My Head
Three Little Words
Three O'clock In The Morning

October 18, 1957   **"The Frank Sinatra Show"**   ABC

With Bob Hope, Peggy Lee, Kim Novak. Orchestra arranged and conducted by
Nelson Riddle.
The Lonesome Road
I Get A Kick Out Of You
Comedy (with Bob Hope)
I Could Write A Book
Pal Joey discussion (with Kim Novak)

The Lady Is A Tramp
The Autumn Leaves
All The Way
Comedy Sketch (with B. Hope & Kim Novak)
Bewitched
Put Your Dreams Away

October 25, 1957   **"The Frank Sinatra Show"**   ABC
Drama - "That Man Hogan" with Sinatra, Jessie White and Reba Waters.

The following are all ABC **"Frank Sinatra Shows"** except where noted.

November 1, 1957   - With Nancy Sinatra, Janie Ross and Belinda Burrell
You'd Be So Nice To Come Home To
The Girl Next Door
I've Got You Under My Skin

With Dean Martin and Mickey Rooney — 1957.

With Jesse White — 1958.

Side By Side (with Nancy & The Girls)
All The Way
Violets For Your Furs
The Lonesome Road

November 8, 1957   - With Peggy Lee
Pennies From Heaven
The Autumn Leaves
Nice Work If You Can Get It (with Peggy Lee)
You Brought A New Kind Of Love To Me
Our Love Is Here To Stay (with Peggy Lee)
I Thought About You
I'll Be Seeing You

November 15, 1957   - With the McGuire Sisters

From This Moment On
Three Coins In The Fountain
Where Are You
I Got It Bad
Something's Gotta Give (with McGuire Sisters)
Baby Won't You Please Come Home

November 22, 1957   - With Erin O' Brien
Wrap Your Troubles In Dreams
Everything Happens To Me
My Funny Valentine
Let's Get Away From It All (with O' Brien)
I Wish I Were In Love Again
I'm Gonna Sit Right Down
She's Funny That Way

November 23, 1957   **"Texaco Star Theatre"**
Ethel Barrymore Tribute
I've Grown Accustomed To Your Face

November 29, 1957   - With Dean Martin

Night And Day
That Old Devil Moon
SINATRA - MARTIN MEDLEY -
Sunday, Monday Or Always
Saturday Night
The Girl That I Marry
I've Got A Crush On You
Don't Cry Joe (with Martin)
The House I Live In
Put Your Dreams Away

December 6, 1957   Drama - **"A Gun At His Back"**

With Sinatra, Celia Lovsky, Maurice Manson and Sidney Smith

December 6, 1957   Drama - **"Take Me To Hollywood"**
With Sinatra, Celia Lovsky, Maurice Manson and Sidney Smith

December 20, 1957   **"The Frank Sinatra Christmas Show"**   ABC

Special guest, Bing Crosby. Orchestra conducted by Nelson Riddle and the Ralph Brewster Singers.

> Mistletoe and Holly
> Jingle Bells (with Bing Crosby)
> It Came Upon A Midnight Clear
> O' Little Town of Bethlehem (with Crosby)
> Santa Claus Is Coming To Town
> The Christmas Song (with Crosby)
> White Christmas (with Crosby)

December 27, 1957   Drama - **"The Feeling Is Mutual"**

With David Wayne, Janice Rule and Hugh Sanders.

January 3, 1958   - With Dinah Shore

> Come Fly With Me
> April In Paris
> London By Night
> Autumn In New York (with Dinah Shore)
> On The Road To Mandalay
> It's Nice To Go Traveling

January 10, 1958   - With Robert Mitchum and his son Jim.
> I Won't Dance
> Withcraft
> Comedy Sketch (with Mitchum and his son)
> All The Way
> Hey Mr. Mitchum (with Mitchum)
> Hey Jealous Lover

January 17, 1958   - With Louis Prima and Keely Smith

> I'm An Old Cowhand
> Birth Of The Blues (with Keely Smith)
> Bewitched
> I Can't Believe That You're In Love With Me (with K. Smith)
> Put Your Dreams Away

January 18, 1958   **"Club Oasis"**   NBC

Starring Sinatra with Stan Freeberg and Pat Suzuki.

> I've Got The World On A String
> All The Way
> Tell Her I Love Her
> Come Fly With Me

January 24, 1958   - With Joe Stafford

    Wrap Your Troubles In Dreams
    This Love Of Mine
    I'll Never Smile Again (with Jo Stafford)
    SINATRA - STAFFORD MEDLEY
    Street Of Dreams
    Violets For Your Furs
    The One I Love
    Our Love Is Here To Stay

January 26, 1958   **"The Chevy Show"**   NBC

Starring Dinah Shore with Sinatra and Peter Lawford, as guests.

    All The Way
    Tea For Two (with Dinah Shore)
    You Make Me Feel So Young
    A Foggy Day
    Side By Side (with Dinah Shore)

January 31, 1958   - With Sammy Davis Jr.

    The Isle Of Capri
    You Make Me Feel So Young
    Tell Her You Love Her
    Me And My Shadow (with Sammy Davis)
    I've Got You Under My Skin

February 1, 1958   **"Club Oasis"**   NBC

Starring Dean Martin with Sinatra and Danny Thomas as guests.

    When You're Smiling (with Martin and Thomas)
    Last Night When We Were Young
    Squeeze Me (with Martin)
    The Tender Trap
    Three Coins In The Fountain
    Tammy (with Martin and Thomas)

February 7, 1958   - With Jeane Carson

    South Of The Border
    They Can't Take That Away From Me
    From This Moment On
    Witchcraft
    Put Your Dreams Away

February 14, 1958   - With Shirley Jones, Tina Sinatra and Alice Pearce

    I Love You
    P.S. I Love You
    If I Love You (with Shirley Jones)

My Funny Valentine (Singing To Tina)
Put Your Dreams Away

February 21, 1958   Drama - **"A Time To Cry"**

With Anne Bancroft, Lloyd Bridges.

February 28, 1958   - With Van Johnson and Jesse White

Come Fly With Me
There's No You
Comedy Sketch (with Van Johnson)
I Could Write A Book
Nothing In Common (with Van Johnson)
At Long Last Love

March 7, 1958   - With Eydie Adams and Stan Freeberg

I'm Gonna Love Till I Die
This Can't Be Love
All Of Me
I'm Gonna Sit Right Down (with Stan Freeberg)
One For My Baby

March 14, 1958   - With Eydie Gorme and Joey Bishop

It Happened In Monterey
The Most Beautiful Girl In The World
Comedy Sketch (with Gorme and Bishop)
Moonlight In Vermont
Nature Boy
Where Are You (with Gorme)
How About You (with Gorme)
Saturday Night

March 21, 1958   Drama - **"The Man On The Stairs"**

With Marisa Pavan and Michael Rennie

March 28, 1958   - With Eddie Fisher

Taking A Chance On Love
Time After Time

SINATRA - FISHER MEDLEY -
All The Way
A Foggy Day
Learnin' The Blues
Young At Heart
It's Nice To Go Traveling (with Eddie Fisher)
Put Your Dreams Away

April 4, 1958   - With Spike Jones and Helen Grayco

You Brought A New Kind Of Love To Me
Autumn Leaves
Baby Won't You Please Come Home
Chloe (with Spike Jones)
Too Marvelous For Words

April 18, 1958   Drama - **"The Brownstone Incident"**

With Cloris Leachman, Ann Seymour.

April 25, 1958   - With Ethel Merman

Just One Of Those Things
You're Getting To Be A Habit With Me
Comedy Sketch (with Ethel Merman)
You're The Top (with Ethel Merman)
I Get A Kick Out Of You

May 2, 1958   - Repeat of February 7, 1958 show.

May 9, 1958   - With Ella Fitzgerald

Jeepers Creepers
On The Road To Mandalay
We'll Be Together Again
Moonlight In Vermont (with E. Fitgerald)
I May Be Wrong (with E. Fitzgerald)

May 16, 1958   Drama - **"The Green Grass Of St. Therese"**

With Frank Albertson, Tim Butler, Wally Cox, Anne Barton and Pat Collins.

May 23, 1958   - With Natalie Wood and Pat Suzuki

Night And Day
Lonely Town
I Believe
Them There Eyes (with Natalie Wood)
How Are You Fixed For Love (with Pat Suzuki)
Put Your Dreams Away

May 30, 1958   Drama - **"A Face Of Fear"**

With Glynis Johns, Michael Pate, Eugene Partin and Katherine Warren.

June 6, 1958   Drama - **"The Seedling Doubt"**
With Phyliss Thaxter and MacDonald Carey.

June 13, 1958   Repeat of **"A Gun At His Back"**

June 20, 1958   Repeat of **"Take Me To Hollywood"**

June 27, 1958   Repeat of **"The Feeling Is Mutual"**

September 28, 1958   Repeat of January 24, 1958 Musical Show with Jo Stafford.

March 3, 1959   **"Some Of Manie's Friends"**   NBC

Special color presentation in tribute to the late Manie Sacks - Sinatra seen via videotape.

This Love Of Mine

SINATRA - DINAH SHORE MEDLEY -
You Make Me Feel So Young
A Foggy Day
Taking A Chance On Love
All Of Me
I Can't Give You Anything But Love
You Must Have Been A Beautiful Baby

September 27, 1959   **"The Bing Crosby Show"**   NBC

With Sinatra, Peggy Lee and Louis Armstrong.

We're Glad We're Not Young Anymore (with Crosby, Lee and Armstrong)
Willow Weep For Me
I Love A Piano (with Crosby and Lee)
The One I Love (with Crosby and Lee)
If I Could Be With You
Up A Lazy River

October 19, 1959   **"The Frank Sinatra Timex Show"**   ABC

With Bing Crosby, Dean Martin and Mitzi Gaynor.

High Hopes (with entire cast)
Day In, Day Out
Together (with Crosby and Martin)
Talk To Me
Cheek To Cheek (with Mitzi Gaynor)

SINATRA-CROSBY-MARTIN MEDLEY -
The Good Old Songs
The Old Grey Mare
That Old Feeling
Ol' Man River
Just One Of Those Things
Angel Eyes
The Lady Is A Tramp
Parody of Jimmy Durante Songs (by Sinatra, Martin, Crosby, Gaynor)
It's Gotta Come From The Heart
Who Will Be With You When I Am Far Away
Inka Dinka Do
Bill Bailey

—259—

November 3, 1959   **"Ford's Star Time"**

Dean Martin Show with Sinatra and Mickey Rooney as guests.

> When You're Smiling
> I Can't Get Started With You
> Dream
>
> SINATRA-MARTIN MEDLEY -
> Lover
> Where Or When
> There's A Small Hotel
> This Can't Be Love
> My Funny Valentine
> My Romance
> Soon
> It's Easy To Remember
> Manhattan

December 13, 1959   **"An Afternoon With Frank Sinatra"**   ABC

With Ella Fitzgerald, Peter Lawford, Juliet Prowse, Hermione Gingold, The Hi-Lo's and Red Norvo and His Jazz Group.

> You're Invited To Spend The Afternoon
> I've Got The World On A String
> Come's Love (with Gingold and Lawford)
> It's Alright With Me
> Too Marvelous For Words
> Here's That Rainy Day
> I'll Never Smile Again (with The Hi-Los)
> Can't We Be Friends (with E. Fitgerald)
> Our Love Is Here To Stay
> Love Is Sweeping The Country (with the Entire cast)

February 15, 1960   **"The Frank Sinatra Timex Show"**   ABC

"Here's To The Ladies" with Lena Horne, Mary Costa, Juliet Prowse, Barbara Heller and Eleanor Roosevelt.

> Here's To The Ladies
> I've Got You Under My Skin
> Lonely Town
>
> SINATRA-LENA HORNE MEDLEY -
> It's Only A Paper Moon
> Accentuate The Positive
> Get Happy
> Between The Devil And The Deep Blue Sea
> My Heart Stood Still
> Here's To The Ladies

*With Joey Bishop and
Elvis Presley — 1960.*

With Bing Crosby — 1964.

| May 12, 1960 | "The Frank Sinatra Timex Show" | ABC |

"Welcome Back Elvis" with Elvis Presly, Sammy Davis Jr., Peter Lawford, Nancy Sinatra and Joey Bishop.

    It's Nice To Go Traveling (with entire cast)
    Witchcraft
    Gone With The Wind
    Love Me Tender
    You Make Me Feel So Old (with Nancy Sinatra)
    It's Nice To Go Traveling

| November 1, 1960 | "The Dean Martin Show" | NBC |

With Dorothy Provine, Don Knotts and Sinatra who arrives a half hour late. Orchestra conducted by David Rose.

    Ol' McDonald
    This Is Your Life Sketch (wtih Dean Martin)

    SINATRA-MARTIN MEDLEY -
    This Love Of Mine, I'll Never Smile Again
    Young At Heart
    Ce'st Magnifique
    I Love Paris
    Night And Day
    The Tender Trap
    Learnin' The Blues
    Bewitched
    Love And Marriage
    All Of Me

| November 23, 1960 | "The Perry Como Show" | NBC |

Sinatra reads a letter to Tommy Sands.

| November 30, 1960 | Red Skeleton's Hollywood Tour Broadcast | |

| January 15, 1961 | "The Gershwin Years" | CBS |

Sinatra as special guest in a star studded tribute to George Gershwin.

| February 25, 1962 | "The Judy Garland Show" | CBS |

With Sinatra and Dean Martin as guests.

    Too Marvelous For Words
    You Do Something To Me (with J. Garland)
    I See Your Face Before Me
    The One I Love (with Dean Martin)
    Let There Be Love (with Garland and Martin)
    You're Nobody Till Somebody Loves You (with Garland and Martin)

April 26, 1962   **"The Bob Hope Show"**   NBC

Sinatra as special guest.

    Goody, Goody
    Small Fry (with Bob Hope)

June 2, 1962   **"This Is Sinatra"**   ABC

Taped from a live concert the night before at the Royal Festival Hall in
England.

    Goody, Goody
    Imagination
    At Long Last Love
    Moonlight In Vermont
    Day In, Day Out
    F. S. Monologue
    They Can't Take That Away From Me
    All The Way
    Chicago
    One For My Baby
    The Lady Is A Tramp
    Ol' Man River
    You Make Me Feel So Young
    Nancy
    Come Fly With Me

December 9, 1962   **"The Dinah Shore Show"**   NBC

With Sinatra as special guest.

    SINATRA-SHORE MEDLEY -
    It's A Good Day
    Almost Like Being In Love
    Get It Day
    Please Be Kind
    Autumn In New York

    SINATRA-SHORE MEDLEY -
    Where Or When
    I See Your Face Before Me
    That Face
    You're Sensational
    The Best Things In Life Are Free (with Dinah Shore)

December 8, 1963   **"The Best On Record"**   NBC

Sinatra introduces Steve Lawrence and Eydie Gorme and exchanges quips with
Bing Crosby.

February 15, 1964   **"The Bing Crosby Show"**   CBS

Sinatra as special guest along with Bob Hope, Dean Martin, Kathryn Crosby, Rosemary Clooney and Peter Gennaro. Orchestra conducted by John Scott Trotter. The oldest established floating crap game (with Crosby and Dean Martin).

June 28, 1964   **"The Ed Sullivan Show"**   CBS

With Sinatra as special guest.

July 27, 1964   **"Hollywood And The Stars"**

Brief Sinatra segment as a young teenage idol.

March 14, 1965   **"The Wonderful World of Burlesque"**   NBC

Color. A Danny Thomas comedy special with Sinatra in a brief cameo comedy spot.

April 4, 1965   **"Cavalcade of Amateurs"**   CBS

Includes two filmed segments of Sinatra on the Major Bowes Amateur Hour Show.

September 16, 1965   **"The Dean Martin Show"**   NBC

Sinatra as special guest star.

October 16, 1965   **"The Hollywood Palace"**   ABC

Starring Sinatra as host with Count Basie and his Orchestra, Jack Leonard Peter Gennaro and the Kessler Twins.

     Luck Be A Lady (with Count Basie)

October 18, 1965   **"The Tonight Show"**   NBC

With Sinatra, Joey Bishop, Sammy Davis Jr., Juliet Prowse and Phil Foster.

November 16, 1965   A news special titled **"Sinatra An American Original"**   CBS

Sinatra is interviewed by Walter Cronkite along with a film essay of the life, times and talent of Sinatra. Frank is also seen in the recording studios taping "The September Of My Years" album.

November 24, 1965   **"Frank Sinatra - A Man And His Music"**   NBC

Color. The first of the justly famous full-hour specials as he sings the songs he has been identified with during the past 25 years. This program won a George Foster Peabody Award for television entertainment and an Emmy Award for the outstanding musical program of the year. It was produced by Dwight Hemion with the orchestra conducted by Gordon Jenkins and Nelson Riddle.

     Without A Song

Don't Worry 'Bout Me
I Get A Kick Out Of You
Nancy
My Kind Of Town
It Was A Very Good Year
Young At Heart
The Girl Next Door
Last Night When We Were Young
This Is All I Ask
Come Fly With Me
The Lady Is A Tramp
I've Got You Under My Skin
I've Got The World On A String
Witchcraft
You Make Me Feel So Young
Angel Eyes
Put Your Dreams Away

Repeated on May 16, 1966

November 27, 1966   **"What's My Line"**   CBS

Sinatra is the first mystery guest and then becomes a member of the panel. He correctly guesses Mia Farrow as the celebrity mystery guest.

December 1, 1966   **"The Dean Martin Show"**   NBC

Color. Sinatra appears as surprise guest.

December 7, 1966   **"A Man And His Music"**   CBS

A new full-hour musical program inspired by the great success of Part I. Daughter Nancy is the lone guest. Produced by Dwight Hemion with the orchestra conducted by Nelson Riddle and Gordon Jenkins.

Fly Me To The Moon
The Most Beautiful Girl In The World
Moonlight In Vermont
You're Nobody Till Somebody Loves You
Yes Sir That's My Baby (with Nancy)
These Boots Are Made For Walking (with Nancy)
Downtown (with Nancy)

SINATRA MEDLEY - Just One Of Those Things, My Heart Stood Still, But Beautiful, When Your Lover Has Gone.
Luck Be A Lady
That's Life
Granada
My Kind Of Town

Repeated on April 3, 1967

November 13, 1967   **"A Man And His Music Plus Ella And Jobim"**
                                                                   NBC

Sinatra in a full-hour tribute to rhythm. His third major television presented by Budweiser with Ella Fitzgerald and Antonio Carlos Jobim. Produced by Robert Scheerer with the orchestra conducted by Nelson Riddle.

   Day In, Day Out
   Get Me To The Church On Time
   What Now My Love
   Ol' Man River
   SINATRA-FITZGERALD MEDLEY - Up, Up and Away, Don't Dry Joe, Tony Rome, Going Out Of My Head
   SINATRA-JOBIM MEDLEY - Quiet Nights, Change Partners, I Concentrate On You, The Girl From Ipanema.
   SINATRA-FITZGERALD MEDLEY - The Song Is You, They Can't Take That Away From Me, Stompin At The Savoy.
   At Long Last Love
   The Lady Is A Tramp (with Fitzgerald)

Repeated on April 21, 1968

December 11, 1967   **"Movin' With Nancy"**   NBC

Color. Sinatra is shown in Hollywood singing "Younger Than Springtime".

December 18, 1967   **"The Dean Martin Christmas Show"**   NBC

With the families of Dean Martin and Frank Sinatra.
   Marshmallow World (with Dean Martin)
   We Wish You The Merriest (with both families)
   Do Re Mi (with Dean Martin)
   SINATRA-MARTIN MEDLEY - I Can't Give You Anything But Love, Too Marvelous For Words, Pennies From Heaven, A Foggy Day, Embraceable You, The Lady Is A Tramp, Where Or When, I've Got The World On A String, All Of Me, When You're Smiling.
   Have Yourself A Merry Little Christmas
   Silent Night (with Dean Martin)

May 19, 1968   **Emmy Awards - 20th Anniversary Show.**

May 29, 1968   **"The Bob Hope Birthday Show"**

Sinatra as special guest
   Happy Birthday

October 2, 1968   **"World Series Baseball"**   NBC

Brief interview in stands with Tony Kubek.

November 4, 1968   **Hubert Humphrey Telethon**

November 25, 1968   **"Francis Albert Sinatra Does His Thing"** CBS

Color. Sinatra's fourth full-hour special in as many years, featuring songs old and new. With special guest stars Diahann Carroll and the 5th Dimension Pop Vocal Group. Produced and directed by Saul Ilson and Ernest Chambers. Orchestra conducted by Don Costa.

> Baubles, Bangles and Beads
> Hello Young Lovers
> Cycles
> Lonesome road (with D. Carroll)
> Here's That Rainy Day
> It Never Entered My Mind
> Gone With The Wind
> Sweet Blindness (with The 5th Dimension)
> Nice 'N Easy
> How Little We Know
> Lost In The Stars

January 20, 1969   **"Rowan and Martin's Laugh In"**   NBC

Color. Sinatra in a cameo appearance on film dressed as Artie Johnson's Nazi character and saying "Very Interesting".

February 24, 1969   **Academy Awards Telecast**

Sinatra sings an Oscar nominee song titled - "Star".

October 19, 1969   **"Frank Sinatra with Family and Friends"** CBS

Orchestra conducted by Billy Strange.
> All Or Nothing At All (with Sinatra Jr.)

November 5, 1969   **"Sinatra"**   CBS

Color. This is his fifth full-hour special for Budweiser Beer. Produced by Carolyn Raskin with orchestra conducted by Don Costa.

> For Once In My Life
> Please Be Kind
> My Way
> I Couldn't Sleep A Wink Last Night
> You're Sensational
> All The Way
> The Tender Trap
> Little Green Apples
> Out Beyond The Window (Poem)
> A Man Alone
> Didn't We
> Forget To Remember
> Fly Me To The Moon
> Street Of Dreams
> Love's Been Good To Me

Goin' Out Of My Head
My Kind Of Town

August 24, 1970   German Television - **"Romeo and Juliet - 1970"**

Sinatra is interviewed and two recordings are played - "That's Life" and "Shadow Of The Moon".

September 9, 1970   **"Dinah's Place"**   NBC

Sinatra demonstrates his talent for cooking (preparing his own fresh tomato sauce).
　　Fly Me To The Moon
　　They Can't Take That Away From Me (with Dinah Shore)

November 16, 1970   **"Jack Benny's 20th T.V. Anniversary Special"**
                                                                NBC

Color. Sinatra among many other guest stars.
　　I Get A Kick Out Of You

November 18, 1970   **"Make Room For Grandaddy"**   ABC

Color. Sinatra as guest on Danny Thomas Show.

　　All The Way

December 31, 1970   **"New Years Eve With Dean And Frank"**   NBC

Color. Sinatra as special guest star on Dean Martin Show along with Ruth Buzzi and Actress Kay Medford. Sinatra does impressions of Bogart and Cagney.

　　SINATRA-MARTIN MEDLEY - Love Is Just Around The Corner, My Kind Of Girl, But Beautiful, L.O.V.E., I Get A Kick Out Of You, Goody Goody, Guys And Dolls.
　　SINATRA-MARTIN MEDLEY - What Is This Thing Called Love, Did You Ever See A Dream Walking, I Can't Give You Anything But Love.
　　Comedy Sketch (with Martin)
　　Something
　　New Years Party Sketch (with Martin and Buzzi)
　　SINATRA-MARTIN MEDLEY - Welcome To My World, Now Is The Hour, So Long Its Been Good To Know You, Auld Lang Syne (with the Goldiggers also)

April 15, 1971   **Academy Awards T.V. Show**

Sinatra makes an acceptance speech for the Jean Hersholt Humanitarian Award.

June 16, 1971   - ABC News - Bill Beutel reports on Sinatra
                              "Retirement".

| February 13, 1972 | Bob Hope Desert Golf Classic. | NBC |

February 13, 1972   Bob Hope Desert Golf Classic.   NBC
Sinatra interviewed on golf course.

February 17, 1973   - Public Service T.V. announcement for "Prevent Blindness.

March 27, 1973   **Academy Awards**

Sinatra presents special award to Rosalind Russell.

November 18, 1973   **"Ol' Blue Eyes Is Back"**   NBC

Presented by Magnavox and produced by Howard W. Koeh with Gene Kelly as special guest. Orchestra conducted by Gordon Jenkins and Don Costa.

You Will Be My Music
I Get A Kick Out Of You
Street Of Dreams
I've Got You Under My Skin
I've Got The World On A String
Last Night When We Were Young
Violets For Your Furs
Here's That Rainy Day
We Can't Do That Anymore (with Gene Kelly)
Nice 'N Easy (with Gene Kelly)
Let Me Try Again
Send In The Clowns
You Will Be My Music

November 27, 1973   Show business honors Milton Berle with Sinatra as guest.

March 14, 1974   **"A Salute To James Cagney"**   CBS

The show is hosted by Sinatra and he also sings a parody of "My Way" dedicated to Cagney.

July 9 & July 11, 1974   Television News coverage of Sinatra's Australian Tour.   BBC T.V.

August, 1974   Public Service T.V. Announcement for "Foster Parent Plan".

October 12, 1974   Fred Astaire salutes Fox Musicals

Sinatra is seen in a brief segment as he presents an Academy Award to Alfred Newman.

October 13, 1974   **"Sinatra - The Main Event - Live from Madison Square Garden"**

Produced by Jerry Weintraub with introduction by Howard Cosell. Woody Hermans Thundering Herd conducted by Bill Miller.

With Dionne Warwick — 1975.

Cooking spaghetti on T.V. with host, Dinah Shore - 1970.

The Lady Is A Tramp
I Get A Kick Out Of You
Let Me Try Again
Autumn In New York
I've Got You Under My Skin
Bad, Bad Leroy Brown
Angel Eyes
You Are The Sunshine Of My Life
The House I Live In
My Kind Of Town
My Way

January 19, 1975   **"The Don Rickles Show"**   CBS

Comedy Sketch (with Rickles)

February 17, 1975   **"A Salute To Orson Welles"**   CBS

The show is once again hosted by Sinatra and sings a parody of "The Lady Is A Tramp" dedicated to Welles.

March 9, 1975   **"The Dionne Warwick Special"**

Sinatra and Danny Thomas make cameo appearances.

June 15, 1975   **"United Cerebral Palsy 20 Hour Telethon"**

My Kind Of Town
They Can't Take That Away From Me (with Carol Lawrence)
Happy Fathers Day To You

September 1, 1975   **"Jerry Lewis Telethon"** for the Muscular
                          Dystrophy Association. Sinatra appeared three
                          separate times.

Midnight - E.S.T.
You Are The Sunshine Of My Life
Bad, Bad Leroy Brown
In The Wee Small Hours
I Believe I'm Gonna Love You
They Can't Take That Away From Me
The Lady Is A Tramp

10:00 a.m. - E.S.T.
Nice 'N Easy
Let Me Try Again
I Believe I'm Gonna Love You
Parody Of Nancy
But Beautiful
Where Or When
I've Got You Under My Skin

4:00 p.m. - E.S.T.
Something

I Believe I'm Gonna Love You
Send In The Clowns
This Love Of Mine
I've Got You Under My Skin

September 20, 1975   **"The Howard Cosell Show"**   ABC

Sinatra appears at the beginning and wishes Cosell good luck.

September 27, 1975   **"Bob Hope's 25th Anniversary Show"**   NBC

Sinatra appears in extracts on film from earlier shows.
Parody Of Nancy (April 1951) (subtitled "Goodbye Old Buddy")
Comedy Sketch (with Hope - live)
The Lady Is A Tramp (1957)

November 30, 1975   **"A Conversation With Frank Sinatra"**   NBC

Bill Boggs talks to Frank Sinatra about his recent engagement at the Uris Theatre and discusses his vocalizing. Sinatra also reminisces about his early days. This show was repeated on December 2, 1975 with comments by Robert Merrill.

January 25, 1976   **"Celebration - The American Spirit"**   ABC

The House I Live In (with military chorus sung in front of the Jefferson Memorial).
Talks about the American spirit.

March 8, 1976   ABC T.V. News - Geraldo Rivera - "Goodnight America"

Scenes from pre-roast activities at Friars Tribute to Sinatra.

March 26, 1976   **"John Denver and Friend"**   ABC

Various orchestras as noted.
I've Got You Under My Skin (with Nelson Riddle)
All Or Nothing At All (with Harry James)
I'll Never Smile Again (with T. Dorsey Orchestra)
SINATRA-DENVER MEDLEY - Let's Get Away From It All, Imagination, There Are Such Things, Saturday Night, Come Fly With Me, Love And Marriage, High Hopes, Learnin' The Blues, Witchcraft, All The Way.
All Of Me (with Count Basie on piano)
My Kind Of Town (with Denver)
The Lady Is A Tramp (with Denver)
I Get A Kick Out Of You (with Denver)
My Way

September 6, 1976   **Jerry Lewis Telethon**

Sinatra appears twice - orchestra conducted by Bill Miller.

First Appearance
    Stargazer
    Never Gonna Fall In Love Again
    Re-unites Martin & Lewis after 20 years of separation.

SINATRA-DEAN MARTIN MEDLEY - I Can't Give You Anything But Love, Too Marvelous For Words, Pennies From Heaven, A Foggy Day, Embraceable You, The Lady Is A Tramp, I've Got The World On A String, Where Or When, All Of Me, When You're Smiling

Second Appearance
    For Once In My Life
    Embraceable You
    Night And Day

November 12, 1976   **"The Tonight Show"**   NBC

    I Sing The Songs
    Sinatra Talks With Johnny Carson
    Sinatra Jokes With Don Rickles
    Where Or When

November 26, 1976   **"All Star Tribute To John Wayne"**

Sinatra is host.

    You Are The Sunshine Of My Life

April 21, 1977   **"Sinatra And Friends"**   ABC

Presented by Sears, with Natalie Cole, Robert Merrill, Dean Martin, Loretta Lynn, Tony Bennett, Leslie Uggams and John Denver. Produced by Paul W. Keyes and directed by Bill Davis. Orchestra conducted by Nelson Riddle.
    Where Or When (while introducing guest stars)
    I've Got You Under My Skin
    I Get A Kick Out Of You (with Natalie Cole)
    The Oldest Established (with Martin and Merrill)
    Night And Day
    All Or Nothing At All (with Loretta Lynn)
    Chicago (with Tony Bennett)
    The Lady Is A Tramp (with Leslie Uggams)
    Everybody Ought To Be In Love
    Put Your Dreams Away

May 24, 1977   **"Suzy Interviews Ol' Blue Eyes"**   NBC

Journalist Suzy Knickerbocker interviewing Sinatra at his home in Palm Springs.

June 20, 1977   Sinatra appeared on Channel 5 newscast.

Scene shows him walking the streets of New York City, filming the movie "Contract on Cherry Street".

— 273 —

September 5, 1977   **Jerry Lewis Telethon**

All Or Nothing At All (disco version)
It Was A Very Good Year
Everybody Ought To Be In Love

SONG INDEX - TELEVISION - CHAPTER X

Accentuate The Positive - (Harold Arlen - Johnny Mercer)
February 15, 1960

All Of Me - (Seymour Simons - Gerald Marks)
March 7, 1958; March 3, 1959; December 18, 1967; March 26, 1976; September 6, 1976

All Or Nothing At All - (Arthur Altman - Jack Lawrence)
October 19, 1969; March 26, 1976; April 21, 1977; September 5, 1977

All The Way - (Sammy Cahn - Jule Styne)
October 18, 1957; November 1, 1957; January 10, 1958; January 18, 1958; January 26, 1958; March 28, 1958; June 2, 1962; November 5, 1969; November 18, 1970; March 26, 1976

All Through The Night - (Cole Porter)
November 8, 1953

Almost Like Being In Love - (Frederick Loewe - Alan Lerner)
December 9, 1962

Amen - (Shoen - Segure - Hardy)
November 25, 1968

Angel Eyes - (Matt Dennis - Earl Brent)
October 19, 1959; November 24, 1965; October 13, 1974

April In Paris - (Yip Harburg - Vernon Duke)
January 3, 1958

At Long Last Love - (Cole Porter)
February 28, 1958; June 2, 1962; November 13, 1967

Auld Lang Syne - (Burns)
December 31, 1970

Autumn In New York - (Vernon Duke)
December 9, 1962; October 13, 1974

Autumn Leaves, The - (Joseph Kosman - Johnny Mercer - Jacques Prevert)

Baby Won't You Please Come Home - (Charles Warfield - Clarence Williams)
October 13, 1974; September 1, 1975

Bad, Bad Leroy Brown - (Jim Croce)
October 13, 1974; September 1, 1975

Baubles, Bangles And Beads - (Robert Wright - George Forrest)
November 25, 1968

Bess, Oh Where's My Bess - (George and Ira Gershwin)
February 17, 1951

Best Things In Life Are Free, The - (Buddy DeSylva - Lew Brown - Ray Henderson)
December 9, 1962

Between The Devil And The Deep Blue Sea - (Harold Arlen - Ted Koehler)

Bewitched - (Richard Rodgers - Lorenz Hart)
January 17, 1958, November 1, 1960

Bill Bailey - (Hughie Cannon)
October 19, 1959

Birth Of The Blues, The - (Buddy DeSylva - Lew Brown - Ray Henderson)
October 13, 1957; January 17, 1958

But Beautiful - (Johnny Burke - Jimmy Van Heusen)
December 7, 1966; December 31, 1970; September 1, 1975

Can't We Be Friends - (Kay Swift - Paul James)
December 13, 1959

C'est Magnifique - (Cole Porter)
November 1, 1960

Change Partners - (Irving Berlin)
November 13, 1967

Cheek To Cheek - (Irving Berlin)
October 19, 1959

Chicago - (Fred Fisher)
June 2, 1962; April 21, 1977

Chloe - (Neil Moret - Gus Kahn)
April 4, 1958

Christmas Song, The - (Mel Torme - Bob Wells)
December 20, 1957

Come Fly With Me - (Sammy Cahn - Jimmy Van Heusen)
January 3, 1958; January 18, 1958; February 28, 1958; June 2, 1962; November 24, 1965; March 26, 1976

Come's Love - (Les Brown - Charles Tobias - Sam Stept)
December 13, 1959

Cycles - (Gayle Caldwell)
November 25, 1968

Day In, Day Out - (Rube Bloom - Johnny Mercer)
October 19, 1959; June 2, 1962; November 13, 1967

Did You Ever See A Dream Walking - (Harry Ravel)
December 31, 1970

Didn't We - (Jim Webb)
November 5, 1969

Ding Dong Ding -
October 5, 1956

Don't Cry Joe - (Joe Marsala)
November 29, 1957; November 13, 1967

Don't Worry 'Bout Me - (Rube Bloom - Ted Koehler)
November 24, 1965

Do Re Mi - (Richard Rodgers - Oscar Hammerstein II)
December 18, 1967

Downtown - (Tony Hatch)
December 7, 1966

Dream - (Johnny Mercer)
November 3, 1959

Embraceable You - (George and Ira Gershwin)
December 18, 1967; September 6, 1976

Everybody Ought To Be In Love - (Paul Anka)
April 2, 1977; September   , 1977

Everything Happens To Me - (Matt Dennis - Tom Adair)
February 3, 1951; November 22, 1957

Faithful - (Leo Robin - Ralph Grainger)
March 17, 1951

Fly Me To The Moon - (Bart Howard)
December 7, 1966; November 5, 1969; September 9, 1970; December 18, 1967;
September 6, 1976

Foggy Day, A - (George and Ira Gershwin)
January 26, 1958; March 28, 1958; March 3, 1959

Forget To Remember - (Teddy Randazzo - Vinny Pike)
November 5, 1969

For Once In My Life - (Ronald Miller - Orlando Murden)
November 5, 1969; September 6, 1976

From This Moment On - (Cole Porter)
November 15, 1957; February 7, 1958

Gal That Got Away, The - (Harold Arlen - Ira Gershwin)
November 7, 1954

Get Happy - (Harold Arlen - Ted Koehler)
February 1, 1951; March 17, 1951; February 15, 1960

Get Me To The Church On Time - (Frederick Loewe - Alan Lerner)
November 13, 1967

Getting To Know You - (Richard Rodgers - Oscar Hammerstein II)
January 1, 1952

Girl From Ipanema, The - (Antonio Carlos Jobim - Gene Lees)
November 13, 1967

Girl Next Door, The - (Hugh Martin - Ralph Blane)
November 1, 1957; November 24, 1965

Girl That I Marry, The - (Irving Berlin)
November 29, 1957

Going Out Of My Head - (Teddy Randazzo - Bobby Weinstein)
November 13, 1967; November 5, 1969

Gone With The Wind - (Allie Wrubel - Herb Magidson)
May 12, 1960; November 25, 1968

Goodbye Old Buddy - (Parody of "Nancy")
September 27, 1975

Good Old Songs, The -
October 9, 1959

Goody, Goody - (Johnny Mercer - Matty Malneck)

Granada - (Augustin Lara - Dorothy Dodd)
December 7, 1966

Great Day - (Vincent Youmans - Edward Elisen - Billy Rose)
January 1, 1952; December 9, 1962

Grovers Corner - (Sammy Cahn - Jimmy Van Heusen)
September 19, 1955

Guys And Dolls - (Frank Loesser)
December 31, 1970

Happy Birthday -
May 29, 1968

Happy Father's Day To You - (Parody of "Happy Birthday")
June 15, 1975

Have Yourself A Merry Little Christmas - (Hugh Martin - Ralph Blane)
December 18, 1967

Hello Young Lovers - (Richard Rodgers - Oscar Hammerstein II)
May 5, 1951; November 25, 1968

Here's That Rainy Day - (Johnny Burke - Jimmy Van Heusen)
December 13, 1959; November 25, 1968; November 18, 1973

Here's To The Ladies - (Sammy Cahn - Jimmy Van Heusen)
February 15, 1960

Hey Jealous Lover - (Sammy Cahn - Jimmy Van Heusen)
February 15, 1960

Hey Mr. Mitchum -
January 10, 1958

High Hopes - (Sammy Cahn - Jimmy Van Heusen)
October 19, 1959; March 26, 1976

House I Live In, The - (Lewis Allen - Earl Robinson)
November 29, 1957; January 25, 1976

How About You - (Arthur Freed - Burton Lane)
March 14, 1958

How Are You Fixed For Love - (Sammy Cahn - Jimmy Van Heusen)
May 23, 1958

How Little We Know - (Philip Springer - Carolyn Leigh)
November 25, 1968

I Believe - (Sammy Cahn - Jule Styne)
May 23, 1958

I Believe I'm Gonna Love You - (Gloria Sklerov - Harry Lloyd)
September 1, 1975

I Can't Believe That You're In Love With Me - (Clarence Gaskill - Jimmy McHugh)
January 17, 1958

I Can't Give You Anything But Love - (Dorothy Fields - Jimmy McHugh)
October 13, 1957; March 3, 1959; December 18, 1967; December 31, 1970; September 6, 1976

I Can't Get Started With You - (Vernon Duke - Ira Gershwin)
November 3, 1959

I Concentrate On You - (Cole Porter)
November 13, 1967

I Couldn't Sleep A Wink Last Night - (Jimmy McHugh - Harold Adamson)
November 5, 1969

I Could Write A Book - (Richard Rodgers - Lorenz Hart)
October 18, 1957; February 28, 1958

If - (Robert Hargreaves - Stanley Damerell - Tolchard Evans)
February 17, 1951; May 5, 1951

If I Could Be With You - (Henry Creamer - Jimmy Johnson)
September 27, 1959

If I Loved You - (Richard Rodgers - Oscar Hammerstein II)
February 14, 1958

I Get A Kick Out Of You - (Cole Porter)
November 8, 1953; October 18, 1957; April 25, 1958; November 24, 1965; April 21, 1977

I Got It Bad And That Ain't Good - (Paul Frances Webster - Duke Ellington)
November 15, 1957

I'll Be Seeing You - (Sammy Fain - Irving Kahal)
November 8, 1957

I'll Never Smile Again - (Ruth Lowe)
January 24, 1958; December 13, 1959; November 1, 1960; March 26, 1976

I Love A Piano - (Joe Buskin)
September 27, 1959

I Love Paris - (Cole Porter)
October 13, 1957; November 1, 1960

I Love You - (Harry Archer - Harlan Thompson)
February 10, 1951; February 14, 1958

Imagination - (Johnny Burke - Jimmy Van Heusen)
June 6, 1962; March 26, 1976

I'm An Old Cow Hand - (Johnny Mercer)
January 17, 1958

I May Be Wrong - (Harry Ruskin - Henry Sullivan)
May 9, 1958

I'm Always Chasing Rainbows - (Harry Carroll - Joseph McCarty)
January 27, 1951; October 13, 1957

I'm Gonna Live Till I Die - (Al Hoffman - Walter Kent - Mann Curtis)
January 8, 1952; April 24, 1955; March 7, 1958

I'm Gonna Sit Right Down And Write Myself A Letter - (Fred Ahlert - Victor Young)
November 22, 1957; March 7, 1958

I'm No Pretender -
January 27, 1951

Impatient Years, The - (Sammy Cahn - Jimmy Van Heusen)
September 19, 1955

Inka, Dinka, Doo - (Ben Ryan - Jimmy Durante)
October 19, 1959

In The Wee Small Hours - (Dave Mann - Bob Hilliard)
September 1, 1975

I See Your Face Before Me - (Howard Dietz - Arthur Schwartz)
February 25, 1962; December 9, 1962

I Sing The Songs - (Bruce Johnston)
November 12, 1976

Isle Of Capri - (Walter Grosz - Jimmy Kennedy)
January 31, 1958

It Came Upon The Midnight Clear - (Traditional)
December 20, 1957

It Had To Be You - (Gus Kahn - Isham Jones)
February 3, 1951

It Happened In Monterey - (Mabel Wayne - Billy Rose)
March 14, 1958

I Thought About You - (Jimmy Van Heusen - Johnny Mercer)
November 8, 1957

It Never Entered My Mind - (Richard Rodgers - Lorenz Hart)
November 26, 1968

It's A Good Day - (Peggy Lee - Dave Barbour)
December 9, 1962

It's Alright With Me - (Cole Porter)
December 13, 1959

It's Easy To Remember - (Richard Rodgers - Lorenz Hart)
November 3, 1959

It's Gotta Come From The Heart - (Sammy Cahn - Jule Styne)
October 19, 1959

It's Nice To Go Traveling - (Sammy Cahn - Jimmy Van Heusen)
January 3, 1958; March 28, 1958

It's Only A Paper Moon - (Yip Harburg - Billy Rose - Harold Arlen)
February 15, 1960

It's The Same Old Shillelagh - (White)
March 17, 1951

It Was A Very Good Year - (Ervin Drake)
November 25, 1965; September 2, 1977

I've Got A Crush On You - (George and Ira Gershwin)
February 10, 1951; November 29, 1957

I've Got The World On A String - (Harold Arlen - Ted Koehler)

September 29, 1953; January 18, 1958; December 13, 1959; November 25, 1965; September 6, 1976

I've Got You Under My Skin - (Cole Porter)
October 13, 1957; November 1, 1957; January 31, 1958; February 15, 1960; November 24, 1965; November 18, 1973; October 13, 1974; September 1, 1975; March 26, 1976; April 21, 1977

I've Grown Accustomed To Her Face - (Alan Lerner - Frederick Loewe)
November 23, 1957

I Whistle A Happy Tune - (Richard Rodgers - Oscar Hammerstein II)
May 12, 1951

I Wish I Were In Love Again - (Richard Rodgers - Lorenz Hart)
November 22, 1957

I Won't Dance - (Jerome Kern)
January 10, 1958

Jeepers Creepers - (Harry Warren - Johnny Mercer)
May 9, 1958

Jingle Bells - (James Pierpoint)
December 25, 1953; December 20, 1957

Just One Of Those Things - (Cole Porter)
November 8, 1953; April 25, 1958; December 7, 1966

Just Say I Love Her - (Kalmanoff - Ward - Dale - Falvo)
February 10, 1951

Lady Is A Tramp, The - (Richard Rodgers - Lorenz Hart)
October 18, 1957; October 19, 1959; June 2, 1962; November 24, 1965; November 13, 1967; December 18, 1967; October 13, 1974; February 17, 1975; September 1, 1975; September 25, 1975; March 26, 1976; September 6, 1976; April 21, 1977

Last Night When We Were Young - (Yip Harburg - Harold Arlen)
February 1, 1958; November 24, 1965; November 18, 1973

Learnin' The Blues - (Dolores Vicki Silvers)
April 24, 1955; March 28, 1958; November 1, 1960; March 26, 1976

Let Me Try Again - (Sammy Cahn - Paul Anka - Michelle Caravelli)
November 18, 1973; October 13, 1974; September 1, 1975

Let There Be Love - (Robert Wright - George Forrest)
February 25, 1962

Let's Do The Town Tonight -
September 29, 1953

Let's Get Away From It All - (Matt Dennis - Tom Adair)
November 22, 1957; March 26, 1976

Let's Take An Old Fashioned Walk - (Irving Berlin)
January 27, 1951

Little Bit Of Heaven, A - (Ernest Ball)
March 17, 1951

Little Green Apples - (Bobby Russell)
November 5, 1969

London By Night - (Carroll Coates)
January 3, 1958

Lonely Town - (Leonard Bernstein - Betty Comden - Adolph Green)
May 23, 1958; February 15, 1960

Lonesome Man Blues - (Sy Oliver)
January 1, 1952

Lonesome Road, The - (Gene Austin - Nathaniel Shilkret)
October 18, 1957; November 1, 1957; November 25, 1968

Look To Your Heart - (Sammy Cahn - Jimmy Van Heusen)
September 19, 1955

Lost In The Stars - (Maxwell Anderson - Kurt Weill)
November 25, 1968

L.O.V.E. - (Bert Kaempfert - Milt Gabler)
December 31, 1970

Love And Marriage - (Sammy Cahn - Jimmy Van Heusen)
September 19, 1955; December 2, 1955; October 13, 1957; November 1, 1960;
March 26, 1976

Love Is Just Around The Corner - (Leo Robin - Lewis Gensler)
December 31, 1970

Love Is Sweeping The Country - (George and Ira Gershwin)
December 13, 1959

Love Me Tender - (Elvis Presley - Vera Matson)
May 12, 1960

Lover - (Richard Rodgers - Lorenz Hart)
January 8, 1952; November 3, 1959

Love's Been Good To Me - (Rod McKuen)
November 5, 1969

Luck Be A Lady - (Frank Loesser)
October 16, 1965; December 7, 1966

Man Alone, A - (Rod McKuen)
November 5, 1969

Manhattan - (Richard Rodgers - Lorenz Hart)
November 3, 1959

Me And My Shadow - (Al Jolson - Dave Dryer)
January 31, 1958

Mistletoe And Holly - (Hank Sanicola - Frank Sinatra - Dak Stanford)
December 20, 1957

Moonlight In Vermont - (Karl Suessdorf - John Blackburn)
March 14, 1958; May 9, 1958; June 2, 1962; December 7, 1966

Most Beautiful Girl In The World, The - (Richard Rodgers - Lorenz Hart)
March 14, 1958; December 7, 1966

My Funny Valentine - (Richard Rodgers - Lorenz Hart)
November 22, 1957; February 14, 1958; November 3, 1959

My Heart Stood Still - (Richard Rodgers - Lorenz Hart)
February 15, 1960; December 7, 1966

My Kind Of Girl - (Leslie Bricusse)
December 31, 1970

My Kind Of Town - (Sammy Cahn - Jimmy Van Heusen)
November 24, 1965; December 7, 1966; November 5, 1969; October 13, 1974; June 15, 1975; March 26, 1976

My Romance - (Richard Rodgers - Lorenz Hart)
May 5, 1951; November 3, 1959

My Way - (Paul Anka - C. Francois - J. Revaix - Gilles Thibault)
November 5, 1969; March 14, 1974; October 13, 1974; March 26, 1976

Nancy - (Phil Silvers - Jimmy Van Heusen)
June 2, 1962; November 24, 1965; September 1, 1975; September 27, 1975

Nature Boy - (Eden Ahbez)
March 14, 1958

Never Gonna Fall In Love Again - (Eric Carmen)
September 6, 1976

Nice N' Easy - (Marilyn Keith - Alan Bergman - Lew Spence)
November 25, 1968; November 18, 1973; September 1, 1975

Nice Work If You Can Get It - (George and Ira Gershwin)
November 8, 1957

Night And Day - (Cole Porter)
November 19, 1957; May 23, 1958; November 1, 1960; September 6, 1976; April 21, 1977

Night Is Young And You're So Beautiful, The - (Billy Rose - Irving Kahal -

Dana Suesse)
February 10, 1951

Nothing In Common - (Sammy Cahn - Jimmy Van Heusen)
February 28, 1958

Now Is The Hour - (Clement Scott - Dorothy Stewart - Maewa Kaihau)
December 31, 1970

Oh Look At Me Now - (Joe Bushkin - John DeVries)
May 5, 1951; January 1, 1952

Oldest Established Permanent Floating Crap Game - (Frank Loesser)
February 15, 1964; April 21, 1977

Old Grey Mare, The -
October 19, 1959

O' Little Town Of Bethlehem - (Traditional)
December 20, 1957

Ol' MacDonald - (Marilyn Keith - Alan Bergman - Lew Spence)
November 1, 1960

Ol' Man River - (Jerome Kern - Oscar Hammerstein II)
October 15, 1959; June 2, 1962; November 13, 1967

One For My Baby - (Harold Arlen - Johnny Mercer)
March 7, 1958; June 2, 1962

One I Love, The - (Gus Cahn - Isham Jones)
January 24, 1958; September 27, 1959; February 25, 1961

On The Great Come And Get It Day - (Yip Harburg - Burton Lane)
December 9, 1962

On The Road To Mandalay - (Oley Speaks - Rudyard Kipling)
January 3, 1958

Our Love Is Here To Stay - (George and Ira Gershwin)
November 8, 1957; January 24, 1958; December 13, 1959

Our Town - (Sammy Cahn - Jimmy Van Heusen)
September 19, 1955

Out Beyond The Window - (Rod McKuen)
November 5, 1969

Pennies From Heaven - (Johnny Burke - Arthur Johnston)
November 8, 1957; December 18, 1967

Penthouse Serenade - (Will Jason - Val Burton)
January 8, 1952

Please Be Kind - (Sammy Cahn - Saul Chaplin)
November 5, 1969

P.S. I Love You - (Gordon Jenkins - Johnny Mercer)
February 14, 1958

Put Your Dreams Away - (Ruth Lowe - Stephan Weiss - Paul Mann)
October 18, 1957; January 17, 1958; February 7, 1958; February 14, 1958; March
28, 1958; May 23, 1958; November 24, 1965; April 21, 1977

Quiet Nights Of Quiet Stars - (Antonio Carlos Jobim - Gene Lees)
November 13, 1967

Remember Me - (Al Dubin - Harry Warren)
October 5, 1956

Road To Morocco, The - (Johnny Burke - Jimmy Van Heusen)
October 13, 1957

Santa Claus Is Coming To Town - (Haven Gillespie - Fred Coots)
December 20, 1957

Saturday Night - (Sammy Cahn - Jule Styne)
November 29, 1957; March 14, 1958; March 26, 1976

Send In The Clowns - (Stephen Sondheim)
November 18, 1973; September 1, 1975

September Of My Years, The - (Sammy Cahn - Jimmy Van Heusen)
November 16, 1965

September Song - (Kurt Weill - Maxwell Anderson)
September 29, 1953; October 13, 1957

Shadow Of The Moon, The - (Kiessling - Brown)
August 24, 1970

She's Funny That Way - (Niel Moret - Richard Whiting)
May 12, 1951; November 22, 1957

Side By Side - (Harry Woods)
November 1, 1957; January 26, 1958

Silent Night - (Franz Gruber)
December 18, 1967

Smack Dab In The Middle - (Charles Calhoun)
October 5, 1956

Small Fry - (Frank Loesser - Hoagy Carmichael)
April 26, 1962

So Long, It's Been Good To Know You -
December 31, 1970

Something - (George Harrison)
December 31, 1970; September 1, 1975

Something's Gotta Give - (Johnny Mercer)
November 15, 1957

Song Is You, The - (Jerome Kern - Oscar Hammerstein II)
November 13, 1967

Soon - (Richard Rodgers - Lorenz Hart)
November 3, 1959

South Of The Border - (Jimmy Kennedy - Michael Carr)
December 25, 1953; October 13, 1957; February 7, 1958

Squeeze Me - (Fats Waller - Earl Williams)
February 1, 1958

Star - (Sammy Cahn - Jimmy Van Heusen)
February 24, 1969

Stargazer - (Neil Diamond)
September 6, 1976

Stompin' At The Savoy - (Benny Goodman - Chick Webb - Edgar Sampson - Andy Razaf)
November 13, 1967

Street Of Dreams - (Victor Young - Sam Lewis)
January 24, 1958; November 5, 1969; November 18, 1973

Sunday, Monday Or Always - (Johnny Burke - Jimmy Van Heusen)
November 29, 1957

Sweet Blindness - (Laura Nyro)
November 25, 1968

Sweetheart of Sigma Chi - (Dudleigh Vernor)
October 13, 1957

Sweet Leilani - (Harry Owens)
October 13, 1957

Take My Love - (Jack Wolf - Herron - Frank Sinatra)
February 3, 1951

Taking A Chance On Love - (Vernon Duke - John LaTouche - Ted Fetter)
March 28, 1958; March 3, 1959

Talk To Me - (Snyder - Kahan - Valee)
October 19, 1959

Tammy - (Jay Livingston - Ray Evans)
February 1, 1958

Tea For Two - (Irving Caesar - Vincent Youmans)
January 26, 1958

Tell Her You Love Her - (Denison - Parker - Halliday)
January 18, 1958; January 31, 1958

Tender Trap, The - (Sammy Cahn - Jimmy Van Heusen)
December 2, 1955; February 1, 1958; November 1, 1960; November 5, 1969

That Face - (Allan Bergman - Lew Spence)
December 9, 1962

That Old Black Magic - (Johnny Mercer - Harold Arlen)
March 17, 1951; January 8, 1952

That Old Feeling - (Lew Brown - Sammy Fain)
October 19, 1959

That Old Devil Moon - (Yip Harburg - Burton Lane)
November 29, 1957

That's Life - (Kay Gordon)
December 7, 1966; August 24, 1970

Them There Eyes - (Maceo Pinkard - William Tracy - Doris Tauber)
February 17, 1951; October 5, 1956; May 23, 1958

There Are Such Things - (Stanley Adams - Abel Baer - George Meyer)
March 26, 1976

There'll Be Some Changes Made - (Higgins - Evans - Overstreet)
January 27, 1951

There's A Long Long Trail Awinding - (Zo Elliot)
October 13, 1957

There's A Small Hotel - (Richard Rodgers - Lorenz Hart)
November 3, 1959

There's No You - (Hal Hopper - Bullets Durgom - Tom Adair)
February 28, 1958

These Boots Were Made For Walking - (Lee Hazelwood)
December 7, 1966

These Foolish Things - (Jack Strachey - Harry Link - Holt Marvel)
February 17, 1951

They Can't Take That Away From Me - (George and Ira Gershwin)
February 7, 1958; June 2, 1962; November 13, 1967; September 9, 1970; June 15, 1975; September 1, 1975

They Didn't Believe Me - (Michael Rourke - Jerome Kern)
January 27, 1951

This Can't Be Love - (Richard Rodgers - Lorenz Hart)
September 29, 1953; March 7, 1958

This Is All I Ask - (Gordon Jenkins)
November 24, 1965

This Love Of Mine - (Sol Parker - Hank Sanicola - Frank Sinatra)
January 24, 1958; March 3, 1959; November 1, 1960; September 1, 1975

Three Coins In The Fountain - (Sammy Cahn - Jule Styne)
November 15, 1957; February 1, 1958

Three Little Words - (Bert Kalmar - Harry Ruby)
October 13, 1957

Three O'Clock In The Morning - (Dorothy Terriss - Julian Robledo)
October 13, 1957

Together - (Buddy DeSylva - Ray Henderson - Lew Brown)
October 19, 1959

Tony Rome - (Lee Hazelwood)
November 13, 1967

Too Marvelous For Words - (Richard Whiting - Johnny Mercer)
April 4, 1958; December 13, 1959; February 25, 1962

Two Sleepy People - (Frank Loesser - Hoagy Carmichael)
October 5, 1956

Up A Lazy River - (Hoagy Carmichael - Sidney Arodin)
September 27, 1959

Up, Up And Away - (Jimmy Webb)
November 13, 1967

Violets For Your Furs - (Matt Dennis - Tom Adair)
November 7, 1954; November 1, 1957; January 24, 1958

Walking My Baby Back Home - (Fred Ahlert - Harry Richmond)
March 17, 1951

We Can't Do That Any More - (Fred Ebb - John Kander)
November 18, 1973

We Kiss In The Shadow - (Richard Rodgers - Oscar Hammerstein II)
May 12, 1951

Welcome To My World - (Gerhard Winkler - Hathcock)
December 31, 1970

We'll Be Together Again - (Frankie Laine - Carl Fischer)
May 9, 1958

We're Glad We're Not Young Any More - (Alan Lerner - Frederick Loewe)
September 27, 1959

We Wish You The Merriest - (Les Brown)
December 18, 1967

What Is This Thing Called Love - (Cole Porter)
December 31, 1970

What Now My Love - (Gilbert Becaud - Carl Sigman)
November 13, 1967

When I Stop Loving You - (Cates - Allan Copeland - Greene)
November 7, 1954

When Your Lover Has Gone - (Edgar Swan)
April 24, 1955; December 7, 1966

When You're Smiling - (Larry Shay - Mark Fisher - Joe Goodwin)
May 5, 1951; February 1, 1958; November 3, 1959; December 18, 1967; September 6, 1976

Where Are You - (Jimmy McHugh - Harold Adamson)
November 15, 1957; March 14, 1958

Where Or When - (Richard Rodgers - Lorenz Hart)
November 3, 1959; December 9, 1962; December 18, 1967; September 1, 1975; September 6, 1976; November 12, 1976; April 21, 1977

Where The Blue Of The Night - (Roy Turk - Bing Crosby - Fred Ahlert)
October 13, 1957

White Christmas - (Irving Berlin)
December 20, 1957

Who Will Be With You When I Am Far Away -
October 19, 1959

Why Shouldn't I - (Cole Porter)
February 17, 1951

Willow Weep For Me - (Ann Ronell)
September 27, 1959

Witchcraft - (Cy Coleman - Carolyn Leigh)
January 10, 1958; February 7, 1958; May 12, 1960; November 24, 1965; March 26, 1976

Without A Song - (Vincent Youmans - Billy Rose - Edward Eliscu)
February 17, 1951; November 24, 1965

Wrap Your Troubles In Dreams - (Ted Koehler - Billy Moll - Harry Barris)
April 24, 1955; November 22, 1957; January 24, 1958

Yes Sir, That's My Baby - (Walter Donaldson - Gus Kahn)
December 7, 1966

Yetta I Can't Forget Her -
September 18, 1955

You Are The Sunshine Of My Life - (Stevie Wonder)
October 13, 1974; September 1, 1975; November 26, 1976

You Brought A New Kind Of Love To Me - (Sammy Fain - Irving Kahal - Pierre Norman)
November 8, 1957; April 4, 1958

You Do Something To Me - (Cole Porter)
November 8, 1953; February 25, 1962

You Go To My Head - (Haven Gillespie - Fred Coots)
October 13, 1957

You'd Be So Nice To Come Home To - (Cole Porter)
February 3, 1951; November 1, 1957

You Make Me Feel So Young - (Mack Gordon - Josef Myrow)
October 5, 1956; January 31, 1958; March 3, 1959; June 2, 1962; November 24, 1965

You Make Me Feel So Old - (Parody of "You Make Me Feel So Young")
May 12, 1960

You Must Have Been A Beautiful Baby - (Harry Warren - Johnny Mercer)
March 3, 1959

Young At Heart - (Carolyn Leigh - Johnny Richards)
March 28, 1958; November 1, 1960; November 24, 1965

Younger Than Spring Time - (Richard Rodgers - Oscar Hammerstein II)
December 11, 1967

You're Getting To Be A Habit With Me - (Harry Warren - Al Dubin)
April 25, 1958

You're Invited To Spend The Afternoon - (Sammy Cahn - Jimmy Van Heusen)
December 13, 1959

You're Nobody Till Someone Loves You - (Russ Morgan - Larry Stock - James Cavanaugh)
February 25, 1962; December 7, 1966

You're Sensational - (Cole Porter)
December 9, 1962; November 5, 1969

You're The Top - (Cole Porter)
November 8, 1953; April 25, 1958

You Will Be My Music - (Joe Raposo)
November 18, 1973

Zip-A-Dee-Do-Da - (Allie Wrubel - Ray Gilbert)
February 3, 1951

ORCHESTRAS, ARRANGERS, COMPOSERS, SOLOISTS, VOCALISTS AND VOCAL GROUPS INDEX FOR TELEVISION CHAPTER X

Armstrong, Louis - (Trumpeter, Vocalist)
January 1, 1952; October 13, 1957; September 27, 1959

Bankhead, Tallulah - Vocalist, Actress
September 29, 1953

Basie, Count - Orchestra Leader
October 16, 1965; March 26, 1976

Bennett, Tony - Vocalist
April 21, 1977

Berle, Milton - Comedian, Vocalist
September 29, 1953

Brewster Singers, Ralph - Vocal Group
December 20, 1957

Britton, Barbara - Actress, Vocalist
February 10, 1951

Carroll, Diahann - Vocalist
November 25, 1968

Clooney, Rosemary - Vocalist
October 13, 1957

Cole, Natalie - Vocalist
April 21, 1977

Costa, Don - Arranger, Conductor
November 25, 1968; November 5, 1969

Crosby, Bing - Vocalist
October 13, 1957; December 20, 1957; September 27, 1959; October 19, 1959;
February 15, 1964

Davis, Sammy, Jr. - Vocalist
January 31, 1958

Dean, Dizzy - Baseball Player, Broadcaster
October 5, 1956

DeCarlo, Yvonne - Actress
January 1, 1952

Denver, John - Vocalist
March 26, 1976

Dimension, Fifth - Vocal Group
November 25, 1968

Dorsey Orchestra, The (Fronted by Warren Covington)
March 26, 1976

Fisher, Eddie - Vocalist
March 28, 1958

Fitzgerald, Ella - Vocalist
May 9, 1958; December 13, 1959; November 13, 1967

Freeberg, Stan - Comedian, Vocalist
March 7, 1958

Garland, Judy - Vocalist
February 25, 1962

Gaynor, Mitzi - Actress, Vocalist
October 19, 1959

Gingold, Hermione - Actress, Vocalist
December 13, 1959

Golddiggers, The - Vocal Group
December 31, 1970

Gorme, Eydie - Vocalist
March 14, 1958

Heathertones, The - Vocal Group
February 10, 1951; March 17, 1951

Herman, Woody - Orchestra Leader
October 13, 1974

Hi Lo's, The - Vocal Group
December 13, 1959

Hope, Bob - Comedian, Vocalist
April 26, 1962

Horne, Lena - Vocalist
February 15, 1960

Hutton, June - Vocalist
January 27, 1951; February 3, 1951; February 10, 1951; March 17, 1951; May 5, 1951; January 8, 1952

James, Harry - Orchestra Leader
March 26, 1978

Jenkins, Gordon - Arranger, Conductor
November 24, 1965, December 7, 1966; November 18, 1973

Jobim, Antonio Carlos - Vocalist, Composer
November 13, 1967

Johnson, Van - Actor, Vocalist
February 28, 1958

Jones, Shirley - Actress, Vocalist
February 14, 1958

Jones, Spike - Orchestra Leader
April 4, 1958

Kelly, Gene - Dancer, Vocalist
November 18, 1973

Lawford, Peter - Actor, Vocalist
December 13, 1959

Lawrence, Carol - Vocalist
June 15, 1975

Lee, Peggy - Vocalist
November 8, 1957; September 27, 1959

Lynn, Loretta - Vocalist
April 21, 1977

McGuire Sisters, The - Vocal Group
November 15, 1957

Martin, Dean - Vocalist
November 29, 1957; February 1, 1958; October 19, 1959; November 3, 1959;
November 1, 1960; February 25, 1962; February 15, 1964; December 18, 1967;
December 31, 1970; September 6, 1976; April 21, 1977.

Merman, Ethel - Vocalist
November 8, 1953; April 25, 1958

Merrill, Robert - Vocalist
April 21, 1977

Miller, Bill - Pianist, Conductor
October 13, 1974; September 6, 1976

Mitchum, Jim - Actor, Vocalist
January 10. 1959

Mitchum, Robert - Actor, Vocalist
January 10, 1958

O 'Brien, Erin - Vocalist
November 22, 1957

Riddle, Nelson - Arranger, Conductor
September 19, 1955; December 20, 1957; November 24, 1965; December 7, 1966;
November 13, 1967; March 26, 1976; April 21, 1977

Rose, David - Arranger, Conductor
November 1, 1960

Shore, Dinah - Vocalist
October 5, 1956; January 3, 1958; January 26, 1958; March 3, 1959; December 9, 1962; September 9, 1970

Silvers, Phil - Comedian, Vocalist
January 27, 1951

Sinatra, Nancy - Vocalist
November 1, 1957; May 12, 1960; December 7, 1966

Smith, Keely - Vocalist
January 17, 1958

Stafford, Jo - Vocalist
January 24, 1958

Stordahl, Alex - Arranger, Conductor
October 7, 1950

Suzuki, Pat - Vocalist
May 23, 1958

Thomas, Danny - Actor, Comedian, Vocalist
February 1, 1958

Trotter, John Scott - Orchestra Leader
February 15, 1964

Uggams, Leslie - Vocalist
April 24, 1977

Wood, Natalie - Actress, Vocalist
May 23, 1958

Chapter XI

FRANK SINATRA - MOTION PICTURES
OCTOBER, 1935 -

Sinatra's activities in films closely parallels that of his recording career. His first appearance on film was with Major Bowes who had a fifteen minute "Short Soundies" made with his amateur hour winners. He next appears some six years later with the Tommy Dorsey Orchestra at the height of his popularity with the band in 1941 and 1942. When he left Dorsey to go out on his own, motion pictures beckoned him to Hollywood. He made a one song appearance in a mild musical and the public clamored for more.

R.K.O. presented him in his first speaking and acting role and Frank went on from there to over fifty more additional films of varying musical and dramatic quality. In 1948 through 1952 his recording sales were taking a disastrous downhill slide and the films he made in that era seemed to coincide with the general feeling that Sinatra was finished.

With great effort and determination he won the role of "Maggio" in "From Here To Eternity" and Hollywood bestowed upon him his second Academy Award. (He previously received a special Oscar for his racial tolerance short film called "The House I Live In"). His film stock shot sky-high and the name of Frank Sinatra listed in the cast of a motion picture practically assured financial success. In the past few years since he has come out of retirement he has not made any feature films outside of narrating a segment of "That's Entertainment". *

He has stated often enough that a desirable role has not come to his attention but we feel that the Motion Picture Industry will surely suffer if he continues to abstain from making new films. He has a marvelous feel for applying himself to a role when he considers the script worthwhile and despite some hurriedly made fiascos, many of his films will be deservedly remembered and appreciated and certainly enjoyed.

* During the printing of this book, Sinatra was filming *"Contract On Cherry Street."*

In our listings we will include the film, the studio which released it and the date of the release. We will also include the cast, a short synopsis and the songs, if any, that Frank sang in the film.

MAJOR BOWES' AMATEUR HOUR MOVIE SHORTS - October 1935

Produced at Biograph Studios by Biograph Productions, Inc. Produced and Directed by John H. Auer. Photography by Larry Williams and Tommy Hogan. Released by R.K.O. Radio Pictures.

Cast
Major Bowes and The Hoboken Four
Skelly Lewis   - (James Petrozelli)
Fred Tamby   - (Tamburro)
Patty Prince   - (Princepe)
Frank Sinatra

"Las Vegas Nights" - Sinatra at left next to Connie Haines — 1941.

"Ship Ahoy" - Sinatra at extreme right — 1942.

Frank Sinatra appears for the first time on the motion picture screen. He is seen harmonizing with three other Hobokenites in **two** film shorts. Collectively they had been given the name "The Hoboken Four" by Mr. Bowes. In one short they do a minstrel show in blackface, singing the song *"Shine"*. In another Frank solos on part of the tune called *"The Curse of an Aching Heart"*. There may have been a few more shorts made for there are tapes of the group singing *"Shine"* in different tempos.

LAS VEGAS NIGHTS

Paramount - March 24, 1941

Produced by William Le Baron; Directed by Ralph Murphy. Original story by Ernest Pogano and Harry Clark with additional dialogue by Eddie Welch. Songs by Frank Loesser, Burton Lane, Louis Alter and Ruth Lowe. Musical Director Victor Young with arrangements by Axel Stordahl, Victor Young, Charles Bradshaw, Leo Shuken and Max Terr. Camera by William Mellor.

Running Time - 90 Minutes

Cast

Bill Stevens	- Phil Regan	Hank Bevis	- Hank Ladd
Stu Grant	- Bert Wheeler	Maitre'D	- Eddie Kane
Norma Jennings	- Constance Moore	Hatcheck Girl	- Eleanor Stewart
Patsy Lynch	- Virginia Dale	Gloria Stafford	- F. Malloy
Mildred Jennings	- Lillian Cornell	Cigarette Girl	- Wanda McKay
Katy	- Betty Brewer	Judge	- Richard Carle

Mexican Trio
Guitar & Violin   - Nick Moro
Concertina   - Frank Yoconelli
Guitar   - Earl Douglas
Red Donohue and His Mule - "Uno"

And

The Tommy Dorsey Orchestra featuring Frank Sinatra, The Pied Pipers, Buddy Rich, Ziggy Elman, Jo Stafford, Connie Haines and Joe Buskin.

Synopsis

A troupe of Vaudevillians land in Las Vegas without a cent, but with a claim to an Uncle's Estate. If Tommy Dorsey didn't appear playing *"Son Of India"* featuring Ziggy Elman and Buddy Rich; and Frank Sinatra and The Pied Pipers didn't sing the beautiful * *"I'll Never Smile Again"*, the film would have been a total loss. The band also performs *"On Miami Shores"* and a wee bit of *"Dolores."*

* In the studio credits, Axel Stordahl is listed as the lone Dorsey arranger, but in reality the arrangement of *"I'll Never Smile Again"* is by Fred Stulce.

SHIP AHOY

M.G.M. - May 1942

Produced by Jack Cummings, Directed by Edward Buzzell. Screenplay by Harry Clork, based on a story by Matt Books, Bradford Ropes and Bert Kalmar. Music conducted by George Stoll. Music and lyrics by Burton Lane, E.Y. Harburg, Margery Cummings and Walter Ruick. Vocal and orchestral arrangements by Axel Stordahl, Sy Oliver, Leo Arnaud, George Bassmann and Conrad Salinger. Musical presentation by Merrill Pye. Dance direction by Bobby Connolly. Directors of photography - Leonard Smith and Robert Planek. Art direction by Cedric Gibbons.

Running Time - 97 Minutes

Cast

Tallulah Winters	- Eleanor Powell	Art Higgins	- Stuart Crawford
Merton K. Kibble	- Red Skelton	Dr. Farno	- John Emery
"Skip" Owens	- Bert Lahr	Pietro Polesi	- Bernard Nedell
Fran Evans	- Virginia O'Brien	Inspector Davis	- Moronsi Olsen
H.V. Bennet	- William Post Jr.	Grimes	- Ralph Dunn
"Stump"	- James Cross	Flammer	- William Tannen
"Stumpy"	- Eddie Hartman	Nurse	- Mary Treen

Also the Tommy Dorsey Orchestra featuring Frank Sinatra, Jo Stafford, Connie Haines, Pied Pipers, Buddy Rich and Ziggy Elman.

Synopsis

An entertaining but trite little musical about a girl who is unwittingly helping enemy agents. Dancing and music are very worthwhile, however. Frank sings *"The Last Call For Love"*, *"Poor You"* and joins with the Pied Pipers and the band to sing a rousing *"I'll Take Tallulah"*. *. A short version of *"Moonlight Bay"* sung again with The Pied Pipers rounds out his singing chores in the film.
   * This rendition was deleted from film.

REVEILLE WITH BEVERLY

Columbia - February 4, 1943

Produced by Sam White; Directed by Charles Barton. Screenplay by Howard J. Green, Jack Henley and Albert Duffy. Musical Director, Morris Stoloff. Director of photography, Philip Tannura. Sinatra's arrangements originally by Axel Stordahl adapted by Stoloff.

Running Time - 83 Minutes

"Reveilli with Beverly" — 1943.

"Higher and Higher" - Dooley Wilson, Sinatra, Michelle Morgan — 1943.

Cast

Beverly Ross	- Ann Miller	Mrs. Ross	- Barbara Brown
Barry Lang	- William Wright	Mr. Ross	- Douglas Leavitt
Andy Adams	- Dick Purcell	Canvassback	- Walter Sande
Vernon Lewis	- Franklin Pangborn	Stamp Meloy	- Wally Vernon
Mr. Kennedy	- Tim Ryan	Mr. Smith	- Andrew Tombes
Eddie Ross	- Larry Parks	Evelyn Ross	- Adele Mara

And

Bob Crosby And His Orchestra
Duke Ellington And His Orchestra
Count Basie And His Orchestra
Freddie Slack And His Orchestra With Ella Mae Morse
The Mills Brothers
The Radio Rogues
Frank Sinatra

Synopsis

A switchboard operator becomes a popular lady disc-jockey. Appearances by Sinatra, Ellington, Basie, etc., save this mild musical. Frank sings Cole Porter's *"Night And Day"*, surrounded by six girl violinists and six girl pianists.

MUSIC AT WAR

March Of Time - Summer 1943

Photographed at Hunter College, New York while Sinatra was appearing before a group of WAVES. Frank sang the tune *"The Song Is You"* which was deleted when the short was finally released in December of 1943. It seems that he was then under contract to R.K.O. Radio Pictures who claimed that this appearance was a direct violation of his contract. The short was eventually retitled *"Upbeat In Music."*

HIGHER AND HIGHER

R.K.O. Radio Pictures - December 18, 1943

Produced and directed by Tim Whelan; Screenplay by Jay Drather and Ralph Spence. Additional dialogue by William Bowers and Howard Harris. Based on the musical play of the same name with book by Gladys Hurlbut and Joshua Logan. Musical director, Constantin Bakaleinikoff. Orchestral arrangements by Gene Rose. Musical arrangements for Frank Sinatra by Axel Stordahl. Vocal arrangements by Ken Darby. Musical numbers staged by Ernest Matray. Music and lyrics by Jimmy McHugh and Harold Adamson.

Running Time - 90 Minutes

"Higher and Higher" — Sinatra, Marcy McQuire, Mel Torme — 1943.

"Step Lively" - Sinatra's first screen kiss - the lucky girl, Gloria DeHaven. George Murphy watches — 1944.

Cast

Millie	- Michelle Morgan	Mrs. Keating	- Elizabeth Risdan
Mike	- Jack Haley	Katherine	- Barbara Hale
Frank	- Frank Sinatra	Marty	- Mel Torme
Drake	- Leon Errol	Byngham	- Paul Hartman
Mickey	- Marcy McGuire	Hilda	- Grace Hartman
Sir Victor	- Victor Borge	Oscar	- Dooley Wilson
Sandy	- Mary Wickes	Mrs. Whiffin	- Ivy Scott
Mr. Green	- Rex Evans	Bing Crosby	- Bing Crosby

Bridesmaids - Elaine Riley, Shirley O'Hara, Dorothy Malone, Daun Kennedy.

Synopsis

An entertaining musical comedy about a man who is unable to pay his servants and forms a corporation with them. This is Frank Sinatra's first speaking role in a full length feature. He sings some fine tunes and is in excellent voice as he warbles *"I Couldn't Sleep A Wink Last Night"*, *"A Lovely Way To Spend An Evening"*, *"The Music Stopped"*, *"You Belong In A Love Song"*. He also teams up with Marcy McGuire on *"I Saw You First"* and with the rest of the cast sings *"You're On Your Own."*

THE ROAD TO VICTORY

Warner Brothers - February 1944

Produced by Warner Brothers for the U.S. Treasury Department. A war activities committe release no. 98. Directed by Leroy Prinz. Executive producer, Jack L. Warner. Produced by Gordon Hollingshead and Arnold Albert. Screenplay by James Bloodworth. Based on an original story by Mannie Manheim. Musical director, Leo. F. Forbstein.

Running Time - 10 Minutes

Cast

Olive Blakeney, Jack Carson, Bing Crosby, Cary Grant, James Lydon, Irene Manning, Dennis Morgan, Charles Ruggles and Frank Sinatra.

Sinatra sings *"There's Gonna Be A Hot Time In The Town Of Berlin"*. This film short was an abbreviated version of *"The Shining Future"* originally produced in two reels for Canada's Sixth Victory Loan and included more stars such as Benny Goodman, Harry James and Deanna Durbin.

STEP LIVELY

R.K.O. Radio Pictures - June 27, 1944

Produced by Robert Fellows; Directed by Tim Wlean and screenplay by Warren Duff and Peter Milne. Based on the play *"Room Service"* by John Murray and Alan Boretz. Musical arrangements for Frank Sinatra by Axel Stordahl. Vocal

"Step Lively" - *Walter Slezak, George Murphy, Sinatra — 1944.*

"The House I Live In" — 1945.

arrangements by Ken Darby.

Running Time - 88 Minutes

Cast

Glenn Russell	- Frank Sinatra	Harry	- Alan Carney
Gordon Miller	- George Murphy	Miss Abbott	- Anne Jeffries
Christine	- Gloria DeHaven	Dr. Glass	- Grant Mitchell
Wagner	- Adolph Menjou	Mother	- Frances King
Gribble	- Walter Slezak	Father	- Harry Noble
Jenkins	- Eugene Pallette	Doorman	- Frank Mayo
Binion	- Wally Brown	Tel. Operator	- Dorothy Malone

Synopsis

A fast thinking, theatrical producer gets his show on despite financial problems. Lively, enjoyable musical. Sinatra again sings very fine material here and of course, his specialized treatments make them early classics. The tunes are: *"As Long As There's Music", "Where Does Love Begin", "Some Other Time"* and *"Come Out Wherever You Are."*

ALL STAR BOND RALLY

20th Century Fox - February 1945

Produced by 20th Century Fox for the U.S. Treasury Department. War Activities Committe release no. 120. Directed by Michael Audley. Produced by Fanchon. Script by Don Quinn. Music supervised by Alfred Newman. Music conducted by Emil Newman. Musical arrangements for Frank Sinatra by Axel Stordahl.

Running Time - 19 Minutes

Cast

Vivian Blaine, Jeanne Crain, Bing Crosby, Linda Darnell, Betty Grable, June Haver, Bob Hope, Faye Marlowe, Harpo Marx, Fibber McGee and Molly, Carmen Miranda, Frank Sinatra, Harry James and His Orchestra.

This is a two reeler made for the Seventh War Loan Drive and Sinatra sings *"Saturday Night"* backed by the James Band.

THE HOUSE I LIVE IN

R.K.O. Radio Pictures - March 1945

Produced by Frank Ross and directed by Mervyn Leroy. Original screenplay by Albert Maltz. Musical director, Axel Stordahl. Incidental score by Roy Webb. Film Editor, Philip Martin, Jr.

Running Time - 12 Minutes

Sinatra stars in a racial tolerance short that he personally talked R.K.O. into

"Anchors Aweigh" — Sinatra, Gene Kelly, Kathryn Grayson — 1945.

"Anchors Aweigh" - Sinatra, Gene Kelly — 1945.

producing. It won him and the studio a special Academy Award. He sings *"If You Are But A Dream"* (adapted from Rubenstein's *"Romance"*) and *"The House I Live In."*

ANCHORS AWEIGH

M.G.M. - August 15, 1945 - Color

Produced by Joe Pasternak. Directed by George Sidney. Screenplay by Isobel Lennart, based on a story by Natalie Marcin. Music supervised and conducted by George Stoll. Sinatra's vocal arrangements by Axel Stordahl. Dance sequences created by Gene Kelly. Art Directors, Cedric Gibbons and Randall Duell. *"Tom and Jerry"* cartoon directed by Fred Quimby. Musical score by Sammy Cahn and Julie Styne.

Running Time - 140 Minutes

Cast

Clarence Doolittle	- Frank Sinatra	Carlos	- Carlos Ramirez
Susan Abbott	- Kathryn Grayson	Police Captain	- Edgar Kennedy
Joseph Brady	- Gene Kelly	Bertram Kraler	- Grady Sutton
Jose Iturbi	- Himself	Admiral's Aide	- Leon Ames
Donald Martin	- Dean Stockwell	Little Girl	- Sharon McManus
Girl from Brooklyn	- Pamela Britton	Radio Cop	- James Flavin
Police Sergeant	- Rags Ragland	Hamburger Man	- Henry Armetta
Cafe Manager	- Billy Gilbert	Asst. Dir.	- Ray Teal
Admiral Hammond	- Henry O'Neill	Movie Dir.	- William Forrest

Synopsis

A tuneful, gay lively musical about three sailors on leave in Hollywood. This is Sinatra's first co-starring picture with Kathryn Grayson and Gene Kelly. The cast is great, the songs are wonderful and you'll love it. Frank sings *"I Fall In Love Too Easily"*, *"What Makes The Sunset"*, *"I Begged Her"*, *"The Charm Of You,"* *"Brahms Lullaby"* and joins the rest of the cast in *"We Hate To Leave."* He certainly was in splendid voice here.

SPECIAL CHRISTMAS TRAILER

M.G.M. - December 1945

Produced by Metro-Goldwyn-Mayer. Directed by Harry Loud. Musical directors, Axel Stordahl and Nathaniel Shilkret.

Running Time - 3 Minutes

This special Christmas short was distributed by M.G.M. during December 1945 and Sinatra sings, *"Silent Night, Holy Night"* written by Franz Gruber and Father Joseph Mohr.

TILL THE CLOUDS ROLL BY

M.G.M. - December 1946 - Color

"Till The Clouds Roll By" - Sinatra singing "Ol Man River" — 1966.

"It Happened In Brooklyn" - Sinatra and Jimmy Durante — 1947.

Produced by Arthur Freed. Directed by Richard Whorf. Story by Guy Bolton. Screenplay by Myles Connolly and Jean Holloway. Adapted by George Wells, based on the life and music of Jerome Kern. Music supervised and conducted by Lennie Hayton. Orchestrations by Conrad Salinger. Vocal arrangements by Kay Thompson. Musical numbers staged and directed by Robert Alton. Costumes designed by Helen Rose and supervised by Irene.

Running Time - 137 Minutes

Cast

Jerome Kern	- Robert Walker	Victor Herbert	- Paul Maxey
Marilyn Miller	- Judy Garland	Cecil Keller	- Rex Evans
Sally	- Lucille Bremmer	Hennessy	- Bill Philips
Sally As A Girl	- Joan Wells	Julie Sanderson	- Dinah Shore
James Hessler	- Van Heflin	Bandleader	- Van Johnson
Oscar Hammerstein	- Paul Langton	Orch. Con.	- Ray Teal
Mrs. Jerome Kern	- Dorothy Patrick	Secretary	- Byron Foulger
Mrs. Muller	- Mary Nash	Miss Laroche	- Ann Codee
Charles Frohman	- Harry Hayden	Producer	- Russell Hicks

Special Guest Stars

June Allyson, Angela Lansbury, Ray McDonald, Cyd Charisse, Gower Champion, Sally Forest, The Wilde Twins, Tony Martin, Kathryn Grayson, Virginia O'Brien, Lena Horne, Caleb Patterson, Johnny Johnston, Bruce Cowling, Maurice Kelly and **Frank Sinatra.**

Synopsis

A fictional biography of great composer Jerome Kern is a muddy mess, but the delightful music makes most of the film a treat. You'll probably remember Frank Sinatra in a white tuxedo standing on a pedestal singing *"Ol' Man River"*.

IT HAPPENED IN BROOKLYN

M.G.M. - March 14, 1947

Produced by Jack Cummings. Directed by Richard Whorf. Screenplay by Isobel Lennart, based on an original story by John McGowan. Musical supervision, direction and incidental scoring by Johnny Green. Sinatra's vocal orchestrations by Axel Stordahl. Piano solos arranged and played by Andre Previn. Musical score by Sammy Cahn and Julie Styne.

Running Time - 105 Minutes

Cast

Danny Miller	- Frank Sinatra	Digby John	- Aubrey Mather
Anne Fielding	- Kathryn Grayson	Mrs. Kardos	- Tamara Shayne
James Shellgrove	- Peter Lawford	Leo Kardos	- Billy Roy
Nick Lombardi	- Jimmy Durante	Johnny O'Brien	- Bobby Long
Nurse	- Gloria Grahame	Police Sergeant	- Bill Haade
Rae Jakobi	- Marcy McGuire	Cop	- Dick Wessel

Synopsis

A pleasant inconsequential musical about an ex-soldier (Frank) who moves in with a janitor (Durante) in Brooklyn. Frank sings a few bars of an uninspired tune called *"Whose Baby Are You"* and also clowns with Durante on *"It's Gotta Come From The Heart."* He duets with Miss Grayson on *"La Ci Darem La Mano"*. The rest of the songs are showcases for Frank and include *"The Brooklyn Bridge"*, *"Time After Time"*, *"I Believe"* and *"It's The Same Old Dream"*. He also sang *"Black Eyes."*

THE MIRACLE OF THE BELLS

R.K.O. Radio Pictures - March 27, 1948

Produced by Jesse L. Lasky and Walter MacEwen. Directed by Irving Pickel. Screenplay by Ben Hecht and Quenton Reynolds. Additional material for Sinatra's sequences by Dewitt Bodeen. Based on the novel by Russell Janney. Music by Leigh Harline, and musical direction by C. Bakaleinikoff. Theme melody by Pierre Norman and Russell Janney. Special effects by Russell Silvera and Clifford Stine. Church bell effects by Liberty Carillon, Inc.

Running Time - 120 Minutes

Cast

Father Paul	- Frank Sinatra	Father Spinsky	- C. Meredith
Bill Dunnigan	- Fred MacMurray	Anna Klowna	- V. Patasky
Olga	- Valli	Ming Gow	- Philip Ahn
Marcus Harris	- Lee J. Cobb	Dolan	- Frank Ferguson
Orloff	- Harold Vermilyea	Dr. Janning	- Frank Wilcox
Tod Jones	- Jim Nolan	Commentator	- Quenton Reynolds

Synopsis

A sophisticated press agent comes to a drab mining town in Pennsylvannia to carry out a promise to a young actress. The promise was to have her buried next to that of her father in the town church. She died of Tuberculosis and a miracle happens. The agent sees a story in it and gets involved. It's really a long, terribly trite and sentimental drama. Frank portrays the town priest and sings one song, *"Ever Homeward"*. Written by Sammy Cahn and Julie Styne adapted from an old Polish Folksong by K. Lubromirski.

"The Miracle Of The Bells" - Fred MacMurray, Valli, Sinatra — 1948.

"The Kissing Bandit" — 1948.

LUCY STRIKE SALESMAN'S MOVIE - No. 48-A

Summer 1948

Produced by The American Tobacco Co.

Running Time - 10 Minutes

The film describes the cultivation, harvesting, storing, buying and manufacturing of tobacco and shows the work of three auctioneers, a warehouseman and a buyer. Sinatra appears on screen with The Lucky Strike Singers and The Hit Parade Orchestra, conducted by Axel Stordahl. He sings *"Embraceable You"*.

THE KISSING BANDIT

M.G.M. - November 19, 1948 - Color

Produced by Joe Pasternak; Directed by Laslo Benedek. Original screenplay by Isobel Lennart and John Braird Harding. Music supervised and conducted by George Stoll. Musical arrangements by Leo Anaud. Additional arrangements by Calvin Jackson, Conrad Salinger and Bobby Van Epps. Special effects by Arnold Gillespie.

Running Time - 102 Minutes

Cast

Ricardo	- Frank Sinatra	General Torro	- Billy Gilbert
Teresa	- Kathryn Grayson	Bianco	- Sono Osato
Chico	- J. Carrol Naish	Colonel Gomez	- Clinton Sundberg
Isabella	- Mildred Natwick	Count Belmonte	- Carlton Young
Don Jose	- Mikhail Rasumny	Juanita	- Edna Skinner

Mexican Guitarist - V. Gomez

Fiesta Dance Specialists - Ricardo Montalban, Cyd Charisse, Ann Miller.

Synopsis

One of Sinatra's least inspired films. It is a story of a nice chap who is forced to go out west and enter his father's business. His father turns out to be an outlaw and in spite of the potential the film becomes a complete bore. Frank sings *"What's Wrong With Me"*, *"If I Steal A Kiss"*, *"Senorita"*, and *"Siesta"*. P.S. Frank finally gets to keep Kathryn Grayson.

TAKE ME OUT TO THE BALLGAME

M.G.M. - March 10, 1949 - Color

Produced by Arthur Freed. Directed by Busbey Berkely. Screenplay by Harry Tugend and George Wells; based on a story by Gene Kelly and Stanley Donen. Music supervised and conducted by Adolph Deutsch. Orchestral arrangements for Sinatra by Axel Stordahl. Vocal arrangements by Robert Tucker. Art directors, Cedric Gibbons and Daniel B. Cathcart.

"On The Town" -
Sinatra,
Jules Munshin,
Gene Kelly,
Betty Garrett,
Ann Miller,
Vera Ellen — 1949.

"Take Me Out To The Ballgame" - Sinatra, Gene Kelly, Jule's Munshin — 1949.

Running Time - 93 Minutes

Cast

Dennis Ryan	- Frank Sinatra	Steve	- Saul Gross
K.C. Higgins	- Esther Williams	Karl	- Douglas Fowley
Eddie O'Brien	- Gene Kelly	Dr. Winston	- Eddie Parkes
Shirley Delwyn	- Betty Garrett	Cop In Park	- James Burke
Joe Lorgan	- Edward Arnold	Specialty	- Blackburn Twins
Nat Goldberg	- Jules Munshin	Senator Catcher	- G. Jones
Michael Gilhuly	- Richard Lane	Reporter	- Frank Scannell
Slappy Burke	- Tom Dugan	Acrobat	- Henry Kulky
Zalinka	- Murray Alper	Girl Dancer	- D. Abbot
Henchman	- Mark Gray	Girl On Train	- Joi Lansing
Henchman	- Charles Regan	DAncer	- Sally Forrest
Nick Donford	- Will Graff	Roosevelt	- Ed Cassidy

Synopsis

A vaudeville song and dance team of 1906 are sensational big league baseball players. This promising musical comedy falters because of forced comedy and of course Miss Williams finds a swimming pool where she can do a water ballet. Sinatra sings the title song *"Take Me Out To The Ballgame"* with Kelly, *"The Boys Said No"*, *"O'Brien, To Ryan, To Goldberg"*, with Kelly and Munshin. A pretty ballad *"She's The Right Girl For Me"* is sung to Miss Williams and *"It's Fate Baby It's Fate"* with Betty Garrett. *"It's Strictly U.S.A."* is sung as a dance production number with everyone joining in. A very pretty song titled *"Boys and Girls Like You"* was deleted in the released version. Also sang *"Yes Indeedy."*

ON THE TOWN

M.G.M. - December 4, 1949 - Color

Produced by Arthur Freed. Directed by Gene Kelly and Stanley Donen. Screenplay by Adolph Green and Betty Comden, based on their play of the same name from an idea of Jerome Robbins. Music supervised and conducted by Lennie Hayton with orchestral arrangements by Conrad Salinger, Robert Franklyn and Wally Heglin. Vocal arrangements by Saul Chaplin. Filmed in New York City.

Running Time - 98 Minutes

Cast

Gabey	- Gene Kelly	Lucy Schmeeler	- Alice Pearse
Chip	- Frank Sinatra	Professor	- George Meader
B. Esterhazy	- Betty Garrett	Working Girl	- B. Benaderet
Claire Hudderson	- Ann Miller	Spud	- Sid Melton
Ozzie	- Jules Munshin	Headwaiter	- Hans Conreid
Ivy Smith	- Vera-Ellen	Cab Co. Owner	- M. Alper
Mme. Dilyovska	- Florence Bates	Dancer In Green	- Carol Haney
		Cop	- Frank Hagney

"Double Dynamite" — *Groucho Marx, Sinatra, Jane Russell* — *1951.*

"Double Dynamite" - *Sinatra, Groucho Marx* — *1951.*

Synopsis

A story of three sailors who hit New York on a 24 hour leave with two intentions: to see the sights and meet three girls. The overall picture flits and frolics with care-free delight, a bulging package of slap-stick and wit, of musical numbers both gagged up and graceful. Frank sings two duets with Betty Garrett; *"Come Up To My Place"* and *"You're Awful"*. He also joins with the others to sing *"New York, New York"*, *"On The Town"* and *"Count On Me."*

DOUBLE DYNAMITE

R.K.O. Pictures - November 7, 1951

An Irving Cummings production; Directed by Irving Cummings. Screenplay by Melville Shavelson; added dialogue by Harry Crane. Story by Leo Rosten, based on the characters created by Mannie Manheim. Songs by Julie Styne and Sammy Cahn and musical score by Leigh Harline.

Running Time - 80 Minutes

Cast

Johnny Dalton	- Frank Sinatra	Bookie	- Nestor Paiva
Mildred	- Jane Russell	Mr. Kofer	- Frank Orth
Emil J. Keck	- Groucho Marx	McKissach	- Harry Hayden
Bob Pulsifer	- Don McGuire	Baganucci	- William Edmunds
R.B. Pulsifer, Jr.	- Howard Freeman	Tailman	- Russ Thorson

Synopsis

Sinatra and Russell are bank clerks in love but too poor to tackle matrimony. By chance Sinatra breaks up an attack on a bigshot bookie who contrives to have the hero win $60,000 betting the ponies. At the same time the bank discovers the shortage of an equal amount, forcing Sinatra to keep his good fortune undercover. A lightweight hodge-podge with comedic intentions. Frank sings *"It's Only Money"* with Groucho Marx and *"Kisses And Tears"* with Jane.

MEET DANNY WILSON

Universal Inernational - February 12, 1952

Produced by Leonard Goldstein; Directed by Joseph Pevney. Story and screenplay by Don McGuire. Musical director, Joseph Gershenson with musical numbers staged by Hal Belfer.

Running Time - 88 Minutes

"Meet Danny Wilson" - Sinatra, Raymond Burr, Shelly Winters, Alex Nicol
— 1952.

"From Here To Eternity" - Ernest Borgnine, Burt Lancaster, Sinatra — 1953.

Cast

Danny Wilson	- Frank Sinatra	Sergeant	- Donald MacBride
Joy Carroll	- Shelly Winters	Marie	- Barbara Knudson
Mike Ryan	- Alex Nicol	Cab Driver	- Carl Sklover
Nick Driscoll	- Raymond Burr	Gus	- John Day
Tommy Wells	- Tommy Farrell	Heckler	- Jack Kruschen
T.W. Hatcher	- Vaughn Taylor	Turnkey	- Tom Dugan

Night Club Patron - Tony Curtis

Synopsis

A down at the heels entertainer is befriended by a girl whose protector is a racketeering nightclub owner. He immediately becomes successful and takes off for Hollywood believing he is going to marry the girl. Miss Winters, however, is in love with Sinatra's piano player, Alex Nicol. Frank sings quite a few fine standards such as: *"You're A Sweetheart"*, *"That Old Black Magic"*, *"I've Got A Crush On You"*, *"All Of Me"*, *"When You're Smiling"*, *"She's Funny That Way"*, *"Lonesome Man Blues"*, *"How Deep Is The Ocean"* and a duet with Miss Winters, *"A Good Man Is Hard To Find."*

FROM HERE TO ETERNITY

Columbia - August 17, 1953

Producer, Buddy Adler and directed by Fred Zinnemann; Screenplay by Daniel Taradash, based on the novel by James Jones. Music supervised and conducted by Morris Stoloff. Background by Arthur Morton. Song *"Re-enlistment Blues"* by James Jones, Fred Karger and Fred Wells. Technical advisor, Brig. General Kendall J. Fielder, U.S. Army.

Running Time - 120 Minutes

Cast

Sgt. Milton Warden	- Burt Lancaster	Mrs. Kipher	- B. Morrison
Robert E. Lee Prewitt	- Montgomery Cliff	Georgette	- K. Miller
Karen Holmes	- Deborah Kerr	Annette	- Jean Willes
Angelo Maggio	- Frank Sinatra	Sal Anderson	- M. Travis
Alma	- Donna Reed	Treadwell	- A. Keegan
Capt. Dana Holmes	- Philip Ober	Sgt. Baldy Thorn	- C. Akins
Sgt. Leva	- Mickey Shaughnessy	Sgt. Tuep Thornhill	- Rob. Karnes
Mazzioli	- Harry Bellaver	Sgt. Henderson	- R. Wilke
Sgt. "Fatso" Judson	- Ernest Borgnine	Cpl. Champ Wilson	- Douglas Henderson
Sgt. Maylon Stark	- George Reeves	Friday Clark	- D. Dubbins
Sgt. Ike Galovitch	- John Dennis		
Sgt. Pete Karlson	- Tim Ryan		
Cpl. Paluso	- John Casor		
Capt. Ross	- John Bryant		

"From Here To Eternity" — *1953.*

"Suddenly" - *Sinatra, Sterling Hayden* — *1954.*

Synopsis

A powerful dramatization of phases of military life in a peaceful army at Scholfield barracks in Hawaii. Tough and brawling but at the same time, a tenderly moving and vivid motion picture. Frank Sinatra, as Maggio, the tough little Italian-American soldier played his part exactly right, rich in comic vitality and genuine pathos. He proved once and for all that he was more than just a singer, much more. He won the Academy Award for best supporting actor for his fine effort. Among other awards were:

Best Production
Donna Reed - Best Supporting Actress
Fred Zinnemann - Direction
Daniel Taradash - Writing (Screenplay)
Burnett Guffey - Cinematography (Black & White)
John P. Livadary - Sound Director
Columbia Studio Sound Dept. - Sound Recording
William Lyon - Film Editing

SUDDENLY

United Artist - September 24, 1954
Produced by Robert Bassler and Directed by Lewis Allen. Assistant Director, Hal Klein and Erick Von Stroheim Jr. Screenplay by Richard Sale.

Running Time - 77 Minutes

Cast

John Baron	- Frank Sinatra	Benny Conklin	- Paul Frees
Tod Shaw	- Sterling Hayden	Bart Wheeler	- Christopher Dark
Pop Benson	- James Gleason	Dan Carney	- Willis Bouchey
Ellen Benson	- Nancy Gates	Slim Adams	- Paul Wexler
Pidge	- Kim Charney	Jud Hobson	- Jim Lilburn

Synopsis

Frank portrays a professional killer who hits a small town bent on assasinating the President of the United States. Sinatra's bravado performance as a cold blooded thug, plus crisp direction make this thriller above average.

FINIAN'S RAINBOW - (Unfinished and unreleased)

Distributors Corporation of America - 1954

Produced and directed by John Hubley. Musical direction by Lyn Murray with songs by Burton Lane and E.Y. Harburg.

This was planned as a full-length animated film featuring the voices of Sinatra, Ella Fitzgerald, Ella Logan, Barry Fitzgerald, Louis Armstrong and Jim Backus. None of the animation was filmed but the scoring and recording were completed and due to lack of financing this potentially entertaining enterprise is now an unrealized project. One consolation, however is that the vocals

"Suddenly" - *Nancy Gates, Sinatra, James Gleason.*

"Young At Heart" - *Doris Day, Sinatra, Ethel Barrymore — 1965.*

contributed by Sinatra along with Miss Fitzgerald and the late Louis Armstrong have recently been presented on an album. They are:
"Necessity" - (Sinatra in a duet with Ella Fitzgerald),
"Ad Lib Blues" - (Sinatra in a duet with Louis Armstrong),
"That Great Come And Get It Day" and a solo version of *"Necessity"*.
Also sang *"If This Isn't Love"*, and *"Old Devil Moon"*.

They all appear on Chairman 6009 titled *"The Definite Sinatra"*.

YOUNG AT HEART

Warner Bros. - January 15, 1955 - Color

Produced by Henry Blanke and Directed by Gordon Davis with Screenplay by Joseph J. Epstein and Lenore Coffe. Adaptation by Liam O'Brien from a story by Fannie Hurst. Music supervised, arranged and conducted by Ray Heindorf. Piano solos by Andre Previn. Wardrobe by Howard Shoup. Assistant Director, Al Alleborn. An Arwin Production in Warner Color.

Running Time - 117 Minutes

Cast

Laurie Tuttle	- Doris Day	Amy Tuttle	- E. Fraser
Barney Sloan	- Frank Sinatra	Gregory Tuttle	- Robert Keith
Alex Burke	- Gig Young	Robert Neary	- A. Hale, Jr.
Aunt Jessie	- Ethel Barrymore	Ernest Nichols	- L. Chapman
Fran Tuttle	- Dorothy Malone	Bartell	- Frank Ferguson
		Mrs. Ridgefield	- M. Bennett

Synopsis

A frankly sentimental tale of a family of modern little women in a peaceful town, whose happy home is invaded by masculine disturbers and by one lonely stray in particular. Frank plays the latter character, a rude and bitter misfit with splendid talents in the musical line, who is the one who does the most disrupting and who is radically reconstructed in the end. Frank sings the title song *"Young At Heart"*, *"She's Funny That Way"*, *"Just One Of Those Things"*, *"Someone To Watch Over Me"* and a duet with Doris Day, *"You My Love."*

In 1955 Sinatra was to appear in the 20th Century Fox Production of *"Carousel"* It was to be a lavish presentation with a great score by Rodgers and Hammerstein and although Sinatra did make recordings he bowed out of the actual film due to the studio's insistence that he film the scenes twice, once in conventional 35 mm. cinescope and again in its new process, 55 mm. cinescope. He refused and was replaced by Gordon MacCrae and the irony of it all was the fact that the studio discovered later on that it could indeed film both processes in one sequence, and even more ironical was the final decision to film in only the larger process. Sinatra recorded nine takes of *"Soliloquy"* and four takes of *"If I Loved You."*

"Not As A Stranger" - Sinatra, Robert Mitchum, Olivia DeHaviland — 1955.

"Guys And Dolls" - Sinatra, Marlon Brando, Jean Simmons, Vivian Blaine — 1955.

NOT AS A STRANGER

United Artists - July 2, 1955

Producer-Director, Stanley Kramer. Screenplay by Edna and Edward Anhalt, based on a novel by Morton Thompson. Music by George Antheil; Song by Jimmy Van Heusen and Buddy Kaye. Assistant Director, Carter DeHaven Jr.; Gowns by Don Loper.

Running Time - 135 Minutes

Cast

Kristina Hedvigson	- Olivia DeHaviland	Joe Marsh	- L. Chaney
Lucas Marsh	- Robert Mitchum	Ben Cosgrove	- J. White
Alfred Boone	- Frank Sinatra	Oley	- Harry Morza
Harriet Lang	- Gloria Grahame	Brundage	- Lee Marvin
Dr. Aarons	- Broderick Crawford	Bruni	- V. Christine
Dr. Runkleman	- Charles Bickford	Dr. Dietrich	- W. Bissel
Dr. Snider	- Mryon McCormick	Dr. Lettering	- J. Raine
		Miss O'Dell	- M. Clarke

Synopsis

A story about a poor man obsessed with the drive to become a great doctor, who practiced medicine, but didn't know how to handle or treat people. Frank Sinatra as a loyal fellow doctor gives the movie its few flashers of humor and most of its compassion. He also recorded the title song.

GUYS AND DOLLS

M.G.M. - November 14, 1955 - Color

Produced by Samuel Goldwyn; Directed by Joseph L. Mankiewicz and also Screenplay by Mankiewicz. From the musical play by Jo Swerling and Abe Burrows based on a story by Damon Runyon. Music and lyrics by Frank Loesser; Supervised and conducted by Jay Blackton. Orchestral arrangements by Skip Martin, Nelson Riddle, Alexander Courage and Albert Sendrey. Dances and musical numbers staged by Michael Kidd. Costumes by Irene Sharoff. In Cinemascope and Eastman Color.

Running Time - 150 Minutes

"The Tender Trap" - Sinatra, Debbie Reynolds, Celeste Holm, David Wayne — 1955.

"The Man With The Golden Arm" - Robert Strauss, Sinatra, Arnold Stang — 1956.

Cast

Sky Masterson	- Marlon Brando	Rusty Charlie	- Dan Layton
Sarah Brown	- Jean Simmons	Society Max	- G.E. Stone
Nathan Detroit	- Frank Sinatra	Arvid Abernathy	- R. Toomey
Miss Adelaide	- Vivian Blaine	Gen. Cartwright	- Kathryn Givney
Lt. Brannigan	- Robert Keith	Laverne	- Veda Ann Borg
Nicely-Nicely Johnson	- Stubby Kaye	Agatha	- Mary Alan Hokanson
Big Jule	- B.S. Pully	Angie The Ox	- Joe McTurk
Benny Southstreet	- Johnny Silver	Calvin	- Kay Kuter
Harry The Horse	- Sheldon Leonard	Mission Member	- S. Kent
Cuban Singer	- Renee Renor		

And The Goldwyn Girls

Synopsis

Based on the Broadway play of the same name, the story revolves around the efforts of Nathan Detroit (Sinatra) to hold a safe crap game for the big time gamblers in town. Brando sings, Sinatra sings, Simmons sings and dances and Vivian Blaine plays the same role (Adelaide) she made famous on Broadway - a lotta fun. Sinatra sings *"Adelaide"*, *"I've Got A Horse Right Here"*, *"Fugue For Tinhorns"*, *"The Oldest Established"*, and *"Sue Me."*

THE TENDER TRAP

M.G.M. - November 17, 1955 - Color

Produced by Laurence Weingarten; Directed by Charles Walters; Assistant Director, Joel Freeman. Screenplay by Julius Epstein, based on the play by Max Schulman and Robert Paul Smith. Background music by Jeff Alexander. Songs by Sammy Cahn and James Van Heusen. Costumes by Helen Rose. In Cinemascope and Technicolor.

Running Time - 113 Minutes

Cast

Charlie Y. Reader	- Frank Sinatra	Helen	- Carolyn Jones
Julie Gillis	- Debbie Reynolds	Mr. Sayers	- Howard St. John
Joe McCall	- David Wayne	Sol Z. Steiner	- Joey Faye
Sylvia Crewes	- Celeste Holm	Mr. Loughran	- Tom Helmore
Jessica	- Jarma Lewis	Director	- Wiliard Sage
Poppy	- Lola Albright	Ballet-Actor	- Marc Wilder

Synopsis

A comical dissertation on the fun a bright fellow can have by merely remaining single in the gutted marriage market of New York, is a vastly beguiling entertainment even for guys who already are hooked. Frank plays this enterprsing bachelor who has the world on a string or at least has half a dozen lovely girls dangling. The title tune *"Love Is The Tender Trap"* is sung by Sinatra.

"Johnny Concho" - Sinatra, Phyliss Kirk — 1956.

"High Society" - Sinatra, Bing Crosby — 1957.

THE MAN WITH THE GOLDEN ARM

United Artists - January 15, 1956

Produced and Directed by Otto Preminger. Screenplay by Walter Newman and Lewis Meltzer from the novel of the same name by Nelson Algren. Music by Elmer Bernstein; Designed by Joe Wright. Assistant to the producer, Maximilian Slater; Costume Supervisor, Mary Ann Nyberg. Assistant Directors, Horace Hough and James Engle. Jazz by Shorty Rogers and his Gants.

Running Time - 119 Minutes

Cast

Frankie Machine	- Frank Sinatra	Mominowski	- Leonard Kinskey
Zosh	- Eleanor Parker	Bedmar	- Emile Meyer
Molly	- Kim Novak	Shorty Rogers	- Himself
Louie	- Daren McGavin	Piggy	- Frank Richards
Schwiefka	- Robert Straus	Lane	- Will Wright
Drunky	- John Conte	Kvorka	- Tommy Hart
Vi	- Doro Merende	Axtek	- Frank Marlowe
Markette	- George E. Stone	Chester	- Ralph Neff
Williams	- George Matthews	Vangie	- Martha Wentworth

Synopsis

Sinatra plays a fabulous poker dealer named Frankie Machine, who can control a card game with instinctive skill. He had returned from a federal narcotics hospital where he has supposedly shaken the habit and studies to be a jazz drummer. Circumstances and pressures force him back into the habit which he eventually kicks for good. Well acted by everyone involved. It contains one Sammy Cahn, Jimmy Van Heusen song *"Molly 'O"*. The title song was recorded by Frank and never released although Capitol records claim they know nothing about it.

JOHNNY CONCHO

United Artists - July 24, 1956

Producer, Frank Sinatra; Director, Don McGuire. Screenplay by David P. Harmon. Assistant director, Emmett Emerson. Music by Nelson Riddle. Associate producer, Henry Sanicola and costumes by Gwen Waherling - A Kent Production.

Running Time - 84 Minutes

Cast

Johnny Concho	- Frank Sinatra	Judge Tyler	- Dan Russ
Barney Clark	- Keenan Wynn	Sheriff Henderson	- Willis Bouchey
Tallman	- William Conrad	Duke Land	- Robert Osterloh
Mary Dark	- Phyliss Kirk	Pearl Lang	- Jean Byron
Albert Dark	- Wallace Ford	Mason	- Leo Gordon
Sarah Dark	- Dorothy Adams	Lem	- Claude Akins
Walker	- Christopher Dark	Jake	- John Quelem
Helgeson	- Howard Petrie	Pearson	- Wilfrid Knapp
Sam Greer	- Harry Bartell	Benson	- Ben Wright
		Bartender	- Joe Bassett

Synopsis

A story of a young bully in a frightened western town who thrives in the shadow of his brother, a famous gunman, until the latter is killed. Then when a genuine bully arrives to take over, he turns coward and tries to make tracks out of that region. This film marks Sinatra's debut as a producer and he also made a recording of the theme *"Wait For Me"* for Capitol Records.

MEET ME IN LAS VEGAS

M.G.M. - 1956 - Color

Produced by Joe Pasternak and Directed by Roy Rowland. Music supervised and conducted by George Stoll.

Sinatra in an unbilled walk-on performance playing a slot machine (and hitting the jackpot). Also in brief appearances are Frankie Laine, Debbie Reynolds, Tony Martin, Peter Lorre, Vic Damone, Lena Horne and Elaine Stewart.

AROUND THE WORLD IN 80 DAYS

United Artists - October 12, 1956 - Color

A guest performance in the fabled Mike Todd production of the faithful adaptation of the popular Jules Verne classic. It was filmed all over the world in authentic locales and relates the daring attempt to circle the globe in recordbreaking time in the year 1872. Sinatra portrays a honky-tonk pianist.

HIGH SOCIETY

M.G.M. - February 16, 1957 - Color

Produced by Sol C. Siegel; Directed by Charles Walters. Screenplay by John Patrick based on a play by Philip Barry. Music and lyrics by Cole Porter, with Johnny Green conducting the M.G.M. Orchestra. Music supervised and adapted by Johnny Green and Saul Chaplin, orchestrated by Conrad Salinger, Nelson Riddle and Skip Martin.

Running Time - 107 Minutes

"High Society" - Bing Crosby, Grace Kelly, John Lund, Mary Gilmore, Lydia Reed, Celeste Holm — 1957.

"The Pride And The Passion" - Sophia Loren, Sinatra, Gary Grant — 1957.

Cast

C.K. Dexter-Haven	- Bing Crosby	Seth Loard	- Sidney Blackmer
Tracy Lord	- Grace Kelly	Louis Armstrong	- Himself
Mike Connor	- Frank Sinatra	Mrs. Seth Lord	- M. Gillmore
Liz Imbrie	- Celeste Holm	Caroline Lord	- Lydia Reed
George Kittredge	- John Lund	Dexter-Haven's	
Uncle Willie	- Louis Calhern	Butler	- Gordon Richards
		Lord's Butler	- Richard Garrick

Synopsis

The *"Philadelphia Story"* brought back here as a musical. An urbane tale about a frosty main line heiress who was narrowly prevented from marrying the wrong man. Whenever the script gets dull and this happens once in a while, the music starts and all is well again. The real hero is Cole Porter who has written an exceptional score that gives the movie its special flair. Sinatra sings *"Who Wants To Be A Millionaire"* with Celeste Holm; *"Well Did You Evah"* with Bing Crosby and two solo stints *"You're Sensational"* and *"Mind If I Make Love To You."*

THE PRIDE AND THE PASSION

United Artists - June 17, 1957 - Color

Produced and directed by Stanley Kramer; a Stanley Kramer presentation. Screenplay and screenstory by Edna and Edward Anhalt, based on the novel by C.S. Forester called *"The Gun"* . Musical Director, Muir Mathieson, music composed by Richard Addinsell. Filmed in Spain. In Cinemascope and DeLuxe Color.

Running Time - 132 Minutes

Cast

Capt. Anthony			
Trumbull	- Cary Grant	Ballinger	- Jay Novello
Miguel	- Frank Sinatra	Carlos	- Jose Nieto
Juana	- Sophia Loren	Jose	- Carlos Larranaga
General Jouvet	- Theodore Bikel	Vidal	- Phillip Van Zandt
Sermaine	- John Wengrof	Manalo	- Paco el Laberinto

Synopsis

Sinatra plays a straight dramatic role in a film set in Spain during the Napoleonic era. It has to do with the moving of a giant cannon halfway across wartorn Spain. Frank portrays the Spanish guerrilla leader who is a constant thorn in Bonaparte's army side. Not one of the better Sinatra films of fairly recent vintage.

"The Joker Is Wild" - Mitzi Gaynor, Sinatra — 1957.

"Pal Joey" - Sinatra, Bobby Sherwood, Rita Hayworth — 1957.

THE JOKER IS WILD (Reissued as *"All The Way"* in 1966)

Paramount - September 12, 1957

Produced by Samuel J. Briskin. Directed by Charles Vidor. Screenplay by Oscar Paul; based on the book by Art Cohn on the life of Joe E. Lewis. Art directors, Hal Periera and Roland Andreson. Music scored and conducted by Walter Scharf. Costumes by Edith Head. Dances staged by Josephine Earl. Photography by Daniel L. Fapp. Special effects, John P. Fulton. Editor, Everett Douglas. An A.M.B.L. Production. In Vista Vision.

Running Time - 126 Minutes

Cast

Joe E. Lewis	- Frank Sinatra	Heckler	- Wally Brown
Letty Page	- Jeanne Craine	Harry Bliss	- Harold Huber
Martha Stewart	- Mitzie Gaynor	Johnson	- Ned Glass
Austin Mack	- Eddie Albert	Dr. Pierson	- Ned Weaver
Cassie Mack	- Beverly Garland	Mr. Page	- Walter King
Swifty Morgan	- Jackie Coogan	Runner	- Sid Melton
Capt. Hugh McCarthy	- Barry Kelly	Man Shaving	- Dick Elliot
George Parker	- Ted DeCorsia	Allen	- John Harding
Tim Coogan	- Leonard Graves	Girl	- Lucy Knoch
Flora	- Valerie Allen	Letty's Husband	- William Pullen
Burlesque Comedian	- Hank Henry	Judge	- F. Oliver McGowan
Photographer	- Dennis McMullen	Butler	- Eric Wilton

Synopsis

A story of a cocky young prohibition era singer almost ruined by a gangster, who switches to comedy and drinks his way to night club fame, as two lovely ladies lose him to show business legend. In reality, the life of Joe E. Lewis, with excellent dialogue, was peppery, amusing and sensitive in turn. Fine acting by Sinatra who appears in virtually every scene. Frank sings *"All The Way"*, written by Sammy Cahn and James Van Heusen especially for this film. *"Chicago"* written by Fred Fisher, *"I Cried For You"* and *"If I Could Be With You."*

PAL JOEY

Columbia - December, 1957 - Color

Essex - George Sidney production, produced by Fred Kohlmer, Directed by Sidney. Screenplay by Dorothy Kingsley from the play of the same title with book by John O'Hara. Music by Richard Rogers; Lyrics by Lorenz Hart. Stage produced by George Abbott; Choreography by Hermes Pan; Music supervised and conducted by Morris Stoloff with arrangements and adaptation by Nelson Riddle and George Dunning. In Technicolor.

"Pal Joey" - Sinatra, Kim Novak — 1957.

"Kings Go Forth" - Sinatra, Tony Curtis — 1957.

Running Time - 112 Minutes

Cast

Joey Evans	- Frank Sinatra	Bartender	- Robin Morse
Vera Simpson	- Rita Hayworth	Col. Langley	- Frank Wilcox
Linda English	- Kim Novak	Mr. Forsythe	- Pierre Watkin
Gladys	- Barbara Nichols	Anderson	- Barry Bernard
Ned Galvin	- Bobby Sherwood	Carol	- Ellie Kent
Mike Miggins	- Hank Henry	Sabrina	- Mara McAfee
Mrs. Carey	- Elizabeth Patterson	Patsy	- Betty Utey
		Lola	- Bek Nelson

Synopsis

Film version of John O'Hara's 1940 Broadway musical drama with a hit score by Rodgers and Hart. The story focuses on a brash singer (Sinatra) who dreams of opening his own nightclub. Frank Sinatra is ideal as the irreverent, free-wheeling glib, Joey, delivering the rapid fire cracks in a fashion that brings out full deeper-than-pale blue comedy potentials. He sings *"A Small Hotel"*, *"I Could Write A Book"*, *"What Do I Care For A Dame"*, *"I Didn't Know What Time It Was"* and a swinging powerhouse rendition of *"The Lady Is A Tramp"*. Many consider this to be Sinatra's greatest musical. (*"Bewitched"*) also sung.

KINGS GO FORTH

United Artists - July 30, 1958

A Ross-Eton Production. Distributor United Artists. Producer: Frank Ross; Director: Delmer Davis. Screenplay by Merle Miller, based on the novel by Joe David Brown. Associate producer: Richard Ross. Music: Elmer Bernstein. Filmed partially on location in Touretler-sur-Loup near Nice, France.

Running Time - 109 Minutes

Cast

Sam Loggins	- Frank Sinatra
Britt Harris	- Tony Curtis
Monique Blair	- Natalie Wood
Mrs. Blair	- Leora Dana
Colonel	- Karl Swenson
Mme. Brieux	- Anne Codee
Jean Francoise	- Jackie Berthe
Old Woman With Wine	- Marie Ilsnard
Jazz Combo	- Trumpet, Pete Candoli; Vibraphone, Red Norvo; Drums, Mel Lewis; Sax, Richie Kamuca; Bass, Red Wooten; Guitar, Jimmy Weible.

Synopsis

A story of two American soldiers who fall for a beautiful French born girl they meet while on leave. Later they learn that her mother is white and her father,

"Some Came Running" - Martha Hyer, Dean Martin, Shirley MacLaine, Sinatra, Nancy Gates, Arthur Kennedy, Leora Dana — 1957.

"A Hole In The Head" - Thelma Ritter, Sinatra, Eddie Hodges, Edward G. Robinson — 1959.

now dead, was a negro. It is the different reactions of the two men that set of the story's conflicts. The performances are effective and the settings picturesque. Sammy Cahn and Elmer Bernstein wrote the new song *"Monique"* which is the theme played throughout the film.

INVITATION TO MONTE CARLO

Valiant Films - Late 1958 - Color

Running Time - 45 Minutes

A Travel feature about Monaco showing Sinatra on the Riviera while attending the premiere of *"Kings Go Forth"*.

SOME CAME RUNNING

M.G.M. - February 4, 1959 - Color

A Sol C. Siegel Production for M.G.M. Producer Sol C. Siegel. Directed by Vincente Minnelli. Screenplay by John Patrick and Arthur Sheekman. Based on the novel by James Jones. Photography: William H. Daniels. Music: Elmer Bernstein. Song: *"To Love And Be Loved"* - Sammy Cahn lyrics and James Van Heusen music. Location scenes filmed in Madison, Indiana in Cinemascope and Metrocolor.

Running Time - 134 Minutes

Cast

Dave Hirsh	- Frank Sinatra	Dawn Hirsh	- Betty Lou Keim
Bama Dillert	- Dean Martin	Professor Robert	
Ginny Morhead	- Shirley MacLaine	French	- L. Gates
Given French	- Martha Hyer	Raymond	
Frank Hirsh	- Arthur Kennedy	Lanchok	- S. Peck
Edith Barclay	- Nancy Gates	Rosalie	- Carmen Phillips
Agnes Hirsh	- Leora Dana	Jane Barclay	- C. Gilchrist
		Smitty	- Ned Weaver
		Wally Dennis	- John Brennan

Synopsis

Frank plays a lonely and skeptical army corporal who returns to his home in Indiana a few years after World War II. He is beautifully casual with a bottle, bullseye sharp with a gag and shockingly frank and impertinent in making passes at dames. The picture really explores the confusion of a writer unable to come to working terms with his social background. The film had several advance bookings late in 1958 and was eligible for the '58 Academy Awards.

A HOLE IN THE HEAD

United Artists - August 26, 1959 - Color

Produced and directed by Frank Capra. Screenplay by Arnold Shulman; based on the T.V. play - *"The Heart's A Lonely Hotel"* and the 1957 stageplay by

Shulman. Assistant Directors Arthur Black Jr. and Jack Berne. Art director - Eddie Imazu. Cinematographer - William H. Daniels. Costumes by Edith Head. Editor - William Hornbeck. Music - Nelson Riddle.

Main titles on a banner carried by Goodyear Blimp. Filmed in Cypress Gardens and Miami Beach, Florida. A Sincap Production in Panovision, DeLuxe Color.

Running Time - 120 Minutes

Cast

Tony Manetta	- Frank Sinatra	Julius Manetta	- J. Kamack
Mario Manetta	- Edward G. Robinson	Fred	- Dub Taylor
Ally Manetta	- Eddie Hodges	Miss Wexler	- Connie Sawyer
Mrs. Rogers	- Eleanor Parker	Abe Diamond	- Benny Rubin
Shirl	- Carolyn Jones	Sally	- Ruby Dandridge
Sophie	- Thelma Ritter	Hood N1	- B.S. Pully
Jerry Marks	- Keenan Wynn	Alice	- Joyce Nizzari
Dorine	- Joi Lansing	Sheriff	- Emory Parnell
Mendy	- George DeWitt	Andy	- Bill Waler

Master of Ceremonies - Pupi Campo

Synopsis

Frank Sinatra plays a care free but broke Miami hotel owner who has high hopes of wheedling some cash out of his older brother, a staid and practical New York businessman. Frank sings *"High Hopes"* which won an Oscar for James Van Heusen and Sammy Cahn and *"All My Tomorrows."*

NEVER SO FEW

M.G.M. - February 12, 1960 - Color

A Canterbury Production for M.G.M.; Producer; Edmund Grainger; Director: John Sturges; Screenplay: Millard Kaufman; Music: Hugo Friedhofer. Location scenes filmed in Burma, Thailand and Ceylon. Cinemascope - Metrocolor.

Running Time - 126 Minutes

Cast

Capt. Tom C. Reynolds	- Frank Sinatra	Nautaung	- Philp Ahn
Carla Vesari	- Gina Lollabrigida	Col. Fred Parkson	- Robert Bray
Capt. Grey Travis	- Peter Lawford	Margaret Fitch	- Kip Hamilton
Bill Ringa	- Steve McQueen	Col. Reed	- John Hoyt
Capt. Danny DeMortimer	- Richard Johnson	Capt. Alofson	- W. Bissell
Nikko Regas	- Paul Henreid	Mike Island	- R. Lupino
Gen. Sloan	- Brian Donlevy	Bellingsly	- A. Aleong
Sgt. Jim Norby	- Dean Jones	Nurse	- Maggie Pierce
Sgt. John Danforth	- Charles Bronson		

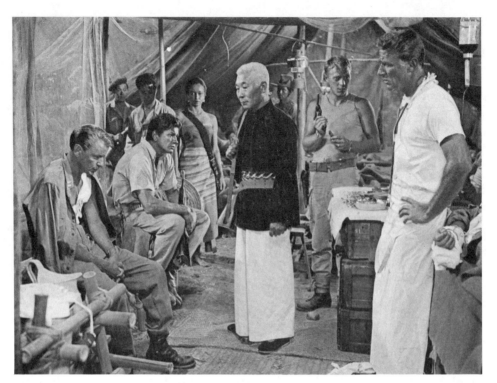

"Never So Few" - Sinatra, Charles Bronson, Philip Ahn, Steve McQueen, Peter Lawford — 1960.

"Can Can" - Sinatra, Shirley MacLaine, Maurice Chevalier — 1960.

Synopsis

Frank Sinatra plays an American Captain who leads a tough band of guerillas assigned to harass Japanese troops in Burma during World War II. Good action and colorful scenery.

CAN-CAN

Twentieth Century Fox - April 1, 1960 - Color

A Suffolk-Cummings Production. Produced by Jack Cummings. Directed by Walter Lang. Associate producer - Saul Chaplin. Screenplay by Dorothy Kingsley and Charles Lederer; based on the musical comedy of 1953 by Abe Burrows. Choreography by Hermes Pan. Art Directors - Lyle Wheeler and Jack Martin Smith. Cinematography - William H. Daniels. Editor - Robert Simpson. Music arranged and conducted by Nelson Riddle. Songs by Cole Porter. In Deluxe Color, TODD-AO

Running Time - 134 Minutes

Cast

Francois Durnais	- Frank Sinatra	Adam	- Marc Wilder
Simone Pistache	- Shirley MacLaine	Policeman Dupont	- P. Coe
Paul Barriere	- Maurice Chevalier	Plainclothesman	- M. Broesse
Philippe Forrestier	- Louis Jourdan	Dowager	- Rene Godfrey
Claudine	- Juliet Prowse	Dowager	- Lili Valenty
Andre	- Marcel Dalio	Gigi	- Carole Bryan
Orch. Leader	- Leon Belasco	Camille	- Barbara Carter
Bailiff	- Nestor Paiva	Renee	- Jane Earl
Photographer	- John Neris	Julie	- Ruth Earl
Judge Merceaux	- Jean Del Val	Germine	- Laura Fraser
League President	- Ann Codee	Gabrielle	- Vera Lee
Chevrolet	- Eugene Borden	Fifi	- Lisa Mitchell
Recorder	- Jonathan Kidd	Maxine	- Wanda Shannon
Knife Thrower	- Charles Carman	Butler	- Alphonse Martell
Gisele	- Darlene Tittle	Secretary	- Genevieve Aumont
Lili	- Wilda Taylor	Judge	- Edward Le Veque
Apache Dancer	- Ambrogio Malerba	Bailiff	- Maurice Marsac

Synopsis

Set in the Montmartre district of Paris at the turn of the century, *"Can-Can"* follows the adventures of an attorney (Frank Sinatra) and his client, (Shirley MacLaine) owner of the Cafe Le Bal du Parides, in their lively encounter with the Paris courts; Represented by judges Maurice Chevalier and Louis Jourdan. Frank sings *"It's All Right With Me"*, *"Let's Do It"* with Shirley MacLaine, *"C'est Magnifique"* and *"Montmart"* with Chevalier and *"I Love Paris"* with Chevalier and chorus. A Cole Porter score.

OCEANS ELEVEN

Warner Bros. - September 16, 1960 - Color

"Oceans Eleven" - Sinatra, Dean Martin, Peter Lawford,
Sammy Davis, Jr. — 1960.

"The Devil At 4 O'Clock" - Spencer Tracy, Sinatra — 1961.

A Dorchester (Frank Sinatra) Production for Warner Bros. Produced and directed by Lewis Milestone. Screenplay by Harry Brown and Charles Lederer. Based on the story by George Clayton Johnson and Jack Golden Russel. Music composed and conducted by Nelson Riddle. Songs by Sammy Cahn and James Van Heusen. Filmed in Las Vegas, Nevada in Panavision and Technicolor.

Running Time - 127 Minutes

Cast

Danny Ocean	- Frank Sinatra
Sam Harmon	- Dean Martin
Josh Howard	- Sammy Davis, Jr.
Jimmy Foster	- Peter Lawford
Beatrice Ocean	- Angie Dickinson
Anthony Bergdorf	- Richard Conte
Duke Santos	- Cesar Romero
Adele Ekstrom	- Patrice Wymore
Mushy O'Connors	- Joey Bishop
Spyros Acebos	- Akim Tamiroff

And

Roger Corneal - Henry Silva; Mrs. Restes - Ilka Chase; Vincent Massler - Buddy Lester; Curly Steffans - Richard Benedict; Mrs. Bergdorf - Jean Willes; Peter Rheimer - Norman Fell; Louis Jackson - Clem Harvey; Mr. Kelly - Hank Henry; Young Man - Lew Gallo; Deputy Sheriff - Hoot Gibson; Sheriff Wimmer - Robert Faulk; Shopkeeper - George E. Stone; Miss Allenby - Majorie Bennett; Orchestra Leader - Red Norvo; Night Club Owner - Donald Barry; Dancers - Laura Cornell and Shiva.

And

Red Skelton - George Raft - Shirley MacLaine

Synopsis

Eleven war-time buddies get together for the purpose of robbing five Vegas casinos on New Year's Eve. All goes according to schedule when one member suffers a fatal heart attack after the holdup. They hide the money in the coffin of their deceased buddy, planning to remove it after the funeral, but ironically his widow has her husband cremated and the boys are left penniless. This film is an uninhibited romp.

THE DEVIL AT 4 O'CLOCK

Columbia - July 16, 1961 - Color

Produced by Fred Kohlmer; Directed by Mervyn LeRoy. Screenplay by Liam O'Brien, based on the novel by Max Cato. Music by George Dunning. Assistant Directors, Carter De Haven Jr. and Floyd Joyer. In Eastman Color.

Running Time - 126 Minutes

Cast

Father Mathew Doonan	- Spencer Tracy	Paul	- Tom Middleton
Harry	- Frank Sinatra	Clarisse	- Ann Duggan
Father Joseph Perreau	- Kerwin Mathews	Corporal	- L. Mercier
Jacques	- Jean Pierre Aumont	Margot	- M. Montau
Marcel	- Gregoire Aslan	Fleur	- N. Tanaka
The Governor	- Alexander Scourby	Antoine	- T. Maxwell
Camille	- Barbara Luna	Louis	- Jean De Val
Matron	- Cathy Lewis	Sonia	- Moki Hana
Charlie	- Bernie Hamilton	Napoleon	- Warren Hsieh
Dr. Wexler	- Martin Brandt	Constable	- W. Keaulani
Astride	- Lou Merrill	Cap. Olsen	- "Lucky" Luck
Gaston	- Marcel Dalio	Fouquette	- N. Wright
		Marianne	- R. Shimatsu

Synopsis

Frank plays one of three convicts dropped off on a tiny volcanic island while en route to Tahiti. A volcano erupts and threatens to destroy the entire island. The convicts are offered paroles if they volunteer to help in a rescue mission. Sinatra falls in love with a blind nurse and marries her during the struggle. A first time meeting in films of two giants - Spencer Tracy and Frank Sinatra.

PEPE

Columbia - August, 1961 - Color

Another guest appearance in which Sinatra is seen in the sequences filmed at the Sands and Tropicana Hotels in Las Vegas.

SERGEANTS THREE

United Artists - January 7, 1962 - Color

An Essex - Claude Production - Released through United Artists. Executive Producer: Howard W. Koch; Producer: Frank Sinatra; Director: John Sturges; Screenplay: W.R. Burnett; Music: Billy May; Song: *"And The Night Wind Sang."* Music by Johnny Rotella; Lyrics by Franz Steininger. In Panavision and Technicolor.

Running Time - 113 Minutes

"Sergeants Three" - Sinatra, Joey Bishop, Dean Martin — 1962.

"The Manchurian Candidate" - Sinatra, Laurence Harvey, James Edwards — 1962.

Cast

1st Sgt. Mike Merry-	Frank Sinatra	Mountain Hawk -	H. Silva
Sgt. Chip Deal	- Dean Martin	Willie Sharpknife-	Buddy Lester
Johan Williams	- Sammy Davis, Jr.	Amelia Parent	- R. Lee
Sgt. Larry Barrett	- Peter Lawford	Corporal Ellis	- Philip Crosby
Sgt. Major Roger Boswell	- Joey Bishop		
Private Wills	- Linsay Crosby		
Blacksmith	- Hank Henry		

Synopsis

A reuniting of the "Clan" in an obvious remake of Rudyard Kipling's *"Gunga Din"*. The three cronies befriend a trumpet playing former slave (Sammy Davis, Jr.) who one day dreams of becoming a trooper. When a fanatical tribe of Indians begin terrorizing the area, Dean Martin decides to capture the chief and takes Sammy with him. They get caught and their friends come to the rescue. Tongue-in-cheek drama.

ROAD TO HONG KONG

United Artists - March 1962 - Color

A typical "Road" picture starring the inseperable trio of Bob Hope, Bing Crosby and Dorothy Lamour with special guest appearance by Frank Sinatra who is dressed as a spaceman with a toy propeller on his hat.

SINATRA IN ISRAEL

May 1962

Produced by the Israeli Federation of Histradruth and narrated by Frank Sinatra.

Running Time - 23 Minutes

This short was filmed in 1962 during Sinatra's nine-day tour of Israel where he performed several concerts. He sings *"In The Still Of The Night"* and *"Without A Song"*.

THE MANCHURIAN CANDIDATE

United Artists - October 12, 1962

Producers - George Axelrod and John Frankenheimer. Director John Frankenheimer, with screenplay by George Axelrod, based on the novel by Richard Condon. Executive producer - Howard W. Koch. Music by David Amram. Assistant director, Joseph Belm; Costumes by Moss Mabry. An M.C. Production.

Running Time - 126 Minutes

"Come Blow Your Horn" - Sinatra, Jill St. John — 1963.

"Come Blow Your Horn" - Molly Picon, Sinatra, Tony Bill, Lee J. Cobb — 1963.

Cast

Bennett Marco	- Frank Sinatra	Senator Thomas	
Raymond Shaw	- Laurence Harvey	Jordan	- John McGiver
Rosie	- Janet Leigh	Yen Fo	- Kligh Dhiegh
Shaw's Mother	- Angela Lansbury	Corporal Melvin	- J. Edwards
Chunjin	- Henry Silva	The Colonel	- D. Henderson
Senator John Iselin	- James Gregory	Zilkokv	- Albert Paulson
Jocie Jordan	- Leslie Parrish	Secretary of	
Berezovo	- Madame Spivy	Defense	- Barry Kelly
		Holborn Gaines	- L. Corrigan

Synopsis

The Chinese Red brainwash an American non-com captured in the Korean War and make him into a psychological time-bomb. The non-com's Lieutenant (Sinatra), becomes suspicious and starts his own private investigation. The plot is to have the non-com (Harvey) kill the presidential candidate so his mother who is in with the reds can make her husband the president. In the windup, Harvey shoots his mother and her husband and himself. This is an absorbing film and the characterizations have a razor edge.

COME BLOW YOUR HORN

Paramount - June, 1963 - Color

Producers, Norman Lear, Bud Yorkin; Executive Producer, Howard W. Koch; Director, Bud Yorkin; Screenplay, Norman Lear; From the play by Neil Simon; Song, Sammy Cahn, James Van Heusen; Music, Nelson Riddle; Costumes; Edith Head; Choreography, Jack Baker; Assistant Director, Daniel J. McCauley; An Essex-Tandem Production in Panavision and Technicolor.

Running Time - 113 Minutes

Cast

Alan	- Frank Sinatra	Mr. Eckman	- Dan Blocker
Mr. Baker	- Lee J. Cobb	Mrs. Eckman	- Phyllis McGuire
Mrs. Baker	- Molly Picon	Eunice	- Carole Wells
Connie	- Barbar Rush	Waiter	- Herbie FAy
Peggy	- Jill St. John	Barber	- Romo Vincent
Buddy	- Tony Bill	Manicurist	- Charlotte Fletcher
		Tall Girl	- Greta Randall
		Wino	- Dean Martin

Synopsis

A broadened film version of the long-running stage success, with Frank Sinatra dominating this Jewish family comedy and moulding it into an extemely entertaining piece of cinema. Sinatra sings the title song.

"Four For Texas" - Anita Ekberg, Sinatra, Dean Martin, Ursula Andress — 1963.

"Robin And The Seven Hoods" - Hank Henry, Dean Martin, Sammy Davis Jr., Sinatra, Richard Bakalayan, Phil Crosby, Bing Crosby — 1964.

THE LIST OF ADRIAN MESSENGER

Universal-International - August, 1963

An excellent British-type murder mystery in which a number of stars appear as guests in various disguises including of course, Frank Sinatra.

FOUR FOR TEXAS

Warner Bros. - December, 1963 - Color

Producer-Director, Robert Aldrich; Executive Producer, Howard W. Koch; Associate Producer, Walter Blake; Screenplay, Teddi Sherman, Robert Aldrich; Story, Robert Aldrich; Music, Nelson Riddle; Orchestrations by Gilgrau; Costumes, Norma Koch; Assistant Directors, Tom Connors, Dave Salven; A Sam Company Production in Technicolor.

Running Time - 124 Minutes

Cast

Zack Thomas	- Frank Sinatra	Trowbridge	- Wesley Addy
Joe Jarret	- Dean Martin	Miss Ermaline	- M. Bennett
Elya Carlson	- Anita Ekberg	Dobie	- Jack Elam
Maxine Richter	- Ursula Andress	Maitre D'	- Fritz Feld
Matson	- Charles Bronson	Ansel	- Percy Helton
Harvey Burden	- Victor Buono	Renee	- Jonathan Hale
Prince George	- Edric Connor	Monk	- Jack Lambert
Angel	- Nick Dennis	Beauregard	- Paul Langton
Mancini	- Richard Jaeckel	Wido	- Jesslyn Fax
Chad	- Mike Mazurki	Teddy Buckner and All Stars and Three Stoogies	

Synopsis

Two of the famous clan, Frank and Dean, in an amusing, tongue-in-cheek sendup of the conventional cowboy story. The duo fight each other for .possession of a hundred thousand stolen dollars and finally see the error of their ways and join forces to oust nast Victor Buono and hs cruel henchman, Charles Bronson, from power. All in all - good fun.

ROBIN AND THE SEVEN HOODS

Warner Bros. - June 27, 1964 - Color

Producer, Frank Sinatra; Director, Gordon Douglas; Screenplay, David R. Schwartz. Director of Photography and Associate Producer, William H. Daniels; Executive Producer, Howard W. Koch; Music, Nelson Riddle; New songs, Sammy Cahn, James Van Heusen; Costumes, Don Field; Assistant Directors, David Salven, Lee White. A P-C Production in Panavision and Technicolor.

Running Time - 123 Minutes

Cast

Robbo	- Frank Sinatra	Tomatoes	- Jack La Rue
John	- Dean Martin	Sheriff Glick	- Robert Faulk
Wil	- Sammy Davis, Jr.	Hood	- Phil Crosby
Guy Gisborne	- Peter Falk	Blue Jaw	- Robert Carricart
Marian	- Barbara Rush	Hatrack	- Phil Arnold
Sheriff Potts	- Victor Buono	Big Jim	- Edward G. Robinson
Allen A. Dale	- Bing Crosby	Hood	- Sonny King
Six Seconds	- Hank Henry	Bananas	- Bernard Fein
Vermin	- Allen Jenkins	Waitress	- Carol Hill
Hood	- Richard Bakalyan	Soupmeat	- Harry Swoger
		Judge	- Milton Rodin

Synposis

The Time:	The Late 20's
The Place:	Chicago, Illinois

Gunhappy gangsters, gambling girls, bullets in the air, bombs in the streets and a frolicking madcap tour of a Chicago gone wild. A swinging new Robin Hood makes that Sherwood Forest version older than history. Frank sings *"My Kind Of Town"*, *"I Like To Lead When I Dance"*, *"Don't Be A Do Badder"* with Crosby, Martin and Davis; *"Style"* with Crosby and Martin. Also *"Mr Booze."*

NONE BUT THE BRAVE

Warner Bros. - January, 1965 - Color

A Tokyo Eiga Co., Ltd., Toko Film and Artanis Productions, Inc. Co-production. A Sinatra Enterprises Production, released by Warner Bros. Producer: Frank Sinatra. Executive Producer: Howard W. Koch. Story by Kikumaru Oluda. Director: Frank Sinatra. Music supervised and conducted by Morris Stoloff.

Running Time - 105 Minutes

Cast

Maloney	- Frank Sinatra	Lt. Kuroki	- Tatsuya Mihashi
Capt. Borch	- Clint Walker	Sgt. Tamura	- Taheshi Kato
Lt. Blair	- Tommy Sands	Cpl. Craddock	- Sammy Jackson
Sgt. Bleeker	- Brad Dexter	Cpl. Ruffino	- Richard Bakalyn
Killer	- Tony Bill	Pvt. Johnson	- Rafer Johnson

Synopsis

A plane carrying raw marine recruits to the front is shot down on an island with a small marooned Japanese force. Then it involves the slow evolution of a truce and ultimately of understanding and friendship between the two forces. Frank plays a hard-drinking cynical medic who saves the gangrenous leg of a Japanese soldier. This was Frank's first directional chore and it was filmed

"None But The Brave" — 1965.

"Von Ryans Express" — 1965.

entirely in Hawaii.

WILL ROGER'S HOSPITAL TRAILER

March, 1965

Sinatra narrated this 2½ minute trailer film appealing for funds for the O'Donnell Memorial Research Laboratories.

VON RYANS EXPRESS

Twentieth Century Fox - June 24, 1965 - Color

Produced by Saul David. Directed by Mark Robson. Based on the novel by David Westheimre. Screenplay by Weldell Mayes and Joseph Landon. Art directors - Jack Martin Smith and Hilyard Brown. Cinematographer - William H. Daniels. Special Photographic effects - L.B. Abbott and Emil Kosa. Music - Jerry Goldsmith. Orchestration by Arthur Morton. Jr. Editor - Dorothy Spencer. In Cinemascope, Deluxe Color.

Running Time - 117 Minutes

Cast

Col. Joseph Ryan	- Frank Sinatra	Battaglia	- Adolfo Celi
Maj. Eric Fincham	- Trevor Howard	Italian Train	
Gabriella	- Raffaella Carra	Engineer	- Vito Scotti
Sarg. Bostick	- Brad Dexter	Corp. Giannini	- R. Bakalayan
Capt. Oriani	- Sergio Fantoni	Capt. Stein	- M. Goodliffe
Orde	- John Leyton	Sarg. Dunbar	- M. St. Clair
Constanzo	- Edward Mulhare	Von Lkiest	- Ivan Triesauslt
Maj. Von Klemment	- Wolfgang Preiss	Gortz's Aide	- J. Stanilavski
Ames	- James Brolin	Ranson	- Eric Micklewood
Col. Gortz	- John Van Dreelan	Oriani's Aide	- J. Mitory
		Italian Nobleman	- Mike Romanoff

And

Al Wyatt, Buzz Henry, John Day, James Sikking as American Soldiers.

Synopsis

A Colonel in the United States Army Air Force is shot down in Italy and is taken prisoner. He encounters resistance when he attempts to take command inside the prison camp. When Italy surrenders they break free only to be captured by the Germans and shipped north. Led by Sinatra (Col. Ryan), they take over the train and by tricking the Nazis they proceed to escape to the Swiss border. The novel was a best seller for David Westheimer.

MARRIAGE ON THE ROCKS

Warner Bros. - October 9, 1965 - Color

"Marriage On The Rocks" - Sinatra, Deborah Kerr, Dean Martin — 1965.

"Assault On The Queen" - Richard Conte, Sinatra — 1966.

An Atanis Production. Producer, William Daniels, Director, Jack Donohue. Assistant Director, Richard Lang. Costume Designer, Walter Plunkett. Screenplay, Cy Howard. In Technicolor and Panavision.

Running Time - 114 Minutes

Cast

Dan Edwards	- Frank Sinatra	Tracy Edwards	- Nancy Sinatra
Valerie Edwards	- Deborah Kerr	Lisa Sterling	- D. Davidson
Ernie Brewer	- Dean Martin	David Edwards	- M. Petit
Miguel Santos	- Cesar Romero	Lola	- Joi Lansing
Jeannie	- Hermoine Badderley	Bunny	- Tara Ashton
Jim Blake	- Tony Bill	Miss Blight	- K. Freeman
Shad Nathan	- John McGiver	Rollo	- Flip Mark
Mr. Turner	- DeForrest Kelley	Kitty	- Sigrid Valdis
		Trini Lopez	- Guest Star

Synopsis

Frank plays the part of a well married, financially successful tycoon. Dean Martin plays the part of a happy highliving, playboy bachelor. Through some implausible misunderstandings, Dean suddenly has Frank's wife and Frank has the girls. Watch for some tender scenes between Sinatra and his daughter, Nancy. Needless to say, all turns out well in the end.

CAST A GIANT SHADOW

United Artists - March 19, 1966 - Color

A personalized biography of West Pointer, Colonel Mickey Marcus. Plenty of action, humor and romance. Sinatra is effective in a featured cameo role as a happy-go-lucky aviator.

THE OSCAR

Paramount - May, 1966 - Color

Sinatra appears as the happy recipient of an Academy Award in a brief appearance near the end of this fairly good film.

ASSAULT ON A QUEEN

Paramount - July 27, 1966 - Color

Seven Arts - Sinatra Enterprise - Paramount Picture Release. Produced by William Goetz. Directed by Jack Donohue from a screenplay by Rod Sterling. Based on the novel by Jack Finny. Duke Ellington - music with orchestrations by Van Cleave. In Panavision and Technicolor.

Running Time - 107 Minutes

Cast

Mark Brittain	- Frank Sinatra
Rosa Lucchesi	- Virna Lisi
Vic Rossiter	- Tony Franciosa
Tony Moreno	- Richard Conti
Eric Lauffnauer	- Alf Kjellin
Linc Langley	- Errol John
Captain	- Murray Matheson
Master-at-Arms	- Reginald Denney

Synopsis

A sea story of an ex-submarine commander who gathers up a motley crew including a drunkard, an ex-German naval officer and dishonorably discharged navy man and talks them into a fantastic scheme. They dredge up a World War II German submarine, secretly recondition it and are on their way to hold up the Queen Mary. They threaten to sink her if she doesn't surrender all her money and gold bullion. What could have been a very exciting adventure film turns out to be just so-so. To their credit the cast fights a commendable but losing battle against poor direction and a surprisingly poor screenplay.

THE NAKED RUNNER

Warner Bros. - July 7, 1967 - Color

A Sinatra (Artanis) Enterprises Production. Produced by Brad Dexter and directred by Sidney J. Furie. Screenplay: Stanley Mann; based on the novel by Francis Clifford. Photography: Otto Heller. Music composed by Harry Sukman; conducted by Morris Stoloff. Art Direction: Peter Proud. Assistant Director: Michael Dryhurst. Location scenes filmed in London and Copenhagen. In Techniscope and Technicolor.

Running Time - 104 Minutes

Cast

Sam Laker	- Frank Sinatra
Martin Slattery	- Peter Vaughan
Colonel Hartman	- Darren Nesbitt
Karen Gisevuis	- Nadia Gray
Ruth	- Toby Robbins
Anna	- Inges Stratton
Cabinet Minister	- Cyril Luckham
Ritchie Jackson	- Edward Fox
Joseph	- J. Dubin-Behrmann
Patrick Lakes	- Michael Newport

Synopsis

A British Spy thriller with Sinatra as an intelligence agent whose goal it is to rub out a defector headed for Russia. In order to induce him, they have told him

"The Naked Runner" - Sinatra, Toby Robins — 1967.

"Tony Rome" - Sinatra, Jill St. John — 1967.

that the defector has murdered his son. Sinatra plays his role diligently and Furie's tricky direction adroitly manipulates the colorful backgrounds.

TONY ROME

20th Century Fox - November 16, 1967 - Color

Produced by Aaron Rosenberg, directed by Gordon Douglas. Screenplay by Richard L. Breen. Based on the novel "Miami Mayhem" by Marvin H. Albert. Art Direction: Jack Martin Smith and James Roth. Assistant Director, Richard Lang. Stunt Director, Buzz Henry; Photography, Joseph Biroe; Editor, Robert Simpson. Sound, Howard Warren and David Dockendorf. Music by Billy May. Song *"Tony Rome"* by Lee Hazelwood, sung by Nancy Sinatra. Sons *"Hard Times"* and *"Something Here Inside Me"* by Billy May and Randy Newman. An Arcola-Millfield Production, filmed in Miami in Panavision and Deluxe Color.

Running Time - 109 Minutes

Cast

Tony Rome	- Frank Sinatra	Donald Pines	- R. Krisher
An Archer	- Jill St. John	Jules Langley	- L. Gough
Lt. Dave Santini	- Richard Conte	Oscar	- Babe Hart
Diana Kosterman	- Sue Lyon	Sam Boyd	- Stanley Ross
Rita Kosterman	- Gina Rowlands	Sally Bullock	- V. Vincent
Rudy Kosterman	- Simon Oakland	Packy	- Rocky Graziano
Adam Boyd	- Jeffry Lynn	Sal - Maitre'D	- M. Romanoff
Vic Rood	- Llyod Bochner	Catleg	- Shecky Greene
Ralph Turpin	- Robert Wilke	Lorna	- Jeanne Cooper
Goergia Makay	- Deanna Lund	Ruyter	- Harry Davis
Irma	- Elizabeth Fraser	Bartender	- Joe E. Ross
Fat Candy	- Joan Shawlee	Card Player	- Jilly Rizzo
		Girl	- Tiffany Bolling

Synopsis

Sinatra as a hard-nosed private eye, Bogart style, sprinting about in Miami Beach in search of a missing piece of jewelry. This leads to a murder in which our sleuth gets naturally involved not to mention cut up, shot at, kicked and almost seduced. It flows along at a rapid clip and a running patter of gags.

THE DETECTIVE

20th Century Fox - June 3, 1968 - Color

An Arcola-Millfield Production. Produced by Aaron Rosenberg and directed by Gordon Douglas. Screenplay: Abby Mann; Based on the novel by Roderick Thorp. Photography: Joseph Birou. Music: Jerry Goldsmith. Orchestration: Warren Barker. Art Direction: Jack Martin Smith and William Creber. Assistant Director: Richard Lang. Location scenes filmed in New York City and the Los Angeles area. In Panavision and color by Deluxe.

"The Detective" - Sinatra, Jacqueline Bisset — 1968.

"Lady In Cement" - Sinatra, Raquel Welch — 1968.

Running Time - 114 Minutes

Cast

Joe Leland	- Frank Sinatra	Felix Tesla	- Tony Musante
Karen Leland	- Lee Remick	Robbie Loughren	- A. Freeman, Jr.
Norma MacIver	- Jacqueline Bisset*	Nestor	- Robert Duvall
Lieut. Curran	- Ralph Meekes	Mercidis	- Pat Henry
Dave Schoenstein	- Jack Klugman	Kelly	- Sugar Ray Robinson
Farrell	- Horace McMahon	Rachel	
Dr. Wendell Roberts	- Lloyd Bochner	Schoenstein	- R. Taylor
Colin MacIver	- William Windom	Bartender	- Jilly Rizzo
Desk Sergeant	- Mark Dawson		

* Mia Farrow was originally set for the role of Norma, but she withdrew after a few days of shooting and the part was retailored for Miss Bisset.

Synopsis

Frank Sinatrat portrays a hard bitten detective who pushes for a fast conviction in a grisly murder case. The victim is the homosexual son of a politically influential department store owner, and in his haste for recognition and promotion Sinatra sends an innocnet man to his death. Upon realizing this he removes his badge and decides to expose the corruption among both police and government officials.

LADY IN CEMENT

20th Century Fox - November 20, 1968 - Color

An Arcola-Millfield Production. Produced by Aaron Rosenberg and Directed by Gordon Douglas. Screenplay by Marvin H. Albert and Jack Guss, based on the novel by Martin H. Albert. Photography by Joseph Birou with special photographic effects by L.B. Abbott and Art Cruckshank. Underwater sequences staged by Ricou Browning. Music composed and conducted by Hugo Montenegro with orchestration by Billy May. Art Direction, Leroy Deane. Set decorations by Walter M. Scott and Jerry Wunderlich. Editor: Robert Simpson and sound by Howard Warren and David Dockendorf. Costumes, Moss Mabry; Makeup, Dan Striepke and Layne Britton; Hairstyles by Edith Lindon. Assistant to the producer, Michael Romanoff. Production Manager, David Silver. Assistant Director, Richard Lang. Filmed on location in Miami, Florida in Panavsion, color by Deluxe.

Running Time - 93 Minutes

Cast

Tony Rome	- Frank Sinatra	Danny Yale	- Frank Raiter
Kit Forrest	- Raquel Welch	Frenchy	- Peter Hock
Gronsky	- Dan Blocker	Shev	- Alex Stevens
Lt. Santini	- Richard Conte	Sandra Lomax	- Christine Todd
Al Mungar	- Martin Gabel	Sid the Organizer	- M. Robbins

"Dirty Dingus McGee" — 1970.

Maria Baretto	- Laine Kazan	The Kid	- Tommy Uhlar
Hal Rubin	- Pat Henry	Paco	- Ray Baumel
Paul Mungar	- Steve Peck	McComb	- Pauly Dash
Audry	- Virginia Wood	Pool Boy	- Andy Jarrel
Arnie Sherwin	- Richard Deacon	Himself	- Joe E. Lewis

Synopsis

This is a follow-up to Tony Rome with Frank Sinatra once more as a private eye in Miami. He is hired by a smalltime hood (Dan Blocker) to find his missing girlfriend and when it is discovered that she is on the bottom of Biscayne Bay, he sets out to find her murderer.

DIRTY DINGUS MAGEE

M.G.M. - November 16, 1970 - Color

A Burt Kennedy Production, produced and directed by Burt Kennedy from a screenplay by Tom Waldman, Frank Waldman and Joseph Heller. Based on the book *"The Ballad Of Dingus Magee"* by David Markson. In Panavision and Metrocolor.

Running Time - 91 Minutes

Cast

Dingus Magee	- Frank Sinatra	Troopers	- Terry Wilson
Hoke Birdsil	- George Kennedy		- David Burk
Belle	- Anne Jackson		- David Cass
Prudence Frost	- Lois Nettleton		- Tom Fadden
John Hardin	- Jack Elam	Old Cronies	- Mae Coyote
Anna Hotwater	- Michele Carey		- Lillian Hogan
The General	- John Dehner		- Ina Bad Bear
Rev. Green	- Henry Jones	Belle's Girls	- Myra Christen
Stuart	- Harry Carey, Jr.		- Mina Martinez
Chief Crazy Blanket	- Paul Fix		- Sheila Foster
Shotgun	- Donald Barry		- Irene Kelly
Driver	- Mike Wagner		- Diane Sayer
			- Jean London
			- Lisa Todd

Synopsis

Another tongue-in-cheek western with Frank playing an endearing rogue who steals from friend and foe alike. This is light entertainment with plenty of slapstick action and also a few very funny bits of dialogue. It will not, of course, be considered one of Sinatra's great film roles but despite the critics' unmerciful panning, he seems to be enjoying himself and movie fans will too.

THAT'S ENTERTAINMENT - PART I

M.G.M. - 1974 - Color and Black & White

Produced by Jack Haley Jr. An assemblage of past highlights taken directly from M.G.M.'s most famous musicals. Sinatra handles the opening and closing narrations, visually and introduces the film itself. He is seen in the following exerpts from the various films named.

"IT HAPPENED IN BROOKLYN" - with Jimmy Durante vocalizing on the tune *"It's Gotta Come From The Heart"*.

TAKE ME OUT TO THE BALLGAME - with Gene Kelly dancing and singing the title song.

ON THE TOWN - with Jules Munshin and Gene Kelly sings *"New York, New York"* and dances.

HIGH SOCIETY - sings *"Well Did You Evah"* with Bing Crosby.

Sinatra is also seen at a luncheon given to all M.G.M. employees in 1945.

THAT'S ENTERTAINMENT — PART II

M.G.M. - July 1976 - Color and Black & White

Produced by Jack Haley Jr. More highlights from M.G.M.'s famous musicals. Sinatra is seen in the following:

ANCHORS AWEIGH - sings *"I Begged Her."*

TILL THE CLOUDS ROLL BY - sings *"Ol' Man River"*

HIGH SOCIETY - sings *"You're Sensational"*

TENDER TRAP - sings Title song

ANCHORS AWEIGH - sings *"I Fall In Love Too Early"*

He also appears in a short film clip on stage at the Paramount Theatre in 1944, singing *"I'll Walk Alone"* and some brief scenes from several dramatic M.G.M. films.

In July of 1977, Sinatra was to start filming *"Contract On Cherry Street"*. It will be filmed mainly on the streets of New York City.

ON THE SOUNDTRACK

This is a listing of films in which only Sinatra's voice is heard but he is not seen.

A THOUSAND AND ONE NIGHTS - Columbia - 1945

Sinatra sings *"All Or Nothing At All"* * **For** Phil Silvers.

ADAM'S RIB - M.G.M. - 1949

Sinatra sings a few bars of *"Farewell Amanda"** on the radio.

THREE COINS IN THE FOUNTAIN - Twentieth Century Fox - 1954

Sinatra sings the title song * as the opening credits are shown.

ADVISE AND CONSENT - Columbia - 1962

Sinatra sings *"The Loser's Song"* * during a sequence in a homosexual bar.

THE VICTORS - Columbia - 1963

Sinatra sings an edited version of a commercially made recording of *"Have Yourself A Merry Little Christmas"*. It plays while an American Soldier is being led to execution for desertion.

PARIS WHEN IT SIZZLES - Paramount - 1964

Sinatra sings a song titled *"The Girl Who Stole The Eiffel Tower"** - a parody of main screen titles.

A NEW KIND OF LOVE - Paramount - 1964

Sinatra sings the title song* as the opening screen credits are shown.

THE AMBUSHERS - Columbia - 1967

Sinatra sings the opening line of *"Strangers In The Night"* - Record on phonograph.

RABBIT, RUN - Warner Bros. - 1970

Sinatra sings *"My Kind Of Town"* - Heard on car radio.

THE PRIEST'S WIFE - Warner Bros. - 1971

Sinatra sings *"Going Out Of My Head"*. - Record on phonograph.

CARNAL KNOWLEDGE - Avco/Embassy - 1971

Sinatra sings *"Dream"* - Capitol version.

* These are specially made recordings for their individual film use.

Frank Sinatra, throughout his acting career looked into many film projects which for one reason or another never materialized. We thought a listing that follows would be of interest and so present them.

THE FILMS SINATRA DID NOT MAKE

1953 - **PINK TIGHTS** - with Marilyn Monroe for 20th Century Fox.

1954 - **ST. LOUIS WOMAN** - with Ava Gardner for M.G.M.

FINIAN'S RAINBOW - (Animated Cartoon). He did record some of the songs.

1955 - **CAROUSEL** - for 20th Century Fox. He was on location the 20th - 24th of August but a dispute over filming in two processes resulted in Sinatra walking out. He did however, record part of the soundtrack - *"Soliloquy"* and *"If I Loved You"*.

1958 - **PARIS BY NIGHT** - For Raoul Levy in Paris. His co-star was to be Bridget Bardot.

1960 - **THE EXECUTION OF PRIVATE SLOVAK** - by Albert Maltz.

   BORN YESTERDAY - by Garson Kanin, with Marilyn Monroe for Frank's own film company.

1962 - **THE GREAT TRAIN ROBBERY** - with Peter Lawford.

1963 - **THE ACTOR** - by Clifford Oddets for M.G.M.

1964 - **THE ODD COUPLE** - with Jack Lemmon for Paramount.

   JUDITH - with Sophia Loren in Israel.

   THE THIRD DAY - by Joseph Hayes for Warner Bros.

1965 - **ANY WEDNESDAY** - by Muriel Resnick.

   ADAM - for Embassy Pictures with Kid Ory and Louis Armstrong. To be produced by Ike Jones.

   FUNNY GIRL - with Barbara Streisand for Columbia.

1966 - **FAVOR THE RUNNER** - by Jay Richard Kennedy with Sammy Davis Jr.

   CASINO ROYALE - a cameo part.

1967 - **SHAMUS** - by Martin Albert for 20th Century Fox. To be produced by Aaron Rosenberg and directed by Gordon Douglas.

1968 - **THE ONLY GAME IN TOWN** - with Elizabeth Taylor.

1970 - **CALAHAN** - for Warner Bros.

   WHERE THE DARK STREETS GO - to be produced by Otto Preminger.

1972 - **THE LITTLE PRINCE** - a Lerner and Lowe Musical.

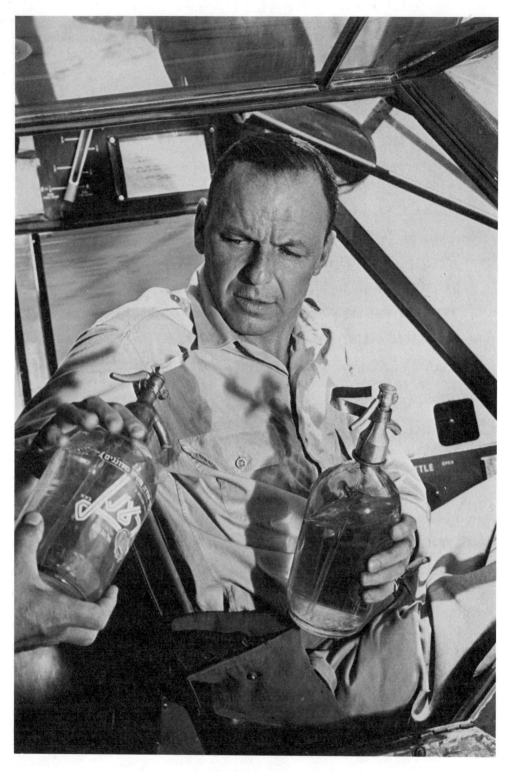

"Cast A Giant Shadow" — *1966.*

SONG INDEX FOR MOTION PICTURES - CHAPTER XI

Adelaide - (Frank Loesser)
Guys and Dolls - November 14, 1955

Ad Lib Blues - (Yip Harburg - Burton Lane)
Fininans Rainbow - 1954

All My Tomorrows - (Sammy Cahn - Jimmy Van Heusen)
A Hole In The Head - August 26, 1959

All Of Me - (Seymour Simons - Gerald Marks)
Meet Danny Wilson - February 12, 1952

All Or Nothing At All - (Arthur Altman - Jack Lawrence)
A Thousand And One Nights - 1945 (Soundtrack Only)

All The Way - (Sammy Cahn - Jimmy Van Heusen)
The Joker Is Wild - September 12, 1957

As Long As There's Music - (Sammy Cahn - Jule Styne)
Step Lively - June 27, 1944

Bewitched - (Richard Rodgers - Lorenz Hart)
Pal Joey - December, 1957

Black Eyes (Dark Eyes) - (Traditional Russian Folk Song)
It Happened In Brooklyn - March 14, 1947

Boys And Girls Like You And Me - (Richard Rodgers - Oscar Hammerstein II)
Take Me Out To The Ballgame - March 10, 1949 (Deleted)

Boys Said No, The - (Roger Edens - Betty Comden - Adolph Green)
Take Me Out To The Ballgame - March 10, 1949

Brahms Lullaby - (Johannes Brahms)
Anchors Aweigh - August 15, 1945

Brooklyn Bridge, The - (Sammy Cahn - Jule Styne)
It Happened In Brooklyn - March 14, 1947

C'est Magnifique - (Cole Porter)
Can-Can - April 1, 1960

Charm Of You, The - (Sammy Cahn - Jule Styne)
Anchors Aweigh - August 14, 1945

Chicago - (Fred Fisher)
The Joker Is Wild - September 12, 1957

Come Blow Your Horn - (Sammy Cahn - Jimmy Van Heusen)
Come Blow Your Horn - June 1963

Come Out Wherever You Are - (Sammy Cahn - Jule Styne)
Step Lively - June 27, 1944

Come Up To My Place - (Leonard Bernstein - Adolph Green - Betty Comden)
On The Town - December 4, 1949

Count On Me - (Roger Edens - Adolph Green - Betty Comden)
On The Town - December 4, 1949

Curse Of An Aching Heart, The - (Henry Fink - Al Piantadosi)
Major Bowes Movie Short - October 1935

Dolores - (Frank Loesser - Louis Alter)
Las Vegas Nights - March 24, 1941

Don't Be A Do Badder - (Sammy Cahn - Jimmy Van Heusen)
Robin And The Seven Hoods - June 27, 1964

Embraceable You - (George & Ira Gershwin)
Lucky Strike Movie Short - Summer of 1948

Ever Homeward - (Sammy Cahn - Jule Styne - Kasimierz Lubomirski)
Miracle Of The Bells, The - March 27, 1948

Farewell Amanda - (Cole Porter)
Adams Rib - 1949 (Soundtrack Only)

Fugue For Tin Horns - (Frank Loesser)
Guys And Dolls - November 14, 1955

Girl Who Stole The Eiffel Tower - (Sammy Cahn - Jimmy Van Heusen)
Paris When It Sizzles - 1964 (Soundtrack Only)

Goin' Out Of My Head - (Teddy Randazzo - Bobby Weinstein)
The Priest's Wife - 1971 - (Soundtrack Only)

Good Man Is Hard To Find, A - (Eddie Green)
Meet Danny Wilson - February 12, 1952

Guys And Dolls - (Frank Loesser)
Guys And Dolls - November 14, 1955

Have Yourself A Merry Little Christmas - (Hugh Martin - Ralph Blane)
The Victors - 1963 (Soundtrack Only)

High Hopes - (Sammy Cahn - Jimmy Van Heusen)
A Hole In The Head - August 26, 1959

The House I Live In, The - (Lewis Allen - Earl Robinson)
The House I Live In - March 1945

How Deep Is The Ocean - (Irving Berlin)
Meet Danny Wilson - February 12, 1952

I Begged Her - (Sammy Cahn - Jule Styne)
Anchors Aweigh - August 14, 1945, That's Entertainment Part II - 1976

I Believe - (Sammy Cahn - Jule Styne)
It Happened In Brooklyn - March 14, 1947

I Couldn't Sleep A Wink Last Night - (Jimmy McHugh - Harold Adamson)
Higher And Higher - December 18, 1943

I Could Write A Book - (Richard Rodgers - Lorenz Hart)
Pal Joey - December 1957

I Cried For You - (Arthur Freed - Gus Arnheim - Abe Lyman)
The Joker Is Wild - September 12, 1957

I Didn't Know What Time It Was - (Richard Rodgers - Lorenz Hart)
Pal Joey - December 1957

I Fall In Love Too Easily - (Sammy Cahn - Jule Styne)
Anchors Aweigh - August 15, 1945, That's Entertainment Part II - 1976

If I Could Be With You - (Jimmy Johnson - Henry Creamer)
The Joker Is Wild - September 12, 1957

If I Loved You - (Richard Rodgers - Oscar Hammerstein II)
Carousel - 1955

If I Steal A Kiss - (Nacio Herb Brown - Edward Heyman)
The Kissing Bandit - November 19, 1948

If This Isn't Love - (Yip Harburg - Burton Lane)
Finian's Rainbow - 1954

If You Are But A Dream - (Nathan Bonx - Jack Fulton - Moe Jaffe)
The House I Live In - March 1945

I Like To Lead When I Dance - (Sammy Cahn - Jimmy Van Heusen)
Robin And The Seven Hoods - June 27, 1964

I'll Never Smile Again - (Rute Lowe)
Las Vegas Nights - March 24, 1941

I'll Take Tallulah - (Yip Harburg - Burton Lane)
Ship Ahoy - May 1942 (Deleted from released film)

I'll Walk Alone - (Sammy Cahn - Jule Styne)
That's Entertainment Part II - 1976

I Love Paris - (Cole Porter)
Can-Can - April 1, 1960

In The Still Of The Night - (Cole Porter)
Sinatra In Israel Movie Short - May 1962

I Saw You First - (Jimmy McHugh - Harold Adamson)
Higher And Higher - December 18, 1943

It's All Right With Me - (Cole Porter)
Can-Can - April 1, 1960

It's Fate, Baby It's Fate - (Roger Edens - Betty Comden - Adolph Green)
Take Me Out To The Ballgame - March 10, 1949

It's Gotta Come From The Heart - (Sammy Cahn - Jule Styne)
It Happened In Brooklyn - March 14, 1947; That's Entertainment Part I - 1974

It's Only Money - (Sammy Cahn - Jule Styne)
Double Dynamite - November 7, 1951

It's The Same Old Dream - (Sammy Cahn - Jule Styne)
It Happened In Brooklyn - March 4, 1947

I've Got A Crush On You - (George & Ira Gershwin)
Meet Danny Wilson - February 12, 1952

I've Got A Horse Right Here - (Frank Loesser)
Guys And Dolls - November 14, 1955

Just One Of Those Things - (Cole Porter)
Young At Heart - January 15, 1955

Kisses And Tears - (Sammy Cahn - Jule Styne)
Double Dynamite - November 7, 1951

La Ci Darem La Mano - (Mozart)
It Happened In Brooklyn - March 14, 1947

Lady Is A Tramp, The - (Richard Rodgers - Lorenz Hart)
Pal Joey - December 1947

Last Call For Love, The - (Yip Harburg - Burton Lane - Margery Cummings)
Ship Ahoy - May 1942

Let's Do It - (Cole Porter)
Can-Can - April 1, 1960

Lonesome Man Blues - (Sy Oliver)
Meet Danny Wilson - February 12, 1952

Losers Song, The - (Sammy Cahn - Jimmy Van Heusen)
Advise And Consent - 1962 (Soundtrack Only)

Lovely Way To Spend An Evening, A - (Jimmy McHugh - Harold Adamson)
Higher And Higher - December 18, 1943

Mind If I Make Love To You - (Cole Porter)
High Society - February 16, 1957

Mon'tmart - (Cole Porter)
Can-Can - April 1, 1960

Moonlight Bay - (Edward Madden - Percy Wenrich)
Ship Ahoy - May 1942

Mr. Booze - (Sammy Cahn - Jimmy Van Heusen)
Robin And The Seven Hoods - June 27, 1964

Music Stopped, The - (Jimmy McHugh - Harold Adamson)
Higher And Higher - December 18, 1943

My Kind Of Town - (Sammy Cahn - Jimmy Van Heusen)
Robin And The Seven Hoods - June 27, 1964; Run Rabbit - 1970 (Soundtrack Only)

Necessity - (Yip Harburg - Burton Lane)
Finian's Rainbow - 1954

New Kind Of Love, A - (Irving Kahal - Sammy Fain - Pierre Norman)
A New Kind Of Love - 1954 (Soundtrack Only)

New York, New York - (Leonard Bernstein - Betty Comden - Adolph Green)
On The Town - December 4, 1949; That's Entertainment Part I, 1974

Night And Day - (Cole Porter)
Reveille With Beverly - February 4, 1943

O'Brien, To Ryan, To Goldberg - (Roger Edens - Betty Comden - Adolph Green)
Take Me Out To The Ballgame - March 10, 1949

Old Devil Moon - (Yip Harburg - Burton Lane)
Finian's Rainbow - 1954

Oldest Established Permanent Floating Crap Game, The - (Frank Loesser)
Guys And Dolls - November 14, 1955

Ol' Man River - (Jerome Kern - Oscar Hammerstein II)
Till The Clouds Roll By - December 1946, That's Entertainment Part II - 1976

One For My Baby - (Johnny Mercer - Harold Arlen)
Young At Heart - January 15, 1955

On The Town - (Roger Edens - Betty Comden - Adolph Green)
On The Town - December 4, 1949

Poor You - (Yip Harburg - Burton Lane)
Ship Ahoy - May 1942

Right Girl For Me, The - (Roger Edens - Betty Comden - Adolph Green)
Take Me Out To The Ball Game - March 10, 1949

Saturday Night - (Sammy Cahn - Jule Styne)
All Star Band Rally Movie Short - February 1945

Senorita - (Nacio Brown - Edward Heyman)
The Kissing Bandit - November 19, 1948

She's Funny That Way - (Neil Moret - Richard Whiting)
Meet Danny Wilson - February 12, 1952

Shine - (Cecil Mack - Lew Brown - Ford Dabney)
Major Bowes Movie Short - October, 1935

Siesta - (Nacio Herb Brown - Earl Brent)
The Kissing Bandit - November 19, 1948

Silent Night - (Franz Gruber)
Special Christmas Movie Short - December 1945

Small Hotel - (Richard Rodgers - Lorenz Hart)
Pal Joey - December 1957

Soliloquy - (Richard Rodgers - Oscar Hammerstein II)
Carousel - 1955

Someone To Watch Over Me - (George & Ira Gershwin)
Young At Heart - January 15, 1955

Some Other Time - (Sammy Cahn - Jule Styne)
Step Lively - June 27, 1944

Song Is You, The - (Jerome Kern - Oscar Hammerstein II)
March Of Time Movie Short - "Music At War" ' Later changed to "Upbeat In Music" - Summer - 1943

Strangers In The Night - (Bert Kaempfert - Charles Singleton - Eddie Snyder)
The Ambushers - 1967 (Soundtrack Only)

Strictly U.S.A. - (Roger Edens)
Take Me Out To The Ballgame - March 10, 1949

Style - (Sammy Cahn - Jimmy Van Heusen)
Robin And The Seven Hoods - June 27, 1964

Sue Me - (Frank Loesser)
Guys And Dolls - November 14, 1955

Take Me Out To The Ballgame - (Albert Von Tilzer - Jack Norworth)
Take Me Out To The Ballgame - March 10, 1949; That's Entertainment Part I - 1974

Tender Trap, The - (Sammy Cahn - James Van Heusen)
The Tender Trap - November 17, 1955; That's Entertainment Part II - 1976

That Great Come And Get It Day - (Yip Harburg - Burton Lane)
Finian's Rainbow - 1954

That Old Black Magic - (Johnny Mercer - Harold Arlen)
Meet Danny Wilson - February 12, 1952

There's Gonna Be A Hot Time In The Town Of Berlin - (John DeVries - Joe Bushkin)
The Road To Victory Movie Short - February 1944

Three Coins In The Fountain - (Sammy Cahn - Jule Styne)
Three Coins In The Fountain - 1954 (Soundtrack Only)

Time After Time - (Sammy Cahn - Jule Styne)
It Happened In Brooklyn - March 14, 1947

We Hate To Leave - (Sammy Cahn - Jule Styne)
Anchors Aweigh - August 15, 1945

Well Did You Evah - (Cole Porter)
High Society - February 16, 1957; That's Entertainment Part I - 1974

What Do I Care For A Dame - (Richard Rodgers - Lorenz Hart)
Pal Joey - December 1957

What Makes The Sunset - (Sammy Cahn - Jule Styne)
Anchors Aweigh - August 15, 1945

What's Wrong With Me - (Nacio Herb Brown - Edward Heyman)
The Kissing Bandit - November 19, 1948

When You're Smiling - (Mark Fisher - Joe Goodwin - Larry Shay)
Meet Danny Wilson - February 12, 1954

Where Does Love Begin - (Sammy Cahn - Jule Styne)
Step Lively - June 27, 1944

Whose Baby Are You - (Sammy Cahn - Jule Styne)
It Happened In Brooklyn - March 14, 1947

Who Wants To Be A Millionaire - (Cole Porter)
High Society - February 16, 1957

Without A Song - (William Rose - Edward Eliscu - Vincent Youmans)
Sinatra In Israel Movie Short - May 1962

Yes Indeedy - (Roger Edens - Betty Comden - Adolph Green)
Take Me Out To The Ballgame - March 10, 1949

You Belong In A Love Song - (Jimmy McHugh - Harold Adamson)
Higher And Higher - December 18, 1943

Young At Heart - (Carolyn Leigh - Johnny Richards)
Young At Heart - January 15, 1955

You, My Love - (Mack Gordon - Jimmy Van Heusen)
Young At Heart - January 15, 1955

You're A Sweetheart - (Jimmy McHugh - Harold Adamson)
Meet Danny Wilson - February 12, 1952

You're Awful - (Roger Edens - Betty Comden - Adolph Green)
On The Town - December 4, 1949

You're On Your Own - (Jimmy McHugh - Harold Adamson)
Higher And Higher - December 18, 1943

You're Sensational - (Cole Porter)
High Society - February 16, 1957; That's Entertainment Part II - 1976

"Around The World In 80 Days" — 1956.

Chapter XII
AIR CHECKS

These are nonauthorized Sinatra tapes and recordings by nonprofessionals from radio broadcasts and are not subject to valid assessment. The quality of these depend upon the professionalism of the recordist and while they may lack studio clarity, they offer an insight into how his voice and style matured, mellowed and progressed in settings other than the rigidly controlled confines of a recording studio.

The authors are aware that this listing cannot be complete when one realizes that Sinatra appeared as vocalist in 191 Hit Parade programs between 1943 and 1948, while simultaneously appearing on numerous Armed Forces Radio Shows (AFRS), and as guest star on many other shows headlined by Bing Crosby, Bob Hope, Jack Benny and the Lux Radio Theater during the same period.

Subsequently, with the advent of miniature equipment, fans were able to record stage appearances, benefits and even political electioneering. What we deal with in this chapter are primarily performances taken directly from radio broadcasts starting with his in-person appearance on the *Major Bowes Amateur Hour* in 1935 and the authors believe that this is the first publication to have attempted to inform the public of what is being traded among "noncommercial Sinatra collectors."

Rarities still exist; but pride and ownership of certain collectors have, of course, created a small void in our listings, but we do wish to thank the many fans who have cooperated and assisted us in the following compilation.

MAJOR BOWES AMATEUR HOUR   September 8, 1935
                                                 Capitol Theatre, New York

Shine - As a member of a singing group called The Hoboken Four (Jimmy Petrozelli, Fred Tamburro and Patty Principal).

MAJOR BOWES AMATEUR HOUR   Late 1935

The Curse Of An Aching Heart - with Hoboken Four.

HARRY JAMES AND HIS ORCHESTRA   June 30, 1939
                                        Hippodrome, Theatre, Baltimore, Maryland

Wishing
My Love For You

HARRY JAMES AND HIS ORCHESTRA   August, 1939

Unknown Broadcast over CBS

To You
From The Bottom Of My Heart

HARRY JAMES AND HIS ORCHESTRA   September 14, 1939
                                                 World's Fair, New York CBS

All Or Nothing At All

TOMMY DORSEY AND HIS ORCHESTRA

January 25, 1940
Rockford, Illinois

Marie (with Band Chorus)
My Prayer

TOMMY DORSEY AND HIS ORCHESTRA

February 2, 1940
Lyric Theatre, Indianapolis

My Prayer
Careless
All The Things You Are
South Of The Border (Comedy Routine)
Marie (with The Pied Pipers)

TOMMY DORSEY AND HIS ORCHESTRA

February 20, 1940
Frank Dailey's Meadowbrook,
Cedar Grove, New Jersey NBC

I've Got My Eyes On You
Careless
A Lover Is Blue

TOMMY DORSEY AND HIS ORCHESTRA

February 24, 1940
Frank Dailey's Meadowbrook
Cedar Grove, New Jersey, NBC

A Lover Is Blue
Careless
I've Got My Eyes On You
East Of The Sun
My Melancholy Baby

TOMMY DORSEY AND HIS ORCHESTRA

March 2, 1940
Frank Dailey's Meadowbrook,
Cedar Grove, New Jersey, NBC

After All
I've Got My Eyes On You
Polka Dots And Moonbeams
Deep Night
Whispering (with Pied Pipers)

TOMMY DORSEY AND HIS ORCHESTRA

March 9, 1940
Frank Dailey's Meadowbrook,
Cedar Grove, New Jersey, NBC

The Sky Fell Down
On The Isle Of May
The Fable Of The Rose
Marie (with Band Chorus)

It's A Blue World
I'll Get By

TOMMY DORSEY AND HIS ORCHESTRA   May 28, 1940
                                "America Dances", New York City, CBS

Polka Dots And Moonbeams
I'll Never Smile Again (with Pied Pipers)
East Of The Sun

TOMMY DORSEY AND HIS ORCHESTRA   June 23, 1940
                                      Hotel Astor, New York City

Midnight On The Trail
I Live The Life I Love
Devil May Care
When We're Alone
Learn To Croon

TOMMY DORSEY AND HIS ORCHESTRA   October 15, 1940
                                      Hotel Astor, New York City

When You Awake
Fools Rush In
Love Lies
In My Dreams

TOMMY DORSEY AND HIS ORCHESTRA   October 17, 1940
                                        Hollywood, California

Marie (with Band Chorus)

TOMMY DORSEY AND HIS ORCHESTRA   November 7, 1940
                                        Hollywood, California

Yearning

TOMMY DORSEY AND HIS ORCHESTRA   November 26, 1940
                                      Palladium Ballroom Cafe,
                                      Hollywood, California, NBC

Our Love Affair
The One I Love (with Connie Haines and Pied Pipers)
Shadows On The Sand
That's How It Goes (with Connie Haines and Pied Pipers)

TOMMY DORSEY AND HIS ORCHESTRA   November 28, 1940
                                        Hollywood, California

How Am I To Know

TOMMY DORSEY AND HIS ORCHESTRA   February 11, 1941
                                      Frank Dailey's Meadowbrook,
                                      Cedar Grove, New Jersey, CBS

Everything Happens To Me
Oh! Look At Me Now
Let's Get Away From It All (with Pied Pipers)
The Moon Won't Talk

TOMMY DORSEY AND HIS ORCHESTRA   February 15, 1941
                              Frank Dailey's Meadowbrook,
                              Cedar Grove, New Jersey, CBS

Do I Worry?
Let's Get Away From It All (with Pied Pipers)

TOMMY DORSEY AND HIS ORCHESTRA   September 20, 1941
                              Spotlight On The Bands,
                              Hollywood, California, NBC

Free For All
The Sunshine Of Your Smile
This Love Of Mine

TOMMY DORSEY AND HIS ORCHESTRA   January 17, 1942
                              Spotlight On The Bands,
                              Hollywood, California, NBC

Blues In The Night
Free For All
This Love Of Mine

TOMMY DORSEY AND HIS ORCHESTRA   March 14, 1942
        "Leo Is On The Air" - Promo Broadcast for Film "Ship Ahoy"

The Last Call For Love

TOMMY DORSEY AND HIS ORCHESTRA   May 3, 1942
                              Band Remote - New York City

My Melancholy Baby

TOMMY DORSEY AND HIS ORCHESTRA   July 30, 1942
                              Band Remote - New York City

I'll Take Tallulah (with Jo Stafford, Tommy Dorsey and The Pied Pipers)

TOMMY DORSEY AND HIS ORCHESTRA   August 18, 1942
                              Capitol Theatre, Washington D.C., NBC

Just As Though You Were Here (with Pied Pipers)
Snootie Little Cutie (with Jo Stafford and The Pied Pipers)

TOMMY DORSEY AND HIS ORCHESTRA   August 25, 1942
                              Youngstown, Ohio, NBC

Only Forever

Promotional Ad For "Your Hit Parade" — 1943.

TOMMY DORSEY AND HIS ORCHESTRA   September 2, 1942
                                        Band Remote - New York City

Sinatra spoke a "Farewell To The Band" and sang "The Song Is You." He did
not leave the band on September 2nd and stayed on for at least another month,
possibly longer. Information gathered from members of the orchestra brings
forth the fact that three were a few more farewells as his replacement, Dick
Haymes, was breaking in.

THE TREASURY SONG PARADE   January, 1943

With David Brookman conducting The Treasury Ensemble these were four
minute shows that featured one song. The following is a collective list of the
songs sung by Sinatra:

That's My Affair	Starlight Sonata
It Started All Over Again	You'll Never Know
I Don't Believe In Rumors	There Are Such Things
As Time Goes By	Rosanne Of Charing Cross
Moonlight Mood	In The Blue Of Evening
Weep No More My Lady	Kiss Me Again
She's Funny That Way	Embraceable You
Every Night About This Time	Close To You
If Loveliness Were Music	

WAR JOBS   January, 1943

With Mark Warnow conducting and Hilo Jack and the Chorus.

Close To You
It Can't Be Wrong
Embraceable You

AMERICA SALUTES THE PRESIDENT'S BIRTHDAY
WITH SAMMY KAYE AND HIS ORCHESTRA   January 29, 1943, CBS

Night And Day

Frank appeared for the first time on "Your Hit Parade", a program that featured
the top tunes of the week. He replaced Barry Wood and his co-performers were
Joan Edwards, Ethel Smith, Lynn Murray and The Hit Parader and mark
Warnow conducting the orchestra.

YOUR HIT PARADE   March 27, 1943
                                                New York City, CBS

Moonlight Becomes You
There Are Such Things
You'd Be So Nice To Come Home To
That Old Black Magic

YOUR HIT PARADE   April 10, 1943, CBS

    As Time Goes By
    You'd Be So Nice To Come Home To
    That Old Black Magic

CBS premiered a new program on Friday nights and they called it the "Broadway Bandbox", and it was natural that they desired to obtain the services of the new "very hot" vocalist - Sinatra. Frank was certainly very busy these days and nights between singing at Nightclubs, The Paramount Theater, Your Hit Parade and this new show, but he was bursting with energy and the desire to reach the top, and top the top he was going. All of these early tapes and recordings show him in complete control of his voice and he sure knew how to get the most out of his predominantly young audience--they were in the palm of his hand and he knew it.

BROADWAY BANDBOX   May 14, 1943
Raymond Scott Orchestra   New York City

    All Or Nothing At All

BROADWAY BANDBOX   May, 1943
Raymond Scott Orchestra   New York City

    I Get A Kick Out Of You - (1)
    People Will Say We're In Love - (1)
      (1) with the Bobby Tucker Singers

BROADWAY BANDBOX   May, 1943
Raymond Scott Orchestra   New York City

    This Love Of Mine (short version)
    Comin' In On A Wing And A Prayer - (1)
      (1) with the Bobby Tucker Singers

YOUR HIT PARADE   May 29, 1943

    Let's Get Lost
    You'll Never Know
    That Old Black Magic
    As Time Goes By

YOUR HIT PARADE   June 5, 1943

    That Old Black Magic
    Let's Get Lost
    As Time Goes By
    You'll Never Know

BROADWAY BANDBOX   June, 1943
Raymond Scott Orchestra   New York City

    The Right Kind Of Love
    Paper Doll

YOUR HIT PARADE

    I Heard You Cried Last Night
    All Or Nothing At All
    People Will Say We're In Love
    You'll Never Know

COMMAND PERFORMANCE No. 80 AFRS   September 5, 1943

    Embraceable You
    Night And Day
    Duffy's Tavern Sketch With Ed. Gardner

YOUR HIT PARADE   September 25, 1943

    In The Blue Of Evening
    You'll Never Know
    Sunday, Monday And Always
    All Or Nothing At All

BROADWAY BANDBOX   October 3, 1943
Axel Stordahl Orchestra   New York City

    Falling In Love With Love
    If You Please
    Are We From Dixie (with Milton Berle)
    I Only Have Eyes For You
    There'll Be A Hot Time In The Town Of Berlin
    That Old Black Magic

YOUR HIT PARADE   October 9, 1943

    Paper Doll
    Pistol Packin' Mama
    If You Please
    Sunday, Monday And Always

BROADWAY BANDBOX   October 10, 1943
Axel Stordahl Orchestra

    Pistol Packin' Mama
    From Taps Till Reveille (with Bert Wheeler)
    Ol' Man River
    Close To You
    Where Or When

YOUR HIT PARADE   October 16, 1943

    All Or Nothing At All

I Heard You Cried Last Night
Pistol Packin' Mama
Sunday, Monday And Always

SONGS BY SINATRA   October 24, 1943

Unknown Tunes

YOUR HIT PARADE   November 6, 1943

I Heard You Cried Last Night
If You Please
Sunday, Monday And Always
Paper Doll

YOUR HIT PARADE   November 27, 1943

My Heart Tells Me
Oh! What A Beautiful Morning
Little Did I Know
Paper Doll

SONGS BY SINATRA   November 28, 1943
Axel Stordahl Orchestra

Just One Of Those Things
I Couldn't Sleep A Wink Last Night - (1)
My Heart Tells Me
My Heart Stood Still
   (1) with Bobby Tucker Singers

YOUR HIT PARADE   December 4, 1943

Sunday, Monday And Always
Oh! What A Beautiful Morning
Pistol Packin' Mama
People Will Say We're In Love

YOUR HIT PARADE   December 18, 1943

My Ideal
Speak Low
My Heart Tells Me

YOUR HIT PARADE   December 25, 1943

People Will Say We're In Love
Oh! What A Beautiful Morning
My Heart Tells Me

THE TREASURY STAR PARADE #307   December, 1943
David Brookman Orchestra

  Falling In Love With Love
  The Music Stopped
  I Couldn't Sleep A Wink Last Night

YOUR HIT PARADE   January 15, 1944

  People Will Say We're In Love
  Oh! What A Beautiful Morning
  Speak Low
  My Heart Tells Me

YOUR HIT PARADE   January 22, 1944

  Paper Doll
  My Shining Hour
  No Love, No Nothin'
  My Heart Tells Me

AMERICA SALUTES THE PRESIDENT'S BIRTHDAY January 29, 1944
Paul Whiteman Orchestra   CBS

  Speak Low

YOUR HIT PARADE   February 5, 1944

  People Will Say We're In Love
  Oh! What A Beautiful Morning
  Beseme Mucho
  My Heart Tells Me

VIMMS VITAMIN SHOW   February 9, 1944
With W.C. Fields and Bert Wheeler

  Falling In Love With Love
  Comedy Sketch With Wheeler
  No Love, No Nothin'
  Long Ago And Far Away
  Comedy Sketch With Fields
  My Heart Stood Still

YOUR HIT PARADE   February 12, 1944

  Beseme Mucho
  Speak Low
  No Love, No Nothin'
  Shoo Shoo Baby

COMMAND PERFORMANCE #104 AFRS   February 20, 1944

    Speak Low
    Scottish Sketch with D. Shore & B. Crosby
    If I Had My Way - with B. Crosby

YOUR HIT PARADE   February 26, 1944

    A Lovely Way To Spend An Evening
    No Love, No Nothin'
    I Couldn't Sleep A Wink Last Night
    My Shining Hour
    Beseme Mucho

COMMAND PERFORMANCE #106 AFRS   March 5, 1944

    The Song Is You
    Desert Island Sketch - with B. Hope & Judy Garland
    Embraceable You - with Judy Garland

THE FRONT LINE THEATRE AFRS   March 6, 1944

    Night And Day
    I'll Follow My Secret Heart
    As Time Goes By
    Time On My Hands
    The Continental

COMMAND PERFORMANCE #110 AFRS   April 2, 1944

    Kiss Me Again
    Dancing In The Dark
    Frankie & Johnnie Sketch - with Dinah Shore and Ginny Simms

YOUR HIT PARADE   April 8, 1944

    I'll Get By
    Poinciana
    Long Ago And Far Away
    I Love You

YOUR HIT PARADE   May 6, 1944

    I Love You
    Long Ago And Far Away
    I'll Be Seeing You
    Poinciana

VIMMS VITAMIN SHOW   May 17, 1944
with Bob Burns & Jerry Lester

Exactly Like You
Some Other Time (V-Disc #241)
Comedy Sketch with G. Burns & J. Lester
Come Out Wherever You Are (V-Disc #241)
The Way You Look Tonight

YOUR HIT PARADE   May 20, 1944

I'll Be Seeing You
I Love You
Long Ago And Far Away

VIMMS VITAMIN SHOW   May 24, 1944
with Judy Garland

San Fernando Valley
And They You Kissed Me (V-Disc #262)
Embraceable You - with Judy Garland

LIFEBOUY MUSICAL VARIETY SHOW   May 25, 1944
with Bob Burns, Cass Daley and Spike Jones

Vitamin Sketch - with B. Burns & C. Daley
South Of The Border
Girlfriend Sketch - with S. Jones

YOUR HIT PARADE   June 3, 1944

Amour
How Blue The Night
Long Ago And Far Away

YOUR HIT PARADE   June 10, 1944

San Fernando Valley
Swinging On A Star
I'll Be Seeing You

YOUR HIT PARADE   June 17, 1944

Amour
I Love You
Long Ago And Far Away

COMMAND PERFORMANCE #122 AFRS   June 25, 1944
with Bob Hope, Bing Crosby & Judy Garland

Comedy Sketch - with rest of cast
All The Things You Are
You Are My Sunshine - with Crosby
Bingy Boy - with Crosby
You're The Top - with Crosby

YOUR HIT PARADE   July 1, 1944

    I'll Get By
    San Fernando Valley
    Goodnight Wherever You Are
    I'll Be Seeing You

COMMAND PERFORMANCE #123 AFRS   July 3, 1944
with Connie Haines, Lena Horne, Shirley Ross, Lotte Lehman and Frances
Langford

    If I Had My Way - with B. Crosby & B. Hope

YOUR HIT PARADE   July 8, 1944

    I'll Get By
    Swinging On A Star
    I'll Be Seeing You

PERSONAL ALBUM   July 12, 1944

    I'll Walk Alone
    I'll Be Seeing You
    Close To You
    I Couldn't Sleep A Wink Last Night

YOUR HIT PARADE   July 15, 1944

    Milkman, Keep Those Bottles Quiet
    Goodnight Wherever You Are
    I'll Be Seeing You

YOUR HIT PARADE   July 22, 1944

    Sweet Lorraine
    And Then You Kissed Me
    Swinging On A Star

SOMETHING FOR THE GIRLS   July 22, 1944

    It Had To Be You
    I'll Be Seeing You
    All The Things You Are

COMMAND PERFORMANCE #126 AFRS   July 23, 1944

    San Antonio Rose
    Western Sketch - with Roy Rogers, Bob Hope and The Andrew Sisters

SOUND OFF   July 28, 1944

    Swinging On A Star

MAIL CALL #104 AFRS   July 29, 1944

Comedy Sketch - with Rudy Vallee & Fred Allen
Begin The Beguine
Come Out Wherever You Are - with Gloria DeHaven
Comedy Sketch about Maine

YOUR HIT PARADE   August 5, 1944

Long Ago And Far Away
It Could Happen To You
I'll Be Seeing You

YOUR HIT PARADE   August 19, 1944

I'll Walk Alone
It Could Happen To You
Amor

YOUR HIT PARADE   August 26, 1944

It Had To Be You
It Could Happen To You
I'll Be Seeing You

YOUR HIT PARADE   September 2, 1944

Is You Is Or Is You Ain't My Baby
I'll Walk Alone
Swinging On A Star

YOUR HIT PARADE   September 9, 1944

It Had To Be You
It Could Happen To You
I'll Be Seeing You

YOUR HIT PARADE   September 16, 1944

Is You Is Or Is You Ain't My Baby
It Could Happen To You
I'll Walk Alone

ALL TIME HIT PARADE   September 17, 1944

I'll Walk Alone
If You Are But A Dream - with the Tommy Dorsey Orchestra (V-Disc #393)

YOUR HIT PARADE   September 30, 1944

Swinging On A Star
It Could Happen To You
I'll Walk Alone

YOUR HIT PARADE   October 7, 1944

Swinging On A Star
Let Me Love You Tonight
I'll Walk Alone

THE JACK BENNY SHOW   October 7, 1944
Sinatra is in New York on "Your Hit Parade"

All The Things You Are
Benny Phones Frank In New York

THE FRANK SINATRA SHOW   October 10, 1944
with guest stars Ginny Simms, Frances Langford and the Pied Pipers
                                                   CBS, AFRS #15

All Of Me
Just Close Your Eyes
Let Me Love You Tonight
Together (Vocal duet with Ginny Simms)
(Medley) Thine Alone And A Kiss In The Dark

YOUR HIT PARADE   October 14, 1944

How Many Hearts Have You Broken
It Could Happen To You
I'll Walk Alone

LUX RADIO THEATER   October 15, 1944
"Wake Up And Live"

I Don't Want To Walk Without You
I've Heard That Song Before
Wake Up And Live
Embraceable You
Dancing In The Dark
Wake Up And Live (Reprise)

YOUR HIT PARADE   October 21, 1944

Is You Is Or Is You Ain't My Baby
Always
I'll Walk Alone

VIMMS VITAMIN SHOW   October 25, 1944
with Milton Berle

It's Only A Paper Moon
What A Difference A Day Makes
I'm In The Mood For Love
Come Out Wherever You Are

YOUR HIT PARADE   October 28, 1944

Together

Let Me Love You Tonight
I'll Walk Alone

PHILCO HALL OF FAME   October 29, 1944

There's No You
Ol' Man River

MAIL CALL #117   October 30, 1944
with Mae West

Comedy Sketch with Mae West on "Romeo and Juliet"
I Love You

ROOSEVELT ELECTION SPECIAL   November 6, 1944
                                                              CBS

Sinatra talks from Hollywood

YOUR HIT PARADE   November 11, 1944

Together
Strange Music
The Trolley Song

VIMMS VITAMIN SHOW   November 15, 1944

Button Up Your Overcoat
Sunday, Monday And Always
I Guess I'll Hang My Tears Out To Dry

THE BING CROSBY SHOW   November 16, 1944
Show is from Hollywood, but Sinatra is in Buffalo   NBC

These Foolish Things

YOUR HIT PARADE   November 25, 1944

How Many Hearts Have You Broken
The Very Thought Of You
The Trolley Song

YOUR HIT PARADE   December 2, 1944

Always
There Goes That Song Again
The Trolley Song

VIMMS VITAMIN SHOW   December 4, 1944
with Tallulah Bankhead

You Brought A New Kind Of Love To Me
Kiss Me Again
The Trolley Song

Sinatra and Fred Allen

Sinatra and Laurence Tibbett — 1945.

YOUR HIT PARADE   December 9, 1944

    Let Me Love You Tonight
    I Dream Of You
    The Trolley Song

THE EIGHT TO THE BAR RANCH   December 12, 1944
Vic Schoen Orchestra

    Western Sketch (with The Andrew Sisters, Gabby Hayes and Bill Elliot)
    Home On The Range (with The Andrew Sisters)

YOUR HIT PARADE   December 16, 1944

    There Goes That Song Again
    I Dream Of You
    The Trolley Song

VIMMS VITAMIN SHOW   December 18, 1944

    Just One Of Those Things
    Going Home
    Put Your Dreams Away

YOUR HIT PARADE   December 23, 1944

    I Dream Of You
    White Christmas
    Don't Fence Me In

YOUR HIT PARADE   December 30, 1944

    Always
    I Dream Of You
    Don't Fence Me In

Sinatra left "Your Hit Parade" after this show and his place was taken by Lawrence Tibbett.

PERSONAL ALBUM   January, 1945
Axel Stordahl Orchestra

    I'll Walk Alone
    Over The Rainbow
    If You Are But A Dream
    Close To You

JUBILEE #146 AFRS   January, 1945

    Saturday Night
    Blue Skies (with Louis Armstrong)

GLOBE THEATER AFRS   January, 1945

"Too Many Husbands"

Embraceable You (sung in comedy sketch with Donna Reed and Bill Goodwin)

SUSPENSE   January 18, 1945

   Sinatra plays handyman for Agnes Moorehead

THE CHARLIE McCARTHY SHOW   January 28, 1945

   There's No You
   The Very Thought Of You

MARCH OF DIMES   January 30, 1945
with Bing Crosby and Judy Garland

   When Your Lover Has Gone

THE MAX FACTOR SHOW   February 5, 1945
with Diana Lynn

   Strange Music
   I'm Beginning To See The Light
   All The Things You Are

G.I. JOURNAL #65   February 18, 1945
with Roy Rogers

   Mighty Lak' A Rose

A DATE WITH JUDY   February 20, 1945
                                                         CBS

   Night And Day
   I Don't Know Why

G.I. JOURNAL #77   February 25, 1945
with Fibber McGee and Molly and Ginger Rogers

   My Ideal
   Comedy Sketch (with Ginger Rogers)
   Shine On Harvest Moon (with Les Paul Trio)

THE ANDREW SISTERS' SHOW   March 4, 1945

   I Didn't Know About
   Empty Saddles (with The Andrew Sisters)

COMMAND PERFORMANCE #159 AFRS   March 11, 1945

   Comedy Sketch (with Frank Morgan, Nelson Eddy and The Andrew
Sisters)
   Saturday Night
   Sing's a bit of "Shortnin' Bread"

Sinatra and Orson Welles.

Sinatra and Rise Stevens — 1944.

G.I. JOURNAL #105   March 14, 1945
with Bing Crosby and Claudette Colbert

> Good, Good, Good
> Mademoiselle From Parley-Vous

THE FRANK SINATRA SHOW   April 4, 1945
with Fred Allen and Bill Goodwin

> The One I Love
> What Makes The Sunset
> Radio Sketch (with Fred Allen)
> I Begged Her
> Detective Sketch (with Allen & Goodwin)
> I'll Walk Alone

COMMAND PERFORMANCE #165 AFRS   April 22, 1945
with Elizabeth Taylor, Margaret O'Brien, Roddy McDowall, Peggy Ann Garner
and Bing Crosby's children.

> The Trolley Song
> Comedy Sketch (with E. Taylor)
> Comedy Sketch (with M. O'Brien)
> Brahm's Lullaby
> Comedy Sketch (with entire cast)

MAIL CALL #142 AFRS   April 24, 1945

> I Can't Give You Anything But Love
> School Sketch (with Vivian Blaine and Betty Hutton)
> Dream

THE FRANK SINATRA SHOW   April 25, 1945
with Danny Kaye and Bill Goodwin

> Good, Good, Good
> Laura
> Lonely Love
> Lulu's Back In Town
> Candy
> Comedy Sketch (with Danny Kaye)
> Memories (with Danny Kaye)
> Ol' Man Crosby (with Danny Kaye)

COMMAND PERFORMANCE #166 AFRS   April 29, 1945
Satire on Dick Tracy

> You Are A Brute* (with Bing Crosby)
> We Three Pin-Up Boys** (with Crosby & Bob Hope)
> My Bride*
* All The Things You Are
** Sunday, Monday And Always

HOLLYWOOD VICTORY SHOW - V-Day   May 8, 1945
                                                             CBS

    You'll Never Walk Alone
    If You Are But A Dream

THE BOB HOPE SHOW #96 AFRS   May 29, 1945
with Frances Langford, Jerry Colonna, Skinnay Ennis and Vera Vague

    Comedy Sketch (with Bob Hope)
    I'm Beginning To See The Light
    Don't Fence Me In (with Bob Hope0
    Western Sketch (with entire cast)

THE DANNY KAYE SHOW   June 14, 1945
with Judy Garland and the orchestra of Axel Stordahl (Danny Kaye is away)

    That's Judy
    Gotta Be This Or That (with J. Garland)
    Till The End Of Time
    Comedy Sketch (with J. Garland)
    My Romance (with J. Garland)
    Long Ago And Far Away
    Suddenly It's Spring

COMMAND PERFORMANCE   August 14, 1945

    You Are My Sunshine (with Crosby)
    Bingy Boy (with Crosby)
    You're The Top (with Crosby)
    The House I Live In

V-J DAY SHOW   September 2, 1945

    The House I Live In
    Monologue

MUSIC FOR MILLIONS AFRS   September 9, 1945

    Night And Day
    Nancy
    If You Are But A Dream
    Buy A Piece Of The Peace

At this point we would like to list the numerous and extremely productive "Songs By Sinatra" programs that were broadcast from 1945 to 1947. The shows featured The Pied Pipers, June Hutton and the resident orchestra of Axel Stordahl. They were sponsored by Old Gold Cigarettes.

SONGS BY SINATRA   September 12, 1945
with Martha Tilton and Bing Crosby's sons   CBS

Stars In Your Eyes
If I Loved You
Comedy Sketch (with Crosby's sons)
Embraceable you (with Martha Tilton)
Song Medley (with Tilton & Pied Pipers)

SONGS BY SINATRA   September 19, 1945
with Peggy Lee   CBS

On The Atchison Topeka And The Santa Fe
My Melancholy Baby
The Surrey With The Fringe On Top (with Pied Pipers)
I Fall In Love Too Easily
The House I Live In

SONGS BY SINATRA   September 26, 1945
with Dinah Shore   CBS

I'm Gonna Love That Girl
Begin The Beguine
Homesick - That's All
Three O'Clock In The Morning (with D. Shore)
Show Me The Way To Go Home (with D. Shore)
The Night Is Young And You're So Beautiful (with Dinah Shore) - V-Disc
564

THE VICTORY CHEST PROGRAM   September 29, 1945
Meredith Wilson Orchestra

Don't Fence Me In (with Jack Carson)
Night And Day
The House I Live In

COMMAND PERFORMANCE #189 AFRS   September 30, 1945

What Makes The Sunset
Kidnap Sketch (with Humphrey Bogart and Lauren Bacall)
Nancy - V-Disc 323

SONGS BY SINATRA   October 10, 1945
with Frances Langford and Ginny Simms

There's No You
All The Things You Are
Frankie And Johnny Sketch (with F. Langford and G. Simms)

SONGS BY SINATRA   October 17, 1945
with Gene Kelly

What Makes The Sunset
"Anchors Aweigh" sketch (with Kelly)
I Fall In Love Too Easily

I Begged Her (with Kelly)
The Charm Of You

THE FRED ALLEN SHOW   October 21, 1945
Al Goodman Orchestra   NBC

Comedy Sketch (with Fred Allen)
It Might As Well Be Spring
Open Up Them Pearly Gates (with Allen)

SONGS BY SINATRA   October 24, 1945
with Tommy Dorsey

I'll Buy That Dream
Without A Song
This Love Of Mine (with Dorsey & Pied Pipers)
Oh! Look At Me Now (with Dorsey & Pied Pipers)
I'll Never Smile Again (with Pied Pipers)

SONGS BY SINATRA   October 31, 1945
with Fred Allen

It's Only A Paper Moon
Don't Forget Tonight Tomorrow
Bess Oh Where's My Bess (with Pied Pipers)
Comedy Sketch (with Fred Allen)
On the Atchison Topeka (with Fred Allen)
It's Been A Long Long Time (with Pied Pipers)
Nancy

SONGS BY SINATRA   November 7, 1945
with Lawrence Tibbett

Just One Of Those Things
Homesick That's All
The Last Time I Saw You
Camptown Races (with L. Tibbett)
Beautiful Dreamer (with L. Tibbett)
It Might As Well Be Spring

SONGS BY SINATRA   November 14, 1945
with The Andrew Sisters

That's For Me
A Kiss Goodnight (with Patty Andrews)
How Deep Is The Ocean
Paramount Sketch (wit The Andrew Sisters)
Empty Saddles (with The Andrew Sisters)

SONGS BY SINATRA   November 21, 1945
with Marilyn Maxwell and Louis Prima

America The Beautiful

— 398 —

Till The End Of Time
Home On The Range (with M. Maxwell)
Oh! What A Beautiful Morning (with M. Maxwell)
The House I Live In

COLGATE'S SPORTS NEWSREEL   November 23, 1945
with Bill Stern   NBC

    Sinatra talks about his youth

SONGS BY SINATRA   November 28, 1945
with Lillian Romondi and Nat King Cole

    One More Dream
    Nancy
    Lover Come Back To Me (with L. Romondi)
    I Found A New Baby (with N. Cole)

SONGS BY SINATRA   December 5, 1945
with Earl Wilson

    Let It Snow
    I'm Always Chasing Rainbows
    Along The Navajo Trail
    Kentucky Home
    If I Loved You
    O Little Town Of Bethlehem (with The Pied Pipers)
    Silent Night (with The Pied Pipers)

THE JEROME KERN MEMORIAL SHOW   December 9, 1945
Al Goodman Orchestra   CBS

    The Song Is You

SONGS BY SINATRA   December 12, 1945

    Aren't You Glad You're You
    It Might As Well Be Spring
    Button Up Your Overcoat (with June Hutton)
    Day By Day
    Lilly Belle
    Ol' Man River

SONGS BY SINATRA   December 19, 1945
with Ella Mae Morse

    I'm An Old Cowhand
    Along The Navajo Trail
    White Christmas

COMMAND PERFORMANCE AFRS   December 25, 1945

    Comedy Sketch (with B. Crosby & B. Hope)

Sinatra and Elleen Barton

If I Loved You

SONGS BY SINATRA   December 26, 1945
with The Bob Mitchell Choir

    Great Day
    Symphony
    Medley Of Songs (with The Pied Pipers)
    Let's Start The New Year Right (with The Bob Mitchell Choir)
    You'll Never Walk Alone

SHOWTIME #157 AFRS   December 28, 1945
with Dinah Shore

    I Begged Her
    I Fall In Love Too Easily
    Dancing In The Dark (with D. Shore)

In 1945, Sinatra did a series of "MARCH OF DIMES" programs with Axel Stordahl. They were five minute broadcasts and featured one song. We have uncovered 12 of these programs but it is possible that there were at least 20 such charity shows.

SHOWTIME AFRS   January 1, 1946
Louis Silvers Orchestra

    I Begged Her (with Gene Kelly)
    What Makes The Sunset
    The Charm Of You

SONGS BY SINATRA   January 2, 1946
with Peggy Lee

    Chickery Chick
    Dearest Darling
    It's Been A Long, Long Time
    You Brought A New Kind Of Love (with P. Lee)
    Over The Rainbow

SONGS BY SINATRA   January 9, 1946
with Lina Romay and Skitch Henderson

    Some Sunday Morning
    Slowly
    Medley Of Songs (with S. Henderson)
    No Can Do (with Lina Romay)
    Day By Day

SALUTE TO AL JOLSON   January 10, 1946
Morris Stoloff Orchestra

    Rock-A-Bye Your Baby

SONGS BY SINATRA   January 16, 1946
with Andy Russell and Clark Dennis

    Aren't You Glad You're You
    Oh What It Seemed To Be
    Medley Of Songs (with Andy Russell)
    Bess, Oh Where's My Bess

SONGS BY SINATRA   January 23, 1946
with Skitch Henderson

    You Must Have Been A Beautiful Baby
    If I Loved You
    It's Been A Long, Long Time (with P. Pipers)
    Chickery Chick (with Pied Pipers)
    Symphony
    Medley Of Songs (with S. Henderson)
    Begin The Beguine

THE BOB HOPE SHOW AFRS #131   January 29, 1946
                                                            CBS

    Comedy Sketch (with Bob Hope)
    Nancy
    Skinnay Ennis, Frances Langford, Jerry Colonna, all join Hope and Frank
in "The Life Of Frank Sinatra"

SONGS BY SINATRA   January 30, 1946
with The Benny Goodman Sextet

    One More Dream
    Dearest Darling
    I Only Have Eyes For You (with B.G. Sextet)
    It Might As Well Be Spring
    Along The Navajo Trail
    Great Day
    Home On The Range

SONGS BY SINATRA   February 6, 1946
with Bob Hope

    Don't Forget Tonight Tomorrow
    That Old Black Magic
    These Foolish Things (with B. Hope)
    Medley Of Songs
    Day By Day

SONGS BY SINATRA   February 13, 1946
with Jack Carson

    Somebody Loves Me
    Oh What It Seemed To Be

Comedy Sketch (with J. Carson)
Don't Bring Lulu (with J. Carson)
The Song Is You

SONGS BY SINATRA   February 20, 1946
with Governor Jimmy Davis of Louisiana

Aren't You Glad You're You
Comedy Sketch (with Axel Stordahl)
Full Moon And Empty Arms
You Are My Sunshine (with J. Davis)
All The Things You Are

THE JACK CARSON SHOW   February 23, 1946
Freddy Martin Orchestra

Comedy Sketch (with J. Carson)
Onesy Twosy (with J. Carson and Norma Jean)
Brahms Lullaby

SONGS BY SINATRA   February 27, 1946
with Jimmy Durante

Sweet Loraine
All Through The Day
Who Will Be With You (with J. Durante)
I Fall In Love Too Easily
Day By Day

SONGS BY SINATRA   March 6, 1946
with Skinnay Ennis and Carlos Ramirez

Gimme A Little Kiss
Full Moon And Empty Arms
  Embraceable You
  Il Rrovatore Aria
  San Antonio Rose   Medley
  Brahms Lullaby
Whispering (with Skinnay Ennis)
Figaro (with Carlos Ramirez)
I'm Always Chasing Rainbows

ANNUAL ACADEMY AWARDS   March 7, 1946

Sinatra accepts special award for "The House I Live In"

SONGS BY SINATRA   March 13, 1946
with Nat King Cole

Some Sunday Morning
A Little Bit Of Heaven
Exactly Like You (with Nat Cole)
The House I Live In

Sinatra and Dinah Shore

SONGS BY SINATRA   March 20, 1946
with Van Johnson

    Personality
    Embraceable You
    Comedy Sketch (with Van Johnson)
    Personality (with Van Johnson)
    From This Day Forward

SONGS BY SINATRA   March 27, 1946
with Skitch Henderson

    One More Dream
    Begin The Beguine
    Spring Is Here
    Medley Of Songs (with S. Henderson)
    All Through The Day

SONGS BY SINATRA   April 3, 1946
with Skitch Henderson

    Aren't You Glad You're You
    Dearest Darling
    The House I Live In
    It Might As Well Be Spring
    Lilly Belle
    All The Things You Are

COMMAND PERFORMANCE   April 7, 1946

    Oh What It Seemed To Be
    You're The Top (with B. Crosby and B. Hope)

SONGS BY SINATRA   April 10, 1946
with Gene Kelly

    Two Hearts Are Better Than One
    I Fall In Love With You Everyday
    Don't Forget Tonight Tomorrow
    Comedy Sketch (with Gene Kelly)
    Down By The Old Mill Stream (with G. Kelly)
    Summertime
        It Ain't Necessarily So   Medley
        Bess, Oh Where's My Bess

COMMAND PERFORMANCE #217 AFRS   April 14, 1946
Johnny Green And His Orchestra

    The House I Live In

SONGS BY SINATRA   April 17, 1946
with Shirley Ross

    You Won't Be Satisfied
    Day By DAy
    The Surrey With The Fringe On Top
    Homesick That's All
    San Antonio Rose
    Without A Song

DINAH SHORE'S OPEN HOUSE   April 19, 1946

    Comedy Sketch (with D. Shore)
    Day By DAy
    Tea For Two (with Dinah Shore)

SONGS BY SINATRA   April 24, 1946
with The Slim Gaillard Trio

    Who's Sorry Now
    They Say It's Wonderful
    All Through The Day
    Cement Mixer (with Slim Gaillard)
    Slowly
    You Are Too Beautiful

HERE'S TO VETERANS   May 14, 1946
Axel Stordahl Orchestra

    Night And Day
    The House I Live In
    From This Day Forward
    All Through The Day
    Put Your Dreams Away

SONGS BY SINATRA   May 15, 1946
with Skitch Henderson

    How Cute Can You Be
    Don't Marry That Girl (Lil' Abner0
    Comedy Sketch (with Pied Pipers)
    Tea For Two (with June Hutton)
    Full Moon And Empty Arms
    You Are Too Beautiful

SONGS BY SINATRA   May 29, 1946
with Rise Stevens

    They Say It's Wonderful
    Day By Day
    Shoofly Pie
    Strange Music (with Rise Stevens)
    Full Moon And Empty Arms

FATHER'S DAY AWARD PROGRAM   June 16, 1946

Sinatra narrates three brief dramatizations on housing, jobs and understanding the veteran. He is also named Radio's Father Of The Year.

PERSONAL ALBUM AFRS   July, 1946
with Axel Stordahl

> Let It Snow
> If You Are But A Dream
> Begin The Beguine
> That's For Me
> Without A Song
> Put Your Dreams Away

JUBILEE #172 AFRS   July, 1946

> How Cute Can You Be
> The House I Live In

SONGS BY SINATRA   September 18, 1946
with Andre Previn and Frances Robinson

> The Coffee Song
> Somewhere In The Night
> South America Take It Away (with The Pied Pipers)
> They Say It's Wonderful (with F. Robinson)
> Come Rain Or Come Shine

STARS IN THE AFTERNOON   September 22, 1946
Al Goodman's Orchestra

> Tea For Two (with Dinah Shore)
> You'll Never Walk Alone

COMMAND PERFORMANCE #241   September 29, 1946

> Movie Star Sketch (with Judy Garland and Phil Silvers)
> The Girl That I Marry

SONGS BY SINATRA   October 9, 1946
with Andre Previn

> Five Minutes More
> This Is Always
> Wait Till The Sun Shines Nellis (with Previn)
> My Melancholy Baby (with Previn)
> If You Were The Only Girl In The World
> Full Moon And Empty Arms
> There's No Business Like Show Business

Sinatra was voted the most popular film star of 1946 by Motion Picture

Magazine and on this show was presented the award by Louis B. Mayer, head of the M.G.M. studio. The award was a bronze bust of himself sculptured by Jo Davidson at a cost of $10,000.

SONGS BY SINATRA   October 16, 1946
with Andre Previn

    Great Day
    Eastside, Westside
    Call Me Up Some Rainy Afternoon
    If I Had My Way
    South American Take It Away (with the Pied Pipers)
    Lost In The Stars

SONGS BY SINATRA   October 30, 1946

    Old Buttermilk Sky
    This Time
    This Is Always
    Comedy Sketch (with The Pied Pipers)
    You'll Always Be The One I Love
    Love Is Just Around The Corner
    Embraceable You

SONGS BY SINATRA   November 6, 1946
with Jimmy Durante

    My Sugar Is So Refined
    Pretending
    Oh How I Miss You Tonight
    All The Things You Are

SONGS BY SINATRA   November 13, 1946
with Martha Tilton

    Shoofly Pie
    Full Moon And Empty Arms
    Nancy
    Little Jack Horner
    Frere Jacques
    Oh What It Seemed To Be

SONGS BY SINATRA   November 20, 1946
with Peggy Mann

    Ole Buttermilk Sky
    Somewhere In The Night
    The Girl That I Marry
    Blue Moon
    Someone To Watch Over Me
    They Didn't Believe Me (with Peggy Mann)
    Begin The Beguine

SONGS BY SINATRA   November 27, 1946

    Let It Snow
    You'll Always Be The One I Love
    I Concentrate On You
    Glory, Glory Hallelujah
    Zip-A-Dee-Doo-Dah
    The House I Live In

SONGS BY SINATRA   December 4, 1946
with Page Cavanaugh Trio

    The Whole World Is Singing My Song
    Pretending
    Ma, He's Making Eyes At Me
    Dear Little Boy Of Mine
    There's No Business Like Show Business

SONGS BY SINATRA   December 11, 1946
with Fred Allen

    It's All Over Now
    You Keep Coming Back Like A Song
    Come Rain Or Come Shine
    Among My Souvenir
    Comedy Sketch (with Fred Allen)
    In My Merry Oldsmobile
    Ol' Man River

SONGS BY SINATRA   December 18, 1946
with Peggy Mann

    Jingle Bells
    You'll Always Be The One I Love
    Parade Of The Wooden Soldiers
    Have Yourself A Merry Little Christmas
    Embraceable You (with Peggy Mann)
    Silent Night

RADIO'S READER'S DIGEST   December 19, 1946
The Hallmark Playhouse   CBS

Silent Night

SONGS BY SINATRA   December 25, 1946
with Jane Powell

    Zip-A-Dee-Doo-Dah
    Let It Snow
    Pretty Baby
    It's All Over Now
    Put On Your Old Grey Bonnet

Sinatra and Benny Goodman

The Song Is You (with Jane Powell)
When Day Is Done

COMMAND PERFORMANCE #254 AFRS   December 29, 1946
with Carole Landis and Jimmy Durante

I Got A Gal I Love
Comedy Sketch (with Carole Landis)
Comedy Sketch (with Jimmy Durante)
The Things We Did Last Summer

SONGS BY SINATRA   January 1, 1947
"Songs Of The Century"

The Coffee Song
My Melancholy Baby
Atlantic City
Soliloquy

SONGS BY SINATRA   January 15, 1947
with Jane Powell - "Jerome Kern Show"

I Won't Dance
The Touch Of Your Hand
Why Was I Born
All Through The Day
Make Believe (with Jane Powell)
The Song Is You (with Jane Powell)
All The Things You Are (with Jane Powell)

MAIL CALL #283 AFRS   February 12, 1947

The Anniversary Song
Begin The Beguine

COMMAND PERFORMANCE #261 AFRS   February 25, 1947

The House I Live In

SONGS BY SINATRA   March 19, 1947
with Jane Powell

Linda
Roses In The Rain
If You Are But A Dream
The Song Is You (with Jane Powell)
It's The Same Old Dream

SONGS BY SINATRA   March 26, 1947
with Jane Powell and The Page Cavanaugh Trio

If This Isn't Love
Time After Time

—411—

Sinatra and Jane Powell

That's How Much I Love You Baby
The Anniversary Song (with Jane Powell)
If There Is Someone Lovelier Than You

U.S. SAVINGS BOND SHOW   March 30, 1947

Powder Your Face With Sunshine
Once In Love With Amy
Why Was I Born

SONGS BY SINATRA   April 9, 1947
with Jane Powell

Managua Nicaragua
A Million Times A Day
Nancy
My Romance (with Jane Powell)
It's The Same Old Dream

SONGS BY SINATRA   April 23, 1947
with Jane Powell and Irving Berlin

Blue Skies
The Girl That I Marry
Call Me Up Some Rainy Afternoon
Always
Help Me To Help My Neighbor

COMMAND PERFORMANCE #272 AFRS   May 4, 1947

Ol' Man Crosby

SONGS BY SINATRA   May 14, 1947
with Jane Powell and Burns and Allen

You Can't See The Sun
Time After Time
Why Shouldn't It Happen To Us (with George Burns)
All The Things You Are (with Jane Powell)
Begin The Beguine

SONGS BY SINATRA   May 21, 1947
with Jane Powell

That's How Much I Love You Baby
As Long As I'm Dreaming
The Anniversary Song
Stella By Starlight
Ain' Cha Ever Comin' Back

SONGS BY SINATRA   June 4, 1947
with Jane Powell

Soon

Embraceable You
Bess You Is My Woman Now (with Jane Powell)
Someone To Watch Over Me
Love Walked In

THE COLGATE SPORTS NEWSREEL   August 1, 1947
                                                        NBC

Sinatra substitutes for the vacationing Bill Stern.

MAIL CALL #274 AFRS   September 1, 1947
with Doris Day, Marvin Miller and The Pied Pipers

Stella By Starlight
Comedy Sketch
Tea For Two (with Doris Day)

Sinatra sang once again on The Hit Parade program and this is when he started
to state his opinions of the songs he was forced to sing and even though he tried
to select the most musical tunes, you will see in the listing that follows that he
did not have much choice. He did institute an all-time favorit format so as to
include one or two decent selections and these were presented as "extras", but
try as he did, it became a losing battle. His old friend, Axel Stordahl, conducted
the orchestra and Doris Day joined on the same date and stayed until November
29, 1947. She was replaced by Beryl Davis.

YOUR HIT PARADE   September 6, 1947
                                                        NBC

Feudin' And Fightin'
That's My Desire
That Old Black Magic
I Wonder Who's Kissing Her Now

YOUR HIT PARADE   October 11, 1947

Peg O' My Heart
The Lady From 29 Palms
I Wish I Didn't Love You So
I Wonder Who's Kissing Her Now

YOUR HIT PARADE   October 25, 1947

Over The Rainbow
You Do
Peg O' My Heart
If There Is Someone Lovelier Than You

Near You

HERE'S TO VETERANS #78   October 27, 1947

Great Day
You'll Never Walk Alone

—414—

HERE'S TO VETERANS #83   November 14, 1947

    The House I Live In
    From This Day Forward
    All Through The Day
    Put Your Dreams Away

COMMAND PERFORMANCE #300 AFRS   November 16, 1947
with Doris Day

    I Wonder Who's Kissing Her Now
    Tea For Two (with Doris Day)
    Comedy Sketch (with Doris Day)
    The House I Live In

YOUR HIT PARADE   November 22, 1947

    Civilization
    And Mimi
    The Whiffenpoof Song
    Laura
    Soon
    You Do

YOUR HIT PARADE   November 29, 1947

    Civilization
    So Far
    And Mimi
    The Girl That I Marry
    Hear You

YOUR HIT PARADE   December 13, 1947

    Let Is Snow
    I Wish I Didn't Love You So
    And Mimi
    Civilization

MARCH OF DIMES SHOW   December 28, 1947
                                                    CBS

    Falling In Love With Love
    Over The Rainbow
    You Can Take My Word For It Baby

YOUR HIT PARADE   January 10, 1948

    I'll Dance At Your Wedding
    Civilization
    Serenade Of The Bells
    Just One Of Those Things
    Ballerina

YOUR HIT PARADE   January 17, 1948

    Civilization
    So Far
    Serenade Of The Bells
    April Showers
    How Soon

TRUTH OR CONSEQUENCES   January 31, 1948

    I'll Dance At Your Wedding
    Civilization
    The Song Is You
    Golden Earrings

STARS IN THE SPOTLIGHT   March 11, 1948
                                                           NBC

Sinatra is interviewed by Harold Collins

DUFFY'S TAVERN   March 28, 1948

    I've Got A Crush On You
    Comedy Sketch

THE JACK BENNY PROGRAM   May 2, 1948

But Beautiful
    Sinatra and Benny argue about his fee

YOUR HIT PARADE   May 8, 1948

    Lili Bolero
    But Beautiful
    The Dickie Bird Song
    Now Is The Hour

YOUR HIT PARADE   May 22, 1948

    Lili Bolero
    Haunted Heart
    The Dickie Bird Song
    Nature Boy

YOUR HIT PARADE   May 29, 1948

    You Can't Be True Dear
    Lili Bolero
    Haunted Heart
    Nature Boy

THE LUX RADIO THEATER   May 31, 1948
"The Miracle Of The Bells"   CBS

A radio presentation of the film of the same name. Starring Sinatra, Fred

Sinatra and Shirley Ross

MacMurray and Valli.

COMMAND PERFORMANCE   June 20, 1948

    Comedy Sketch (with Bob Burns)
    Superman Sketch (with Bob Burns)
    All Of Me
    Priest Sketch (with Bob Burns and Beryl Davis)

YOUR HIT PARADE   June 26, 1948

    Little White Lies
    You Can't Be True Dear
    Haunted Heart
    Nature Boy

YOUR HIT PARADE   July 10, 1948

    Haunted Heart
    Nature Boy
  My Happiness
    Woody Woodpecker

YOUR HIT PARADE   July 17, 1948

    Little White Lies
    My Happiness
    Nature Boy
    You Can't Be True Dear

YOUR HIT PARADE   July 24, 1948

    It's Magic
    A Tree In The Shadow
    My Happiness
    Woody Woodpecker

YOUR HIT PARADE   July 31, 1948

    Little White Lies
    A Tree In The Meadow
    It's Magic
    You Can't Be True Dear

SYMPHONIES UNDER THE STARS   August 5, 1948
"Music For The Wounded"   Hollywood Beach

    Time After Time
    That Old Black Magic
    Bess, Oh Where's My Bess

YOUR HIT PARADE   August 7, 1948
with Lynn Murray and The Lucky Strike Orchestra

    Just One Of Those Things

My Happiness
A Tree In The Meadow

It's Magic

YOUR HIT PARADE   August 14, 1948

  You Call Everybody Darling
  My Happiness
  Woody Woodpecker
  It's Magic

YOUR HIT PARADE   August 28, 1948

  Love Somebody
  Maybe You'll Be There
  It's Magic
  A Tree In The Meadow

YOUR HIT PARADE   September 11, 1948

  Hair Of Gold
  My Happiness
  It Only Happens When I Dance With You
  A Tree In The Meadow

COCA COLA SPOTLIGHT REVIEW   October 1, 1948
with Spike Jones and Dorothy Shay   CBS

  Everybody Loves Somebody

COCA COLA SPOTLIGHT REVIEW   December 3, 1948
with Spike Jones and Dorothy Shay   CBS

  Once In Love With AMy
  Prisoner Of Love

GUEST STAR #91   December 19, 1948
David Rose Orchestra

  White Christmas
  Goin' Home

HERE'S TO VETERANS   Late 1948

Axel Stordahl Orchestra

  A Little Bird Told Me
  Buttons And Bows

COMMAND PERFORMANCE AFRS   January 4, 1949
with Gloria DeHaven and Phil Moore Four

  Bop Goes My Heart
  Detective Sketch (with G. DeHaven)

Sinatra and Lina Romay — 1946.

When Is Sometime

GUEST STAR   January 12, 1949
Axel Stordahl Orchestra

    Powder Your Face With Sunshine
    Once In Love With Amy
    Why Was I Born

YOUR HIT PARADE   February 5, 1949

    So In Love
    On A Slow Boat To China
    I've Got My Love To Keep Me Warm
    Far Away Places

ARTHRITIS AND RHEUMATISM FOUNDATION BROADCAST
                                                   March 16, 1949
"A Dream Come True" with Bob Hope, Dorothy Shay and Les Brown and His
Orchestra

    On A Slow Boat To China
    Anything You Can Do (with Hope and Shay)

YOUR HIT PARADE   April 30, 1949

    Far Away Places
    Again
    Sunflower
    So In Love

U.S. SAVINGS BOND SHOW   May 16, 1949
                                                   CBS

All star cast with Sinatra

YOUR HIT PARADE   May 28, 1949

    Red Roses For A Blue Lady
    Bali Hai
    Some Enchanted Evening
    Again

This was Sinatra's last show on "YOUR HIT PARADE". He was constantly in
conflict with the entire presentation especially the popular hits of the day and
eventually disagreed with George Washington Hill as to arrangment tempos. In
September he began a new three year contract with Lucky Strike on a show
called "LIGHT UP TIME". They were fifteen minute broadcasts with Dorothy
Kirsten and Jeff Alexander conducting the orchestra until Februarty of 1950
when Skitch Henderson replaced Alexander.

LIGHT UP TIME   September 5, 1949

    Night And Day
    It All Depends On You
    Where Are You Now That I Need You
    Some Enchanted Evening (with Kirsten)

LIGHT UP TIME   September 12, 1949

    You Do Something To Me
    Nancy
    I Only Have Eyes For You

LIGHT UP TIME   September 20, 1949

    At Sundown
    Younger Than Springtime
    Full Moon And Empty Arms

LIGHT UP TIME   September 22, 1949

    You Are My Sunshine
    Clementine
    Hey Lollie, Lollie Low (with Kirsten)
    Wagon Wheels

LIGHT UP TIME   September 27, 1949

    Wrap Your Troubles In Dreams
    Maybe It's Because
    If There Is Someone Lovelier Than You

LIGHT UP TIME   October 14, 1949

    The One I Love
    Mad About You
    I'm Comin Virginia (with Kirsten)

LIGHT UP TIME   October 24, 1949

    I Found A New Baby
    Just One Of Those Things
    All Of Me (with Kirsten)
    Baby It's Cold Outside
    The Hucklebuck

LIGHT UP TIME   November 8, 1949
with Ziggy Elman Orchestra

    You Must Have Been A Beautiful Baby
    On A Dreamers Holiday
    Maybe Its Because
    A Man Wrote A Song

LIGHT UP TIME   November 22, 1949

My Blue Heaven
The Touch Of Your Hand
Meadows Of Heaven
On The Island Of Stromboli

LIGHT UP TIME   November 24, 1949

The Best Things In Life Are Free
Don't Cry Joe
The House I Live In

LIGHT UP TIME   December 5, 1949
with Ziggy Elman Orchestra

A Foggy Day
Don't Cry Joe
Full Moon And Empty Arms (with Kirsten)

LIGHT UP TIME   December 24, 1949

Winter Wonderland
My Romance (with Kirsten)
Our Father

LIGHT UP TIME   December 27, 1949

It All Depends On You
A Man Wrote A Song
You're The Cream In My Coffee
I Think Of You (with Jane Powell)

The following "Light Up Times" are listed without any dates* and were broadcast between 1949 through May of 1950. *Except where possible.

LIGHT UP TIME #1

Someday
Just One Way To Say I Love You
The First Time
Strange Music (with Kirsten)

LIGHT UP TIME #2

Them There Eyes
If I Loved You (with Kirsten)
Envy
The Huckle Buck

LIGHT UP TIME #3

The One I Love
Katrina

Sinatra and Jimmy Durante.

At Sundown
Bali Hai

LIGHT UP TIME #4

It All Depends On You
You're Breaking My Heart
The Old Master Painter
Nothing Less Than Beautiful

LIGHT UP TIME #5

You Told A Lie
Stromboli
Don't Cry Joe
You'll Never Walk Alone

LIGHT UP TIME #6

There's Yes Yes In Your Eyes
If I Ever Love Again
If I Could Be With You
Why Do I Love You

LIGHT UP TIME   January 22, 1949

For You
Easy To Remember
You Do Something To Me
O Solo Mio

LIGHT UP TIME #7

Wrap Your Troubles In Dreams
Be Goody Good Good
Every Time I Meet You, I Meet You For The First Time
You're Breaking My Heart
My Romance (with Kirsten)

LIGHT UP TIME #8
with Eileen Wilson

On The Sunny Side Of The Street
The Meadows Of Heaven
A Fine Romance (with Eileen Wilson)

LIGHT UP TIME #9
with Margaret Whiting

The Old Master Painter
If I Ever Love Again
You're In Love With Someone
This Can't Be Love (with M. Whiting)

LIGHT UP TIME #10

    What Is This Thing Called Love
    A Dream Is A Wish
    I've Got A Crush On You
    The Very Thought Of You

LIGHT UP TIME #11

    Then I'll Be Happy
    Isn't It Romantic (with Kirsten)
    Bye, Bye Baby

LIGHT UP TIME   January 19, 1950

    Wrap Your Troubles In Dreams
    Embraceable You
    I Love You
    Chattanoogie Shoe Shine Boy

LIGHT UP TIME #12

    I Beeped When I Should Have Bopped
    Why Remind Me
    Where Or When
    Oh Look At Me Now

LIGHT UP TIME #13

    I Beeped When I Should Have Bopped
    I Must Have Done Something Wonderful
    Bye, Bye Baby
    Poineiana

LIGHT UP TIME #14

    Just You, Just Me
    Sorry
    I've Got A Crush On You
    What A Day, I'm In Love (with Kirsten)
    Somebody Loves Me

LIGHT UP TIME   February 10, 1950

    Don't Do Something To Someone Else
    Strange Music (with Kirsten)
    Brahms Lullaby
    You're My Thrill

LIGHT UP TIME   February 13, 1950

    Chattanoogie Shoe Shine Boy
    A Fine Romance (with Kirsten)
    White Christmas

My Foolish Heart

LIGHT UP TIME #15

Don't Do Something To Someone Else
Sitting By The Window
Sorry
Where Or When

LIGHT UP TIME #16

Lover
Sorry
I Don't Know Whether To Laugh Or Cry
Don't Worry, 'Bout Me
What A Day I'm In Love (with Kirsten)

LIGHT UP TIME #17

Doncha Go Away Mad
I Gotta Have My Baby Back
You're Awful (with Kirsten)

LIGHT UP TIME #18

The Old Master Painter
Sunshine Cake
Let It Snow
Lullaby Of Broadway

LIGHT UP TIME #19
Skitch Henderson Orchestra From Now On

A Foggy Day
Sure Thing
I Gotta Have My Baby Back
Full Moon And Empty Arms (with Kirsten)

LIGHT UP TIME   March 16, 1950

Doncha Go Away Mad
Gods Country
While We're Young (wiht Kirsten)
Let's Fall In Love (with Kirsten)

LIGHT UP TIME   March 24, 1950

Should I
Why Remind Me
A Little Bit Of Heaven
Sunshine Cake (with Kirsten)

—427—

LIGHT UP TIME #20

> Doncha Go Away Mad
> It Isn't Fair
> If I Knew You Were Coming I'd A Baked A Cake
> Body And Soul (with Bobby Hackett on trumpet)

LIGHT UP TIME #21

> If I Knew You Were Coming I'd A Baked A Cake
> I Gotta Have My Baby Back
> Why Do I Love You (with Kirsten)
> At Sundown

LIGHT UP TIME #22

> Chattanoogi Shoe Shine Boy
> Why Remind Me
> Can I Come In For A Second
> Dearie (with Kirsten)

LIGHT UP TIME #23

> That Old Black Magic
> Kisses And Tears
> When You're Smiling
> Penthouse Serenade (with Kirsten)

LIGHT UP TIME   April 20, 1950

> Lover
> It Isn't Fair
> All Or Nothing At All
> Dearie (with Kirsten)

LIGHT UP TIME   April 24, 1950

> This Can't Be Love
> One Hundred Years From Today
> Where Or When
> All Or Nothing At All

LIGHT UP TIME   April 27, 1950

> American Beauty Rose
> Kisses And Tears
> A Dream Is A Wish
> The Way You Look Tonight (with Kirsten)

LIGHT UP TIME   May 1, 1950

> American Beauty Rose
> My Foolish Heart

Lets Fall In Love (with Kirsten)

THE BOB HOPE SHOW   December 25, 1951
with Bing Crosby and the Orchestra of Les Brown   NBC

Sinatra is a surprise guest and sings "Silent Night" with Crosby.

STARS FOR DEFENSE   February 12, 1952
Axel Stordahl Orchestra

    Walking In The Sunshine
    My Girl
    I Hear A Rhapsody

THE JACK BENNY PROGRAM   March 4, 1952
with Danny Kaye, George Burns and Groucho Marx

    Then I'll Come Back To You (with whole cast)

GUEST STAR #319   May 3, 1953
Harry Sosnick Orchestra

    Why Try To Change Me Now
    Birth Of The Blues

SHOW BAND SHOW   June 11, 1953
Cyril Stapleton Orchestra   BBC - Radio England

    Birth Of The Blues
    Ol' Man River
    I'm Walking Behind You

SHOW BAND SHOW   July 16, 1953
Cyril Stapleton Orchestra   BBC - Radio England

    I've Got The World On A String
    Day In, Day Out
    London By Night

When Sinatra returned from England he appeared once again on radio in a drama series titled "The Rocky Fortune Show". He does not sing on these shows and a total of twenty-four dramatizations were broadcast.

The Rocky Fortune Show

Oyster Shucker/Pearl Smuggling	October 6, 1953
Chauffeur/Double Indemnity	October 13, 1953
Ships Steward/From The Bottom	October 20, 1953
All Night Hamburger Diner/$50.00 Shoe Box	October 27, 1953
$100 Per Hour Messenger Boy	November 3, 1953
A Bass Player	November 10, 1953
Body Guard To A Drama Critic	November 17, 1953
Art Shop Of Statues	November 24, 1953
Fortune Teller At A Carnival	December 1, 1953

Sinatra and Bob Hope — 1946.

Paid Companion To A Monkey Named "Senator"	December 8, 1953
"Gondolfo" The Prize Fighter	December 15, 1953
Sister Ellie Is Dead	December 22, 1953

THE BOB HOPE SHOW   December 24, 1953
Les Brown Orchestra

    Christmas Gift Sketch (with Bob Hope)
    South Of The Border
    Jingle Bells (with Bob Hope)

Body Guard At A Rodeo	December 29, 1953
Tour Guide At A Museum	January 5, 1954
Nitroglycerine Truck Driver	January 12, 1954
The Casey Affair/Football Scandal	January 19, 1954
Social Director At The Catskills	January 26, 1954
Blonde From New Orleans Has Too Many Husbands	February 2, 1954
Grinder Escapes	February 9, 1954
Process Server Gets Involved With Doctor's Son	February 16, 1954
Actuary Probabilities/Insurance Salesman	February 23, 1954
Witness To A Will Of An Insane Woman	March 2, 1954
Zenith Foundation/Trip To The Moon	March 9, 1954
Rents A Room (Final Show)	March 16, 1954

Sinatra's new radio show "To Be Perfectly Frank" was a mixture of recordings and live performances. It was a fifteen minute show and was broadcast twice weekly. On the "live" vocals he was generally accompanied by five pieces (piano, clarinet, guitar, bass and drums), called the "Sinatra Symphonette." Bill Miller was the solo pianist. We will list only the "live" selections.

TO BE PERFECTLY FRANK #1   November 27, 1953

    The Most Blues

#2   December 1, 1953

    All Of Me
    The Can't Take That Away From Me

#3   December 4, 1953

    It All Depends On You

#4   December 8, 1953

    I Can't Believe That You're In Love With Me

#5   December 11, 1953

    They Can't Take That Away From Me

#6   December 15, 1953

    Wrap Your Troubles In Dreams

#7   December 18, 1953

   I've Got My Love To Keep Me Warm
   Platinum Blues
   This Can't Be Love

#8   December 22, 1953

   My Funny Valentine

#10   December 29, 1953

   It All Depends On You

#12   1954

   If I Could Be With You

#13   1954

   I Don't Know Why

#15   1954

  I've Got My Love To Keep Me Warm

#16   1954

   Somebody Loves Me

#17   1954

   On The Sunny Side Of The Street

#18   1954

   You Must Have Been A Beautiful Baby

#19   1954

   I'm In The Mood For Love

#20   1954

   What Can I Say After I Say I'm Sorry

#21   1954

   I'll String Along With You

#22   1954

   The One I Love
   Love Is Here To Stay

#23   1954

  Should I
  This Can't Be Love

#24   1954

  What Is This Thing Called Love
  They Can't Take That Away From Me

#26   1954

  One Hundred Years From Today (Bill Miller)

#35   1954

  Between The Devil And The Deep Blue Sea

#37   1954

  This Can't Be Love

#38   1954

  Don't Blame Me

#40   1954

  Just You, Just Me

#41   1954

  S'Wonderfull

#42   1954

  Them There Eyes

#43   1954

  Thou Swell
  I Can't Believe That You're In Love With

#44   1954

  You Took Advantage Of Me
  September Song (Bill Miller)

#45   1954

  Lets Fall In Love

#47   1954

  Out Of Nowhere
  Where Or When

#48   1954

    Tenderly (Bill Miller)

#49   1954

    I'm Confessin'
    As Time Goes By

#50   1954

    If I Had You

#52   1954

    That Old Black Magic
    Under A Blanket Of Blue

#53   1954

    Them There Eyes
    Don't Blame Me

#56   1954

    Sometimes I'm Happy
    Its Only A Paper Moon

#57   1954

    Love Me Or Leave Me

#58   1954

    Should I
    Hello Young Lovers (Bill Miller)

#60   1954

    I'm In The Mood For Love

#62   1954

    Nevertheless
    She's Funny That Way (Bill Miller)

#64   1954

    Taking A Chance On Love
    This Love Of Mine

#91   1954

    You'd Be So Nice To Come Home To

#97   1954

    Hands Across The Table

#108 1955

    Come Rain Or Shine
    Love Is Here To Stay

#116 1955

    Try A Little Tenderness

#117 1955

    One For My Baby (Bill Miller)

#123 1955

    Someone To Watch Over Me

THE BING CROSBY SHOW   March 21, 1954
John Scott Trotter Orchestra   NBC

    Young At Heart
    Among My Souvenirs (with Crosby)
    September Song (with Crosby)
    As Time Goes By (with Crosby)

THE BING CROSBY SHOW   March 28, 1954
John Scott Trotter Orchestra   NBC

    Take A Chance
    Till We Meet Again
    There's A Long, Long Trail Awinding (with Crosby)

Frank appeared on the "Bobbi Show" in the form of recorded music taken from the Columbia and Capitol Sessions and also some "live" selections from "Perfectly Frank" shows. These were broadcast in late 1954 and early 1955.

TOP TUNES OF THE WEEK   June 25, 1955
Host - Andre Baruch with the McGuire Sisters, Georgia Gibbs, Eddie Fisher, Sarah Vaughan and Frank Sinatra.

HERE'S TO VETERANS #437 AFRS   July 12, 1955
Capitol Recordings

    Young At Heart
    All Of Me
    When I Stop Loving You
    You My Love

HERE'S TO VETERANS #511 AFRS   August 14, 1955
Capitol Recordings

    You Make Me Feel So Young

BIOGRAPHY IN SOUND   September 19, 1955
"The Kenton Era"

Stan Kenton's life narrated by Sinatra including excerpts from records.

ALL STAR REVUE   April 4, 1958

Extracts from previous shows with Sinatra singing duets with Bing Crosby.

SONS OF ITALY PRESENTATION   July 26, 1959

   High Hopes

UNKNOWN SOURCE   January 15, 1961

   Let's Call The Whole Thing Off
   I've Got A Crush On You
   A Foggy Day
   Nice Work If You Can Get It
   Let's Call The Whole Thing Off

BBC - RADIO ENGLAND   October 21, 1962

Frank Siantra personally presents Reprise Album R 1006, "Great Songs From Great Britain."

CANCER CRUSADE   April 4, 1963

   I'm Beginning To See The Light (Reprise)

HERE'S TO VETERANS #936   January 12, 1965

   All Of Me (Capitol)

CANCER CRUSADE   April, 1966

   Three Promo's For The Cancer Crusade

NATIONAL GUARD TRANSCRIPTION   September 28, 1967

   Hey Jealous Lover
   Street Of Dreams

SOUNDTRACK FIVE   October 11, 1967
Veterans Administration

   The World We Knew (Reprise)

GOLDEN DAYS OF RADIO   October 20, 1967

   Pistol Packin Mama (Your Hit Parade)

HERE'S TO VETERANS #1126   September 10, 1968

   The World We Knew (Reprise)
   You Are There (Reprise)
   Drinking Again (Reprise)

KGIL INTERVIEW   June 15, 1970
48 Hour Tribute

    Includes "Curse Of An Aching Heart"
    By The Original Hoboken Four.

KNEW TRIBUTE   August 4, 1970
91 Hour Tribute

HERE'S TO VETERANS #1231   September 15, 1970

    The Summer Wind (Reprise)
    Something Stupid (Reprise)
    It Was A Very Good Year (Reprise)

SINATRA THE MAN-RADIO LUXEMBOURG   March 27, 1971

Retirement tribute, including interviews with Harold Davidson and John Gee.

WILLIAM B. WILLIAMS SHOW   March 29, 1971
Tribute with Jonathan Schwartz   WNEW

HERE'S TO VETERANS #1260   April 6, 1971

    Goodbye (Reprise)
    Michael and Peter (Reprise)
    The Train (Reprise)

THREE DECADES OF A STAR (1939 - 1949)   June 17, 1971
Australian Broadcast
Narrator - Peter Young

THREE DECADES OF A STAR (1949 - 1959)   June 24, 1971
Same As Last

THREE DECADES OF A STAR (1959 - 1969)   July 1, 1971
Same As Last

NELSON RIDDLE INTERVIEW   July 8, 1971
Canadian Interview

SPIRO AGNEW TRIBUTE   May 19, 1972
Broadcast From Baltimore

    Sinatra sings parodies of:
    The Lady Is A Tramp
    But Beautiful

SINATRA SPECIAL   May 27, 1972
Albany, New York   WQBK

Ed O'Brien plays many selections from his vast collection.

TOP OF THE MARK   June 9, 1972

Guest Paul Compton in an in-depth discussion on Frank Sinatra.

MORNING MELODIES   August 10, 1972
Birmingham, England   BBC

Duncan Gibbons, J. Ridgeway and R. Purslow talk about Sinatra.

A MAN ALONE   August 28, 1972
with Harry James and Buddy Rich

Allan Dell and Fred May in a Retirement Tribute.

BIG BAND SOUNDS   November 4, 1972

Intro by Allan Dell who discusses the Sinatra/Dorsey Boxed Set.

RADIO COMMERCIAL   December 25, 1972
                                                             KPOL

Sinatra does a commercial for a record shop.

UN UOMO SOLO   January 5, 1973
Swiss - Italian Radio Broadcast

Narrated by Giuliano Fournier - easily understood description of several recordings.

HERE'S TO VETERANS #1419   March 4, 1973

        You Will Be My Music (Reprise)
        You're So Right (Reprise)
        Let Me Try Again (Reprise)
        Dream Away (Reprise)

PERSONAL CHOICE   April 20, 1973
Australian Broadcast
        Skitch Henderson talks about Sinatra.

THE SONG STYLISTS   July 2, 1973
Radio, England   BBC
        I Wish I Were In Love Again

JONATHAN SCHWARTZ SHOW   July 3, 1973
                                                            WNEW
        Plays and Discusses Sinatra Recordings.

JONATHAN SCHWARTZ SHOW   July 10, 1973
                                                            WNEW
        Talks about Sinatras Capitol
reissues and forthcoming new record.

JONATHAN SCHWARTZ SHOW   July 17, 1973
                                                              WNEW
    Talks about Sinatras' Basie's backing. There are many more shows of Mr. Schwartz in which he plays and discusses Sinatra, and in fact, the broadcasts continue to this present day, every Sunday morning.

WELCOME BACK SINATRA   October 1, 1973
    Radio KGIL in a 24 hour tribute with non-commercial material supplied by Joseph Memoli.

SINATRA NOW   December 2, 1973
RADIO MELBOURNE
    Presented by Geoff Manion and includes tracks from the "Ol' Blue Eyes" albums.

Sinatra and Lana Turner — 1944.

SONG INDEX - AIR CHECKS - CHAPTER XII

ACCENTUATE THE POSITIVE

(Harold Arlen - Johnny Mercer) December 26, 1945 (Medley with Pied Pipers)

AFTER ALL

(Joseph Meyer - Lee Roberts - Walter Scharf) March 2, 1940

AGAIN

(Dorcas Cochran - Lionel Newman) April 30, 1949, May 28, 1949

AIN'CHA EVER COMIN' BACK

(Paul Weston - Axel Stordahl - I. Taylor) May 21, 1947

ALL OF ME

(Seymour Simons - Gerald Marks) October 10, 1944, June 20, 1948, October 24, 1949, December 1, 1953, July 12, 1955, January 12, 1965

ALL OR NOTHING AT ALL

(Arthur Altman - Jack Lawrence) September 14, 1939, May 14, 1943, August 28, 1943, September 25, 1943, October 16, 1943, April 20, 1950, April April 24, 1950

ALL THE THINGS YOU ARE

(Jerome Kern - Oscar Hammerstein II) June 25, 1944, July 22, 1944, October 7, 1944, February 5, 1945, April 29, 1945, February 20, 1946, April 3, 1946, November 6, 1946, January 15, 1947, May 14, 1947

ALL THROUGH THE DAY

(Jerome Kern - Oscar Hammerstein II) February 27, 1946, March 27, 1946, April 24, 1946, May 14, 1946, January 15, 1947, November 14, 1947

ALONG THE NAVAJO TRAIL

(Larry Markes - Dick Charles - Eddie Delange) December 5, 1945, December 19, 1945, January 30, 1946

ALWAYS

(Irving Berlin) October 21, 1944, December 2, 1944, December 30, 1944, April 23, 1947

AMERICA THE BEAUTIFUL

(Katherine Bates - Samuel Ward) November 21, 1945

AMERICAN BEAUTY ROSE

(Ray Evans - Mack David - Arthur Altman) April 27, 1950, May 1, 1950

AMONG MY SOUVENIRS	(Edga Leslie - Horatio Nicholls) December 11, 1946, March 21, 1954
AMOR	(Gabriel Ruiz - Sunny Skylar) June 3, 1944, June 17, 1944, August 19, 1944, January 16, 1946 (Medley with Andy Russell)
AND MIMI	(Nat Simon - Jimmy Kennedy) November 22, 1947, November 29, 1947, December 13, 1947
AND THEN YOU KISSED ME	(Sammy Cahn - Jule Styne) May 24, 1944, July 22, 1944
ANNIVERSARY SONG, THE	(Al Jolson - Saul Chaplin) February 12, 1947, March 26, 1947, 1947, May 21, 1947
ANYTHING YOU CAN DO	(Irving Berlin) March 16, 1949
APRIL SHOWERS	(Buddy Desylva - Louis Silvers) January 17, 1948
ARE WE FROM DIXIE	(Jack Yellin - George Cobb) October 3, 1943
AREN'T YOU GLAD YOU'RE YOU	(Johnny Burke - Jimmy Van Heusen) December 12, 1945, January 16, 1946, February 20, 1946, April 3, 1946
AS LONG AS I'M DREAMING	(Johnny Burke - Jimmy Van Heusen) May 21, 1947
AS TIME GOES BY	(Herman Hupfield) January 1943, April 10, 1943, May 29, 1943, June 5, 1943, March 6, 1944, March 21, 1954, Mid 1954 (T.B.P.F. # -49)
ATLANTIC CITY	(Mack Gordon - Josef Myrow) January 1, 1947
AT SUNDOWN	(Walter Donaldson) September 20, 1949 Light Up Time # 3
BABY ITS COLD OUTSIDE	(Frank Loesser) October 24, 1949
BALI HAI	(Richard Rodgers - Oscar Hammerstein II) May 28, 1949, Light Up

BALLERINA   (Bob Russell - Carl Sigman)
January 10, 1948

BEAUTIFUL DREAMER   (Stephen Foster)
November 7, 1945

BEDELA   (Jean Schwartz - Billy Jerome)
October 16, 1946
Omitted from our listing on that date
and discovered later)

BEGIN THE BEGUINE   (Cole Porter)
July 29, 1944, September 26, 1945,
January 23, 1946, March 27, 1946,
July 1946, November 20, 1946, February 12, 1947, May 14, 1947

BE GOOD GOOD GOOD   (James Shelton)
Light Up Time # 7

BELL BOTTOM TROUSERS   (Moe Jaffe) February 6, 1946
(Included in song medley)

BESEME MUCHO   (Consuello Valazquez - Sunny Skylar)
February 5, 1944, February 12, 1944,
February 26, 1944

BESS, OH WHERES BY BESS   (George & Ira Gershwin - DuBose
Heyward) October 31, 1945, January
16, 1946, April 10, 1946, June 14,
1947, August 5, 1948

BEST THINGS IN LIFE ARE FREE   (Buddy De Sylva - Lew Brown - Ray
Henderson)
November 24, 1949

BETWEEN THE DEVIL AND THE   (Harold Arlen - Ted Koehler)
DEEP BLUE SEA   T.B.P.F. #35

BINGY BOY   (
June 25, 1944, August 14, 1945

BIRTH OF THE BLUES, THE   (Buddy Desylva - Lew Brown - Ray
Henderson)
May 3, 1953, June 11, 1953

BLUE MOON   (Richard Rodgers - Lorenz Hart)
November 20, 1946

BLUE SKIES   (Irving Berlin)
January 1945, January 9, 1946,

	(included in song medley) April 23, 1947
BLUES IN THE NIGHT	(Harold Arlen - Johnny Mercer) January 17, 1942
BODY AND SOUL	(Edward Heyman - Robert Sour - Frank Eyton - Johnny Green) Light up Time #20
BOP GOES MY HEART	(Walter Bishop - Jule Styne) January 4, 1949
BRAHMS LULLABY	(Johannes Brahms) April 22, 1945, February 23, 1946, March 6, 1946, February 10, 1950
BUT BEAUTIFUL	(Johnny Burke - Jimmy Van Heusen) May 2, 1948, May 8, 1948, May 19, 1972
BUTTONS AND BOWS	(Jay Livingston - Ray Evans) Late 1948 Heres To Veterans
BUTTON UP YOUR OVERCOAT	(Buddy De Sylva - Lew Brown - Ray Henderson) November 15, 1944, December 12, 1945
BUY A PIECE OF THE PEACE	(Sammy Cahn - Jimmy Van Heusen) September 9, 1945
BYE BYE BABY	(Leo Robin - Jule Styne) Light Up Time #11 and #13
BY THE LIGHT OF THE SILVERY MOON	(Gus Edwards) March 27, 1946 (included in song medley)
CALL ME UP SOME RAINY AFTERNOON	(Irving Berlin) October 16, 1946, April 23, 1947
CAMPTOWN RACES	(Stephen Foster) November 7, 1945
CANDY	(Mack David - Joan Whitney - Alex Kramer) April 25, 1945
CAN I COME IN FOR A SECOND	(Sammy Cahn - Jule Styne) Light up Time #22
CARELESS	(Lew Quadling - Eddy Howard - Dick Jurgens)

	February 2, 1940, February 20, 1940, February 24, 1940
CEMENT MIXER	(Slim Gaillard - Lee Ricks) April 24, 1946
CHARM OF YOU, THE	(Sammy Cahn - Jules Styne) October 17, 1945, January 1, 1946
CHATTANOOGIE SHOE SHINE BOY	(Harry Stone - Jack Stupp) January 19, 1950, February 13, 1950 Light up Time #22
CHICKERY CHICK	(Sylvia Dee - Sidney Lippman) January 2, 1946, January 23, 1946
CIVILIZATION	(Bob Hilliard - Carl Sigman) November 22, 1947, November 29, 1947, January 10, 1949, January 17, 1948, January 31, 1948
CLEMENTINE	(Percy Montrose) (September 22, 1949)
CLOSE TO YOU	(Al Hoffman - Jerry Livingston - Carl Lampl) January 1943, October 10, 1943, July 12, 1944, January 1945
COFFEE SONG, THE	(Bob Hilliard - Dave Miles) January 1, 1947
COME OUT WHEREVER YOU ARE	(Sammy Cahn - Jule Styne) May 17, 1944, July 29, 1944, October 25, 1944
COME RAIN OR COME SHINE	(Harold Arlen - Johnny Mercer) September 18, 1946, December 11, 1946, T.B.P.F. #108
COME WITH ME	(Catalani) March 27, 1946 (included in song medley)
COMIN' IN ON A WING AND A PRAYER	(Harold Adamson - Jimmy McHugh) May 1943
CURSE OF AN ACHING HEART, THE	(Henry Fink - Al Piantadosi) Late 1935, June 15, 1970
DANCING IN THE DARK	(Arthur Schwartz - Howard Dietz) April 2, 1944, October 15, 1944,

	December 28, 1945
DAY BY DAY	(Sammy Cahn - Axel Stordahl - Paul Weston) December 12, 1945, January 9, 1946, February 27, 1946, April 17, 1946, April 19, 1946, May 29, 1946
DAY IN - DAY OUT	(Rube Bloom - Johnny Mercer) July 16, 1953
DEAREST DARLING	(James Cavanaugh - Robertson - Frank Weldon) January 2, 1946, January 30, 1946, April 30, 1946
DEARIE, DO YOU REMEMBER	(Fred Coots - Raymond Klages) Light up Time #22, April 20, 1950
DEAR LITTLE BOY OF MINE	(Ernest Ball - J. Kiern Brennan) December 4, 1946
DEEP NIGHT	(Rudy Vallee - Ray Henderson) March 2, 1940
DEVIL MAY CARE	(Johnny Burke - Harry Warren) June 23, 1940
DICKY BIRD SONG, THE	(Howard Dietz - Sammy Fain) May 8, 1948, May 22, 1948
DO I WORRY	(Stanley Cowan - Bobby Worth) February 15, 1941
DON'CHA GO AWAY MAD	(Jimmy Munday - Al Stillman - Illinois Jacquet) Light up Time #17 and #20, March 16, 1950
DON'T BLAME ME	(Dorothy Fields - Jimmy McHugh) T.B.P.F. #38, T.B.P.F. #53
DON'T BRING LULU	(Ray Henderson - Billy Rose - Lew Brown) February 13, 1946
DON'T CRY JOE	(Joe Marsala) November 24, 1949, December 5, 1949 Light up Time #5
DON'T DO SOMETHING TO SOMEONE ELSE	(February 10, 1950, Light up Time #15

DON'T FENCE ME IN	(Cole Porter) December 30, 1944, May 29, 1945, September 29, 1945
DON'T FORGET TONIGHT TOMORROW	(Jay Milton - Manny Sherwin) October 31, 1945, February 6, 1946, April 10, 1946
DON'T MARRY THAT GIRL	(Johnny Mercer - Gene DePaul) May 15, 1946
DON'T WORRY 'BOUT ME	(Rube Bloom - Ted Koehler) Light up Time #16
DOWN BY THE OLD MILL STREAM	(Tell Taylor) April 10, 1946
DREAM	(Johnny Mercer) April 24, 1945
DREAM AWAY	(Paul Williams - J. Williams) March 4, 1973
DREAM IS A WISH, A	(Mack David - Al Hoffman - Jerry Livingston) Light up Time #10, April 27, 1950
DREAMERS HOLIDAY, (ON), A	(Kim Gannon - Mabel Wayne) November 8, 1949
DRINKING AGAIN	(Johnny Mercer - Doris Tauber) September 10, 1968
EAST OF THE SUN	(Brooks Bowman) February 24, 1940, May 28, 1940
EAST SIDE WEST SIDE	(Charles Lawler - Jas Blake) October 16, 1946
EMBRACEABLE YOU	(George & Ira Gershwin) January 1943, September 5, 1943, March 5, 1944, May 24, 1944, January 1945, September 12, 1945, March 6, 1946, March 20, 1946, October 30, 1946, December 18, 1946, June 4, 1947, January 19, 1950
EMPTY SADDLES	(Billy Hill) March 4, 1945, November 14, 1945
ENVY	(Light up Time #2

EVERY NIGHT ABOUT THIS TIME   (James Monaco - Ted Koehler)
January 1943

EVERYBODY LOVES SOMEBODY   (Irving Taylor - Ken Lane)
October 1, 1948

EVERYTHING HAPPENS TO ME   (Matt Dennis - Tom Adair)
February 11, 1941

EVERY TIME I MEET YOU   (Joseph Myrow - Mack Gordon)
Light up Time #7

EXACTLY LIKE YOU   (Dorothy Fields - Jimmy McHugh)
May 17, 1944, March 13, 1946

FABLE OF THE ROSE, THE   (Bickley Reichner - Josef Myrow)
March 9, 1940

FALLING IN LOVE AGAIN   (Frederick Hollander - Sammy
Lerner)
March 27, 1946, (included in song
medley)

FALLING IN LOVE WITH LOVE   (Richard Rodgers - Lorenz Hart)
October 3, 1943, December 1943,
December 28, 1947

FAR AWAY PLACES   (Joan Whitney - Alex Kramer)
February 5, 1949, April 30, 1949

FEUDIN' AND FUSSIN' AND   (Burton Lane - Al Dubin)
FIGHTIN'   September 6, 1947

FIGARO   (Mozart)
March 6, 1946

FINE ROMANCE, A   (Jerome Kern)
Light up Time #8
February 13, 1950

FIRST TIME, THE   (Nathaniel Shilkret)
Light up Time #1

FIVE MINUTES MORE   (Sammy Cahn - Jule Styne)
October 9, 1946

FLY ME TO THE MOON   (Bart Howard)
April, 1966

FOGGY DAY, A   (George & Ira Gershwin)
December 5, 1949
Light up Time #19
January 15, 1961

FOOLS RUSH IN   (Johnny Mercer - Rube Bloom)
                                       October 15, 1940

FOR YOU   (Johnny Burke - Al Dubin)
                                       January 22, 1950

FREE FOR ALL   (Matt Dennis - Tom Adair)
                                       September 20, 1941, January 17, 1942

FRERE JACQUES   (
                                       November 13, 1946

FROM TAPS TO REVEILLI   (Bert Wheeler)
                                       October 10, 1943

FROM THIS DAY FORWARD   (Leigh Harline - Greene)
                                       March 20, 1946, May 14, 1946,
                                       November 14, 1947

FULL MOON AND EMPTY ARMS   (Buddy Kaye - Ted Mossman)
                                       February 20, 1946, May 15, 1946, May
                                       29, 1946, October 9, 1946, November
                                       13, 1946, September 20, 1949,
                                       December 5, 1949, Light up Time #19

GIMMIE A LITTLE KISS   (Maceo Pinkard - Toy Turk - Jack
                                       Smith)
                                       March 6, 1946

GIRL OF MY DREAMS   (Sunny Clapp)
                                       January 23, 1946 (included in song
                                       medley)

GIRL THAT I MARRY, THE   (Irving Berlin)
                                       September 29, 1946, April 23, 1947,
                                       November 29, 1947

GLORY GLORY HALLELUJAH   (William Steffe)
                                       November 27, 1946

GOD'S COUNTRY   (Harold Arlen - Yip Harburg)
                                       March 16, 1950

GOIN' HOME   (Richard Addinsell)
                                       December 18, 1944, December 19, 1948

GOLDEN EARINGS   (Jay Livingston - Ray Evans - Victor
                                       Young)
                                       January 31, 1948

GOODBYE (SHE QUIETLY SAYS)   (Bob Gaudio - Jake Homes)
                                       April 6, 1971

GOOD GOOD GOOD	(Allan Roberts) March 14, 1945
GOODNIGHT WHEREVER YOU ARE	(Dick Robertson - Al Hoffman - Frank Weldon) July 1, 1944
GOTTA BE THIS OR THAT	(Sunny Skylar) June 14, 1945
GREAT DAY	(Vincent Youmans - Edward Eliseu - Billy Rose) December 26, 1945, January 30, 1946, October 16, 1946, October 27, 1947
HAIR OF GOLD	(Sunny Skylar) September 11, 1948
HANDS ACROSS THE TABLE	(Jean De Lettro - Mitchell Parish) T.B.P.F. #97
HAUNTED HEART	(Howard Dietz - Arthur Schwartz) May 22, 1948, May 29, 1948, June 26, June 26, 1948, July 10, 1948
HAVE YOURSELF A MERRY LITTLE CHRISTMAS	(Hugh Martin - Ralph Blane) December 18, 1946
HELLO YOUNG LOVERS	(Richard Rodgers - Oscar Hammerstein II) T.B.P.F. #58
HELP ME TO HELP MY NEIGHBOR	(Irving Berlin) April 23, 1947
HEY LOLLIE LOLLIE LOW	(September 22, 1949
HIGH HOPES	(Sammy Cahn - Jimmy Van Heusen) July 26, 1959
HOME ON THE RANGE	(Traditional) December 12, 1944, November 21, 1945
HOMESICK THAT'S ALL	(Gordon Jenkins) November 7, 1945
HOUSE I LIVE IN, THE	(Lewis Allen - Earl Robinson) August 14, 1945, September 2, 1945, September 19, 1945, September 29, 1945, November 21, 1945, April 3, 1946, April 14, 1946, May 14, 1946,

	July 1946, February 25, 1947, November 14, 1947, November 16, 1947, November 24, 1949
HOW AM I TO KNOW	(Dorothy Parker - Jack King) November 29, 1940
HOW BLUE THE NIGHT	(Jimmy McHugh - Harold Adamson) June 3, 1944
HOW CUTE CAN YOU BE	(Carl Fishcer - Bill Carey) May 15, 1946
HOW DEEP IS THE OCEAN	(Irving Berlin) November 14, 1945
HOW MANY HEARTS HAVE YOU BROKEN	(Marty Symes - Mel Kaufman) November 25, 1944
HOW SOON	(Clarence Lucas - Jack Owens) January 17, 1948
HUCKLEBUCK, THE	(Roy Alfred - Andy Gibson) October 24, 1949
I BEEPED WHEN I SHOULD HAVE BOPPED	Light up Time #12 Light up Time #13
I BEGGED HER	(Sammy Cahn - Jule Styne) April 4, 1945, October 17, 1945, December 28, 1945, January 1, 1946
I CAN'T BEGIN TO TELL YOU	(James Monaco - Mack Gordon) February 6, 1946 (included in song medley)
I CAN'T BELIEVE THAT YOU'RE IN LOVE WITH ME	(Clarence Gaskill - Jimmy McHugh) December 8, 1953
I CAN'T GIVE YOU ANYTHING BUT LOVE	(Dorothy Fields - Jimmy McHugh) April 24, 1945
I CONCENTRATE ON YOU	(Cole Porter) November 27, 1946
I COULDN'T SLEEP A WINK LAST NIGHT	(Jimmy McHugh - Harold McHugh - Harold Adamson) November 28, 1943, December 1943, February 26, 1944, July 12, 1944
I CRIED FOR YOU	(Arthur Freed - Gus Arnheim - Abe Lyman) January 16, 1946 (included in song medley)

I DIDN'T KNOW ABOUT YOU   (Duke Ellington - Bob Russell)
March 4, 1945

I DON'T BELIEVE IN RUMORS   (
January 1943

I DON'T KNOW WHETHER TO   (Bernie Wayne - Margarite James)
LAUGH OR CRY   Light up Time #16

I DON'T KNOW WHY   (Roy Turk - Fred Ahlert)
February 20, 1945, T.B.P.F. #13

I DON'T WANT TO WALK WITHOUT   (Frank Loesser - Jule Styne)
YOU   October 15, 1944, September 12, 1945
(Included in song medley)

I DREAM OF YOU   (Marjorie Goetsehius - Edna Osser)
December 9, 1944, December 16, 1944,
December 23, 1944, December 30, 1944

I FALL IN LOVE TOO EASILY   (Sammy Cahn - Jule Styne)
September 19, 1945, October 17, 1945,
December 28, 1945, February 27, 1946

I FALL IN LOVE WITH YOU   (Mamy Sherwin - Arthur Altman)
EVERYDAY   April 10, 1946

IF I COULD BE WITH YOU   (Harry Creamer - James Johnson)
Light up Time #6, T.B.P.F. #12

IF I EVER LOVE AGAIN   (Carlyle - Reynolds)
Light up Time #6
Light up Time #9

IF I HAD MY WAY   (James Monaco)
February 20, 1944, July 3, 1944,
October 16, 1946

IF I HAD YOU   (Ted Shapiro - Jimmy Campbell - Reg
Connelly) T.B.P.F. #50

IF I KNEW YOU WERE COMING I'D   (Al Hoffman - Bob Merrill - Clem
HAVE BAKED A CAKE   Watts)
Light up Time #20
Light up Time #21

IF I LOVE YOU   (Richard Rodgers - Oscar
Hammerstein II)
September 12, 1945, December 5, 1945,
December 25, 1945

IF LOVELINESS WERE MUSIC   Mickey Stoner - Bert Reisfeld)
January 1943

IF THERE IS SOMEONE LOVELIER THAN YOU

(Howard Dietz - Arthur Schwartz)
March 26, 1947, September 27, 1949

IF THIS ISN'T LOVE

(Yip Harburg - Burton Lane)
March 26, 1947

I FOUND A NEW BABY

(Jack Palmer - Spencer Williams)
October 24, 1949, November 28, 1945

IF YOU ARE BUT A DREAM

(Moe Jaffe - Jack Fulton - Nathaniel Bonx)
September 17, 1944, January 1945, May 8, 1945, September 9, 1945, July 1946, March 19, 1947

IF YOU PLEASE

(Johnny Burke - Jimmy Van Heusen)
October 3, 1943, October 9, 1943, November 6, 1943

IF YOU WERE THE ONLY GIRL IN THE WORLD

(Nat Ayer)
October 9, 1946

I GET A KICK OUT OF YOU

(Cole Porter)
May, 1943

I GOT A GAL I LOVE

(Sammy Cahn - Jule Styne)
December 29, 1946

I GOTTA HAVE MY BABY BACK

(Floyd Tilman)
Light up Time #19, #20

I GUESS I'LL HANG MY TEARS OUT TO DRY

(Mickey Stoner - Martin Block - Harold Greene)
November 15, 1944

I HEAR A RHAPSODY

(George Fragos - Jack Baker - Dick Gasparre)
February 12, 1952

I HEARD YOU CRIED LAST NIGHT

(Ted Grouya - Jerry Kruger)
August 28, 1943, October 16, 1943, November 6, 1943

I LIVE THE LIFE I LOVE

(Clay Boland)
June 23, 1940

I'LL BE SEEING YOU

(Sammy Fain - Irving Kahal)
May 6, 1944, May 20, 1944, June 10, 1944, July 1, 1944, July 12, 1944, July 22, 1944, August 5, 1944, September 9, 1944

I'LL BUY THAT DREAM	(Herb Magidson - Allie Wrubel) October 24, 1945
I'LL DANCE AT YOUR WEDDING	(Ben Oakland - Herb Magidson) January 10, 1948, January 31, 1948
I'LL FOLLOW MY SECRET HEART	(Noel Coward) March 6, 1944
I'LL GET BY	(Roy Turk - Fred Ahlert) March 9, 1940, April 8, 1944, July 1, 1944, July 8, 1944
I'LL NEVER SMILE AGAIN	(Ruth Lowe) May 28, 1940, October 24, 1945
I'LL STRING ALONG WITH YOU	(Harry Warren - Al Dubin) T.B.P.F. #21
I'LL TAKE TALLULAH	(Yip Harburg - Burton Lane) July 30, 1942
I'LL WALK ALONE	(Sammy Cahn - Jule Styne) July 12, 1944, August 19, 1944, September 2, 1944, January 1945, April 4, 1945
IL TROVATORE	(Verdi) March 6, 1946
I LOVE YOU	(Cole Porter) April 8, 1944, May 6, 1944, May 20, 1944, June 17, 1944
I LOVE YOU	(Harry Archer - Harlan Thompson) January 19, 1950
I LOVE YOU DEAR	(Webb - Grieg) October 30, 1944
I'M ALWAYS CHASING RAINBOWS	(Harry Carroll - Joseph McCarty) December 4, 1945, March 6, 1946
I'M AN OLD COWHAND	(Johnny Mercer) December 19, 1945
I'M BEGINNING TO SEE THE LIGHT	(Harry James - Johnny Hodges - Duke Ellington - Don George) February 5, 1945, May 29, 1945, April 4, 1963
I'M COMIN' VIRGINIA	(Donald Heywood - Will Cook) October 14, 1949

I'M CONFESSIN'	(Doc Doughty - Ellis Reynolds - Al Neiburg) T.B.P.F. #49
I'M GONNA LOVE THAT GIRL	(Frances Ash) September 26, 1946
I'M IN THE MOOD FOR LOVE	(Dorothy Fields - Jimmy McHugh) T.B.P.F. #19
I MUST HAVE DONE SOMETHING WONDERFUL	(Light up Time #13
I'M WALKING BEHIND YOU	(Billy Reid) June 11, 1953
IN MY DREAMS	(October 15, 1940
IN MY MERRY OLDSMOBILE	(Vincent Bryan - Gus Edwards) December 11, 1946
IN THE BLUE OF EVENING	(Tom Adair - Alfred D'Artega) January 1943, September 25, 1943
IN THE GLOAMIN	(Annie Harrison) January 23, 1946 (included in song medley)
I ONLY HAVE EYES FOR YOU	(Al Dubin - Harry Warren) October 3, 1943, January 30, 1946
IRISH LULLABY	(Owen) December 26, 1945 (included in song medley)
IS YOU IS OR IS YOU AIN'T MY BABY	(Ray Austin - Louis Jordan) September 2, 1944, September 16, 1944, October 21, 1941
ISN'T IT ROMANTIC	(Richard Rodgers - Lorenz Hart) Light up Time #11
IT AIN'T NECESSARILY SO	(George and Ira Gershwin - Dubose Heyward) April 10, 1946
IT ALL DEPENDS ON YOU	Buddy DeSylva - Lew Henderson - Ray Brown) December 27, 1949, Light up Time #4, December 4, 1953, December 29, 1953
IT CAN'T BE WRONG	(Kim Gannon - Max Steiner)

January 1943 (Move to "W" Wrong
Can It Be Wrong To Love

IT COULD HAPPEN TO YOU   (Johnny Mercer - Jimmy Van
                          Heusen)
                          August 5, 1944, August 19, 1944,
                          August 26, 1944, September 9, 1944

IT HAD TO BE YOU   (Gus Kahn - Isham Jones)
                          July 22, 1944, August 26, 1944,
                          September 9, 1944

I THINK OF YOU   (Jack Elliot - Don Marcotte)
                          December 27, 1949

IT ISN'T FAIR   (Richard Himber - Frank Warshaver -
                          Sylvester Sprigate)
                          Light up Time #20, April 20, 1950

IT MIGHT AS WELL BE SPRING   (Richard Rodgers - Oscar
                          Hammerstein II)
                          October 21, 1945, November 7, 1945,
                          December 12, 1945

IT ONLY HAPPENS WHEN I DANCE (Irving Berlin)
YOU   September 11, 1948

IT STARTED ALL OVER AGAIN   (Carl Fischer - Bill Carey)
                          January 1943

IT'S A BLUE WORLD   (Chet Wright - Bob Forrest)
                          March 9, 1940

IT'S ALL OVER   (Woodhouse)
                          December 25, 1946

IT'S BEEN A LONG LONG TIME   (Sammy Cahn - Jule Styne)
                          October 31, 1945, January 2, 1945,
                          January 23, 1946

IT'S EASY TO REMEMBER   (Richard Rodgers - Lorenz Hart)
                          January 22, 1950

IT'S MAGIC   (Sammy Cahn - Jule Styne)
                          July 24, 1948, July 31, 1948, August
                          August 7, 1948, August 14, 1948,
                          August 28, 1948

IT'S ONLY A PAPER MOON   (Harold Arlen - Billy Rose - Yip
                          Harburg)
                          October 31, 1945, T.B.P.F. #56

IT'S THE SAME OLD DREAM	(Sammy Cahn - Jule Styne) March 19, 1947, April 9, 1947
I'VE GOT A CRUSH ON YOU	(George & Ira Gershwin) Light up Time #10, Light up Time #14, January 15, 1961
I'VE GOT MY EYES ON YOU	(Cole Porter) February 20, 1940, February 24, 1940, March 2, 1940
I'VE GOT MY LOVE TO KEEP ME WARM	(Irving Berlin) December 18, 1953, T.B.P.F. #15
I'VE GOT THE WORLD ON A STRING	(Harold Arlen - Ted Koehler)
I'VE HEARD THAT SONG BEFORE	(Jule Styne - Sammy Cahn) October 15, 1944
I WISH I DIDN'T LOVE YOU SO	(Frank Loesser) October 11, 1947, December 13, 1947
I WISH I WERE IN LOVE AGAIN	(Richard Rodgers - Lorenz Hart) July 2, 1973
I WONDER WHO'S KISSING HER NOW	(Frank Adams - Will Hough - Joseph Howard) September 6, 1947, October 11, 1947, November 16, 1947
I WON'T DANCE	(Jerome Kern - Dorothy Fields - Jimmy McHugh) January 15, 1947
JINGLE BELLS	(James Pierpont) December 18, 1946, December 24, 1953
JUST AS THOUGH YOU WERE HERE	(Eddie De Lange - John Brooks) August 18, 1942
JUST CLOSE YOUR EYES	(Bernice Petkere) October 10, 1944
JUST ONE OF THOSE THINGS	(Cole Porter) November 7, 1945, January 10, 1948, August 7, 1948, October 24, 1949
JUST ONE WAY TO SAY I LOVE YOU	(Irving Berlin) Light up Time #1
JUST YOU, JUST ME	(Raymond Klages - Jesse Greer) Light up Time #14, T.B.P.F. #40

KATRINA	(Don Raye - Gene De Paul) Light up Time #3
KISSES AND TEARS	(Sammy Cahn - Jule Styne) Light up Time #23 April 27, 1950
KISS GOODNIGHT, A	(Freddie Slack - Paul Victor - Woody Herman) November 14, 1945
KISS ME AGAIN	(Victor Herbert - Henry Blossom) January 1943, April 2, 1944
KISS IN THE DARK, A	(Buddy De Sylva - Victor Herbert) October 10, 1944
LADY FROM 29 PALMS	(Allie Wrubel) October 11, 1947
LADY IS A TRAMP, THE	(Richard Rodgers - Lorenz Hart) May 19, 1972
LAST CALL FOR LOVE, THE	(Yip Harburg - Margery Cummings - Burton Lane) March 14, 1942
LAST TIME I SAW YOU, THE	(Marjorie Goetschius - Edna Osser) November 7, 1945
LAURA	(Johnny Mercer - David Raskin) April 25, 1945, December 26, 1945, (included in song medley) November 22, 1947
LEARN TO CROON	(Arthur Johnson - Sam Coslow) June 23, 1940
LET IT SNOW	(Sammy Cahn - Jule Styne) December 5, 1945, July 1946, November 27, 1946, December 25, 1946, December 13, 1947, Light up Time #18
LET ME LOVE YOU TONIGHT	(Mitchell Parish - Rene Touzet) October 7, 1944, October 10, 1944 October 28, 1944, December 9, 1944
LET ME TRY AGAIN	(Paul Anka - Caravelli - Sammy Cahn) March 4, 1973

LET'S CALL THE WHOLE THING OFF	(George & Ira Gershwin) January 15, 1961
LET'S FALL IN LOVE	(Harold Arlen - Ted Koehler) March 15, 1960, May 1, 1950, T.B.P.F. #45
LET'S GET AWAY FROM IT ALL	(Matt Dennis - Tom Adair) February 11, 1941, February 14, 1941
LET'S GET LOST	(Frank Loesser - Jimmy McHugh) May 29, 1943, June 5, 1943
LET'S START THE NEW YEAR RIGHT	(Irving Berlin) December 26, 1945
LILLI BOLERO	(Sidney Lippman - Sylvia Dee - Moore) May 8, 1948, May 22, 1948, May 29, 1948
LILLY BELLE	(Dave Franklin - Irving Taylor) December 12, 1945, April 3, 1946
LINDA	(Jack Lawrence) March 18, 1947
LITTLE BIRD TOLD ME, A	(Harvey Brooks) Late 1948
LITTLE BIT OF HEAVEN, A	(Ernest Ball - Keirn Brennan) March 13, 1946, March 24, 1950
LITTLE DID I KNOW	(Abner Silver - Charles Kenny - Nick Kenny) November 27, 1943
LITTLE JACK HORNER	November 13, 1946
LITTLE WHITE LIES	(Walter Donaldson) June 26, 1948, July 17, 1948, July 31, 1948
LONDON BY NIGHT	(Carroll Coates) July 16, 1953
LONELY LOVE	April 25, 1945
LONG AGO AND FAR AWAY	(Ira Gershwin - Jerome Kern) February 9, 1944, April 8, 1944, May 6, 1944, May 20, 1944, June 3, 1944, June

17, 1944, August 5, 1944, June 14, 1945

LOST IN THE STARS	(Kurtweill - Maxwell Anderson) October 16, 1946
LOVE IS HERE TO STAY	(George & Ira Gershwin) T.B.P.F. #22, #108
LOVE IS JUST AROUND THE CORNER	(Leo Robin - Lewis Gensler) October 30, 1945
LOVE LIES	(Joseph Meyer - Carl Sigman - Ralph Freed) October 15, 1940
LOVE ME OR LEAVE ME	(Walter Donaldson - Gus Kahn) T.B.P.F. #57
LOVELY WAY TO SPEND AN EVENING, A	(Harold Adamson - Jimmy McHugh) February 26, 1944
LOVER	(Richard Rodgers - Lorenz Hart) Light up Time #16, April 20, 1950
LOVER COME BACK TO ME	(Oscar Hammerstein II - Sigmund Romberg) November 28, 1945
LOVER IS BLUE, A	(Jimmy Mundy - Trummy Young - Charles Carpenter) February 20, 1940, February 24, 1940
LOVE SOMEBODY	(Joan Whitney - Alex Kramer) August 28, 1948
LOVE WALKED IN	(George & Ira Gershwin) June 4, 1947
LULLABY OF BROADWAY	(Harry Warren - Al Dubin) Light up Time #18
LULU'S BACK IN TOWN	(Harry Warren - Al Dubin) April 25, 1945
MA, (HE'S MAKING EYE'S AT ME)	(Con Conrad - Sidney Clare) December 4, 1946
MAD ABOUT YOU	(Ned Washington - Victor Young) October 14, 1949
MADEMESELLE FROM PARLEY-VOUS	(March 14, 1945

MAGIC IS THE MOONLIGHT (Charles Pasquale - Maria Grever)
January 16, 1946 (included in song
medley)

MAKE BELIEVE (Jerome Kern)
January 15, 1947

MANAGUA NICARAGUA (Irving Fields - Albert Gamse)
April 9, 1947

MAN WROTE A SONG, A (Dave Franklin)
November 8, 1949, December 27, 1949

MARIE (Irving Berlin)
January 25, 1940, February 2, 1940,
March 9, 1940, October 17, 1940

MAYBE IT'S BECAUSE (Harry Ruby - John Scott)
September 27, 1949, November 8,
1949

MAYBE YOU'LL BE THERE (Rube Bloom - Sammy Gallop)
August 28, 1949

MEADOWS OF HEAVEN, THE

November 22, 1948, Light up Time
#81

MEMORIES OF YOU (Andy Razaf - Eubie Blake)
April 25, 1945

MICHAEL AND PETER (Bob Gaudio - Jake Holmes)
April 6, 1971

MIDNIGHT ON THE TRAIL

June 23, 1940

MIGHTY LAK' A ROSE (Ethelbert Nevin - Frank Stanton)
February 18, 1945

MILKMAN KEEP THOSE BOTTLES (Gene De Paul - Don Raye)
QUIET July 15, 1944

MILLION TIMES A DAY, A

April 9, 1947

MOONLIGHT BECOMES YOU (Johnny Burke - Jimmy Van
Heusen)
March 27, 1943

MOONLIGHT MOOD (Harold Adamson - Peter De Rose)
January 1943

MOON WON'T TALK, THE (Charlie Hathaway - Helen Bliss)

February 11, 1941

MOST BLUES, THE

(Sy Oliver)
T.B.P.F. #1

MUSIC STOPPED, THE

(Harold Adamson - Jimmy McHugh)
December 1943

MY BLUE HEAVEN

(Walter Donaldson - Gus Whiting)
November 22, 1949

MY BRIDE

(Parody of "All The Things You Are")
April 29, 1945

MY FOOLISH HEART

(Ned Washington - Victor Young)
February 13, 1950, May 1, 1950

MY FUNNY VALENTINE

(Richard Rodgers - Lorenz Hart)
December 22, 1953

MY GIRL

(Arthur Freed)
February 12, 1952

MY HAPPINESS

(Betty Peterson - Borney Bergantine)
July 10, 1948, July 17, 1948, July 24,
1948, August 1, 1948, August 14, 1948,
September 11, 1948

MY HEART STOOD STILL

(Richard Rodgers - Lorenz Hart)
November 28, 1943, February 9, 1944

MY HEART TELLS ME

(Harry Warren - Mack Gordon)
November 27, 1943, November 28,
1943, December 18, 1943, December
25, 1943, January 15, 1944, January
22, 1944, February 5, 1944

MY IDEAL

(Newell Chase - Richard Whiting -
Leo Robin)
December 18, 1943, February 25,
1945

MY LOVE FOR YOU

(Harry Jacobson - Edward Heyman)
June 30, 1939

MY MELANCHOLY BABY

(George Norton - Ernie Burnett)
February 24, 1940, May 3, 1942,
September 19, 1945, October 9, 1946,
January 1, 1947, July 2, 1973

MY OLD KENTUCKY HOME

(Stephen Foster)
December 5, 1945

MY PRAYER

(Jimmy Kennedy - George
Boulanger)
January 25, 1940, February 2, 1940

MY ROMANCE

(Richard Rodgers - Lorenz Hart)
June 14, 1945, April 9, 1947, December
24, 1949, Light up Time #7, February
13, 1950

MY SHINING HOUR

(Johnny Mercer - Harold Arlen)
January 22, 1944, February 26,
1944

MY SUGAR IS SO REFINED

(Sidney Lippman - Sylvia Dee)
November 6, 1946

NANCY

(Phil Silvers - Jimmy Van Heusen)
September 9, 1945, September 30,
1945, November 28, 1945, November
13, 1946, April 9, 1947, September 12,
1949

NATURE BOY

(Eden Abhez)
May 28, 1949, May 29, 1948, June 26,
1948, July 17, 1948

NEAR YOU

(Francis Craig - Kermit Goell)
October 24, 1947, November 29, 1947

NEVERTHELESS

(Bert Kalmar - Harry Ruby)
T.B.P.F. #62

NICE WORK IF YOU CAN GET IT

(George & Ira Gershwin)
January 15, 1961

NIGHT AND DAY

(Cole Porter)
January 29, 1943, September 25, 1943,
March 6, 1944, February 26, 1944,
February 20, 1945, September 9, 1945,
May 14, 1946, September 5, 1949

NIGHT IS YOUNG, THE

(Vincent Rose - Ivring Kahal - Diana
Suesse)
September 26, 1945

NO CAN DO

(Charles Tobia - Nat Simon)
January 9, 1946

NO LOVE, NO NOTHIN'

(Harry Warren - Leo Robin)
January 22, 1944, February 9, 1944,
February 12, 1944

Sinatra, Beryl Davis, Axel Stordahl — 1948.

NOTHING LESS THAN BEAUTIFUL	(Murray Will) Light up Time #4
NOW IS THE HOUR	(Clement Scott - Dorothy Stewart - Maewa Kaihav) May 8, 1948
OH HOW I MISS YOU TONIGHT	(Benny Davis - Joe Burke - Mark Fisher) November 6, 1946
OH LOOK AT ME NOW	(John DeVries - Joe Bushkin) February 11, 1941, October 24, 1945, Light up Time #12
OH WHAT A BEAUTIFUL MORNING	(Richard Rodgers - Oscar Hammerstein II) November 27, 1943, December 4, 1943, December 25, 1943, January 15, 1944, February 5, 1944, November 21, 1945
OH WHAT IT SEEMED TO BE	(Stephen Weiss - Bennie Benjamin - Frankie Carle) January 16, 1946, February 13, 1946, April 7, 1946, November 13, 1946
O' LITTLE TOWN OF BETHLEHEM	(Philip Brooks - Lawrence Rodner) December 5, 1945
OLE BUTTERMILK SKY	(Hoagy Carmichael - Jack Brooks) November 20, 1946
OL' MAN CROSBY	(Parody of "Ol Man River) April 25, 1945, May 4, 1947
OL' MAN RIVER	(Jerome Kern - Oscar Hammerstein II) October 29, 1944, December 12, 1945, December 11, 1946, June 11, 1953
OLD MASTER PAINTER	(Haven Gillespie - Beasley Smith) Light up Time #4, #9, #18
ON A SLOW BOAT TO CHINA	(Frank Loesser) February 5, 1949, March 16, 1949
ONCE IN LOVE WITH AMY	(Frank Loesser) March 30, 1947, December 8, 1948, January 12, 1949

ONE FOR MY BABY	(Harold Arlen - Johnny Mercer) T.B.P.F. #117
ONE HUNDRED YEARS FROM TODAY	(Victor Young - Ned Washington) April 24, 1950, T.B.P.F. #26
ONE I LOVE, THE	(Gus Kahn - Isham Jones) November 26, 1940, April 4, 1945, October 14, 1949, Light up Time #3, T.B.P.F. #22
ONE MORE DREAM	November 28, 1945, January 30, March 27, 1946
ONESY TWOSY	(Dave Franklin) February 23, 1946
ONLY FOREVER	(Johnny Burke - James Monaco) August 25, 1942
ON THE ISLAND OF STROMBOLI	(Irving Taylor - Ken Lane) November 22, 1949, Light up Time #5
ON THE ISLE OF MAY	(Peter De Rose) March 9, 1940
ON THE ATCHISON TOPEKA AND THE SANTA FE	(Harry Warren - Johnny Mercer) September 19, 1945
ON THE SUNNY SIDE OF THE STREET	(Dorothy Fields - Jimmy McHugh) Light up Time #8, T.B.P.F. #17
OPEN UP THEM PEARLY GATES	(Carson Robinson) October 21, 1945
O' SOLO MIO	(Edward Di Capua) January 22, 1950
OUR FATHER	(Peter Cornelius) December 24, 1949
OUR LOVE AFFAIR	(Arthur Freed - Roger Evans) November 26, 1940
OUT OF NOWHERE	(Johnny Green - Edward Heyman) T.B.P.F. #47
OVER THE RAINBOW	(Yip Harburg - Harold Arlen) January 1945, January 2, 1946, October 25, 1947, December 28, 1947
PAPER DOLL	(Johnny Black)

June 1943, October 9, 1943, November 6, 1943, November 27, 1943, January 22, 1944, January 9, 1946 (included in song medley)

PARADE OF THE WOODEN SOLDIERS
(Leon Jessel)
December 18, 1946

PEG O' MY HEART
(Alfred Bryan - Fred Fisher)
October 11, 1947, October 25, 1947

PENTHOUSE SERENADE
(Will Jason - Val Burton)
Light up Time #23

PEOPLE WILL SAY WE'RE IN LOVE
(Richard Rodgers - Oscar Hammerstein II)
May 1943, August 28, 1943, December 4, 1943, December 25, 1943, January 15, 1944, February 5, 1944

PERSONALITY
(Johnny Burke - Jimmy Van Heusen)
March 20, 1946

PISTOL PACKIN' MAMA
(Al Dexter)
October 9, 1943, October 10, 1943, October 16, 1943, December 4, 1943, October 20, 1967

PLATINUM BLUES

December 18, 1953

POINCIANA
(Nat Simon - Buddy Bernier)
April 8, 1944, May 6, 1944, Light up Time #13

POLKA DOTS AND MOONBEAMS
(Johnny Burke - Jimmy Van Heusen)
March 20, 1940, May 28, 1940

POWDER YOUR FACE WITH SUNSHINE
(Carmen Lombardo - Stanley Rochinski)
March 30, 1947, January 12, 1949

PRAISE THE LORD AND PASS THE AMMUNITION
(Frank Loesser)
September 12, 1945
(Included in song medley)

PRETENDING
(Harry Porter - Mel Ball - Mabby Cohen)
November 6, 1946, December 4, 1946

PRETTY BABY   (Tony Jackson - Egbert Van
                                    Alstyne)
                                    December 25, 1946

PRISONER OF LOVE   (Russ Columbo - Clarence Gaskill -
                                    Leo Robin)
                                    December 3, 1948

PUT ON YOUR OLD GREY BONNET (Percy Wenrich - Stanley Murphy)
                                    December 25, 1946

PUT YOUR DREAMS AWAY   (Ruth Lowe - Stephen Weiss - Paul
                                    Mann)
                                    December 18, 1944, May 14, 1946, July
                                    1946, November 14, 1947

RED ROSES FOR A BLUE LADY   (Sid Tepper - Roy Brodsky)
                                    May 28, 1949

ROCK-A-BYE YOUR BABY   (Al Jolson - Jean Schwartz)
                                    January 10, 1946

ROSANNE OF CHARING CROSS   (Mabel Wayne - Kermit Goell)
                                    January 1943

ROSES IN THE RAIN   (Frankie Carle - Al Frisch - Fred Wise)
                                    March 19, 1947

SAN ANTONIO ROSE   (Bob Wills)
                                    July 23, 1944, March 6, 1946,
                                    April 17, 1946

SAN FERNANDO VALLEY   (Gordon Jenkins)
                                    May 24, 1944, June 10, 1944, July 1,
                                    1944

SANTA CLAUS   (Parody of "Jingle Bells")
                                    December 5, 1945 (included in song
                                    medley)

SATURDAY NIGHT   (Sammy Cahn - Jule Styne)
                                    January 1945, March 11, 1945

SEPTEMBER SONG   (Kurt Weill - Maxwell Anderson)
                                    T.B.P.F. #44, March 21, 1954

SERENADE OF THE BELLS   (Kay Twomey - Al Goodhart - Al
                                    Urband)
                                    January 10, 1948

SHADOWS OF THE SAND   (Stanely Adams - Cross)
                                    November 26, 1940

SHE'S FUNNY THAT WAY   (Neil Moret - Richard Whiting)

	January 1943, T.B.P.F. #62
SHINE	(Cecil Mack - Lew Brown - Ford Dabney) September 8, 1945
SHINE ON HARVEST MOON	(Nora Bayes - Jack Norworth) February 25, 1945
SHOOFLY PIE AND APPLE PAN DOWDY	(Sammy Gallop - Guy Woods) May 29, 1946, November 13, 1946
SHOO SHOO BABY	(Phil Moore) February 12, 1944
SHORTNIN' BREAD	(Clement Wood - Jacques Wolfe) Mardh 11, 1945
SHOULD I	(Nacio Herb Brown - Arthur Freed) March 24, 1950, T.B.P.F. 23, T.B.P.F. 58
SHOW ME THE WAY TO GO HOME	(Irving King) September 26, 1945
SILENT NIGHT	(Franz Gruber) December 5, 1945, December 18, 1946, December 19, 1946, December 25, 1951
SITTING BY THE WINDOW	(Paul Insetta) Light Up Time #15
SKY FELL DOWN, THE	(Edward Heyman - Louis Alter) March 9, 1940
SLOWLY	(David Raskin - Kermit Goell) January 9, 1946, April 24, 1946
SNOOTIE LITTLE CUTIE	(Bobby Troup) August 18, 1942
SO FAR	(Richard Rodgers - Oscar Hammerstein II) November 29, 1947, January 17, 1948
SO IN LOVE	(Cole Porter) February 5, 1949, April 30, 1949
SOLILOQUY	(Richard Rodgers - Oscar Hammerstein II) January 1, 1947
SOMEBODY LOVE'S ME	(Buddy Desylva - Ray Henderson -

Lew Brown)
Light up Time #14, T.B.P.F. #16

SOMEDAY   (Fred Godfrey - Harry Gifford - Robert Wright)

SOME ENCHANTED EVENING   (Richard Rodgers - Oscar Hammerstein II)
May 28, 1949, September 5, 1949

SOME OTHER TIME   (Sammy Cahn - Jule Styne)
May 17, 1944

SOMEONE TO WATCH OVER ME   (George & Ira Gershwin)
November 20, 1946, June 4, 1947, T.B.P.F. #123

SOME SUNDAY MORNING   (Richard Whiting - Ray Egan - Gus Kahn)
January 9, 1946, March 13, 1946

SOMETHING STUPID   (Richard Whiting - Ray Egan - Gus Kahn)
January 9, 1946, March 13, 1946

SOMETIMES I'M HAPPY   (Vincent Youmans - Irving Caesar)
T.B.P.F. #56

SOMEWHERE IN THE NIGHT   (Mack Gordon - Joseph Myrow)
September 18, 1946, November 20, 1946

SONG IS YOU, THE   (Jerome Kern)
September 2, 1942, March 5, 1944, December 9, 1945, February 13, 1946, December 25, 1946, January 15, 1947, March 19, 1947, January 31, 1948

SOON   (George & Ira Gershwin)
June 4, 1947, November 22, 1947

SORRY   (Buddy Pepper - Richard Whiting)
Light up Time #14, 15, 16

SOUTH AMERICA TAKE IT AWAY   (Harold Rome)
September 18, 1946, October 16, 1946

SOUTH OF THE BORDER   (Jimmy Kennedy - Michael Carr)
February 2, 1940, May 25, 1944, December 24, 1953

SPEAK LOW   (Kurt Weill - Ogden Nash)

December 18, 1943, January 15, 1944,
January 29, 1944, February 12, 1944,
February 20, 1944

SPRING IS HERE
(Richard Rodgers - Lorenz Hart)
March 27, 1946

STARDUST
(Hoagey Carmichael - Mitchell
Parish)
March 27, 1946 (included in song
medley)

STARLIGHT SONATA

January 1943

STARS IN YOUR EYES
(Gabriel Ruiz - Johnny Green)
September 12, 1945

STELLA BY STARLIGHT
(Ned Washington - Victor Young)
May 21, 1947, September 1, 1947

STRANGE MUSIC
(Edvard Grieg - Robert Wright -
George Forrest)
November 11, 1944, February 5, 1945,
May 29, 1946, Light up Time #1,
February 10, 1950

STREET OF DREAMS
(Victor Young - Sam Lewis)
September 28, 1967

SUDDENLY ITS SPRING
(Johnny Burke - Jimmy Van
Heusen)
June 14, 1945

SUMMERTIME
(George & Ira Gershwin - Dubose
Howard)
April 10. 1946

SUMMER WIND
(Johnny Mercer - Henry Mayers)
September 15, 1970

SUNDAY, MONDAY OR ALWAYS
(Johnny Burke - Jimmy Van
Heusen)
September 25, 1943, October 9, 1943,
October 16, 1943, November 27, 1943,
December 4, 1943, November 6, 1944

SUNFLOWER
(Mack David)
April 30, 1949

SUNSHINE CAKE
(Johnny Burke - Jimmy Van
Heusen)
Light up Time #18, March 24, 1950

SUNSHINE OF YOUR SMILE, THE	(Leonard Cooke - Lillian Ray) September 20, 1941
SURETHING	(Johnny Burke - Jimmy Van Heusen) Light up Time #19
SURREY WITH THE FRING ON TOP, THE	(Richard Rodgers - Oscar Hammerstein II) September 19, 1945
SWEET LORRAINE	(Mitchell Parish - Cliff Burwell) July 22, 1944, February 27, 1946
SWINGING ON A STAR	(Johnny Burke - Jimmy Van Heusen) June 10, 1944, July 8, 1944, July 22, 1944, July 28, 1944, September 2, 1944, September 30. 1944, October 7, 1944
S'WONDERFUL	(George & Ira Gershwin) T.B.P.F. #41
SYMPHONY	(Alex Alstone - Jack Lawrence) January 23, 1946
TAKE A CHANCE	(David Raskin - Dak Stanford) March 28, 1954
TAKING A CHANCE ON LOVE	(Vernon Duke - John Latouette - Ted Fetter) T.B.P.F. #64
TEA FOR TWO	(Vincent Youmans - Irving Caesar) April 10. 1946, May 15, 1946, September 22, 1946, September 1, 1947, November 16, 1947
TENDERLY	(Walter Gross) T.B.P.F. #48
THAT OLD BLACK MAGIC	(Johnny Mercer - Harold Arlen) March 27, 1943, April 10, 1943, May 29, 1943, June 5, 1943, February 6, 1946, September 6, 1947, August 5, 1948, Light up Time #23, T.B.P.F. #52
THAT'S FOR ME	(Richard Rodgers - Oscar Hammerstein II) November 14, 1945, July, 1946

THAT'S HOW IT GOES
November 26, 1940

THAT'S HOW MUCH I LOVE YOU
(Arnold - Fowler - Hall)
March 26, 1947, May 21, 1947

THAT'S JUDY
(Hoagy Carmichael - Allan Lerner)
June 14, 1945

THAT'S MY AFFAIR
(Irving Weiser)
January, 1943

THAT'S MY DESIRE
(Helma Kresa - Carroll Lindsay)
September 6, 1947

THEM THERE EYES
(Maceo Pinkard - William Tracy - Doris Tauber)
Light up Time #2, T.B.P.F. #42, #53

THEN I'LL BE HAPPY
(Cliff Friend - Lew Brown - Sidney Clare)
Light up Time #11

THEN I'LL COME BACK TO YOU
(Jack Benny)
March 4, 1954

THERE ARE SUCH THINGS
(Stanley Adams - Abelbaer - George Meyer)
January 1943, March 27, 1943

THERE GOES THAT SONG AGAIN
(Sammy Cahn - Jule Styne)
December 2, 1944, December 16, 1944

THERE'LL BE A HOT TIME IN THE TOWN OF BERLIN
(John DeVries - Joe Bushkin)
October 3, 1943

THERE'S A LONG, LONG TRAIL AWINDING
(Zo Elliot)
March 28, 1954

THERE'S NO BUSINESS LIKE SHOW BUSINESS
(Irving Berlin)
October 9, 1946, December 4, 1946

THERE'S NO YOU
(Hal Hopper - Bullets Durgom - Tom Adair)
October 29, 1944, January 28, 1945, October 10, 1945

THERE'S YES YES IN YOUR EYES
(Joseph Santly)
Light up Time #6

THESE FOOLISH THINGS
(Jack Strachey - Harry Link - Holt Marvel
November 16, 1944, February 6, 1946

THEY CAN'T TAKE THAT AWAY FROM ME	(George & Ira Gershwin) December 1, 1953, December 11, 1953 T.B.P.F. #24
THEY DIDN'T BELIEVE ME	(Jerome Kern - Michael Rourke) November 20, 1946
THEY SAY IT'S WONDERFUL	(Irving Berlin) April 24, 1946, May 29, 1946, September 18, 1946
THINE ALONE	(Henry Blossom - Victor Herbert) October 10, 1944
THINGS WE DID LAST SUMMER, THE	(Sammy Cahn - Jule Styne) December 29, 1946
THIS CAN'T BE LOVE	(Richard Rodgers - Lorenz Hart) Light up Time #9, April 24, 1950, December 18, 1953, T.B.P.F. #23, #37
THIS IS ALWAYS	(Harry Warren - Warren Bregman) October 30, 1946
THIS LOVE OF MINE	(Sol Parker - Hank Sanicola - Frank Sinatra) September 20, 1941, January 17, 1942, May 1943, October 24, 1945
THIS TIME	(Irving Berlin) October 30, 1946
THOU SWELL	(Richard Rodgers - Lorenz Hart) T.B.P.F. #43
THREE O'CLOCK IN THE MORNING	(Julian Robledo - Dorothy Terriss) September 26, 1946
TILL THE END OF TIME	(Buddy Kaye - Ted Mossman) June 14, 1945, November 21, 1945
TILL WE MEET AGAIN	(Richard Whiting) March 28, 1954
TIME AFTER TIME	(Sammy Cahn - Jule Styne) March 26, 1947, May 14, 1947, August 5, 1948
TIME ON MY HANDS	(Vincent Youmans - Mack Gordon - Harold Adamson) March 6, 1944
TOGETHER	(Buddy De Sylva - Ray Henderson - Lew Brown)

	October 10, 1944, October 28, 1944, November 11, 1944
TOUCH OF YOUR HAND, THE	(Jerome Kern) January 15, 1947, November 22, 1949
TRAIN, THE	(Bob Gaudio - Jake Holmes) April 6, 1971
TREE IN THE MEADOW, A	(Billy Reid) July 24, 1948, July 31, 1948, August 7, 1948, August 28, 1948, September 11, 1948
TROLLEY SONG, THE	(Hugh Martin - Ralph Blane) November 11, 1944, November 25, 1944, December 2, 1944, December 4, 1944, December 9, 1944, December 16, 1944, April 22, 1945
TRY A LITTLE TENDERNESS	(Harry Woods - Jimmy Campbell - Reg Connelly) (January 9, 1946 (included in song medley), T.B.P.F. #116
TWO HEARTS ARE BETTER THAN ONE	(Johnny Mercer - Jerome Kern) April 10, 1946
UNDER A BLANKET OF BLUE	(Marty Symes - Jerry Livingston - Al Neiburg) T.B.P.F. #52
VERY THOUGHT OF YOU, THE	(Ray Noble) November 25, 1944, Light up Time #10, November 28, 1945
WAGON WHEELS	(Peter DeRose) September 22, 1949
WAIT TILL THE SUN SHINES NELLIE	(Harry Von Tilzer - Andrew Sterling) October 9, 1946
WAKE UP AND LIVE	(Mack Gordon - Harry Revel) October 15, 1944
WAKING IN THE SUNSHINE	(Bob Merrill) February 12, 1952
WAY YOU LOOK TONIGHT, THE	(Dorothy Fields - Jerome Kern) May 17, 1944, April 27, 1950

Sinatra and Bing Crosby.

WEEP NO MORE MY LADY	(Johnny Green) January 1943
WE THREE PIN-UP BOYS	(Parody of "Sunday Monday Or Always") April 29, 1945
WHAT A DAY I'M IN LOVE	(Robert Stolz) Light up Time #14, #16
WHAT A DIFFERENCE A DAY MADE	(Stanley Adams - Maria Grever) October 25, 1944
WHAT CAN I SAY AFTER I SAY I'M SORRY	(Walter Donaldson - Abe Lyman) T.B.P.F. #20
WHAT IS THIS THING CALLED LOVE	(Cole Porter) Light up Time #10, T.B.P.F. #24
WHAT MAKES THE SUNSET	(Sammy Cahn - Jule Styne) April 4, 1945, September 30, 1945, October 17, 1945, January 1, 1946
WHEN DAY IS DONE	(Robert Katscher) December 25, 1946
WHEN IS SOMETIME	(Johnny Burke - Jimmy Van Heusen) January 4, 1949
WHEN I STOP LOVING YOU	(Cates - Copeland - Greene) July 12, 1955
WHEN WE'RE ALONE	June 23, 1940
WHEN YOU AWAKE	(Henry Nemo) October 15, 1940
WHEN YOU COME TO AN END OF A PERFECT DAY	March 27, 1946 (Included in Song Medley)
WHEN YOU WORE A TULIP	(Percy Wenrich) January 23, 1946 (included in song medley)
WHEN YOUR LOVE HAS GONE	(Edgar Swan) January 30, 1945
WHEN YOU'RE SMILING	(Larry Shay - Mark Fisher - Joe Goodwin) Light up Time #23

WHERE ARE YOU, NOW THAT I NEED YOU	September 5, 1949
WHERE OR WHEN	(Richard Rodgers - Lorenz Hart) Light up Time #12, #15, April 24, 1950, T.B.P.F. #47
WHERE THE BLUE OF THE NIGHT	(Roy Turk - Bing Crosby - Fred Ahlert) January 16, 1946 (included in song medley)
WHIFFENPOOF SONG, THE	(Meade Minnigerode - George Pomeroy - Tod Galloway - Rudy Vallee) November 22, 1947
WHILE WE'RE YOUNG	(Alec Wilder - Morty Palitz) March 16, 1950
WHISPERING	(John Schonenburger - Richard Coburn - Vincent Rose) March 2, 1940, March 6, 1946
WHITE CLIFFS OF DOVER	(Harry Leon - Leo Towers) September 12, 1945 (included in song medley)
WHITE CHRISTMAS	(Irving Berlin) December 23, 1944, December 19, 1948, February 13, 1950
WHO'S SORRY NOW	(Ted Snyder - Bert Kalmar - Harry Ruby) April 24, 1946
WHO WILL BE WITH YOU	February 27, 1946
WHOLE WORLD IS SINGING MY SONG, THE	(Mann Curtis - Vic Muzzy) December 4, 1946
WHY DO I LOVE YOU	(Jerome Kern) Light up Time #6, #21
WHY REMIND ME	(Doris Tauber - Willner) Light up Time #12, March 24, 1950, Light up Time #22
WHY SHOULDN'T IT HAPPEN TO US	(Mann Holiner - Alberta Nichols) May 14, 1947
WHY TRY TO CHANGE ME NOW	(Cy Coleman - Joseph McCarthy) May 3, 1953

WHY WAS I BORN	(Jerome Kern - Oscar Hammerstein II) January 15, 1947, March 30, 1947, January 12, 1949
WINTER WONDERLAND	(Felix Bernard - Richard Smith) December 24, 1949
WISHING	(Buddy De Sylva) June 30, 1939
WITHOUT A SONG	(Vincent Youmans - Billy Rose - Edward Eliseu) October 24, 1945, April 17, 1946, July 1946
WOODY WOODPECKER	(George Tibbles - Ramey Idriss) July 10, 1948, July 24, 1948, August 14, 1948
WORLD WE KNEW, THE	(Bert Kaempfert - Carl Sigman - Herbert Rehbein) October 11, 1967, September 10, 1968
WRAP YOUR TROUBLES IN DREAMS	(Ted Koehler - Billy Moll - Harry Barris)
YEARNING	(Benny Davis - Joe Burke) November 7, 1940
YOU ARE A BRUTE	(Parody of "All The Things You Are") April 29, 1945
YOU ARE MY SUNSHINE	(Jimmie Davis - Charles Mitchell) June 25, 1944, August 14, 1945, February 20, 1946, September 22, 1949
YOU ARE THERE	(Harry Sukeman - Paul Francis Webster) September 10, 1968
YOU ARE TOO BEAUTIFUL	(Richard Rodgers - Lorenz Hart) April 24, 1946, May 15, 1946
YOU BROUGHT A NEW KIND OF LOVE TO ME	(Sammy Fain - Irving Kahal - Pierre Norman) December 4, 1944, January 2, 1946
YOU CALL EVERYBODY DARLING	(Sam Martin - Ben Trace - Clem Watts) August 14, 1948

YOU CAN'T BE TRUE DEAR	(Gehard Ebeler - Hal Cotten - Hans Otten) May 29, 1948, June 26, 1948, July 17, 1948, July 31, 1948
YOU CAN'T SEE THE SUN WHEN YOU'RE CRYING	(Allen Roberts - Doris Fisher) May 14, 1947
YOU CAN TAKE MY WORD FOR IT BABY	(Ticker Freeman - Irving Taylor) December 28, 1947
YOU'D BE SO NICE TO COME HOME TO	(Cole Porter) March 27, 1943, April 10, 1943, T.B.P.F. #91
YOU DO	(Mack Gordon - Josef Myrow) November 22, 1947
YOU DO SOMETHING TO ME	(Cole Porter) September 12, 1949, January 22, 1950
YOU GO TO MY HEAD	(Fred Coots - Haven Gillespie) March 27, 1946 (included in song medley)
YOU KEEP COMING BACK LIKE A SONG	(Irving Berlin) December 11, 1946
YOU'LL ALWAYS BE THE ONE I LOVE	(Al Freeman - Sunny Skylar) October 30, 1946, November 27, 1946, December 18, 1946
YOU'LL NEVER KNOW	(Mack Gordon - Harry Warren) January 1943, March 29, 1943, June 5, 1943, August 28, 1943, September 25, 1943
YOU'LL NEVER WALK ALONE	(Richard Rodgers - Oscar Hammerstein II) May 8, 1945, December 26, 1945, September 22, 1946, October 27, 1947, Light up Time #5
YOU MAKE ME FEEL SO YOUNG	(Mack Gordon - Josef Myrow) August 14, 1955
YOU MUST HAVE BEEN A BEAUTIFUL BABY	(Harry Warren - Johnny Mercer) January 23, 1946, November 8, 1949, T.B.P.F. #18
YOU MY LOVE	(Mack Gordon - Jimmy Van Heusen) July 12, 1955

YOUNG AT HEART   (Carolyn Leigh - Johnny Richards)
                                        March 21, 1954, July 12, 1955

YOUNGER THAN SPRINGTIME   (Richard Rodgers - Oscar
                                        Hammerstein II)
                                        September 20, 1949

YOU'RE AWFUL   (Betty Comden - Roger Edens -
                                        Adolph Green)
                                        Light up Time #17

YOU'RE BREAKING MY HEART   (James Cavanaugh - John Redmond -
                                        Arthur Altman)
                                        Light up Time #4, #7

YOU'RE IN LOVE WITH SOMEONE   (Johnny Burke - Jimmy Van
                                        Heusen)
                                        Light up Time #9

YOU'RE MY THRILL   (Jay Gorney - Sidney Clare)
                                        February 10. 1950

YOU'RE THE CREAM IN MY   (Buddy DeSylva - Lew Brown - Ray
COFFEE   Henderson)
                                        December 27, 1949

YOU'RE THE TOP   (Cole Porter)
                                        August 14, 1945, April 7, 1946

YOUR SO RIGHT FOR WHAT'S   (Pike - Randazzo - Joyce)
WRONG IN MY LIFE   March 4, 1973

YOU TOLD A LIE
                                        Light up Time #5

YOU TOOK ADVANTAGE OF ME   (Richard Rodgers - Lorenz Hart)
                                        Light up Time #44

YOU WILL BE MY MUSIC   (Joe Raposo)
                                        March 4, 1973

YOU WON'T BE SATISFIED UNTIL   (Freddie James - Larry Stock)
YOU BREAK MY HEART   April 17, 1946

ZIP A DEE DOO DAH   (Allie Wrubel - Ray Gilbert)
                                        November 27, 1946, December 25,
                                        1946

INDEX OF ORCHETRAS, ARRANGERS, COMPOSERS, SOLOISTS, VOCALISTS AND VOCAL GROUPS FOR CHAPTER XII - AIRCHECKS

Alexander, Jeff - Orchestra Leader, Arranger
September 5, 1949 through February 1950 Light Up Time

Allen, Fred - Comedian, Vocalist
October 21, 1945, October 31, 1945

Andrew Sisters - Vocal Trio
December 12, 1944, March 4, 1945, November 14, 1945

Andrews, Patty - Vocalist
November 14, 1945

Armstrong, Louis - Trumpet, Vocalist
January, 1945

Brookman, David - Orchestra Leader and Conductor
January, 1943, December, 1943

Brown, Les - Orchestra Leader
March 16, 1949, December 25, 1951, December 24, 1953

Burns, George - Comedian, Vocalist
May 14, 1947, March 4, 1952

Carson, Jack - Comedian, Actor, Vocalist
September 29, 1945, February 13, 1946, February 23, 1946

Cavanaugh, Page - Vocal and Instrumental Trio
March 26, 1947

Cole, Nat - Vocalist, Pianist
November 28, 1945, March 13, 1946

Crosby, Bing - Vocalist
February 20, 1944, April 29, 1945, April 7, 1946, December 25, 1951, March 28, 1954

Crosby's Sons - Vocalists
September 12, 1945

Davis, Jimmy - (Governor of Louisiana) - Vocalist
February 20, 1946

Day, Doris - Vocalist
September 1, 1947, November 16, 1947

DeHaven, Gloria - Vocalist, Actress
July 29, 1944

Dorsey, Tommy - Orchestra Leader
January 25, 1940, February 11, 1941, January 17, 1942, September 2, 1942, September 17, 1944, October 24, 1945

Durante, Jimmy - Comedian, Vocalist
February 27, 1946

Elman, Ziggy - Orchestra Leader and Trumpet Soloist
November 8, 1949, December 5, 1959

Ennis, Skinnay - Vocalist, Orchestra Leader
March 6, 1946

Gaillard, Slim - Vocal and Instrumental Trio
April 24, 1946

Garland, Judy - Vocalist
March 5, 1944, May 24, 1944, June 14, 1945

Goodman, Al - Orchestra Leader
October 21, 1945, September 22, 1946

Goodman, Benny - Clarinetist, Sextette Leader
January 30, 1946

Green, Johnny - Orchestra Leader, Conductor
April 14, 1946

Hackett, Bobby - Trumpet Soloist
Light Up Time #20

Haines, Connie - Vocalist
November 26, 1940

Henderson, Skitch - Pianist
January 16, 1946, April 3, 1946, Light Up Time #19 through May 9, 1950

Hoboken Four, The - Vocal Quartet
September 8, 1935, June 15, 1970

Hope, Bob - Comedian, Vocalist
July 3, 1944, April 29, 1945, February 6, 1946, March 16, 1949, December 24, 1953

Hutton, June - Vocalist
December 12, 1945, May 15, 1946

James, Harry - Orchestra Leader
June 30, 1939, September 14, 1939

Jean, Norma - Vocalist
February 23, 1946

Johnson, Van - Actor, Vocalist
March 20, 1946

Kaye, Danny - Actor, Vocalist
April 25, 1945, March 4, 1952

Kaye, Sammy - Orchestra Leader
January 29, 1943

Kelly, Gene - Vocalist, Dancer, Actor
October 17, 1945, April 10, 1946

Kirsten, Dorothy - Vocalist
September 5, 1949, May 1, 1950 through late 1955 (Light Up Time)

Langford, Frances - Vocalist
October 10, 1945

Lee, Peggy - Vocalist
January 2, 1946

Major Bowes - Talent Scout, Coordinator
September 8, 1935

Mann, Peggy - Vocalist
November 20, 1946, December 18, 1946

Martin, Freddy - Orchestra Leader
February 23, 1946

Marx, Groucho - Comedian, Vocalist
March 4, 1952

Maxwell, Marilyn - Vocalist
November 21, 1945

Miller, Bill - Pianist
November 27, 1953 through late 1955

Mitchell, Choir, Bob - Large Vocal Group
December 26, 1945

Moore Four, Phil - Instrumental Quartet
January 4, 1949

Murray, Lynn - Orchestra Leader, Conductor
August 7, 1948

Paul Trio, Les - Instrumental and Vocal Group
February 25, 1945

Pipers, Pied - Vocal Group
February 2, 1940, February 11, 1941, July 30, 1942, September 12, 1945, December 26, 1945, January 23, 1946, October 16, 1946

Powell, Jane - Vocalist
December 25, 1946, January 15, 1947, December 27, 1949

Previn, Andre - Pianist
September 18, 1946, October 9, 1946

Ramirez, Carlos - Vocalist
March 6, 1946

Ramondi, Lillian - Vocalist
November 28, 1945

Robinson, Frances - Vocalist
September 18, 1946

Romay, Lina - Vocalist
January 9, 1946

Russell, Andy - Vocalist
January 16, 1946

Schoen, Vic - Orchestra Leader
December 12, 1944

Scott, Raymond - Orchestra Leader
May 1943, June 1943

Shay, Dorothy - Vocalist
March 16, 1949

Shore, Dinah - Vocalist
February 20, 1944, September 26, 1945, September 22, 1946

Silvers, Lou - Orchestra Leader, Conductor
January 1, 1946

Simms, Ginny - Vocalist
April 2, 1944, October 10, 1944, October 10, 1945

Sosnick, Harry - Orchestra Leader
May 3, 1953

Stafford, Jo - Vocalist
August 18, 1942

Stapleton, Cyril - Orchestra Leader
June 11, 1953, July 16, 1953

Stevens, Rise - Vocalist
May 29, 1946

Stoloff, Morris - Orchestra Leader and Conductor
January 10, 1946

Stordahl, Axel - Orchestra Leader, Arranger
October 3, 1943, January, 1945, September 12, 1945 through June 4, 1977 (Songs by Sinatra), 1949 (Your Hit Parade), February 12, 1952

Symphonette, Sinatra - Instrumental Quintet
November 27, 1953 through late 1955 (To Be Perfectly Frank Shows)

Tibbett, Lawrence - Vocalist
November 7, 1945

Tilton, Martha - Vocalist
September 12, 1945

Tucker Singers, Bobby - Large Vocal Group
May 1943, November 28, 1943

Warnow, Mark - Orchestra Leader, Conductor
January 1943, March 1943 through 1944 (Your Hit Parade)

Wheeler, Bert - Comedian, Vocalist
October 10, 1943

Whiteman, Paul - Orchestra Leader
January 29, 1944

Whiting, Margaret - Vocalist
Light Up Time #9

Wilson, Eileen - Vocalist
Light Up Time #8

Wilson, Meredith - Orchestra Leader, Conductor
September 29, 1945

Sinatra and William B. Williams.

Chapter XIII
CONCERT LISTING

This listing is more than a brief sampling of Sinatra concert dates available on tape which are traded by his many fans. The quality of these tapes vary from poor to excellent but are of interest and are included as they intend to show Sinatra unfettered and uninhibited by recording restrictions. As it progresses through the years you will also note that it includes many nightclub and various "live" appearances and in a sense is not strictly limited to formal concert dates as such.

The authors know that this list is not complete and thereby make no representations as to the following dates, being all that are available, however, we contend that the Forrest Hills date and a few more equally superlative performances, while lacking studio quality, justifies the inclusion of this chapter, and we respectfully solicit correspondence concerning any other privately held concert dates by Frank Sinatra.

In late 1942 and early 1943, Sinatra, after leaving Dorsey, sang in quite a few different clubs and theatres. Most notable are the appearances he made at the Mosque Theater in Newark, New Jersey, The Rio Bamba nightclub in New York City and of course the Paramount Theatre which has a chapter of its own in this book. In the mid-forties he also appeared in the Swank Wedgewood Room in the Waldorf Astoria, but since there are no tapes of these performances we will begin our listing from 1953.

The Opera House, Blackpool, England   July 26, 1953

Billy Terment and His Orchestra

    When You're Smiling
    That Old Black Magic
    You Go To My Head
    Ol' Man River
    Ol' Man Crosby
    Sweet Lorraine
    The Birth Of The Blues
    Embraceable You
    One For My Baby
    Don't Worry 'Bout Me
    I've Got The World On A String
    It Never Entered My Mind
    All Of Me
    Night And Day

From now on Bill Miller will be his pianist and sometimes conductor on almost every appearance.

Bill Miller's Riviera, Paramus, N.J.   September 15, 1953

    I Get A Kick Out Of You
    My One And Only Love

You Go To My Head
They Can't Take That Away From Me
My Funny Valentine
A Foggy Day
Little Girl Blue
It All Depends On You
Violets For Your Furs
This Can't Be Love
The Coffee Song
Spring Is Here
One For My Baby
All Of Me
You'll Never Walk Alone
Don't Worry 'Bout Me
From Here To Eternity
I've Got The World On A String

Long Beach, California   September 5, 1955

On Judy Garland's closing performance Siantra comes on stage and
introduces some friends.

Vancouver, British Columbia   June 8, 1957

You Make Me Feel So Young
It Happened In Monterey
At Long Last Love
I Get A Kick Out Of You
Just One Of Those Things
A Foggy Day
The Lady Is A Tramp
They Can't Take That Away From Me
I Won't Dance
F.S. Monologue
When Your Lover Has Gone
Violets For Your Roses
My Funny Valentine
Glad To Be Unhappy
One For My Baby

Civic Auditorium, Seattle, Washington   June 9, 1957

You Make Me Feel So Young
It Happened In Monterey
At Long Last Love
I Get A Kick Out Of You
Just One Of Those Things
A Foggy Day
The Lady Is A Tramp
They Can't Take That Away From Me

I Won't Dance
When Your Lover Has Gone
Violets For Your Furs
My Funny Valentine
Glad To Be Unhappy
One For My Baby
The Tender Trap
Hey Jealous Lover
I've Got You Under My Skin
Oh Look At Me Now

The Sporting Club, Monte Carlo, Monaco   June 14, 1958

Come Fly With Me
I Get A Kick Out Of You
I've Got You Under My Skin
Where Or When
Moonlight In Vermont
On The Road To Mandalay
When Your Lover Has Gone
April In Paris
All The Way
Monique
Bewitched
The Lady Is A Tramp
You Make Me Feel So Young

West Melbourne Stadium, Australia   April 1, 1959

With Red Norvo Quintet and Stan Freberg
   Red Norvo (Vibes), Bud Shank (Reeds), Nick Bonny (Guitar), Irv Cottler
   (Drums) and Bill Miller (Piano). Plus Australian Brass.

I Could Have Danced All Night
Just One Of Those Things
I Get A Kick Out Of You
At Long Last Love
Willow Weep For Me
I've Got You Under My Skin
Moonlight In Vermont
The Lady Is A Tramp
F.S. Monologue
Angel Eyes
Come Fly With Me
All The Way
Dancing In The Dark
All Of Me
On The Road To Mandalay
Night And Day

The Moulin Rouge, Hollywood   May 14, 1959

Orchestra conducted by Paul Weston

Too Marvelous For Words
A Foggy Day
Come Fly With Me
I Can't Give You Anything But Love (with Dean Martin)
We're Glad We're Italians (with Dean Martin)

New York City, New York   September 5, 1959

Friar's Roast of Dean Martin

500 Club, Atlantic City, New Jersey   August 4, 1960

Too Marvelous For Words
Day In, Day Out
Willow Weep For Me
It's Over, It's Over, It's Over
I Could Have Danced All Night
I Love Paris
River Stay Away From My Door
All The Way
Moonlight In Vermont
I've Got You Under My Skin

National Guard Armory, Washington, D.C.   January 19, 1961

Orchestra conducted by Leonard Bernstein.
Sinatra talks about Presidential campaign
The House I Live In
Sinatra introduces Lyndon Johnson
Sinatra introduces Tony Curtis and Janet Leigh
Siantra talks about Abraham Lincoln
Sinatra introduces John F. Kennedy

This evening was recorded by Reprise Records for release as a two record set but so far has not been issued.

Sydney, Australia   December 21, 1961

Orchestra includes Al (Porky) Porcino (Trumpet), Johnny Markam (Drums) and Bill Miller (Piano).

I've Got The World On A String
In The Still Of The Night
Day In, Day Out
You're Nobody Till Somebody Loves You
F.S. Monologue
Come Fly With Me
April In Paris

A Foggy Day
The Second Time Around
Young At Heart
Witchcraft
The One I Love
My Funny Valentine
My Blue Heaven
One For My Baby
The Lady Is A Tramp

Hibiya Park, Tokyo, Japan   April 20. 1962

With Al Viola (Guitar), Emil Richards (Vibes), Harry Klee (Reeds), Ralph Pena (Bass), Bill Miller (Piano), and Irv Cottler (Drums).

Too Marvelous For Words
Imagination
Moonlight In Vermont
Day In, Day Out
Without A Song
The Moon Was Yellow
I've Got You Under My Skin
I Get A Kick Out Of You
At Long Last Love
My Funny Valentine
In The Still Of The Night
Embraceable You
Night And Day
April In Paris
The Lady Is A Tramp
All The Way
Chicago
I Could Have Danced All Night

The Mikado, Tokyo, Japan   April 21, 1962

Same songs as last concert.

Teatro Manzoni, Milan, Italy   May 25, 1962

Goody, Goody
They Can't Take That Away From Me
Moonlight In Vermont
Without A Song
Day In, Day Out
The Moon Was Yellow
I've Got You Under My Skin
I Get A Kick Out Of You
Too Marvelous For Words
My Funny Valentine
In The Still Of The Night

My Blue Heaven
April In Paris
The Lady Is A Tramp
F.S. Monologue
One For My Baby
All The Way
Chicago
Night And Day
Ol' Man River
I Could Have Danced Alll Night
A Foggy Day

The Ice Palace, Milan, Italy   May 26, 1962

Same songs as last concert except for last tune in which "Nancy" replaces "A Foggy Day."

Paris, France   May 28, 1962

Unknown songs from this appearance but most likely similar to last concert in Italy.

Royal Festival Hall, London, England   June 1, 1962

Goody, Goody
Imagination
At Long Last Love
Moonlight In Vermont
Day In, Day Out
They Can't Take That Away From Me
All The Way
Chicago
One For My Baby
The Lady Is A Tramp
Ol' Man River
You Make Me Feel So Young
Nancy
Come Fly With Me

All in all, Sinatra performed thirty concerts on this world tour to raise money for children's charities.

500 Club, Atlantic City, New Jersey   August 25, 1962

He appeared on behalf of his old time friend "Skinny" D'Amato. He sang and clowned around with pals Dean Martin and Sammy Davis Jr.

Goody, Goody
At Long Last Love
The Lady Is A Tramp
I've Got The World On A String

Concert appearance at Carnegie Hall.

The Birth Of The Blues (with Martin and Davis)
I Can't Give You Anything But Love
Too Marvelous For Words
All Of Me

United Nations, New York September 13, 1963

With Skitch Henderson at the Piano.

Too Marvelous For Words
They Can't Take That Away From Me
I Have Dreamed
F.S. Monologue
A Foggy Day
My Heart Stood Still
I Get A Kick Out Of You

Carnegie Hall, New York October 5, 1963

Concert with Lena Horne

Please Be Kind
Bewitched
In The Still Of The Night
Ol' Man River
Call Me Irresponsible
You're Nobody Till Somebody Loves You
Without A Song
Guess I'll Hang My Tears Out To Dry
On The Road To Mandalay
Luck Be A Lady
Last Night When We Were Young
I Hadn't Anyone Till You

Kiel Opera House, St. Louis, Missouri June 20, 1965

Dismas House benefit with the orchestra of Count Basie conducted by Quincy
Jones.

Get Me To The Church On Time
Fly Me To The Moon
Luck Be A Lady
You Make Me Feel So Young
My Kind Of Town
Please Be Kind
I Only Have Eyes For You
I've Got You Under My Skin
The Birth Of The Blues
Comedy with Dean Martin & Sammy Davis, Jr.

The Newport Jazz Festival, Rhode Island   July 4, 1965

With Count Basie Orchestra

> Get Me To The Church On Time
> Fly Me To The Moon
> I Wish You Love
> Street Of Dreams
> Luck Be A Lady
> It's Easy To Remember
> Too Marvelous For Words
> I've Got You Under My Skin
> F.S. Monologue
> Call Me Irresponsible
> I Only Have Eyes For You
> The Gal That Got Away
> Please Be Kind
> In The Wee Small Hours Of The Morning
> Hello Dolly
> You Make Me Feel So Young
> All The Way
> Where Or When
> My Kind Of Town

Westside Tennis Club, Forest Hills   July 9, 1965

New York

With Count Basie Orchestra

> All the same songs as last concert.

San Francisco Hilton, California   September 7, 1966

Orchestra conducted by Nelson Riddle

Democratic rally for Governor Brown with Joey Bishop, Rowan and Martin, Connie Francis, Trini Lopez and Ella Fitzgerald.

> I've Got The World On A String
> Fly Me To The Moon
> The Shadow Of Your Smile
> I've Got You Under My Skin
> It Was A Very Good Year
> You Make Me Feel So Young

University of Southern California   February 12, 1967

"Town and Gown", friends of the Libraries. Tribute to Cole Porter; "The Life That Late He Led". Guests are Ethel Merman, Fred Astaire, Roger Edens, Gene Kelly, Garsin Kanin, Alan Jay Lerner and Sinatra who sings:

I've Got You Under My Skin
Let's Do It
It's Alright With Me
I Love Paris
I Concentrate On You
Friendship (with entire group)

Convention Hall, Philadelphia   July 13, 1957

With Buddy Rich Orchestra

The Summer Wind
At Long Last Love
Day In, Day Out
The Shadow Of Your Smile
Moonlight In Vermont
A Foggy Day
This Is All I Ask
Fly Me To The Moon
I've Got You Under My Skin
F.S. Monologue
Nancy
You're Nobody Till Somebody Loves You
Ol' Man River
Quiet Nights Of Quiet Stars
My Kind Of Town
That's Life
Strangers In The Night
The Lady Is A Tramp
That's Life (short Reprise)

Sinatra opened a three week engagement at the Sands Hotel in Las Vegas in September 1967, with Buddy Rich's Orchestra plus Strings. On September 9th he has a falling out with the hotel's management and has since appeared exclusively at Caesar's Palace.

Madison Square Garden, New York   October 19, 1967

At Long Last Love
Day In, Day Out
Moonlight In Vermont
Fly Me To The Moon
I've Got You Under My Skin
The Lady Is A Tramp (with Sammy Davis Jr.)

The Fountainbleau, Miami, Florida   May 4, 1968

I Get A Kick Out Of You
In The Still Of The Night
I Have Dreamed
The Lady Is A Tramp

This Is All I Ask
All Or Nothing At All
That's Life
Ol' Man River
F.S. Monologue
Angel Eyes
All I Need Is The Girl
Moonlight In Vermont
It Was A Very Good Year
You're Nobody Till Somebody Loves You
My Kind Of Town

Coliseum Arean, Oakland, California   May 22, 1968

Orchestra conducted by Bill Miller
Concert for Hubert Humphrey

Day In, Day Out
I Get A Kick Out Of You
Moonlight In Vermont
The Lady Is A Tramp
I Have Dreamed
I've Got You Under My Skin
That's Life
Ol' Man River
All I Need Is The Girl
I've Got The World On A String
Willow Weep For Me
Goin' Out Of My Head
Nancy
Fly Me To The Moon
It Was A Very Good Year
My Kind Of Town

Baltimore, Maryland   August 1, 1968

Same selections as last concert except "This Is All I Ask" is substituted for
"It Was A Very Good Year" and "Fly Me To The Moon" is dropped.

The Spectrum, Philadelphia   August 3, 1968

Same selections as last concert.

Caesar's Palace, Las Vegas, Nevada   November 26, 1968

With The Harry James Orchestra - This is Sinatra's initial appearance here and
by no means his last.

I've Got The World On A String
Day In, Day Out
You Make Me Feel So Young
Cycles

Please Be Kind
By The Time I Get To Phoenix
All Or Nothing At All
This Is All I Ask
I've Got You Under My Skin
Little Green Apples
The Lady Is A Tramp
Medley: Strangers In The Night
Young At Heart
Nancy
It Was A Very Good Year
All The Way
That's Life
My Kind Of Town

Caesar's Palace, Las Vegas, Nevada   November 27, 1968
With The Harry James Orchestra

Same selections as last concert.

Caesar's Palace, Las Vegas, Nevada   May 15, 1969
Bill Miller conducts the Nat Brandwynne Orchestra

Mrs. Robinson
Please Be Kind
Cycles
The Lady Is A Tramp
F.S. Monologue
Lost In The Stars
Didn't We
Try A Little Tenderness
I've Got You Under My Skin
Medley: All The Way
Strangers In The Night
Young At Heart
Nancy
It Was A Very Good Year
That's Life
My Kind Of Town

The Astrodome, Houston, Texas   August 16, 1969

The Lady Is A Tramp
Fly Me To The Moon
God Bless America

Civic Hall, Richmond, Virginia   April 29, 1970

Concert for Mitrione Family Benefit Fund. Jerry Lewis appears for first 30 minutes and Frank brings his own musicians and bears the complete cost.

I've Got The World On A String
I Get A Kick Out Of You
Close To You
Don't Worry 'Bout Me
Fly Me To The Moon
Street Of Dreams
Pennies From Heaven
My Kind Of Town
Autumn Leaves
Yesterday
This Is All I Ask
I Would Be In Love Anyway
Try A Little Tenderness
Lady Day
Ol' Man River
Moonlight In Vermont
Angel Eyes
You Make Me Feel So Young
I've Got You Under My Skin
Please Be Kind
The Lady Is A Tramp
On The Road To Mandalay
My Way

Royal Festival Hall, London, England   May 8, 1970
The Count Basie Orchestra with British String Section

    Same songs as last concert

The Hilton Hotel, San Francisco, California   October 5, 1970

    "Californians For Ronald Reagan" - an evening of entertainment with Sinatra, Dean Martin, Pat Henry and Robin Wilson.

I've Got You Under My Skin
I Get A Kick Out Of You
Pennies From Heaven
Don't Worry 'Bout Me
I Get Along Without You Very Well
Spring Is Here
Angel Eyes
That's Life
You Make Me Feel So Young
My Kind Of Town
Nancy
My Way
F.S. introduces Ronald Reagan

Royal Festival Hall, London, England   November 16, 1970
"Nights Of Nights" Bill Miller leader and Pianist Intro by Grace Kelly

    You Make Me Feel So Young
    Pennies From Heaven
    I've Got You Under My Skin
    Something
    The Lady Is A Tramp
    I Get Along Without You Very Well
    This Love Of Mine
    Spring Is Here
    Didn't We
    One For My Baby
    A Foggy Day
    I Will Drink The Wine
    I Have Dreamed
    My Kind Of Town
    My Way

There was also a second performance on the same day with Sinatra repeating the same songs.

Felt Forum, New York City   November 29, 1970

Italian-American Civil Rights League Benefit. Ed McMahon - M.C. with Jerry Vale, The Four Seasons, Ross Martin, Connie Francis, Guy Marks, Vic Damone, The P.J.'s, Morty Storm, Trini Lopez, Pat Henry and Sammy Davis, Jr. Orchestra conducted by Bill Miller.

    You Make Me Feel So Young
    Pennies From Heaven
    I Get Along Without You Very Well
    I Have Dreamed
    Nancy
    Something
    My Way

Memorial Auditorium, Sacramento, California   January 4, 1971

Inaugural gala for Governor Ronald Reagan. Orchestra conducted by Bill Miller.

Essentially the same songs sung for the October 5, 1970 performance.

Palm Springs, California   January 15, 1971

Dedication ceremonies of The Martin Anthony Sinatra Medical Education Center at the Desert Hospital. Attended by the entire Sinatra family plus V.P. Spiro Agnew and Governor Reagan.

Beverly Hills Hotel, California   January 29, 1971

Sinatra did show to raise funds for Democratic Senator John Tunney.

Los Angeles, California   February 5, 1971

Frank Sinatra received the Cecil B. DeMille Award during the Golden Globes Awards ceremony. Award was accepted by daughter Tina.

Hynes Civic Auditorium, Boston, Mass.   March 18, 1971

Testimonial dinner for Frank Fontaine.
Tony Bruno's Orchestra with Bill Miller, Pianist.

> You Make Me Feel So Young
> Pennies From Heaven
> Don't Worry 'Bout Me
> Didn't We
> Angel Eyes
> My Kind Of Town
> My Way

Memphis, Tennessee   May 29, 1971

"Shower Of Stars" - benefit for St. Judes Research Hospital. Orchestra conducted by Bill Miller.

> That's Life
> Fly Me To The Moon
> Ol' Man River
> Nancy
> My Way
> My Kind Of Town
> One For My Baby

Rive Gauche Restaurant, Georgetown, Maryland   June 1, 1971

Henry Kissinger, The President's Foreign Policy expert, honors Sinatra at a dinner party.

U.C.L.A. Royce Hall, Los Angeles   June 7, 1971

Sinatra presents the 5th Annual Musical Performances Awards to students. He also speaks briefly about his coming retirement.

Los Angeles Music Center, California   June 13, 1971

50th Anniversary Celebration - Motion Pictures And Television Relief Fund. There were two shows. First show at the Dorothy Chandler Pavilion with the orchestra of David Rose, Sinatra's portion was conducted by Bill Miller. Second show at the Ahmanson Theater with Nelson Riddle's Orchestra. This was supposedly Sinatra's "farewell" appearance as he announced his retirement.

First Show
    All Or Nothing At All
    I've Got You Under My Skin
    I'll Never Smile Again
    The Lady Is A Tramp
    My Way
    That's Life
    Angel Eyes
Second Show
    All Or Nothing At All
    I've Got You Under My Skin
    I'll Never Smile Again
    Ol' Man River
    That's Life
    Try A Little Tenderness*
    Fly Me To The Moon
    Nancy
    My Way
    The Lady Is A Tramp
    Angel Eyes
* Accompanied by Al Viola (Guitar)

Americana Hotel, New York   May 13, 1972

    Celebrity night salute to Spiro Agnew.
    Sinatra sings parody of "Lady Is A Tramp" and also on "But Beautiful."

Central Plaza Hotel, Los Angeles   November 1, 1972

    State of Israel Commendation Dinner honoring Frank Sinatra.

The White House, Washington, D.C.   April 17, 1973

    White House Concert for Prime Minister Andreotti of Italy. With the U.S.
Marine Band conducted by Nelson Riddle.

    You Make Me Feel So Young
    Moonlight In Vermont
    One For My Baby
    I've Got You Under My Skin
    I Have Dreamed
    Fly Me To The Moon
    Try A Little Tenderness
    Ol' Man River
    I've Got The World On A String
    The House I Live In

Caesar's Palace, Las Vegas, Nevada   January 25, 1974

    Sinatra's first appearance since coming out of retirement. Nat Brandwynne
Orchestra conducted by Gordon Jenkins.

Come Fly With Me
I Get A Kick Out Of You
Bad, Bad Leroy Brown
You Will Be My Music
You Make Me Feel So Young
Last Night When We Were Young*
Violets For Your Furs*
Here's That Rainy Day*
F.S. Monologue
Let Me Try Again
My Kind Of Town
I've Got You Under My Skin
Send In The Clowns
The Summer Knows
That's Life
If
I've Got The World On A String
* Song as a medley

The Caesar's Palace Engagement continued till January 31, 1974 with a few shows cancelled due to a sore throat.

Civic Auditorium, San Jose   March 9, 1974

The 8th Annual Golden Circle Theatre Party for the University of Santa Clara. Orchestra conducted by Gordon Jenkins.

Come Fly With Me
I Get A Kick Out Of You
You Will Be My Music
Bad, Bad Leroy Brown
Send In The Clowns
I've Got You Under My Skin
Let Me Try Again
My Kind Of Town

The Fountainbleau, Miami, Florida   March 28, 1974

"The Miracle Ball" Benefit - Orchestra conducted by Gordon Jenkins. Same songs as Caesar's Palace engagement.

Carnegie Hall, New York   April 8, 1974

With musicians from New York City including Irv Cottler (Drums) and Al Viola (Guitar) with Bill Miller conducting. The concert was recorded by Reprise and was supposed to be released as a "Live" album.

Come Fly With Me
I Get A Kick Out Of You
Don't Worry 'Bout Me
If

Bad, Bad Leroy Brown
Last Night When We Were Young
Violets For Your Furs
Here's That Rainy Day
F. S. Monologue
My Way
You Will Be My Music
I've Got You Under My Skin
Send In The Clowns
That's Life
There Used To Be A Ball Park
My Kind Of Town

Nassau Coliseum, New York	April 9, 1974
Nassau Coliseum, New York	April 10, 1974
Nassau Coliseum, New York	April 11, 1974
Civic Center, Providence, Rhode Island	April 15, 1974
Civic Center, Providence, Rhode Island	April 16, 1974
Olympia Stadium, Detroit	April 18, 1974
The Spectrum, Philadelphia	April 21, 1974
The Spectrum, Philadelphia	April 22, 1974
Capitol Center, Washington, D.C.	April 24, 1974
The Stadium, Chicago, Ill.	April 27, 1974

The above April concert tour was originated to aid the Variety Clubs International; and are all similar to the Carnegie Hall concert given on April 8, 1974.

Caesar's Palace, Las Vegas, Nevada	June 6, 1974

With the Count Basie Orchestra conducted by Bill Miller. Ella Fitzgerald who was also on the bill joined Sinatra on the final number of each show.

Bad, Bad Leroy Brown
Pennies From Heaven
Don't Worry 'Bout Me
If
Here's That Rainy Day
F.S. Monologue
I've Got You Under My Skin
My Way
Sweet Caroline
My Kind Of Town
I Get A Kick Out Of You
The Lady Is A Tramp (with E.F.)

Sinatra performed ten shows at Caesar's and most are similar in content.

Tokyo, Japan   July 3, 1974

Bill Miller (Piano), Al Viola (Guitar), Irv Cottler (Drums), Gene Cherico (Bass), Billy Byers (Trombone), Marvin Stamm (Trumpet) and Bud Shank (Saxaphone).

Come Fly With Me
I Get A Kick Out Of You
I've Got The World On A String
You Will Be My Music
Bad, Bad Leroy Brown
If
You Are The Sunshine Of My Life
Don't Worry 'Bout Me
Ol' Man River
I've Got You Under My Skin
Angel Eyes
My Kind Of Town
Let Me Try Again

Aircraft Carrier U.S.S. Midway, off Japan   July 5, 1974
With same accompaniment.

You Are The Sunshine Of My Life
Sweet Caroline
I Get A Kick Out Of You
Bad, Bad Leroy Brown
If
I've Got You Under My Skin
The Lady Is A Tramp
Nancy
My Way

Festival Hall, Melbourne, Australia   July 9, 1974

I Get A Kick Out Of You
You Are The Sunshine Of My Life
Don't Worry 'Bout Me
If
Bad, Bad Leroy Brown
Ol' Man River
F.S. Monologue
Last Night When We Were Young
Violets For Your Furs
Here's That Rainy Day
I've Got You Under My Skin
My Kind Of Town
Let Me Try Again

The Lady Is A Tramp
My Way

Horden Pavilion, Sydney, Australia   July 16, 1974

I Get A Kick Out Of You
You Are The Sunshine Of My Life
Let Me Try Again
If
Bad, Bad Leroy Brown
F.S. Monologue
Angel Eyes
I've Got You Under My Skin
My Kind Of Town
Send In The Clowns (Piano only)
Nancy
The Lady Is A Tramp
My Way

Harrah's, Lake Tahoe   September 10, 1974

With Nancy Sinatra, Frank Sinatra, Jr., Pat Henry, The Veterans and Woody
Herman's Orchestra.

The Lady Is A Tramp
I Get A Kick Out Of You
Bad, Bad Leroy Brown
Send In The Clowns
Let Me Try Again
F.S. Monologue
My Kind Of Town
Chicago
Angel Eyes
I've Got You Under My Skin
My Way

Caesar's Palace, Las Vegas, Nevada   September 12, 1974

With entire cast from Lake Tahoe.

The Lady Is A Tramp
I Get A Kick Out Of You
Bad, Bad Leroy Brown
Send In The Clowns
Let Me Try Again
F.S. Monologue
My Kind Of Town
Angel Eyes
I've Got You Under My Skin
My Way
Side By Side (with entire cast)

Sinatra continued at Caesar's Palace through September 18, 1974 with essentially the same songs and cast.

Universal Amphitheatre, Los Angeles   September 27, 1974

Benefit for Cedars-Mt. Sinai Medical Center Building Fund. Orchestra conducted by Bill Miller.

> The Lady Is A Tramp
> I Get A Kick Out Of You
> Bad, Bad Leroy Brown
> Let Me Try Again
> Send In The Clowns
> My Kind Of Town
> Ol' Man River
> F.S. Monologue
> Don't Worry 'Bout Me
> If
> I've Got You Under My Skin
> Angel Eyes
> You Are The Sunshine Of My Life
> My Way

Sinatra commenced a nine city tour with Woody Herman's Orchestra. All of these performances were recorded by Reprise and many were included in the "Main Event Album". The tour started in Boston on October 2 and ended in Dallas on October 29.

Boston, Mass.   October 2, 1974

Memorial Auditorium, Buffalo, New York   October 4, 1974

The Spectrum, Philadelphia   October 7, 1974

Madison Square Garden, New York   October 13, 1974

This is the concert that was televised as the "Main Event."

Dallas, Texas   October 29, 1974

Madison Square Garden, New York   November 1, 1974

Rally for Hugh Carey.

The Diplomat, Miami, Florida   December 31, 1974

This New Year's Eve show was billed as "Irv Cowan's Main Even."

> Bad, Bad Leroy Brown
> At Long Last Love
> I Get A Kick Out Of You
> If
> The Lady Is A Tramp

Don't Worry 'Bout Me
I Have Dreamed
I've Got You Under My Skin
Here's That Rainy Day
My Kind Of Town
F.S. Monologue
You Are The Sunshine Of My Life
What Are You Doing The Rest Of Your Life
I've Got The World On A String
My Way

Harrah's, Lake Tahoe   January 10, 1975

The Lady Is A Tramp
At Long Last Love
If
Bad, Bad Leroy Brown
Let Me Try Again
F.S. Monologue
Here's That Rainy Day
You Are The Sunshine Of My Life
Lonely Town
I've Got You Under My Skin
My Way
Send In The Clowns
I Get A Kick Out Of You

Harrah's , Lake Tahoe   January 11, 1975

Harrah's, Lake Tahoe   January 12, 1975

Back to Caesar's Palace for seven more nights with Bill Miller conducting the Nat Brandwynne Orchestra.

Caesar's Palace, Las Vegas, Nevada   January 16, 1975

The Lady Is A Tramp
Bad, Bad Leroy Brown
Let Me Try Again
My Kind Of Town
Last Night When We Were Young
Violets For Your Furs
Here's That Rainy Day
F.S. Monologue
Something
You Are The Sunshine Of My Life
My Way
Send In The Clowns
I've Got You Under My Skin

Caesar's Palace   January 17, 1975

On Tour at New Port.

Concert appearance at Nassau Coliseum.

Caesar's Palace	January 18, 1975
Caesar's Palace	January 19, 1975
Caesar's Palace	January 20, 1975
Caesar's Palace	January 21, 1975
Caesar's Palace	January 22, 1975
South Shore Room, Harrah's, Lake Tahoe	February 25, 1975

With Bill Miller conducting The Brian Farnon Orchestra.

>The Lady Is A Tramp
>Bad, Bad Leroy Brown
>Let Me Try Again
>My Kind Of Town
>Last Night When We Were Young
>Violets For Your Furs
>Here's That Rainy Day
>F.
>F.S. Monologue
>My Way
>You Are The Sunshine Of My Life
>Send In The Clowns
>I Have Dreamed
>I've Got You Under My Skin

Caesar's Palace, Las Vegas, Nevada	March 20, 1975

The Nat Brandwynne Orchestra conducted by Don Costa, plus Octet: Bill Miller (Piano), Charlie Turner (Trumpet), Charles Shoemaker (Vibes), Francisco Aquabello (Bongos), Nino Tempo (Tenor Sax), Pat Rizzo (Alto Sax), Gene Cherico (Bass), Al Viola (Guitar) and Irv Cottler (Drums).

>You Are The Sunshine Of My Life
>Oh Babe What Would You Say
>Bad, Bad Leroy Brown
>But Beautiful
>I See Your Face Before Me
>Something
>Nice N' Easy
>My Way
>F.S. Monologue
>Angel Eyes
>Anytime
>The Saddest Thing Of All
>My Kind Of Town
>Send In The Clowns
>I've Got You Under My Skin
>Put Your Dreams Away

Caesar's Palace	March 21, 1975
Caesar's Palace	March 22, 1975
Caesar's Palace	March 23, 1975
Caesar's Palace	March 25, 1975
Caesar's Palace	March 26, 1975
Civic Arena, San Francisco, California	April 24, 1975

Orchestra conducted by Don Costa.

You Are The Sunshine Of My Life
The Most Beautiful Girl In The World
Bad, Bad Leroy Brown
But Beutiful
Didn't We
Something
Nice N' Easy
My Way
F.S. Monologue
Last Night When We Were Young
Violets For Your Furs
Here's That Rainy Day
Anytime
Cycles
Granada
Send In The Clowns
Let Me Try Again
The Saddest Thing Of All
If
I've Got You Under My Skin
Put Your Dreams Away

The Coliseum, Portland, Oregon	April 26, 1975
Center Arena, Seattle, Washington	April 27, 1975
The Coliseum, Denver, Colorado	May 1, 1975
The Stadium, Chicago, Illinois	May 3, 1975
The Auditorium, St. Louis, Missouri	May 4, 1975
Market Square Arena, Indianapolis	May 6, 1975
Kiel Auditorium, St. Louis, Missouri	May 7, 1975
The Forum, Montreal, Canada	May 9, 1975
Mapple Leaf Gardens, Toronto, Canada	May 10, 1975
Civic Center, Providence, Rhode Island	May 12, 1975

Veteran's Memorial Coliseum, New Haven, Conn.   May 13, 1975

The majority of the songs sung on these various dates are the same as the April 24, 1975 concert.

Sinatra's next embarks on his first European tour since 1962. He contracted an orchestra of British musicians to accompany him and they were conducted by Don Costa but when Costa became ill after the Frankfurt concert, Bill Miller took over the conducting chores. Al Viola (Guitar), Gene Cherico (Bass), and Irv Cottler (Drums) also were with him throughout the tour.

The Sporting Club, Monte Carlo   May 19, 1975

> You Are The Sunshine Of My Life
> Bad, Bad Leroy Brown
> But Beautiful
> Didn't We
> I See Your Face Before Me
> Something
> Nice N' Easy
> My Way
> F.S. Monologue
> Last Night When We Were Young
> Violets For Your Furs
> Here's That Rainy Day
> Cycles
> Strangers In The Night
> Send In The Clowns
> Let Me Try Again
> If
> I've Got You Under My Skin
> The Lady Is A Tramp
> Put Your Dreams Away

Palais De Congress, Paris, France   May 20, 1975

Stadhalle, Vienna   May 22, 1975

Olympiahalle, Munich   May 23, 1975

Festhalle, Frankfurt, Germany   May 25, 1975

Deutsch Landhalle, Berlin, Germany   May 26, 1975
(This concert cancelled)

Royal Albert Hall, London, England   May 29, 30, 1975

Forest National, Brussels   June 1, 1975

Concert Gebouw, Amsterdam   June 2, 1975

The majority of the songs on these various dates are the same as the May 19, 1975 concert.

Frank appears next at Caesar's Palace from June 19, to July 2, substituting for Diana Ross who was ill.

Caesar's Palace, Las Vegas, Nevada   June 19, 1975

    Where Or When
    You Are The Sunshine Of My Life
    My Kind Of Town
    In The Wee Small Hours
    Didn't We
    Something
    Nice N' Easy
    My Way
    F.S. Monologue
    Send In The Clowns
    Cycles
    Granada
    If
    I've Got You Under My Skin
    The Lady Is A Tramp
    Put Your Dreams Away

Harrah's, Lake Tahoe   August 1, 1975
    This was the "Back to back" engagement with John Denver. Sinatra did the midnight show and introduced a new arrangement of "Let Me Try Again".

    Where Or When
    My Kind Of Town
    Let Me Try Again
    You Are The Sunshine Of My Life
    But Beautiful
    Didn't We
    Something
    Nice N' Easy
    F.S. Monologue
    Send In The Clowns
    I Believe I'm Gonna Love You
    Cycles
    Ol' Man River
    I Concentrate On You
    I've Got You Under My Skin
    The Lady Is A Tramp
    Put Your Dreams Away

    Sinatra appeared at Harrah's 'till the 5th of August and then proceeded on a short tour.

Post Pavilion, Merriweather, Washington D.C.   August 19, 1975

National Exhibition Centre, Toronto, Canada   August 21, 1975

Garden State Arts Center, Holmoen, New Jersey	August 22, 1975
Performing Arts Center, Saratoga, New York	August 25, 1975

Next we have the Uris Theater engagement with Count Basie and His Orchestra and Ella Fitzgerald. This ran for two weeks and was sold out for every performance.

Uris Theater, New York City	September 8, 1975

Withe The Count Basie Orchestra conducted by Bill Miller plus Al Viola (Guitar), Gene Cherico (Bass), and Irv Cottler (Drums). Miss Fitzgerald also dueted with Sinatra as will be noted in the listings of selections.

Where Or When
Bad, Bad Leroy Brown
Let Me Try Again
My Kind Of Town
But Beautiful
Didn't We
How Deep Is The Ocean
Something
Nice N' Easy
F.S. Monologue
Just One Of Those Things
When Your Lover Has Gone
I Believe I'm Gonna Love You
Pennies From Heaven
Send In The Clowns
Please Be Kind
I've Got You Under My Skin
The Song Is You*
They Can't Take That Away From Me*
At Long Last Love
The Lady Is A Tramp*

* Duets with Ella Fitzgerald.

The engagement at the Uris Theater ended on September 20, 1975 and the entire show moved on to Philadelphia for one performance.

The Spectrum, Philadelphia	September 22, 1975

Same as Uris Theater performance.

Harrah's, Lake Tahoe	October 17, 1975
Harrah's, Lake Tahoe	October 18, 1975
Harrah's, Lake Tahoe	October 19, 1975
Harrah's, Lake Tahoe	October 20, 1975
Harrah's, Lake Tahoe	October 21, 1975

Harrah's, Lake Tahoe	October 22, 1975
Harrah's, Lake Tahoe	October 23, 1975
Harrah's, Lake Tahoe	October 24, 1975

His next appearance at Caesar's Palace was from October 30 to November 6, 1975 and then on to England once more where he appeared at the London Palladium from November 13 to November 20, 1975.

The Palladium, London, England	November 13, 1975

With The Count Basie Orchestra conducted by Bill Miller, and Sarah Vaughan.

Where Or When
At Long Last Love
My Kind Of Town
Didn't We
Something
Nice N' Easy
F.S. Monologue
Send In The Clowns
I Believe I'm Gonna Love You
My Way
I've Got You Under My Skin
Don't Worry 'Bout Me
Pennies From Heaven
The Song Is You*
They Can't Take That Away From Me*
Let Me Try Again
The Lady Is A Tramp*
* Vocal duets with Sarah Vaughan.

Aryamtir, Tehran	November 24, 1975
Binyanei, Israel	November 29, 1975
Haooma, Israel	November 30, 1975

Benefit for Jewish and Arab children.

The Stadium, Chicago, Illinois	December 31, 1975

Aside from the songs that seem to appear on all his engagements he adds a few more for this appearance and since it is New Year's Eve, includes "Auld Lang Syne."

He returns to Caesar's Palace once again with Bill Miller conducting the Nat Brandwynne Orchestra and introduces a new song which was especially written for him by Johnny Mercer and Jimmy Van Heusen; - "Empty Tables."

Caesar's Palace, Las Vegas, Nevada	January 15, 1976

Chicago

Where Or When
The Lady Is A Tramp
What's New
Didn't We
Empty Tables (solo piano)
Here's That Rainy Day
Witchcraft
My Way
F.S. Monologue
I Sing The Songs
Let Me Try Again
If
Send In The Clowns
My Kind Of Town

He closes at the Latin Casino on February 22, 1976, a few days early because of the "flu."

Harrah's, Lake Tahoe   March 13, 1976
   The Brian Farnon Orchestra conducted by Bill Miller and Sam Butera and The Witnesses featuring Sandy Williams.

Bad, Bad Leroy Brown
For Once In My Life
The Lady Is A Tramp
What's New
Didn't We
Here's That Rainy Day
Witchcraft
I Sing The Songs
F.S. Monologue
Send In The Clowns
The Hungry Years
My Kind Of Town
I've Got You Under My Skin
My Way

Westchester Premier Theater, Tarrytown, N.Y.   April 1, 1976

Night And Day*
For Once In My Life
The Lady Is A Tramp
Imaginations
What's New
Didn't We
Here's That Rainy Day
Witchcraft
All By Myself
F.S. Monologue
If

The Hungry Years
Send In The Clowns
I Sing The Songs
My Kind Of Town
My Way
* New Johnnie Beck arrangement.

Sinatra continues at the Premier Theater until the 11th of April 1976. He then returns to The Latin Casino in Philadelphia to make up for the days he missed in February.

The Latin Casino, Philadelphia, Pa.   May 27, 1976
    The Al Cavanaugh Orchestra conducted by Bill Miller.

    Night And Day
    For Once In My Life
    The Lady Is A Tramp
    Imagination
    Didn't We
    Witchcraft
    My Way
    F.S. Monologue
    All By Myself
    Send In The Clowns
    My Kind Of Town
    I Sing The Songs

The Waldorf Hotel, New York City, N.Y.   June 1, 1976
    Hugh Carey Fund Rally

    Night And Day
    For Once In My Life
    The Lady Is A Tramp
    Imagination
    Didn't We
    Witchcraft
    My Way
    Send In The Clowns
    I Sing The Songs
    F.S. Speech For Carey

Pacific Coliseum, Vancouver, B.C.   August 21, 1976

    Night And Day
    For Once In My Life
    Where Or When
    The Lady Is A Tramp
    Imagination
    Empty Tables
    Didn't We

Here's That Rainy Day
Stargazer
My Way
My Kind Of Town
F.S. Monologue
All By Myself
I've Got You Under My Skin
Send In The Clowns
I Sing The Songs

Harrah's, Lake Tahoe   September 11, 1976

Night And Day
Where Or When
Here's That Rainy Day
For Once In My Life
This Is All I Ask
I Sings The Songs

   Medley with John Denver: Saturday Night, Come Fly With Me, Learnin' The
Blues, Witchcraft, Nancy, Love And Marriage, All The Way, All Of Me, My
Sweet Lady, Leaving On A Jet Plane, Like A Sad Song, September Song.

Memorial Auditorium, Buffalo, N.Y.   October 8, 1976

I Sing The Songs
Where Or When
Stargazer (with Sam Butera)
The Lady Is A Tramp
Embraceable You
My Funny Valentine
I Get Along Without You Very Well
For Once In My Life
F.S. Monologue
Like A Sad Song
This Is All I Ask
Never Gonna Fall In Love Again
Empty Tables
It Was A Very Good Year
Night And Day
My Way

Caesar's Palace, Las Vegas Nevada   January 6, 1977

Bad, Bad Leroy Brown
Where Or When
I Sing The Songs
The Lady Is A Tramp
My Funny Valentine
Embraceable You
I Get Along Without You Very Well

I Love My Life
See The Show Again
For Once In My Life
Like A Sad Song
Send In The Clowns
Night And Day
My Way

The remaining dates of this appearance were cancelled due to the tragic death of Frank Sinatra's mother.

Harrah's, Lake Tahoe   January 15, 1977

Harrah's, Lake Tahoe   January 16, 1977

Harrah's, Lake Tahoe   January 17, 1977

Sunrise Theater, Miami, Florida   January 24, 1977

This appearance lasted through January 30, 1977

Royal Festival Hall, London   March 3, 1977

Night And Day
For Once In My Life
I've Got You Under My Skin
I Love My Wife
Embraceable You
My Funny Valentine
Here's That Rainy Day
Sorry Seems The Hardest Word
I Sing The Songs
The Lady Is A Tramp
Send In The Clowns
Where Or When
It Was A Very Good Year
Bad, Bad Leroy Brown
See The Show Again
A Foggy Day
My Kind Of Town
My Way

Casear's Palace, Las Vegas, Nevada   March 17, 1977

This appearance lasted through March 24, 1977

Harrah's, Lake Tahoe   March 25, 1977

This appearance lasted through March 30, 1977

Circle Star Theater, San Carolos, California   April 12, 1977

Bill Miller, Conductor and Pianist with Al Viola (Guitar), Charlie Turner (Trumpet), Gene Cherico (Bass) and Irv Kottler (Drums)

    Night And Day*
    Sweet Lorraine**
    Spring Is Here
    I Sing The Songs
    Where Or When
    I Love My Wife
    My Kind Of Town
    Sorry Seems To Be The Hardest Word
    All Or Nothing At All
    See The Show Again
    Send In The Clowns
    My Way
    Everybody Ought To Be In Love
    I've Got You Under My Skin
    Here's That Rainy Day
    The Lady Is A Tramp
* Disco Version
**With Small Group

Pat Henry opened each show and wife Barbara attended most performances. While there, Frank threw out the first baseball at the San Francisco Giants versus Los Angeles Dodgers game at Candlestick Park.

Upon hearing the plight of a heroin-addicted newly born baby in the San Francisco area, Sinatra personally brought a check of $3,000.00 to the hospital to care for the child. Of course, this did not appear in any newspaper which is typical. If there had been an altercation with a reporter, it would have been smeared all over the front pages.

So much for the media. All in all there were eight splendid performances here which lasted through April 17, 1977.

Palm Srings, California   April 23, 1977
    Benefit Concert

Carnegie Hall, New York City   April 27, 1977
    Benefit Concert for Lennox Hill Hospital

Latin Casino, New Jersey   April 29, 1977

    This appearance lasted through May 8, 1977

Westchester Premier Theater, New York   May 16, 1977

    With Dean Martin, Pat Henry and the Goldiggers. This appearance lasted through May 29, 1977.

Forest Hills Tennis Stadium, New York   July 15, 1977

Joe Malone Orchestra conducted by Bill Miller with Charlie Turner (Trumpet), Al Viola (Guitar), Gene Cherico (Bass), and Irv Kottler (Drums). Milton Berle special guest.

Night And Day ** ꞏ
Where Or When
For Once In My Life
Spring Is Here
Here's That Rainy Day
My Funny Valentine
I Love My Wife
I Sing The Songs
My Kind Of Town
See The Show Again
Everybody Ought To Be In Love
My Way
I've Got You Under My Skin
Send In The Clowns*
All Or Nothing At All**
It Was A Very Good Year
The Lady Is A Tramp

* with piano only
** Disco version

Concert appearance at Carnegie Hall.

SONG INDEX — CONCERTS — CHAPTER XIII

All By Myself - (Eric Carmen - Rachmaninov)
April 1, 1976; May 23, 1976; August 21, 1976

All I Need Is The Girl - (Stephen Sondheim - Jule Styne)
May 22, 1968

All Of Me - (Seymour Simons - Gerald Marks)
July 26, 1953; September 15, 1953; April 1, 1959; August 25, 1962; September 11, 1976

All Or Nothing At All - (Arthur Altman - Jack Lawrence)
November 26, 1968; June 13, 1971, April 12, 1977; July 15, 1977

All The Way - (Sammy Cahn - Jimmy Van Heusen)
June 14, 1953; April 1, 1959; August 4, 1960; April 20, 1962; May 25, 1962; June 1, 1962; July 4, 1965; November 26, 1968; May 15, 1969; September 11, 1976

Angel Eyes - (Matt Dennis - Earl Brent)
April 1, 1959; May 4, 1968; April 29, 1970; May 7, 1970; October 5, 1970; March 18, 1971; June 13, 1971; July 3, 1974; July 16, 1974; September 10, 1974; September 12, 1974; September 27, 1974; March 20, 1975

Any Time - (Paul Anka)
March 20, 1975; April 24, 1975

April In Paris - (Yip Harburg - Vernon Duke)
June 14, 1958; December 2, 1961, April 20, 1962, May 25, 1962

At Long Last Love - (Cole Porter)
June 8, 1957, June 9, 1957, April 1, 1959, April 20, 1962, June 1, 1962, August 25, 1962, July 13, 1967, October 19, 1967, May 7, 1970, December 31, 1974, January 10, 1975, September 8, 1975, November 13, 1975

Auld Lang Syne - (Burns)
December 31, 1975

Autumn Leaves - (Joseph Kosman - Jacques Prevert - Johnny Mercer)
April 29, 1970

Bad, Bad Leroy Brown - (Jim Croce)
January 25, 1974 through December 31, 1974; January 10, 1975 through September 8, 1974; February 13, 1976 through March 3, 1977

Bewitched - (Richard Rodgers - Lorenz Hart)
June 14, 1958; October 5, 1963

Birth Of The Blues, The - (Buddy DeSylva - Lew Brown - Ray Henderson)
July 26, 1963; August 25, 1962; June 20, 1965

But Beautiful - (Johnny Burke - Jimmy Van Heusen)
April 24, 1975; May 19, 1975; August 1, 1975; September 8, 1975; January 15,

1976

By The Time I Get To Phoenix - (Jim Webb)
November 26, 1968

Call Me Irresponsible - (Sammy Cahn - Jimmy Van Heusen)
October 5, 1963; July 4, 1965

Chicago - (Fred Fisher)
April 20, 1962; May 25, 1962; June 1, 1962; September 10, 1974; January 15, 1976

Close To You - (Burt Bacharach - Hal David)
April 29, 1970

Coffee Song, The - (Bob Hilliard - Dave Miles)
September 15, 1953

Come Fly With Me - (Sammy Cahn - Jimmy Van Heusen)
June 14, 1958; April 1, 1959; May 14, 1959; December 2, 1961; June 1, 1962;
January 25, 1974; March 9, 1974; April 8, 1974; July 3, 1974; September 11, 1976

Cycles - (Gayle Caldwell)
November 26, 1968; May 15, 1969; May 19, 1975; June 19, 1975; August 1, 1975

Dancing In The Dark - (Arthur Schwartz - Howard Dietz)
April 1, 1959

Day In, Day Out - (Rube Bloom - Johnny Mercer)
August 4, 1960; December 2, 1961; April 20, 1962; May 25, 1962; June 1, 1962;
October 19, 1967; May 22, 1968; November 26, 1968

Didn't We - (Jim Webb)
May 15, 1969; November 16, 1970;

May 15, 1969; November 16, 1970; March 18, 1971; April 24, 1975 through
November 13, 1975; January 15, 1976; February 13, 1976; March 13, 1976;
April 1, 1976; May 27, 1976; June 1, 1976, August 21, 1976

Don't Worry 'Bout Me - (Rube Bloom - Ted Koehler)
July 26, 1953; September 15, 1953; April 29, 1970; October 5, 1970; March 28,
1971; April 28, 1974; June 6, 1974; July 3, 1974; September 27, 1974; December
31, 1974; November 13, 1975

Embraceable You - (George & Ira Gershwin)
July 26, 1953; April 20, 1962; October 8, 1976; January 6, 1977; March 3, 1977

Empty Tables - (Johnny Mercer - Jimmy Van Heusen)
January 15, 1976; February 13, 1976; August 21, 1976; October 8, 1976

Everybody Ought To Be In Love - (Paul Anka)
April 12, 1977; July 15, 1977

Fly Me To The Moon - (Bart Howard)
July 4, 1965; September 7, 1966; July 13, 1967; October 19, 1967; May 26, 1968;

August 16, 1969; April 29, 1970; May 29, 1971; June 13, 1971; April 17, 1973

Foggy Day, A - (George & Ira Gershwin)
September 15, 1953; June 8, 1957; June 9, 1957; May 14, 1959; December 2, 1961; May 25, 1962; September 13, 1963; July 13, 1967; November 16, 1970; March 3, 1977

For Once In My Life - (Ronald Miller - Orlando Burden)
March 13, 1976; April 1, 1976; May 27, 1976; June 1, 1976; August 21, 1976; September 11, 1976; January 6, 1977; March 3, 1977; July 15, 1977

Friendship -
February 12, 1967

From Here To Eternity - (Freddie Karger - Robert Wells)
September 15, 1953

Gal That Got Away, The - (Harold Arlen - Ira Gershwin)
July 4, 1965

Get Me To The Church On Time - (Alan Lerner - Frederick Loewe)
July 4, 1965

Glad To Be Unhappy - (Richard Rodgers - Lorenz Hart)
June 8, 1957; June 9, 1957

God Bless America - (Irving Berlin)
August 16, 1969

Goin' Out Of My Head - (Teddy Randazzo - Bobby Weinstein)
May 22, 1968

Goody, Goody - (Johnny Mercer - Matty Malneck)
May 25, 1962; June 1, 1962; August 25, 1962

Granada - (Augustin Lara - Dorothy Dodd)
April 24, 1975; June 19, 1975

Guess I'll Hang My Tears Out To Dry - (Sammy Cahn - Jule Stune)
October 5, 1963

Hello Dolly - (Jerome Herman)
July 4, 1965

Here's That Rainy Day - (Johnny Burke - Jimmy Van Heusen)
January 25, 1974; April 8, 1974; December 31, 1974; January 10, 1975; April 24, 1975; February 13, 1976; August 21, 1976; March 3, 1977; July 15, 1977

Hey Jealous Lover - (Sammy Cahn - Kay Twomey - Beewalker)
June 9, 1957

House I Live In, The - (Lewis Allen - Earl Robinson)
January 19, 1961; April 17, 1973

How Deep Is The Ocean - (Irving Berlin)
September 8, 1975; January 15, 1976

Hungry Years, The - (Neil Sadaka)
March 13, 1976; April 6, 1976

I Believe I'm Gonna Love You - (Gloria Sklerov - Harry Lloyd)
August 1, 1975; September 8, 1975; November 13, 1975

I Can't Give You Anything But Love - (Dorothy Fields - Jimmy McHugh)
May 14, 1959; August 25, 1962

I Concentrate On You - (Cole Porter)
February 12, 1967; August 1, 1975

I Could Have Danced All Night - (Alan Lerner - Frederick Loewe)
April 1, 1959; August 4, 1960; April 20, 1962; May 25, 1962

If - (David Gates)
January 25, 1974 through December 31, 1974; January 10, 1975; April 24, 1975;
May 19, 1975; January 15, 1976; February 13, 1976; April 1, 1976

I Get A Kick Out Of you - (Cole Porter)
September 15, 1953; June 8, 1957; June 14, 1958; April 1, 1959; April 20, 1962;
September 13, 1963; May 4, 1968; April 29, 1970; January 25, 1974; January 10,
1975

I Get Along Without You Very Well - (Hoagy Carmichael)
April 29, 1970; November 29, 1970; October 8, 1976; January 6, 1977

I Hadn't Anyone Till You - (Ray Noble)
October 5, 1963

I Have Dreamed - (Richard Rodgers - Oscar Hammerstein II)
September 13, 1963, May 4, 1968, November 16, 1970, April 17, 1973, December
31, 1974, February 15, 1975

I'll Never Smile Again - (Ruth Lowe)
June 13, 1971

I Love My Wife - (Cy Coleman - Michael Stewart)
January 6, 1977, March 3, 1977, April 12, 1977, July 15, 1977

I Love Paris - (Cole Porter)
August 4, 1960, February 12, 1967

Imagination - (Johnny Burke - Jimmy Van Heusen)
April 20, 1962, June 1, 1962, March 13, 1976, August 21, 1976

In The Still Of The Night - (Cole Porter)
December 2, 1961, April 20, 1962, October 5, 1963, May 4, 1968

In The Wee Small Hours - (Bob Hilliard - Dave Mann)
July 4, 1965, June 19, 1975

I Only Have Eyes For You - (Al Dubin - Harry Warren)
June 20, 1965, July 4, 1965

I See Your Face Before Me - (Arthur Schwartz - Howard Dietz)
March 20, 1975, May 19, 1975

I Sing The Songs - (Bruce Johnston)
January 15, 1976, October 8, 1976, January 6, 1977, March 3, 1977, July 15, 1977

It All Depends On You - (Buddy DeSylva - Lew Brown - Ray Henderson)
September 15, 1953

It Happened In Monterey - (Mabel Wayne - Billy Rose)
June 8, 1957, June 9, 1957

It Never Entered My Mind - (Richard Rodgers - Lorenz Hart)
July 26, 1953, September 8, 1975

It's Alright With Me - (Cole Porter)
February 12, 1967

It's Easy To Remember - (Richard Rodgers - Lorenz Hart)
July 4, 1965

It's Over, It's Over, It's Over - (Matt Dennis - Dak Stanford)
August 4, 1960

It Was A Very Good Year - (Irvin Drake)
September 7, 1966, May 4, 1968, May 15, 1969, October 8, 1976, July 15, 1977

I've Got The World On A String - (Harold Arlen - Ted Koehler)
July 26, 1953, December 2, 1961, August 25, 1962, September 7, 1966, May 22, 1968, April 29, 1970, April 17, 1973, January 25, 1974, December 31, 1974

I've Got You Under My Skin - (Cole Porter)
June 9, 1957, June 14, 1958, April 1, 1959, August 4, 1960, April 20, 1962, June 20. 1965, September 7, 1966, February 12, 1967, May 22, 1968, May 15, 1969, April 20, 1970, June 13, 1971, April 17, 1973, January 25, 1974, January 10, 1975, March 13, 1976, March 3, 1977, July 15, 1977

I Will Drink The Wine - (Paul Ryan)
November 16, 1970

I Wish You Love - (Charles Trenet - Albert Beach)
July 4, 1965

I Won't Dance - (Jerome Kern - Dorothy Fields - Jimmy McHugh)
June 8, 1957

I Would Be In Love Anyway - (Bob Gaudio - Jake Holmes)
May 7, 1970

Just One Of Those Things - (Cole Porter)
June 9, 1957, April 1, 1959, September 8, 1975

Lady Day - (Bob Gaudio - Jake Holmes)
May 7, 1970

Lady Is A Tramp - (Richard Rodgers - Lorenz Hart)
June 8, 1957, June 14, 1958, April 1, 1959, December 2, 1961, April 20, 1962, July 13, 1967, May 4, 1968, May 15, 1969, April 29, 1970, June 13, 1971, June 6, 1974, January 10, 1975, January 15, 1976, April 12, 1977

Last Night When We Were Young - (Yip Harburg - Harold Arlen)
October 5, 1963, January 25, 1974, January 16, 1975, May 19, 1975

Leaving On A Jet Plane - (John Denver)
September 11, 1976

Let Me Try Again - (Sammy Cahn - Paul Anka - Michelle Carravelli)
January 25, 1974, January 10, 1975, February 3, 1976

Let's Do It - (Cole Porter)
February 12, 1967

Like A Sad Song - (John Denver)
September 11, 1976, January 6, 1977

Little Girl Blue - (Richard Rodgers - Lorenz Hart)
September 15, 1953

Little Green Apples - (Bobby Russell)
November 26, 1968

Lonely Town - (Leonard Bernstein - Betty Comden - Adolph Green)
January 10, 1975

Lost In The Stars - (Kurt Weill - Maxwell Anderson)
May 15, 1969

Love And Marriage - (Sammy Cahn - Jimmy Van Heusen)
September 11, 1976

Luck Be A Lady - (Frank Loesser)
October 5, 1963, June 26, 1965, July 4, 1965

Monique - (Sammy Cahn - Elmer Bernstein)
June 14, 1958

Moonlight In Vermont - (Karl Suessdorf - John Blackburn)
June 14, 1958, April 1, 1959, August 4, 1960, April 20, 1962, July 13, 1967, May 4, 1968, April 29, 1970, April 17, 1973

Moon Was Yellow, The - (Fred Ahlert - Edgar Leslie)
April 20, 1962, May 25, 1962

Most Beautiful Girl In The World, The - (Richard Rodgers - Lorenz Hart)
April 24, 1975

Mrs. Robinson - (Paul Simon)
May 15, 1969

My Blue Heaven - (Walter Donaldson - Gus Whiting)
December 2, 1961, May 25, 1962

My Funny Valentine - (Richard Rodgers - Lorenz Hart)
September 15, 1953, June 8, 1957, October 2, 1961, April 20, 1962, October 8, 1976,
January 6, 1977, July 15, 1977

My Heart Stood Still - (Richard Rodgers - Lorenz Hart)
September 13, 1963

My Kind Of Town - (Sammy Cahn - Jimmy Van Heusen)
June 20, 1965, July 13, 1967, May 4, 1968, May 15, 1969, November 16, 1970,
March 29, 1971, January 25, 1974, January 16, 1975, January 15, 1976, March 3,
1977, July 15, 1977

My One And Only Love - (Guy Wood - Robert Mellin)
September 15, 1953

My Way - (Paul Anka - C. Francois - J. Revaix - Gilles Thibault)
April 29, 1970, March 18, 1971, June 6, 1974, December 31, 1974, January 10,
1975, November 13, 1975, January 15, 1976, October 8, 1976, January 6, 1977,
July 15, 1977

Nancy - (Phil Silvers - Jimmy Van Heusen)
June 1, 1962, July 13, 1967, May 22, 1968, May 15, 1969, October 5, 1970, March
29, 1971, July 5, 1974, September 11, 1976

Never Gonna Fall In Love Again - (Eric Carmen)
October 8, 1976

Nice 'N Easy - (Marilyn Keith - Alan Bergman - Lew Spence)
March 20, 1975, May 19, 1975, November 13, 1975

Night And Day - (Cole Porter)
July 26, 1953, April 1, 1959, April 10, 1962, June 1, 1976, October 8, 1976, January
6, 1977, July 15, 1977

Oh Babe What Would You Say - (Hurricane Smith)
March 20, 1975

Oh Look At Me Now - (Joe Bushkin - John DeVries)
June 9, 1957

Ol' Man Crosby - (Parody of "Ol Man River")
July 26, 1953

Ol' Man River - (Jerome Kern - Oscar Hammerstein II)
July 26, 1953, May 25, 1962, October 5, 1963, July 13, 1967, May 4, 1968, April 29,
1970, May 21, 1971, April 17, 1973, July 3, 1974, August 1, 1975

One For My Baby - (Harold Arlen - Johnny Mercer)

July 26, 1953, June 8, 1957, December 2, 1961, May 25, 1962, November 16, 1970, May 29, 1971, April 17, 1973

One I Love, The - (Gus Kahn - Isham Jones)
December 2, 1961

On The Road To Mandalay - (Oley Speaks - Rudyard Kipling)
June 15, 1958, April 1, 1959, October 5, 1963, May 7, 1970

Pennies From Heaven - (Arthur Johnson - Johnny Burke)
April 29, 1970, March 18, 1971, June 6, 1974, November 13, 1975

Please Be Kind - (Sammy Cahn - Saul Chaplin)
October 5, 1963, November 26, 1968, May 15, 1969, May 7, 1970, September 8, 1975

Put Your Dreams Away - (Ruth Lowe - Stephen Weiss - Paul Mann)
March 20, 1975, May 9, 1975, June 19, 1975

Quiet Nights of Quiet Stars - (Antonio Carlos Jobim - Gene Lees)

River Stay Away From My Door - (Harry Woods - Mort Dixon)
August 4, 1960

Saddest Thing Of All, The - (Michel Legrand - Carl Sigman - Eddy Barclay)
March 20, 1975, April 24, 1975

Saturday Night - (Sammy Cahn - Jule Styne)
September 11, 1976

Second Time Around, The - (Sammy Cahn - Jimmy Van Heusen)
December 2, 1961

See The Show Again - (Barry Manilow)
January 6, 1977, March 3, 1977, April 12, 1977, July 15, 1977

Send In The Clowns - (Stephen Sondheim)
January 25, 1974, September 27, 1974, January 10, 1975, November 13, 1975, February 13, 1975, January 6, 1977, July 15, 1977

September Song - (Maxwell Anderson - Kurt Weill)
September 11, 1976

Shadow Of Your Smile, The - (Johnny Mandel - Paul Frances Webster)
September 7, 1966, July 13, 1967

Side By Side - (Harry Woods)
September 12, 1974

Something - (George Harrison)
November 16, 1970, January 16, 1975, November 13, 1975

Song Is You, The - (Jerome Kern)
September 8, 1975, November 13, 1975

Sorry Seems The Hardest Word -
March 3, 1977, April 12, 1977

Spring Is Here - (Richard Rodgers - Lorenz Hart)
September 15, 1953, October 5, 1970, November 16, 1970, April 12, 1977, July 15, 1977

Stargazer - (Neil Diamond)
August 21, 1976, October 8, 1976

Strangers In The Night - (Bert Kaempfert - Charles Singleton - Eddie Snyder)
July 13, 1967, November 26, 1968, May 15, 1969, May 19, 1975

Street Of Dreams - (Victor Young - Sam Lewis)
July 4, 1965, May 7, 1970

Summer Knows, The - (Alan & Marilyn Bergman - Michel Legrand)
January 25, 1974

Summer Wind, The - (Johnny Mercer - Henry Mayer)
July 13, 1967

Sweet Caroline - (Neil Diamond)
June 6, 1975, July 5, 1974

Sweet Lorraine - (Mitchell Parish - Cliff Burwell)
July 26, 1953, April 12, 1977

Tender Trap, The - (Sammy Cahn - Jimmy Van Heusen)
June 9, 1957

That Old Black Magic - (Johnny Mercer - Harold Arlen)
July 26, 1953

That's Life - (Kay Gordon)
July 13, 1967, May 4, 1968, May 15, 1969, October 5, 1970, May 29, 1971, April 8, 1974

There Used To Be A Ballpark - (Joe Raposo)
April 8, 1974

They Can't Take That Away From Me - (George & Ira Gershwin)
September 5, 1953, June 8, 1957, May 25, 1962, September 13, 1963, September 8, 1975, January 15, 1976

This Can't Be Love - (Richard Rodgers - Lorenz Hart)
September 15, 1953

This Is All I Ask - (Gordon Jenkins)
July 13, 1967, May 4, 1968, April 29, 1970, October 8, 1976

This Love Of Mine - (Sol Parker - Hank Sanicola - Frank Sinatra)
November 16, 1970

Too Marvelous For Words - (Johnny Mercer - Richard Whiting)
May 15, 1959, August 4, 1960, April 20, 1962, September 13, 1963, July 4, 1965

Try A Little Tenderness - (Harry Woods - Jimmy Campbell - Reg Connelly)
May 15, 1969, May 7, 1970, June 13, 1971, April 17, 1973

Violets For Your Furs - (Matt Dennis - Tom Adair)
September 15, 1953, June 8, 1957, January 25, 1974, January 16, 1975, May 19, 1975

We're Glad We're Italians -
May 14, 1959

What Are You Doing The Rest Of Your Life - (Alan & Marilyn Bergman - Michel Legrand)
December 31, 1974

What's New - (Bobby Haggart - Johnny Burke)
February 13, 1976, March 13, 1976, April 1, 1976

When You're Smiling - (Mark Fisher - Joe Goodwin - Larry Shay)
July 26, 1953

When Your Lover Has Gone - (Edgar Swan)
June 8, 1955, June 14, 1958, September 8, 1975

Where Or When - (Richard Rodgers - Lorenz Hart)
June 14, 1958, July 4, 1955, June 19, 1975, January 15, 1976, October 8, 1976, January 6, 1977, July 15, 1977

Willow Weep For Me - (Ann Ronell)
April 1, 1959, August 4, 1960, May 22, 1968

Witchcraft - (Carolyn Leigh - Cy Coleman)
December 2, 1961, February 13, 1976, September 11, 1976

Without A Song - (Vincent Youmans - Billy Rose - Edward Eliseu)
April 20, 1962, May 25, 1962

Yesterday - (John Lennon - Paul McCartney)
April 29, 1970, May 7, 1970

You Are The Sunshine Of My Life - (Stevie Wonder)
July 3, 1974, September 27, 1974, January 16, 1975, April 24, 1975, June 19, 1975

You Go To My Head - (Fred Coots - Haven Gillespie)
July 26, 1953, September 15, 1953

You Make Me Feel So Young - (Josef Myrow - Mack Gordon)
June 8, 1955, June 9, 1957, June 14, 1958, June 1, 1962, June 20, 1965, September 7, 1966, November 26, 1968, April 29, 1970, March 18, 1971, April 17, 1973, January 25, 1974

You'll Never Walk Alone - (Richard Rodgers - Oscar Hammerstein II)
September 15, 1953

Young At Heart - (Carolyn Leigh - Johnny Richards)
December 2, 1961, November 26, 1968, May 15, 1969

You're Nobody 'Till Somebody Loves You - (Russ Morgan - Larry Stock - James Cavanaugh)
December 2, 1961, October 5, 1963, July 13, 1967, May 4, 1968

You Will Be My Music - (Joe Raposo)
January 25, 1974, March 9, 1974, April 18, 1974, July 3, 1974

Concert appearance - Bill Miller Conducting at Carnegie Hall.

ORCHESTRA, ARRANGERS, COMPOSERS, SOLOISTS, VOCALISTS AND VOCAL GROUP INDEX - CHAPTER XIII CONCERT APPEARANCES

Aquabella, Francisco - Bongo Soloist
March 20, 1957

Basie, Count - Orchestra Leader
June 20, 1965, July 4, 1965, July 9, 1965, May 8, 1970, June 6, 1974, September 8, 1975, November 12, 1975

Bernstein, Leonard - Conductor
January 19, 1961

Bonney, Nick - Guitarist
April 1, 1959

Brandwynne, Nat - Orchestra Leader
May 15, 1969

Bruno, Tony - Conductor, Orchestra Leader
March 18, 1971

Butera, Sam - Tenor Sax Soloist
March 13, 1976

Byers, Bill - Trombone Soloist
July 3, 1974

Cherico, Gene - Bassist
July 3, 1974, March 20, 1975, September 8, 1975, April 12, 1977, July 15, 1977

Costa, Don - Orchestra Conductor and Arranger
March 20, 1975, April 24, 1975

Cottler, Irv - Drummer
April 1, 1959, April 20, 1962, April 8, 1974, July 3, 1974, March 20, 1975, May 19, 1975, September 8, 1975

Davis, Sammy - Vocalist
August 25, 1962, October 19, 1967

Farnon, Brian - Orchestra Leader and Conductor
February 15, 1975

Fitzgerald, Ella - Vocalist
June 6, 1974, September 8, 1975

Henderson, Skitch - Pianist
September 13, 1963

Henry, Pat - Comedian, Vocalist
September 12, 1974

Herman, Woody - Orchestra Leader
September 10, 1974, October 13, 1974

Horne, Lena - Vocalist
October 5, 1963

James, Harry - Orchestra Leader
November 26, 1968, November 27, 1968

Jenkins, Gordon - Conductor, Arranger
January 25, 1974, March 9, 1974, March 28, 1974

Jones, Quincy - Arranger, Conductor
June 20, 1965

Kottler, Irv - Drummer
April 12, 1977, July 15, 1977

Klee, Henry - Reeds
April 20, 1962

Malone, Joe - Conductor
July 15, 1977

Markham, Johnny - Drummer
December 2, 1961

Martin, Dean - Vocalist
May 14, 1959, August 25, 1962

Miller, Bill - Pianist, Conductor
Featured throughout his concert career

Norvo, Red - Vibist (Soloist)
April 1, 1959

Pena, Ralph - Bassist
April 20, 1962

Porcino, Al (Porky) - Trumpet Soloist
December 2, 1961

Rich, Buddy - Drummer, Orchestra Leader
July 13, 1967

Richards, Emil - Vibist (Soloist)
April 20, 1962

Riddle, Nelson - Conductor, Arranger
June 13, 1971, April 17, 1973

Rizzo, Pat - Alto Sax Soloist
March 20, 1975

Rose, David - Conductor

June 13, 1971

Shank, Bud - Reeds
April 1, 1959, July 3, 1974

Shoemaker, Charles - Vibist (Soloist)
March 20, 1975

Sinatra, Frank, Jr. - Vocalist
September 12, 1974

Sinatra, Nancy - Vocalist
September 12, 1974

Stamm, Marvin - Trumpet Soloist
July 3, 1974

Tempo, Nino - Tenor Sax Soloist
March 20, 1975

Ternent, Billy - Orchestra Leader
July 26, 1953

Turner, Charlie - Trumpet Soloist
March 20, 1975, April 12, 1977, July 15, 1977

Vaughan, Sarah - Vocalist
November 13, 1975

Viola, Al - Guitar Soloist
April 20, 1962, April 8, 1974, July 3, 1974, March 20, 1975, May 19, 1975,
September 8, 1975, April 12, 1977, July 15, 1977

Weston, Paul - Orchestra Leader, Conductor
May 14, 1959

Chapter XIV
ALBUM INDEX

Harry James And His Great Vocalists   Harmony HL 7159
On A Little Street In Singapore
It's Funny To Everyone But Me

The One And Only Tommy Dorsey   Camden CAL-650
The Call Of The Canyon
Too Romantic
A Sinner Kissed An Angel
Be Careful, It's My Heart

Dedicated To You   Camden CAL-800
   With Tommy Dorsey
Snootie Little Cutie
I'd Know You Anywhere
Just As Though You Were Here
Do You Know Why?

Yes Indeed   R.C.A. LPM-1229
   With Tommy Dorsey
Stardust
I'll Never Smile Again

Tribute to Dorsey - Volume I   R.C.A. LPM-1432
   with Tommy Dorsey
Everything Happens To Me

Tribute To Dorsey - Volume II   R.C.A. LPM-1433
   With Tommy Dorsey
East Of The Sun
Street Of Dreams
Violets For Your Furs
Blue Skies
The One I Love (Belongs To Somebody Else)

Tommy Plays, Frankie Sings   R.C.A. LPM-1569
   With Tommy Dorsey
Side I
Oh Look At Me Now   F.S., C.H. & Pied Pipers
This Love Of Mine   Frank Sinatra
Davil May Care   Frank Sinatra
Anything   Frank Sinatra
I Guess I'll Have To Dream The Rest   F.S. & Pied Pipers
How Do You Do Without Me?   Frank Sinatra

Chairman Album

Harry James Album

Side II
How About You?	Frank Sinatra
There Are Such Things	F.S. & Pied Pipers
Our Love Affair	Frank Sinatra
I Could Make You Care	Frank Sinatra
Say It	Frank Sinatra
Polka Dots And Moonbeams	Frank Sinatra

We Three   R.C.A. LPM-1632
    Tommy Dorsey and Axel Stordahl
Side I
Dig Down Deep	T.D., F.S. & P.P.
The Lamplighters Serenade	F.S. & A.S.
Night And Day	F.S. & A.S.
The Night We Called It A Day	F.S. & A.S.
The Song Is You	F.S. & A.S.
Tell Me At Midnight	F.S. & T.D.

Side II
We Three	F.S. & T.D.
I'll Be Seeing You	F.S. & T.D.
It Started All Over Again	T.D., F.S. & P.P.
Fools Rush In	F.S. & T.D.
This Is The Beginning Of The End	F.S. & T.D.
Whispering	T.D., F.S. & P.P.

Having A Wonderful Time   R.C.A. LPM-1643
    With Tommy Dorsey
Head On My Pillow

Satisfying Rhythms   R.C.A. Premium PRM-182
    With Tommy Dorsey
There Are Such Things
Without A Song
Everything Happens To Me
This Is The Beginning Of The End

That Sentimental Gentleman   R.C.A. LPM-6003
    With Tommy Dorsey
My Melancholy Baby
Yearning
I'll Take Tallulah
Marie
How Am I To Know
The Song Is You

Tommy Dorsey, Featuring Frank Sinatra   Coronet CX-186
I'll Buy That Dream
I've Got A Restless Spell
Is There A Chance For Me

I'll Never Smile Again
Without A Song

This Is Tommy Dorsey   R.C.A. VPM-6038
Whispering
Stardust
I'll Never Smile Again
There Are Such Things
Street Of Dreams
Our Love Affair
I'll Be Seeing You
East Of The Sun
The Great Band Era   Reader's Digest RD-25K
  With Tommy Dorsey
Dolores
Fools Rush In
I'll Be Seeing You
Imagination
You And I

Tommy Dorsey And His Orchestra   Reader's Digest RD-76
Polka Dots And Moonbeams
Do I Worry
Let's Get Away From It All
Street Of Dreams

The Incomparable Tommy Dorsey   Reader's Digest RD 4-92
This Love Of MIne
Somewhere A Voice Is Calling
Yours Is My Heart Alone
I'll Never Smile Again
Head On My Pillow
Stardust
Snooty Little Cutie
Street Of Dreams
Dolores
Without A Song
There Are Such Things
The One I Love
East Of The Sun
Whispering
How About You?
I Guess I'll Have To Dream The Best

Ten Great Bands   R.C.A. LPM-6702
  With Tommy Dorsey
Let's Get Away From It All
In The Blue Of Evening
Shake Down The Stars

This Love Of Mine   R.C.A. LPV-583
  With Tommy Dorsey
Side I
The Sky Fell Down
Polka Dots And Moonbeams
Fools Rush In
Imagination
Yours Is My Heart Alone
I Could Make You Care
It's Always You
I Tried

Side II
Without A Song
Everything Happens To Me
This Love Of Mine
A Sinner Kissed An Angel
Violets For Your Furs
How About You
Be Careful, It's My Heart
In The Blue Of Evening

Tommy Dorsey/Sinatra Sessions   R.C.A. SD-1000

   This is a six (6) record Lp box set containing all the sides made by Sinatra
with The Tommy Dorsey Orchestra. It also contains a twelve page informative
booklet compiled by Alen Dell.

This Is Tommy Dorsey - Volume II   R.C.A. VPM-6040
The One I Love
This Love Of Mine
Blue Skies

The Big Band Sound Of Tommy Dorsey   Avenue International 1009
I'll Buy That Dream

Frank Sinatra   Harmony HS-11390
Side I
Autumn In New York
Among My Souvenirs
I Only Have Eyes For You
She's Funny That Way
Begin The Beguine

Side II
I'm Glad There Is You
Oh! What It Seemed To Be
Why Was I Born/
Where Or When

Someone To Watch Over Me   Harmony HS-11277
Side I
Someone To Watch Over Me
I Couldn't Sleep A Wink Last Night
I Have But One Heart
Stella By Starlight
The Nearness Of You

Side II
Put Your Dreams Away
All Of Me
The Girl That I Marry
I Love You

Sinatra Music Of Alec Wilder   Col. CL-884
  (No Vocal)
Theme And Variations
Air For Bassoon
Air For Flute
Air For English Horn
Slow Dance
Air For Oboe
      Reverse - Alec Wilder Octet
NOTE: Reissued on rechanneled stereo for Odyssy Records.

Dedicated To You   Columbia 10 inch CL-6096
Side I
The Music Stopped
The Moon Was Yellow
I Love You
Strange Music

Side II
Where Or When
None But The Lonely Heart
Always
Why Was I Born

Get Happy   Columbia 10 inch CL-2521
Side I
Five Minutes More
The Birth Of The Blues
That's How Much I Love You

Side II
The Huckle Buck
Bim Bam Baby
Let It Snow, Let It Snow, Let It Snow

Tommy Dorsey
Album

Columbia Album

Frankie   Columbia CL-606
Side I
Hello Young Lovers
I Only Have Eyes For You
Falling In Love With Love
You'll Never Know
It All Depends On You
Sposin'

Side II
All Of Me
Time After Time
How Cute Can You Be/
Almost Like Being In Love
Nancy
Oh! What It Seemed To Be

The Voice   Columbia CL-743
Side I
I Don't Know Why
Try A Little Tenderness
A Ghost Of A Chance
Paradise
These Foolish Things
Laura

Side II
She's Funny That Way
Fools Rush In
Over The Rainbow
That Old Black Magic
Spring Is Here
Lover

That Old Feeling   Columbia CL-902
Side I
That Old Feeling
Blue Skies
Autumn In New York
Don't Cry Joe
The Nearness Of You
That Lucky Old Sun

Side II
Full Moon And Empty Arms
Once In Love With Amy
A Fellow Needs A Girl
Poinciana
For Every Man There's A Women
Mean To Me

Ain'tcha Ever Comin' Back
Put Your Dreams Away

Love Is A Kick   Columbia CL-1241
Side I
You Do Something To Me
Bim Bam Baby
My Blue Heaven
When You're Smiling
Saturday Night
Bye, Bye Baby

Side II
The Continental
Deep Night
Should I
American Beauty Rose
Five Minutes More
Farewell, Farewell To Love

Reflections   Columbia CL-1448
Side I
Stella By Starlight
But Beautiful
Body And Soul
Where Or When
When Your Lover Has Gone
Strange Music

Side II
Goodnight Irene
Dear Little Boy Of Mine
Mighty Lak' A Rose
Cradle Song
Nature Boy
All The Things You Are

The Broadway Kick   Columbia CL-1297
Side I
There's No Business Like Show Business
THey Say It's Wonderful
Some Enchanted Evening
You're My Girl
Lost In The Stars
Why Can't You Behave?

Side II
I Whistle A Happy Tune
The Girl That I Marry
Can't You Just See Yourself
There But For You Go I

Adventures Of The Heart   Columbia CL-953
Side I
I Guess I'll Have To Dream The Rest
If Only She'd Look My Way
Love Me
Nevertheless
We Kiss In A Shadow
I Am Loved

Side II
Take My Love
I Could Write A Book
Mad About You
Stromboli
It's Only A Paper Moon
Sorry

Christmas Dreaming   Columbia CL-1032
Side I
White Christmas
Jingle Bells
O' Little Town Of Bethlehem
Have Yourself A Merry Little Christmas*
Christmas Dreaming*

Side II
Silent Night, Holy Night
It Came Upon A Midnight Clear
Adeste Fidelis
Santa Claus Is Comin' To Town
Let It Snow, Let It Snow, Let It Snow
NOTE: These are second takes and not the same as the single issued on
Columbia 37089.

Put Your Dreams Away   Columbia CL-1136
Side I
I Dream Of You
Dream
I Have But One Heart
The Girl That I Marry
The Things We Did Last Summer
Lost In The Stars

Side II
If I Forget You
Mam'selle
The Song Is You
It Never Entered My Mind

The Nearness Of You

Side II
Put Your Dreams Away
All Of Me
The Girl That I Marry
I Love You

Frank Sinatra   Harmony HS-11390
Side I
Among My Souvenirs
Autumn In New York
Begin The Beguine
I'm Glad There Is You

Side II
Oh What It Seemed To Be
I Only Have Eyes For You
She's Funny That Way
Where Or When
Why Was I Born

The Frank Sinatra Story In Music   Columbia C-2L6
Side I
Ciribiribin
All Or Nothing At All
You'll Never Know
If You Are But A Dream
Nancy
You Go To My Head

Side II
Stormy Weather
The House I Live In
If I Loved You
Soliloquy* - Part I and II
How Deep Is The Ocean
Ol' Man River

Side III
You'll Never Walk Alone
I Concentrate On You
Castle Rock
Why Was I Born?
I've Got A Crush On You
Begin The Beguine

Side IV
The Birth Of The Blues
April In Paris
I'm Glad There Is You

Side II
Saturday Night
Five Minutes More
The Coffee Song
Sunday, Monday Or Always
Put Your Dreams Away

The Early Years - Volume II   Columbia CL-2572, CS-9372
Side I
Mean To Me
I Have But One Heart
The Moon Was Yellow
Full Moon And Empty Arms
Time After Time
I'm A Fool To Want You

Side II
Day By Day
I Couldn't Sleep A Wink Last Night
Ol' Man River
People Will Say We're In Love
September Song

In The Beginning - 1943-1951   Columbia KG31358
Contents same as CL-2474, CS-9274, and CL-2572, CS-9372.

Metronome All Stars   Harmony HL-7044
Sweet Lorraine

Romantic Songs From The Early Years   Harmony HL-7405
                                                       HS-11205

Side I
Laura
Spring Is Here
Paradise
I Fall In Love Too Easily
Mam'selle

Side II
Over The Rainbow
If I Had You
The Music Stopped
Try A Little Tenderness
That Old Feeling

Someone To Watch Over Me   Harmony HS-11277
Side I
Someone To Watch Over Me
I Couldn't Sleep A Wink Last Night
I Have But One Heart
Stella By Starlight

Bali Hai
Where Is My Bess

Come Back To Sorrento   Columbia CL-1359
Side I
When The Sun Goes Down
None But The Lonely Heart
Luna Rosa
My Melancholy Baby
Embraceable You
Day By Day

Side II
Come Back To Sorrento
I Hear A Rhapsody
Someone To Watch Over Me
September Song
Among My Souvenirs
Always

Frank Sinatra In Hollywood   Columbia CL-2913
Side I
I Couldn't Sleep A Wink Last Night
The Music Stopped
A Lovely Way To Spend An Evening
I Begged Her
What Makes The Sunset
I Fall In Love Too Easily
The Charm Of You
The House I Live In

Side II
Time After Time
It's The Same Old Dream
The Brooklyn Bridge
I Believe
Ever Homeward
Senorita
If I Steal A Kiss
The Right Girl For Me

Frank Sinatra's Greatest Hits - The Early Years   Columbia CL-2472
                                                        CS-9274

Side I
I've Got A Crush On You
If You Are But A Dream
Nancy
The Girl That I Marry
The House I Live In
Dream

Laura
One For My Baby
Put Your Dreams Away
*Different Takes

The Essential Frank Sinatra   Columbia S3L-42, S3S-842
Side I
From The Bottom Of My Heart
Melancholy Mood
My Buddy
Here Comes The Night
Close To You
There's No You
The Charm Of You
When Your Lover Has Gone

Side II
I Should Care
A Friend Of Yours
My Shawl
Nancy
You Are Too Beautiful
Why Shouldn't I?
One Love
Something Old, Something New

RECORD II

Side I
Blue Skies
Guess I'll Hang My Tears Out To Dry
Why Shouldn't It Happen To Us
It's The Same Old Dream
You Can Take My Word For It Baby
Sweet Lorraine
My Romance
One For My Baby

Side II
It All Came True
Poinciana
Body And Soul
I Went Down To Virginia
If I Only Had A Match
Everybody Loves Somebody
Comme Ci, Comme Ca
If You Stub Your Toe On The Moon

RECORD III

Side I
The Right Girl For Me

Capitol Album

Christmas Album

The Huckle Buck
If I Ever Love Again
Why Remind Me
Sunshine Cake
(We've Got) A Sure Thing
It's Only A Paper Moon
My Blue Heaven

Side II
Nevertheless
You're The One
Love Me
I'm A Fool To Want You
Birth Of The Blues
Walkin' In The Sunshine
Azure-Te
Why Try To Change Me Now

This 3 record set includes a 12 page booklet, including discography of tunes and rare pictures. Produced by Frank Driggs with notes by George T. Simon. A few comments about this set: although it is an excellent collection with over 30 sections which have never appeared before on L.P., we feel that all 48 tunes should have fallen into this category. Secondly, the title itself defeats this purpose, for now, tunes such as 'Nancy', 'Blue Skies', etc., etc., which have been repeated on other L.P.'s have to be included. This necessitates the exclusion of many rare Sinatra sides, aside from their merits, that never seem to appear on reissues.

In The Wee Small Hours   Capitol W-581; DT-58
Side I
In The Wee Small Hours Of The Morning
Mood Indigo
Glad To Be Unhappy
I Get Along Without You Very Well
Deep In A Dream
I See Your Face Before Me
Can't We Be Friends*
When Your Lover Has Gone

Side II
What Is This Thing Called Love
Last Night When We Were Young
I'll Be Around
Ill Wind*
It Never Entered My Mind*
Dancing On The Ceiling
I'll Never Be The Same
This Love Of Mine
*Omitted in later versions of this album.

Swing Easy   Capitol W-587*

Side I
The Girl Next Door
They Can't Take That Away From Me
Violets For Your Furs
Little Girl Blue
Like Someone In Love
A Foggy Day
I Get A Kick Out Of You
My Funny Valentine

Side II
Jeepers Creepers
Wrap Your Troubles In Dreams
Taking A Chance On Love
I'm Gonna Sit Right Down And Write Myself A Letter
Get Happy
All Of Me
Sunday
Just One Of Those Things

*This is the original twelve inch LP issue bearing the title 'Swing Easy'.

Songs For Swingin' Lovers
Side I
You Make Me Feel So Young
It Happened In Monterey
You're Getting To Be A Habit With Me
Too Marvelous For Words
Old Devil Moon
Pennies From Heaven*
Love Is Here To Stay*

Side II
I've Got You Under My Skin
I Thought About You
We'll Be Together Again
Makin' Whoopee*
Swingin' Down The Lane
Anything Goes
How About You?
You Brought A New Kind Of Love To Me

*Omitted in later versions of this album.

Tone Poems Of Color (No Vocal)   Capitol W-735
Frank Sinatra Conducts
Side I
White
Green

Purple
Yellow
Gray
Gold

Side II
Orange
Black
Silver
Blue
Brown
Red

High Society Film Sound Track   Capitol W-750;SW-750

Side I
High Society (Overture)
High Society Calypso
Little One
Who Wants To Be A Millionaire
True Love

Side II
You're Sensational
I Love You Samantha
Now You Has Jazz
Well Did You Evah
Mind If I Make Love To You

This Is Sinatra - Volume I   Capitol T-768; D-768

Side I
I've Got The World On A String
Three Coins In The Fountain
Love And Marriage
From Here To Eternity
South Of The Border
Rain (Falling From The Skies)

Side II
The Gal That Got Away
Young At Heart
Learnin' The Blues
My One And Only Love
(Love Is) The Tender Trap
Don't Worry 'Bout Me

Close To You   Capitol W-789;DW-789

Side I
Close To You
P.S. I Love You

Love Locked Out
Everything Happens To Me
It's Easy To Remember
Don't Like Goodbyes

Side II
With Every Breath I Take
Blame It On My Youth
It Could Happen To You
I've Had My Moments
I Couldn't Sleep a Wink Last Night
The End Of A Love Affair

A Swingin' Affair   Capitol W-803;DT-803
Side I
Night And Day
I Wish I Were In Love Again
No One Ever Tells You
I Got Plenty Of Nothin'
I Guess I'll Have To Change My Plans
Nice Work If You Can Get It
Stars Fell On Alabama
I Won't Dance

Side II
The Lonesome Road
At Long Last Love
You'd Be So Nice To Go Home To
I Got It Bad And That Ain't Good
From This Moment On
If I Had You
Oh! Look At Me Now

Where Are You?   Capitol W-855;SW-855

Side I
Where Are You?
The Night We Called It A Day
I Cover The Water Front
Maybe You'll Be There
Laura
Lonely Town

Side II
Autumn Leaves
I'm A Fool To Want You
I Think Of You
Where Is The One?
There's No You

A Jolly Christmas   Capitol W-894;DT-894

Side I
Jingle Bells
The Christmas Song
Mistletoe And Holly
I'll Be Home For Christmas
The Christmas Waltz
Have Yourself A Merry Little Christmas

Side II
The First Noel
Hark! The Herald Angels Sing
O'Little Town Of Bethlehem
Adeste Fidelis
It Came Upon A Midnight Clear
Silent Night

Pal Joey Sound Track   Capitol W-912;DT-912
Side I
Main Title
That Terrible Rainbow
I Didn't Know What Time It Was
Do It The Hard Way
Great Big Town
There's A Small Hotel
Zip
I Could Write A Book
Bewitched

Side II
The Lady Is A Tramp
Plant You Now, Dig You Later
My Funny Valentine
You Musn't Kid Around
Bewitched
Strip Number
Dream Sequence and Finale
   What Do I Care For A Dame
   Bewitched
   I Could Write A Book

Come Fly With Me   Capitol W-920;ST-920
Side I
Come Fly With Me
Around The World
Isle Of Capri
Moonlight In Vermont
Autumn In New York
On The Road To Mandalay

Side II
Let's Get Away From It All
April In Paris
London By Night
Brazil
Blue Hawaii
It's Nice To Go Traveling

This Is Sinatra - Volume II   Capitol W-982;DT-982
Side I
Hey Jealous Lover
You're Cheatin' Yourself
Everybody Loves Somebody
Something Wonderful Happens In Summer
Half As Lovely Twice As True
How Little We Know
Johnny Concho Theme (Wait For Me)*
You Forgot All The Words

Side II
Time After Time
I Believe
Crazy Love
It's The Same Old Dream
If You Are But A Dream
So Long My Love*
You'll Always Be The One I Love*
*Omitted in later versions of this album.

Only The Lonely   Capitol W-1053;ST-1053
Side I
Only The Lonely
Angel Eyes
What's New
It's A Lonesome Old Town
Willow Weep For Me
Goodbye

Side II
Blues In The Night
Guess I'll Hang My Tears Out To Dry
Ebb Tide
Spring Is Here
Gone With The Wind
One For My Baby

Come Dance With Me   Capitol W-1069;ST-1069
Side I
Come Dance With Me
Somethings Gotta Give

Just In Time
Dancing In The Dark
Too Close For Comfort
I Could Have Danced All Night

Side II
Saturday Night
Day In, Day Out
Cheek To Cheek
Baubles, Bangles And Beads
The Song Is You
The Last Dance

Look To Your Heart
Side I
Look To Your Heart
Anytime, Anywhere
Not As A Stranger
Our Town
You, My Love
Same Old Saturday Night

Capitol W-1164;DT-1164

Side II
Fairy Tale
The Impatient Years
I Could Have Told You
When I Stop Loving You
If I Had Three Wishes
I'm Gonna Live Till I Die

No One Cares
Side I
When No One Cares
Cottage For Sale
Where Do You Go
I Don't Stand A Ghost Of A Chance
Here's That Rainy Day
Stormy Weather

Capitol W-1221;ST1221

Side II
I Can't Get Started
Why Try To Change Me Now
Just Friends
I'll Never Smile Again
None But The Lonely Heart

Can Can Sound Track
Side I
Ent'acte
It's All Right With Me
Come Along With Me

Capitol W-1301;SW-1301

Live And Let Live
You Do Something To Me
Let's Do It

Side II
Main Title
I Love Paris
Montmart
C'est Magnifique
Just One Of Those Things
I Love Paris
Can-Can

Nice N' Easy   Capitol W-1417;SW-1417
Side I
Nice N' Easy
That Old Feeling
How Deep Is The Ocean
I've Got A Crush On You
You Go To My Head
Fools Rush In

Side II
Nevertheless
She's Funny That Way
Try A Little Tenderness
Embraceable You
Mam'selle
Dream

Swing Easy   Capitol W-1429;DT-1429
Side I
Jeepers Creepers
Taking A Chance On Love
Wrap Your Troubles In Dreams
Lean Baby
I Love You
I'm Gonna Sit Right Down And Write Myself A Letter

Side II
Get Happy
All Of Me
How Could You Do A Thing Like That To Me
Why Should I Cry Over You
Sunday
Just One Of Those Things

*This is the second 12 inch LP release bearing the title "Swing Easy".

Songs For Young Lovers   Capitol W-1432; DT-1432

Side I
The Girl Next Door
They Can't Take That Away From Me
Violets For Your Furs
Someone To Watch Over Me
My One and Only Love
Little Girl Blue

Side II
Like Someone In Love
A Foggy Day
It Worries Me
I Can Read Between The Lines
I Get A Kick Out Of You
My Funny Valentine

Swingin' Session   Capitol W-1491;ST-1491
Side I
When You're Smiling
Blue Moon
Sposin'
It All Depends On You
It's Only A Paper Moon
My Blue Heaven

Side II
Should I
September In The Rain
Always
I Can't Believe That You're In Love With Me
I Concentrate On You
You Do Something To Me

All The Way   Capitol W-1538;SW-1538
Side I
All The Way
High Hopes
Talk To Me
French Foreign Legion
To Love And Be Loved
River Stay Away From My Door

Side II
Witchcraft
It's Over, It's Over, It's Over
Ol' MacDonald
This Was My Love
All My Tomorrows
Sleep Warm

Come Swing With Me   Capitol W-1594;ST-1594

Side I
Day By Day
Sentimental Journey
Almost Like Being In Love
Five Minutes More
American Beauty Rose
Yes Indeed

Side II
On The Sunny Side Of The Street
Don't Take Your Love From Me
That Old Black Magic
Lover
Paper Doll
I've Heard That Song Before

Point Of No Return   Capitol W-1676;ST-1676

Side I
When The World Was Young
I'll Remember April
September Song
A Million Dreams Ago
I'll See You Again
There Will Never Be Another You

Side II
Somewhere Along The Way
It's A Blue World
These Foolish Things
As Time Goes By
I'll Be Seeing You
Memories Of You

The Great Years   Three Record Capitol Set -
                                          WCO-1726;STCO-1726

Record One
Side I
Lean Baby
I've Got The World On A String
South Of The Border
From Here To Eternity
Violets For Your Future
Young At Heart

Side II
Three Coins In The Fountain
All Of Me
The Gal That Got Away
Baby Won't You Please Come Home

Witchcraft
When Your Lover Has Gone

Record Two
Side I
In The Wee Small Hours
Learnin' The Blues
Love And Marriage
The Tender Trap
Hey Jealous Lover
No One Ever Tells You

Side II
All The Way
Autumn Leaves
High Hopes
Come Fly With Me
Put Your Dreams Away
Only The Lonely

Record Three
Side I
One For My Baby
Come Dance With Me
The Last Dance
I'll Never Smile Again
Talk To Me

Side II
The Nearness Of You
Dream
How Deep Is The Ocean
Nice N' Easy
Ol' MacDonald
It's Over, It's Over, It's Over

Sinatra Sings Of Love And Things   Capitol W-1729;ST-1729
Side I
The Nearness Of You
Hidden Persuasion
The Moon Was Yellow
I Love Paris
Monique (Songs From £Kings Go Forth£)
Chicago

Side II
Love Looks So Well On You
Sentimental Baby
Mr. Success
They Came To Cordura

I Gotta Right To Sing The Blues
Something Wonderful Happens In Summer

Sinatra Sings Rogers And Hart   Capitol W-1825;DT-1825
Side I
Little Girl Blue
My Funny Valentine
Wait Till You See Her
Spring Is Here
Dancing On The Ceiling
The Lady Is A Tramp

Side II
I Wish I Were In Love Again
Lover
It's Easy To Remember
It Never Entered My Mind
Glad To Be Unhappy
Blue Moon

Tell Her You Love Her   Capitol T-1919;DT-1919
Side I
Tell Her You Love Her
Love Is Here To Stay
I've Got It Bad And That Ain't Good
Pennies From Heaven
I Guess I'll Have To Change My Plans
Night And Day

Side II
Makin' Whoopee
Weep They Will
Ill Wind
It Never Entered My Mind
Can't We Be Friends
When Your Lover Has Gone

Sinatra Sings The Select Johnny Mercer   Capitol W-1894;
DT-1984

Side I
Somethings Gotta Give
Day In, Day Out
Jeepers, Creepers
Fools Rush In
P.S. I Love You
When The World Was Young

Side II
Blues In The Night
Too Marvelous For Words
Laura

I Thought About You
Dream
Autumn Leaves

The Great Hits Of Frank Sinatra   Capitol T-2036;DT-2036
Side I
South Of The Border
Young At Heart
Love And Marriage
Learnin' The Blues
Three Coins In The Fountain

Side II
Hey Jealous Lover
Witchcraft
All The Way
Come Dance With Me
Only The Lonely
Nice N' Easy

Sinatra Sings The Select Harold Arlen   Capitol W-2123
Side I
I've Got The World On A String
Don't Like Goodbyes
The Gal That Got Away
Ill Wind
One For My Baby
It's Only A Paper Moon

Side II
Blues In The Night
That Old Black Magic
Last Night When We Were Young
Get Happy
Stormy Weather
I've Got A Right To Sing The Blues

Sinatra Sings The Select Cole Porter   Capitol W-2301;DT-2301
Side I
I've Got You Under My Skin
I Concentrate On You
What Is This Thing Called Love
You Do Something To Me
At Long Last Love
Anything Goes

Side II
Night And Day
Just One Of Those Things
I Get A Kick Out Of You

You'd Be So Nice To Come Home To
I Love Paris
From This Moment On

Forever Frank   Capitol T-2602
Side I
Can I Steal A Little Love
Your Love For Me
Chicago
Melody Of Love
Two Hearts, Two Kisses
Flowers Mean Forgiveness

Side II
Same Old Song And Dance
If It's The Last Thing I Do
From The Bottom To The Top
Don't Make A Beggar Of Me
You'll Get Yours

The Movie Songs   Capitol T-2700; ST-2700
Side I
Young At Heart
The Tender Trap
To Love And Be Loved
C'est Magnifique
They Came To Cordura
All My Tomorrows

Side II
All The Way
Monique
High Hopes
It's All Right With Me
Three Coins In The Fountain

The Sinatra Touch   Capitol DNFR-7630

    Record One
Side I
Lean Baby
Hey Jealous Lover
From Here To Eternity
Melody Of Love
Wrap Your Troubles In Dreams

Side II
Young At Heart
Learnin' The Blues
The Tender Trap

Close To You
How About You

Record Two
Side I
All The Way
If I Had You
Three Coins In The Fountain
Swingin' Down The Lane
It Happened In Monterey

Side II
Witchcraft
Love And Marriage
How Little We Know
The Girl Next Door
Taking A Chance On Love

Record Three
Side I
The Impatient Years
I Love You
Sunday
Your Love For Me
The Gal That Got Away

Side II
South Of The Border
Tell Her You Love Her
I'll Never Be The Same
This Love Of Mine
I Got It Bad And That Ain't Good

Record Four
Side I
Day By Day
I'm A Fool To Want You
London By Night
To Love And Be Loved
River Stay Away From My Door

Side II
On The Sunny Side Of The Street
My Blue Heaven
Spring Is Here
Just Friends
I've Heard That Song Before

Record Five
Side I
Mr. Success

Talk To Me
High Hopes
It's Over, It's Over, It's Over
Come Dance With Me

Side II
Only The Lonely
Autumn Leaves
Nice N' Easy
Memories Of You
Ebb Tide

    Record Six
Side I
That Old Feeling
All My Tomorrows
Laura
There Will Never Be Another You
Mam'selle

Side II
Come Fly With Me
Try A Little Tenderness
Where Are You
One For My Baby
Put Your Dreams Away

The Nearness Of You   Pickwick PC-3450;SPC-3450
Side I
The Nearness Of You
You Brought A New Kind Of Love To Me
It Could Happen To You
That Old Black Magic
Blue Hawaii

Side II
Lover
Laura
Just In Time
I Get Along Without You Very Well
No One Ever Tells You

Try A Little Tenderness   Pickwick SPC-3452
Side I
My Blue Heaven
Try A Little Tenderness
Stars Fell On Alabama
Moonlight In Vermont
I Can't Get Started

Side II
Paper Doll
September Song
It Never Entered My Mind
Ebb Tide
I Can Read Between The Lines

Look Over Your Shoulder   English Capitol TP-81
Side I
 Not As A Stranger
I'm Walking Behind You
My Lean Baby
Melody Of Love
White Christmas
I'm Gonna Live Till I Die

Side II
How Could You Do A Thing Like That To Me
Don't Change Your Mind About Me
Why Should I Cry Over You?
I Love You
Don't Worry 'Bout Me

Sings Music For Pleasure   English Capitol MFP-1120
Side I
Same Old Saturday Night
Look To Your Heart
From The Bottom To The Top
It Worries Me
Two Hearts, Two Kisses
If I Had Three Wishes

Side II
Take A Chance
I Could Have Told You
Fairy Tale
You'll Get Yours
Flowers Mean Forgiveness
There's No You

This Love Of Mine   Capitol SPC-3458
Side I
This Love Of Mine
From Here To Eternity
I've Got The World On A String
The Girl Next Door
Don't Worry 'Bout Me

Side II
My One And Only Love
I'm A Fool To Want You

Tell Her You Love Her
Your Love For Me

Ring-A-Ding-Ding　　　　　　　　　　　　　Reprise F-1001;9-1001
Side I
Ring-A-Ding-Ding
Let's Fall In Love
Be Careful, It's My Heart
A Foggy Day
A Fine Romance
In The Still Of The Night

Side II
The Coffee Song
When I Take My Sugar To Tea
Let's Face The Music And Dance
You'd Be So Easy To Love
You And The Night And The Music
I've Got My Love To Keep Me Warm

Sinatra Swings　　　　　　　　　　　　　Reprise F-1002,9-1002
Side I
Falling In Love With Love
The Curse Of An Aching Heart
Don't Cry Joe
Please Don't Talk About Me When I'm Gone
Love Walked In
Granada

Side II
I Never Knew
Don't Be That Way
Moonlight On The Ganges
It's A Wonderful World
Have You Met Miss Jones?
You're Nobody Till Somebody Loves You

I Remember Tommy　　　　　　　　　　　　Reprise F-1003, 9-1003
Side I
I'm Getting Sentimental Over You
Imagination
There Are Such Things
East Of The Sun
Daybreak
Without A Song

Side II
I'll Be Seeing You
Take Me
It's Always You

Polka Dots And Moon Beams
It Started All Over Again
The One I Love

Sinatra And Strings   Reprise F-1004, 9-1004
Side I
I Hadn't Anyone Till You
Night And Day
Misty
Stardust
Come Rain Or Come Shine

Side II
It Might·As Well Be Spring
Prisoner Of Love
That's All
All Or Nothing At All
Yesterdays

Sinatra And Swingin' Brass   Reprise F-1005, 9-1005
Side I
Goody, Goody
They Can't Take That Away From Me
At Long Last Love
I'm Beginning To See The Light
Don'tcha Go Away Mad
I Get A Kick Out Of You

Side II
Tangerine
Love Is Just Around The Corner
Ain't She Sweet
Serenade In Blue
I Love You
Pick Yourself Up

Great Songs From Great Britian   British Reprise F-1006
Side I
If I Had You
The Very Thought Of You
I'll Follow My Secret Heart
A Garden In The Rain
London By Night

Side II
Gypsy
A Nightingale Sang In Berkley Square
We'll Meet Again
Now Is The Hour
We'll Gather Lilacs

All Alone

Reprise F-1007, 9-1007

Side I
All Alone
The Girl Next Door
Are You Lonesome Tonight
Charmaine
When I Lost You
What'll I Do

Side II
Oh How I Miss You Tonight
Indiscreet
Remember
Together
The Song Is Ended

Sinatra And Basie

Reprise F-1008, 9-1008

Side I
Pennies From Heaven
Please Be Kind
Love Is The Tender Trap
Looking At The World Through Rose Colored Glasses
My Kind Of Girl

Side II
I Only Have Eyes For You
Nice Work If You Can Get It
Learnin' The Blues
I'm Gonna Sit Right Down And Write Myself A Letter
I Won't Dance

The Concert Sinatra

Reprise F-1009, 9-1009

Side I
I Have Dreamed
My Heart Stood Still
Lost In The Stars
Ol' Man River

Side II
Soliloquy
This Nearly Was Mine
Bewitched
You'll Never Walk Alone

Sinatra's Sinatra

Reprise F-1010, 9-1010

Side I
I've Got You Under My Skin
In The Wee Small Hours
The Second Time Around
Nancy
Witchcraft

Young At Heart

Side II
All The Way
How Little We Know
Pocketful Of Miracles
Oh What It Seemed To Be
Call Me Irresponsible
Put Your Dreams Away

Days Of Wine And Roses   Reprise F-1011,S-1011
Side I
Days Of Wine And Roses
Moon River
The Way You Look Tonight
Three Coins In The Fountain
In The Cool, Cool, Cool Of The Evening
Secret Love

Side II
Swingin' On A Star
It Might As Well Be Spring
The Continental
Love Is A Many Splendored Thing
All The Way

It Might As Well Be Swing   Reprise F-1012, S-1012
Side I
Fly Me To The Moon
I Wish You Love
I Believe In You
More
I Can't Stop Loving You

Side II
Hello Dolly
I Wanna Be Around
The Best Is Yet To Come
The Good Life
Wives And Lovers

Softly (As I Leave You)   Reprise F-1013, S-1013
Side I
Emily
Here's To The Losers
Dear Heart
Come Blow Your Horn
Love Isn't Just For The Young
I Can't Believe I'm Losing You

Side II
Pass Me By
And Suddenly Love
Talk To Me Baby
Available
The Look Of Love
Softly As I Leave You

The September Of My Years
Reprise F-1014, S-1014
Side I
The September Of My Years
How Old Am I
Don't Wait Too Long
It Gets Lonely Early
This Is All I Ask
Last Night When We Were Young
The Man In The Looking Glass

Side II
It Was A Very Good Year
When The Wind Was Green
Hello Young Lovers
I See It Now
Once Upon A Time
September Song

My Kind Of Broadway
Reprise F-1015, S-1015
Side I
Everybody Has The Right To Be Wrong
Golden Moment
Luck Be A Lady
Lost In The Stars
Hello Dolly

Side II
I'll Only Miss Her When I Think Of Her
They Can't Take That Away From Me
Yesterdays
Nice Work If You Can Get It
Have You Met Miss Jones?
Without A Song

A Man And His Music
Reprise 2F-1016, 2S-1016
Side I
Put Your Dreams Away
All Or Nothing At All
I'll Never Smile Again
There Are Such Things
I'll Be Seeing You

The One I Love
Polka Dots And Moonbeams

Side II
Night And Day
Oh What It Seemed To Be
Soliloquy
Nancy
The House I Live In
From Here To Eternity (Extract From Film)

Side III
Come Fly With Me
How Little We Know
Learnin' The Blues
In The Wee Small Hours
Young At Heart
Witchcraft
All The Way
Love And Marriage
I've Got You Under My Skin

Side IV
Ring-A-Ding-Ding-
The Second Time Around
The Summit (Comedy Routine--Sinatra, Dean Martin, and
        Sammy Davis, Jr.)
The Oldest Established
Luck Be A Lady
Call Me Irresponsible
Fly Me To The Moon
Softly As I Leave You
My Kind Of Town
The September Of My Years

Strangers In The Night   Reprise F-1017, S-1017
Side I
Strangers In The Night
Summer Wind
All Or Nothing At All
Call Me
You're Driving Me Crazy

Side II
On A Clear Day
My Baby Just Cares For Me
Downtown
Yes Sir, That's My Baby
The Most Beautiful Girl In The World

Moonlight Sinatra　　　　　　　　　　Reprise F-1018, S-1018

Side I
Moonlight Becomes You
Moon Song
Moonlight Serenade
Reaching For The Moon
I Wished On The Moon

Side II
Oh You Crazy Moon
The Moon Got In My Eyes
Moonlight Mood
Moon Love
The Moon Was Yellow

Sinatra At The Sands　　　　　　　　Reprise 2F-1019, 2S-1019

Side I
Come Fly With Me
I've Got A Crush On You
I've Got You Under My Skin
The Shadow Of Your Smile
One For My Baby

Side II
Fly Me To The Moon
One O'Clock Jump (Basie Instrumental)
'The Tea Break' (Monologue)
You Make Me Feel So Young

Side III
All Of Me (Basie Instrumental)
September Of My Years
Get Me To The Church On Time
It Was A Very Good Year
Don't Worry 'Bout Me
Making Whoopee (Basie Instrumental)

Side IV
Where Or When
Angel Eyes
My Kind Of Town
'A Few Last Words' (Closing Monologue)
My Kind Of Town (Reprise)

That's Life　　　　　　　　　　　　Reprise F-1020, R9-1020

Side I
That's Life
I Will Wait For You
Somewhere My Love
Sand And Sea
What Now My Love

Side II
Winchester Cathedral
Give Her Love
Tell Her (You Love Her Each Day)
The Impossible Dream
You're Gonna Hear From Me

Francis Albert Sinatra
Antonio Carlos Jobim
Side I
Girl From Ipanema
Dindi
Change Partners
Quiet Nights (Corcovado)
Meditation

Side II
If You Never Come To Me
How Insensitive
I Concentrate On You
Baubles, Bangles and Beads
Once I Loved

The World We Knew
Side I
The World We Knew
Something Stupid
This Is My Love
Born Free
Don't Sleep In The Subway

Side II
This Town
This Is My Song
You Are There
Drinking Again
Some Enchanted Evening
Reprise F-1023 was never released or even finished. It was
supposedly a Christmas album.

Francis A., Edward K.
Side I
Follow Me
Sunny
All I Need Is The Girl
Indian Summer

Side II
I Like The Sunrise
Yellow Days
Poor Butterfly

Reprise F-1021
S-1021

Reprise F-1022, S-1022

Reprise FS-1024

Come Back To Me

Frank Sinatra's Greatest Hits   Reprise FS-1025
Side I
Strangers In The Night
Summer Wind
It Was A Very Good Year
Somewhere In Your Heart
Forget Domani
Something Stupid

Side II
That's Life
Tell Her (You Love Her Each Day)
The World We Knew
When Somebody Loves You
This Town
Softly As I Leave You

The Sinatra Family Wish You   Reprise FS-1026
A Merry Christmas
Side I
I Wouldn't Trade Christmas
It's Such A Lovely Time Of The Year
Some Children See Him
O Bambino
The Bells Of Christmas (Greensleaves)

Side II
Whatever Happened To Christmas
Santa Claus Is Comin' To Town
Kids
The Christmas Waltz
The 12 Days Of Christmas

Cycles   Reprise FS-1027
Side I
Rain In My Heart
From Both Sides Now
Little Green Apples
Pretty Colors
Cycles

Side II
Wandering
By The Time I Get To Phoenix
Moody River
My Way Of Life*
Gentle On My Mind
*Substituted for 'Wait By The Fire.'

Sinatra - Jobim   Reprise FSD-1028*
Side I
Sabia
Drinking Water
Someone To Light Up My Life
Triste
This Happy Madness

Side II
One Note Samba
Don't Ever Go Away
Wave
Off Key
Bonita
*Album never released.

My Way   Reprise FS-1029
Side I
Watch What Happens
Didn't We
Hallelujah, I Love Her So
Yesterday
All My Tomorrows

Side II
My Way
A Day In The Life Of A Fool
For Once In my Life
If You Go Away
Mrs. Robinson

A Man Alone   Reprise FS-1030
Side I
A Man Alone
Night
I've Been To Town
From Promise To Promise
The Single Man
The Beautiful Strangers
Lonesome Cities

Side II
Love's Been Good To Me
Empty Is
Out Beyond The Window
Some Traveling Music
A Man Alone (Reprise)

Watertown

Reprise FS-1031

Side I
Watertown
Goodbye (She Quietly Says)
For A While
Michael And Peter
I Would Be In Love (Anyway)

Side II
Elizabeth
What A Funny Girl (You Used To Be)
What's Now Is Now
She Says
The Train

Frank Sinatra's Greatest Hits - Volume II

Reprise RS-1032

Side I
The Shadow Of Your Smile
Yesterday
Blue Lace
For Once In My Life
Born Free
My Way

Side II
Little Green Apples
Both Sides Now
Mrs. Robinson
Call Me Irresponsible
Gentle On My Mind
Love's Been Good To Me

Sinatra And Company

Reprise FS-1033

Side I
Drinking Water
Someone To Light Up My Life
Triste
Don't Ever Go Away
This Happy Madness
Wave
One Note Samba

Side II
I Will Drink The Wine
Close To You
Sunrise In The Morning
Bein' Green
My Sweet Lady
Leaving On A Jet Plane
Lady Day

Sinatra's Greatest Hits - Volume III   Reprise FS'1034
Side I
My Way
A Man Alone
Cycles
Bein' Green
Love's Been Good To Me
I'm Not Afraid

Side II
Goin' Out Of My Head
Something
What's Now Is Now
Star
The September Of My Years

Frank Sinatra Conducts Music   Reprise R-6045
From Pictures And Plays (No Vocal)   9-6045
Side I
All The Way
Affair To Remember
Laura
Tammy
Moon River
Exodus

Side II
Little Girl Blue
Maria
Something Wonderful
I've Grown Accustomed To Her Face
The Girl That I Marry
If Ever I Would Leave You

Robin And The Seven Hoods (Sound Track)   Reprise F-2021,
                                                                  S-2021

Side I
Overture
My Kind Of Town
All For One And One For All
Don't Be A Do Badder
Any Man Who Loves His Mother
Style

Side II
Mister Booze
I Like To Lead When I Dance
Bang, Bang
Charlotte Couldn't Charleston
Give Praise, Give Praise, Give Praise

Don't Be A Do Badder (Finale)

Finian's Rainbow   Reprise F-2015, S-2015
Side I
Overture
This Time Of Year
How Are Things In Glocca Morra?
If This Isn't Love
Look To The Rainbow
Something Sort Of Grandish
Old Devil Moon

Side II
Necessity
When I'm Not Near The Girl That I Love
When The Idle Poor Become The Idle Rich
The Begat
How Are Things In Glocca Morra?
The Great Come And Get It Day

Guys And Dolls   Reprise F-2016, S-2016
Side I
Overture
Fugue For Tin Horns
I'll Know
The Oldest Established
A Bushel And A Peck
Guys And Dolls
If I Were A Bell
I've Never Been In Love Before

Side II
Take Back Your Mink
More I Cannot Wish You
Adalaide's Lament
Luck Be A Lady
Sit Down You're Rocking The Boat
Guys And Dolls (Reprise)

Kiss Me Kate   Reprise F-2017, S-2017
Side I
Overture
Another Opening, Another Show
Why Can't You Behave
We Open In Venice
So In Love
I Hate Men
Too Darn Hot

Side II
Were Thine That Special Face

Where Is The Life That Late I've Led
Wunderbar
Always True To You (In My Fashion)
Bianca
So In Love (Reprise)

South Pacific
Side I
Overture
Dite Moi
A Cockeyed Optimist
Twin Soliloquies
Some Enchanted Evening
A Wonderful Guy
Younger Than Springtime
Bali Hai

Reprise F-2018, S-2018

Side II
There Is Nothing Like A Dame
I'm Gonna Wash That Man
Bloody Mary
Happy Talk
Younger Than Springtime
This Nearly Was Mine
Honeybun
Carefully Taught
Some Enchanted Evening (Reprise)

America I Hear You Singing
Side I
America I Hear You Singing
This Is A Great Country
The House I Live In
Hills Of Home
This Land Is Your Land
Give Me Your Tired, Your Poor

Reprise F-2020, S-2020

Side II
A Lucky Fellow, Mr. Smith
A Home In The Meadow
Early American
You Never Had It So Good
Let Us Break Bread Together
Stars And Stripes Forever

Twelve Songs Of Christmas
Side I
White Christmas
It's Christmas Time Again
Go Tell It On The Mountain

Reprise F-2022, S-2022

An Old Fashioned Christmas
When Angels Sang Of Peace
The Little Drummer Boy

Side II
I Heard The Bells On Christmas Day
Do You Hear What I Hear
The Secret Of Christmas
Christmas Candles
We Wish You The Merriest
The Twelve Days Of Christmas

Sinatra '65 Reprise R-6167, S-6167
Side I
Somewhere In Your Heart
I've Never Been In Love Before
Anytime At All
Main Theme From The Cardinal 'Stay With Me'
When Somebody Loves You
My Kind Of Town

Side II
Tell Her (You Love Her Each Day)
When I'm Near The Girl That I Love
You Brought A New Kind Of Love To Me
I Like To Lead When I Dance
Luck Be A Lady

The Sammy Davis Show Reprise R-6188, S-6188
We Open In Venice

Movin' With Nancy Reprise RS-6277
Younger Than Springtime

Schlagers Warners-Reprise PRO-359
This is a special collection of Warner-Reprise headliners which includes one
selection by Frank Sinatra.
Song Of The Sabia

Ol' Blue Eyes Is Back Reprise FS-2155
Side I
You Will Be My Music
You're So Right
Winners
Nobody Wins
Send In The Clowns

Side II
Dream Away
Let Me Try Again
There Used To Be A Ball Park

Noah

Some Nice Things I Missed   Reprise FS-2195
Side I
You Turned My World Around
Sweet Caroline
The Summer Knows
I'm Gonna Make It All The Way
Tie A Yellow Ribbon 'Round The Old Oak Tree

Side II
Satisfy Me One More Time
If
You Are The Sunshine Of My Life
What Are You Doing The Rest Of Your Life
Bad, Bad Leroy Brown

The Main Event - Live   Reprise FS-2207
Side I
Tribute - Howard Cossell
Overture - Orchestra
The Lady Is A Tramp
I Get A Kick Out Of You
Let Me Try Again
Autumn In New York
I've Got You Under My Skin

Side II
Bad, Bad Leroy Brown
Angel Eyes
You Are The Sunshine Of My Life
The House I Live In
My Kind Of Town
My Way

The Sinatra Collection   English Reprise K44145
Check Reprise section for contents.

The Voice - Volume I   Italian Reprise FS-5238

The Voice - Volume II   Italian Reprise FS-5240

The Voice - Volume III   Italian Reprise FS-5250
Check Reprise section for contents.

Magnovox Presents   PRO-573
Limited Edition
Sinatra performs four selections taken directly from Reprise.
Come Fly With Me
Street Of Dreams
I Get A Kick Out Of You
Put Your Dreams Away

Album Recorded
In England

Christmas Album
with Bing Crosby

Harry Tobias Golden Anniversary Album   Tobey Music T-200
It's A Lonesome Old Town - (Capitol Recording)

Christmas Is   P-11417
Columbia Special Products Christmas Album.
White Christmas - (Columbia Recording)

Christmas Eve With Bing And Frank   HO - HO - HO - 1088
   Sinatra and Crosby do a medley of Christmas songs. Taken from the T.V.
broadcast of December 20, 1957.

Mistletoe And Holly
Jingle Bells -with Crosby
It Came Upon A Midnight Clear
O Little Town Of Bethlehem - with Crosby
Santa Claus Is Coming To Town
The Christmas Song - with Crosby
White Christmas -with Crosby

The Many Moods Of Christmas   P-12013
A Columbia special products album.

Whatever Happened To Christmas (Reprise Recording)

Both Sides Of Crosby   Curtain Calls 100/2
   Sinatra appears with Bob Hope and Crosby in a comedy skit promoting the
movie 'The Great John L.'

Dick Tracy In B-Flat   Curtain Calls 100/1
Taken from the Armed Forces radio service broadcast on February 15, 1945.
(#166)

   Sinatra appears as Shaky in comedy skits. He then sings 'All The Things You
Are' with Crosby with special comedy lyrics. He also does 'Sunday, Monday
And Always' with Hope and Crosby and a tune called 'My Bride'.

Here's To Veterans #110   72383-1
   Program #1419
   Sinatra sings and also talks about V.A. benefits. (Reprise Recordings).

You Will Be My Music
You're So Right
Let Me Try Again
Dream Away

This Land Is Your Land   Harmony H 30931
You Never Had It So Good
The House I Live In
You're A Lucky Fellow Mr. Smith

Sinatra Rarities -   M&M-1

Side I
Old School Teacher
My Love For You
Home On The Range
You'll Know When It Happens
So They Tell Me
It's All Up To You
Catana
Help Yourself To My Heart

Side II
Kisses And Tears
There's Something Missing
Meet Me At The Copa
A Good Man Is Hard To Find
If You Please
Lilly Belle
Don't Forget Tonight, Tomorrow
All Through The Day
* The songs in the album above (M&M-1) are Columbia masters and none have been commercially released prior to this album. For more particulars, check Chapter Six.

Sinatra Like Never Before   Longines SYS 5637
Side I
The One I Love
I Couldn't Care Less
Five Hundred Guys
There's A Flaw In My Flue
Take A Chance

Side II
Day In, Day Out
I'm Walking Behind You
It All Depends On You
Memories Of You
Don't Change Your Mind About Me

Frank Sinatra And His Friends   Reprise Premium 50001
Have Yourself A Merry Little Christmas

The Victors   Colpix CP 509
Have Yourself A Merry Little Christmas

The Young Sinatra   Joker SM 3055
Side I
All Or Nothing At All
Too Romantic
Hear My Song, Violetta
Your's Is My Heart Alone

I'll Never Smile Again
Whispering

Side II
Oh, Look At Me Now
Blue Skies
A Sinner Kissed An Angel
Somewhere A Voice Is Calling
There Are Such Things
I'll Take Tallulah

Sinatra - Volume II   Joker SM 3631
Side I
It All Depends On You   Radio Broadcast 1954
The Gal That Got Away   Capitol
Sunday   Capitol
Violets For Your Furs   Capitol
Get Happy   Capitol
Somebody Loves Me   Radio Broadcast 1946

Side II
Oh What It Seemed To Be   Radio Broadcast 1946
The Song Is You   Radio Broadcast 1946
Begin The Beguine   Radio Broadcast 1945
Homesick, That's All   Radio Broadcast 1945
There's A Flaw In My Future   Capitol

Sinatra - Volume III   Joker SM 3632
Side I
I've Got A Crush On You   Columbia
They Say It's Wonderful   Columbia
The Girl I Marry   Columbia
I Hear A Rhapsody   Columbia
If I Loved You   Columbia
You Do Something To Me   Columbia

Side II
Laura   Columbia
Why Was I Born   Columbia
I Don't Stand A Ghost Of A Chance   Columbia
The Music Stopped   Columbia
I Love You   Columbia
Strange Music   Columbia

Sinatra - Volume IV   Joker SM 3633
Side I
It Might As Well Be Spring   Radio Broadcast 1945
Button Up Your Overcoat   Radio Broadcast 1945
Day By Day   Radio Broadcast 1945
Lilly Belle   Radio Broadcast 1945

Ol' Man River	Radio Broadcast 1945
It Isn't Fair	Radio Broadcast 1949

Side II

Atchison Topeka And The Santa Fe	Radio Broadcast 1945
My Melancholy Baby	Radio Broadcast 1945
Surrey With The Fringe On Top	Radio Broadcast 1945
I Fall In Love Too Easily	Radio Broadcast 1945
The House I Live In	Radio Broadcast 1945
Aren't You Glad You're You	Radio Broadcast 1945

Frank Sinatra And Bing Crosby　　　　　　Joker SM 3612

Side I

Take A Chance	Radio-March 28, 1954
Among My Souvenirs (with Crosby)	Radio-March 28, 1954
September Song (with Crosby)	Radio-March 28, 1954
As Time Goes By (with Crosby)	Radio-March 28, 1954

Side II

Young At Heart	Radio-March 21, 1954
Till We Meet Again	Radio-March 21, 1954
There's A Long, Long Trail A'winding	Radio-March 21, 1954
(with Crosby)	

Sinatra - The Early Days　　　　　Avenue International 1001

Formerly Joker SM 3634

Side I

No Orchids For My Lady	Columbia
Tennessee News Boy	Columbia
All Through The Night	Columbia
I Fall In Love With You Every Day	Columbia
Oh What A Beautiful Morning	Columbia
It All Came True	Columbia

Side II

Neiani	Victor
Daybreak	Victor
I Tried	Victor
April Played The Fiddle	Victor
I Haven't Time To Be A Millionaire	Victor
Two In Love	Victor

The Essential Sinatra　　　　　Avenue International 1002
   Contents same as Joker 3633.

The Song Is You　　　　　Avenue International 1003
   Contents same as Joker 3631.

Sinatra Sings Evergreens　　　　　Avenue International 1004
   Contents same as Joker 3632.

Original Postwar Hits   Avenue International 1008
Chattanooga Shoe Shine Boy
Surry With The Fringe On Top
Get Happy

Stars Of Hollywood   Avenue International 1011
Side I
You Can Take My Word For It Baby   Columbia
Why Was I Born   Columbia
The Song Is You   Columbia
It's Only A Paper Moon   Columbia
One For My Baby   Columbia
I'm Glad There Is You   Columbia

Side II
All Doris Day

The Master Of Song   Avenue International 1012
Side I
While The Angelus Was Ringing   Columbia
When Is Sometimes   Columbia
Bop, Goes My Heart   Columbia
Just For Now   Columbia
My Cousin Louella   Columbia
Life Is So Peculiar   Columbia

Side II
Chattanooga Shoe Shine Boy   Columbia
The Old Master Painter   Columbia
A Fella With An Umbrella   Columbia
It Only Happens When I Dance   Columbia
With You
If You Stub Your Toe On The Moon   Columbia
Sunflower   Columbia

The Romantic Sinatra   Avenue International 1013
Side I
One Finger Melody   Columbia
It Happens Every Spring   Columbia
If I Ever Love Again   Columbia
London By Night   Columbia
If Only She Looked My Way   Columbia
The Stars Will Remember   Columbia

Side II
I'm Sorry I Made You Cry   Columbia
All Of Me   Columbia
My Girl   Columbia
My Love For You   Columbia
Kiss Me Again   Columbia
Somewhere In The Night   Columbia

Reprise Album

Great Stars Of Broadway   Avenue International 1014

Blue Skies	Victor
When You Awake	Victor
Remember Me In Your Dreams	Columbia

Sinatra 1935-1970   Chairman 6008

Side I

Shine	Major Bowes Show - Sept. 8, 1935
All Or Nothing At All	Harry James - Sept. 14, 1939
A Lover Is Blue	Tommy Dorsey - Feb. 20, 1940
I'll Get By	Your Hit Parade - July 1, 1944
Pistol Packin' Mama	Your Hit Parade - October 16, 1943
Speak Low	Your Hit Parade - Dec. 18, 1943
I Found A New Baby	Light Up Time - Oct. 24, 1949
I've Got My Eyes On You	Tommy Dorsey - Feb. 20,1940

Side II

When You're Smiling	Blackpool - July 26, 1953
Tenderly	To Be Perfectly Frank - 1954
Sweet Lorraine	Blackpool - July 26, 1954
Just One Of Those Things	Sinatra Show - April 25, 1958
Night And Day	Sinatra Show - Nov. 29, 1957
The Lady Is A Tramp	Seattle Concert - June 9, 1957
Oh Look At Me Now	Seattle Concert - June 9, 1957
You Make Me Feel So Young	Royal Festival - Nov. 16,1970
My Way	Royal Festival - Nov. 16, 1970

The Definite Sinatra   Chairman 6009

Side I

For You	Sinatra Show - 1951
They Didn't Believe Me	Sinatra Show - Jan. 27, 1951
S' Wonderful	Perfectly Frank - 1954
Under A Blanket Of Blue	Perfectly Frank - 1954
Necessity	Finian's Rainbow - 1955
I'll String Along With You	Perfectly Frank - 1954
Lonesome Man Blues	Sinatra Show - Jan. 1, 1952
(with Louis Armstrong)	
Ad Lib Blues	Finian's Rainbow - 1955
(with Louis Armstrong)	
Sometimes I'm Happy	Perfectly Frank - 1954

Side II

That Great Come And Get It Day	Finian's Rainbow - 1955
Don't Blame Me	Perfectly Frank - 1954
Thou Swell	Perfectly Frank - 1954
You Are Love	Sinatra Show - 1951
I'm Confessin'	Perfectly Frank - 1954
Necessity(with Ella Fitzgerald)	Finian's Rainbow - 1955
Out Of Nowhere	Perfectly Frank - 1954
One Hundred Years From Today	Perfectly Frank - 1954

Between The Devil And The Deep Blue Sea   Perfectly Frank - 1954

To Be Perfectly Frank   Chairman 6010
All the selections on this album derive from the 'To Be Perfectly Frank'
shows. 1953-1955.

Side I
This Can't Be Love
Nevertheless
What Can I Say After I Say I'm Sorry
Hello Young Lovers
Love Me Or Leave Me
I Don't Know Why
You Took Advantage Of Me
September Song
I've Got My Love To Keep Me Warm

Side II
Just You, Just Me
Let's Fall In Love
Them There Eyes
Come Rain Or Come Shine
Somebody Loves Me
I'm In The Mood For Love
On The Sunny Side Of The Street
She's Funny That Way

The Paramount Years   Chairman 6011
Side I
That's For Me   Songs by Sinatra - Nov. 14, 1945
Suddenly It's Spring   Danny Kaye Show - June 14, 1945
Linda   Songs by Sinatra - March 19, 1947
Long Ago And Far Away   Vimm's Show - Feb. 9, 1944
Ole' Buttermilk Sky   Songs by Sinatra - Nov. 20, 1946
My Ideal   Your Hit Parade - December 18, 1943
No Love, No Nothin'   Vimm's Show - February 9, 1944
Pretending   Songs by Sinatra - December 4, 1946
When Day Is Gone   Songs by Sinatra - December 25,1946
You Can't See The Sun   Songs by Sinatra - May 14,1947
When You're Crying

Side II
It's A Good Day   Songs by Sinatra - Dec. 4, 1946
The Anniversary Song   Songs by Sinatra - May 21, 1947
Parade Of The Wooden Soldiers   Songs by Sinatra - Dec. 18,1946
Slowly   Songs by Sinatra - Jan. 9, 1946
My Sugar Is So Refined   Songs by Sinatra - Nov. 6, 1946
Exactly Like You   Songs by Sinatra - March 13, 1946
I Found A New Baby   Songs by Sinatra - Nov. 28, 1945
Till The End Of Time   Danny Kaye Show - June 14, 1945

Let's Get Lost
Lullaby Of Broadway

Your Hit Parade - June 5, 1943
Songs by Sinatra - Dec. 4, 1946

The V-Disc Years - Volume I   My Way 1001
Side I
Sunflower
A Lovely Way To Spend An Evening
She's Funny That Way
There's No You
Come Out Wherever You Are
Some Other Time

Side II
You've Got A Hold On Me
Soliloquy
I'll Be Around
You Brought A New Kind Of Love
Someone To Watch Over Me
One For My Baby

The V-Disc Years - Volume II   My Way 1002
Side I
I Only Have Eyes For You
A Hot Time In The Town Of Berlin
Let Me Love You Tonight
Ol' Man River
I'll Follow My Secret Heart
When Your Lover Has Gone
All The Things You Are

Side II
Falling In Love With Love
The Night Is Young
All Of Me
Nancy
Old School Teacher
Just Close Your Eyes
Put Your Dreams Away
And Then You Kissed Me

Sinatra For The Collector   My Way 1004
The Radio Years - Volume I   Broadway Bandbox
Side I
This Love Of Mine
Coming In On A Wing And A Prayer
All Or Nothing At All
The Right Kind Of Love
I Get A Kick Out Of You
People Will Say We're In Love
Paper Doll

Pistol Packin' Mama
From Taps Till Reveille (with Bert Wheeler)
Ol' Man River
Close To You
Where Or When

My Way 1003 was to be issued as 'The V-Disc Years - Volume III' but at this point has not been released and after many inquiries concerning the album we have been led to understand that it most likely will never be issued.

S' Wonderful
Side I

	Windmill 200
S' Wonderful	To Be Perfectly Frank
Thou Swell	To Be Perfectly Frank
Just You, Just Me	To Be Perfectly Frank
Love Me Or Leave Me	To Be Perfectly Frank
Don't Blame Me	To Be Perfectly Frank
I'll String Along With You	To Be Perfectly Frank

Side II

It's All Up To You	Columbia
You'll Know When It Happens	Columbia
O' Sole Mio	Light Up Time No. 32- 1950
The Dickie Bird Song	Your Hit Parade 1948
You Can't Be True Dear	Your Hit Parade 1948

I'm Confessin'
Side I

	Windmill 214
I'm Confessin'	To Be Perfectly Frank
Sometimes I'm Happy	To Be Perfectly Frank
If I Could Be With You	To Be Perfectly Frank
What Can I Say After I Say I'm Sorry	To Be Perfectly Frank
Blue Moon	To Be Perfectly Frank
Between The Devil And The Deep Blue Sea	To Be Perfectly Frank

Side II

It Could Happen To You	Your Hit Parade - Aug. 26, 1944
Woody, Woodpecker Song	Your Hit Parade - July 24, 1948
It's Magic	Your Hit Parade - Aug. 7, 1949
Platinum Blues	To Be Perfectly Frank - 1954
You Do	Your Hit Parade - 1947

There are three Cobra LPs which have been issued and two of them are duplicates of the last listed Windmill sets. The Cobra numbers are CLP 17001 and CLP 17002.

Cobra number CLP 17003 is an excellent duplicate of My Way 1002.

The Early Years   Windmill 240
Side I
All The Things You Are
All Of Me
Mighty Lak' A Rose
Nancy
There's No You
Someone To Watch Over Me

Side II
Ol' Man River
When Your Lover Has Gone
Falling In Love With Love
None But The Lonely Heart
I'll Never Smile Again
Without A Song

On The Town   Showbiz 5603
Original Motion Picture Soundtrack
Side I
New York, New York   With Gene Kelly & Jules Munshin
Prehistoric Man   With Ann Miller, Gene Kelly, & J. Mushin
Come Up To My Place   With Betty Garrett

Side II
When You Walk Down Main Street   With Gene Kelly & Vera Ellen
You're Awful   With Betty Garrett
Count On Me   With Jules Mushin, Ann Miller
On The Town   With rest of cast

Anchors Aweigh   Curtain Calls 100/17
Original Motion Picture Soundtrack
Side I
We Hate To Leave   With Gene Kelly
Brahms Lullaby
I Begged Her   With Gene Kelly
If You Knew Suzy   With Gene Kelly
What Makes The Sunset

Side II
The Charm Of You
I Fall In Love Too Easily
Anchors Aweigh   With rest of cast

Take Me Out To The Ballgame   Curtain Calls 100/18
Original Motion Picture
Side I
Take Me Out To The Ballgame   With Gene Kelly
Yes Indeedy   With Gene Kelly & J. Mushin
O'Brien To Ryan To Goldberg   With Gene Kelly & J. Mushin
The Right Girl For Me

Boy's And Girls Like You And Me*
* This Sinatra solo was deleted from the released print of the film.

Side II
It's Fate, It's Fate, It's Fate   With Betty Garrett
Strictly U.S.A.   With rest of cast
Take Me Out To The Ballgame   With rest of cast

The Frank Sinatra Television Special*   Reprise R-5004
A Man And His Music Part II
Fly Me To The Moon
The Most Beautiful Girl In The World
You're Nobody Till Somebody Loves You
That's Life
Downtown
Luck Be A Lady
My Kind Of Town
Angel Eyes
Put Your Dreams Away

* We, the editors, have never seen or heard this album, but we do have a Reprise worksheet showing the label listing and most importantly, the times of each selection which do match the exact times of a tape made from the 1966 telecast. Sixteen sides were recorded at the Sands Hotel and were to be issued as a live album, but this project never became a reality. Check concert listings - Nov. 5, 1961 for complete titles.

Sunday And Every Day With Sinatra   Capitol EMI-MFP 5005
Side I
Sunday
I'll Never Be The Same
Tell Her You Love Her
Close To You
River Stay Away From My Door
I'm A Fool To Want You

Side II
How About You
I Got It Bad And That Ain't Good
Your Love For Me
If I Had You
Laura
The Impatient Years

The Famous Fred Allen Show   Memorabilia MLP 712
Taken from a broadcast of October 21, 1945.

It Might As Well Be Spring
Open Up Them Pearly Gates - with Fred Allen

Bogart/Sinatra/Bacall   Memorabilia MPL 734
Taken from the Command Performance show of September 30, 1945.

What Makes The Sunset
Nancy

Hollywood Is On The Air   Radiola 2MR-1718
Taken from the soundtrack of the film 'Ship Ahoy'.

Moonlight Bay

One Night Stand With Tommy Dorsey   Joyce 1002
Taken from the broadcast of November 26, 1940.

The One I Love
Our Love Affair
Shadows On The Sand
That's How It Goes

One Night Stand With Harry James   Joyce 1024
All Or Nothing At All - Sept. 14, 1939.

Anything Goes/Panama Hattie   Larynx LAR 567
Taken from the the telecast of the Colgate Comedy Hour of November 8, 1953.

You Do Something To Me - With Ethel Merman
I Get A Kick Out Of You - With Ethel Merman
You're The Top - With Ethel Merman
Just One Of Those Things
All Through The Night

Your Hit Parade   Startone ST 222
Sinatra sings only one song and introduces Doris Day's song - "The Lady From
29 Palms".

I'll Walk Alone   October 21,1944

Vintage Sinatra - Volume I   Australian CP 12-76

This album is the first long play record release from the Australian Sinatra
Society and they are taken directly from the Columbia Record Sessions.

Side I
No Orchids For My Lady
Always
Tea For Two
It Never Entered My Mind
We Just Couldn't Say Goodbye
Where Is The One
Kisses And Tears

Side II
Peach Tree Street
My Girl
Wedding Of Lilly Marlene
White Christmas
I Got A Gal I Love
I Want To Thank Your Folks
What'll I Do

Vintage Sinatra - Volume II
Australian CP 12-77

This album is the second release from the Australian Sinatra Society and features the Melbourne Concert of April 1, 1959, with the Red Norve Quintet. Norvo is on (Vibes), Bud Shank (Reeds), Nick Bonny (Guitar), Irv Cottler (Drums), and Bill Miller (Piano).

Side I
I Could Have Danced All Night
Just One Of Those Things
I Get A Kick Out Of You
At Long Last Love
Willow Weep For Me
I've Got You Under My Skin
Moonlight In Vermont
The Lady Is A Tramp

Side II
Angel Eyes
Come Fly With Me
All The Way
Dancing In The Dark
All Of Me
On The Road To Mandalay
Night And Day

The Compleat Sinatra
Cameron FS

This was an album that was compiled from 'Your Hit Parade' from late 1947 to late 1948 and was given away free to mail order customers when the first edition of this Sinatra Volume was released.

Side I
I Wonder Who's Kissing Her Now
I Wish I Didn't Love You So
How Soon
The Lady From 29 Palms
You Do
Serenade Of The Bells
Golden Earrings
Ballerina

Side II
I'll Dance At Your Wedding
Lilli Bolero
Haunted Heart
Little White Lies
A Tree In The Meadow
My Happiness
You Call Everybody Darling
Now Is The Hour

The First Times   Cameron CLP 5001
Side I
This Can't Be Love   To Be Perfectly Frank 1953
My Happiness   Your Hit Parade 1948
I'll Get By   Your Hit Parade 1944
Lilli Bolero   Your Hit Parade 1948
Hair Of Gold   Your Hit Parade 1948

Side II
I Wish I Didn't Love You So   Your Hit Parade 1947
I Wonder Who's Kissing Her Now   Your Hit Parade 1947
One Hundred Years From Today   To Be Perfectly Frank 1953
Let Me Love You Tonight   Your Hit Parade 1944
Long Ago And Far Away   Your Hit Parade 1944

The Original Frank Sinatra   Cameron CLP 5002
Side I
Tenderly   To Be Perfectly Frank 1954
Little White Lies   Your Hit Parade 1948
Haunted Heart   Your Hit Parade 1948
The Lady From 29 Palms   Your Hit Parade 1947
I Heard You Cried Last Night   Your Hit Parade 1943

Side II
I'll String Along With You   To Be Perfectly Frank 1953
A Tree In The Meadow   Your Hit Parade 1948
How Soon   Your Hit Parade 1947
Civilation   Your Hit Parade 1947
The Very Thought Of You   Your Hit Parade 1943

The last two albums have also been issued in Spain on Carnaby 15048 and
15049.

Frank Sinatra   Cameron CLP 5003
Side I
Golden Earrings   Your Hit Parade 1948
You Call Everybody Darling   Your Hit Parade 1948
Pistol Packin' Mama   Your Hit Parade 1944
I Found A New Baby   Light Up Time 1949
You Can't Be True Dear   Your Hit Parade 1948

Side II

I'm In The Mood For Love	To Be Perfectly Frank 1953
A Lover Is Blue	Dorsey Broadcast 1940
I'll Dance At Your Wedding	Your Hit Parade 1948
Long Ago And Far Away	Your Hit Parade 1944
My Shining Hour	Your Hit Parade 1944

Sinatra   Cameron CLP 5004

Side I

Speak Low	Your Hit Parade 1944
Between The Devil And	To Be Perfectly Frank 1953
The Deep Blue Sea	
What Can I Say After I	To Be Perfectly Frank 1953
Say I'm Sorry	
Now Is The Hour	Your Hit Parade 1948
It Only Happens When I Dance With You	Your Hit Parade 1948

Side II

Ballerina	Your Hit Parade 1948
You Do	Your Hit Parade 1947
Serenade Of The Bells	Your Hit Parade 1948
My Heart Tells Me	Your Hit Parade 1944
And Mimi	Your Hit Parade 1947

The above two albums have been released in Spain on Carnaby 15050 and 15051.

Frank Sinatra And Tommy Dorsey   Durium BLJ 0819
These selections are from Dorsey broadcasts.

Side I

After All	March 2, 1940
Polka Dots And Moon Beams	March 2, 1940
Deep Night	March 2, 1940
Whispering	March 2, 1940
The Sky Fell Down	March 2, 1940
On The Isle Of May	March 9, 1940
It's A Blue World	March 9, 1940

Side II

The Fable Of The Rose	March 9, 1940
Marie	March 9, 1940
I'll Get By	March 9, 1940
A Lover Is Blue	March 9,1940
Careless	March 14,1940
I've Got My Eyes On You	March 2, 1940

Original Sessions 1940-1950   Festival 195
    Record I
Side I
Little White Lies   Your Hit Parade 1948

Let It Snow	Your Hit Parade 1947
Civilization	Your Hit Parade 1947
You Can't Be True Dear	Your Hit Parade 1948
Lili Bolero	Your Hit Parade 1948
Hair Of Gold	Your Hit Parade 1948
A Tree In The Meadow	Your Hit Parade 1948
Aren't You Glad You're You	Songs by Sinatra 1946

Side II

When You're Smiling	Light Up Time 1950
I've Got A Crush On You	Light Up Time 1950
Full Moon And Empty Arms	Songs by Sinatra 1946
All The Things You Are	Songs by Sinatra 1945
Swinging On A Star	Your Hit Parade 1944
The One I Love	Dorsey Broadcast 1940
Our Love Affair	Dorsey Broadcast 1940
Shadows On The Sand	Dorsey Broadcast 1940

Record II
Side I

American Beauty Rose	Light Up Time 1950
My Foolish Heart	Light Up Time 1950
Great Day	Guest Star 1947
I Wonder Who's Kissing Her Now	Your Hit Parade 1947
Wrap Your Troubles In Dreams	Light Up Time 1950
The Surrey With The Fringe On Top	Songs by Sinatra 1945
Without A Song	Songs by Sinatra 1945
It's Only A Paper Moon	Songs by Sinatra 1945

Side II

The Best Things In Life Are Free	Light Up Time 1950
Polka Dots And Moon Beams	Light Up Time 1950
I Love You	Light Up Time 1950
Why Remind Me	Light Up Time 1950
Just You, Just Me	Light Up Time 1950
Somebody Loves Me	Light Up Time 1950
I Found A New Baby	Light Up Time 1950

Hollywood Story   Festival 214
    Record I
Side II

I've Got My Eyes On You	Dorsey Broadcast - February 20, 1940
A Lover Is Blue	Dorsey Broadcast - February 20, 1940

    Record II
Side I

Strictly U.S.A.	Soundtrack 1949
For You	Frank Sinatra Show 1951
Lonesome Man Blues	Frank Sinatra Show 1952

Side II

Moonlight In Vermont	Sinatra Show (T.V.) - May 9, 1958
I May Be Wrong	Sinatra Show (T.V.) - May 9, 1958
Just One Of Those Things	Sinatra Show (T.V.) - April 25, 1958
Night And Day	Sinatra Show (T.V.) - November 29, 1957

Star Collection With Count Basie   Midi - 34005
Same contents as Reprise FS - 2022

Gems From Your Hit Parade 1944   Oscar OSC 101
Side I

Amor	June 17, 1944
Long Ago And Far Away	June 17, 1944
I'll Walk Alone	October 21, 1944
Is You Is Or Is You Ain't My Baby	October 21, 1944
How Many Hearts Have You Broken	November 25, 1944
The Trolley Song	November 25, 1944

Side II

Don't Fence Me In	December 23, 1944
Speak Low	January 15, 1944
San Fernando Valley	June 10, 1944
My Shining How	January 22, 1944
No Love, No Nothin'	January 22, 1944
My Heart Tells Me	January 22, 1944

Gems From Songs By Sinatra 1945   Oscar OSC 102
All of these selections come from Old Gold Shows.

Side I

One More Dream	November 28, 1945
Lover Come Back To Me	November 28, 1945
(with Lillian Romondi)	
I Found A New Baby	November 28, 1945
(with Nat King Cole Trio)	
Great Day	December 26, 1945
Symphony	December 26, 1945
I'm Gonna Love That Gal	December 26, 1945
On The Atchinson Topeka And The Santa Fe	October 31, 1945
(with Fred Allen)	
It's Been A Long, Long Time	October 31, 1945

Side II

That's For Me	November 14, 1945
A Kiss Goodnight(with Patty Andrews)	November 14, 1945
Empty Saddles(with the Andrew Sisters)	November 14, 1945
I'm Always Chasing Rainbows	December 5, 1945
Somebody Loves Me	December 5, 1945
The Last Time I Saw You	November 7, 1945
Camptown Races(with Laurence Tibbett)	November 7, 1945
Beautiful Dreamer(with Laurence Tibbett)	November 7, 1945

Frank Sinatra   Super Oscar SPO 573
Side I
I've Got My Love To Keep Me Warm   To Be Perfectly Frank 1953
Lover   Columbia
It's Only A Paper Moon   Columbia
My Blue Heaven   Columbia
Blue Skies   Columbia
Somebody Loves Me   Songs by Sinatra

Side II
That Old Black Magic   Light Up Time 1949
People Will Say We're In Love   Broadway Bandbox 1943
I Get A Kick Out Of You   Broadway Bandbox 1943
The Surrey With The Fringe On Top   Songs by Sinatra 1945
Ol' Man River   Songs by Sinatra 1945
Begin The Beguine   Songs by Sinatra 1945

Inimitable   Variety Relst 19185
Side I
Little White Lies   1948
Pistol Packin' Mama   1943
Speak Low   1944
My Ideal   1943
Woody Woodpecker   1948
Almost Like Being In Love   1947

Side II
Jingle Bells   1947
You Do   1947
A Tree In The Meadow   1948
Love Somebody   1948
How Soon   1948
Serenade Of The Bells   1948
All of the above songs come from 'Your Hit Parade'.

1962 World Tour   6013
This was an album made from the charity world tour (April - June 1962)
accompanied by: Bill Miller (Piano), Al Viola (Guitar), Irv Cottler (Drums),
Harry Klee (Saxaphone), Emil Richards (Vibes), and Ralph Pena (Bass).

Side I
Day In, Day Out

A firm named Kat Wisker Productions has recently assembled an 8 hour
biography in song concerning Frank Sinatra. This is offered to radio stations
for commercial use. We will list the songs that Sinatra sings and a few other
interesting facts.

The tape begins with Frank Chacksfields recording of 'All the Way'.

Shine	Hoboken Four featuring Sinatra
Our Love	Sinatra Home Recording
From the Bottom of My Heart	With Harry James
All or Nothing at All	With James
Ciribiribin	With James
The Sky Fell Down	With Tommy Dorsey
I'll Be Seeing You	With Dorsey
Polka Dots and Moonbeams	With Dorsey
East of the Sun	With Dorsey
I'll Never Smile Again	With Dorsey
The One I Love	With Dorsey
We Three	With Dorsey
Our Love Affair	With Dorsey
Oh, Look At Me Now	With Dorsey
Without a Song	With Dorsey
Everything Happens To Me	With Dorsey
This Love of Mine	With Dorsey
The Sunshine of Your Smile	With Stordahl
The Night We Called It a Day	With Dorsey
Poor You	With Dorsey
In the Blue of Evening	With Dorsey
There Are Such Things	With Dorsey
It Started All Over Again	With Dorsey
I'll Buy That Dream	With Dorsey
The Song is You	
I Call It Love	
As Time Goes By	
Close To You	With Tucker Singers
People Will Say We're In Love	With Tucker Singers
I Couldn't Sleep a Wink Last Night	With Tucker Singers
If You Are But A Dream	With Stordahl
Comedy Bit	With W.C. Fields
Ol' Man River	With Stordahl
Put Your Dreams Away	With Stordahl
If I Loved You	With Stordahl
Kiss Me Again	With Stordahl
I Fall in Love Too Easily	With Stordahl
Blue Skies	With Stordahl
Nancy	With Stordahl
I'll Be Around	
Oh What it Seemed to Be	With Stordahl
I Only Have Eyes For You	With Stordahl
Home on the Range	With Stordahl
The House I Live In	With Stordahl
Time After Time	With Stordahl
Sweet Lorraine	With Metronome All-Stars
Someday	

I'm A Fool to Want You	With Stordahl
Birth of the Blues	With Stordahl
Why Try to Change Me Now	With Percy Faith
From Here To Eternity	With Nelson Riddle
Lean Baby	With Stordahl
I've Got the World on a String	With Riddle
Violets For Your Furs	With Riddle
Young at Heart	With Riddle
Tenderly	
Day In, Day Out	With Riddle
Wrap Your Troubles in Dreams	With Riddle
Hands Across the Table	
In the Wee Small Hours	With Riddle
Learnin' the Blues	With Riddle
Love and Marriage	With Riddle
The Tender Trap	With Riddle
I've Got You Under My Skin	With Riddle
Memories of You	With Riddle
The End of a Love Affair	With Riddle
Hey Jealous Lover	
Well Did You Evah	With Bing Crosby
The Lady is a Tramp	With Riddle
Lonely Town	With Gordon Jenkins
Witchcraft	With Riddle
All the Way	With Riddle
Come Fly With Me	With Billy May
Angel Eyes	With Riddle
Nice N' Easy	With Riddle
I Gotta Right to Sing the Blues	With Skip Martin
A Foggy Day	With Johnny Mandel
The Second Time Around	With Felix Slatkin
I'm Getting Sentimental Over You	With Sy Oliver
You're Nobody Till Somebody Loves You	With Billy May
I Hadn't Anyone Till You	With Don Costa
The Girl Next Door	With Gordon Jenkins
They Can't Take That Away From Me	With Neal Hefti
Night and Day	With Costa
Call Me Irresponsible	With Riddle
Soliloquy	With Riddle
Luck Be a Lady	With Billy May
My Kind of Town	With Count Basie
Softly As I Leave You	With Ernie Freeman
It Was a Very Good Year	With Jenkins
Comedy Bit	With Dean Martin
You Make Me Feel So Young	With Count Basie
Strangers in the Night	With Ernie Freeman
That's Life	With Freeman
I Concentrate On You	With Claus Ogerman
Cycles	With Don Costa

Loves Been Good to Me	With Costa
Fly Me to the Moon	With Count Basie
Send in the Clowns	With Costa
My Way	With Costa

In addition to the recordings, there are many interviews with performers who have been associated with Sinatra through the years. These interviews offer a great insight to Frank's fans and are conducted with the following: Jo Stafford, Sy Oliver, Keenan Wynn, Bullets Durgom, Paul Weston, Sammy Cahn, Bing Crosby, Percy Faith, Nelson Riddle, Gordon Jenkins, Matt Denniss, Al Viola, Jimmy Bowen, Bill Miller and Rod McKuen.

Here's To Veterans Album

Chapter XV
SELECT BIBLIOGRAPHY
PART I
BOOKS AND ARTICLES ABOUT SINATRA

METRONOME - Music Magazine - May 1943 - 'Frankly Speaking' by Leonard G. Feather. Also July, 1943 - Under the heading of 'Simon Says'. The very able author, George T. Simon, gives an inside account of the new rising star, Sinatra.

BANDLEADERS MAGAZINE - May, 1945 - Sinatra's Life Story up to that point.

THE VOICE - Hard cover book - by E.J. Kahn, Jr. - Harper & Brothers - 1946.

METRONOME - Music Magazine - February, 1948 - Cover photo and interview with George T. Simon - excellent. Also, June 1948 - Sinatra's review of Harry Ulanovs book, 'The Fabulous Crosby'

TIME - Magazine - August 29, 1955 - Featured article.

LOOK - Magazine - September 6, 1955 - Featured article with photos.

WOMENS HOME COMPANION - May, 1956 - Featured article with photos.

METRONOME - Music magazine - September 1956 - Cover photo - All Star Winner - also December, 1957 - 'Mr Personality' - well written article by Bill Coss.

LOOK - Magazine - May 27, 1957 - featured article with photos.

HI FI STEREO - Magazine - April, 1960 - 'Analysis Of An Idol' by Nat Hentoff - with photos and short album discography.

PLAYBOY - Mens' Magazine - June, 1960 - 'Meeting At The Summit' by Robert Le Care - with photos.

THE REAL AND THE UNREAL - Paperback book - 1961 - by Bill Davidson.

SINATRA AND HIS RAT PACK - Paperback book - 1961 - By Richard Gehman.

FRANKIE - 'The Life and Loves of Frank Sinatra' - paperback book - published in late 1961 - written by Don Dwiggins.

ROGUE - Magazine - October 1, 1962 - 'The Thin One and Hefti' - by Arnold Shaw, who was present for this recording session, relates in detail how Sinatra records an album.

SINATRA - Hard cover book - by Robin Douglas Home - late 1962 - excellent - with many fine photos.

NEWSWEEK - Magazine - September 6, 1965 - 'Where The Action Is' - by Joseph Morgenstern.

BILLBOARD - Magazine - November 20, 1965 - 'The Sinatra Report' - by George T. Simon - excellent biography, discography (albums only) and filmography. Great photos, in our opinion, one of the finest pieces ever written on Sinatra.

CASHBOX - Magazine - November 25, 1965 - 'Sinatra' - life in music and films with discography and filmography - excellent photos - very well done tribute.

T.V. GUIDE - Magazine - May 14 to 20, 1966 - 'The Time Of His Life' - by Leslie Raddatz.

SINATRA - 'TWENTIETH CENTURY ROMANTIC' - 1968 - hard cover book - now in paperback - written by Arnold Shaw and is an excellent blow by blow account of Sinatra's career.

FRANK SINATRA - Discography - 1969 - written and compiled by David Shrimpton - presented by the Music Society in Great Britain. Badly done and contains many errors.

FRANK SINATRA - 'A Man Alone' - 1969 - Limited Edition - by Rod McKuen.

THE COMPLEAT SINATRA - In 1970, the first edition of this book was released on a very limited basis and despite virtually no distribution, it received wide acclaim from those wise enough to seek it out and purchase it. It also received some heated disclaims because of the apparent errors and ommissions. We do hope that now with all of our initial problems solved, it will reach the newly acquired audience that Mr. Sinatra has so deservedly developed in addition to the many fans who have always stood by him.

AUDIO - Magazine - December, 1970 - features an excellent article entitled - 'Have You Heard Sinatra' - by Don Altobell.

AFTERBEAT - Magazine - a series of articles about Sinatra appeared in installments (Jan.); (Feb.); (March); (April) - 1971. Actually a rehash of his life and recordings. Well done even if repetitive.

CORONET - Magazine - February 1971 - containing a good article - 'My Life With Frank Sinatra Since Our Divorce' - by Nancy Sinatra. Plus cover photo.

CRESCENDO — British magazine - February 1971 - has an extremely interesting two page article - 'In Rehearsal With Sinatra' - by Trombonist Don Lusher, who played in the orchestra which accompanied Sinatra on his recent London concert.

LIFE — Magazine - June 25, 1971 - 'Frank Sinatra's Swan Song' - by Thomas Thompson. Fine article concerning Sinatra's farewell performance in Los Angeles on June 13, 1971, excellent insight on the 'Man' as to how he feels and prepares to perform. Also great photos both old and new.

HI FIDELITY — Magazine - August, 1971 - 'Sinatra' - end of a giant - by Arnold Shaw - a Sinatra retrospective.

STEREO REVIEW — Magazine - November, 1971 - 'Sinatra A Great Vocal Artist Retires' - by Henry Pleasants. Another fine retrospective well written with alphabetical discography containing a minimal of errors and also many rare photos.

THE FILMS OF FRANK SINATRA — Hard cover book, now available in paperback - 1972 - by Gene Ringold and Clifford Mc Carty - well done, lavish spread of the motion picture career of Sinatra. Excellent forward and many photos.

SINATRA AND THE GREAT SONG STYLISTS — 1972 - by Ken Barnes and Ian Allan - (London).

SATURDAY REVIEW — August, 1972 - 'Sinatra - That Certain Style', well written by Gene Lees. Author discusses Sinatra's way of singing, especially his phrasing and enunciation - makes good comparisons and gives examples. Great article for those who truly listen to Sinatra's recordings.

SONGS BY SINATRA — 1939 - 1970 - 1973 -Discography by Brian Hainsworth - (London).

POPULAR MUSIC AND SOCIETY - College magazine - May 1973, 'The Sinatra Nobody Hears - Not Even Sinatra', well written discourse concerning rare Sinatra recordings and tapes that circulate among collectors - by John Brady.

THE MAN, THE MYTH AND THE MUSIC — 1973 - Paperback - by Peter Goddard.

PROTECTING SINATRA AGAINST THE BIG BEEF STORY — New York magazine - July 15, 1974 - Christopher Buckley's account of Sinatra's return to Las Vegas to settle some old scores.

BABES, BOOZE, BRAWLS AND SINATRA — Billboard magazine - March 8, 1975 - by Eliot Tiegel. Sinatra recording with Snuff Garrett producing and Frank commenting on how he wants to try newer things. Fine insight on his recent views of the entire music field with a few excellent photos taken at the recording session.

SINATRA — THE MAN AND HIS MUSIC — Paperback book by Hal Shaper with additional material by Stan Britt and Michael Leitch. Sinatra's career is discussed but the article that makes the book worthwhile is the chapter titled 'The Hank Sanicola Story'. Good photos and a song listing of songs of Sinatra's more famous recordings. Published in Great Britain around January, 1976.

SINATRA — Paperback pocketbook - May, 1976 - by Tony Sciacca - Sinatra's life story updated with both sides of his alleged mob connections given. Fairly well done especially for recent Sinatra fans.

SINATRA — An unauthorized biography - hard bound - May, 1976 - written by Earl Wilson - excellent biography with many inside, first hand information articles and yet one gets the feeling that Mr. Wilson is holding back. Still a must for Sinatra fans and foes - very good photos included.

PART II — BOOKS AND ARTICLES BY SINATRA

TIPS ON POPULAR SINGING — 1941 TUNE IN — Radio magazine - January, 1944 - 'Frankly Speaking' - article with some fine early photos.

BANDLEADERS — Magazine - April 1945 - 'I Can't Forget' - recalling the lean years by Sinatra.

ESQUIRE JAZZ YEARBOOK — 1947 - 'I've Got News For You' by Sinatra.

LIFE — Magazine - April 23, 1965 - 'Sinatra talks freely about himself and his music.

PLAYBOY — Magazine - 1967 - interview with Sinatra.

THE BIG BANDS — 1967 - by George T. Simon - with forward by Sinatra.

SOMEONES IN THE KITCHEN WITH DINAH — 1971 - by Dinah Shore - two recipes by Sinatra.

GENE KELLY — 1975 - by Clive Hirschorn - with forward by Sinatra.

PART III — BOOKS CONTAINING MATERIAL ON SINATRA

AVA — 1960 - David Hanna

YES I CAN — 1965 - by Sammy Davis, Jr.

ALL TALKING, ALL SINGING, ALL DANCING — 1966 - by John Springer

KING COHN — The life of Harry Cohn - 1967 - by Bob Thomas.

FADS, FOLLIES AND DELUSIONS OF THE AMERICAN PEOPLE — 1967 - by Paul Sann.

THIS FABULOUS CENTURY — 1940 -1950-1969- Time Life Books

THE HOLLYWOOD CAGE — 1969 - by Charles Hamblett

AMERICAN POP — 1969 - David Sachs

FAME AND OBSCURITY — 1970 - by Gay Talese

DON'T FALL OFF THE MOUNTAIN — 1970 - by Shirley Mac Laine

THE NAME ABOVE THE TITLE — 1971 by Frank Capra

MYSELF AMONG OTHERS — 1971 - by Ruth Gordon

COME BACKSTAGE WITH ME — 1971 - by Benny Rubin

REBELS — 1971 - by Joe Morella & Edward Epstein

SIMON SAYS — 1971 -by George T. Simon

SHOW BUSINESS NOBODY KNOWS — 1971 - by Earl Wilson

TOMMY AND JIMMY — THE DORSEY YEARS — 1972 - by Herb Sanford

THE GREAT MOVIE STARS — 1972 - by Dave Shipman

THE MGM YEARS — 1972 - by Lawrence Thomas

THE MOONS A BALLOON — 1972 - by David Niven

THE MGM STOCK COMPANY — 1973 - by Robert Parish & Ronald Bowers

LAS VEGAS IS MY BEAT — 1973 - by Ralph Pearl

THEY CALL ME THE SHOWBUSINESS PRIEST — 1973 - by Father Robert Perrella

THIS LAUGH IS ON ME — 1973 - by Phil Silvers

THEY'RE PLAYING OUR SONG — 1973 - by Max Wilk

SOME ENCHANTED EGOS — 1973 - by Donald Zec

I SHOULD CARE — 1974- by Sammy Cahn

AVA — 1974 by Charles Nigham

THE GREAT AMERICAN POPULAR SINGERS — 1974 - by Henry Pleasants

HEART THROBS — 1974 - by Jack Tresidder

THE FILMS OF GENE KELLY — 1974 - by Tony Thomas

THE PLATINUM YEARS — 1974 - by Bob Willoughby and Henry Schickel

LIFE GOES TO THE MOVIES — 1975 - Time Life Books

JUDY — 1975 - by Gerold Frank

DORIS DAY — HER OWN STORY — 1976 - by A.E. Hotchner

GENE KELLY — 1976 - by Jeanine Bassinger

HOLLYWOOD IS A FOUR LETTER TOWN — 1976 - by James Bacon

FOR ONCE IN MY LIFE — 1976 - by Connie Haines

OFF GUARD — 1976 - by Ron Galella

New Book 'Sinatra's Women' by Jerry Romero, not reviewed at this printing.

Of course, there have been many other articles and a few more books on Frank Sinatra that have not been included in this listing but we feel that these are the best and most representative of his multiple careers. As a final note we would most certainly recommend the fine British monthly 'Fan' magazine called 'Perfectly Frank' and its American counterpart published in California titled - 'The Sinatra Newsletter'. These are a must for the serious Sinatra devotee as is the Australian Sinatra Society. For those interested in subscribing we list the addressed below.

THE SINATRA NEWSLETTER
c/o Joseph Memoli
P.O. Box 11202
Oakland, California 94611

PERFECTLY FRANK
c/o Brian O'Connor
42 Kestral Way
New Addington
Croydon, Surrey
Lodge Hill 4758, Great Britian

AUSTRALIAN SINATRA SOCIETY
P.O. Box 123
Clayton 3168
Victoria
Australia

RARECORDS
P.O. Box 254
Getzville, New York 14068

SINATRA SOCIETY OF LAS VEGAS
P.O. Box 42343
Las Vegas, Nevada 89104

THE SINATRA SOCIETY OF NEW YORK
P.O. Box 866
Times Square Station
N.Y.C., N.Y. 10108

SPECIAL LISTING

THE SINATRA FILE — PART ONE — Hardbound and paperback - by John Ridgway - printed in Great Britian. A listing of radio shows, television shows, and concert performances in chronological sequence and an album section containing non-commercial recordings. We don't know if the purchasers of this book can really appreciate the work involved in compiling it, but we certainly do, and can heap nothing but praise upon Mr. Ridgway for his outstanding efforts. If you are a Sinatra fan, you should own this book.

Chapter XVI
MAJOR AWARDS AND HONORS

1935 - Wins Major Bowes Amateur Hour Contest Singing "Night and Day."

1941 - Voted best male singer by Down Beat Magazine.

1942 - Voted best male singer by Downbeat Magazine

1943 - Voted best male singer by Downbeat Magazine.

1944 - Voted most popular singer by Metronome Magazine.

1945 - Awarded the Hollywood Womans Press Club Plaque for having made the most constructive contribution to National Welfare of Any Person in the Motion Picture Industry. (For entertaining troops overseas). Named "Chairman of the Young Division of the March of Dimes.

Voted most popular singer by Metronome Magazine.

1946 - Receives "Jefferson Award" from Council against Intolerance in America.
Special Academy Award for "House I Live In".
Voted most popular screen star of 1946 by Modern Screen Magazine.
Voted most popular singer by Metronome and Downbeat Magazines.

1947 - Voted best male singer by Downbeat Magazine.

1949 - Receives Holizer Memorial Award from Los Angeles Jewish Community.

1954 - Academy Award for Best Supporting Actor in "From Here to Eternity".
Metronome Magazine Award for "Singer of the Year." Downbeat Winner through 1962.

1958 - Voted Entertainer of the Year by Al Jolson B'Nai B'Rith.

1959 - Grammy Award for best solo performance for Vocalist - "Come Dance with Me" Album.

1962 - Receives start of solidarity award by the Italian Government.

1965 - Conference of personal managers Man of the Year Award.
Peabody Award, for Television Show - "Frank Sinatra - A Man and His Music."
Emmy Award, for television show - "Frank Sinatra - A Man and His Music."
Receives the "De Gaule Peace Award" from the French Government.
Grammy Award, Best Solo Vocal Performance, "It Was A Very Good Year"
Grammy Award, Album of the Year, "September of My Years".
Recaptures Downbeat Award for Best Male Singer.

1966 - Grammy Award, Best Vocal Performance, "Strangers in the Night".
Grammy Award, Album of the Year, "Sinatra - A Man and His Music."
Grammy Award, Record of the Year, "Strangers in the Night."
Voted Best Male Vocalist by Downbeat Magazine.

Special Academy Award for "The House I Live In".

The Second Oscar For "From Here To Eternity".

1969 - Honorary Alumnus, University of California at Los Angeles.

1971 - Receives Humanitarian Award from Los Angeles.
Receives the Jean Hersholt Humanitarian Award at 43rd Annual Academy Awards.

1972 - Beverly Hills Friars Humanitarian Award.
State of Israel Medalion of Valor Award.

1973 - March of Dimes Man of the Year Award.
Thomas A. Dooley Splendid American Award.
Voted entertainer of the Century by the Songwriters of America.

1975 - Receives Cecil B. DeMille Golden Globe Award.
Becomes Honorary Citizen of Chicago.
Jerusalem Medal from City of Jerusalem, Israel.

1976 - Certificate of Appreciation, from City of New York.
Named Entertainer of the Year by Friars.
Doctor of Humane Letters from University of Las Vegas.
Scopus Award of the American Friends of the Hebrew University.

1977 - Receives Israel Cultural Award.
City of Philadelphia bestows the Freedom Medal upon him.

Chapter XVII
LOOKING BACK

We are one of the faceless pubescent hundreds standing near the bandstand at the Astor Roof. Cornering him between sets while our prom dates, hair like silk softly curling, petition for his autograph. We are one of the swaddling thousands lining up around the Paramount Shrine. Hands in pockets, jingling the quarters we are saving for his opening at the Riobamba. We are one of the tender millions seasoning along with that self assured lost little boy who is Francis Albert Sinatra......

It is another time. The interlude between a great depression and a great war. It is a different world. When we are both young.

It is the age of Henry Wallace and the Brown Bomber, "I'll Never Smile Again" and "Oh Look At Me Now", the cactus needle and four inch lapel, "Polka Dots and Moonbeams" and "The One I Love Belongs To Somebody Else". And most assuredly it is the age of the two cent stamp and "Swing and Sweat with Charlie Barnett"....

Norma Jean Engstrom is not yet Peggy Lee. But Baby Yvonne Marie Jasmine is already Connie Haines. Petula Sally Owen Clark is at a private school in Espen, England and Connie Francis is in her playpen in New York, U.S.A......

It is Wednesday and we will travel by trolley, train and on foot to 42nd and 7th to await the new issue of Downbeat. We will memorize and devour it on the ride home. It is Thursday and Basie is at the Blackhawk in Chicago. The blue network will have a full hour remote at midnight. Downbeat informs that Bix is dead and Jelly Roll is dying. Jazz is the seed and the big band its flower. Artie Shaw with Helen Forest, Tony Pastor and Cliff Leeman is alive at the Lincoln. The days of Cuba Libre and Roses .... Les Brown with Betty Bonney is only 29 miles away at the Log Cabin. It is the early age of the Hasbrouck Heights swooner......It is also the age of the Eberly Brothers, Kitty Kallen, Perry Como, Anita O'Day, Bob Allen, Billie Holliday, Helen O'Connell, Ivie Anderson, Jimmy Rushing, the Haymes Boys, Jo Stafford, Kenny Sargent, Ziggy, Buddy, Heinie and Hymie. It is the era of the most glamorous and startingly beautiful women in our universe. And they are vocalizing to the oscillating, syncopating sounds of the Duke, the Count, the Clouds of Joy, the King, the Sentimental Gentleman, the Rippling Rhythms and the Dawn Patrol.

In a year or two or three he will be the Sultan of Swoon. He will also be the Boudoir Singer, the Larynx, the Lean Lark and Frankie You-Know-Who. In another seven he will be standing in Madison Square Garden, tossing away his prepared speech and pleading for a just cause aleady lost. A national institution and a world phenomenon, there will be theories on how he reached the stars. As many as there are star gazers. In nine years he will be rated among the top twelve drawing cards in Motion Pictures. Confounding the critics who said he wouldn't last. The legends will grow. And two and a half decades after he will still be the heavyweight champ. This vocally articulate kid with the twenty-six inch waistline will be proficiently flailing away, seldom missing his target. At an age when most of us are mere shadows of our pristine selves, he will still be the guy with the golden voice.

It is 1940 no longer. The very good year for city girls and soft summer nights.

It is almost after the fall. The hair thinning arthritic days when rains tumble from eaves into dichondra lawns. When we sit in our stereo pads reaching high for a Bluebird. Waltzing with the ghosts of frail young ballerinas, hair like silk softly curling. Juvenescently zeroing our turntables to seventy-eight. And listening to the echoes of the Pipers tunes.

Reprinted from Cash Box.
December 4th 1965
Written by Mr. Harvey Geller
West Coast Editor

Sinatra with the Tommy Dorsey Orchestra — 1941.

On Stage with the Tommy Dorsey Orchestra — 1942.

Singing at the Waldorf Astoria with Skitch Henderson On Piano.

Discussing an Arrangement with His Close Friend Axel Stordahl.

With Vocalist
June Christy — 1946.

"Frankie".

With Edgar Bergen and Jimmy Durante.

"Feeling" the Song.

With Judy Canova, William Bendix, Kay Kyser, and Ralph Edwards.

With Dinah Shore and Judy Garland.

"Crooning" at C.B.S.

On Stage at the Paramount Theater.

With Bing Crosby — 1943.

Relaxing — 1944.

Signing Autographs with Lovella Parsons.

With Phil Baker.

Sinatra Croons to Tami Mauriello, Boxer.

At Veterans Hospital — 1945.

Publicity Pose.

*Recording Session with the Charioteers and Nick Fatool (Drums), Red Nichols
(Trumpet), Dave Barbour (Guitar), Phil Stevens (Bass) — 1945.*

With Nat "King" Cole — 1946.

Publicity Pose — 1945.

With Columbia Executive and Les Brown — 1947.

Publicity Pose.

*With Slim
Gailard Trio.*

*With Drummer,
Buddy Rich.*

With Claudette Colbert and Bing Crosby — 1945.

With Harry James — 1945.

With Rosemary Clooney and Fan — 1947.

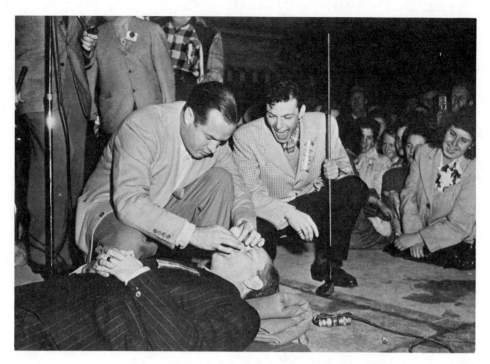

With Bob Hope and Kay Kyser (on floor) — 1946.

With Tex Beneke and Maurice Cohen at the Hollywood Palladium — 1945.

Sinatra, Eddie Cantor, Eddie Fisher.

With Judy Garland.

With First Wife Nancy and Daughter Nancy.

With First Wife Nancy — 1946.

With First Wife Nancy — 1945.

Signing Autographs at Ebbets Field — 1944.

With Sy Oliver, Johnny Hodges, Harry Carney — 1946.

Bing Crosby and Sinatra Duet.

Sinatra at Golden Gate Theater, San Francisco. At far left is Bob Chiappari who became President of the Sinatra Music Society — 1946.

With Van Johnson at Waves Barracks, San Francisco — 1946.

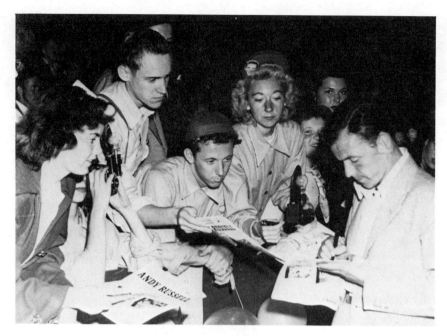

At Gilmore Field, Hollywood Benefit Baseball Game. Sinatra's Team versus Andy Russell's with fan Bob Chiappari with cap — 1948.

With Second Wife, Ava Gardner — 1952.

With Second Wife, Ava Gardner in New York — 1951.

With Toots Shore and Jackie Gleason.

With Tommy Dorsey, Buddy Rich, Ziggy Elman, Jo Stafford, The Pied Pipers, Axel Stordahl, Nancy Sinatra, Manie Sachs and members of The Dorsey Orchestra — 1943.

With Ezzard Charles, Symphony Sid, Sarah Vaugh at Birdland — 1952.

Sinatra at Macy's Department Store — 1949.

Sinatra and Tommy Dorsey Reunited at the Paramount Theater — 1956.

Sinatra with Axel Stordahl — 1946.

With Gracie Allen, George Burns, Mary Healey, and Peter Lind Hayes

Cover of "Tune In" Magazine — 1944.

Sinatra in Hollywood — 1949.

Promo for "Till The Clouds Roll By".

With Trini Lopez.

With Bob Austin of "Record World".

With Buddy Greco.

Cover of "Close To You" Album for Capitol.

At Capitol Records.

At Marine Camp with Dorothy Malone and Doris Day.

With Third Wife, Mia Farrow.

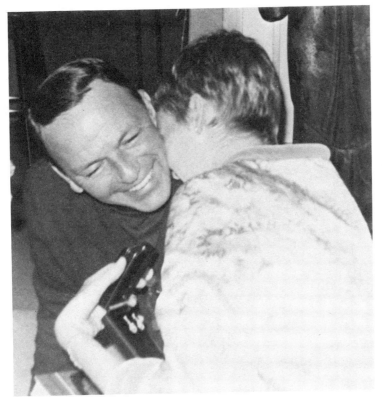

With Mia Farrow.

With Astronauts.

With Grace Kelly on set of "High Society".

Publicity Pose.

At a Concert.

Proposed Album Cover — 1967.

Hand Print Ceremony at
Grauman's Chinese Theater.

At Caesar's Palace, Las Vegas with Daughter Nancy, Nancy Sr., Daughter Tina and Frank Jr. — 1970.

With Daughters Tina, Nancy and Son Frank Jr. in Las Vegas — 1968.

With Cary Grant, Claudette Colbert, Jack Benny and Mrs. Benny.

Sinatra, Mia Farrow and Joe E. Lewis.

Sinatra, Dinah Shore and Burt Reynolds.

With George Burns, Mrs. Jack Benny, Jack and Pearl Bailey.

Sinatra and Jilly Rizzo.

Sinatra and Jilly Rizzo.

With Howard Cossell — 1976.

With Milly Hoffman, Walter Von Hauffe, Bob Chiappari, Isabel Mazzella — 1977.

Promo for "Robin And The Seven Hoods".

A Happy Sinatra.

With Great Fan — Jim Perikle.

With Wife Barbara Marx Sinatra.

Accepting an Oscar in the Movie "The Oscar".

At A T.V. Rehearsal.

At A T.V. Rehearsal.

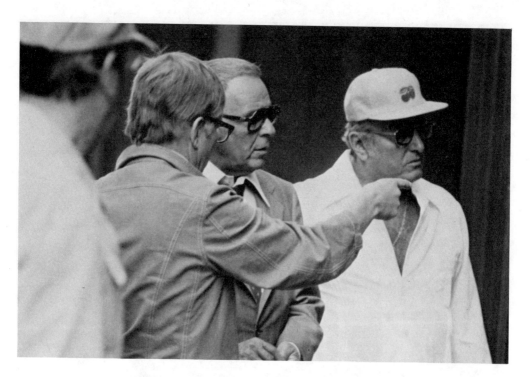

On set of T.V. Movie — "Contract On Cherry Street".

T.V. Movie - "Contract On Cherry Street".

Getting Ready To Swing.

Addenda and Errata
With Space for Corrections and Additions

Chapter I - In The Beginning

Sinatra also sang "The Curse Of An Aching Heart" with Major Bowes.

Chapter II - Harry James

The arrangements on "My Buddy" and "It's Funny To Everyone But Me" are by Jack Mathias **not** Andy Gibson.

Chapter III - With the Sentimental Gentleman

The Pied Pipers at this time were Jo Stafford, Chuck Lowery, Clark Yokun and John Huddleston. Contrary to "The Sinatra File - Part I", Jo Stafford was not replaced by Connie Haines in April, 1940. Miss Haines was simply featured on certain songs and Miss Stafford can be heard on many Pied Piper recordings up until the time they also left Tommy Dorsey in late 1942. Freddie Woolston started arranging for Dorsey String Section on July 6, 1942.

Chapter IV - Four For Bluebird

Chapter V - Appearances At The Paramount Theatre

Add February 12, 1952 - Orchestra Unknown - 1 week with his own movie, "Meet Danny Wilson" - sings many songs from the film.

Chapter VI - The Columbia Years

"Accidents Will Happen", recorded on September 18, 1950, was the first 45 RPM by Sinatra. It retained the original release number but was preceded by the Number 4. Columbia Records had been issuing 7 inch 33-1/3 RPM discs prior to these but they never caught on with the public.

Chapter VII - V-Discs

Chapter VIII - A Fresh Start - Capitol Records

The vocal chorus behind Sinatra on "Don't Change Your Mind About Me" (September 23, 1954) sounds exactly like June Hutton and the Pied Pipers. There is also a vocal chorus on "Five Hundred Guys" (April 9, 1956).

Chapter IX - On His Own - Reprise Records

Chapter X - Television Appearances

"Love and Marriage" sung by Sinatra on September 19, 1955 in the NBC Presentation "Our Town" won the first Emmy award for a song written expressly for television. On the Judy Garland Show, February 25, 1962, the orchestra was arranged and conducted by Mort Lindsey. October 4, 1977 Sinatra throws out first ball (Phillies versus Dodgers).

Among other motion pictures that Sinatra was scheduled to appear in were: "Honey Boy" in 1948 for MGM, based on the novel by Daily Paskman with a completed screenplay by Jack McGowan; "It's Always Fair Weather" in 1954 for MGM and to co-star with Gene Kelly. On the soundtrack he sings "Young At Heart" in the opening and closing three minutes of the Woody Allen and Zero Mostel film "The Front". Sinatra was turned down for the role of "Mr. Roberts" because Leland Hayward thought he was too old.

Chapter XII - Air Checks

Chapter XIII - Concert Appearances

On July 20, 1946 - Hollywood Bowl, Los Angeles, California, Sinatra walked on stage at the last possible moment, during the eight bar introduction, and proceeded to give one of his finest renditions of "Ol' Man River". Orchestra was conducted by Johnny Green.

I Sing The Songs
Reprise (Italian) W54093

Side 1
Empty Tables (with orchestra)
The Saddest Thing Of All
A Baby Just Like You
Christmas Mem'ries
The Only Couple On The Floor

Side II
I Believe I'm Gonna Love You
Anytime (I'll Be There)
The Hurt Doesn't Go Away
I Sing The Songs
The Shadow Of The Moon

Frank Sinatra At His Rarest Of All Rare Performances
Two Record Set
BIAC BRAD 10512 - 10513

Side 1

If I Loved You	Radio Show	December, 1945
Just One Of Those Things	Radio Show	November 28, 1943
I Couldn't Sleep A Wink Last Night	Radio Show	November 28, 1943
My Heart Stood Still	Radio Show	November 28, 1943
Wrap Your Troubles In Dreams	Radio Show	1948

Side II

The Surrey With The Fringe On Top	Radio Show	September 19, 1945
Without A Song	Radio Sow	October 24, 1945
Don't Forget Tonight Tomorrow	Radio Show	October 31, 1945
It's Been A Long Long Time	Radio Show	October 31, 1945
Paper Moon	Radio Show	October 31, 1945

Side III

Aren't You Glad You're You	Radio Show	December 12, 1945
Civilization	Radio Show	December 13, 1945
Lily Bolero	Radio Show	May 22, 1948
You Can't Be True Dear	Radio Show	July 31, 1948
All Of Me	Capitol Recording	April 19, 1954
Haunted Heart	Radio Show	July 10, 1948

Side IV

Nature Boy	Radio Show	May 29, 1948
Hair Of Gold	Radio Show	September 11, 1948
My Happiness	Radio Show	September 11, 1948
A Tree In The Meadow	Radio Show	September 11, 1948
I Wish I Didn't Love You So	Radio Show	December 13, 1947

It Only Happens When I Dance
 With You   Radio Show   September 11, 1948

Frank Sinatra - Bing Crosby - Rarest Of All Rare Performances
Two Record Set   BIAC BRAD 10514 - 10515

Side I
Dearest Darling   Radio Show   January 30, 1946
Medley with Crosby - It Had To Be You, Who, Dear Old Girl, When Day Is
Done, Boy Of Mine, Full Moon and Empty Arms, and Mimi
                                    Radio Shows   January 23, 1946
                                    February 20, 1946, November 22, 1947
You My Love   Capital Recording September 23, 1954
(Unedited Version)

Side II
It Might As Well Be Spring   Radio Show   December 12, 1945
The House I Live In   Radio Show   November 21, 1945
All The Things You Are   Radio Show   October 10, 1945
Lilly Belle   Radio Show   December 12, 1945
Sweet Lorraine   Radio Show   July 22, 1945

The Remainder Of This Two Record Set By Bing Crosby

The Best Of Dinah Shore   Columbia C-34395

One Sinatra Selection

My Romance (with Dinah Shore)   April 25, 1947

Frank Sinatra Classics   Columbia (Holland) 88133
Two Record Set - All Commercially Released Columbia Recordings

Laura	Stormy Weather
Blue Skies	Lover
Autumn In New York	Over The Rainbow
Come Back To Sorrento	They Say It's Wonderful
Poinciana	When You're Smiling
Mam'selle	Paradise
The Continental	Bim Bam Baby
My Blue Heaven	That Old Black Magic
It's Only A Paper Moon	She's Funny That Way
September Song	Some Enchanted Evening
Always	Mean To Me
My Melancholy Baby	Bali-Hai
Begin The Beguine	Should I

The Young Harry James   Jazz Archives JA-31

To You - (Fall, 1939)
From The Bottom Of My Heart - (Fall, 1939)

The Voice Volume IV

Italian Reprise FS 5283

Side I
Early American
The House I Live In
Let Us Break Bread Together
You Never Had It So Good
By The Time I Get To Phoenix
A Day In The Life Of A Fool

Side II
We Open In Venice
Charmaine
When I Lost You
Here's To The Losers
Golden Moments
Shadow Of The Moon

Portrait Of Sinatra
Two Record Set With Booklet

Reprise K64039

Side I
Let's Face The Music And Dance
Nancy
I've Got You Under My Skin
Let Me Try Again
Fly Me To The Moon
All Or Nothing At All
For Once In My Life
Bonita
My Kind Of Town
Call Me Irresponsible

Side II
All The Way
Strangers In The Night
Didn't We
Come Fly With Me
The Second Time Around
In The Wee Small Hours
Bad, Bad Leroy Brown
Softly As I Leave You
Cycles
Send In The Clowns (Piano)

Side III
That's Life
Little Green Apples
Song Of The Sabia
Goody Goody

Empty Tables (Piano)
I Believe I'm Gonna Love You
Stargazer
I Sing The Songs
You Are The Sunshine Of My Life
It Was A Very Good Year

Side IV
You Make Me Feel So Young
Pennies From Heaven
Love's Been Good To Me
Something Stupid
If
Star
Young At Heart
Yesterday
Something
My Way

Capital Records Reissues

Come Fly With Me
SY-4533

Contains the twelve songs from the original release - in true stereo with original cover.

Only The Lonely
SY-4535

In true stereo with the original award winning cover, but "It's A Lonesome Old Town" and "Spring Is Here" have been deleted.

Songs For Swingin' Lovers
SM-653

The original, untampered mono sound has been retained, but "Pennies From Heaven", "Our Love Is Here To Stay" and "Makin' Whoppee" have been deleted. Same cover.

A Swingin' Affair
SM-11502

Good mono sound, but "I Got It Bad", "I Guess I'll Have To Change My Plan" and "Night and Day" have been deleted.

Pal Joey
SM-912

In true stereo with original cover.

Come Dance With Me
SM-1069

Same as original and stereo.

Nice 'N Easy
SM-1417

Same as original and in true stereo.

Can Can
SM-1301

Same as original and in true stereo.

Swingin' Session
SM-1419

Same as original and in true stereo.

All The Way
SM-1538

Same as original except that two songs are in enhanced monophonic sound. The rest are true stereo.

On November 5, 1961, while Sinatra was appearing at the Sands Hotel in Las Vegas, Reprise recorded him "Live" with the orchestra of Antonio Morelli. It was never issued and here are the selections.

April In Paris	The One I Love
Don't Cry Joe	On The Road To Mandalay
Here's The Rainy Day	River Stay Away From My Door
Imagination	The Second Time Around

In The Still Of The Night
Just One Of Those Things
The Lady Is A Tramp
Moonlight In Vermont
The Moon Was Yellow

Witchcraft
Without A Song
You Make Me Feel So Young
Young At Heart
You're Nobody Till Somebody Loves
You

In The Wee Small Hours   English Capitol EMI-CPS-1008

Same as original - excellent mono sound.

Point Of No Return   SM-1676

Same as original except that "A Million Dreams Ago" is deleted.

Sinatra Albums That Were In The Making But For One Reason Or Another Were Never Started, Completed Or Released:

1. A Latin-American Jazz LP arranged and conducted by Tito Puente.

2. A collaboration with Ella Fitzgerald.

3. An LP with the Oscar Peterson Trio.

4. An LP to be produced by Ex-Beatle, George Harrison.

5. A Country-Western LP produced by Snuff Garrett.

6. An album to be titled "Saloon Songs".

7. An album of ballads with Michel Legrand.

8. An album of women's names to be titled "Here's To The Ladies".

There is also an LP currently available entitled "The Adventures of Ali and His Gang Versus Mr. Tooth Decay". Sinatra plays a store keeper who is discouraged from selling candy to children by Muhammad Ali. It is only available at Woolworth and Woolco Stores. Sinatra's picture is on the cover and it sells for $2.98.

Frank Sinatra & Ella Fitzgerald   Zafiro ZV-891
Taken Directly From Television Shows

Side 1
Goin' Out Oof My Head (with Fitzgerald)   November 13, 1967
Don't Be That Way (Fitzgerald alone)   November 13, 1967
I May Be Wrong (with Fitzgerald)   may 9, 1958
Moonlight In Vermont (with Fitzgerald)   May 9, 1958
Angel Eyes (Fitzgerald alone)   May 9, 1958

Side II
They Can't Take That Away From Me (with Fitzgerald) November 13, 1967
Stompin' At The Savoy (with Fitzgerald)   November 13, 1967
Body And Soul (Fitzgerald alone)   November 13, 1967
When You're Smiling (Fitzgerald alone)   May 9, 1958
The Lady Is A Tramp (with Fitzgerald)   November 13, 1967

Frank Sinatra & Judy Garland   Zafiro ZV-892
Taken Directly From Television and Radio Shows

Side I
Garland Medley (Orchestra alone)   February 25, 1962
You're Nobody Till Somebody Loves You (with Garland) February 25, 1962
I Can't Give You Anything But Love (Garland alone)   February 25, 1962
The One I Love (with Dean Martin)   February 25, 1962
Gotta Be This Or That (with Garland)   June 14, 1945

Side II
Get Me To The Church On Time   November 13, 1967
That's Judy   June 14, 1945
My Romance (with Garland)   June 14, 1945
Just In Time (Garland alone)   February 25m 1962
How Deep Is The Ocean (Garland alone)   June 14, 1945

ASI Canta Frank Sinatra   Zafiro ZV-893
Taken From Radio Shows and Unreleased Recordings and One Selection From
Television.

Side I
As You Desire Me   Reprise Recording
A Good Man Is Hard To Find (with Shelley Winters)   Columbia Recording
You're The Top (with Ethel Merman) T.V. Show   November 8, 1953
Lilly Belle   Columbia Recording
Don't Forget Tonight Tomorrow   Columbia Recording

Side II
It's All Up To You (with Dinah Shore)   Columbia Recording
Old School Teacher   Columbia Recording
Long Ago And Far Away   Vims Radio Show, February 9, 1944
Till The End Of Time   Radio Show, June 14, 1945
Suddenly It's Spring   Radio Show, June 14, 1945

Frank Sinatra   Zafiro ZV-894
Taken from Columbia Recordings With One Selection From Radio

Side I
One Hundred Years From Today   Radio Show, 1953
So They Tell Me   Columbia Recording
If You Please   Columbia Recording
You'll Know When It Happens   Columbia Recording
All Through The Day   Columbia Recording

Side II
Meet Me At The Copa   Columbia Recording
My Love For You   Columbia Recording
There's Something Missing   Columbia Recording
Help Yourself To My Heart   Columbia Recording
Kisses And Tears   Columbia Recording

Two new albums have recently been released that have not been reviewed at this time and they seem to be welcome additions to the Sinatra collector. It remains to be seen if the sound quality is acceptable or superior to the tapes of these live performances that have been circulating among Sinatraphiles for many years.

Sinatra Live   Retrospect 505

For contents, check the concert chapter on June 9, 1957 - Civic Auditorium, Seattle, Washington.

Sinatra Live - Volume II   Retrospect 506

There are supposedly taken from his 1962 world tour with Bill Miller (Piano); Al Viola (Guitar); Irv Cottler (Drums); Emil Richards (Vibes); Ralph Pena (Bass); Harry Klee (Reeds).

Chapter XV - Select Bibliography

Tell It To Louella - 1961 - Louella Parsons
The Whole Truth And Nothing But - 1962 - Hedda Hopper
The Jazz Story - 1964 - Dave Dexter, Jr.
Uncle Frank - Biography Of Frank Costello - 1973 - Leonard Katz.

NOTES

NOTES

NOTES

NOTES